Seeing with Free Eyes

SUNY Series in Ancient Greek Philosophy

Anthony Preus, editor

Seeing with Free Eyes
The Poetic Justice of Euripides

Marlene K. Sokolon

Published by State University of New York Press, Albany

© 2021 State University of New York Press

All rights reserved

Printed in the United States of America

No part of this book may be used or reproduced in any manner whatsoever without written permission. No part of this book may be stored in a retrieval system or transmitted in any form or by any means including electronic, electrostatic, magnetic tape, mechanical, photocopying, recording, or otherwise without the prior permission in writing of the publisher.

For information, contact State University of New York Press, Albany, NY
www.sunypress.edu

Library of Congress Cataloging-in-Publication Data

Name: Sokolon, Marlene K., author
Title: Seeing with free eyes : the poetic justice of Euripides / Marlene K. Sokolon, author.
Description: Albany : State University of New York Press, [2021] | Series: SUNY series in Ancient Greek Philosophy | Includes bibliographical references and index.
Identifiers: ISBN 9781438484716 (hardcover : alk. paper) | ISBN 9781438484723 (ebook) | ISBN 9781438484709 (pbk. : alk. paper)
Further information is available at the Library of Congress.

10 9 8 7 6 5 4 3 2 1

For Patrik Marier

Contents

Acknowledgments ix

Introduction 1

Part I: Justice in the City

Chapter 1 The *Medea*: What Justice Conceals 19

Chapter 2 The *Bacchae*: Justice, Dialectics, and Dismemberment 41

Chapter 3 The *Phoenician Women*: Justice is Multicolored 65

Part II: Justice in Sacred Spaces

Chapter 4 The *Ion*: Justice, In and Out of Bounds 91

Chapter 5 The *Children of Heracles*: And Justice for Others 113

Chapter 6 The *Suppliant Women*: Justice among Cities 137

Part III: Justice in the Wilderness

Chapter 7 The *Hecuba*: Justice as Autonomy 161

Chapter 8 The *Alcestis*: Justice as Generosity, or Too Much
of a Good Thing   183

Chapter 9 The *Electra*: The Justice of Good and Bad Judgment   207

Conclusion   227

Notes   243

Bibliography   347

Index   385

Acknowledgments

As this manuscript had many false starts and was interrupted by serving time as departmental chair, it took far too long to write, and there are too many people to thank for finally bringing it to completion. Bookended as it was by two sabbaticals, I especially would like to thank my hosts Jean-Baptiste Gourinat and the Centre Léon Robin for the incredible year at Paris IV/Lettres Sorbonne Université, as well as Tim Hayward of the Just World Institute at the University of Edinburgh. The excellent librarians at the Bibliothèque Historique de la Ville de Paris were wonderful and gracious during the many hours of editing I spent in their beautiful reading room. I also would like to thank the many conference discussants who commented on earlier and alternative versions over the years. In particular, the manuscript has been much improved by the comments of Mary P. Nichols, Ann Ward, Lee Trepanier, Lee Ward, Thornton Lockwood, Bernard Dobski, Dustin Gish, Ryan McKinnell, Michael Di Gregorio, Nina Valiquette Moreau, and Lilly Goren. My ideas also have benefited from the many discussions about Euripides over the years with my patient colleagues and remarkable students at Concordia University. I would also like to thank the anonymous reviewers for their careful reading of the full draft and comments for revisions, as well as Michael Rinella and the team at SUNY Press for their commitment to this manuscript. Finally, thank you to the amazing poet Frederick Turner and the Liberty Fund for inviting me many years ago to the colloquium "Freedom and the Epic," which first inspired this investigation into the political thought of ancient poetry.

Introduction

On February 18, 1992, a cold and cloudy day in Milwaukee, Rita Isbell made a victim impact statement during the sentencing of the notorious serial killer Jeffrey Dahmer.[1] The previous year, Dahmer had murdered and raped her brother Errol Lindsey. After a parade of weeping family members, Isbell is the very image of rage. She opens by declaring: "This is what hate looks like." For several minutes, she starkly lays bare her desire for revenge. She screams obscenities. She calls him "Satan." She wants him to see "what out of control is." Eventually it takes three guards to restrain her from physically attacking her brother's murderer, and the judge orders a recess. Isbell's rage is juxtaposed with the calmness of court proceedings, where participants dressed in pressed suits and ties deliberated on whether the accused was responsible for raping, murdering, and eating seventeen people. Her display of rage also contrasts sharply with our court system's emphasis on logic, argumentation, and material evidence. Yet, somehow her response seems more genuine and more human than an image of justice removed from such private wrath. The pure spectacle of her honesty also likens her to a character in a Greek tragedy: in her rage, she is Hecuba, or Alcmene, or Medea. Such a spectacle also raises questions as to what might be missing or lost when justice becomes institutionalized and is grounded in an understanding of impartial or dispassionate rationality. Might it be important for our comprehension of justice to understand Medea?

This image of justice as requiring some kind of impartial rationality is found across the history of political thought. Although there is certainly no agreement on what kind of rationality is necessary for just decision making, one dominant perspective emphasizes reason as an instrumental ends-means calculation or maximization of a fairly coherent set of preferences.² Rawls, for example, reflects an ideal version of this perspective in his theory of justice, which employs a value-neutral form of rationality that avoids introducing "controversial ethical elements."³ The idea that justice demands objectivity can be found in earlier philosophers, such as Locke's founding of community on the relinquishing private judgment to impartial arbitrators and settled, known laws.⁴ Even earlier, although Aristotle may have labeled our contemporary view of instrumental reason as a form of "cleverness," he emphasized the ends-means deliberation of prudence as essential to ethical decision making.⁵ Importantly, however, like most ancient philosophers, Aristotle stresses that contemplative reasoning, which investigates universal or invariable first principles, is a higher form of rational activity.

Plato placed even greater emphasis on rational contemplation as the highest activity of the soul.⁶ He opens his famous examination in the *Republic* by questioning popular ancient Greek opinions of justice, such as keeping oaths or helping friends and harming enemies. Socrates's own opinion is that justice is found in every member minding their own business and contributing to the community in the role for which they are most naturally suited. Establishing such justice requires not only the famous philosopher-king but holding all things, including the family, in common. This latter point underscores the preference for one's own as a source of injustice. Whether Plato intends this opinion of justice literally, or as merely a segue into justice as a properly ordered soul, is a long-standing scholarly debate.⁷

More relevant for this present discussion, in this same dialogue on justice, Socrates invokes his most derisive critique of his pedagogical rivals: the poets. Hence, in Book III, Socrates censors poetry that depicts gods or heroes as emotionally excessive or deceitful; in Book V, he suggests those drawn to the theater resemble philosophers, but their love of learning results only in opinions and not truth. And, by Book X, the poets and the makers of tragedy are not only censored but banished.⁸ In particular, Socrates dismisses poets as imitators of imitation who do not understand what improves human beings or cities; instead, they manipulate the people with a kind of wizardry that destroys calculative and prudential understanding. Thus, "unconcerned with justice and other virtues," the poets are dangerous to good government and banished.⁹ By contrast, Socrates suggests the philosopher possesses a love of learning, desire for wisdom, and always seeks the truth itself concerning the good and the just. Philosophy is nourished not by shadows and images but by rational calculation, geometry, and dialectic. Like a true pilot, philosophers are useful because they are concerned with the health of the soul and what is truly good for cities. Thus, appearing to set up a strict dichotomy between philosophical truth-seeking and dangerous poetic trickery, Socrates boldly declares that "for a long time, there has been a quarrel (*diaphora*) between poetry and philosophy."[10]

Although this is an extremely crude sketch of Plato's extensive and highly complex assessment of poetry in this text—and throughout many of his dialogues—the question of whether Plato is serious about this quarrel has itself become another ancient debate.[11] In general, the censorship and banning of the poets is taken seriously by scholars who argue that Plato rejects traditional mythology in favor of rational inquiry and proposes an insurmountable distance between poetic inspiration and philosophy.[12] By contrast, the very poetic elements in the dialogues suggest Plato may not be as hostile to the poets as Socrates's critique implies. Socrates frequently quotes the poets, and especially Homer, as authorities in his arguments.[13] Poetic elements, such as dramatic context and narrative, are argued as essential for understanding and interpreting his dialogues.[14] Plato also generously employs many other poetic devices from analogy, myths, and allegories, to outrageous examples likely intended to provoke his audience.[15]

From this perspective, Plato's critique of poetry is ironic or, at least, does not support a strict dichotomy between poetry and philosophy.[16] Scholars who think Plato is being ironic about the quarrel often understand poetry as a useful supplement, when directed by philosophy, to point young men and the masses toward truth.[17] Focusing on the critique of poetry in Book III, this interpretation understands poetry as an important step in education but requiring superior philosophic understanding. Going further, other scholars argue Plato incorporates poetic elements as part of, or essential to, his understanding of philosophy.[18] In this case, poetic devices and other elements are not simply complementary to or guided by rational argumentation but rather a necessary aspect or element of philosophic thinking.

Whether Plato's critique is ironic or serious, at the heart of this ancient quarrel is an important pedagogical question: can poetry provide an education concerning the truth about justice and how to improve citizens and cities? The current scholarly debate concerning Plato's critique of poetry still focuses on this question from the perspective of the philosopher. By contrast, this analysis takes up Socrates's challenge to reverse this polarity by exploring the ancient quarrel from the perspective of a poet.[19] Thus, setting aside the debate as to whether Plato is ironic, it explores the pedagogical questions raised by Plato. Does poetry, for example, lack knowledge concerning what makes people or cities better? Is it destructive of prudence and calculation? Does it really neglect "justice and other virtues"? To investigate such questions, the analysis focuses on the same overarching inquiry of the *Republic*—what is justice?—from the perspective of a contemporary of the historical Socrates: the tragic poet Euripides.

There are several reasons why Euripides is a good "case" for examining whether the poets were serious educators. First, although the poets, and especially Homer, were considered the main educators of Greece, the question of whether Euripides's tragedies provided a serious education was already salient in the fifth century.[20] Aristophanes's *Frogs* dramatizes a competition between the recently deceased Euripides and the more senior Aeschylus concerning who was the greater poet. Their disagreement hinges on whether tragedians ought to dramatize the complexity of human conflicts (Euripides's view) or offer an idealized heroic model of behavior (Aeschylus's view). Aristophanes's Euripides defends his multifaceted approach because his art "leads the people (*dēmos*) to think," by "putting in calculation" so that "they can perceive and understand."[21] Although we do not know whether the real Euripides said anything similar, it is possible such satire reflected the public perception of Euripides's tragedies. In addition, in Aristotle's *Poetics*, Euripides's reputation for pedagogical realism is underscored by a quote attributed to Sophocles: "He [Sophocles] portrayed people as they ought to be and Euripides portrayed them as they are."[22] Thus, by the fifth century, Euripides's reputation already reflected a concern with the education of the common people.

Second, although Euripides was popular in classical antiquity, since at least Hegel's interest in the *Antigone*, contemporary political thought has been comparably more interested in his rival tragedians.[23] It is not clear why political theorists are less interested in Euripides. Nietzsche's criticism of Euripides as destructive of the irrational with a preference for rationality highlights the tragedian's interest in political and philosophic concerns.[24] Euripides's tragedies include, for example, many highly formalized and seemingly superfluous debates on political questions, such as the best regime or relativity of truth. He also incorporates genuine fifth-century political debates, such as the superiority of a "quietist" or isolationist versus "activist" foreign policy. His ideas often reflect the concerns of fifth-century sophists, such as the power of rhetoric or whether morality can be taught.[25] As we will see, Euripides often seems critical of these sophistic views, but he is clearly interested in the intellectual debates of his fifth-century Athens.[26] Importantly, however, Aristophanes's comic portrayal is very revealing: Euripides's audience was not limited to the leisured elite discussing philosophy over glasses of wine at symposiums. Instead, as his tragedies were part of a large community festival, his audience included the average, hardworking democratic citizen.

If Euripides is concerned with the education of average citizens, then the quarrel between philosophy and poetry is politically significant. In a democracy, the citizens—the people—are ultimately responsible for questions of justice and political decision making. Taking Socrates's critique at face value, if poetry is unconcerned with "justice and other virtues," then the tragedies are merely entertainment, and the citizens are corrupted, learn nothing, or at most are only introduced to opinions about justice. Furthermore, since many poorer citizens do not possess the leisure time necessary for a philosophic education, they will always be unable to make truly just decisions. In this case, democracy really would be an inferior regime. By contrast, if Euripides's tragedies take justice seriously and enhance (rather than corrupt) prudential and political reasoning, then democratic citizens receive a real education in distinguishing good from bad or the just from unjust. The implications of the quarrel for the possibility of a just democracy are immeasurable.

Although there are other poetic genres, ancient Greek tragedy may have had an even more crucial connection to Athenian democratic education.[27] As will be discussed later, although the origin of tragedy predates democracy and is found in other nondemocratic regimes, it flourished in Athens during the democratic period. Like all art forms, tragedy can transmit political propaganda that reinforces group cohesion and promotes community exclusiveness or chauvinism. Yet tragedies can also disrupt and question those traditional norms, expose injustice, and present multiple viewpoints that challenge dogmatic thinking.[28] As the audience for tragedy was primarily a gathering of citizens, it provided a valuable pedagogical opportunity for the democratic regime.

This is especially true in Athenian democracy, which did not separate church and state or art and religion. As will be developed below, the Great Dionysia festival provided the leisure and opportunity for the community to come together to watch stories of great heroes and, potentially, to learn about "justice and the other virtues." The importance, however, between poetic art forms and democratic education may not be limited to ancient democracy. Our contemporary citizens may have unlimited sources of information and ways to learn, from public education, traditional media, and town-hall discussions, to various forms of online talks, tutorials, and social media. With so much available information, it is still important that citizens develop and practice their prudential capacity to judge this political information and determine the just from the unjust. If theater and the other contemporary poetic legacies, such as film and television, are crucial to the functioning of democracy, then perhaps we, too, ought to reconsider the pedagogical role of our own storytelling genres.[29]

The "Seeing Place" and the Great Dionysia Festival

Euripides's tragedies were performed as part of the City or Great Dionysia festival in the Athenian month of *Elaphebolion* (roughly late March to early April).[30] Although precious little is known concerning the origins of theater, by tradition, Athenian tragedy began under the tyrant Peisistratus in 534 BCE with the first performances of the innovative poet Thespis.[31] Most likely, tragedy (*tragōdia* or literally "goat-song") developed out of long-established community gatherings of performances of dithyrambs (choral songs and dance), which may have included the sacrifice of goats.[32] If the legendary Thespis existed, he introduced or singled out an actor (called a *hypocritēs* or pretender) from the rest of the chorus. Aeschylus is thought to have introduced a second—and Sophocles a third—speaking actor interacting at the same time. By unifying the many disparate rural festivals, Peisistratus probably introduced the Great Dionysia festival as part of his overall cultural program intended to create and promote a common Athenian identity.[33]

Like the sporting events at the Olympic Games, the tragedies performed at the Great Dionysia festival were competitions, with the city memorializing the winners' names on official monuments throughout the city.[34] In 486 BCE, comedy was added to the Great Dionysia. About twenty years later, the ancient Ionian festival of Lenaea (held in late January) became the second main dramatic competition, especially for the newer genre of comedy. Aristophanes's *Frogs*, for example, won the Lenaea competition in 405 BCE. Smaller Rural Dionysia festivals continued to flourish at the local level, and many of the political subdivisions called "demes" had their own theaters. The popularity of dramatic competitions was found across Greece in other major sites, such as Delphi, Epidaurus, Dodona, and as far away as Macedon and Syracuse.

The theater (*theatron* or literally, the "seeing place") was an open-air space on a natural hill slope that accentuated acoustics. Except for the theater at Epidaurus, what we see today at most other surviving Greek theaters, including the Theater of Dionysus in Athens, reflects later Roman renovations. The earliest theaters had a flat space for the choral dances at the bottom of the hill called the *orchēstra* (the "dancing place") with the actors entering and exiting to the sides. A temporary cloth and later a wooden structure (the *skēnē* or "tent") were placed in front of the *orchēstra* and painted to resemble the setting, with the use of a door for a third entrance. Although evidence is unclear, a small, raised platform may have separated visually (and symbolically) the actors from the *orchēstra*. To enhance dramatic effect, other stage devices were introduced. The *ekkyklēma* (the "roll-out") could be pushed through the doors in the *skēnē* to reveal bodies or something from inside. The more famous *mēchanē* was a crane that suspended actors, especially as gods, from above. The use of the crane in the finale is the origin of the infamous Latin expression: deus ex machina. The actors wore stylized masks with exaggerated facial features and costumes that allowed them to assume the identity of their characters. To complete the dramatic effect, they often employed other stage props, such as crowns, swords, or the special items of the recognition scenes.

As Athenian tragedy developed, temporary wooden benches were built on the sloped hillside of the Acropolis. Special seating (*prohedria*) was reserved for civic officials, the ten democratically elected generals, and probably foreign dignitaries as well.[35] The size and composition of the audience remain a point of considerable debate. In the *Symposium*, Plato hints that thirty thousand people attended the festival; however, since it seems unlikely the hill slope could accommodate such a large number, he might be referring to those attending the various activities of the five-day festival.[36] Such high estimates also may include an unofficial audience who watched from any vantage point, such as higher on the Acropolis or even from strategic positions on trees. Other scholars estimate a number from fourteen hundred to seventeen hundred people, but most recent scholarship proposes a more modest six thousand official ticket holders.

Another source of contention is audience composition. Male citizens, resident foreigners (*metoikoi*), young men undergoing military training (*ephēboi*), and foreign dignitaries certainly were in attendance. Less clear is whether women were allowed to watch productions. Although little empirical evidence confirms this idea, Plato also suggests women, children, and slaves were part of the audience.[37] As the price of official tickets was about two obols (approximately one-third of a day laborer's salary), this certainly would be too high a price for poorer women, children, and slaves. Importantly, possibly as early as Pericles's generalship but definitely by the fourth century, a special civic fund (*theōrika*) subsidized poor male citizens' attendance. Thus, the majority of the audience definitely would have been male Athenian citizens.

The introduction of the *theōrika* also underscores the political dimension of the festival. Planning began early the previous summer, when the ancient civic leader called the *Archon Eponymous* selected three *didaskaloi* (the teachers) for the competition. Each competitor would have one day to present his trilogy of three tragedies, usually but not necessarily on a related mythological story or theme, and a satyr play featuring those half-horse ribald companions of Dionysus and a drunken Heracles.[38] The *didaskaloi* worked with a rich patron called a *chorēgos*, who recruited and paid for the chorus, actors, trainers, masks, costumes, and other dramatic features as part of their liturgy (*leitourgia*), or expected public duties of wealthy Athenians. The festival began with civic processions (*pompē*), which included a parade of war orphans and involved feasts and other choral competitions. During the latter part of the Peloponnesian War, allies presented their tribute during the festival, which was stored in the Acropolis immediately above the theater space. Each of the ten Athenian political tribes sent one judge chosen democratically by lot to form the competition jury. Although the criteria used to determine the winner are unknown, these judges may have been influenced by the audience: unlike our modern silent spectators, they were so loud and boisterous that the city employed a special police force (the *rhabdouchoi* or "rod-holders") to keep the rowdiness under control. In a final act of democratic oversight, after the festival concluded, a special session of the Assembly was held in the theater to discuss festival proceedings.

In years when the Great Panathenaea was not held, the Great or City Dionysia was the largest festival gathering in Athens. For five days, the city suspended the Assembly and all court business, temporarily freed prisoners, forbid the acquisition of debts, and took on a festive atmosphere of animal sacrifices, general mirth, and celebration. After all, Dionysus was a god of fertility, death and rebirth, sexuality, and wine. Yet, the degree to which tragedy has "something to do with Dionysus" is highly contentious.[39] Although many gods are invoked and some appear as characters on stage, Dionysus is rarely mentioned and rarely appears.[40] Tragedies are not an enactment of a specific ritual, although some tragedies may mimic ritual or provide an account of the origin of rituals and cult sites. Although this point will be developed further in the chapter on the *Bacchae*, an important hint may be found in Dionysus's other divine powers as god of paradox, ambiguity, metamorphosis, revelation, and mania. As a liminal god, Dionysus defies boundaries: he has a human mother but is reborn divine; he is Greek and foreign; he is both a new but ancient god. Importantly, he is also the god of *ekstasis*, which literally means "standing outside oneself" and is the root of our word "ecstasy."[41] In donning their mask, the actors "step outside themselves" to become someone else. By watching, the audience members are invited to step outside their own viewpoint to experience another's perspective. Tragedy allows the audience, in Aristotle's words, to see and learn by inferring similarities in these "representations of life."[42] Thus, the god of the "seeing place" provides a crucial opportunity for the community to come together to think about the complexities of social life and to practice prudential reasoning by seeing from different viewpoints and inferring similarities with one's own circumstances.

The Life of Euripides and Transmission of His Plays

Little is reliably known about Euripides.[43] By tradition, he was born on the island of Salamis on the same day the Athenians defeated the Persians off its coast in 480 BCE; he is said to have died in self-imposed exile at the court of Archelaus of Macedon in 407 BCE, when he was unintentionally torn apart by the king's hunting dogs. Probably from Aristophanes, who made frequent fun of Euripides, comes the legend of humble origins, such as his shopkeeper father's insolvency and subsequent exile from Boeotia or his vegetable-selling mother. Other accounts suggest he was impoverished or lived a kind of hermit life by writing his plays in seclusion in a cave on Salamis. There are typical salacious reports about marital troubles, including a series of unfaithful wives. He is associated with virtually every famous intellectual figure of his day from Anaxagoras and Protagoras to Prodicus and Socrates. This tradition, however, is highly untrustworthy. Derived from later sources, it rather conveniently supports subsequent interpretations of his tragedies, such as his supposed negative view of women or suspected atheism.

Unfortunately, what is known about Euripides's life is thin. He was born sometime between 480–485 BCE and registered in the Athenian deme *Phlya*, which confirms his parents were Athenian. Aristotle mentions that Euripides was involved a lawsuit concerning property, which suggests he was quite wealthy.[44] Although it is not certain whether he went into exile or to Macedon, he must have died sometime between 407–406 BCE as he is in Hades in Aristophanes's *Frogs* in 405 BCE and won the Great Dionysia posthumously later that same year.[45] Unlike his rivals Aeschylus and Sophocles, we have no mention of military or political exploits, even though he would have fought in the war and performed typical citizenship duties. He was popular enough to be frequently quoted, even in his own lifetime. Most famous was the widespread anecdote that during the disastrous Sicilian Expedition, the Syracusans freed Athenian prisoners who sang his choruses.[46] From the Alexandrian scholars, we have evidence of about ninety-two plays starting with the *Daughters of Pelias* in 455 BCE. From the same sources we also know that he took part in approximately twenty-three competitions; however, including his posthumous victory, he won the Great Dionysia prize only five times.

Compared with seven extant tragedies each from Aeschylus and Sophocles, nineteen of Euripides's plays (including the likely spurious *Rhesus*) survived, as well as countless fragments.[47] That we have more of his manuscripts attests to his popularity in antiquity but also to fortuitous circumstances. Around 250 CE Alexandrian scholars selected and widely circulated seven tragedies of the other two playwrights but chose ten of Euripides's tragedies (counting the *Rhesus*) for the teaching of Greek in schools.[48] Along with the even more popular Byzantine Triad (*Hecuba*, *Orestes*, and *Phoenician Women*), these tragedies were transmitted in medieval manuscripts accompanied by *hypotheseis* (short introductions) and *scholia* (explanatory margin notes). We also have an additional nine other Euripidean plays, all copies of which can be traced to a single manuscript.[49] Known as the "alphabet plays" because their Greek titles are in alphabetical order (epsilon, eta, iota, kappa), this sole manuscript somehow miraculously survived; one can only imagine some medieval scholar scooping up the scrolls as he fled a burning library. Unfortunately, the alphabet plays are transmitted without *scholia* or any other information, including the other tragedies in the trilogy or date of performance. Although imperfect, contemporary scholarship attempts to date these plays using metrical analysis on the flexibility of Euripides's poetic style.[50] As the alphabet plays were not chosen for educational purposes, they are important examples of tragedy that often break expected tragic convention and provide a useful glimpse into Euripides's artistic ingenuity.

Outline of the Book

The purpose of this analysis is to explore the question of justice from the perspective of a poet. As such, it is important at the outset to stress the limits of this analysis. First, as tragedy involves and questions cultural norms, it engages with common opinions concerning justice in ancient Athens. Some of these opinions of justice reflect the new thinking of the sophists, but other perspectives are more traditional and found in earlier Homeric epics. Later Greek philosophers, such as Plato, Xenophon, or Aristotle, often explore and question the same or similar ideas of justice. To place Euripides in his historical context and intellectual environment, I will note points of contact between these philosophic accounts and Euripides but refrain from further exploring the meaning and significance of these points of contact. As the goal of this analysis is to provide a poetic account of justice, a respectable or comprehensive comparison between Euripides and these philosophic authors would fundamentally shift the focus of this investigation. Admittedly, some of these points of contact are interesting, surprising, and sometimes enticing, which hopefully invites further research. Secondly, as the goal is to explore Euripides's portrayal of justice, this analysis does not engage in Plato's critique of poetry, nor does it directly evaluate the ancient quarrel as to whether poetry or philosophy offers a better political education. Finally, similar to the points of contact with ancient philosophy, the conclusion of each chapter highlights potential connections of Euripidean justice with ideas in the history of political thought and contemporary political theory. Again, these points of contact are not developed or analyzed; instead, they are intended to highlight connections between Euripides and subsequent ways of thinking about justice. Although the development of Euripides and these other lines of thinking are important, they remain beyond the scope of this investigation into Euripides's understanding of justice.

Similarly, it is important at the outset to stress that this analysis does not assume there really was an ancient quarrel between poetry and philosophy or that Euripides intentionally addressed such a quarrel—or even deliberately explored the concept of justice. It is reductionist to assume a tragedy is "about" justice or "about" any one particular theme.[51] Like all tragedies, Euripides's plays are highly complex and resist conclusive interpretations. Instead, the following chapters investigate justice in tragedies that often have other significant themes or avenues of interpretation. In addition, as with all storytelling genres, tragedy does not present a systematic, linear, or rational argument: Euripides offers no theory of justice, no thesis statement, and never directly answers the question "what is justice?" Instead, as Segal stresses, "to discuss Euripides is to speak in paradox," since his plots are full of reversals of anticipated outcomes and the unexpected realism of characters and settings.[52] Going beyond the paradoxes Segal outlines as dramatized within his tragedies (such as paradoxical endings, settings, or characterization), Euripides also reflects the god of theater in his approach to understanding justice. Thus justice, like Dionysus, cannot be defined, pinned down, and fully recognized; instead, it mirrors the god's ambiguity, metamorphosis, and moments of revelation that are part of the experience of human social community.

Dedicated to one tragedy, each chapter explores three intertwined questions. First, what concepts or ideas of justice are identified in the plot, and how are they depicted in his tragedy? Second, does Euripides's exploration reveal limitations, shortcomings, or raise further questions concerning the various understandings of justice in each play? Third, what lessons does Euripides's portrayal reveal about ancient conceptions of justice, and how might these lessons be useful for our own efforts to determine the just from unjust. Euripides's tragedies engage with the main competing perspectives of justice in fifth-century Athens. All plays to some extent address the ancient understanding of justice as helping friends and harming enemies. Certain tragedies focus on the still-relevant perspective of justice as merit, including equality or fairness, as well as some kind of proportional corrective for past injury. Euripides also engages with fifth-century sophistic views that justice is relative and ultimately reducible to unadulterated power. In addition, he includes a dimension of justice as it relates to the recognition, meaning, and enforcing of individual and community boundaries.

By carefully examining the nuances of his complex stories, Euripides reveals contradictions, paradoxes, and limitations of all these various perspectives of justice. His tragedies do not endorse any one perspective; rather, using the tragedy's dramatic context, Euripides presents a nuanced exploration of competing understandings of justice.[53] He reveals the true human cost of institutional failures and our lack of knowledge; he explores the inevitable bias of our judgment and irresolvable impulses at the heart of our desire for justice. Taken together, Euripides's portrayal of justice reveals the limitations of a perspective that relies on institutional solutions and impartial judgment to distinguish the just from unjust. Instead, Euripides presents justice as imprecise and lacking clear boundaries. It appears to reflect something more akin to the ancient Greek idea of a *sōros* or "pile" than an exact measurement.[54] Such opaqueness reveals why the concept of justice resists classification and definition. It also explains why Euripides does not offer any definitive statement on what the best idea of justice is. Instead, he indicates the important questions to ask about any view of justice, including our own ideas of social justice, restorative justice, or justice as fairness. If he offers any advice on how to create a more decent society, it is to remember with humility that all perspectives of justice are partial, incomplete, and precarious enough to become its opposite.

The chapters cover nine of Euripides's surviving tragedies. To provide a representative sample, the analysis covers five of the tragedies saved for pedagogical purposes (*Medea, Phoenician Women, Bacchae, Hecuba,* and *Alcestis*) and four alphabet plays (*Ion, Children of Heracles, Suppliant Women,* and *Electra*). Some of these plays, such as the *Medea* or the *Bacchae*, are more familiar to political theorists; others, such as the *Ion, Hecuba, Children of Heracles* and *Suppliant Women*, have blatant political themes, such as the plight of refugees or fate of political prisoners. Certain plays offer unique or unexpected storytelling, such as the *Alcestis, Phoenician Women,* and *Electra*, which reveals the range of Euripides's innovative artistry. In order to assess whether space or location is crucial to his idea of justice, the chapters are organized into three sections of three plays, according to the tragedy's setting: the city, sanctuary or sacred space, and outlying areas (or the wilderness). As Euripides does not present a linear argument, each chapter is designed as a standalone analysis with no expectation that the reader will follow consecutively. There is also no expectation that readers would be familiar with ancient Greek mythology or the specific tragic plots under investigation. To ensure contextual understanding, prior to analysis, each chapter includes an overview of the tragedy's broader mythological background, the main details of the dramatic plot, and Euripides's potential narrative innovations. Unlike our own expectation of narrative continuity in sequels and prequels, the ancient Greeks did not view mythological stories as canonical or static, and all the playwrights altered aspects of their stories.[55] Most of the tragedies retold stories developed out of long oral traditions with multiple versions of the same stories existing simultaneously.[56] Some of the great heroes had more stable life stories, but even the great Heracles's labors varied widely in different times and regions of Greece.[57] Such mythical innovations are important to note, as they reveal Euripides's narrative choices, which are important for understanding and interpreting his tragedies.

The first three plays, *Medea*, *Bacchae*, and the *Phoenician Women*, are set in the civilized space of a city. In chapter one, Medea's story of an abandoned woman highlights the limitations of the ancient ethic of helping friends and harming enemies, especially the difficulty of distinguishing friends from enemies. Medea's anger is central, but her desire to reverse wrongdoing reveals justice as limited by the impossibility of true rectification. The *Bacchae*, in chapter 2, is one of the posthumous plays produced in 405 BCE. A rare dramatization of the ambiguous god Dionysus onstage, this tragedy explores the shocking and horrific consequences of failing to recognize the role of the divine in human community. It also exposes a necessary but potential danger inherent in investigating the meaning of justice. Focusing on the *Phoenician Women*, chapter 3 retells the story of Oedipus's sons' mutual slaughter before the Seven-gated Thebes. In this complicated and difficult plot, Euripides explores justice as merit in opposition to the sophistic assertion of the relativity of justice. Through this brothers' war, Euripides exposes the consequences of our inadequate and fallible understanding of the just.

The central section focuses on Euripides's most political plays, all set in the inviolable sacred spaces of temples and sanctuaries: *Ion*, *Children of Heracles*, and *Suppliant Women*. Chapter 4 presents the *Ion*, an innovative retelling of Athens's foundation myth set in the sanctuary of Delphi. Focusing on justice as a belief that the good can be dichotomously separate and autonomous from the bad, this play also exposes the limitations of human perspective and the value of respecting traditional boundaries. The *Children of Heracles*, in chapter 5, is set in a rural sanctuary not far from the site of the famous battle of Marathon. The story turns to the question of justice between political communities and asks the still-relevant question of whether and how much a political community is obligated to help refugees fleeing persecution. The tragedy reveals the oft-blurred line between justice as merit and political gain, as well as the dark side of justice found in the enjoyment of watching our enemies suffer. In chapter 6, set in Eleusis, the *Suppliant Women* builds on this question of justice between nations by focusing on the Athenian hero Theseus. After debating whether to help noncitizens, Theseus is convinced to retrieve the unburied bodies of the Argive generals who died with Polynices at the famous battle of the Seven against Thebes. This tragedy highlights the boundaries of international law and warns against excessive identification with cosmopolitanism.

The final section includes three plays set in the wilderness, far from the civilization of city and sanctuary: *Hecuba*, *Alcestis*, and *Electra*. Chapter 7 on the *Hecuba* tells the horrific fate of Priam's Queen after the fall of Troy. After discovering that her son has been murdered by her friend and her daughter sacrificed to Achilles, Hecuba's anger draws attention to the limitations of justice as merit, especially when political leadership and institutions are self-serving. It also highlights the complications of justice in warfare when there are no clear demarcations between victim and persecutor. Chapter 8 is dedicated to the most innovative of Euripides's plays: the *Alcestis*. In a departure from traditional myth and reflecting a satyr play, this tragedy tells the story of a woman who agrees to die in place of her husband. Connecting justice to appropriate boundaries, the play reveals that too much virtue becomes its opposite. Since the line between enough and too much is often opaque, the *Alcestis* exposes the search for justice as limited and incomplete. In the final chapter, in the *Electra*, Euripides returns to the famous story of Electra and Orestes's retaliation against their mother for murdering their father. Importantly, unlike Aeschylus's famous *Oresteia* trilogy, this time no divinity intervenes to establish justice in the form of political institutions; instead, Euripides leaves us with the shortcomings of all authority and standards of judgment, including the bias of institutions and our own judgment.[58]

The conclusion sums up the analyses of all nine chapters to assess the seriousness of Euripides's portrayal of justice and his insights on the limitations of these overlapping but differing perspectives. Reflecting an experience of identifying justice in the conditions of limited knowledge, Euripides's tragedies force a thoughtful and serious investigation into the meaning of justice and its role in a political community. His tragedies reveal nuances and limitations of competing conceptions of justice across every setting or environment. As many of these ideas of justice still resonate, his tragedies raise questions for our own contemporary opinions of justice. Most importantly, Euripides challenges a vision of justice that replaces the centrality of the individual with institutionalized, impartial arbitrators calculating objective outcomes. Justice appears to be not something that one possesses but, reflecting the paradoxical god of the theater himself, it is imprecise and eternally open to inquiry and deliberation.

Part I
JUSTICE IN THE CITY

Chapter 1

The *Medea*

What Justice Conceals

> The flow of holy rivers turns backwards to their source
> And justice and all things have turned around.[1]

The *Medea* is a truly disturbing play. Initially, Medea invites sympathy. She gave up everything—her family and her country—for a charming Greek hero on a foreign adventure of incredible labors. Although Jason brings Medea to Greece as his wife, he eventually succumbs to the heroic archetype and abandons her for the greener pastures of a Greek princess. For anyone who has ever been dumped, it is easy to relate to Medea's grief and rage. As the play unfolds, Medea drifts farther and farther away from our sympathy by murdering not only her rival and the king but also her own children. For this, she stands apart from Euripides's other heroines, such as Hecuba, who kills her enemy's children, or the *Bacchae*'s Agave, who kills her son in a fit of madness. Most disturbingly, rather than facing human or divine punishment, or even a prophesied metamorphosis, Euripides's finale presents Medea as victorious as she soars off on the sun-god's chariot to an Athenian sanctuary. It is no wonder that many contemporary readers find the play nihilistic and an abandonment of hope and justice.

Unlike the uncertainties of the plot, evidence dates the tragedy to the Great Dionysia Festival in 431 BCE.[2] For us this date resonates, as the tragedy was produced shortly before the outbreak of the Peloponnesian War. Although neither Euripides nor his audience could predict how long and devastating this war would be, the tragedy's dark pessimism seems to reflect the anxiety of that prewar spring before the hostile Corinthians (who figure prominently in the *Medea*) prompted the normally reticent Spartans into all-out war.[3] We also know the names of his other plays presented at that festival: the *Philoctetes*; the *Dictys*; and the *Theristae*, which was a satyr play. Although only the *Medea* survived in its entirety, fragments of the other two tragedies reveal a focus on "displaced" or abandoned persons: Medea is an exile rejected by her husband; Philoctetes is abandoned by the Greek army on a deserted island; and Danae is discarded by her *oikos* only to be saved by the fisherman Dictys.[4] The play's *hypothesis* also notes that Euripides's entry came in third, after Sophocles and Aeschylus's son Euphorion (who may have used his father's plays). Although it is tempting to assume this ranking is a rejection of the trilogy's theme, it may simply reflect the quality of his competition.[5] The *Medea* is the second-oldest surviving Euripidean play, after the *Alcestis* (produced in 438 BCE). Included in his first competition at the 455 BCE Great Dionysia festival was his *Daughters of Pelias*; since the theme of that first play interconnects with the *Medea*, Euripides seems to have been thinking about Medea's troubling story for some time.

The *Medea* has been the subject of many diverse and contradictory interpretations. A tradition of scholarship views the play as a warning against the threat of the "other" in the form of irrational women and dangerous foreigners.[6] By contrast, McDermott argues Medea personifies the disorder that undermines ethical grounding and leaves behind a nihilistic worldview.[7] Other scholars praise Medea as a heroic figure on par with the likes of Heracles and Achilles, or as a protofeminist heroine seeking justice for the plight of women.[8] Despite these differing viewpoints, scholarship certainly has moved beyond Page's comment that Medea's filicide is so abhorrent because it is "unknown in human experience." The unfortunate reality is that there are over two hundred annual cases of maternal filicide in the United States alone.[9] This chapter focuses on the relevance of Medea's filicide as central to Euripides's exploration of justice. Specifically, the tragedy locates her filicide within the twin ancient moral codes of justice: helping friends and harming enemies—and punishing oath breakers. Most importantly, Medea's violent act reveals more than a simple desire to get even with her wayward husband; it uncovers the underlying longing to rejuvenate or undo the past, which lies at the heart of justice.

The Mythological Context and Plot of the *Medea*

BACKGROUND MYTH

Euripides's version of Medea's story draws upon and is embedded within a much older context of fluid ancient Greek mythology.[10] Although Euripides's version shaped later accounts, such as Apollonius of Rhodes's *Argonautika* or Seneca's play also titled *Medea*, he likely drew upon a pre-Homeric version of *Argonautika* that may also have influenced Homer's *Odyssey*.[11] As with all Greek myths, conflicting versions of Medea's story coexisted, but one consistency is her connection to Jason's famous quest to recover the Golden Fleece.

What varies across her mythology is the extent to which Medea aids this hero and what happens to the couple in the aftermath. In one version, her father, King Aeetes of Colchis (in the vicinity of modern Georgia), comes to possess the Golden Fleece because he provided sanctuary to the children of the Boeotian King Athamas. These children were escaping the murderous intentions of their stepmother Ino on a magical flying golden ram. Jason's uncle Pelias (who usurped the political power of Iolcus from Jason's father Aeson) sends Jason on his quest with a promise to forfeit the throne if Jason brings him the Fleece. After many adventures with his heroic crew of Argonauts, the typical story has Jason aided in Colchis by Medea, who fell in love with the panther-skin clad young man or, in some cases, was tricked by Aphrodite.[12] In any case, Medea provided Jason with magical aid, such as potions that allow him to harness fire-breathing bulls and defeat the horrific Sown Men who sprung from sown dragon's teeth.[13] During their escape, Medea's brother Apsyrtos is killed. In this play, Euripides adopts the version where Medea kills her infant brother at the family hearth. In another account, to facilitate their escape, she dismembers a fully-grown Apsyrtos to force her father to stop and pick up the pieces. In still another version, Jason, not Medea, commits this horrific crime.[14]

What happens to the couple upon their return to Iolcus also varies. In one story, she uses her magical powers to rejuvenate the aging Aeson; in another, she rejuvenates Jason. Euripides tells another story of Medea's use of magical rejuvenation powers in his *The Daughters of Pelias*.[15] In this tragedy, despite Jason's retrieval of the Fleece, Pelias still refused to hand over the throne. In retaliation, Medea decides to trick Pelias's daughters into committing parricide. She demonstrates her rejuvenation powers by dismembering and cooking an old ram, which emerges from the pot as a young lamb. In hopes of a similar rejuvenation, his daughters kill, dismember, and cook Pelias. Medea, however, either cannot or refuses to revitalize him.[16] For this crime, the people of Iolcus exile the couple, and they find sanctuary in Corinth. It is here, living after several years with two unnamed sons (but by tradition called Mermerus and Pheres), where we find them at the beginning of Euripides's play. In other versions of Medea's story, the couple has only one son. In another, they have seven sons and seven daughters. And in still another, they have a son and a daughter.

Although our play ends with Medea flying off in triumph on her grandfather's chariot, the Athenian audience would have known her continuing story. In the most famous version, she bears Athens's King Aegeus a son called Medus. Years later, a stranger arrives in Athens whom Medea recognizes as Aegeus's older son Theseus.[17] In our play, Medea met Aegeus on his journey to visit King Pittheus of Troezen, where he will have the fateful romantic encounter with Theseus's mother Princess Aethra. Later in her exile in Athens, Medea tries to trick Aegeus into poisoning young Theseus, but at the last minute, Aegeus recognizes his son, and Medea is exiled once again.

There are several conflicting versions of what happens to her after this. Some say she returns to Colchis and reconciles with her father, Aeetes. In another version, she reconciles with Jason. In Herodotus's *Histories*, she and Medus find sanctuary with an Aryan people who are called the "Medes," after her son. As the Athenians often conflated the Persians with the Medes, this tradition connects the Athenians by common ancestry to their Persian archenemies.[18] Importantly, in no extant version does Medea ever receive punishment for filicide, nor do we know exactly how she dies. In fact, since she is a granddaughter of the Sun, it is not certain whether the partially divine Medea dies at all. In a version where she does die, she (and not Helen, as is more typical) marries Achilles and dwells in the Elysian Fields with the blessed. Jason, in contrast, always dies some sort of ignoble death: sometimes he is crushed by timber falling from his disintegrating ship the Argo (as Medea prophesizes in our play); sometimes, he is burned alive with his new princess by the poisoned robe; and, in other cases, he hangs himself.[19]

As confusing and varied as Medea's life story appears, she and Jason are connected by even broader kinship ties to larger narratives significant to the events of this play. Although, as scholars note, until she appears in the miraculous chariot of the Sun, Euripides downplays Medea's exotic and divine origins, magical abilities, and "foreignness."[20] Older stories of Medea stress her divinity and connection to both Titanic gods and the Olympians.[21] In Hesiod's *Theogony*, for example, Medea is listed as one of the goddesses who had sex with mortal men.[22] Importantly, through her father, she is the granddaughter of Helios, the Titan sun-god whose chariot is drawn through the sky each day. She is also the grandniece of Circe, the sorceress of the *Odyssey* who seduces Odysseus and turns his men into pigs.[23] During the return journey of the Argonauts, Apollonius describes a stopover on Circe's island where this sorceress performs a rite of atonement for the murder of Apsyrtos.[24] In some versions, Medea's mother is not Iduia but Hekate, the ancient goddess of magic, witchcraft, necromancy, and the crossroads.[25] In this play, at line 395, Medea invites such comparison by invoking Hekate as helper and protector of the hearth (a role usually given to the goddess Hestia). Similar to Hekate, Medea is famous for her skill in medicinal and magical arts, including necromancy and the use of drugs and poisons (*pharmakon*). By the Roman period, Medea was able to summon the power of the "evil eye" and destroy her enemies by creating "images of death" with her mind.[26]

Jason's lineage is also complicated and connects the play to events surrounding his great-grandfather's House of Aeolus. Again, there are confusing, contradictory, and divergent lineages, but three connections are important for Euripides's play. First, the tyrant Pelias (who sent Jason to Colchis and was killed by his daughters) was the son of Poseidon and Jason's grandmother Tyro, which makes him Jason's half-uncle.[27] Second, Jason is a distant cousin to the Creon in our play and his daughter (who by tradition is called either Creusa or Glauce), since their (great-)grandfather Sisyphus was also Jason's grand-uncle. Finally, Jason is related to Ino who, at line 1285, the chorus claims is the only female filicide in memory. In Ino's case, she did not deliberately choose to kill her children but was driven mad by Hera.[28] Ino was Jason's great-aunt through marriage to his great-uncle, King Athamas. Importantly, prior to her committing filicide, Ino also attempted to kill her stepchildren; these were the children who escaped to Colchis on the golden ram. It is because he is sent to retrieve this ram's Golden Fleece that Jason meets Medea.

Finally, Jason's lineage is important to the story since his great-grandfather's House of Aeolus has a family curse.[29] Extant mythology does not fix the curse to any particular event, but Jason's great-grandfather Aeolus was known for general ill-treatment of his children (such as forcing daughters and sons to marry). His grandfather Sisyphus has a more well-known fate: as punishment from Zeus, he spends eternity unsuccessfully trying to push a stone up a hill. Of the many impieties of Sisyphus, he raped his niece Tyro, which resulted in twin boys. Although our chorus claims not to remember, these twin boys are also killed by their mother. Significantly, Tyro also attempted to kill the older sons she had with Poseidon, but they (one of whom is Jason's half-uncle Pelias) were rescued by their divine father. Tyro eventually remarries another uncle, Cretheus, and has a son named Aeson, who is Jason's father. Jason is thus related to two filicides: his grandmother and his great-aunt. In this version of the myth, Medea is only one in a list of family women who personify an avenger (*alastōr*) fulfilling the curse to bring childlessness upon the House of Aeolus.[30]

Euripides's *Medea*

All the action of Euripides's *Medea* takes place before a *skēnē* representing Jason's "House that is not."[31] The plot indicates a path running past the House with one direction toward the royal palace and the other leading away from Corinth to Delphi and beyond. The drama is best understood as divided into two parts (both in action and emotionally) with the scene involving the Athenian King Aegeus representing the middle section.[32] The first part of the play (lines 1–660) focuses on the misfortune of abandoned Medea. The prologue opens with her elderly nurse wishing "that the ship Argo had not flown through the inky Symplegades to the land of Colchis" to Jason's fateful encounter with Medea. Until Jason breached this "boundary" (with more than a little help from Athena), the treacherous moving rocks of the Symplegades prevented sailing from Greece into the barbarian lands beyond the Bosporus.[33] From Colchis, Jason brought Medea to Iolcus, then into exile in Corinth, and now, to utter grief.[34] In the only extant dialogue between two slaves in the tragic corpus, the tutor enters and learns of Medea's unceasing grief. Offstage, Medea's lamentations continue as she calls for the deaths of her children, the destruction of Jason and his House, and the decimation of the House of Corinth.

Yet, when she finally appears on stage, Medea appears absolutely composed and dismisses advice to leave punishment to Zeus; instead, starting at line 213, she makes her famous speech on the plight of women as the most wretched "of all ensouled and thinking creatures" as they are subject to the whims of men. Creon, the King of Corinth, enters and pronounces immediate exile for her and her children. Supplicating and appealing to his paternal love, Medea manages to gain a reprieve of one day to organize her departure. With her added grief of new exile, Jason appears: their encounter quickly degenerates into a viperous debate (*agōn*) of insult and finger pointing for current and past woes. Jason finally exits when Medea rejects his monetary aid for her impending exile.

Just as all seems lost, King Aegeus of Athens unexpectedly appears on his way from Delphi (where he was seeking advice for childlessness) to visit his friend Pittheus in Troezen. Since Aristotle, this turning point (lines 663–763) has been criticized for its seemingly abrupt disconnect to the plot.[35] The turning point, however, does invoke several crucial plot devices. First, Aegeus provides an additional unbiased confirmation that Jason's behavior is unjust and shameful (*aischros*).[36] Second, he provides the soon-to-be-exiled Medea with a place of refuge. Medea convinces Aegeus to make an oath to protect her from her enemies in exchange for her cure for his childlessness.[37] Importantly, for later plot developments, Aegeus's oath echoes the now-broken oath that Jason took to secure her aid in Colchis. Medea's only remaining obstacle is that she must find her own transportation to Athens.

With this new harbor secured, the final section (lines 764–1419) begins with Medea's revelation of her whole plan (*panta bouleumata*). First, she will call Jason back and pretend to be won over as a ruse to trick him into allowing their children to present a poisoned robe to the Corinthian princess. Second, and more horrifyingly, to destroy the House of Jason, she announces her intention to kill her own children. Although the chorus strongly protests that such an act violates the "laws of mortals" (*nomoi brotōn*) and will pollute Athens, the play unfolds exactly according to Medea's plans.[38] Easily mollified by her fake obsequiousness, Jason takes the children with their poisoned gifts to his new princess. With the first part of her plan in place, Medea initially hesitates: on the one hand, she looks upon her sons with loving (*philois*) eyes; on the other hand, her spirit (*thumos*) cannot allow her enemies' laughter to go unpunished.[39] In the end, she announces that her *thumos* is "the master" of her plans, and she resolves to follow through even though she will mourn her sons.

A messenger arrives to announce the gruesome death of not only the Corinthian princess but also of King Creon, who is engulfed by the poisonous flames when he embraces his dying daughter. In what looks like a case of malicious enjoyment, Medea rejoices at their fate and enters the palace.[40] Horrifically, we hear the offstage pleading of her children as she stabs them. Rushing to save his children from what he thinks will be Corinthian retribution, Jason discovers Medea with their corpses in the chariot of her grandfather Helios.[41] Now from above, most likely on the *mēchanē*, she and Jason reverse the first *agōn*.[42] This time, Medea abandons him to start anew, and Jason is left behind to lament. The tragedy closes with standard Euripidean choral lines that god finds a way to bring about the unexpected.[43]

Euripides's Potential Innovations

Euripides's *Medea* alludes to events and storylines from several different sources of known myth, including Medea's murder of Apsyrtos (similar to a Sophoclean version) and her tricking of Pelias's daughters.[44] Although Euripides's Medea may overstate her role in Jason's adventure, her aid of Jason was firmly established by the late fifth century. Importantly, there are three potential innovations in Euripides's version of her story. First, although Medea's story continues in Athens, it is possible that Euripides invents the much-criticized scene where Medea meets the Athenian Aegeus on his way to Troezen.[45] Second, Euripides also appears to be the first to provide a magical resolution to his play with Medea's escape on the chariot of the Sun. Such a means of escape was unknown prior to Euripides. Third, and most significant, it is possible that Euripides invents the crucial event of his tragedy: Medea's filicide.[46]

Prior to Euripides's play, at least two other versions of the children's deaths were in circulation. The Corinthian poet Eumelus (who lived in either the eighth or sixth century BCE) provides an account where Medea's father, Aeetes, originally ruled Corinth but migrated to Colchis after leaving the city in the care of a regent. In this case, Jason rules Corinth through Medea's legitimate authority (and she is not a barbarian, and he does not abandon her). In this version, Medea kills her children accidentally while attempting to make them immortal by using her magical powers.[47] In another version attributed to Creophylus (either the poet from the Homeric age or possibly the fourth-century historian), the children are killed by the people of Corinth in an act of retribution for Medea's murder of their King Creon. The fragmentary evidence does not explain why Medea kills Creon, but it could be to enable Jason to take power. Later in the second century BCE, Parmeniscus tells a similar story where in retaliation for their king's death, the Corinthians kill her children in Hera's temple. This focus on the Corinthian responsibility provides a mythical explanation for Corinth's cult of guilt atonement, the Hera Akraia, which is mentioned in Euripides's play.[48]

Prior to Euripides's play, no firm evidence exists for Medea's deliberate filicide or for Jason abandoning her. Of potential importance, in a comment in the text's *hypothesis*, Euripides is accused of stealing the story of the filicide from a lesser-known playwright named Neophron.[49] Although previous scholarship tended to uncritically accept this statement, more recent analyses, such as that by McDermott, Mastronarde, and Mossman, argue that the *hypothesis* comment is unreliable and that the filicide had to be Euripides's innovation.[50] In particular, McDermott provides metatextual evidence that Euripides anticipates the "newness" of Medea's action within the play's dialogue (see, for example, lines 35–7; 790–93).[51] Although this debate may never be resolved, even if Euripides did not invent the deliberate filicide, it is "the central and indeed defining element of the play."[52] In particular, it proves central to the question of justice.

Justice: How to Distinguish Friends and Enemies

One important issue raised by the *Medea* concerns the ancient code of justice: helping friends and harming enemies. The Greek understanding of *philoi* (friends) included not only our view of close, unrelated individuals but also anyone connected by ties of kinship (*genetēs*) or formalized relationships, such as guest-friendship (*xenia*), supplication, or oath making.[53] Similar to later philosophic accounts, most famously Plato's presentation of Polemarchus in the *Republic*, the play exposes this ethic as problematic.[54] In particular, the tragedy reveals how these traditional categories of friend (*philos*) and enemy (*ekhthros*) become confused, subverted, and transgressed. Such subverted categories result in a confounding of the code, in which one harms the closest and most natural of *philoi*: one's own children.[55] That the *Medea* is working in and around this heroic ethic is not surprising, since harm to *philoi* is "a central element in the plot structures of nearly all of the extant tragedies."[56] Aristotle echoes this observation in the *Poetics* where he notes that tragedy is "within the sphere of the natural affections, such as when a brother kills or is on the point of killing his brother."[57] What makes a play tragic for the Greeks is not that the story is sad or ends badly (another of Aristotle's ideas for tragic plots) but that there is a disruption of this ancient ethic.[58] Importantly, even if Euripides did not invent Medea's deliberate filicide, he could have chosen an alternative version where she does not kill her children—or at least not deliberately. Thus, Medea's actions draw attention to the consequences of confusing this ethic for the family and political communities.

Importantly, Medea is not the only character in the play to subvert the categories of friends and enemies. As she points out several times, Jason is ultimately to blame because he is the first to harm friends. In the final scene, for example, when accused of being a bad (*kakos*) mother, she retorts: the children "perished from the disease (*nosos*) of their father."[59] The chorus also identified Jason's injustice as a disease in the prologue: "now all is hatred and the most loved (*philotata*) is sickened (*nosos*)." Two other characters confirm the injustice of Jason's betrayal of his *philoi*. First, the Athenian King Aegeus calls his action "most shameful" (*aischiston*) and "bad" (*kakos*); second, the tutor declares that "this man here [Jason] is no friend (*philos*) to his House." Certainly, Jason would protest this characterization, since in his own estimation he is a "great friend," to his House: his new marriage will improve the status of his "outsider" family by connecting it to new royal brothers.[60] Medea, however, rejects his argument as specious (*euschēmos*) and asserts that his primary concern is not his family but self-interest. The only legitimate reason, she argues, for leaving their marriage would be childlessness (*apaias*).[61] One might add (even though Medea does not) that his marriage to a Greek princess is no improvement to a match with the granddaughter of the Sun.[62]

Although we might side with Medea, whether Jason's new marriage would improve the precarious situation of the exiles and their children is a valid question. Some scholars argue that the fifth-century Athenian audience would find Jason's argument more convincing. Athenian men often had second families with foreign concubines, but only Athenian wives could bear legitimate Athenian citizens.[63] Significantly, however, Jason's reasoning appears specious from the perspective of the plot.[64] First, Jason does not appear overly concerned for his children's welfare: for example, although he offered Medea financial support, he did nothing to prevent their exile, even though from the perspective of an Athenian, legally his children should have remained with him.[65] Second, it is not Jason but Medea who secures amnesty for the boys by bribing his new wife. Finally, only after the princess is murdered does Jason try to save the boys. The tutor's assessment that Jason took a new bride because "each man loves (*philei*) himself more than others," seems a more genuine description of his motivation.[66] By "wronging loved ones," he reveals the worst of all human diseases: his shamelessness (*anaideia*). Thus, Medea appears correct: he is the first to harm friends for his own narrow self-interest.[67]

Although Medea identifies Jason's betrayal as the cause of sickness, her act of filicide is also a clear violation of justice as helping friends and harming enemies.[68] Importantly, her act of retribution against an external "enemy"—the princess—is never judged by anyone in the play as impious or unjust; it is only her act of filicide that violates "the laws of mortals" (*nomoi brotōn*) and condemns her an "abomination" (*musara*). Notably, her decision to turn against her own children is not the first time Medea harmed *philoi*; rather, it is the first time she has done so against Jason's interests. In the backstory to this play, the couple originally met during Jason's quest to steal the Golden Fleece. As she tells us in the play, she saved his life from the fire-breathing bulls, fields of murderous Sown Men, and it is she who killed the dragon who guarded the Fleece. She accomplished these things for his sake and, in doing so, betrayed her *oikos* and her polis. Most importantly, as the couple fled, she left her natal family heirless as she murdered her brother to escape. That was the first time she had been an *oikos* destroyer.[69]

Medea's actions are also symbolic of the conflicting status of women in any patriarchal society that adopts the heroic ethic of helping friends and harming enemies.[70] When a woman is transferred from her natal home to her husband's family, she is expected to transfer allegiance to this new family.[71] Thus, it was safest if daughters were married to loyal friends; otherwise, your own daughter could become an enemy. It was equally dangerous to one's own *oikos* every time a new bride was introduced: as an outsider or "other," the daughter-in-law could undermine her new House from within. As an epic character, Medea represents this potential conflict. In her speech on the plight of women, she draws attention to the prophetic power needed to survive the unfamiliar customs (*nomoi*) of a new family.[72] What Medea fails to mention is that her father neither consented to her marriage nor was she a foreign concubine taken as "war-booty." By contrast, Medea chose her own husband.[73] In addition, unlike divorced women of fifth-century Athens, who returned to their natal families for protection, Medea cannot go home. She is utterly alone, as she puts it, "without family (*aphiloi*), without political community (*apolis*)."

Despite her famous speech on the plight of women, Medea is a poor example of a fragile woman at the mercy of the patriarchy. By contrast, her deliberate choices and actions expose an underlying problem of the heroic ethic.[74] In her intentional act of destroying her father's House for her father's enemy, she literally dislocates *philoi* and *echthroi*: friends became enemies and enemies became friends. Importantly, Medea is fully cognizant of her categorical disruption of friends and enemies. She intentionally harms friends. In her first exchange with Jason, she states: "This is how things are now: to my friends, I have become an enemy, and though actions for your benefit, I have gone to war with those whom I should not have harmed."[75] Most significantly, Medea is also fully conscious that the category of friend and enemy has reversed again: her father's enemy, who became her best friend, has now "become [her] worst enemy (*echthistos*)." For Medea, the categories of friend and enemy are unclear, unstable, and porous.[76]

Consequently, the tragedy challenges and raises questions concerning the meaning and stability of ethical categories such as friend and enemy.[77] In particular, this play highlights the problematic nature of friendship based on kinship ties (and, as will be developed later, oaths). Medea's situation reveals the potential weakness of kinship bonds: it may be shameless, as noted by Aegeus, for Jason to abandon his kin; but it is also, as noted by the tutor, common for mortals to do so.[78] Aristotle may be right that kinship ties are the strongest and most natural, but such ties are still fragile.[79] In addition, Medea is an expert in manipulating these natural feelings and bonds of kinship, especially the parent-child bond.[80] She manipulates others, such as the daughters of Pelias in her backstory and Creon, by appealing to this parent-child bond; she manipulates Aegeus with the mere promise of future children. At the very epicenter of the play, Euripides draws attention to this Greek fear of childlessness, which was alarming, not only for epic kings but also for the average fifth-century Greek. The Spartans, for example, in their famous battle at Thermopylae sent only men who had already fathered a son.[81] Medea recognizes and accepts this cultural norm, since she admits childlessness is the only legitimate reason for seeking a new wife. As terrible as it sounds, Medea's filicide is directed at Jason's fear of childlessness. He did only come to his sons' aid after the mother of his future sons was murdered. And Medea knew him all too well. Jason's first words upon seeing their corpses were that she "destroyed [his] life with childlessness."[82]

This tragedy also reveals other problematic features of heroic justice. Medea, as Knox famously argued, can be understood in heroic terms as "one of those great individuals whose intractable firmness of purpose, whose defiance of threats and advice, whose refusal to betray their ideal vision of their own nature, were central."[83] As a heroic figure, Medea is comparable to Sophocles's Ajax who also fears, above all, the laughter of enemies. Both she and Ajax have great speeches exploring possible courses of action, and both resolve to pursue honor. As much as Medea fears enemy laughter, she rejoices with "double pleasure" at the report of the princess's "dripping flesh."[84] Luschnig also points out that Medea's famous comparison between the dangers of war and childbirth underlines her identification with the fact that "in war, men will sacrifice anything: their marriages, their daughters, their sons, themselves."[85] What matters most is honor, victory, renown, and reputation. Medea fully embraces this heroic ethic of justice: "Let no one think me insignificant, weak, or silent, but the just the opposite: harmful to enemies but kind to friends."[86]

Even within the world of the play, unlike the silent and discreet wife celebrated by Pericles's oration, Medea has a reputation (*doxa*): she is talked about.[87] Unlike most husbands, Jason proudly calls attention to her reputation and argues that it is a benefit of their union. Medea, at times, tries to minimize her reputation for cleverness or wisdom (*sophia*). Although Creon, for example, softens when she appeals to their shared parenthood, he is not suspicious enough to exile her immediately: she is really planning a great deed of harm against him and his daughter.[88] Importantly, unlike Ajax, Medea is neither driven mad nor deceived into her acts of violence. She fully recognizes the consequences of following her heroic temper (*thumos*) and self-will (*authadia*).[89] Despite the fact that many scholars read the famous lines of 1079–80 (*thumos de kreissōn tōn emōn bouleumatōn*) to refer to a struggle between her passion and reason, Medea's reason is not overwhelmed by passion, nor is she a slave to her base desires.[90] As Mossman and Foley assert, this line refers to her deliberation (*bouleuesthai*) between two different passions: love for her children (*philoi*) versus heroic anger (*thumos*) toward her enemies (*echthroi*).[91] In other words, hers is not a struggle between passion and reason but between the desire to harm an enemy and the desire to protect a loved one.[92] This is the crux of the play: the reality is that she cannot have both. A more helpful translation of the line 1079–80 might be: "My anger is the master of my plans." Medea has chosen anger over love, or chosen what is most harmful to her enemy, even though it equally harms friends.[93] Most importantly, Medea fully understands that her action will also end in self-harm. As she makes her decision, she tells herself: "Weep afterwards. For even though you kill them, you brought forth these loved ones. I am a misfortunate woman." Medea's decision, therefore, represents the potential self-destruction embedded in this heroic code.[94]

As many scholars have pointed out, because she is a woman, Medea is not the ideal heroic figure.[95] At the beginning of the play, for example, she behaves with a "typical" feminine response to a departed lover: she refuses to eat, she weeps all day, she will not look up from the ground, and she is deaf to all advice.[96] Even after she regains her composure, she is too nervous to kill the princess with a sword and opts for the female weapon of poison. Medea also displays characteristic Greek feminine vices of deception and manipulation to achieve her goals. Importantly, however, Medea appears to be self-conscious of these expectations of female behavior. This is seen in her obsequious interactions with both Creon and Aegeus but most vividly in her second interaction with Jason. Unlike their first encounter, in this second scene, she no longer challenges Jason but conforms to his expectation that a woman should not disagree or be at "variance" with her husband. She is literally "performing gender."[97] Medea turns out to be a peculiar kind of heroic character because she satisfies neither masculine nor feminine ideals. Instead, she seems more of a liminal figure and neither masculine nor feminine: or, alternatively, both masculine and feminine. This liminality also connects Medea with the divine patron of the dramatic festival, as Dionysus similarly embodied both male and female traits.[98]

Medea's liminality draws attention to the problematic nature of justice understood as helping friends and harming enemies. The key problem of this ethic as it unfolds in this tragedy is threefold. First, as the chorus points out: "Anger (*orgē*) is terrible and incurable when beloved is thrown with beloved into animosity."[99] In other words, if categories of friends and enemies are not stable, the worst anger is reserved and directed toward former friends. As Medea's life history clearly reveals, she slips between categories and makes friends of enemies and enemies of friends. She made a friend of the stranger who came to Colchis to steal her father's Golden Fleece, but now the same man is her greatest enemy. Eventually, as the audience knew, she again will turn against her new Athenian friend Aegeus when she tries to kill his son Theseus. Medea's liminality reveals the categories of enemies and friends as fluid and unstable. Second, the ethic is also problematic because, as Medea reveals, harming an enemy may be inseparable from harming friends. Her action is considered "unholy" and "against the laws of mortals" specifically because she kills her own beloved children.[100] In addition, she is also fully aware that she harms herself by killing those most dear; thus, she even violates the tutor's claim that everyone loves themselves the most.[101] Medea reveals the impossibility of a strict delineation between harming and helping, or between friend and enemy; instead, she harms everyone—self, friend, and enemy alike.

Third, even though Medea's story is about a woman harming her family (*oikos*), the lessons apply equally to a political community. In ancient Greece, there was less distinction between public and private. The ancient Greek family (*oikos*) was not considered separate from the public but formed the basic building block of the city (polis). In democratic Athens, the male citizens of each *oikoi* were registered in local subdivisions called *dēmes*, which were collected into the ten tribes of the *politeia*—the community of citizens.[102] Second, like other Greek poleis, Athens traced its foundation to an autochthonous origin in which all citizens descended from those who literally sprang from the soil. Such civic mythology created a symbolic kinship, not only in name but as fact.[103] Hence, the polis is as susceptible to the confusion of friends and enemies as the *oikos*. It also was susceptible to the degree of anger and kind of damage wrought by Medea against former friends.[104] In the year following this tragedy, Athens would experience the first of many breakdowns in community as a plague devastated the city. As Thucydides describes it, the civic turmoil during this plague parallels the destructiveness of civil war; in both situations, there was a general breakdown in morality, and citizens brutally turned against each other.[105]

Justice: Oath Making and Oath Breaking

In addition to justice as helping friends and harming enemies, the Medea explores a second idea of justice: keeping one's word or oaths (*horkos*). Oath making was also significant for both the heroic time of the tragedy and for its fifth-century audience.[106] Although one could swear an oath to any god, Zeus (in his guise as Zeus Horkios) was the primary deity responsible for ensuring adherence to one's sworn word. A variety of punishments existed for oath breakers, but Zeus often punished violators with childlessness by "rooting out all traces of a man who had sworn falsely."[107] In this tragedy, Euripides focuses on two oath events: the oath breaking of Jason and the oath making of Aegeus. In both cases, the oath provides a form of security that justifies Medea's harm to *philoi*. In her scene with Aegeus, his oath provides a new sanctuary and permits her to enact her whole plan. Significantly, Medea's strategic use of oaths as part of the larger calculation of her plan reflects her deliberate choice or rational goal-directed risk evaluation.[108] Additionally, she uses curses to call upon Zeus and other gods to punish oath violators. She becomes, through her understanding of the power of language, the manifestation of Pindar's description of her as the "deathless mouth."[109]

From Medea's perspective, Jason's main crime was to break his sworn oath. In the prologue, immediately after relating the story of their love affair, the nurse reports that Medea laments "most of all" Jason's breaking of his oath (made by the assurance of his right hand).[110] She also calls the gods as witnesses to "the kind of recompense (*amoibes*)" she received in return for his oath. Medea, herself, calls upon the goddesses Themis and Artemis to witness Jason's violation of his "great oath" (*megalois horkois*) to be her husband. Themis (whose name means "Law") was also a deity who guarded oaths. In some versions of Themis's myth, she was a second wife of Zeus and the mother of Dikē (Justice). Artemis, one of the twelve Olympians, was a special protector of women and an associate of Medea's patroness Hekate.[111]

Jason's oath is central to Medea's situation because it makes their breakup more significant in comparison to an average divorce in fifth-century Athens.[112] As noted above, Medea could not return to her natal guardian (*kurios*) for protection and, more importantly, her marriage to Jason was made of stronger stuff than an Athenian marriage. Although marriage ceremonies varied across Greece, they did not typically include a declaration of sworn vows. In Athens, for example, the bride underwent several rituals, such as sacred baths, sacrifices, and a special ceremony dedicating toys to Artemis as symbolic of leaving childhood. Finally, the bride would appear veiled to be transferred by the right hand to her husband and her husband's House.[113] These rituals were considered sacred, but they did not include any kind of oath to Zeus Horkios. In Medea's case, there was no marriage ritual of this kind, nor did her father arrange, consent to, or transfer her into this union; instead, Medea received an oath from Jason that, in exchange for her aid in Colchis, he would take her to Greece as his wife.

Although scholars point out that their marriage departed from Athenian practice, no character in the play challenges the legitimacy of this union or of their children.[114] In fact, since the oath that fashioned Medea's marriage more commonly created allegiances between men, the bond could be seen as stronger than a typical marriage.[115] These alliance oaths were highly sacrosanct and, if violated, would entail the wrath of Zeus Horkios. The chorus wonders why the sacred power of oaths has departed, and Medea questions whether Jason thinks the gods (to whom he swore) no longer rule or that some new law allows him to ignore his oath. Hence, since Jason swore an oath, it was not a simple matter for him to leave Medea. Whatever the complications of a Greek divorce were, it was not the same as a broken oath, nor did it incur the wrath of Zeus's divine justice.

Significantly, the play contains a similar dramatization to Jason's pledge in Colchis. In her conversation with Aegeus, Medea supplicates him for an exchange: he will provide her sanctuary, and she will use her wisdom of *pharmakon* (drugs) to cure his childlessness.[116] Aegeus agrees to protect her, but Medea requests he swear an oath to this effect. He is slightly taken aback by this request, as it reveals a lack of trust (*pistis*) in her supplication; however, Medea argues that such an oath will allow him to withstand diplomatic requests to give her up (either to Corinth or to still hostile Iolcus): it will provide him with the power to keep his word. Importantly, Medea's demand highlights the role of trust and ability to keep one's word as core to the formation of new relationships, as trust allows for the possibility of the dynamics of exchange.[117]

Aegeus declares that her argument is persuasive and reveals foresight (*promētheia*). Therefore, Aegeus swears by the Earth, by the Sun, by the whole race of gods, never to banish her from the land nor willingly hand her to her enemies. As punishment if he breaks his word, he swears to suffer "such things that happen to those who are impious among mortals."[118] As the chorus later notes, this oath binds Aegeus and his city "favored by the gods" to a woman whose hands will be stained with the pollution of filicide.[119] Medea, however, in exacting this oath does reveal her foresight. Without the oath, both she and Aegeus recognize how easily promises are broken for diplomatic or political advantage. Medea uses her knowledge of the power of binding language to secure a stronger commitment that allows her to deliberately choose and enact her plans. Without Aegeus's oath and a more secure refuge, she would have been foolish to go ahead with her plans.

Similar to the oath she made with Jason, the oath between Aegeus and Medea is an alliance that cannot be broken without incurring the wrath of Zeus Horkios. Hence, with the departure of Aegeus, Medea freely calls upon "Zeus, and both the Justice of Zeus and the Light of the Sun, now to be most victorious over my enemies."[120] With a calculated haven secured, she finally reveals "the whole plan" (*panta bouleumata*): first, to kill the princess with the poisoned robe; second, to utterly destroy Jason's House by killing her own children. By calling upon Zeus and his daughter Justice, Medea takes up the mantle of punishing the oath breaker and becomes herself the "agent of Zeus's revenge."[121] For Medea, these two acts of justice are intertwined and necessary to achieve the same goal: Jason's childlessness. If Medea killed only the princess, her sons would live on and through them Jason's lineage; if she killed only their sons, the princess would simply bear him new sons.

Medea's actions fulfill both divine punishment and her own curse at the beginning of the play: she dooms her children, their father, and his House.[122] Yet, working on a larger mythological scale, she also enacts the curse of childlessness on the House of Aeolus: in concert with other women in this family—Ino and Tyro—her actions bring childlessness upon Jason and other descendants of Sisyphus (King Cleon and the princess). Medea's filicide reveals how much she rejects the chorus's earlier advice to wait patiently for Zeus to punish the oath breaker; in contrast, she assumes for herself the divine authority to become her own avenger (*alastōr*). Taking on this mantle, she punishes violations of binding language by transforming her curses into deeds.[123]

Justice: Retribution and Rejuvenation

The *Medea* leaves little doubt that Jason's broken oath and abandonment of Medea is unjust (*adikos*) and most shameful (*aischiston*).[124] Although Euripides never uses the Greek word for revenge (*timōria*), her reaction can be seen as a form of reciprocal or retributive justice in which she exchanges a harm for harm. Despite the underlying justice of her cause, however, Medea's retribution is not unambiguous. Jason, the oath breaker, deserved childlessness; but, simultaneously, her action is "most unholy" (*anosiōtaton*). The chorus declares the filicide "against the laws of mortals"; and Jason has reason to believe the children will live on as "avenging spirits." Similar to the difficulty in making clear and definitive distinctions between friends and enemies, her retribution is an act that is simultaneously both just and unholy.[125] Her actions reveal potential contradictions of retributive justice. More significantly, the motivations underlying Medea's retribution expose a hidden desire at the heart of justice.

Medea's retribution has several motivations. First, as developed previously, as female avenging agent (*alastōr*), her retribution is an enactment of Zeus's punishment of oath breakers. Second, her retribution involves the ancient Greek understanding of blood price. The ancient concept of blood price, which could be the exchange of a life for a life, was most often financial compensation offered to resolve disputes arising from murder, theft, or insult to one's honor.[126] McHardy suggests that women like Medea tended to reject financial compensation because they had less to gain than men by forgoing blood retribution. One of the earliest depictions of blood price is the scene of public justice described on Achilles's shield in the *Iliad*.[127] In this scene, a quarrel has broken out over whether the compensation of blood price was equitable to the loss. Thus, blood price was an attempt to refund, restore, or reset the original balance. Importantly, since Medea is motivated by dishonor, her act of retribution reflects the concerns of a Greek hero.[128] Combining these two motives, Medea becomes simultaneously a female avenger ending the bloodline of an oath breaker and a male avenger defending her honor.[129] As such, she again defies firm categorization and crosses boundaries between male and female.

At the core of retributive justice is an attempt to find a measure to restore a previous harm. This desire to restore or reset draws attention to the core motivation behind Medea's revenge. Medea, as noted above, was a granddaughter of the Sun whose patron goddess (or, in some accounts, mother) was Hekate. This ancient goddess of magic, the crossroads, and necromancy held power in the in-between space of crossovers, such as between life and death. Medea possessed some of Hekate's knowledge of medicinal and magical arts, including her knowledge and power of rejuvenation.[130] As discussed previously, in several versions of Medea's larger mythology she uses this power to rejuvenate Jason's father or even Jason himself. The play draws attention to her former deed of manipulating Pelias's daughters into killing their father because Medea tricked them by rejuvenating a ram. She may also derive this power from her grandfather, who in the ultimate act of rejuvenation disappears each evening on his chariot, only to be reborn anew the next day. Significantly, unlike simple resurrection that brought back the dead like Alcestis, Medea's power of rejuvenation brought back the dead in their youth or prime.[131] Thus, Medea had the power to turn back, reset, and restore time.

Medea's power of rejuvenation is symbolic of what is at stake in retributive or corrective justice: the desire to either restore circumstances to their former balance or replace the consequence of a crime with an action that erases its effect. Medea is driven onward because, as Nussbaum points out, she wants "payback" as a way to "counterbalance" her pain and restore her status or control in a situation of perceived helplessness.[132] Her retribution may punish an oath breaker or be a form of compensation for dishonor, but what she really exposes in her desire for rejuvenation is a reconfiguration of her relationship with Jason. With the death of the children, Medea sends us back in time or rewinds the story to the point in Colchis where the original oath was taken. It was as if her marriage and children had never occurred.[133] As Burnett notes, Jason is simply "erased."[134]

This desire to turn back time or rejuvenate the past is found throughout the play. Most significantly, it is the desire which bookends this tragic story. In the prologue, the nurse opens the play with the lines:

> Would that the ship Argo had not flown through the dark blue Symplegades to the land of Colchis. Would that fir-trees not fallen in the woods of Pelion to make oars for the hands of the best of men, whom Pelias commanded to gain the Golden Fleece. For then, my lady Medea would not have sailed away.[135]

Again, immediately before the traditional final lines of the chorus, Jason's parting words are: "Would that I had not begotten them [the children] to see slain by you." Hence, both the opening and closing highlight the same wishful desire to reverse Medea's sailing away from her natal home. Finally, in the middle of the tragedy at line 410, after Medea announces her plan to harm her enemies (and friends), the chorus marks the moment when events begin to reverse: "The flow of holy rivers turns backwards to their source and justice and all things have turned around." In other words, the ending of the tragedy has turned itself into the beginning. Jason, now, is left to lament the sorrow of his empty House that is no more.[136] Instead of Jason abandoning her for a new union, Medea abandons him for a new family and flies away triumphantly, having enacted this rejuvenation on the very same chariot her grandfather used to renew each day.

Conclusion

As much distance as we have traveled from the heroic world of the *Medea*, the tragedy remains disturbing as many aspects of its portrayal of justice endure. Although the ancient ethic of helping friends and harming enemies is no longer thought of as "justice," relatives becoming enemies is still "a terrible and difficult anger to heal," and it is still easy to identify with the depth of bitterness between these divorcing spouses.[137] Like Medea, we make mistakes and exchange binding oaths with those who prove faithless. The *Medea* also draws attention to the fact that—despite the rhetoric to the contrary—it is often not foreign enemies who do the greatest harm; by contrast, the community breaks down from within when citizens can no longer trust each other. The community collapses when citizens begin to regard other citizens as "enemies." Medea's situation may be an excessive example of the collapse of distinctions between friends and enemies, but all less extreme retributive acts on former *philoi* and fellow citizens contain a similar kind of collateral and self-inflicted damage.

Most significantly, this tragedy focuses our attention on the hidden desire embedded in retributive or other forms of justice that attempt to make up for past injustices. As the tragedy unfolds and refolds back in upon itself, Medea's desire for retribution reveals a deeper, more hidden yearning: to return to and obliterate the mistakes of the past. This desire underlies the act of killing her own children, which restores Jason to that very moment in time when he was nothing and allows her to fly away to begin life anew. Our own attempts at justice reveal the same hidden desire. It is found in our judicial institutions with punishments designed to "fit the crime" or financial compensation to balance past grievances. It motivates political apologies as an "act of moral repair" for long past historic crimes.[138] This desire also underlies justice as reconciliation or an attempt to rebuild from past injustice. As defined by the International Center for Transitional Justice, reconciliation includes "restoring victims to their position as rights bearers and citizens."¹³⁹ All such perspectives reveal an underlying desire to return to some original position before damage was done. Yet, the damage cannot be undone. True rejuvenation is impossible. And this impossibility explains why we are never satisfied, even when we appear to achieve some form of justice, be it restorative, redistributive, or corrective.

True rejuvenation is impossible even for Medea. She achieved all her plans; yet, for all the turning back of rivers, she did betray her natal family, Jason did break his oath, and she did kill her own children. Even for the granddaughter of the Sun, the past cannot be undone. Nussbaum calls the impossibility of fulfilling her desire for rejuvenation a "type of magical thinking," which she argues should be replaced by an appropriate "transitional anger" and a rational, future-oriented form of justice.¹⁴⁰ Yet, the desire to replace Medea's anger (and our own) with such emotional detachment seems inhuman and equally impossible. It simply conceals another kind of magical thinking to undo the past by denying grief and anger. The story of Medea does not reveal that there is no justice in the world, only that justice will always be inadequate. Medea's desire for justice, like our own, is tragic because it conceals within it this impossible and unattainable longing to undo or correct the past.

Chapter 2

The *Bacchae*

Justice, Dialectics, and Dismemberment

> And even if the god is not,
> as you say,
> you should speak a beautiful lie
> and say that he is.[1]

Euripides's drama of madness, cross-dressing, voyeurism, and bloody murder has long fascinated theatrical audiences. Against the backdrop of this excitement, the *Bacchae* is the story of the god Dionysus's triumphant return to Thebes, the land of his birth. As the god of wine, Dionysus brings with him a sweet forgetfulness; as god of fertility, he represented the cycle of life and birth. As a god of mania, metamorphosis, and paradox, his worship included a literal departure from traditional norms to celebrate beyond the city in the uncultivated wilderness. As the god of the theater, worshiped in the very festival for which this play was probably written, he was celebrated in the freedom to "be what is not."[2] In this, one of his final tragedies, Euripides brings this mysterious god of theater on stage and reminds us of the dangers of attempting to understand and control the primordial forces of human experience.

Written shortly before the final defeat of the Athenians at Aegospotami, which finally ended the Peloponnesian War, along with *Iphigenia at Aulis* and a lost play, possibly *Alkmeon at Corinth*, Euripides's *Bacchae* posthumously won first prize at (probably) the 405 BCE Great Dionysia Festival.[3] As noted in the introduction, by tradition Euripides left Athens around 409–8 BCE for the court of the Macedonian tyrant Archelaus.

This may have been a self-imposed exile for wealthy patronage, but it is possible he was avoiding prosecution for exploring nontraditional ideas in his tragedies.[4] The years toward the end of the Peloponnesian War were turbulent times in Athens: the Oligarchy of the 400 was deposed in 411 BCE, the Athenians surrendered to Sparta in 404 BCE, and Socrates was executed in 399 BCE. Euripides is thought to have died in Macedonia around 406 BCE, although it is doubtful he was torn apart by hunting dogs as held by traditional accounts.[5] Regardless of the reason for his exile, he wrote this play about Dionysus's return from a similar barbarian exile. *Iphigenia at Aulis* was likely unfinished, and we know very little about the *Alkmeon*. The trilogy may have been united by themes of family dysfunction, separation, and sacrifice. Euripides is said to have never returned to Athens, and it was Euripides the Younger (his son or perhaps a nephew) who produced his final play about Dionysus for the festival of Dionysus.[6]

As with all of Euripides's plays, there is a wide range of interpretations.[7] Influenced by Nietzsche's famous analysis, the story has been read as a conflict between reason and emotion, with Pentheus representing the "rational" and Dionysus as the triumph of the "irrational."[8] Other interpretations see Dionysus's victorious return ex machina as indicating that the irreligious Euripides experienced some kind of "death bed" change of heart and finally recognized Aeschylus as possessing the "truer" tragic vision of learning through suffering.[9] Another possibility is that the "hard divine justice" of the *Bacchae* reflected "the Athenian mentality as they found themselves at the end of a long and devastating war."[10] Still other scholars focus on how the story confounds traditional binaries, such as god and human, human and nature, male and female, old and new.[11] Such interpretative variation is unsurprising, as it is impossible to "pin down" this tragedy to one particular theme or overarching lesson.[12] In the face of this kaleidoscope of potential interpretations, this chapter focuses on Euripides's portrayal of justice. Despite, or perhaps due to, the instability of interpretation, the tragedy highlights two important ideas. First, traditional norms may have an important stabilizing role mediating between inflexible and formless perspectives of justice. Second, the tragedy focuses less on the question of what justice is than on the process (or what is involved with it) and the potential dangers to the self and community in exploring such a question.

The Mythological Context and Plot of the *Bacchae*

Background Myth

The *Bacchae* retells the archaic myth of the House of Cadmus against the backdrop of fifth-century Athenian concerns.[13] Dionysus's story begins in Thebes. His mother, the Theban princess Semele, was a daughter of the Phoenician Cadmus. Sent to Greece to find his sister Europa (who was abducted by Zeus), Cadmus is famous for two things. First, he founded the city of Thebes after killing the dragon son of Ares who guarded its sacred spring. Following the advice of Athena, he sowed this dragon's teeth into the earth from which sprang his fellow Theban founders: the famous Sown Men.[14] Second, Cadmus introduced the alphabet and writing into the previous oral Greek culture. Semele's mother, Harmonia, was even more famous as she was the daughter of Aphrodite's illicit affair with Ares. As was often the case, the beautiful young Semele was noticed by Zeus and became pregnant. As was also typical, Hera discovered her husband's affair and designed a way to destroy her human rival: in the guise of an old woman, she tricked Semele into asking Zeus to reveal his true form. As the god of lightning, Zeus obliterated Semele, but he was able to rescue their son by hiding him in a "womb" he created in his immortal thigh. Thus, Dionysus was born twice: once from the human Semele and a second time from immortal Zeus.[15] Hundreds of years later, Pausanias reported that Semele's room in Thebes was still a shrine covered in ivy and lit by a perpetual fire.[16]

There are various versions of Dionysus's childhood, and all are violent. In one account, Dionysus is fostered by his aunt Ino. Consequently, Hera drives Ino's husband Athamas insane: thinking he was hunting an animal, Athamas kills and dismembers their son Learchos. In other versions, such as the one remembered in the *Medea*, Ino kills their children in a fit of divine madness.[17] In yet another variation, jealous of this new god, the Titans kill young Dionysus by tearing apart his body and boiling the pieces; he is reborn (again) when the goddess Demeter, or sometimes her daughter Persephone, reassembles his body. Eventually, Zeus gives Dionysus to Hermes who hides him in the barbarian lands of Mount Nysa, where he is disguised as a girl and raised by nymphs and satyrs. Although the exact location of Mount Nysa is disputed (it is variously located in Thrace, northern Africa, northwest India, or, as identified in our play, in Lydia), it is always somewhere in the east.[18] Different accounts relate his journey homeward: sometimes he is captured by pirates whom he turns into dolphins; sometimes he meets and marries the Cretan princess Adriane after Theseus abandons her; or, as Homer tells us, he is the one who betrays Adriane.[19]

All these stories underscore Dionysus's foreign upbringing and his return. It is in the east where he introduced the vine and taught humanity to make wine and where he first taught women to untie their hair and dance in the hills under the cover of night. Importantly, even though he is a son of Zeus and grandson of the Theban founder, Cadmus, in his myth Dionysus always arrives from elsewhere.[20] He is the god of paradox. He has a human mother but is divine. He is male but raised as a female. He is and is not a foreigner—an "other."[21] Like Apollo, with whom he shares the sacred site of Delphi, he is a prophetic god.[22] Most importantly for this analysis, Dionysus represents ecstasy or "the force that takes possession of our minds and places us outside ourselves (*ekstasis*)."[23] Dionysus, thus, is the god of wine, metamorphosis, mania, forgetfulness, prophecy, epiphany, and truth-telling; he is the god of the theater and represents a separation from and transformation of ourselves.

Euripides's *Bacchae*

The tragedy begins shortly after Dionysus returns home to introduce his sacred rites. In this version, there is no mention of his being raised by an aunt, as his family believed his mother lied about her affair with Zeus. In this case, too, the elderly King Cadmus abdicated in favor of his young grandson Pentheus (rather than, more typically, his son Polydorus). The young king, adolescent enough to be described as "beardless," happens to be out of the city when Dionysus and his followers, the chorus of Asian Bacchae, arrive there. In the prologue (lines 1–60), Dionysus tells us he has returned incognito (in the play, he is "disguised" in the mask of a priest) to introduce his rites and claim recognition as the son of Zeus.[24] In retaliation for the slander against his mother, he "stings" his aunts and the women of Thebes with a mania that inspires them to run wild performing his rites (*orgia*) beyond the city's boundaries. In the first ode, the chorus sings the ecstatic tale of the triumphant return of the god.

As an aside, there is no scholarly agreement as to whether the *orgia* in the tragedy represents actual historical practices.[25] As many elements of Dionysiac *orgia* were secretive, there is little external evidence and likely wide variations in cultic practice. We do know more about official Athenian public rituals in celebration of Dionysus. As the god of wine, for example, Dionysus shared a twin harvest festival with his half-brother Apollo.[26] Called the Oschophoria (*ōschoi*: "bunch of grapes"), this festival involved a procession of young men (*ephēboi*) dressed in the clothing of adolescent girls. Dionysus shared with Hermes another festival, the Anthesteria, which was a three-day flower and "new wine" celebration that, like our Halloween, was a time when the boundary between the dead and living was permeable. The many theatrical festivals, including the Great Dionysia, also encouraged his followers to "cross boundaries" or "take on new identities."[27] Although little is uncontroversial concerning Dionysiac rites, his *orgia* probably involved some sort of secret activities on the mountains, such as women letting down their hair, dressing in animal skins, and dancing with Dionysus's sacred symbol—the *thyrsus* or ivy-twinned fennel stick.

At line 215, Pentheus returns to find the women have abandoned the city and, dressed as bacchantes, Cadmus and the blind prophet Teiresias prepared to worship the new god beyond the city walls. Young Pentheus and these two old men have a debate (*agōn*) concerning whether to permit something new—a new god—into the normal life of the city. Pentheus rejects this new god as a fraud and threatens to stone him and "separate his head from his body."[28] By contrast, Teiresias extols this new god who also "shares a part" of the violence associated with the war-god Ares, and cautions the young man against thinking "political rule holds the most power in human life." Cadmus tries Pascal's wager approach by suggesting that "even if the god does not exist, as you say, you should speak a beautiful lie (*kalōs katapseudou*) and say that he is."[29] Cadmus also adds political expediency, as it would be honorable to have a son of Zeus in the royal family, and he cautions as to the fate of Pentheus's cousin Actaeon who Artemis ordered to be torn apart by hunting dogs.[30] Although Cadmus refers to the version where Actaeon boasts he was a better hunter than Artemis, in other versions Artemis kills Actaeon because he saw her bathing. Convinced the women and elderly men have some sort of disease (*nosos*), Pentheus orders the effeminate "Stranger," who is described with typical feminine traits of long flowing curly hair, to be arrested and stoned to death. This scene ends with the chorus proclaiming the power of their new god and warning that "unbridled mouths and unthinking lawlessness will end in misery."[31]

The middle section of the play (lines 435–810) focuses on the struggle between Pentheus and "the Stranger." Although the imprisoned chorus miraculously escapes, Pentheus interrogates the Stranger with a series of questions to discover his identity.[32] The disguised Dionysus is evasive concerning the form (*idea*) of the god's rites or the identity of a god who can take "whatever look he wishes." In response, the Stranger mocks Pentheus's attempt "to bind" him; instead, he replies that he "sees" Pentheus as the one "who does not know who he is."[33] After the disguised god is led away, the chorus sings an ode to stop the insolence of Pentheus, whom they compare to a Giant battling the power of the Olympians. The Stranger returns by creating apparitions that cause Pentheus to stab the air with a sword and concocting visions of an earthquake and fire burning the palace to the ground.

Meanwhile, at line 665, a messenger arrives to report on the women who continue their worship of the new god beyond the city walls. Spying on them like Actaeon watching Artemis bathe, he reports their rites were initially peaceful (and not at all sexual) but turned violent when threatened by male trespassers. Driven to frenzy, the bacchantes seize, dismember, and eat raw cattle; impervious to manmade metal weapons, they pillage nearby villages and snatch babies. Fearing more violence and personal disgrace, Pentheus is about to send troops to stop the carnage. At this ripe moment, Dionysus intervenes with an alternative: he asks, "do you wish to see the form (*idein*) of them [the women] sitting together?"[34]

From this point forward, like a theatrical director, Dionysus controls the action of the play, and Pentheus is completely under his influence.[35] Shamed, but overwhelmed by his curiosity to see the secret female *orgia*, Pentheus agrees to alter his "look" and take on the appearance of a woman. The chorus sings again: "Never should man's thoughts and actions rule over law (*nomos*)"; and what is lawful comes from the gods, from long-established tradition, and is upheld by nature. Pentheus reemerges in his new gender-reversal disguise to "see what he should not see." With this new "look," he also begins to see double: two suns in the sky, two cities of Thebes, and two versions of Dionysus—a man and a horned bull.[36] Concerned with whether he is the "image" of his aunts, Pentheus takes up Dionysus's symbolic *thyrsus* and leads the procession, like the young *ephēboi* of the Oschophoria, through the city and into the hills.[37] Dionysus declares that Pentheus will bear "the burden alone," and the young king departs with his final words: "I grasp onto what I deserve."

As Pentheus is led into the mountains, the chorus sings again: "Let justice (*dikē*) become visible" against this man who is without god or law.[38] Two messengers arrive. Cautioned against enjoying the suffering of others, the chorus still rejoices in hearing of the terrifying deeds in the wilderness.[39] After leading Pentheus to the now peaceful bacchantes, he is still unable to "to see without being seen." Dionysus bends down the top of a fir tree "like a circle of a wheel" and raises Pentheus into the air.[40] Having their rites once more invaded, the Theban women become manic and, all foaming at the mouth, their revelry again turns violent. This time, it is not cattle but Pentheus whom the Theban women stone, tear apart, and behead with their bare hands. Thinking she has killed a lion; his mother Agave impales his head on her *thyrsus* and joyfully dances with her trophy to the city.

In the final scene of the play (lines 1165–1393), Cadmus returns to Thebes with the remainder of Pentheus's body, which was strewn around the same place where Actaeon was torn apart by his dogs. In what is now often referred to as "the psychoanalysis scene," through a series of questions focusing on self-recognition, Cadmus slowly returns Agave back to her senses, and she recognizes what she has done.[41] Unfortunately, and ironically, at this point our extant text is no longer intact, and more than fifty lines of the tragedy's ending are lost: thus reflecting Pentheus, our text is "dismembered."[42] One possible ending sees Agave reassemble the parts of her son's corpse. Dionysus appears in divine glory and prophesizes a final punishment: Cadmus and his wife Harmonia will be turned into snakes that bring a great barbarian army against Greece until destroyed at Delphi. Only after this final atrocity will Ares escort them to the Isle of the Blessed. The rest of the family will also be dismembered, as Agave and her sisters will wander in exile deprived of home and city.[43] The play ended with the typical Euripidean warning that "the god finds achievement [by performing] the unexpected."[44]

EURIPIDES'S POTENTIAL INNOVATIONS

It is always difficult to establish Euripides's poetic innovations, but the *Bacchae* proves especially difficult as there were many contradictory stories concerning Dionysus. Much of the tragedy follows typical mythological patterns, such as disguised gods establishing cults (similar to Demeter at Eleusis) or offspring returning "home" to claim their birthright (i.e., Theseus or Oedipus).[45] Other thematic elements are reflective of other chapters of Dionysus's story. King Lycurgus of Thrace, for example, also denied Dionysus's divinity. To retaliate, the god drove the king into a frenzy and, mistaking his son for a vine, he chopped him into pieces.

In other versions, Lycurgus is encouraged by Hera and Ares to capture Dionysus with a net; instead, the god catches Lycurgus with a vine and lifts him spread-eagled above the ground. In another Dionysus rejection story, the daughters of King Minyas of the ancient town of Orchomenos refuse to join his *orgia*. In retribution, the god inflicted them with a mad desire for human flesh, and so they dismembered and ate one of their sons. They were eventually transformed into bats and owls. Thus, there are several elements of Euripides's version, such as divine punishment for refusing to recognize the god, capture by net, suspension on high, familial dismemberment, and metamorphoses that are similar to other events in Euripides's Dionysus story.

Although Euripides's *Bacchae* is the only extant tragedy concerning Pentheus's resistance, we know of other theatrical accounts of the god's return home to Thebes. The supposed first dramatist Thespis was reputed to have produced a *Pentheus*. We have fragments of plays entitled *Semele*, *Pentheus*, and a *Bacchae* attributed to Aeschylus. In what we know of Aeschylus's versions, Dionysus is similarly portrayed as effeminate and captured but escapes by causing an earthquake. Sophocles, as well as the playwrights Xenocles and Iophon, are also thought to have produced versions of the *Bacchae*. Despite the potential similarities, Euripides may be the origin of three important potential innovations in his myth.[46] First, it is possible that Euripides invented Pentheus's procession, unarmed and dressed as a woman, to spy on the bacchantes. Although such cross-dressing was part of the Dionysian festival of Oschophoria, other images from ancient Greek vase painting show Pentheus armed and not disguised as a female bacchante. Second, Euripides may be the first to represent Agave as responsible for Pentheus's gruesome murder: in the earliest painted representation on vase pottery of his death, from around 520 BCE, his killer is identified as "Galene." Finally, other versions do not appear to mention Cadmus or Teiresias, so it is possible that Euripides invented the abdication and included a role for these two old men. In Ovid's later Roman version, for example, Cadmus and Harmonia are turned into snakes because Cadmus wishes it, without any connection to Dionysian vengeance.[47]

Justice: Dualism and the God of Wine

In Euben's seminal work on the political theory of the *Bacchae*, he suggests that "there is no talk of justice in the *Bacchae*, expect talk that identifies it with the vengeance the *Oresteia* rejects."[48] From Euben's perspective, rather than Aeschylus's triumph of legal institutionalism over the primitive drive for vengeance, the *Bacchae* reveals how instinctive and primitive urges overwhelm such political structures.[49] By contrast, other scholars see the chorus representing the "humanity of the herd" or a mob following the demagoguery of triumphing over one's foes without reflection, pity, or understanding.[50] Yet the characters in the tragedy speak more often of justice than vengeance. The chorus refers to Pentheus's fate as a coming of "justice" (*dikē*) for an "unjust" man (*adikos*). The old King Cadmus admits to Dionysus that "we have committed an injustice (*ēdikēkamen*)."[51] Even Pentheus connects his fate to justice with his final words in the play: he "grasps what he deserves (*axiōn*)."

This statement, that Pentheus will get what he deserves, echoes the ancient view of justice as desert, merit, or what is owed. As we know from Aristotle, although there was some agreement that justice concerns merit, there is no agreement on why someone is deserving or what constitutes the proper measure they deserve.[52] The *Bacchae* further complicates the quarrels associated with justice as merit by connecting it to questions of piety. Hence, Pentheus's refusal to give what is "owed" to the god—recognition and worship—means he is not simply impious but also unjust.[53] Furthermore, Pentheus's rejection of the god reveals an additional nuance to justice as merit. His rejection is violation of the relationship between, or proper measure of, the cosmic order between man and god.[54] Thus, instead of giving a god what is owed him, Pentheus subverts this order and places human cleverness and political power above all things.[55] Finally, Pentheus's failure to recognize the god and his rejection of the proper order highlight another dispute concerning justice as merit: when it is unclear who deserves what, which authority should determine what is deserved? Since Pentheus defies the god of paradox, contradictions, and the freedom to "be what is not," Euripides's exploration of justice in this tragedy reveals that in any attempt to understand the "right measure," nothing is what it seems.

Justice: By Whose Authority?

Starting with the question of which authority should determine justice, a straightforward interpretation associates Pentheus and Dionysus with the conflict between political and religious authorities. In this case, Pentheus represents political authority, especially the tyrannical rule of a young, inexperienced king. Described as having an "unbridled tongue," Pentheus is impatient, prone to anger, and stubbornly rejects all advice or counsel.[56] Both Cadmus and Teiresias note that the young king thinks he is wiser than he really is. In addition, Pentheus's refusal to accept their advice highlights another opposition or duality in the play: age and youth. Many of Pentheus's traits, such as his irascibility, hubris, love of honor, and immoderation, reflect the typical Greek view of youth.[57] Thus, Pentheus's youth may explain his certainty about the women in the hills being sexually promiscuous and his excessive curiosity in observing the bacchantic rituals.

Yet Pentheus's rigid response to this new god cannot be simply explained by his youth and inexperience. Similar to the messenger in the *Antigone* who feared Creon, our messenger hesitates to speak frankly (*parrhēsia*): "I fear your harsh nature, lord, very much kingly and too quick to anger."[58] Although Pentheus allows the messenger to speak freely, he actually runs little risk as his message confirms what Pentheus already believes (i.e., that the women have gone wild in the hills). By contrast, Pentheus's anger is reserved for those who tell him what he does not want to hear. Like a tyrant who refuses contrary advice, he literally brushes aside, for example, the old men who caution against his imprudence. He imprisons the chorus who "fear to speak freely before the tyrant." Openly frustrated by Dionysus's evasive answers, he asserts political power that makes him *kuriōteros*—the more authoritative man. Pentheus confirms Teiresias's critique that he thinks human authority is the most important power in human life.[59]

Pentheus's desire for control also reveals his understanding of justice as an extension of his own authority. Much has been written concerning Pentheus's resistance to the "formless god" in his several attempts to bind, enclose, and (re)secure those who have escaped his orders.[60] Upon returning home, he imprisoned the bacchantes, but his main target was the Stranger whom he also attempts to "overturn," "catch in the net," and keep "penned up."[61] He does manage "to capture" the disguised god but is unable to control Dionysus, who is evasive and easily shakes off all bonds. The language Pentheus uses is significant. He talks of "catching," "binding," "enclosing," and "shutting," which reveals his preference for control, order, and, as Saxonhouse points out, "form" (*idein*).[62] This language of binding and enclosing also reveals Pentheus's self-understanding as the sole creator and enforcer of boundaries, especially the boundary between the city and what lies outside.

Although his main target is the disguised Dionysus, Pentheus also desires to capture and control the city's women who have escaped from their roles in the *oikos* to wander freely outside the polis.[63] Their activities reflect a Hesiodic "golden age" before civilization, in which human beings lived in harmony with nature.[64] Until threatened by the prying men, the women are described as living in a communion with nature that flows with milk and honey. Pentheus believes they are engaged in illicit sexual acts, but they are actually chaste and calm. Importantly, however, instead of performing their civilized role of childcare and working the loom, they now are out of their "minds," dwelling in the untamed wilderness, wearing animal skins, suckling wolf cubs and gazelles, and eating raw meat. Their worship of Dionysus is transformative; it is a literal relocation of both place and state of mind.

Pentheus's desire to capture, chain, and enclose the women and the effeminate stranger "in nets" represents encircling them spatially, mentally, and behaviorally: literally and figuratively, they would be controlled by him. They would lack freedom of thought and movement. Significantly, they would be bound by the will of the tyrant who, as Thumiger puts it, "embodies state control and the stability of mind."[65] As the political authority, Pentheus is determined to control all the boundaries that delineate order and justice in the city. And Pentheus's vision of justice remains closed: "I order all the gates of the walls to be shut, enclosing us in a circle."

In contrast to this idea of political control is Dionysus, the multifaceted god of wine, prophecy, paradox, and metamorphosis. In the prologue, he tells us his plan to reveal his godhood to a doubting Pentheus, his aunts, and the city.[66] He comes to demonstrate his divine right and authority. Thus, in the straightforward duality, he represents religion to Pentheus's politics. As noted above, his typical mythology represents him as a "new" god who arrives from some foreign elsewhere. In this version, like his cousin, he is young and "beardless." He is also described with typical feminine traits: he has long, curly strawberry blond hair and pale skin.[67] He never displays the typical male warrior virtue of violence; instead, he uses disguise and manipulation and invites cross-dressing and the communion with nature. He is emblematic of what is outside civilization and its political boundaries.[68]

If Pentheus embodies civic control, boundary making, and political justice, his cousin appears to be a negation, or reversal, of the referents of this ordering. As much as Pentheus uses the language of control in "catching," "binding," "enclosing," and "shutting," Dionysus responds with the language of "freedom," "mania," "ecstasy," "release," "escape," and "turning upside down."[69] Teiresias praises the virtue of this god of wine who, twinned with Demeter the goddess of grain, brings the gift of wine that "frees" us from pain and allows us to "forget" our troubles.[70] Also twinned with Apollo, Dionysus's prophetic power possesses with frenzy and mania. The god easily escapes Pentheus's attempts to enclose and can make those things on high, like Pentheus's palace, appear to be crashing down; at the same time, he can put those things that are grounded, like Pentheus, suspended on high. As he tells the chorus, those who attempt to enclose are doomed, as they only "think" they create boundaries but in reality do not; just as Pentheus thought he was tying up the stranger when he was really tying up a bull; or when he thought he was attacking the stranger but actually slashing at the air. Thus, despite all Pentheus's efforts to confine, control, and enclose within the walls of the city, Dionysus easily steps over or transgresses (*huperbainō*) such imagined human boundaries.

In this way, this "elusive god" of paradox, metamorphosis, or "being what is not," blurs or confounds the accepted boundaries of the civic order, including distinctions between old and young, male and female, appearance and reality, and justice and injustice.[71] He challenges the dichotomy of old and young by calling Cadmus and Teiresias to his dance. Cadmus, who was too old to rule the city, declares: "how joyful to forget our age."[72] Teiresias replies that he "too is young and eager to dance." Despite their age, they dress in the god's disguise of fawn skin and shake his *thyrsus*, a phallic symbol that emphasized the god's connection to fertility and sexuality.[73] As we know from Plato's Cephalus, the ancient Greeks thought old men were normally beyond the madness of sexual desire.[74] Importantly, Dionysus "makes no distinction between old and young" and unites everyone together in his worship. Thus, one of the first dichotomies invalidated by the god's call to worship is the blurring of the boundary of age and youth.

Importantly, it is not the confusion of old and young in Dionysus's ritual that causes Pentheus the most concern but the god's subversion of gender roles and its subsequent distorting of human and animal.[75] As noted above, the women have abandoned their traditional looms and hearths to wander freely without confinement or the supervision of men. It is only when confronted by men that their peaceful behavior turns violent.[76] They tear animals to pieces with their bare hands and, "rising like birds," snatch away children. In their violent revelry, they easily defeat armed men. This description, and the later sacrifice of Pentheus, may suggest the god transforms the women into beasts; however, his blurring of the human/animal occurs much earlier. Even while at peace, the women have the appearance of animals: they literally take on animal skins and suckle wild beasts. Thus, it is not only gender but the dichotomy of animal and human that is undermined by the women's relocation to uncivilized space outside the city walls.[77]

Significantly, when provoked, the women appear to respond not like animals but like men in battle. Describing the ferocious women, the messenger announces: "They threw their *thyrsoi* at them inflicting wounds. And then the men *ran* routed by women."[78] Such language echoes Homer's epic battles, such as the Trojan Echepolus who died with a bronze spearhead "lodged in his forehead, smashing through his skull."[79] In their mania, the women also mimic the madness of the Greek hero Ajax by ripping apart cattle with their bare hands.[80] Their frenzy in battle was predicted by Teiresias who stressed that Dionysus also shares in the violence of the war-god Ares. Thus, at first, living in harmony with nature, the women were virtually indistinguishable from animals; but when threatened by men, they come to resemble men by becoming hunters in the woods and marauders of villages.

Famously, this blurring of gender also works in reverse in what is often referred to as the "cross-dressing" scene.[81] Easily enticed by his desire to spy on the women's secret rituals (*orgia*), Pentheus agrees to disguise himself as a woman.[82] Just as the women appear animalistic because they took on the "skin" of animals, Pentheus takes on the appearance of a woman: his hair magically grows, and he is clothed in the feminine costume of a long dress and headdress. He puts on the bacchantic fawn skin and picks up the *thyrsus*. Beyond his physical appearance, Pentheus's overt male violence is transformed into feminine "self-concealment."[83] In this new state (where he begins to see double), Pentheus also takes on other stereotypical behavioral characteristics, or "performs gender," by fussing with his clothing and worrying about his appearance. He is, on all accounts, the very "image" of his female relatives.

This scene could represent Pentheus's liberation from "repressed sexuality" by revealing what was already "hidden within" him.[84] Like the women released from their "repressed rage," Pentheus's metamorphosis confirms that the god cannot transform someone into something they are not, only into something they really are. Although god's ultimate triumph occurs outside the city, Pentheus's initial metamorphosis begins with this transformation, within the city, from a tyrant into a subordinate. Thus, the tyrant, who demanded to control and restrain, is transformed into the very image of what he subjugates. Mirroring the Theban women who now act like men, the king is led as a woman beyond civic order and outside the city boundaries to his punishment for "attempting to rule with force what cannot be ruled."

Thus, at first glance, the story confirms a straightforward triumph of divine authority over human political rule. From this perspective, as "champion of permanence and stability," Pentheus is undone by the god of "excitement, formlessness, and instability."[85] All his attempts to establish order by enclosing or shutting off the city are upended by this god of freedom who undermines all boundaries: he blurs the distinction between human and animal, male and female, and old and young. From this perspective, Dionysus's victory establishes the superiority of divine justice over human hubris and ensures human beings respect the proper order of the gods. The chorus celebrates this victory over the failed belief that human beings are the center of all things: "mouths without bridles lead to misfortune . . . [and] thinking not as a mortal, leads to a short life." Importantly, Dionysus is not content with simply gaining his proper recognition; instead, in a play on words, the god brings complete grief (*penthos*) to Pentheus.[86] Pentheus's punishment begins with subjection, increases to violent dismemberment by his own mother, and ends in the annihilation of his entire House.[87] From the perspective of the god, Pentheus's punishment is merited, as he overstepped human limits and failed to give what is owed to the gods: recognition and worship. In other words, as Pentheus demanded: he does "grasp what he deserves." With the triumph of Dionysus, divine justice utterly "rips apart" the human attempt to control, bind, or define absolute boundaries.

Justice and the God of "What Is Not"

Although the play appears to support this clear opposition between Pentheus's civic authority and Dionysus's divine authority, it is unsurprising in a tragedy about the paradoxical god that this simple distinction between Pentheus (the rational or ordered) and Dionysus (the irrational and amorphous) does not hold. Instead, like Pentheus stabbing at the air, this clear demarcation is only an illusion. The first way the tragedy undermines the strict duality between competing human and divine rule is by incorporating a third vision of authority: traditional custom (*nomos*). As represented by the old men, this third way suggests justice is found neither in the rigidity of Pentheus's tyrannical dictates nor in the formlessness of the boundary blurring of Dionysus. In contrast to these extremes, the flexibility or plasticity of *nomos* allows it to incorporate the "new" yet be so ancient that it is mistaken for the natural.[88] Second, the tragedy also challenges and collapses a strict one-to-one correspondence between Pentheus as civic boundary enforcer and Dionysus as shapeless divine annihilator of boundaries. Pentheus and Dionysus are revealed not to be opposing sides of a dualism; instead, in their resemblance, the cousins and their corresponding referents of control and formlessness blur into one another.

A Third Way: Traditional Authority

The first way the tragedy undermines the straightforward triumph of divine justice is by introducing authority of tradition. Representing neither political control nor divine fluidity are the two old men: Cadmus and Teiresias. Unlike the two young men whose conflict dominates the story, these two old men perform a very small "bookend" role.[89] Cadmus and Teiresias appear together immediately following the choral *parodos*; Cadmus alone reappears at the end with the pieces of Pentheus's dismembered body. In his short role, Teiresias comes to the palace to remind Cadmus of their oath to worship the new god together; hence, unlike the women who worship "whether they want to or not," the old men consent to incorporate this new god into the city's long-established divine rituals. Thus, although Pentheus is "sightless" in his inability "to recognize" this new god, the old, blind Teiresias "can see."[90] This is the first clue that tradition and custom have insights lacking in strict political authority.

Teiresias represents this customary or traditional view of justice with an eye to the limitations of human understanding concerning questions of justice. First, Teiresias stresses that "no rational argument or cleverness (*sophon*) invented by the highest thinkers can overthrow traditions (*paradochas*) of our fathers, founded and equal in age with time."[91] Teiresias emphasizes that tradition honors the gods and avoids Pentheus's error of thinking that "human authority (*kratos*) holds power over human beings." *Nomos* or the tradition of custom and law, in this case, is opposed to dependence on individualistic rational analysis and clever speech.⁹² Instead, represented by prophet Teiresias himself, age-old tradition emphasizes a different kind of flexible wisdom found in foresight or prudence. Cadmus also identifies Pentheus's rejection of the god as a rejection of tradition: "Make your home with us," he advises his grandson, "do not stand outside the walls of custom (*nomos*)." This traditional *nomos* does not set up human justice in opposition to divine authority but is able to recognize the new divinity and the limitations of political power and human understanding.

In addition, the flexibility of *nomos* is highlighted in its ability to hold the tension between antiquity and novelty. On the one hand, as Teiresias notes, traditional opinions and customs are "equal in age with time."⁹³ The chorus makes a similar point: "That which has been customary (*nomimon*) for such a long time is nourished by nature." Yet, on the other hand, this particular cult of Dionysus and the god himself is called "new" (*neos*).⁹⁴ In the timeline of the play, Dionysus's rites have not yet been nourished by age, and all rites take place in the mountains "outside the limits of the city." What is traditional custom or "equal in age with time" is in the paradoxical position of simultaneously being "new." Thus, reflecting the paradoxical god himself, linear time is destabilized or undermined by this "old-new" *nomos*. What this indicates, as Dionysus himself points out, is that "customs or laws (*nomos*) are variable." Custom is powerful because it is plastic enough to incorporate what was "outside the walls" and bring it "inside" the city as if it were always there. This powerful flexibility appears valid, even if the motives for incorporating new traditions might appear suspect: neither Cadmus (who suggests honoring the new god is a good political move) nor Teiresias (who finds rational explanations for Dionysus's miraculous birth) appear genuinely committed to this new divinity. Nevertheless, in contrast to Pentheus's unyielding political opposition, the longevity of custom may be its potential for accommodation, even if in doing so it requires "beautiful lies."⁹⁵

PENTHEUSIAN DIONYSUS OR DIONYSIAN PENTHEUS?

The strict dichotomy or opposition between political and divine authority also collapses in the identification of Pentheus with control and boundary making and Dionysus with the formless undermining of boundaries. As noted above, Pentheus understands his authority as that which defines, encloses, and controls by closing the city off from what is "outside."

Unlike his grandfather or the *nomos* of tradition, Pentheus is inflexible in his enforcement and delineation of boundaries. Pentheus is certain that the city's women should behave like proper Greek women and return to their looms and life under male domination.[96] His belief in the self-sufficiency of human reason is never shaken, even in the face of conflicting evidence; he maintains, for instance, his belief that Dionysus *orgia* is sexual despite accounts to the contrary. Reflecting Protagoras's famous statement that "man is the measure of all things," Pentheus's assertion of human cleverness ignores the proper order between man and god.[97] Thus, even though Pentheus appears to be the enforcer of order and boundaries, he simultaneously undermines another dualism: human and divine. By the end of the tragedy, his attempt to enclose the city and enforce human judgment ultimately fails as Dionysus destabilizes not only Pentheus's authority but his very being.

Significantly, as much as Pentheus's actions simultaneously demand and undermine boundaries, the formless and disordered Dionysus similarly works to enforce order. Dionysus has come to Thebes, he tells us in the prologue, to establish or "erect all things properly."[98] What is not "proper" in Thebes is the denial of his divinity. His order destroys civic control and can reverse the expected course of nature as the ground can sprout milk and women can be immune to metal weapons. Yet, Dionysus's disorder is actually his order: his rites, once established, collapse the typical dichotomies of male and female, old and young, human and animal; but in doing so, he "erects" the proper order between god and man.[99] Reflecting Pentheus, he captures and controls those who try to step beyond his order; Dionysus controls the women by driving them into madness on the hillside. In addition, like Apollo with whom he shares Delphi, Dionysus knows the future: all that has occurred, he tells Cadmus at the end of the tragedy, was "foretold long ago by his father Zeus." Such prophecy underscores that in his "disordering," all things occurred exactly as they must. Thus, the disordered new god returns to Greece to erect a preordained new order of formlessness, which ultimately seeks to enforce the most ancient of all ordering: the proper order of man and god.

The reversal of the polarity or blurring of the boundaries between these two characters reveals that Dionysus and Pentheus are not in opposition but, as each cousin blurs into his opposite, they become the other's "double." After Pentheus's metamorphosis, he also begins to see double: two suns, two cities of Seven-gated Thebes, and Dionysus as a man and a bull.[100] Scholars have long noted the use of "doubles" in ancient mythology and Greek tragedy.[101] In his seminal work, for example, René Girard views Pentheus's dismemberment as a sacrificial scapegoat, which is necessary to end repetitions of violence and establish civilization.[102] Euripides makes liberal use of the double in other tragedies, such as his *Ion*, to collapse things that appear to be two into "one" or "the same."[103] In this tragedy, this collapse occurs by mirroring Dionysus and Pentheus: although appearing opposite, they reflect the other in their simultaneous establishing and undermining of order. The blurring of Dionysus and Pentheus into "one" is also reproduced in Dionysus's violent victory over Pentheus. The stoning and beheading of Pentheus replicate the exact same threats he issued at Dionysus. If Pentheus had been victorious, the sacrifice would have been identical: the victim is interchangeable.[104]

Another such blurred distinction also challenges equating the opposition of a rational Pentheus with an irrational Dionysus.[105] Again, rather than a strict dichotomy, Pentheus's claim to rational cleverness is undermined by his emotional desire to spy on the women; and, although Dionysus stings his followers into emotional revelry, he is unemotional or "profoundly serious" throughout the story.[106] Even after his complete victory, he remains unmoved by Cadmus's appeal to pity.[107] Both characters also appear equally rigid and excessive in their claims to authority. Both are equally unbending in their certitude of judgment: as Nikolopoulou puts it, the tragedy is "less a struggle of right versus wrong than a struggle of right versus right or maybe even more aptly wrong versus wrong."[108] In their "sameness" or equality, the strict opposition between Dionysus and Pentheus, order and formlessness, reason and emotion, religious and political authority, male and female, or any other such dichotomies completely collapses. With this collapse, so too goes the straightforward interpretation of a conflict between dualistic forces or the victory of divine justice over human hubris.

Justice: Dialectics and Mutilated Endings

If this collapse of opposing forces undermines divine justice, it is not clear what to make of the *Bacchae*'s particularly violent ending.[109] Even though most (but not all) Greek tragedies end with some kind of horrible suffering, the *Bacchae* is overtly gruesome. Cadmus returns with the pieces of his grandson's body and reports his "endless searching . . . since no piece was found together on the same ground."[110] On stage, Agave is slowly brought back to herself to "see" that it is her son's head that she joyously impaled. In contrast to this horror, Dionysus reveals himself in all his divine glory and proclaims his final revelation: the entire House of the great Cadmus will be scattered, like Pentheus's body, with none living on the same ground. The terrible spectacle of Dionysus shining in his victory contrasted with the bloodied ground of Thebes seems only to reveal one final twinning in the "inexorable interdependence of the cruelty and the beauty."[111]

The meaning behind the triumph of this formless god, who is as "tragic as human existence," remains obscure.[112] Did Pentheus really get what he deserved?[113] As noted previously, to get what one deserves requires a judgment of proper "measure." In the logic of the play, Cadmus agrees that Pentheus was wrong, but he suggests the god punished "too harshly."[114] In other words, the punishment did not fit the crime. By contrast, however, Pentheus's punishment could be a proper balance because he received exactly what he threatened. Or the punishment could be just if Dionysus is understood as punishing a vicious tyrant. These options raise the important question: how do we determine what is deserved if this formless god undermines the boundaries that allow us to compare, measure, or balance? Furthermore, even if Pentheus had grasped what he deserved, was the punishment of scattering the entire House of Cadmus just? In the prologue, Dionysus revealed his purpose to be recognized as a god; however, even though he achieves this goal, it is not enough. Even though Cadmus and his aunts danced in the hills, they are all dispersed, as they "understood the god too late." Yet how does one recognize an amorphous god who reveals himself "in whatever look he wishes" and ensures we see only what he reveals? Furthermore, as Saxonhouse asks, what does it even mean that Dionysus revealed himself "when he has no form to reveal?"[115]

This type of questioning raises the possibility that we cannot know or see the boundaries between things. Such incapacity to make distinctions until too late could suggest a proto-nihilist interpretation of the tragedy: in this case, because human reason is insufficient and divine law is unknowable until it is "too late," human beings are ultimately unable to distinguish between the just and unjust. Yet this nihilistic reading reintroduces a new dualism: either questions of justice are determined by knowable fixed boundaries, or without such secure knowledge, there is no justice.[116] Since the formless god asserts order and the ordered tyrant is disordered, this opposition between knowable justice and moral relativism seems equally unstable. Hence, it seems too simplistic to flatten the tragedy's message to one saying there is no justice, only power.

Importantly, Euripides may provide a clue to the question of justice in a world without knowable, firm boundaries. Throughout the tragedy, there has been an excess of the language of "seeing," "looking," "recognizing," and "understanding." Dionysus demands recognition. Pentheus wants "to look on" the women's rituals; in the "look" of a woman, he sees double: he is "seen" on high in the treetops. Horrifically, Agave comes to "see" the impaled head as that of her son.[117] In addition, it should not be forgotten that all of this took place in the theater—the *theatron* or "seeing place."[118] Instead of focusing on the question of "what is justice?" the tragedy can be seen as turning our eyes to the question of "how?" How, in our world in which human reason is always limited and divine justice is not perfectly knowable, do we come to "see" or recognize justice?

From this perspective, the story of Pentheus and Dionysus symbolizes the experience of thinking about justice. As the philosophers—those clever thinkers of Teiresias—would point out, this involves a process of identifying what distinguishes one thing from another. What distinguishes a god from a human being, a human being from an animal, or a man from a woman? The Greeks called this process of distinguishing one thing from another "dialectics." Understood as part of a conversation or discussion, dialectic literally means "a picking apart of one thing from another."[119] What happens to Pentheus is symbolic of the human experience of dialectics as seeing, recognizing, or understanding: he begins the process with denial and resistance but then, inexplicably, is seduced by a deep curiosity to "see." He feels shame at taking on a new way of looking. He begins to see "the double" or that what appears to be one thing is really more than one: he sees, for example, Dionysus appearing both human and animal.[120] One way we come to know is by moving beyond appearances, to recognize what something "is" by distinguishing it from what it "is not."[121] For the Greeks, to know (*oida*) is connected etymologically and logically to the "look" (*eikos*) and the "form" (*idea*). This dialectical experience turns inward with questions that require self-examination, such as "who am I," "what is the difference between human and animal," or "what is justice?"[122] Thus, Pentheus's dismemberment is symbolic of the dialectical experience of understanding, which is itself a kind of dismemberment or a taking apart of one's ideas, one's assumptions, and oneself.

Significantly, the mutilated ending may have portrayed Agave attempting to reassemble the pieces of her son to make him whole. This (possible) reassembly may also symbolize the potential risks inherent in the human experience of questioning or taking apart, distinguishing, and understanding.[123] First, there is a potential danger to the questioner. Led by his desire to "see," Pentheus is destroyed as he comes to understand the reality of the limits of human authority too late. Second, there is a danger to the political community as the ruling family is also dismembered and dispersed; as Euben points out, the city is no longer a place of "diversity within unity" but is fragmented like Pentheus.[124] Importantly, unlike similar stories of Dionysus, who is also dismembered, Pentheus cannot be miraculously reassembled. Like us, Agave lacks the divine knowledge of Demeter.[125] In other words, the dialectical questioning of "picking out one thing from another," reflects what happens to Pentheus and Thebes: it is a disintegration that cannot be put back together. Finally, despite the risks of permanent fragmentation, the tragedy also reveals that the search for understanding does not end in certain knowledge of what distinguishes one thing from another. Human investigations into what something "is" may allow us to "see" parts but not necessarily the whole.[126]

Thus, one lesson of this tragedy is its warning that experience of investigating what something "is," like justice and injustice, is not easy nor ever definitively resolved. To define requires that we know something's "fines" or literally the boundaries of where something begins and ends.[127] If the play is a warning that we cannot definitively know boundaries, the best we may be able to do is follow the "beautiful lie" of Cadmus. We may not always believe what our tradition says is "just," but sometimes we "dance" anyway.[128] Importantly, as Cadmus was also destroyed, the tragedy also reveals that we cannot dance with pretense all the time. To do so would mean denying the desire of seeking knowledge, even if partial, of the important questions at the heart of what it means to be human. It would mean failing to challenge the claims to truth of any authority be it political, religious, or traditional. It would mean there can be no experience of revelation, no metamorphosis, and no transformation of self or of politics.[129] At a minimum, Pentheus's suffering is a warning that we ought to tread carefully in questioning the meaning of things or in taking apart "beautiful lies." It is easier to transgress boundaries and venture outside the meanings established by our city than it is to "cross-back" and return to the commonly held distinctions that make judgment possible.[130]

Conclusion

Whatever we make of Dionysus's triumph, it challenges Pentheus's view that man is the measure of all things or that we can be certain of divine dictates that are often understood too late. Despite this seeming hopelessness, one of Euripides's last tragedy hints at important aspects of justice that remain relevant to our own attempts to distinguish the just from the unjust. First, Euripides reveals an important mediating role for custom or tradition. Since tradition is flexible enough to incorporate what is new while remaining ancient, it avoids the excesses of both Pentheus's rigid certitude and Dionysus's formlessness. Although currently very unpopular in much contemporary discourse on justice, the importance of tradition is reflected in the history of political thought. In Burke's *Reflections on the Revolution in France*, for example, the respect for tradition stands in contrast to the "clan of enlightened men . . . who have a very full measure of confidence in their own [wisdom]" to enforce something new.[131] Burke's understanding reflects the blurred Dionysus-Pentheus, as such "enlightened men" of the French Revolution combine Pentheus's tyrannical impulses and Dionysus's destructive creativity. More recently, Oakeshott echoes the importance of tradition found in the *Bacchae*. He suggests that tradition has no changeless center or model that can be followed; instead, it contains the potential of continuity with an authority "diffused between past, present, and future" in which "everything is temporary, but nothing is arbitrary."[132]

In the end, the story of the cousins may be symbolic not only of the perilous experience of asking important questions but also of living with the partiality of our provisional answers. If Euripides is indicating that human beings will not hold a definite understanding of justice, then he is suggesting some kind of pluralism. Importantly, Euripides's vision is not a kind of relativistic pluralism in which all competing claims to justice are equally valid. Certainly, Pentheus as representative of the view that man is the measure of all things is utterly dismantled. Instead, Euripides seems to suggest a kind of pluralism personified by Cadmus's metamorphosis into a snake at the end of the play. Unlike the unbending Pentheus, whatever justice is in the *Bacchae*, it appears flexible and coiled.[133] It is an understanding of justice in which the Phoenician Cadmus is fated to mix into Greece more new barbarian things, comparable to his introduction of written language.

This approach to justice exposes and ultimately breaks those, like Pentheus, who are rigid in their views. Importantly, it is a kind of pluralism that requires recognizing boundaries. As Seligman and Weller describe it, "Boundaries delineate an entity, defining it, giving it a place from which we can access its relation to other entities . . . we cannot measure or balance anything, let alone justice, without boundaries."[134] Finally, it is a kind of pluralism that reminds us that Dionysus is the god of wine, which as Teiresias noted early in the play, brings a "sweet forgetting."[135] Thus, in our pursuit of truth, or, in Greek, *alētheia* (which literally means an "unforgetting"), we should not expect a straight and uncoiled path either. Maybe in our pursuit of what justice might mean, once in a while we are supposed to disengage from this potentially overwhelming experience of "seeing" and "knowing," since "humans cannot attend continuously."[136] For this the god is crucial: we need only to remember to have a glass of wine.

Chapter 3

The *Phoenician Women*

Justice is Multicolored

> If everyone brought forth the same thing
> Concerning the beautiful and wisdom,
> There would be no debate or strife among human beings.
> As it is, except in the names,
> Such things are not the same nor equal for mortals;
> But, action is not like this.[1]

Although titled the *Phoenician Women*, this tragedy is a Theban story. It focuses on the final chapter of the tragedy of Oedipus as his two sons go to war in the famous Battle of the Seven against Thebes. The plot is so complicated, as Wyckoff notes, it covers "more stages of the Oedipus legend than one would have thought a single play could hold."[2] In antiquity it was so popular it followed the *Iliad* in status, and Byzantine scholars selected it (along with the *Hecuba* and *Orestes*) for special study.[3] Despite this status, as early as Aristophanes's *Frogs*, the play's poetic style was parodied and medieval *hypotheseis* criticized its "highly emotional" style and found it "overstuffed" (*paraplērōmatikon*).[4] Nineteenth-century classicists considered it to be an exemplar of Euripides's destruction of the grandeur of Greek tragedy.[5] Even in the twentieth century, the play has been disparaged as "cluttered and confused," without "single artistic conception," or "pageantry . . . devoid of tragic coloring."[6] Complicating current interpretation, our extant texts are corrupted with several suspect passages, including the *teichoskopia* (scene from the walls) and *exodos*, thought to be later interpolations.⁷ It is no wonder that Sophocles's version of this famous family is more popular with our contemporary audiences.⁸

In contrast to such critiques, other scholars find Euripides's dense plot and multiple characterizations as central to his art. Mastronarde, for example, argues that the play's open form presents "a complex but well-organized dramatic structure" that brings together simultaneous themes, such as political duty, loyalty, and the limitation of human wisdom.⁹ Ringer suggests it concurrently "pushes innovation with the upholding of tradition to the point of no return."¹⁰ Podlecki sees several themes coalescing, such as the joyless dance of darkness and light, which center on the chorus.¹¹ Other interpretations locate the main theme in the role of exile or in the city's hub-and-spoke relationship to its various human associations.¹² Adopting this approach of appreciating the importance of the play's complicated plot and numerous characters, this chapter focuses on Euripides's dramatization of competing, contradictory, excessive, and often irresolvable perspectives on justice. Reflecting the complexity of his multifaceted story, Euripides exposes both our inability to see the variegated form of justice as well as the potentially fatal consequences of failing to recognize our own inadequate and limited understanding.

Although the first production of the *Phoenician Women* (in Greek *Phoinissai* or Latin *Phoenissae*) is unknown, many factors point to a date late in Euripides's career.¹³ Several elements, such as metrical analysis, the play's length, and number of characters, echo later tragedies such as *Helen* (produced in 412 BCE) and *Iphigenia among the Taurians* (between 414–412 BCE). Other evidence suggests a date closer to his death in 407 BCE: *scholia* from Aristophanes's *Frogs* (performed in 405 BCE) question why Aristophanes refers to Euripides's *Andromeda* (produced in 412 BCE) rather than a more recent play like the *Phoenician Woman*. A fragment from the *hypothesis* of Aristophanes of Byzantium (the Grammarian) names the other two plays in this trilogy as *Oinomaos* and *Chrysippos*. Although this might indicate a unifying theme of curses, this reference is unreliable as it attributes the play to an unknown Archon named Nausikrates.¹⁴ Most scholars date the first performance as sometime between 411 and 409 BCE. This puts the date of the first production about a war among brothers roughly to the period of violence and upheaval of the Athenian oligarchic crisis of 411 BCE.

The Mythological Context and Plot of the *Phoenician Women*

Background Myth

Euripides's *Phoenician Women* retells the notorious story of the cursed royal family of Thebes.[15] So dominant is the Theban myth that almost 20 percent of extant plays deal with the story of Oedipus and his children.[16] As is often the case, this story really begins when Zeus takes an interest in the Phoenician princess Europa and, in the form of a white bull, carries her off to Crete. Sent by his father to retrieve his sister, Cadmus travels to Greece but is redirected by Apollo to establish a city where a sacred cow comes to rest. She stops at a spring guarded by the dragon son of Ares. Cadmus kills this dragon and plants its teeth in the ground, from which emerge the fully armed Sown Men (Spartoi), who immediately attack each other: only five survive this initial battle to establish the noble families of Thebes. In our play, Jocasta and her brother Creon (and his family) are the last surviving full-blooded descendants of these autochthonous founders.[17]

As penance for killing his dragon son, Cadmus was forced to serve Ares. In most versions, his service is so exceptional that he is given Harmonia (Ares's daughter with Aphrodite) as his wife.[18] They have five children: Semele (the mother of Dionysus), Agave (the mother of Pentheus whose story is told in the *Bacchae*), Autonoë, Ino (who figures in the backstory of the *Medea*), and Polydorus. At this point, there are many variations (such as the *Bacchae*'s skipping a generation with Pentheus succeeding Cadmus), but usually Polydorus succeeds his father and begets Labdacus, who in turn begets Laius.[19] When his throne is usurped, Laius finds refuge with Pelops in the southern Peloponnese. He violates this hospitality by raping Pelops's son Chrysippus; the angry father curses Laius's line, establishing another source of familial affliction.

Returning to Thebes, Laius regains his throne and marries Jocasta (or Epicaste), a descendant of the Spartoi, but a prophecy warns that his son is fated to kill his father (and marry his mother).[20] For a while he abstains from his wife, until one drunken night results in Oedipus. Laius pierces the ankles of the baby and exposes him on Mount Cithaeron. The baby is saved and given to King Polybus of Corinth. In Sophocles's version, after learning his fate but unaware he is adopted, Oedipus leaves Corinth.[21] On the road to Delphi, in the first recorded act of road rage, Oedipus kills Laius, whom he thinks is an old man trying to force him off the road. Making his way to Thebes, Oedipus solves the Sphinx's riddle and, in reward, receives the kingdom and widowed Jocasta as wife.[22]

From here on, versions vary widely.[23] In the *Odyssey*, the marriage is short lived and childless: they quickly discover the incest, and Jocasta kills herself.[24] In the *Iliad*, Oedipus is not blinded but dies honorably in battle. In other accounts, after Jocasta commits suicide, Oedipus remarries Eurygania, the mother of his warring sons. By contrast, in Sophocles's *Oedipus the King*, before discovering the truth he and Jocasta have four children: Eteocles, Polynices, Antigone, and Ismene. In that play, Jocasta commits suicide, and the self-blinded Oedipus begs for exile.[25] In other accounts, Oedipus does not blind himself but is blinded by the servants of Laius. In Sophocles's *Oedipus at Colonus*, after wandering for many years in exile with his daughter Antigone, Oedipus finds refuge and is buried on Athenian soil.

The story of what happens to their children also varies, but Polynices's siege of Thebes was second only to Troy in mythological importance.[26] Aeschylus's *Seven against Thebes* is the first version that openly suggests the children were born of incest and Aeschylus probably innovated the strategy of seven champions defending seven gates.[27] This play also presents Eteocles as undoubtedly the more noble son and Polynices as clearly in the wrong.[28] Euripides echoes this view in his *Suppliant Women*, as Theseus concludes the Argives unjustly allied with Polynices.[29] Typically, the battle of the Seven against Thebes is a fulfillment of a curse (either the general curse on the House of Thebes or, as in this play, because Oedipus cursed his own sons) and the brothers kill each other in combat.[30] Their uncle Creon assumes power and decrees that the corpses of Polynices and his Argive allies remain unburied.[31] In Sophocles's *Antigone*, their sister's defiance culminates in the suicides of Eurydice, Haemon, and Antigone.[32] Euripides's *Suppliant Women* recounts the Athenian involvement in retrieving the bodies of the Argive generals and ends with the prophecy that their sons (the *Epigoni*) return to destroy Thebes.

EURIPIDES'S *PHOENICIAN WOMEN*

Euripides's cast includes most of the usual suspects: Jocasta, Oedipus, three of their children (Antigone, Polynices, and Eteocles), Jocasta's brother

Creon, and the blind prophet Teiresias.[33] As Jocasta and Oedipus are both still alive in this version, they are older, and Oedipus is described as frail and elderly.[34] The play is divided roughly into six episodes interposed with six choral odes that coalesce around the brothers' mutual slaughter. The setting is the royal palace at Thebes with one exit leading to the city gates and the other to the city interior.[35] Euripides also includes several exciting visual effects, such as exotic foreign costumes, multiple stage props such as swords, many extras including dead corpses, and possibly the spectacle of the tutor and Antigone on stage scaling a ladder onto the *skēnē* roof.[36]

The play opens with the matriarch Jocasta's *monody* (lines 1–90) tracing the story back to the founding by the Phoenician Cadmus then to the more recent events of Oedipus's rule: the drunken conception and exposure to avoid prophesied patricide (with no mention of incest); his salvation in Corinth; the murder of the old man at the crossroads to Delphi; and his marriage to his mother (unknowingly) as reward for triumph over the Sphinx.[37] Upon learning the truth, Oedipus blinded himself but was locked up by his sons; in return, he cursed them to mutual self-destruction. To avoid this fate, the brothers agreed to share power by exchanging rule and exile in alternating years; however, after the first year, when it was Eteocles's turn to relinquish power, he refused. The current situation is imminent war: Polynices has returned with his powerful Argive allies to lay siege to the city. Jocasta has brokered a parley between her quarreling sons and exits to prepare for Polynices's arrival.

Although the audience must have expected the choral *parodos* or the meeting between Oedipus's sons, the second episode (lines 90–205) is an encounter between Antigone and her tutor.[38] This scene is called the *teichoskopia* ("the viewing from the walls") because it mirrors the *Iliad* passage where, standing on the walls of Troy, Helen identifies the Greek heroes to Priam. In this case, the identification is in reverse, with the old tutor helping Antigone identify the seven Argive warriors.[39] The tutor helps her recognize Polynices, whom she cannot see clearly and only identifies as a glittering "shape" reflecting the sun. As the tutor sees foreign women of the chorus approaching, he advises Antigone to return to her proper place indoors.

At line 203, the chorus finally makes its *parodos*. The young Phoenician women were on their way to serve as attendants in Delphi when they stopped to visit their extended kin in Thebes. Now stranded in the siege, their song traces their (and Cadmus's) journey from Phoenicia to the beauty of the precinct of Delphi. Stressing their shared kinship misfortune, they take sides by declaring that Polynices's "war is not unjust." Polynices arrives in the third episode (lines 261–637), which builds from a discussion with his mother to the infamous truce-conference with Eteocles. Fearful of a trap, Polynices laments exile as friendless suffering, without the advantage of noble birth, citizenship, or freedom to speak frankly (*parrhēsia*); forced by necessity to marry a foreigner, he blames his brother's injustice for the siege on the city.[40] In response, Eteocles dismisses his brother's claim to justice as meaningless talk; instead, since tyranny is "the greatest gift of the gods," he will not give up power. Jocasta chastises them both: Eteocles for failing to see the advantage of equality and lawfulness and Polynices for his willingness to enslave his own city in pursuit of justice.[41] The parley breaks down into insults. War will not be avoided.

The second choral ode (lines 635–690) retraces Cadmus's steps in founding the city to the murder of Ares's dragon son and the Sown Men's mutual slaughter. By bringing the past into the present, their song is a reminder that the violence of Thebes's founding survives in the present anxious circumstances. In the next episode, Creon appears for a debate on military strategy with Eteocles (690–785). Unlike Aeschylus's strategic leader, our Eteocles suggests several rash or ignoble stratagems: immediate confrontation, ambushing the Argives by night, or attacking at dinner.[42] Creon wisely cautions Eteocles that he must "share joint command, because one man cannot see all things." And Creon, not Eteocles, proposes the famous strategy of seven generals defending seven gates. This episode ends with Eteocles agreeing to the strategy and usurping his father's rights by arranging his sister's marriage to Creon's son Haemon.[43] He departs with the command that whatever happens, Polynices should never be buried on Theban ground.

The third choral ode (784–830) repeats the layers of curses on the House of Thebes: Ares's curse on its violent founding; the curse on Atreus and his son; the curse of the Sphinx; and Oedipus's curse that results in the brothers' war. Guided by his daughter and Creon's son Menoeceus, the blind prophet Teiresias enters the stage (lines 850–1015). Fresh from helping the Athenians defeat Eumolpus, the prophet tells Creon that the best action is to banish Oedipus's sons; however, he admits a second "redeeming medicine" is the blood sacrifice of a pure Spartoi descendant as compensation for the death of Ares's dragon son.[44] As it turns out, the only pure-blooded virgin candidate in this line is Menoeceus.[45] Although Creon refuses to save his city by sacrificing his youngest son, the young man only pretends to obey. Rejecting exile and cowardice, Menoeceus chooses to sacrifice his own life to save his city.

After repeating the layered curses of the House of Thebes, the fourth choral ode focuses on the Sphinx as the harbinger of Oedipus's doom (lines 1015–1065). They are also amazed at Menoeceus's willing sacrifice. Highlighting the darkness of Thebes's salvation, their song emphasizes that each moment of joy or hope calls forth a new doom. The first messenger arrives (lines 1065–1285) and narrates the offstage violence to Jocasta. Beginning with Menoeceus's plunge from the battlements, the messenger's description mirrors the carnage of the *Iliad*: shining like "the rising and setting of stars," armor clashed with armor, the ground covered with "bloodied cheeks" of shattered skulls, and Zeus's holy fire rained down on the Argive Capaneus. The seven gates hold, but the brothers have agreed to stand in a single "winner-take-all" combat. Panicking, Jocasta calls Antigone from the safety of her maiden room, and the two rush to prevent the brothers' mutual destruction.

Finally abandoning the past and their passive role as witnesses, the chorus sings briefly (lines 1280–1330) about the savagery of the brothers, and they report the impending duel to the grieving Creon. In the second messenger scene (1330–1479), Creon receives the full report that like "wild boars" the brothers matched each other blow for blow.[46] Using a Thracian trick, Eteocles finally got the upper hand and stabbed his brother; yet, as he prematurely began to strip his armor, Polynices rose to kill him. Thus, the brothers finally divided equally the land of Thebes: each dying with "a mouthful of its soil." Seeing this fresh doom, Jocasta fell upon her son's sword.[47] As the mutual slaughter left no clear victor, battle erupted again. Since the Thebans sneakily kept their armor nearby during the truce, they had the advantage over the Argives and were ultimately victorious.[48]

In the final (and textually disputed) episode (1480–1765), Antigone returns with her dead.[49] Echoing her own summoning from inside the House, she calls Oedipus forth to tell him of the fate of his sons and mother/wife.[50] Arriving on stage, Creon asserts his new authority given "as dowry for Antigone" with three decrees. First, claiming to follow Teiresias's prophecy to rid the city of pollution, he exiles the blind Oedipus; second, he confirms Eteocles's order that Polynices remain unburied beyond the city borders; finally, he orders Antigone to return to maiden seclusion to prepare for her marriage to Haemon. A now defiant Antigone refuses: she insists she will bury Polynices as Creon's decree is "a justice which is not lawful." In addition, she threatens to kill Haemon on their wedding night and chooses, despite Oedipus's protest, to join her father in exile.[51] Creon dismisses her as "noble but foolish." The play ends with the seemingly contradictory finale in which father and daughter depart, even while Antigone vows to remain and die burying her brother.[52]

Euripides's Potential Innovations

Since modern readers are more familiar with Sophocles's or Aeschylus's version of events, Euripides's tragedy has several startling portrayals and sequences of plot.[53] Such differences may have been less startling to his first audience who were familiar with now lost tragedies and epic poems, such as the *Oedipodea* and *Thebaid*. With such diverse mythological variations, it is difficult to assess whether Euripides is innovative or is merely reflecting these lost sources. In our extant versions, for example, Jocasta typically commits suicide immediately after the discovery of incest: however, in a fifth-century poem attributed to Stesichorus, she is alive and mediates a parley between her sons.[54] Similarly, the fact that Oedipus is in Thebes during the epic battle and curses his sons reflects what is known from the *Thebaid*. Other surprising elements, such as the *teichoskopia* and the lengthy messenger reports of blood-soaked battles, are not genuine innovations but are familiar scenes from epic poetry.

Yet despite the lack of firm evidence, Euripides appears to have made three important innovations. First, his chorus of young Phoenician women, who lend their name to the title, is unique to this story of the House of Thebes.[55] As remote kin, however, the chorus symbolizes (and in their odes constantly reinforces) the foreign contribution and past crimes that will require the sacrifice of Menoeceus. Secondly, although Sophocles refers to a dead son of Creon named Megareus, Euripides most likely invented the character of Menoeceus (who assumes the name of his paternal grandfather) and the plot device of his voluntary sacrifice to save the city.[56] Finally, Euripides appears to offer a unique twist on the brothers' quarrel. Although the political strife and their fate of mutual slaughter are typical, in other versions Eteocles has the stronger claim to rule: Polynices voluntarily agrees to take his inheritance in property and leave; or Eteocles wins the right to rule after they agree to determine who rules by democratic lot.[57] In this play, however, the brothers swear a mutual oath to exchange rule and exile annually, and Eteocles breaks his word.

This last innovation also modifies the characterization of the two brothers.[58] The typically heroic Eteocles now is an oath breaker who openly rejects justice and embraces tyranny. In his exchange with Creon, Eteocles also reveals poor military judgment and usurps his father's rights. In contrast, the wild and ruthless Polynices is brought on stage and given the opportunity to present the justice of his cause, which is supported by the chorus and his mother. Thus, Euripides once again confounds the expected characterization of these well-known heroes: Polynices (whose name means "all-strife") has sympathy and justice on his side; and Eteocles (whose name is "truly glorious") is an imprudent tyrant.[59] This altering of sympathy for characters also extends to Jocasta and Oedipus. In Jocasta's retelling of the Delphic prophecy, Apollo mentions only Oedipus's murder of his father but nothing about marrying his mother.[60] Thus, the unfortunate couple has diminished culpability, as they are ignorant of any potential problem of Oedipus marrying a woman old enough to be his mother. Whatever justice will be in this play, it will be neither expected nor straightforward.

The Justice *Agōn*: When Being Right Is Not Enough

The tragedy's most obvious presentation of the question of justice is found in the parley debate (*agōn*) between Eteocles and Polynices. Although Euripides is infamous for his generous use of debates that mimic formal political speech and appear superfluous to the plot, this debate is atypical; first, Jocasta is not the arbitrator of the case ("one of the gods," she tells us, "ought to judge") but offers a rare third position.[61] In addition, although logically the battle could have taken place (and in other versions does) without this parley, the debate reveals the inner thinking of the protagonists. Finally, Euripides also uses the opportunity to explore intellectual debates of classical Athens, including ideas of justice as merit, sophistic accounts of relativism, and justice as equality and moderation. Importantly, the *agōn* highlights how conflicting views of justice converge on questions of self-interest as well as the potential consequences of refusing to recognize opposing opinions of the just cause.

Polynices opens the debate with the typical flourish of Athenian forensic speech. "Speech about the truth," he says, "is singular (*aplous*), and it is unnecessary to provide elaborate (literally, multicolored: *poikilōn*) explanations, for it holds the proper measure (*kairos*)."[62] Thus, rejecting the "clever medicines" required of unjust speech, Polynices's case is based on two typical ancient Greek understandings of justice: keeping oaths and right measure or merit. First, like Medea, Polynices stresses the injustice of Eteocles's broken oath.[63] Due to their shared interest ("his and mine") in escaping their father's curse, he tells us: they agreed and "swore by the gods" to exchange rule and exile yearly. Polynices does not mention to which gods they swore, but keeping oaths was an important ethical obligation protected by Zeus Horkios.[64] As Eteocles broke his oath, Polynices's exile is unjust; he suffers in poverty and ignoble reliance on foreigners. In addition, as he told his mother earlier, exile is "the greatest suffering" because one cannot speak frankly (*parrhēsia*) and must abide the ignorance (*amathia*) of those who rule. Thus, Polynices stresses the ability to speak openly (or as we might now say: speak truth to power) limits tyranny and poor decision making.[65]

Second, Polynices argues a claim of justice as merit. Justice as merit was a contested idea in ancient Greece but often referred to a judgment or assessment of what another deserves or is owed. It can, as in the case of the *Children of Heracles*, be conflated with the obligation of helping friends (i.e., a friend merits what is good and an enemy what is bad); or, as in the *Hecuba*, merit can be based on a judgment of character or actions.[66] In this case, Polynices's claim to merit is connected to his claim of equality: he merits or is owed his equal portion of the inheritance. Hence, Polynices demands "his turn to rule (*meros archein*)," "his equal measure (*ton ison chronon*)," "my own (*tamautou*)," and "his portion of the House (*ton emon oikon meros*)."[67] This idea of the brother's equal inheritance is not unique to Euripides. As noted above, other versions reveal attempts to balance their equal inheritance: Polynices sometimes takes his share in terms of property into exile; or the right to rule was determined under the equalitarian practice of lot. In Euripides's version, for all Polynices's talk of poverty, what he really demands is the justice of his equal share of power.

Polynices's argument reflects ideas popular in the intellectual tradition of ancient Greece. His comment on straightforward truth reflects not only Plato's *Apology* but also Greek cultural preference for the frank speech (*parrhēsia*) of Achilles to the wily Odysseus.[68] Polynices's interpretation of justice as merit reflects the idea of what one possesses by right, such as what one owns or inherits. This idea can be found, for example, in Xenophon's famous passage in the *Cyropaedia* where justice as merit reinforces rightful ownership.[69] In the *Nicomachean Ethics*, Aristotle explains that justice as merit involves distributions of "things that are divisible," and disputes, such as the one portrayed in this play, occur "whenever people who are equal have or are given things that are not equal, or people who are not equal have or are given things that are."[70] In this case, Polynices's claim emphasizes the injustice of equals having been given unequal amounts. In a final example, in Plato's *Republic*, Cephalus defines justice as "speaking the truth and giving back what one takes . . . or giving what is owed."[71] Again, echoing the same sentiments, Polynices's argument stresses Eteocles is unjust because he broke his oath (i.e., told an untruth) and failed to give what was owed (Polynices's equal turn at rule).

By contrast, Eteocles brazenly dismisses the relevance of these claims to justice. Instead, he is the voice of the opening epigraph:

> If everyone brought forth the same thing concerning the beautiful and wisdom, there would be no debate or strife among human beings. As it is, except in the names, such things are not the same nor equal for mortals; but, an action (*ergon*) is not like this.[72]

In other words, Eteocles argues that what is agreed upon is the use of a word, such as "the beautiful" or "the just," but we do not agree on what these words signify or mean. Nor does our understanding of ideas reflect actions in the real world.[73] Human conflict, therefore, results from our failure to agree on the meaning of the standards of behavior that govern sociopolitical life. As such, Eteocles posits a strict dichotomy between ideas and reality or thoughts and deeds. In addition, like contemporary international relations realists, what ultimately matters in the real world are not abstract concepts like justice but action.

Eteocles understands the conflict with his brother, therefore, not as a question of justice as oaths or merit but purely in terms of power. As he tells us: he would do anything, including "go to where the stars rise or travel beneath the earth," to secure tyranny, which he calls "the greatest gift of the gods."[74] As such, he would never willingly yield this "good thing" (*to chrēston*) but will preserve it for himself alone. Significantly, unlike other Greek terms such as *agathon* (the good) or *kalon* (the beautiful), *chrēston* implies something that is considered good because of its benefit or utility. Related words, such as the noun *chreia* indicate advantage or want. Thus, tyrannical power is not an abstract concept with an insecure meaning but a real tangible and useful good. To stress his position that tyranny matters where abstract terms do not, Eteocles suggests that if tyranny is unjust, it is "the more beautiful (*kalliston*) injustice." What matters more than talking about injustice is engaging in cowardly or disgraceful actions. Hence Polynices may talk of injustice but acts "disgracefully" by attacking his own city. Eteocles ends his short speech with the concession that Polynices can remain in Thebes but only if he dismisses the allies and abandons his claim to rule.

Eteocles's position echoes the arguments of many fifth-century Greek sophists. Although few texts of these disparate intellectuals survive, they challenged orthodox ideas by investigating, among other topics, the distinction between custom and nature, the precision of moral terms, and the relativity of virtue.[75] In particular, Eteocles's rejection of moral values as imprecise and unrelated to real action is reflected in several accounts of sophistic thinking. In Thucydides's Melian Dialogue, for example, the Athenian envoys similarly dismiss the Melian argument from justice: "You know that justice is determinative only under the compulsion of equality, but those superior do what they are able to and the weak accede."[76] In addition, Eteocles agrees with the sophist Thrasymachus in Plato's *Republic* who argues that everyone calls successful tyrants happy and blessed, no matter how wicked their actions. This is because "injustice is stronger, freer, and more powerful than justice, and . . . injustice is what is what profits or is useful for oneself."[77] In another example, in Plato's *Gorgias*, Callicles distinguishes conventional justice (it is more shameful to do harm than suffer harm) from the natural justice that the strong rule and take from the weak.[78] Also like Eteocles, Callicles argues that what is truly shameful and slavish is to submit to conventional justice, rather than doing what is advantageous. Thus, Eteocles's moral relativism justifies his own claim to power as rooted in the idea that might makes right.

In her rare third position, Jocasta stakes the middle ground. She chastises Eteocles's celebration of tyranny as following not "the greatest god" but "the worst of the *daimons*": Philotimia or the love of honor.[79] In particular, she thinks tyranny is "empty" because power and wealth are merely borrowed until the gods take it back. In contrast, Jocasta suggests Eteocles should honor the goddess Isotēta (Equality), who is truly "more beautiful" because she binds together friends, cities, and allies.[80] Unlike the hostility engendered toward those with more, she says, equality of what is merited is conducive to lawfulness. Thus, Jocasta rejects Eteocles's relativist argument as specious and counsels her son to seek moderation (*sōphrosin*) and true kingship for the sake of the city.[81] Turning to Polynices, she cautions against the foolishness of returning to sack Thebes with his Argive allies. Such a war against his own city, she argues, is a "double-evil": if he is victorious, he accomplishes the destruction of his own people, his own city, and his own shrines; if he loses, he will be blamed for a "foolish" war that cost his allies countless lives. She ends by stressing that both brothers are "together" in the wrong and cautions them to "let go of their excess (*lian*) . . . because when two foolish positions come together, both are hostile evils."

Jocasta's position also reflects prevalent classical Greek intellectual ideas. Her argument supporting temperance or self-control (*sōphrosin*) mirrors Greek cultural norms that celebrated such moderation as the greatest of virtues.[82] Her critique of Eteocles's support of tyranny reflects Socrates who, in the *Gorgias*, also rejects tyranny as the greatest life because the tyrant is enslaved to his own desires.[83] Her dismissal of the greatness of tyranny is also found in Aristotle's description of the tyrant who rules in his own self-interest but lives without security or friends.[84] Finally, although Jocasta praises equality as more beautiful than love of honor, this is not so much democratic equality but the arithmetical equality of Polynices's argument that justice demands equals be given equal portions.[85] Yet, like the Farmer in the *Electra* or Theseus in the *Suppliant Women*, Jocasta's idea that equality stabilizes regimes echoes Aristotle's discussion of the "middling" class as a corrective to the excesses of both the poor and the rich.[86] Most importantly, however, the idea that moderation counteracts excess is emphasized in her last line: both her sons are in the wrong because they equally refuse to let go of the excessiveness (*lian*) of their own view of justice.

As is typical of Euripides, the debate ends in a stalemate. Eteocles declares the discussion as a waste of time, and the discussion deteriorates into mutual name calling.[87] At first glance, it appears that the parley failed because the brothers' positions are diametrically opposed. Their speeches are incommensurate: Polynices's speech is forensic, as it focuses on what happened in the past in terms of justice and injustice; by contrast, his brother makes a deliberative speech that prioritizes the future with concerns for utility over questions of justice.[88] Hence the brothers are speaking past each other. Second, although Eteocles claims that "speech can capture everything that the iron of war can do," such comment seems ironic, as nothing would convince him to trade the "lesser [situation] for the higher."[89] Eteocles may be wrong about many things, but he is not wrong that conflicts over the meanings of abstract ideas create animosity.[90] Unsurprisingly, the *agōn* ends in failure.

Yet despite their seemingly contrary views, the brothers' positions share much in common. First, they both ground their arguments in individual or private good: their language of "the greatest," either in the good (tyranny) or evil (exile), reveals that what is most important is personal experience. Second, although Polynices may have justice and sympathy on his side, his arguments and goals are not so dissimilar from his brother. Polynices claims, for example, that he will speak simply about justice; yet, like his brother, he often speaks in contradictions that betray his self-interest.[91] Polynices may argue that exile is the greatest evil, but he rejects Eteocles's offer to let him return to Thebes; he will do anything, even destroy his own city, to gain personal power. On the same note, despite all his bravado, Eteocles is an uncommitted relativist who uses abstract principles to justify his actions, such as the "greatest good" of power.[92] Although Eteocles celebrates it, both brothers fit Aristotle's definition of a tyrant: they desire power for their own self-interest, not the common good.[93] Thus, their positions merge: in their pursuit of self-interest, they become equal and interchangeable.[94]

The first revelation of Euripides's tragedy is the consequence of opinions of justice that are grounded in self-interest and taken to an extreme "winner-take-all" perspective. If Eteocles is correct and what really matters is not debate about the meaning of justice but actions in the real world, the brothers' positions are undifferentiated in their twin fate. Despite their seemingly contrary intellectual positions (justice as oath keeping and merit versus relativism and power), the rigidity of brothers' understanding of justice blurs and converges on a mutual willingness to ignore the common good. As Luschnig eloquently points out: the community literally is absent from this play.[95] Significantly, however, instead of one winner taking all, Euripides dramatizes that uncompromising self-interested justice ends in mutual self-destruction. Such inflexible certitude, as Eteocles's notes, brings nothing but quarreling and strife among men.

Justice as Self-Sacrifice:
Blood Price and the Needs of the Many

In stark contrast to the self-interested perspective of the two rival brothers, the following episode explores an opposite view of justice:

selfless action for the sake of the community good. This episode also provides a crucial link between the current curse of the brothers' quarrel to the more ancient curse of the city's violent founding. Although exotic outsiders, the chorus is a reminder of the city's bloody origin in the Phoenician Cadmus's murder of the dragon and the violent birth of the Sown Men.[96] As Teiresias prophesied, this very ancient curse on the land can be removed if the war-god Ares receives a "similar" compensation for his murdered son. Removing this ancient curse requires an ancient form of justice: reciprocal blood price. Intermingling the current crisis with this ancient debt, this episode exposes the multiple tensions between self-interest and self-sacrifice, questioning whether the good of the many always outweighs the good of the one.

Although blood price can be an eye-for-an-eye form of retributive justice, it typically meant the "price" or compensation paid to the victim's family. The idea of blood price is one of the oldest understandings of justice in Western political thought and described in Book 18 of Homer's *Iliad*.[97] In this epic, after the loss of Patroclus and his armor, Achilles receives a new shield from the smith-god Hephaestus. This shield depicts scenes of human civilization from agriculture and marketplaces, music and dance, to siege and warfare. It also contains one of the very first depictions of public justice: a quarrel has broken out over the payment of blood price for a murdered kinsman. Two men press the independent judges to determine the "straightest justice" (*dikēn ithuntata*) of compensation.[98]

In this play, the theme of justice as a form of blood price is introduced by the prophet Teiresias. Led by his daughter and Menoeceus, Teiresias confirms the brothers' extreme self-interest is impious: he would not provide a prophecy for Eteocles, he tells Creon, as both brothers made an "ignorant mistake" of hiding their father away.[99] Although he tries to leave before providing the city with "its salvation medicine (*pharmakon*)," Creon forces him to speak. "The best medicine," Teiresias finally admits, would be to banish those belonging to Oedipus from "its land as either leader or citizen" because they are cursed. When pressed further, however, Teiresias reveals another way to save the city: to cleanse the ancient curse of Thebes's founding requires "a libation of blood" or the "blood for blood" of a pure-blooded virgin Spartoi in compensation for the death of Ares's son. As Haemon is betrothed, Teiresias tells the shocked father, only young Menoeceus can save Thebes.[100]

Teiresias leaves Creon with a stark exemplar of the public versus private dilemma: "You must release one of two of these two destinies:

save either your child or your city."[101] Unlike other fathers in Greek mythology, such as Agamemnon's sacrifice of Iphigenia, Creon refuses to sacrifice his son. To this horrific prophecy he claims to have "not heard, not listened—I say, good-bye city!" Creon also emphasizes that everyone loves their children and that "no one would give his own child to be killed." In response, Creon willingly offers himself as a substitute to save the city; yet, in the end, he can only urge Menoeceus to escape before the Thebans kill him to save themselves.[102] Echoing Polynices's description of exile as the worst thing to befall man, Menoeceus wonders how he will live and what city, gods, or friend shall protect him. In the end, he appears to yield to his father's wishes. Yet, in the choice between city and family, Creon chooses self-interest over the good of the city.

Menoeceus, however, lied to his father. Once Creon exits, Menoeceus reveals his true plan to save the city by sacrificing himself in payment of the blood price. It is forgivable for an old man like his father to be a "coward," but he will not betray "the fatherland that gave birth to [him]."[103] From Menoeceus's perspective, his father's choice of personal interest, rather than the good of the city, is disgraceful. In contrast, he sees his sacrifice as commensurate to the free, deliberate choice of soldiers defending their city: such soldiers are "under no compulsion from fate or the gods," he says, "but willingly die to save others."[104] His perspective of justice is not merit, fulfillment of oaths, or the relativism of power. The right choice for Menoeceus is that "each person ought to consider what useful thing (*chrēston*) they can bring to community of the fatherland." He parts with the comment that if citizens did so, there would be less evil, and communities would flourish.

Menoeceus's view of "right action" as contributing to the common good also reflects a current of intellectual ideas in ancient Athens. Comparing his sacrifice to the deliberate choice of soldiers in battle, Menoeceus echoes Aristotle's later description of courage in the *Nicomachean Ethics*: as with all Aristotelian virtues, courage is a habitual, voluntary, deliberate choice about possible actions.[105] In particular, Aristotle defines courage as "fearlessness regarding a noble death" in defense of one's city. Thus, in direct contrast with his cousins' self-interest that puts the community at risk, Menoeceus understands proper action as a selfless prioritization of the common good. In addition, his comment that "it would be unforgivable to abandon the fatherland which gave birth to him," echoes Socrates in the *Crito*.[106] In that dialogue, Socrates refuses to escape because "if the Laws were to come and confront us . . . [would they not say] did we not give you life in the first place? . . . did we not bring you into this world and raise you?" Like Socrates, Menoeceus argues that self-exile is comparable to abandoning the community that provides the conditions to live. Finally, Menoeceus's insistence that each person should contribute whatever useful thing they can to the community echoes Socrates's definition of justice in Book IV of the *Republic*: for Socrates, justice is "each one pursuing the one thing the city needs; that one which is naturally suited to him."[107] And like Socrates, Menoeceus suggests cities prosper when individuals contribute what they can to the good of the community.

Menoeceus's sacrifice contrasts with the brothers' individualistic view that reduces the idea of justice to self-interest. From Menoeceus's perspective, what causes political instability is not disputes regarding the meaning of justice (as Eteocles claimed) but when individuals such as Eteocles, Polynices, or Creon choose self-interest above the common good. Unlike his cousins who are willing to destroy the city for private gain, Menoeceus voluntarily and deliberately chooses to destroy himself to save the city.[108] Or, put another way, in contrast to how one man (or two men) can destroy a city, his sacrifice is an example of how "one man can save a city."[109] Menoeceus's payment of ancient blood price may seem an archaic plot device, but his death is not so dissimilar from the countless young soldiers who we continue to sacrifice to the god of war. Such sacrifice is a reminder of the real cost of excessive self-interest and extreme certitude of one's own just cause. Importantly, despite his extreme altruism, Menoeceus's parting comment reminds us that each contribution need not be as extreme as his: right action is contributing what one can to the common good.

Justice: Irreconcilable Good Things

Euripides does not end his play with this tragic but sanguine view of justice as a kind of selfless altruism for the common good. Following Menoeceus's sacrifice, the bloodshed continues until the brothers' curse of mutual slaughter is fulfilled, the Thebans defeat the invaders, and the House of Oedipus is destroyed. Rather than endorsing altruistic justice, Euripides exposes additional complications for any understanding of justice that collapses the tension between public and private.[110] Menoeceus made the ultimate sacrifice, but the final scene reveals the limits to which we can justify sacrificing the one (or the few) for the good of the many. It also reveals that justice understood as purely a public or private good remains complicated by irresolvable ethical dilemmas. Although the final scene is textually disputed, if approached as transmitted, this finale highlights the inherent and irresolvable tensions in understanding justice and the limitations of enacting those understandings in the world.[111]

The final episode involves the characters left standing after the bloody carnage: Creon, Antigone, and yet unseen Oedipus. After the second messenger reports the final battle to Creon, Antigone brings the corpses on stage and calls her father "into the light" to lament their "threefold grief."[112] This is a very different Antigone than the girl who excitedly watched soldiers from rooftop or hesitantly followed her mother onto the battlefield.[113] Claiming his right to rule Thebes as "dowry" for Antigone's marriage to Haemon, Creon makes his three declarations: first, he exiles Oedipus because "Teiresias clearly said that the city would not do well if you lived on the land." He insists this action is for the common good: "I do not say this out of insult . . . but to prevent the avengers who pursue him from suffering evil upon the land." Second, respecting Eteocles's orders, Polynices is to be thrown "unburied" and "unwept" outside the city boundaries, and anyone caught burying him will be put to death. Finally, he commands Antigone to return to her maiden rooms to await her upcoming marriage.

Once again, Eteocles's remark about the meaning of abstract words proves prophetic as a quarrel erupts between Creon and Antigone. Exercising the frank speech (*parrhēsia*) of those who do not suffer foolish rulers, our new bold Antigone challenges the justice of Creon's three proclamations.[114] She demands Creon justify the outrage (*hubrizeis*) of banishing her elderly blind father and the reasons for his "law against a pathetic corpse."[115] Although Creon reasserts that he is only following Eteocles's orders, Antigone retorts that only "foolish men follow senseless decisions" or "perform wicked deeds by following evil orders." Finally, refusing to return to her maiden chambers, Antigone threatens to kill Haemon on their wedding night.[116] Instead of marriage, she reasserts her desire both to accompany her blind father into exile and to die defiantly burying Polynices.

Antigone's argument that Creon's decrees are unlawful and wicked turns the tragedy back to the question of justice. Perhaps influenced by Menoeceus's sacrifice, Creon's view of justice now appears centered on community good. Based on Teiresias's prophecy, he exiles Oedipus to protect "the land from evil," and he leaves Polynices unburied because it is "just" (*dikaiōs*) for enemies of the city to be "thrown to the dogs."[117] By contrast, now occupying Creon's former role as protecting family interests over community good, Antigone reiterates Polynices's just claim to his equal share and the "unlawfulness" of insulting a corpse.[118] In response, Creon introduces a new dimension of justice in the play. He asserts: "A divine being (*daimōn*) determines justice, young lady, which is not simply what seems good to you." By appealing to higher, divine standards of justice, Creon appears to reject Eteocles's relativism. Justice is not simply a word that can mean whatever Antigone (or anyone else) wants it to mean; instead, Creon suggests divine judgment is associated with justice understood as community good.

Although Antigone does not object on these grounds, Creon's argument seems disingenuous. First, as is often the case, it is rather convenient that Creon's view of divine judgment aligns perfectly with his new decrees. As we know from other plays, such as Euripides's *Suppliant Women*, refusal to bury the dead violated divine law and Panhellenic norms.[119] Historically, fifth-century Athenian law did prohibit formal burial rites for traitors, who were cast out from the community into permanent exile in "Deadman's Pit."[120] This was a positive law of Athens, however, and not divinely sanctioned. Second, all of Creon's decrees are inconsistent with earlier comments in the text. Although Teiresias prophesied salvation by exiling those belonging to Oedipus, nothing is said about Oedipus himself; in fact, Teiresias was particularly critical of past improper treatment of Oedipus. In addition, according to Teiresias's "other way," Menoeceus's self-sacrifice already purified the city, so no further banishment should be necessary.[121] Additionally, Creon's second command to not bury Polynices is also problematic. He claims to be following Eteocles's command that "the body of Polynices never be buried on Theban soil." Creon interprets this to mean any burial whatsoever, as his body is to be thrown to the dogs. This new punishment of Polynices's corpse appears to be Creon's own idea.

As for the three decrees, since Antigone is exiled with her father, Creon may have undermined his own claim to rule, which he asserts was given to him as her dowry. Yet by exiling Oedipus and Antigone, his rule seems secure, as there is no one left to challenge it. Furthermore, his willingness to protect Haemon echoes the same motivation underlying his desire to save Menoeceus. Creon appears still motivated by concern for private self-interest and not community good. Finally, despite his suggestion that divine beings are responsible for justice, he provides no evidence for why the gods would support his decrees. Thus, unlike his son who sacrificed himself to save the city, Creon exposes himself as willing to sacrifice others (Oedipus and Antigone) to secure his own power. With specious arguments and unlucky scapegoats, Creon maintains only the pretense that his decrees are the will of the gods or for the sake of the city.[122]

Importantly, Creon's disingenuousness does not validate Antigone's understanding of justice; instead, his underlying concern for Haemon actually reflects Antigone's own view of the good. Antigone's desire both to accompany her father into exile and die burying her brother, although contradictory, reveal her sole interest in acting for the good of herself and her family. In addition, by rejecting the role of wife, she further underscores the political problem intrinsic to Oedipus's incestuous House. As Creon noted, it is part of human life to love and want to protect one's family.[123] Yet all political communities require intermarriage of families and the extension of obligations beyond the individual and natal family to the community. In Antigone's situation, because her family is so insular and self-identical, her disproportionate attachment to family does not allow her to see beyond family interest to community good. As her brothers were excessive in private self-interest, Antigone is also excessive in her self-identification with family interests. In other words, she avoids the choice of public or family good that Teiresias presents to Creon by seeing only one dimension: family obligation.

The play ends with one final reflection on the complexity of understanding justice. Although Antigone has collapsed the public and private dilemma by considering only the good of her family, this disintegration does not resolve inherent tensions in questions of justice. As Creon departs, Antigone remains torn by incompatible and irreconcilable familial obligations: to live in exile as a guide to her elderly blind father but also to die in the noble cause of burying her brother.[124] The impossibility of accomplishing both may indicate textual corruption; it is possible, however, that Antigone's contradictory declarations are a dramatic presentation of the impossibility of choosing between different and contradictory right actions.[125] In other words, even in her exclusive and excessive familial worldview, Antigone still cannot fulfill all actions that she declares just. She is a symbol of the stark reality that, as limited creatures, human beings cannot accomplish all good things. Human beings are, as Oedipus reminds the audience in the penultimate lines of the play, "mortal beings that must endure the necessity of the gods."

Conclusion

This tragedy is definitely "overstuffed" with many competing perspectives of justice, including keeping oaths, equality of merit, relativism of abstract words, might makes right, reciprocal blood price, altruistic self-sacrifice, giving what one can to the common good, divine sanctions, and political self-interest disguised as the common good. With so many competing perspectives and no clear definition, it is easy to see why this play is criticized as "a pessimistic evaluation of the conditions for civilized life."[126] Yet this dramatization of so many competing perspectives is not an endorsement of Eteocles's relativism that justice is only an empty concept. Certain views of justice appear to have a stronger claim. Jocasta and the chorus originally support Polynices's claim that justice requires upholding oaths and equality of merit. Polynices's position only becomes unjust when he is willing to sacrifice the good of the community for his own self-interest. By contrast, the chorus also celebrates Menoeceus's altruistic willingness to sacrifice himself for the common good. Yet, Creon's rationalizations expose the potential deceptiveness of justifying wrongdoing in the name of common good. Thus, actions that might be recognized as justice do occur in this play, but similar to Antigone squinting over the walls of the city, it is not easy to see and correctly name what justice is.[127]

This overstuffed tragedy leaves behind at least three lessons for our own attempts to see and identify justice. First, there is something seemingly just in Menoeceus's willing self-sacrifice for the good of the community and his assertion that all citizens should do what they can for the common good. His sacrifice can be seen from different perspectives. Is it some form of utilitarianism or maximization of the welfare or utility of the greatest number?[128] Is it just because it recognizes the greater importance of the needs of the many? After all, Menoeceus understands his action in terms of utility (*chrēston*). Or, following Nagel, is Menoeceus's action just because it is altruistic?[129] Is his altruism purely a selfless action or, as Lerner might suggest, can self-interest encompass aims beyond individual good.[130] Or, is justice motivated at least partly by some kind of self-interest? The latter seems to describe Menoeceus, who sacrifices himself not only for the common good but also to avoid being seen as a coward (and perhaps the wretchedness of exile). This sacrifice, seemingly the most unambiguous act of justice in the play, hints at a more complicated interrelationship between justice and self-interest. Most importantly, Euripides also raises the potential deceptiveness of claims of justice on behalf of the common good. Creon's securing his own power by exiling a blind old man reveals how suspicious we ought to be of any political rhetoric that sacrifices individuals or groups under the justification of public good.

Second, the tragedy highlights that any claim to justice requires recognizing the tension among competing claims to the good. A common characteristic of all Jocasta's children is their flattened, one-sided vision of justice.[131] Polynices and Eteocles destroy each other for individualistic gain; Antigone rejects the community for familial good; and her adopted son Menoeceus's sacrifice emphasizes the common good. To some extent, Euripides reflects the idea of competing goods found in Socrates's *Antigone*, at least as interpreted by Hegel. In Hegel's understanding, Sophocles's tragedy represents a collision of familial and state rights: neither Antigone nor Creon are in the wrong to claim the good for either family or community, but they are nonetheless unjust because each claim is one sided.[132] Although Euripides's version is not reducible to a straightforward dualism (and admittedly neither is Sophocles), he reveals the potential destructiveness of a monoscopic view of justice that looks past competing claims to a narrow claim for only individual, familial, or public good.

Finally, Euripides's "open form" points to another potentially destructive consequence of the many competing views of justice in the tragedy.[133] Eteocles was correct to stress that quarrels erupt because we do not agree the meaning of justice; yet even more damaging is what Eteocles fails to mention. The greatest quarrels in the tragedy occur because of the certitude or excessiveness in holding to one's own one-sided view of justice. These great conflicts occur because no one heeds Jocasta's advice to "let go of excess" and seek moderation (*sōphrosin*).[134] Although often understood as temperance or self-control, *sōphrosin* can also mean prudence or sound-mindedness. In Plato's *Charmides*, one possible definition is "knowing oneself and being able to examine well what one knows and does not know."[135] Thus, perhaps hardest to hear as we, too, are certain we know what justice is, the play offers a lesson in humility. It is a dramatic presentation of the consequences of holding tightly to our monoscopic, short-sighted vision of justice, especially when enacted in tandem with the competing perspectives of others who are equally certain. This is not to suggest Euripides rejects justice as having something to do with equality of merit, or keeping one's word, or doing what one can for the common good. Instead, the play reveals that all such perspectives are incomplete. And, most importantly, there are consequences for overconfidence in our worldview and a high cost to forgetting Creon's advice to the doomed Eteocles: "No one man can see everything."

Part II
JUSTICE IN SACRED SPACES

Chapter 4

The *Ion*

Justice, In and Out of Bounds

> Tutor: Do you carry them mixed together or apart?
> Creusa: Separately. For the good does not
> blend together with the bad.[1]

The *Ion* is an unfamiliar play about an even lesser-known myth concerning Ion, the eponymous founder of the Ionian tribe of Greek peoples. The tragedy has a complicated plot involving divine misinformation, mistaken identities, and murder prevented in the nick of time by the intervention of the gods. It does not end with the expected tragic reversal from good to bad fortune but contains the opposite reversal from bad to seemingly good fortune. Ever since Aristotle, scholars have criticized such atypical reversals as presenting more of a "tragicomedy" than tragedy proper.[2] More recent scholarship, however, has begun to question this straightforward interpretation of a patriotic "happy ending."[3] Focusing on the implications of the *Ion*'s reformulation of the Athenian foundation myths, much of this scholarship has explored the play's portrayal of civic identity, especially as it relates to the predominantly Ionian subject states of the empire or the city's large foreign (*metic*) population.[4] Other scholarship concentrates on the significance of the play's exploration of gender as the "other" in community foundation myths.[5]

This chapter follows the interpretation that Euripides's tragedy is far more complicated than the patriotic "happy ending" acknowledges. Without such an easy resolution, the *Ion* becomes a difficult and complex tragedy to interpret, especially since we have little information on the dating or other tragedies in its trilogy. As one of the "alphabet plays," it has been transmitted without any accompanying information.[6] Zacharia dates the play to 412 BCE, as she understands its mythological reworking as a response to the failed Athenian expedition in Sicily.[7] Even if we take the less controversial chronology for production as sometime between 420–410 BCE, the tragedy may still be responding to issues resulting from declining support from the subject states of the Athenian empire. With this theme of nationalism in mind, the following analysis focuses on the significance of two ancient interconnected ideas of justice: the ancient ethic of helping friends and harming enemies and the belief that good is dichotomously separate from the bad. It is Euripides's use of doubling and duality in this tragedy that exposes several limitations and characteristic problems in exploring ideas of justice, especially the insufficiency of knowledge, the bias of perspective, and the need to acknowledge and respect the ancient goddesses of the boundaries.

The Mythological Context and Plot of the *Ion*

Background Myth

Even within the tradition of Greek mythological stories, Ion was a relatively obscure figure.[8] He was the eponymous founder of the "Ionian" Greek tribal group. The Greek people in the classical period consisted of several different "tribes" with distinctive dialects, cultural norms, and religious rituals. The Spartans, for example, identified as Dorian. The other major tribe was the Aeolians of central Greece. The Athenians identify as "Ionian" as early as 600 BCE. In his archeology, for example, Thucydides points to long-established Ionian cultural practices, costumes, and religious festivals.[9] Who exactly Ion was, however, is not well established in the extant stories. There is, for example, no mention of Ion in the typical lineage of the kings of Athens. There are no stories before Euripides about Ion's offspring or their connection to the founding leaders of the ancient tribes. Fragments from Hesiod tell a version of events where, after being expelled from Thessaly, Xuthus marries a daughter of the Athenian king Erechtheus and had two sons called Achaeus and Ion.[10] In another account, Herodotus indicates that Ion was not a king but a general who gave his name to the people who migrated with him to Attica after being forced out of their native Peloponnesian territory.[11] In a much later version, Pausanias indicates that Ion became king after the Ionians were expelled from their homeland of Aegialia.[12] Although it is not likely Ionians inhabited Attica from the heroic age, in none of these versions is Ion connected to significant mythological events. Compared to other well-trodden myths with many contradictory versions, Ion is virtually unknown.

A little more is known about Creusa and the autochthonous foundation of Athens. For the ancient Greeks, autochthony had a double meaning. On the one hand, as ancient historians and rhetoricians stressed, Athenian autochthony emphasized the uninterrupted continuity of its people who "ruled always (*aei*)"; that is, they ruled their land without external invasion over successive generations.[13] On the other hand, mythology stressed literal autochthony: the Athenians are men born from the earth itself (*auto-chthōn*).[14] Both understandings stressed the brotherhood and equality of Athenian citizens.[15] Such myths of autochthonous beginnings were not unique to Athens.[16] More famous, for example, were the Sown Men (Spartoi) of Thebes. In this myth, referred to in the *Phoenician Women*, the peripatetic Phoenician Cadmus killed the dragon son of Ares and sowed its teeth in the soil; from these teeth sprang fully armed soldiers who attacked each other.[17] Only five survived to found Thebes with Cadmus. We also know of other autochthon founders such as Pelasgos, the founder of the Arcadia; Anax, the founder of Miletos; and Lelex, the founder of Lakonia.

In the case of Athenian mythology, there are two autochthonous origin stories.[18] The first Athenian founder was Cecrops, who was portrayed as having the upper body of a man and the lower body of a snake or fish. He marries Aglaurus with whom he had several daughters. He was celebrated as the founder of Athenian institutions such as marriage, political organization, religious rituals to the Olympic gods, and its judicial system. Cecrops was also the arbitrator who chose Athena as patron god of the city over Poseidon. A second autochthonous founding began when Hephaestus attempted to rape Athena; managing to escape, Athena impregnated the earth when she wiped his semen from her leg and it fell to the ground. Significantly, unlike the warrior Theban Sown Men, Erechtheus (sometimes known as Erichthonius) was born as a helpless baby. Hiding him in a basket surrounded by protective snakes, Athena gave the baby to be fostered by Cecrops's daughters. Although they were told not to look in the basket, they disobeyed and, driven mad as a consequence, they leaped to their death (and thus ended Cecrops's first founding). Although there are different versions of the succession,

Erechtheus/Erichthonius usually succeeded Cecrops. He also has only daughters whom he sacrifices (all except newborn Creusa) to save the city when it is invaded by Eleusis.[19] In this same battle, in retaliation for the death of his son Eumolpus, Poseidon hit the earth with his trident and Erechtheus/Erichthonius was swallowed by the earth.[20] In most accounts, his surviving daughter Creusa marries the Thessalian Xuthus after this foreigner helps save Athens in another invasion. They have the two sons: Achaeus and Ion.

Euripides's *Ion*

Although the *Ion* is set before the Temple of Apollo in Delphi, it tells the story of the heirs of Athens's second autochthonous founder Erichthonius.[21] It is told in three parts: the first encounter and the Delphic "prophecy"; the plot to kill Ion; and the recognition and deus ex machina scene. The first part (1–675) opens with the prologue of the messenger god Hermes telling the backstory: Apollo raped the Athenian Creusa but secretly rescued their exposed son (Ion) to be raised in Delphi.[22] The audience also learns that Creusa and her foreign-born husband Xuthus are coming to Delphi to seek a cure for their childlessness. As for the future, Hermes prophesizes the plot: Apollo plans to give Ion to Xuthus as his own child so that the boy will gain his rightful place, but the god's shameful liaison with Creusa will remain concealed. After exposing these secrets, Hermes hides in Apollo's sacred laurel grove to watch this plot unfold.

Carrying Apollo's symbols of the bow and laurel branch, Ion enters the stage to sing the purification rites of Apollo; he is interrupted, first, by birds sacred to Apollo and Zeus, whose droppings defile the temple: he wards them off with threats from his bow.[23] Second, he is interrupted by the choral *parodos* of Athenian maidservants who provide a vivid description of the images representing the battle between the gods and monstrous Giants adorning the Delphic architecture.[24] Ion ensures that in their excitement, the chorus does not cross the boundary of sacred space. Creusa arrives in advance of her husband and encounters Ion; their meeting is sympathetic, but they do not recognize their familial bond. Although Creusa hesitates because of her shame (a "do-nothing goddess" according to Ion), she eventually reveals her desire to consult a secret oracle on behalf of a "friend" who was raped by Apollo. Ion defends the god from such salacious accusations. Xuthus's arrival prevents her from cross-examining the god to expose "what the god is not willing [to reveal]."[25] After consulting the oracle, Xuthus announces the prophecy that his son will be the first person he sees: this person is Ion. At first, Ion resists Xuthus's interpretation of the oracle. He argues, as the son of a foreigner, that life as a temple servant is superior to being rejected by the pure-blood Athens.[26] Echoing Polynices in the *Phoenician Women*, Ion argues such foreigner status will prevent him from speaking freely (*parrhēsia*).[27] Xuthus convinces Ion to come to Athens but agrees to conceal the boy's "true" identity from Creusa (to spare her feelings, he says) by disguising Ion as a guest-friend (*xenos*).

The second part (675–1110) begins with plans for a banquet in celebration of Ion's departure.[28] Angered by the deceit of a foreign king, the chorus members vow "to be ruled by none except the noble Erechtheids" and expose Xuthus's "secret harvest of a child" to Creusa. At this unfortunate news, she reveals the true story of what happened in Pan's grotto: she was raped by Apollo and exposed the child. Refusing her citizens' impious suggestion to burn Apollo's Temple or kill Xuthus (because, she says, "he has been a good husband"), a plot is hatched to kill the new usurper with Creusa's inheritance: a gift given by Athena to Erichthonius that contains two separate vials of Gorgon blood: one cures, and the other kills. These drops of blood, she says, are kept separate "because good does not blend together with the bad." It is determined that the old tutor will use the poisonous blood to kill Ion at the banquet. The chorus sings an ode to Enodia, the Thracian goddess of crossroads, for the success of their plan.

The third part (1110–1620) begins with the arrival of a servant report.[29] After setting up a tent with tapestries depicting the starry sky, half-beast men, and the first autochthonous Athenian king Cecrops and his daughters, Ion invites all of Delphi to enjoy the feast. The old tutor manages to poison Ion's wine with a drop of the bad blood. After hearing a disrespectful oath, however, Ion pours it out. The plot is exposed when a bird dies from drinking this spilled wine. With support from the Delphian people, Ion reappears on stage to enact revenge. At the last minute, he is prevented by Apollo's priestess from impiously killing Creusa as she claims sanctuary in the temple. The priestess reveals the tokens of his birth left with him at the temple steps: a basket, a living olive branch, a cloth woven with the Gorgon and serpents, and a golden necklace of snakes. By these signs, Creusa and Ion come to recognize each other as "one's own." Ion, still unconvinced that he is divine progeny, is prevented from confronting the god by Athena's deus ex machina arrival.

In the finale, the Athenian patron goddess admits Apollo sent her to avoid direct confrontation and confirms Ion's divine paternity.[30] In addition, she prophesizes that Ion will father four sons (Geleon, Hopletes, Argades, and Aigikores) who establish the four ancient Athenian tribes as well as the colonies in the Cyclades, Asia, and Europe: all these people will be called "Ionian" after their common forefather. Creusa will go on to bear two sons with Xuthus: Dorus and Achaeus. These half-brothers will establish the Dorian and Achaean tribes of Greek peoples. Finally, she commands that no one, especially not Xuthus, should be told the truth of Ion's paternity; instead, he is to continue to believe the god's "sweet belief (*hēdeōs dokēsis*)." The play ends with Creusa reconciling with Apollo, Athena admitting that the "right time" of gods may be considered slow by human standards, and the chorus praising that "in the end the good get what they deserve, but those who do bad, just as is natural, never prosper."[31]

Euripides's Potential Innovations

Euripides's version contains three probable innovations. First, and most importantly, he reinvents the obscure Ion who is revealed to be both the true descendant of the autochthonous lineage of Athens and the half-divine progenitor of the Ionian peoples of their empire.[32] With such upgrades, Ion is now in the rarified air of the great hero Heracles whose children refound Spartan territory as the Heracleidae.[33] In addition, this revamped genealogy makes Ion the older, half-brother of Dorus and Achaeus; the former who is now the child (and not brother) of Xuthus.[34] Euripides's new version of the family tree marks the Ionians as primary to their Dorian enemies, especially the Spartans, Corinthians, and Syracusans.[35] In addition, since Ion's sons are the founders of the ancient Athenian tribes and Ionian colonies, Athens is transformed into the mother city of all the Ionian Greeks. As noted by several scholars, Ion's new lineage provides a convenient justification for Athenian rule over their empire and mythical superiority to rival their Spartan archenemies.[36] As noted previously, although the exact date is unknown, the tragedy definitely was performed during the Peloponnesian War. With this perilous atmosphere in mind, Euripides turns the stage into a space to explore the rhetoric of Athenian political identity.

Second, Euripides also establishes a more coherent genealogical lineage for the competing foundation myth to Ionianism: the autochthonous founding of Athens.[37] Importantly, as several scholars have noted, there was always a darker side to autochthonous birth.[38] The monstrous Giants (*gigantes*) were autochthons whom Mother Earth (*gē*) bore from drops of blood that fell when the Titan Chronos castrated his father Ouranos (Sky) to seize divine power. Euripides draws attention to these Giants in the *parodos* when the chorus describes the Delphic architecture depicting their battle with the Olympian gods. In most mythology this Battle of the Giants represents the establishment of these new Olympian gods, who overthrew Chronos to create civilized order. Other monstrous earthborn creatures alluded to in the play include the original prophetic force at Delphi: the Python. Apollo killed this giant snake, which encircled the earth, to establish his own cult at the Delphic site.[39] Not all these early monstrous autochthons were dangerous; for example, there are several references to Cecrops, the first autochthonous founder and civilizer of Athens. Yet, such allusions highlight past transitions in which early autochthons are replaced in order to establish the more civilized rule of the Olympian gods and their half-human refounding offspring.

By the fifth century, the Athenians took great pride in their status as autochthonous people who were born of the earth and ruled their land over generations.[40] As the son of Creusa, Ion is the last surviving descendant of the second earthborn founder of Athens: Erechtheus/ Erichthonius. There is considerable scholarly debate concerning the relationship between these two figures, as it is not clear if they represent the same or separate individuals.[41] In some versions, Erechtheus represents an adult version of Erichthonius. Euripides's tragedy reconstructs this confusing lineage by making Erechtheus not the adult version but the son of Erichthonius.[42] With this innovation, Euripides provides an unambiguous lineage from the earthborn Erichthonius to the now demigod Ion; this innovation not only orders the family ancestry but also reconciles the two competing Athenian foundation myths of Ionian migration into Attica with the opposing narrative of autochthonous origins.[43]

Euripides's final innovation concerns the role of Athena in the killing of the Gorgon Medusa. Certain monstrous creatures, such as the Gorgon sisters, were considered *chthonic* (subterranean gods); however, like the Giants, they were symbolic of the violence, chaos, and panic of the time during the transition to civilization.[44] The Gorgons were three sisters: Stheno, Euryale, and Medusa. Although the first two were immortal, Medusa was not. In the classical Greek era, these sisters were depicted with scaly heads, boars' tusks, and wings.[45] Importantly, one glance at Medusa's face was believed to turn a human being into stone. In Euripides's version, he changes the lineage of the Gorgons: Creusa notes that "the Mother Earth (*gē*) gave birth to the Gorgon" in Phlegra, the site of the famous Giant-Olympian war.[46] In more common mythology, the Gorgon sisters were daughters of the Sea Titans Phorkys and Keto. With Euripides's innovation, Medusa is no longer simply a *chthonic* Titan but an autochthon born directly of the earth like Cecrops, Erichthonius, or the Giants. In addition, in more typical mythology, it is the great Peloponnesian hero Perseus who slays Medusa, albeit with the help of Athena. In our play, Creusa notes "the goddess Pallas Athena, child of Zeus, slayed her" and gave to Erichthonius the twin vials of good and bad blood. Significantly, this innovation destabilizes the heroism of the rival Dorian Perseus and highlights the patron of Athens as the separation of good and bad.

Justice: Only Helping My Friends

In her first speech, Creusa introduces the question of justice by exclaiming: "To what court should we go for a decision, if we are perishing by the injustice of those who rule?"[47] In contrast to questions of justice, more obvious themes in the tragedy concern political identity, such as reconciling the two competing Athenian origin myths. Read as a political play, this new and improved mythical founding appears to be a patriotic victory of Athenian superiority over their largely Ionian empire and Dorian rivals. These overt political themes, however, are not disconnected but embedded in a broader narrative of justice. Early in the story, Ion identifies political legitimacy with the rule of "one's own." The Athenians, he tells Xuthus, will reject him because "they are no race from abroad" but a "pure-bred" city.[48] Ion's opinion is confirmed by the old tutor's outrage that a foreigner's child could claim the throne or the chorus's complaint that too many outsiders have been allowed to live in Athens.

Within the plot, the celebration of this xenophobic "pure-bred" Athenian rule receives its strongest support in the chorus's parting words: "In the end, the good (*esthloi*) get what they deserve and the bad (*kakoi*), as is natural (*pephukas'*), never prosper."[49] Significantly, this patriotic celebration of the Athenian refounding identifies the prosperous and good with "one's own," and the bad and ill-fated with those who would now be called the "other." This one-to-one correspondence of "my own" with the good and the "other" with the bad reflects one of the most ancient understandings of justice: helping friends and harming enemies.[50] This ancient view of justice can be traced far back through Homer and, as Socrates notes in the *Republic*, the poet Simonides.[51] It is found across ancient literature. Hesiod suggests that when friends violate this ethic through betrayal, the payback should be "twice as much" as the original harm.[52] Like our chorus, Xenophon calls the desire to benefit friends and defeat enemies "natural" and "most pleasant."[53] Even the rhetorician Lysias argues that the worst men are those who make an art of doing no harm to enemies but harm to friends.[54] Echoing a similar view, Aristotle argues that plots involving friends harming friends make the best tragedies because this is what most incites our poetic emotions of fear and pity.[55] In the case of the *Ion*, only divine intervention prevents Creusa and Ion from violating the ethic and causing harm to kin or friends by killing each other.

Although this one-to-one correspondence between "my own" and the good justifies the happy ending interpretation, it is not clear whether the chorus's celebration should be taken at face value. In general, the ancient Greeks considered friends (*philia*) anyone who was a family member, extended kin, close associate, or those connected by formalized relationships, such as *xenia* (guest-friends) and supplication.[56] In the case of *Ion*, however, there is an even narrower chauvinistic or xenophobic interpretation of friends: those who are identified as "good" are limited solely to blood relations. All others, even the ally Xuthus (who normally would be identified as a friend), are considered bad and unworthy. Yet similar to Polemarchus in the *Republic*, the chorus celebrates that friends are worthy of good things without any examination of the important questions associated with this assumption: What makes someone a friend or an enemy?[57] How do you know if you are helping or harming? Or, since the chorus brings up the idea of "nature," what is good or bad by nature? The serious problem with this ancient ethic is that it can result in benefiting friends who are truly bad men and harming good men who have done nothing wrong.

In light of the events of the play, there are several reasons to doubt the veracity of the chorus's parting comment. First, despite the chorus's outburst that foreigners are treacherous, the main foreigner Xuthus is the object and not the agent of the most important deception in the plot.[58] To be fair, Xuthus is not entirely blameless, as he intended to conceal his false prophecy regarding Ion's "paternity" (to protect, he says, Creusa from grief). Although this intended lie exposes his capacity for deception, Xuthus is portrayed mainly positively throughout the story. Even the old tutor, who suspects Xuthus lied about the prophecy, admits that he does not hate Xuthus but simply loves Creusa—the earthborn Athenian—more. Creusa also refuses to kill Xuthus because he has been a good husband and past savior of Athens. Thus, if this foreigner had not saved the city, Athenian autochthonous self-rule or proud *parrhēsia* would not be possible among its pure-bred citizens.

By contrast, as the object of Apollo's "sweet belief," the foreigner Xuthus will unknowingly accept a false child into his *oikos*. The reason for Athena's insistence on this continued deception is not entirely clear, although it is doubtful that Athena's intention is to protect Xuthus from grief. It was common in Greek mythology that mortal men raised the illegitimate sons of gods, which was often considered an honor.[59] We also know that with Creusa he will father more sons, so it is not to protect him from the grief of childlessness. By contrast, this act of duplicitously "hiding" another man's child in one's *oikos* was a very real anxiety in ancient Greece and may explain female segregation in Athenian society.[60] In addition, we also know from Hermes that the old tutor is wrong regarding Xuthus. It was not Xuthus who lied about the prophecy: it was the god who lied to him. Thus, the decent foreigner, who by all accounts is a good husband and invaluable ally, is the target of a harmful divine deceit.

Importantly, the tragedy also hints that there is something amiss in the one-to-one correspondence between Ion and good men getting what they deserve. Importantly, for the Athenians, the one and only thing that changed their former murderous rage into celebration is the recognition of Ion as "one's own." This is not to suggest that Ion has not changed throughout the course of the play; in fact, it is possible to understand the tragedy as Ion's transition from a boy into a young man.[61] We do see a transition from a pious youth who protects his temple from pollution of birds, the haphazard overstepping of choral tourists, and Creusa's desire to force the god to reveal all. What is revealed in his transition to adulthood, however, is not necessarily the qualities of a good ruler. In his *agōn* with Xuthus, for example, Ion revealed a preference for political apathy or "quietism" that would be at odds with political leadership.⁶² Despite being the autochthonous heir, he is ignorant regarding Athenian culture and dubious of its traditions. Furthermore, by the finale, he reveals his own capacity for impiety by attempting to kill the suppliant Creusa and, like her, demanding the god reveal what he wishes to remain hidden.

This potential act of impiety toward a suppliant, in particular, stands in stark contrast to the Athenian self-image as savior of suppliants. In other tragedies, Euripides portrays Athenian kings as helping suppliants, such as Theseus who fought a war on behalf of the Argive suppliants or Demophon who saved the suppliant exiled children of Heracles.⁶³ Rather than a righteous king, Ion behaves more like the Argive herald in the *Children of Heracles*; he must be prevented from physically forcing suppliants from the altar. Yet, Ion goes even further than this herald, as he attempts to make demands of the gods: it is only the priestess and Athena's deus ex machina that prevents him from such acts of impiety.⁶⁴ Although still a young man with much to learn, there is little indication that he will become a wise and pious ruler. Hence, the Athenian reversal from hostility to elation is based solely on their desire to be ruled by "one's own blood" without any assessment of this person's qualities, qualifications, or past service to the city.⁶⁵ Despite the chorus's xenophobic celebration, the tragedy has not silenced the lingering question: if Ion is being judged solely by his blood, is his blood good or bad?

Justice: Separating Good from Bad

Euripides also raises questions regarding this xenophobic identification of friends with the good in a second perspective of justice: the belief that the good is dichotomously distinct and separable from the bad. This perspective is vividly represented in Creusa's autochthonous inheritance of the twin vials of Gorgon's blood. In the version told in the *Ion*, these vials were given to Creusa's grandfather Erichthonius by Athena after she killed this monstrous Gorgon. The vials contain two drops of her blood: the blood from her principal vein "keeps away diseases and provides nourishment for life"; the second vial contains bad blood that has the power to kill.⁶⁶ In this story, only the bad blood is used in the ill-conceived plot to kill Ion at his banquet; the good blood performs no role.⁶⁷ Symbolically, this lack of good blood could indicate that the good, or actions on behalf of the good, are not part of the unfolding events of the play. Conversely, it could hint that the autochthon descendants are the good blood. Creusa wears the goddess's double-gift on a golden chain around her wrist. Significantly, she stresses that the two fluids should never mix but be kept separate because "the good does not mix together (*summeignutia*) with bad."

This idea that the good and bad should be kept separate is a repeating theme in this tragedy. It appears again in the scene where Ion attacks Creusa after the failed attempt on his life. Fearing for her life, Creusa takes sanctuary on the altar of Apollo.[68] An action such as sitting on a god's altar was a rite of supplication (*hiketeia*) that made the person, including exiles and criminals, inviolable and under the protection of Zeus.[69] By divine law, no person or thing could be removed from the sacred space, which was considered divine property. Frustrated, Ion criticizes this divine law as unintelligible or "without the wisdom of intelligence" (*apo gnōmēs sophēs*) because it allows bad men to be protected by the gods; by contrast, he asserts that only righteous men should receive divine shelter. It is wrong, he stresses, "that good and bad men receive the same thing from the gods."[70] Thus, Ion appears to be supporting some kind of proportional distributive justice in which those who are unequal are not treated as equals.[71] By complaining about equal treatment under the principle of inviolability of sanctuary, Ion also is implying that the bad literally should not mix or be on the same ground with the good.

This is not the first time that Ion labels as "unintelligible" the laws and treatment of the gods. Earlier in the play, when he first met Creusa, he found it unbelievable that Apollo could rape a woman and conceive a child who was left to be eaten by birds.[72] Rationalizing Creusa's story, he insists the woman must be lying to disguise a commonplace human indiscretion. Importantly, Ion recognizes the injustice of rape, as he also might be the offspring of such "an injustice done to a woman." After he is left alone with his thoughts, Ion develops this idea further: "I must chastise Phoebus" he says, "since those who write the laws for men should not be found guilty of lawlessness."[73] In addition, he surmises divine bad behavior is incomprehensible because the gods always have the power to be good. It is human beings that lack resources and are sometimes "helpless" to fight against injustice or do the right thing. Instead, as our educators, the gods should not mix good and bad behaviors in their own actions or treat equally such actions among mortals.[74]

For Ion, what is incomprehensible or "without wisdom of intelligence" is that good and bad are mixed together. Instead, the good should be unadulterated and pure, similar to the Delphic Temple, which he swept daily with holy laurel branches and protected from the pollution of the birds and blundering tourists. Confirming Athena's standard, set by her gift of the twin vials, Ion's perception of justice draws attention to the important function of knowing and respecting boundaries.[75] The first boundary, introduced in the choral *parodos*, was a separation between the sacred and profane.[76] This *parodos*, most famous for its description of Delphic architecture, concludes when the Athenian maidservants have walked the long winding path of the Sacred Way to the temple precinct. Here, encountering Ion in his task of purification, they ask permission to step or pass beyond (*huperbēnai*) into the shrine. Ion replies that they cannot cross into the innermost recesses without performing certain rituals. The chorus complies: "I do not transgress (*parabainomen*) the law of the god: my eyes can enjoy the things outside." And to this, Ion replies, "Look upon all things that is [permitted by] divine law (*themis*)."

This exchange is connected to the theme of keeping separate the good from bad in two ways. First, it establishes the idea that the boundaries between the sacred and profane are intelligible and tangible. In this case, as Apollo's temple was a well-established sacred site, there was a literal boundary marking the inside or sacred space of the temple from what was outside; it is this inner space that Ion keeps pure by sweeping and warding off birds.[77] Importantly, only after performing a series of ritual actions can one move from the secular human space to the inner consecrated sanctum. In this way the sacred and the good was kept pure and isolated from the profane. Second, anyone who entered the shrine without performing such ritual action was, as the chorus indicates, "passing or going beyond" or "transgressing" the boundary between the sacred and profane. As Ion insinuates, such transgressions were punished by the goddess Themis. This ancient goddess was the personification of divine law and established social order (*nomos*); as her name implies—she is the one that "puts in place (*tithēmi*)."[78]

As much as the chorus indicates their willingness to respect the proper place of things, they abandon this view after they witness Xuthus's plan to conceal Ion's "paternity." Together with the old tutor, they encourage Creusa's rage and hatch the plot to kill Ion with the Gorgon's bad blood. The old tutor, charged with the actual deed, departs with the comment, "Whenever someone wishes to bring evil upon an enemy, no law (*nomos*) is an impediment."[79] This comment underscores the vengeful anger of retaliation for perceived wrongs underlying justice understood as harming enemies. At this point, the chorus begins to sing their Ode to Enodia.[80] A more obscure goddess, Enodia was often conflated with other goddesses, such as Artemis, Selene, or the liminal goddess Hekate. In this tragedy, the chorus calls Enodia the "daughter of Demeter," which conflates her with Persephone, another dark, *chthonic* goddess celebrated in the life and death rituals of the Eleusinian Mysteries.[81] Their summoning of Enodia marks the moment of the tragedy's transition: no longer are these Athenian women content merely to look upon what is permitted, but they have crossed over or "gone beyond."[82] Echoing the chorus in the *Medea*, our chorus also declares, "Let the song begin to sing backwards." In this case, it is not time that is transgressed but moral space.

Justice: Boundaries and the Double

The significance of "the double" in this play as well as in ancient tragedy in general is well established.[83] The concept of "the double" appears in various forms: it can denote something similar that repeats, like a replication; it can also suggest the idea of something close, confused with (but not identical to) the original. In literature, "the double" often indicates double meanings or the dualities of opposite or mirrored images. As a genre, Greek tragedy itself is a form of doubling in which the new retelling of a story is a double or image of events from mythical time.[84] The innovations of Greek playwrights are also a kind of doubling: Ion's new paternity, for example, is experienced as an unexpected surprise by the characters in the story as well as by the audience.[85] Doubling in the *Ion* also points to the violent repetitions of political origins. This view, argued most famously by René Girard, sees the sacrifice of a "double" as a way to break endless cycles or repetitions of violence.[86] The *Ion* draws attention to such foundational violence in its cycles of autochthonous foundings that require an "other," such as women or foreigners to break the cycle of impotent beginnings.[87] The necessity of this "other" also highlights the conflicts that gave birth to the city and the limitations of a myopic view of the political self.[88] Beyond these elements of political self-understanding, the *Ion's* doubling reveals the limitations of understanding justice either as helping friends and harming enemies or in the attempt to ensure strict, unmitigated boundaries between good and bad.

It is impossible to escape the layers of doubling, repetition, and duality at work in the *Ion*. The entire structure of the tragedy, similar to the *Alcestis* or *Helen*, is a mirrored opposite of the tragedy's expected reversal from good to bad fortune. The plot contains many structural doublings or repetitions: two entrance scenes with two gods bearing prophecies, two recognition scenes, two attempted murders, two versions of Ion's birth, and Ion's two sets of parents (Apollo/Creusa and stepparents of Xuthus/Pythia).[89] Several elements hint at doubles of the "self": Athena arrives in the deus ex machina but has previously appeared as her stone double in the *parodos*; Creusa invents a double in her story of a "friend"; and Ion becomes an imposter or hidden double in Xuthus's *oikos*.[90] Such examples indicate two forms of doubling at work: on the one hand, there is a doubling as a form of repetition, in which the same thing repeats or occurs again, albeit always with an important variation; on the other hand, there is also the form of doubling in which what appears as one is revealed to be two or a duality.

The most vivid double is Ion himself, who embodies both kinds of doubling: he is a repetition of the autochthonous founding and, revealed as a demigod, he has a dual nature. Both kinds of doubling are unveiled through the tokens of his birth: a basket, golden snake necklace, a garland of olive leaves, and double weaving of a Gorgon.[91] These tokens are symbolic of the doubling of Erichthonius and Ion: both were conveyed in baskets to their foster mothers (Erichthonius to Cecrops's daughters and Ion to the Pythia in Delphi); the snake necklace is a symbolic reminder of Cecrops, the half-snake autochthonous first founder; the garland was from the sacred olive tree given by Athena after Cecrops chose her as patron of the city; and the Gorgon weaving points to the double vial of blood. The effect of repetition is a duplication of the original founding: as Creusa so elegantly puts it: "Erechtheus is young once more."[92] Importantly, this refounding of the city seems to be accomplished by the exclusion of the "other"—the foreigner Xuthus. And this time, rather than a false and impotent start, Athena prophesizes that this new foundation will find posterity.

Examining this refounding more closely, other forms of doubling undermine this straightforward exclusionary founding. Most importantly, Ion himself represents dualism. As noted previously, Ion's story also mimics the rites of passage that marked the transition from childhood to a member of the Athenian political community.[93] As with all such transitions, the passage between youth and adulthood was considered perilous as the young *ephēboi* were neither boys nor men—they were both or neither. Ion also lives a double life or exists in duality in other ways: he is an Athenian and a foreigner; he is earthborn and born of a woman; and, most significantly, he is both human and divine. As a semidivine founder king, he is equal to and a rival of the famous heroes of Greece, in particular Heracles, the progenitor of their Spartan and allied Peloponnesian enemies.

As a rival to Heracles, Ion's newfound status reflects back to the allusions made by the chorus in their *parados* to the Gigantomachy adorning the Delphic architecture.[94] In this famous battle, Heracles fought alongside the new Olympian gods against these ancient autochthonous Giants. Heracles was also famous, of course, for killing other monstrous creatures, like the Hydra or man-eating horses, as part of his laborious civilizing process. Other semidivine heroes also fought hybrid liminal creatures, such as Perseus's typical slaying of the Gorgon Medusa. Although some of these hybrid creatures were dangerous, others like Cecrops or the wise centaur Chiron (who trained heroes), were also liminal figures that symbolize a "crossing over" to civilizing norms, such as marriage rites and legal systems.[95] The autochthons and other kinds of liminal creatures were not necessarily good or bad. Thus, unlike Athena's gift of the twin vials, which artificially separated the Gorgon blood, the living Gorgon contained both good and bad as part of her nature.

The sort of duality raised by the autochthons' mingled nature repeats several times. Most colorful is the dual role of birds. In his monody, Ion threatens and chases away Apollo's sacred birds because they pollute the sanctuary.[96] Creusa also reveals her greatest fear is that a rapacious bird ate her exposed child. In contrast to this image of birds as impure and vicious, a bird drinks the poisoned wine to become the scapegoat in the attempt on Ion's life.[97] Generally, in ancient Greece, birds were sacred messengers in the divination of prophecy. Birds also were instrumental in establishing sacred boundaries: it was two eagles, for example, that Zeus let fly in opposite directions, which met at Delphi marking it as the center of the earth. Although Ion chases the sacred birds away, Apollo protected birds as suppliants at his altars.[98] Birds are symbolic of a dual nature of purity and pollution.

In other Greek stories, birds are associated with magical or medicinal plants as a kind of guardian spirit.[99] In Greek culture, medicinal plants also had a dual essence as *pharmakon*, a word that can be translated as either drug or poison. Thus, similar to Creusa's vial, a *pharmakon* could heal or kill. Ion's name, which Xuthus associates with the verb "to go" (*iōn*), is also related to the noun *iamos*, which was a species of medicinal but potentially toxic plants.[100] Such medicinal plants connect the story again to the goddesses of magic, such as Hekate or Enodia, who used knowledge of such plants in their craft. The *pharmakon* also was connected to Apollo in his guise as a god of healing.[101] In particular, Apollo was associated with the laurel tree, which is mentioned seven times in the play; although highly toxic, laurel was used in ceremonies of divine purification (such as Ion's sweeping of the temple) and awarded in ritualistic contests.

The question of whether Ion is good or bad can be understood in the same way. He is celebrated as an autochthonous descendant who, as kin, is considered good and worthy of prospering. In his monody, he reveals his capacity for piety, and his resistance to Xuthus's plan to bring him to Athens reveals some regard for Athenian customs. Yet like the Sown Men of Thebes, Ion has a similar potential for violence, exhibited in his impious attempt to remove Creusa from the altar. Ion's doubling with the liminal and autochthonous creatures symbolizes his similar dual nature: he is good mingled or mixed with bad. Thus, the monstrous Giants, liminal creatures, birds, plants, and the children of the earth who "grew from her like weeds" symbolize a kind of duality that proves Ion wrong: good is mixed with bad.[102]

There is one final important kind of doubling highlighted in the tragedy: words can have a double meaning. The most significant example of this is autochthony. As noted previously, for the Greeks, autochthony could mean literally "born of the earth," or simply "uninterrupted continuous rule." Hoffer points to Euripides's careful use of other double meanings throughout the story, especially with Greek words like *dikē* and *nomos*.[103] As an abstract concept, for example, *dikē* can mean "justice," but it also can refer to the institutions of justice, such as courts, trials, or penalties. Thus, Creusa's famous exclamation that there is no *dikē* to appeal to when you are destroyed by the injustices (*adikiais*) of those in power has two meanings: she could mean there is no physical court of law; or, she could mean there is no such thing as justice (even if there are "courts") when those in power are unjust.[104] Similarly, Ion uses the term *nomos* in his critique of the gods as unjust: "Those who write the laws (*nomous*) for men should not be found guilty of lawlessness (*anomian*)." In this case, the term *nomos* can mean law or legal decrees but can also mean unwritten customary practices or principles. Thus, Ion could also mean that gods who establish customary practices for mortals should not be immoral.

It is hardly controversial to suggest that language can be used to deliberately conceal meaning or the truth. Ion draws attention to the limitation of speech, when he argues against accompanying Xuthus, since foreigners cannot speak freely (*parrhēsia*).[105] The ancient Athenian democracy celebrated their equality of *parrhēsia*, which means not only freedom to speak but to speak frankly or honestly. Such honestly allowed the democrats to "uncover" themselves and say what they really think.[106] Importantly, much of the language in the tragedy is not honest: Creusa makes up a "friend"; or, Apollo purposefully conceals Ion's identity. Finally, it cannot be ignored the tragedy takes place at Delphi, the site of the most famous Oracle in the ancient world.[107] Here, even when not deliberately misdirecting, the god also spoke in a prophetic language of riddles that simultaneously exposes and conceals meaning. Like dual beings of hybrid creatures and half-divine heroes, language itself is part of liminal space.

The *Ion's* confrontation with doubling is not surprising, as theatrical performances took place in open, public spaces that invited the community to explore such dualities and uncover new meanings.[108] Such public explorations and challenges simultaneously can re-create and re-form new boundaries. As Rusk suggests, ancient drama functioned as a religious experience that reconciled the dichotomies, such as the mingling of good and bad, of human existence.[109] To illustrate, the story of *Ion* reconciles the two competing myths of Athenian foundation: the autochthonous story that they were born of the earth and the Ionian story that they migrated into Attica and as far as Asia Minor. In other words, there is a doubling effect in which what was considered two (stories) is revealed to be one. Some scholars, most notably Loraux, understand this reconciliation as re-creation that reinforces the democratic myth in which all Athenians, as descendants of the earthborn, are equal.[110] Yet, as other scholars point out, this reestablishment of new boundaries remains problematic as the reconciliation between autochthony and Ionianism is never fully accomplished.[111] Since the tragedy's chorus is made up of already xenophobic proud Athenians, for example, "Athenians" exist prior to Ion and his Ionian progeny; in other words, there are Athenians who are pre-Ionian. Thus, the reconciliation effected by this refounding is partial, and like the insistence of Apollo, much remains concealed and eternally open to new possibilities and new challenges.

This continual problematizing of boundaries can suggest that without some ultimate scapegoat or final autochthonous heir, there is no hope of unequivocally distinguishing good blood from bad blood, or right from wrong. The loss of delineated meaning is symbolized by the absent god of the play: Apollo. This missing god is a literal "dis-embodiment" that signifies a lack of center or authoritative voice. Instead, always speaking through others, Apollo's speech is constantly distorted and sometimes intentionally false. Importantly, even Apollo's prophetic foresight is limited, as we know he planned to reveal Ion's true identity after they arrived in Athens.[112] It was the righteous indignation of Creusa and her old tutor that set in motion the impious actions that even the prophetic Apollo could not foresee.[113] Athena's deus ex machina appears to reestablish divine authority, yet her gift of the twin vials of good and bad blood is revealed to be an artificial separation. Thus, the secure distinction of good from bad is mere artifice and not, as the chorus stresses, "natural." From this perspective, Euripides again seems to support some sort of proto-nihilist position that questions whether meaning, boundaries, or justice exist.

The doublings at work in this tragedy, however, do not necessarily take this nihilist turn. The strict identification of "my own" or friend with blood kin seems an easy answer to the question of who a friend is, but the story reveals that it is not: Creusa does not know her child, and Ion does not know his parents.[114] Instead, the meaning of "my own" and the boundary between "friend" and "enemy" appears fluid and unstable because all the characters, including the gods, have a limited perspective. Although this could suggest there is no truth, it could also emphasize the importance of what Zacharia calls a "dialogistic discourse."[115] Such discourse requires the recognition that because all viewpoints and experience are limited, any attempt to understand the truth of who is "my own" or the boundary between good and bad requires us to listen and pay attention to the plurality of worldviews in seeking the truth.

Conclusion

The *Ion*, despite being a rather obscure play about a rather obscure myth, is a treasure trove of storytelling. It explores the ancient view of justice as helping friends and harming enemies through the question of "my own"; it challenges the certainty of a firm boundary between friends and enemies by revealing the extent to which our perception and ignorance (and also deliberate deceptions) contribute to erroneous judgment. The multiple forms of doubling and repetition in the play also point to our limited perception in distinguishing the one from the many, the friend from the enemy, the just from the unjust. It the lack of knowledge of the duality in things that lead Ion to almost kill the very birds that will be his salvation in the end.[116] It is the inability to definitively recognize "my own" that almost leads Creusa and Ion to mutual destruction. The lingering lesson—that our partial viewpoints require listening to a plurality of voices—adds at least two important ideas to our contemporary discussion of justice.

First, it is impossible to think about the *Ion* without its implications for contemporary accounts of nationalism, citizenship, and immigration. The straightforward interpretation that the tragedy celebrates the rule of "one's own" reflects a type of modern nationalism that locates political identity in a people's distinctiveness (religion, cultural, history, and language) to the exclusion of all others.[117] Like modern nationalism, the tragedy also emphasizes the claim of a distinctive people to their land (*chthōn*): for the Athenians, the soil is literally their mother. Yet, as discussed previously, there are numerous problems with this straightforward xenophobic perspective, as the new refounding continues to conceal truth and ignores the reality of preexisting Athenians. Such tensions between narrow and broader visions of "my own" were also reflected in Athenian political history, which revised what counted as "my own" many times.[118] The reforms that led to democracy, for example, created new citizens. After the massive losses in the latter part of the Peloponnesian War, exemptions were made to the famous law that restricted citizenship to those with two Athenian parents by expanding suffrage to resident foreigners (metics) and slaves who volunteered for the navy. There is also some evidence that large numbers of citizens were struck from the citizen lists following the restoration of democracy in 403 BCE. Thus, as hinted at in the tragedy, the process of determining "my own" is not an event, but like the repetitions of autochthonous founders, it is a continuous process of renewal.

This continued need for renewal also exposes the injustice of the concealed falsehoods of excluding those, like Xuthus, who contribute to the common good. In our contemporary politics, the injustice of the exclusion of the "other" from political identity and decision making is shared in the arguments of postcolonial analysis and the politics of immigration.[119] It is also at the root of many social movements that speak out for those marginalized in our social and political spaces. Importantly, Euripides's ancient story adds an important "voice" to this contemporary debate. One of the most important lessons of the tragedy is the recognition of our limited vision of "my own" and the need to listen to multiple viewpoints in the continuing renewal and updating of political identity. Thus, it is not only this ancient Athenian story but also our own story of who is "my own," that is part of the ever-evolving process in which the political community is "founded and re-founded over time by narratives with reference to new cultural exigencies."[120]

Second, and in a final word, Euripides's *Ion* also reminds us of the role shame plays in our exploration of boundaries and meaning.[121] In contemporary political thought, shame is at the heart of a debate about authenticity and civility in public discourse. On one side are scholars who see shame, especially in a legal context, as dubious for promoting justice; instead, shame is seen to "pathologize radical democratic political activity" or police diverse ways of being.[122] On the other hand, other scholars argue that the lack of shame or respect for moral boundaries, especially in interactions on social media, is damaging to individuals but also the community.[123] At the heart of this debate is the question of whether shame, which can be used to stigmatize, oppress, and control others, is necessary for the community. In other words, is there a way that shame is valuable, even if it can be used in oppressive ways?

In the *Ion*, shame or respect for others is always present but seems to linger in the shadows.[124] It is respect for divine law that prevents the chorus from transgressing the sanctuary boundaries.[125] Creusa invents her story of a "friend" out of a sense of shame. Even the gods might feel shame: Apollo remains absent in order to avoid reproach. This suggests the real reason the god continues to lie to Xuthus is to keep his bad behavior concealed. Of course, shame is not all powerful, as the tutor stresses in his outrage at his enemies. There are times when the boundaries should be transgressed and "sweet opinions" revealed for the lies they conceal. Importantly, however, Ion is proven wrong: shame is not a "do nothing goddess." By contrast, this goddess and others invoked in the tragedy, such as Enodia and Themis, remind us to pause for introspection and due reverence in our questioning and crossing of boundaries between the just and unjust. It is easy, like the old tutor, to be moved by righteous indignation and act without full knowledge against perceived injustices in the world. Yet the tragedy reminds us to revere the goddesses who can lead us carefully through the difficult task of distinguishing the commingled form of the just from the unjust. They can also guide us through the dangerous transitions of how and when to "cross beyond" legal and cultural norms.

Chapter 5

The *Children of Heracles*

And Justice for Others

> For a long time, I have held this expectation:
> A man can be just by nature to neighbors,
> But, holding without restraint the will for gain
> He can be entirely useless to the city
> And burdensome to associate with,
> Because he is best only to himself.[1]

Euripides's *The Children of Heracles* has all the earmarks of a good story: evil kings, child refugees, human sacrifice, and miraculous rejuvenation—all culminating in an act of bloodthirsty vengeance. Traditional scholarship tended to dismiss the play as textually problematic, careless, or a straightforward patriotic piece.[2] Yet, Euripides's tragedy highlights the complexity and volatility of political decision making concerning questions of justice, especially in light of the enduring conflict between domestic politics and wider obligations to aid others in need. This chapter builds on scholarship, such as that by Zuntz, Burian, and Bernett, which argues that suspect passages of this tragedy are integral to its coherent and complex dramatic form.[3]

    This tragedy, about the orphaned children of the great hero Heracles, remains relevant as it concerns the question of a community's moral obligation to support refugees. Although the tragedy's ending appears triumphant in its defeat of a tyrant, there is something amiss or uncomfortable in this victorious celebration. One way the finale is unnerving is its reminder of the joy we feel at watching friends succeed but also the pleasure of seeing enemies suffer. The ending also lays bare the narrow and often blurred line between an understanding of justice as merit and our desire for self-interested gain. In this tragedy, this narrow line turns out to be at its thinnest and most mutable outside the bonds of political community in the relationship between citizens and members of other communities. This theme, about the proper relationship with foreigners, may have been in the air. As one of Euripides's alphabet plays, the production date and titles of the other tragedies in its trilogy are not identified. Metrical dating, however, places it somewhere near the *Medea*, which is more firmly dated at 431 BCE.[4] This means that the *Children of Heracles* was likely produced sometime early in the Peloponnesian War with Heracles's descendants: the Spartans.[5] As is typical, Euripides does not present a clear resolution to the question of justice between noncitizens; rather, he exposes the flaws of rooting justice in friendship (*philia*) and reciprocal obligations (*kharis*), and he reveals the dark desires often underlying our pursuit of justice, especially with those who are not "our own."

The Mythological Context and Plot of the *Children of Heracles*

Background Myth

Euripides's *Children of Heracles* picks up the story shortly after the death of Heracles, the greatest and most Panhellenic of all the ancient heroes. As Heracles's story is so widespread, there exist many different and conflicting versions of his life and adventures.[6] In most accounts, Heracles was conceived when Zeus tricked the Mycenean princess Alcmene into having intercourse with him by disguising himself as her husband, Amphitryon. On the same night, she also slept with her real husband. From this fateful encounter, Alcmene bore twins: Iphacles, who was the mortal son of Amphitryon, and Heracles, son of Zeus. Although Zeus had many illegitimate children, like his half-brother Dionysus, Heracles becomes immortal. In one account, Zeus tricked Hera into breastfeeding Heracles, which made him immortal; perhaps for this reason, and certainly for his bastardy, Hera became Heracles's lifelong enemy. As a baby she tried to kill him by sending snakes into his crib, but the infant simply strangled them. Heracles did live happily for a while with his first wife Megara until, in a fit of madness brought on by Hera, he kills their children (and in some versions Megara as well).[7]

Typically, in recompense for these murders, the Delphic Oracle sent him to Hera's beloved Eurystheus (the King of Argos), who tasked him with his famous labors.[8] Embarking on these labors with his nephew Iolaus, among other deeds, Heracles killed the nine-headed Lernaean Hydra, retrieved the girdle of the Amazon Queen Hippolyte, and miraculously cleaned the stables of Augeas. Generally, these labors are considered civilizing acts that freed all of Greece from monstrous or dangerous creatures. In some versions of his story, for successfully carrying out these labors, Apollo and/or Athena reward him with the gift of future immortality. Heracles also participated in other famous events, such as allying with the Olympian gods in the Gigantomachy against the autochthonous Giants. In most accounts, he at least begins the journey with Jason as part of the team of Argonauts who went to retrieve the Golden Fleece. There are stories that he may have freed the Titan Prometheus, who famously gave art and fire to human beings (and was punished by Zeus for doing so by being chained and having his liver eaten and rejuvenated daily).[9] Importantly, for our story, Heracles also rescued the Athenian hero Theseus from Hades following that hero's failed attempt to kidnap Persephone.

His mortal life, however, characteristically ends at the hands of his last human wife, Deianira. Jealous of Heracles's new interest in another princess (Iole of Euboea), she uses the "love potion" given to her by Heracles's enemy, the centaur Nessos. Unaware that this potion is really his poisonous blood (much like Creusa's vial of bad Gorgon blood), Deianira pours it on a cloak, which she gives to Heracles: it burns him alive. In some versions, while watching his son burn, Zeus finally decides Heracles has suffered enough and grants him divine immortality. Also, of importance for our story, the kings of Sparta all traced their ancestry to Hyllus, the eldest of Heracles's children with Deianira.

Euripides's *Children of Heracles*

Euripides's version begins when Heracles's children (in the plural: the Heracleidae), under the protection of his mother Alcmene and Iolaus (his partner in the twelve labors), arrive as refugees and suppliants at the Temple of Zeus of the Marketplace in Marathon. This temple was located in Athenian territory near the site of the famous defeat of the Persians in 490 BCE. This past imbues the settling with the symbolism of the Battle of Marathon, which the Athenians saw as another great act that saved all of Greece.[10] In the prologue, an elderly Iolaus tells of the fugitive plight of the Heracleidae, who have been chased from polis to polis because Eurystheus threatens any city that offers them protection.[11] They finally arrive at the extreme boundary (*termōn*) of Athenian territory because the Athenian king Demophon is kin to the Heracleidae. Not confident of Athenian support, however, the eldest son Hyllus has gone ahead to find alternative allies.

Unlike many of Euripides's tragedies, and despite the speculation that the text may be corrupted, the *Children of Heracles* does have fairly tight plot development and action. The story as it has been transmitted is told in four segments. The first part, from lines 50–350, focuses on the arrival of a herald sent by Eurystheus, who disrespectfully pushes the elderly Iolaus from the sanctuary of Zeus's altar.[12] Immediately following this act of violence is the *parodos* arrival of the chorus of Marathonian elders.[13] They send for the sons of the great Athenian hero Theseus: King Demophon and his brother Acamas (in a nonspeaking role) who adjudicate an *agōn* or dispute between Iolaus and the herald regarding the children's supplication.[14] The herald's argument for rejecting the suppliants is straightforward politics: first, legality dictates the refugees should be rejected, as they were sentenced in accordance with the laws of Argos; second, expediency confirms only "unnecessary trouble" and nothing to "gain" (*kerdos*) from helping these suppliants. In reply, Iolaus counters with a more complicated argument that reinforces "political idealism."[15] He starts with a competing claim to legality: since the Argives exiled the children, they no longer have legal authority, and Argos has no authority to command the rest of Greece. Second, Demophon has a duty to aid the children based both on kinship obligations and as repayment of the debt of *kharis* (gratitude) because Heracles rescued Demophon's father from Hades.[16]

After hearing both sides, Demophon is convinced to support supplication. He provides three reasons: first, out of piety for Panhellenic laws protecting sanctuary; second, out of the duty of kinship and *kharis* obligation; and third, which he says is "most important," to avoid the disgrace of allowing a foreign power to command Athens, which is a free city.[17] The herald persists and suggests Demophon simply place the refugees beyond Athenian borders. The king rejects such clever speaking as impious. At this point, rational dialogue breaks down. The herald refuses to accept Demophon's decision and tries to forcibly claim the children.[18] The chorus has to restrain Demophon from attacking the herald and violating another Panhellenic law protecting the sanctity of heralds. This section ends with Iolaus telling the children to remember Athens as their savior, and the chorus sings an ode celebrating the Athenian self-identity of justly helping the weak.[19]

The hope embedded in this first episode reverses in the second, from lines 350–630, when Demophon returns with an oracular prophecy stating that victory over Eurystheus requires the sacrifice of a noble virgin to Persephone. Demophon declares that a citizen cannot be expected to commit such a horrific act. The city is now divided to the point of civil war over whether to aid the refugees. At the moment when all seems lost, an unnamed daughter of Heracles presents a solution. She offers herself, "of my own choice without being asked," also for three reasons: first, to prove her courage as a noble daughter of Heracles; second, to demonstrate the worthiness of the Heracleidae; and third, to be remembered for her glorious death.[20] Iolaus suggests that it would be more just to choose a daughter by lottery, but the maiden refuses. There is no gratitude (*kharis*), she stresses, for those who die under compulsion. Departing to her fate, she reminds her brothers to honor their elderly relatives, their hosts, and the memory of her sacrifice.

The third episode, from 630–890, begins with Iolaus prostrate with grief over the maiden's death. Suddenly the pace of the action accelerates. A servant sent from the absent son Hyllus reports to Alcmene, who has appeared onstage, that Hyllus has brought a large army of allies. Despite Alcmene's greater concern to see her grandson, she is informed the battle is already underway. Hearing this, the elderly Iolaus decides to join the fight. Plundering Zeus's temple for weapons—some so heavy that the servant must carry them—he totters off to battle. A messenger arrives with news from the battlefield: Eurystheus rejected Hyllus's offer to fight one on one. And, most astonishingly, "from the lips of others," the messenger heard that the now divine Heracles and his new wife Hēbē (the goddess of youth) miraculously rejuvenated Iolaus.[21] With his newfound youth, Iolaus captured Eurystheus. The prisoner is being brought to Alcmene so that she may see her enemy's suffering "with her own eyes."

The final episode, from 890–1055, begins with a celebration of victory. The chorus opens by suggesting that "it is delightful to see the success of friends who previously did not prosper" and asserts that Zeus always strips the unjust of their hubris.[22] The servant echoes: "there is nothing more pleasing than to see an enemy turn from success to misfortune." Alcmene, particularly, is delighted to lash out at this enemy who sent her son on his dangerous civilizing labors and persecuted her grandchildren. She announces that he will die "evilly . . . for causing so much misery." At this point, the servant interrupts by reminding her that Athenian law forbids the execution of prisoners of war.

This announcement initiates the tragedy's second *agōn* between Alcmene and Eurystheus over his fate. At first, Alcmene dismisses Athenian law and expresses her intention to kill him anyway. In response, Eurystheus attempts to defend himself by justifying his actions as self-defense: he sent Heracles on his labors under the divine compulsion of Hera and persecuted the children to protect himself from their inevitable retaliatory revenge.[23] Echoing the herald in the opening scene, Alcmene resorts to clever argumentation: by giving up his corpse, she argues, Athens would "obey" their laws because they would still "return" his body to the Argives. Since all seems lost, Eurystheus reveals his knowledge of a future prophecy: if the Athenians bury his body by the shine of Athena, he will rise to destroy the descendants of the Heracleidae if they ever invade Athens. Alcmene uses this prophecy to suggest an even shrewder argument: the Athenians should disobey their own laws, since his death will secure their future "gain" (*kerdos*). The chorus agrees and departs by declaring that Eurystheus's death will bring no pollution or taint upon those who rule the city.

Euripides's Potential Innovations

Euripides's retelling of the fate of Heracles's children presents a unique version with four important potential innovations. First, in Euripides's version, the character of Iolaus has aged two generations.[24] In the more typical account, Iolaus was the son of Heracles's half-brother Iphicles, which would make him a nephew and closer in age to Hyllus, Demophon, and the maiden than to Alcmene.[25] Second, since all similar references are dated after this play, Euripides may have invented the maiden and her self-sacrifice.[26] As will be developed in this chapter, in the extant manuscripts of Euripides's *Heracleidae*, she is never identified by name. It is possible that Euripides did not "name" her because theatrical custom prohibited the creation of wholly new mythological personas in tragedy; in any case, identifying her as Macaria was a later addition to the myth.[27] Third, Euripides most likely invented Demophon as the king of Athens during the Heracleidae supplication. Demophon and his brother Acamas are minor figures in mythology, and this is the only known tragedy that mentions him by name.[28]

Euripides's final scene is also exceptional. In versions prior to Euripides's, Eurystheus was killed in battle and buried far from Athens under the Skironian Cliffs.[29] In no other version is he taken prisoner of war and executed by Alcmene. The inclusion of the prophecy and an alternative burial site near Athena's shrine is another reason the play may have been performed in the early days of the war.[30] Such a prophecy would make more sense during this period, when the Spartans attacked the Attic countryside each summer but before such foretelling would seem spurious.

Importantly, all four of these potential innovations are at the heart of the traditional criticism of Euripides's tragedy. The maiden scene, for example, has been dismissed either as an interpolation or as evidence that there is a major lacuna in the manuscript. McLean, for example, argues that this scene is "not essential" as the servant could arrive with Iolaus prostrate in grief over the denial of Athenian support and not over a girl who is "a prig."[31] Other scholars have suggested that there must be a missing scene in which the sacrificed girl receives a proper tragic lament.[32] In addition, the entire last scene is argued as mutilated since it reverses the mood: Alcmene proves savagely vengeful and Eurystheus becomes sympathetic.[33] Similarly, scholars criticize the chorus for abandoning their former righteousness for the sake of future gain (*kerdos*).[34] In short, this traditional line of scholarship suggests our extant text suffers from textual corruption, including a possible deus ex machina scene, in which this sour ending is reversed possibly by Heracles himself.

Another critique of the innovations centers not on the aging of Iolaus per se but on the two scenes resulting from this portrayal. Much is made of Iolaus's awkward departure for battle with the servant carrying him and the looted weapons; this scene, as Burian points out, is "perhaps the most overtly comic in extant tragedy."[35] Second, it is not clear what to make of the hearsay reports of Iolaus's miraculous rejuvenation and heroic capture of Eurystheus. Fitton notes that the whole rejuvenation takes place "without a word of criticism or irony" as if it were a "fairy tale."[36] This rejuvenation scene also disrupts Athenian patriotism, since it turns the Heracleidae into their own saviors.[37] Much of this critique assumes the tragedy's reversal, and inconsistencies are problematic because they do not meet the criteria of a "straight" or "closed" play with an uncomplicated patriotic theme.[38]

More recent scholarship has focused on the same scenes not as problematic but as key to interpreting its complexity. Zuntz championed this more sympathetic interpretation by arguing the tragedy has the "ambiguous conclusion of a Platonic dialogue, [which] leaves the spectator with disquieting questions and thus stirs him to thinking."[39] For Zuntz, the play represents the difficulty of living up to such high Athenian ideals "of the right, the just, and the noble" in the uncertainty and "overwhelming insecurity which characterizes our lives." In another approach, Avery suggests the play's title "the descendants of Heracles" signifies not the genealogical Spartans but all those characters (Iolaus, the maiden, and Demophon) that support Heracles's moral view of sacrifice on behalf of others.[40] In a less optimistic line, Burian argues that the disquieting ending reveals a rather proto-nihilistic view in which all terms such as "violence and nobility, profit and justice, piety and gratitude . . . no longer have unequivocal referents and fixed meanings."[41] Despite the different interpretations, this line of analysis takes the complexity as a sign of Euripides's serious approach to confronting difficult moral questions.

Building on this latter approach to interpretation, this analysis focuses on the ways in which the tragedy confronts the question of how to determine the boundary between obligations to others and individual gain or political necessity. This question is highlighted by Iolaus in the opening words of the tragedy, where he suggests that "by nature" we can be just to those nearby, but interest in individual profit makes one "useless" to the political community.[42] This statement sets up an opposition between natural justice and self-interested gain. Even more interesting, since this is a story about justice pertaining to foreign refugees and prisoners of war, the opening lines beg the question of whether the same natural justice is at work in our relationship with foreigners. Euripides's complicated tragedy reveals the distinction between citizen and noncitizen, or justice and self-interested gain becomes easily blurred, especially at the very edge, both spatially and conceptually of the boundaries of community.

Justice as Friendship: Helping Those in Need

The opening scene deals directly with the question of a community's obligation to help outsiders, especially if such aid is without self-interested gain or could be potentially harmful to the political community. This question brings to the forefront two important political debates in Euripides's fifth-century Athens. First, it highlights the use of helping the weak as a moral justification against the common critique that Athens was a "busybody" or interfered in the political affairs of other states. In Thucydides's *Peloponnesian War*, for example, the Corinthians make a forceful argument that Athenian interference in the affairs of others is due to their "active" nature.[43] From this perspective, the tragedy confronts fifth-century political debates concerning the sphere of politics we call "international relations." Second, this question of helping others is related to the traditional heroic understanding of justice: helping friends and harming enemies.[44] The ancient Greeks called "friends" (*philoi*) anyone closely associated with them (such as family members and close associates) or related via formalized institutions, such as guest-friendship or supplication (*hiketeia*). This ancient code of helping friends and harming enemies is ubiquitous in ancient tragedy.[45]

In this tragedy, the importance of helping friends and harming enemies is raised in the rhetorical debate (*agōn*) between Iolaus and Eurystheus's herald. Demophon cites it as one reason to support the suppliants, and it is reiterated in the uncomfortable ending.[46] As this first *agōn* appears at the very beginning of this tragedy, Euripides dramatizes the significance of political leadership. Such leadership, faced with an aggressive herald and politically motivated decision to help others, mimics Demophon's father, Theseus, in the *Suppliant Woman*.[47] Like Demophon, in that play Theseus is convinced to aid foreigners based on the principle of protecting Panhellenic customs. Also similar to Demophon, Theseus does not disconnect principle from political interest. Unlike Theseus's successful example, however, Demophon loses political support in the following episode of this tragedy.

The herald is a personification of the twin faces of politics: force and persuasion.[48] From his entrance on stage, the herald arrives with the pretense of diplomacy but readily resorts to violence in his threats against the Heracleidae and physical removal of the elderly Iolaus from the altar's sacred space.[49] This threat of violence continues in the exchange between Demophon and the herald. The herald's persuasive appeal indicates pure expediency: "No one will choose to have your [the Heracleidae] worthless strength in preference to Eurystheus."[50] This argument, which Zuntz suggests is Realpolitik, stresses that refugees are subject to an interstate calculation of "national interest."[51] As the herald puts it: it is neither prudent nor profitable to help because taking "foolish pity on the [Heracleidae] misfortunes" or preferring "weak to noble friends" would bring "unnecessary trouble." The herald also dismisses any reference to justice since Argos did not attack Athens or their allies. In other words, the only just war would be in self-defense. Finally, the herald objects to claims of sanctuary. Such claims would interfere with the power rulers have over their subjects by allowing criminals to take advantage of the sacred space.[52] The gist of his argument is that it would not be politically expedient for Athens to aid the suppliants rather than make new friendships with powerful allies.

Iolaus counters the herald's arguments of pure political expediency by emphasizing arguments based on religious, familial, and alternative political reasoning. Immediately after being dragged off the altar, Iolaus calls for someone to witness to such "dishonor[ing] of your gods."[53] With this comment, Iolaus draws attention to the duty of any sanctuary site in ancient Greece, which was to offer protective asylum to refugees and exiles. Victims of war, like the Heracleidae, were protected by the religious tenet that such sacred territory was owned by the gods, which meant nothing could be removed because the boundaries of the temple were inviolate.[54] As Iolaus emphasizes, such a violation was politically shameful, since sanctuaries were maintained by the political authority of the region. Iolaus reinforces this political aspect of sanctuary in the *agōn* by pointing out that Athenian sovereignty would be compromised if they allow the herald to take the suppliants by force.

Second, Iolaus counters the herald's legal argument that the suppliants are under Argive authority. He points out that since they are exiles, Argos no longer has political authority over them. Iolaus's point is also in line with Athenian norms, which historically protected exiles since the ancient laws of Draco.[55] Most significantly, Iolaus turns the debate away from political expediency to Demophon's private obligations. The king is obligated to help the suppliants because of the ancient ties of "birth and blood."[56] In addition, Demophon owes a personal debt (*kharis*) because Heracles rescued his father during Theseus's failed attempt to abduct Persephone.[57] The Greek idea of *kharis* is complex, but it emphasized a reciprocal relationship founded in the benevolence of helping others as well as the gratitude that inspired future repayment.[58] Finally, Iolaus makes a typical rhetorical appeal to pity when he implores Demophon to "look at" the children and prove to be a true kinsman, friend, father, brother, and master.

Significantly, the chorus is not neutral but participates in the debate with clear support for Iolaus. Representing the old men of Marathon, the chorus symbolizes those men who fought in that famous battle and personify the Athenian self-image of standing up to invaders in a just cause. Their contribution underscores three of Iolaus's arguments. The old men resist the herald's violence by pointing out that his actions "mock justice" and even the powerful are bound to respect the "rights of those the gods protect."[59] Also, like Iolaus, they point to the herald's disrespect of Athenian sovereignty as he did not follow protocol by consulting the king before making demands. Finally, most swayed by the Heracleidae's misfortune, they express their sorrow: "I pity these [children] for what has befallen them . . . [they] are suffering undeserved misfortune."[60] Aiding those who suffer undeservedly, the chorus stresses, is achieved by "helping the weak" and "toiling on behalf of friends."

Unlike the chorus, which is influenced by pity for the Heracleidae, Demophon seems immune to pity; however, as noted previously, he supports the supplication for the other three reasons. The "most important" was respect for the divine law of supplication; second was obligation to kin and reciprocity (*kharis*); and third (and what "concerned him the most") was to uphold Athenian sovereignty.[61] Demophon completely ignores the legal wrangling concerning Eurystheus's authority over the exiles as well as the question of whether the Heracleidae merit their suffering. By contrast, although he recognizes claims of justice in familial obligations, his most important concern is political independence and obligations to protect sanctuary. Significantly, he is also unmoved by the herald's critique that sanctuary protects criminals; instead, he upholds the Panhellenic principle that all suppliants should be protected by sanctuary. Demophon's view, of course, foreshadows Eurystheus's own situation at the end of the play when that king, too, claims sanctuary on the altar of Zeus.[62]

Importantly, Demophon's support for such Panhellenic principles is not absolute. When the herald persists even after losing the argument, Demophon has to be restrained by the chorus from physically abusing him: "By the gods," they shout, "don't dare to hit a herald!"[63] In ancient Greece, the rules protecting the sanctity of heralds were derived from the same prohibitions that guaranteed safety to suppliants and safe passage to travelers.[64] This safe conduct applied to envoys on diplomatic missions but also artists, athletes, and spectators on their way to religious ceremonies or pilgrimage sites. In his willingness to strike a herald, Demophon confirmed that he really is "most concerned with" upholding his political authority, and not the "most important" reason of safeguarding the sanctity of divine space.

In contrast to Demophon, the chorus and Iolaus emphasize the injustice of unmerited suffering of the Heracleidae. They also celebrate the renewed friendship and reciprocity arising from Demophon's decision. Join hands with the chorus, Iolaus tells the children, and "consider for all time [the Athenians] as your saviors and friends . . . never raise a hostile force against this land . . . [for] the Athenians are worthy of your reverence."[65] Demophon echoes that he is confident that Heracleidae always "will remember this favor (*kharis*)." All of this praise is very ironic, of course, considering that the invading Spartans in the Peloponnesian War are the future descendants of the Heracleidae.

The potential consequence of Demophon's primary concern for political freedom creates the conditions that bring to fruition his second (but less important) reason for helping the children: the obligation of *kharis*.[66] Protecting Athenian political sovereignty generates cyclical reciprocity of potential future alliance, friendship, and enduring respect. Hence, this is the initial answer to the question of what kind of action, in contrast to self-interested gain, is useful and not burdensome to the community. It is simply "helping others." Importantly, this version of helping others includes helping foreigners in need. Such aid, beyond the concerns of immediate expediency, can potentially establish more enduring bonds with positive long-term benefits, both for the individual and the political community. Or, in contemporary language, those who are useful to their political systems are individuals, and especially leaders, who delay immediate private gain for long-term common good.

The protection of the refugees, however, brings not only a promise of future benefits but also immediate danger and risk. By the end of the play, of course, even this promise will collapse with Alcmene's violation of Athenian law and Eurystheus's prophecy to protect against future invasions. If the play was performed shortly after 430 BCE, when those descendants of Heracles ravaged Attica without any intervention from a ghostly Eurystheus, then the trust in such future promises proves doubly ill-considered. The *kharis* of future reciprocity is, even at this point in the tragedy, already questionable.[67] Only the chorus and Iolaus genuinely appear to celebrate this new friendship; Demophon has made it clear that, above all, his concern is for Athenian authority and not *kharis*, which was a distant third in his reasoning. Helping others may facilitate long-term benefits for the community, but political self-interest is not absent from Athenian motivations.

Justice as Merit: Helping Friends by Saving Oneself

Although many scholars regard Alcmene's revenge as a reversal of the positive ideal of "not being best only to oneself," Euripides begins to confound and problematize this value early in the second episode.[68] Immediately after the chorus celebrates the Athenian defense of the defenseless, Demophon reappears from war preparations to announce the "bad news." The typical conflicting oracles this time all agree: "To destroy the enemies and save the city . . . a virgin who is of a noble father must be sacrificed to Demeter's daughter."[69] Demophon stresses his earlier "eagerness to help" cannot include such a horrific sacrifice; instead, other political considerations are more important, as the city is on the brink of civil war over the question of protecting the refugees. In effect, Demophon's hands are now tied: if the Heracleidae want his help, they must help him first. This scene also reflects the historically "favored method" of using oracles as a convenient justification to renege on the sacred law to protect suppliants.[70] Thus, the tragedy begins to reveal the tension between Athens's self-identity of helping the weak and political necessity.[71] Both Iolaus and Demophon approach this new situation with calm practicality. Iolaus readily agrees that Demophon must think of his "own city first." Demophon easily rejects Iolaus's offer to be the sacrificial victim, as this would neither satisfy the oracle, nor Eurystheus.

Into this panicked atmosphere, the young maiden daughter of Heracles appears "outside" from the inner sanctuary. This nameless daughter is the only child of Heracles given a voice in the tragedy, and she proves to be "the seed of the divine Heracles" both in lineage and noble action.[72] A female equivalent of her famous father, she is thus determined to take on this heroic labor. Although she appears similar to other Euripidean sacrificial women, such as Iphigenia, Polyxena, or Evadne, in her emboldened choice she most resembles Menoeceus in the *Phoenician Women*.[73] She also resembles an archaic hero by rejecting the democratic principle of choosing among equals (i.e., her sisters) by the lottery method. As she stresses: "I won't be butchered as a gambling debt."[74] By contrast, the maiden calmly outlines the reasoning for her choice: first, reciprocity for the requests the Heracleidae placed on others; second, proof of her family's worthiness of such benevolence; third, to avoid the dishonorable life of an exiled orphan; and, finally, to fulfill the oracular prophecy that by sacrificing herself she will save both her family and Athens. She ends by stressing that her deliberate choice will win her everlasting glory. As she is led off to Hades, she reminds her brothers to always remember her.

The meaning of the maiden's sacrifice is highly controversial. Scholars have variously dismissed her as a "prig," or endorsed her character as representing either "the moral center of the play" or "a community surrogate."[75] She does, at first glance, seem to embody the two principles celebrated by the chorus and Iolaus as reasons for supporting supplication: her voluntary choice proves the Heracleidae worthy of Athenian support; and, she confirmed that Heracleidae would return Athenian benevolence since her action saves Athens both from a possible civil war and the foreign enemy descending on the plains of Attica.[76] Yet despite this proof of merit, the maiden's sacrifice is also based on self-interest; as Burnett puts it, she is more "tribally focused" than concerned with proving the merit of reciprocal justice.[77] The main reason for her sacrifice and refusal of a lottery is self-glorification. As she stresses, it is not by "loving the spirit too much but [by] leaving life beautifully" that we are remembered.[78] Thus, she rejects the idea of democratic lot, precisely because glory and reciprocity (*kharis*) cannot arise from random chance among equals. Instead, more like her heroic father, her death transforms her into a glorious heroine whose noble action guarantees eternal remembrance.[79]

With the maiden's departing words, the action begins a slow unraveling of the tragedy's celebration of helping others as a way to benefit the community. Her sacrifice establishes the maiden's nobility, but her rationale for sacrificing herself stresses self-interested gain or those "best to themselves." Like Demophon, she is concerned with the reciprocity of *kharis*; however, also like Demophon, such concerns are subordinate to more important ones. In the maiden's case, she stresses personal justifications of avoiding a dishonorable life and gaining personal glory and eternal remembrance.

Yet, unlike Demophon, the maiden does not include in her list of reasons to "leave life beautifully" any reference to Panhellenic or divine law. Her lack of interest in the divine highlights the irony of her sacrifice. The oracles demanded a maiden girl be sacrificed to Demeter's daughter Persephone, the Queen of Hades. As our maiden is led away to be slaughtered, she is openly skeptical of such an afterlife; as she puts it: "If indeed there is anything beneath the earth, but I think there is nothing."[80] The strange logic at work here is that the oracles ask for a sacrifice to a goddess who rules the underworld, a divine being whose existence is doubted by the sacrificial victim. If she doubts the source of the oracle, then she must not believe her sacrifice will really win the war. This means her reason for dying must be embedded in her desire to be remembered for her glorious action in this world. This desire leads to the most disheartening irony of all in the tragedy: as many scholars have pointed out, this final view of herself as a glorious heroine is completely undermined in the plot.[81] She is never even given a name, never receives proper tragic lament, and she is not remembered by anyone in the tragedy, not even her own grandmother. She vanishes without a trace.

Although she is easily forgotten, with the maiden's self-sacrifice, "the crisis is averted," and the Heracleidae transform themselves from submissive suppliants to active participants in their own salvation.[82] The maiden's sacrifice is the beginning of the rejuvenation of the Heracleidae that culminates in Iolaus's miraculously recovered youth and Alcmene's triumph over her son's persecutor. The second step of this self-salvation is the announcement that Hyllus has returned leading an allied army. At this point, Alcmene makes her debut and provides the audience with a glimpse of what is to come: she demands to see Hyllus immediately because the ensuing battle to save Athens "is nothing to us."[83] Alcmene has not only already forgotten her granddaughter's sacrifice but also the Athenian's favor of granting refuge.

In contrast, Iolaus is exhilarated to hear of the impending battle. In this much-criticized scene, he loots the temple and, buttressed by his servant, totters off to war.[84] Although this scene appears comic with the doddering Iolaus unable to hold his plundered weapons, it does set the stage for his imminent rejuvenation. Without, for example, a vision of his extreme fragility, Iolaus's victory over their old enemy would be less miraculous.[85] It is not clear, however, whether Iolaus's rejuvenation was entirely unexpected by Euripides's audience. It is possible Euripides incorporates a long-standing Theban tradition concerning Iolaus's recovered youth, which was reflected in their youth cult of Iolaus.[86] It is also possible that our discomfort with this scene was not shared by Euripides's original audience. Culturally such stories of miraculous rejuvenations were part of ancient Greek mythology, such as Laertes's rejuvenation to aid his son against the suitors in the *Odyssey* or Medea's notable powers that rejuvenated Aeson and that she withheld in the death of Pelias.[87]

It is nevertheless Iolaus's rejuvenation from an old man into his younger self that most symbolizes the reversal of the Heracleidae's fortunes.

His literal reversal from old to young overturns the familial archenemy Eurystheus, and the Heracleidae emerge as triumphant self-saviors. Hyllus, on the left flank of the Athenians, turns the battle, and the now youthful Iolaus captures Eurystheus. With the "triumph belong[ing] to themselves," the Heracleidae so eclipse the Athenians that the children alone set up the victory tripod.[88] Although the gods support the Heracleidae's success, it is still a family affair. It is Heracles and his new wife Hēbē, the goddess of youth, who guarantee their success.[89] The outcome of the battle is, as Iolaus puts it: A victory of "better gods."

Despite the absence of clear reports of Athenian participation, the battle could be interpreted as a patriotic success supported by Heracles, the defender of civilization. The symbol of a rejuvenated Iolaus may even be a stand-in for the heroism of Heracles himself.[90] As king, Demophon protected the suppliants and reinforced the Athenian self-image as champion of the weak who suffer undeservedly.[91] Iolaus's claim that the Heracleidae would remember the Athenians' benevolence was fulfilled almost immediately by the maiden's sacrifice. Demophon appears vindicated by his "most concerned" reason to support the supplication: the political independence of Athens. Hence, with such a victory, the Athenians must be those who are "just by nature." Their action of aiding others without immediate gain is justified by the victorious outcome of the war. But this celebratory note is not Euripides's last word concerning justice in this tragedy.

Justice as Merit: Harming Enemies

The story, at this point, does appear to celebrate Athens as a city that supports the principles of righteousness and helping others. As Tzanetou puts it, Athens is revealed as a "benevolent *hēgemōn.*"[92] With such a high point, many scholars suggest the tragedy should have ended here rather than with its hastily drawn reversal of these high ideals.[93] But does the ending really represent a reversal of the tragedy's main themes, especially its treatment of justice? There is no doubt that there is reversal of the mood in the showdown between Alcmene and Eurystheus. The messenger brings the joyous news of victory but also Eurystheus to face the wrath of his enemy. Alcmene immediately demands blood retribution, despite protests from both the messenger and the chorus that Athenian law protects prisoners of war. Although her actions appear to undermine moral certainty, Alcmene brings to fruition a form of justice that has been at work throughout the play. In other words, is the finale merely a long-delayed reciprocal penalty, whereby the enemy truly "gets what he deserves"?[94]

Alcmene's action appears to be a reversal because she violates the three reasons Demophon sets forth as justification for aiding her grandchildren. First, she violates the "most important" reason to respect the inviolability of sanctuary. As Eurystheus is brought to Zeus's temple, it would be as much a violation of divine space to kill him as it would have been for the herald to drag off the suppliants.[95] As Demophon had pointed out earlier, sanctuary is "a common defense for all," which meant that even Eurystheus is protected in the sacred space. Second, she violates the reason that "most concerned" Demophon: since protecting prisoners of war was Athenian law, it would violate Athenian sovereignty for her to break this law, even with her clever sophistry of ransoming a corpse. As such, she undermines Iolaus's promise that Athens will be the master of the Heracleidae.[96] Finally, Alcmene ignores, without even comment, Demophon's reason for supporting reciprocal obligations of *kharis* and bonds of friendship so recently celebrated by the chorus and Iolaus.

Therefore, by the end of this tragedy, promises to "remember always" the favor (*kharis*) of the Athenians have been as easily forgotten as the maiden's sacrifice. Alcmene's lapse of memory reveals the fragility of such reciprocal friendships and may explain why, in the *Suppliant Women*, Athena descends deus ex machina to demand the stronger stuff of oath taking.[97] In addition, her action transforms Eurystheus into a future benefactor. By the finale, it is possible to question whether the chorus was right to urge support for the Heracleidae; they have already disrespected the sanctity of sacred space, reciprocal bonds of friendship, and the sovereignty of Athens. On one level, Alcmene's action could reveal the moral superiority of Athens over the Heracleidae and all their Spartan descendants; yet, it also reveals the futility and danger of helping others.[98] Most importantly, with Eurystheus's prophecy that the descendants of the Heracleidae will invade Athens, there is one final reversal of justice understood as helping friends and harming enemies: the Heracleidae who were friends will become the enemies, and the enemy Eurystheus will become the friend.[99] Understood as a straight reversal, this ending confounds or undermines the certainty of moral values, such as justice, reciprocity, and friendship.[100]

Yet, the ending is not so much a reversal of the plot but the zenith of the Heracleidae's own actions. Two of the three reasons provided by

Demophon for helping the Heracleidae were undermined long before Alcmene violated Athenian sovereignty by ignoring their law and reciprocal expectations of friendship. The maiden's sacrifice may have provided a reciprocal benefit for Athens (i.e., without her sacrifice, civil war may have erupted, or Argos may have been victorious), but her main concern was self-glory, and her sacrifice set into motion the resurrection of the Heracleidae as self-saviors. From her sacrifice onward, the entire family has no regard for justice as reciprocity or respecting divine norms and Athenian law. Even Iolaus, who argued so vehemently for the sanctity of divine space, has no qualms about the impiety of taking the inviolable weapons from the altar. By doing so, Iolaus breaks the same divine law of *asylia* or "prohibition against stealing" for which he condemned the herald or Demophon held up as the "most important" reason for protecting the suppliants. Hyllus is reported to erect the victory tripod on Athenian soil, in the absence of the Athenians. Alcmene stands out, not because she is more willing to violate the principles that aided the Heracleidae but because her actions most unreservedly challenge those principles. "I love this city," and she tells the messenger, "but since this man has come into my hands, there is no mortal man who will take him away."[101] Her desire to destroy her enemy is above regard for others and for all law. She does not hide that her only consideration is unrestrained self-interest. She does not hide that she is best only to herself.

Although most vivid in Alcmene's final revenge, the primacy of her self-interest is unsurprising. Alcmene ignored the maiden's sacrifice and demanded to see Hyllus, even though an army marched on Athenian soil. The maiden's sacrifice also celebrated her self-interested glory. In addition, Hyllus's tripod celebrates the Heracleidae alone. On the side of the Athenians, Demophon revealed an underlying self-interest in his concern for Athenian sovereignty. The city almost erupted in civil war over sacrificing one of their own. Thus, it is not really Alcmene who disappoints with such self-interest in the finale; instead, it is the chorus of Marathonian men. Unlike all the other characters, the chorus always supported principles of justice and was restrained in its desire for gain. The chorus never wavered in helping the weak who suffer undeservedly and were always willing to "bear without number labors on behalf of friends."[102] Importantly, the chorus was also the loci of the tragedy's two conceptions of justice: justice as merit derived from aiding those who suffer undeservedly and justice found in the older heroic code of helping friends and harming enemies. These two conceptions of justice become intertwined, since aiding those who suffer undeservedly fosters future bonds of reciprocal friendship, which in turn, becomes a form of helping (future) friends. From this perspective, aiding the Heracleidae could be also useful to the community as potential reciprocal friendship would be "always remembered." With the news of the Argive victory, the chorus celebrates this new success by singing an ode not only for the safety of their city but also to the "delight of seeing the good luck of friends who, in the past, had nothing."[103]

This newfound delight highlights another kind of reversal at work in the story. In this case, the chorus's former pity for the undeserved sufferings of the Heracleidae turns into joy at the sight of their friends' deserved success.[104] The servant echoes this joy of seeing friends prosper by adding: "There is no more pleasant a vision than to see a man's enemy fallen from good luck into misfortune." Thus, the destruction of an enemy reveals the obverse side of justice as helping friends: the harming of enemies. What remains is the question of whether this "more pleasant vision" of watching enemies suffer is also tied to questions of justice as merit. In other words, since Eurystheus has already lost the battle and is protected by Athenian law, does he deserve Alcmene's final retribution?

On the one hand, there is considerable objection to interpreting the final scene as portraying the just execution of Eurystheus.[105] Significantly, Euripides gives Eurystheus the opportunity to defend himself against Alcmene. Many scholars and potentially some audience members are sympathetic to his case. His actions, Eurystheus pleads, were not voluntary but done under distress. As Eurystheus argues: Hera, not he, was the inventor of the troubles of Heracles and he only persecuted the children out of fear that they would grow up to avenge their father.[106] Furthermore, he emphasizes that the Athenians are under legal and divine obligation to protect him, as he was not killed on the battlefield and has claimed sanctuary. Some of these arguments are valid in the logic of the play; for example, Demophon earlier rejected Iolaus's offer to be the sacrificial victim because the children's deaths are necessary to prevent future revenge. Furthermore, political necessity did win the day when Demophon reneged on his promise to help the children. Hence, Eurystheus appears to be following the same kind of statecraft by arguing for the priority of saving oneself: no city and no ruler would do otherwise. This leads to the conclusion that Alcmene's actions are without provocation and represent "an insatiable thirst for revenge," which elicits "the stern, self-perpetuating, and apparently endless cycle of retribution."[107] According to this view, she does not represent justice as merit. At best, she represents a "primitive" or "old morality" as opposed to the high moral principles of the Athenians.[108] The celebration of her enemy's reversal of fortune is, therefore, "indecent joy over the fate of her victim, [which] excites more repulsion than sympathy."[109]

On the other hand, it is not so clear that Eurystheus has established an indisputable case or that Alcmene's actions are not without due provocation. Eurystheus was guilty of planning to destroy the Heracleidae; he sent Heracles on his labors; he exiled and unlawfully persecuted anyone who aided the children. Eurystheus did act as a tyrant who demanded absolute deference from all political regimes, as if they were not free and independent. He did bring an army to destroy Athens, which had an autonomous and divine right to protect suppliants. Finally, it was Eurystheus's agent, the herald, who proposed the most amoral of moral codes that "might makes right" and "political gain" is all. Thus, his argument of persecuting the children for the sake of political necessity stresses a meaningless moral code in which all and any action becomes permissible for the sake of political expediency and "security" of the city. What, after all, could not be justified on those terms?

Alcmene's actions are also less harsh than some of her poetic companions. Euripides's Hecuba, for example, is often severely criticized, not for her actions against Polymestor (who did, after all, kill her son for gold) but for killing Polymestor's sons in retaliation.[110] Similarly, scholars censure Medea not because she harms Jason's new wife but because she kills their own children.[111] In this tragedy, Alcmene does not harm innocent children but an enemy deserving of punishment. The chorus certainly thinks Alcmene is justified; as they sing: "I know well, oh lady, the victory you have over this man is dreadful but forgivable."[112] If it is not her action that is so problematic, perhaps it is the sheer joy she takes from watching her enemy suffer? The joy of harming enemies who suffered deserved punishment, however, may be intertwined with the pity that inspires helping those who suffer undeservedly. In other words, without the joy of watching bad men suffer, perhaps there can be no pity for the weak who are suffering from such men. From this perspective, Alcmene's joy is not indecent, as she brings to fruition a version of justice as merit established earlier by the chorus's pity for her grandchildren.

If Alcmene's actions are consistent with the development of the plot, why does this final scene of her joyful triumph remain so disturbing? This unease could simply be modern sensitivity, since the ancient Greeks possibly were not at all disturbed by an enemy facing utter destruction.[113] Alcmene's joy, however, is problematic within the logic of the play. Her actions blur the distinction between justice and an excessive concern with gain. Everyone, including Eurystheus, believes justice would have been served if he had been killed in battle (as he was in typical mythology). Yet in her desire to exact punishment at all costs, Alcmene reveals herself more interested in satisfying her will than in recognizing divine law, reciprocity, or the political authority of Athens. She even jumps at the chance to doom her descendants, since Eurystheus would save Athens from future attack. Euripides has portrayed Alcmene as consistently and singularly concerned with her own individualistic good: for example, her first thought on stage was for Hyllus to desert a battle that is of "no concern to us."[114] It is not that there is no justice in Alcmene's single-minded destruction of Eurystheus: the problem is that she is so excessive in this self-interested pursuit that she becomes what the chorus prayed would never befall them. She, like Eurystheus, is insatiable.[115]

In the final evaluation of all the uncomfortable truths in this play, what proves most troublesome is not that Alcmene is excessively self-interested (as she has been all along) but that the line between justice and self-interest becomes blurred in the greatest proponent of justice in the play—the chorus. Importantly, the chorus proposed justice as merit as the reason to help the Heracleidae. The chorus has unwaveringly supported the weak in the face of political and opportunistic gain. This support did foster a potential (even if unfulfilled in the longer term) foundation for reciprocal friendship between the Athenians and the Heracleidae. Yet, as the Heracleidae reverse their fortune with increasing violations of reciprocal friendship, sanctity of law, and Athenian autonomy, the chorus remains silent. The chorus says nothing when Iolaus loots the temple's weaponry; it is not they but the servant who initially points out that Athenian law protects Eurystheus. By the end of the tragedy, the chorus expresses not an ounce of outrage at Alcmene's clever attempt to circumvent both divine (i.e., the inviolability of sanctuary) and Athenian law (sanctity of prisoners of war); instead, they acquiesce to the illegal execution of Eurystheus and announce that such actions will not contaminate Athenian leadership.

There are at least two possible reasons why the chorus allows Eurystheus to be killed. First, the chorus may simply think that Eurystheus deserves what he gets. After all, as they noted earlier, the gods supported his defeat, and they justify Alcmene's anger. They report feeling only joy at his demise. From this perspective, Burnett may be right to see the tragedy as exposing our irrational obligations and that "the state, just because it is the expression of man's reason, is powerless to fulfill them."[116] Hence, try as we might, law is incapable of stopping the demands of vengeance and the overwhelming joy at seeing our enemies suffer.

In contrast, the chorus could allow Eurystheus's illegal execution because they are willing to abandon their position as champion of the weak and defender of sacred space when it proves in their self-interest to do so. In this final scene, the chorus initially is hesitant to supersede their laws. Surprising, it is Eurystheus who rewards their hesitation by announcing the oracular prophecy that he will be the future savior of Athens. Alcmene pounces on this statement and asks why the chorus would continue to hesitate "if you can secure this savior for the city."[117] Unlike their restraint of Demophon when he threatened to strike a herald for his clever sophistry, the chorus encourages her twisting of their own laws as long as "our royal house is unsoiled." Thus, by the end of the play, those elder Marathonian men who defended all of Greece from invasion seize upon the chance to gain (*kerdos*) from Eurystheus's death, even if this gain violates their own law and political autonomy. If Vernant is correct in his supposition that this chorus can express through its "fears, hopes, questions and judgements, the feelings of the spectators who make up the civic community," this conclusion takes on an added dimension of anguish. In this case, the very audience is implicated in this violation of law for profit.[118] In the end, this is the true and final reversal in the tragedy since no one is left untainted by the will for gain.

Conclusion

If this tragedy ends on a false note for so many modern commentators, it is because it cannot be reduced to a simple patriotic play, an encomium of Athens, or celebration of a clear case of justice. In contrast, Euripides explores the difficult issues involved in determining what we owe those who are not "nearby" or noncompatriots. Although the story seems to present an easy case for helping noncitizens, as the Heracleidae are refugee children of a great Panhellenic hero, this "easy case" is still not so easy. Athenian security and self-interest trump Demophon's initial support of the weak; the maiden's self-sacrifice begins the reversal from this weak position into one of strength; the steadfast chorus swaps their concern for justice for future gain; and despite his illegal execution, the tyrant Eurystheus is turned into a friend who will benefit the city. As none of the categories of friends and enemy or victim and persecutor are fixed, the tragedy fails to provide a clear example of who might be just "by nature" and more useful to the community than to himself.

The tragedy does reveal how such questions of justice are even more complicated on the international or global level. Unlike certain contemporary political theorists who locate helping others in a natural duty of care owed to persons as persons, this ancient story suggests that justice concerning those not "nearby," whether innocent child or prisoner of war, is not disconnected from questions of community self-interest.[119] Thus, Euripides reflects more Goodin's argument: considering the great needs of so many others, supporting co-nationals can be justified. Euripides, therefore, is in contrast to Pogge's moral cosmopolitanism that argues human beings as individuals are the ultimate units of concern and not family, tribe, religion, or political community.[120] Iolaus is unsurprised, for example, by Demophon's reneged support for the children, which demands too much sacrifice from Athens. Our more steadfast chorus did an easy about-face and violated their own law and principles for future community gain. In the end, it is important that the Heracleidae really save themselves. The herald was proven correct in his suggestion that helping the children was connected to political expediency. Such questions of political expediency continue to be reflected in contemporary debates about the justice of helping or aiding refugees, such as concerns about limited resources in potential host countries.[121]

Second, it is not simply that the tragedy reveals limits to benevolence for noncitizens, but Euripides highlights the fragility of institutions and moral standards in maintaining any kind of "cosmopolitan" justice. At some point in the tragedy, every character from the herald and Demophon to Alcmene and the chorus, breaks or attempts to break either divine or positive law. Political authority, the reason that Demophon admits "concerned him the most," is undermined, even by the chorus, who previously chastised the herald "for disrespecting the freedom of this land."[122] This collapse of law and principle is even more vivid in the weaker bonds of reciprocity, as the opportunity to form lasting friendship slips away when the chorus reverses friends and enemies. Thus, all legal, cultural, and divine institutions and bonds of obligations and friendship prove unable to withstand the transgressions of those who pursue gain. If this tragedy has a message to contribute to modern refugee crises, it is that citizens will help noncitizens in need, but pragmatic self-interest will always be a necessary part of the calculation.

Finally, this tragedy dramatizes not only the plight of refugees but the difficult question of how to treat the tyrants who persecute such victims. The tragedy reveals that pity for those who suffer is mirrored with the twin joys at the success of friends and the failure of enemies. Alcmene is a troubling character because she reminds us of this powerful joy that delights in seeing those who persecute the weak punished: as the tragedy points out, it is not enough that Eurystheus dies but that he suffers in front of "her own eyes." She is willing to do anything—trample on the inviolability of the divine sanctuary or violate the laws of the city that protected them—to satisfy this desire. Righteous anger or, as Montaigne would put it, "the cruel hatred of cruelty is the ultimate vice."[123] It underlies Martha Nussbaum's argument that such payback anger ought to be replaced with some kind of forward-looking "transition-anger" that is not derived from retaliatory instincts.[124] It also inspires contemporary forms of transitional justice to find new ways, such as truth-telling or reparations, to assuage such "accusing anger" in the lingering trauma of "unreconciled" societies.[125] Unfortunately, Euripides's example of Alcmene offers little hope for such solutions as antidotes to the joy of watching enemies suffer.

The question of whether there is an obligation to aid the refugee children or how to reconcile the wrath of Alcmene remains a crucial political issue. According to the UN Refugee Agency, more than 79.5 million people were among the forcibly displaced in 2019, with approximately 26 million refugees.[126] Approximately half of these refugees are children like the Heracleidae. The problem of what to do with Eurystheus has also not gone away, as we still have many examples, such as Charles Taylor, Ratko Mladić, Joseph Kony, and Bashar al-Assad. If Euripides leaves us with a final lesson, it is that institutions, laws, and bonds of obligation always have to contend with individual self-interest and political advantage; and pity and concern for the plight of refugees also sit alongside the dark joy of gaining power over one's enemies. Such anger can turn victims into criminals and tyrants into victims. In such a volatile situation at the very boundary of community, perhaps we can only attempt to distinguish the "just man" by his restraint in the pursuit of justice.

Chapter 6

The *Suppliant Women*

Justice among Cities

> Justice calls for justice,
> Like murder calls forth murder.[1]

Euripides's *Suppliant Women* encompasses familiar tragic elements, including a confrontation over unburied bodies, rash young rulers, quarrelsome Thebans, and heroic Athenians fighting on behalf of the weak. The tragedy deals with themes of enduring interest to political theorists, such as the question of whether justice simply reflects a regime's positive law or broader universal principles. Euripides dramatizes a debate (*agōn*) concerning what the best form of government is. There is a long history of scholarship focusing on these political ideas, especially in light of possible allusions to historical events of Euripides's own time.[2] The following analysis builds on interpretations that explore such political themes but focuses attention on what Euripides reveals about the role of justice in the relationship between political communities.[3] This tragedy is not hopeful about the possibility of a just and peaceful international community but highlights the problems and limitations of durable solutions to repeating patterns of war. In particular, the tragedy serves as a warning against identifying too closely with noncitizens or other regimes in the international community.

As one of Euripides's alphabet plays, the *Suppliant Women* (in Greek: *hiketides*) deviates from the common expectations of ancient tragedy. As will be developed later, many plot elements, such as the deus ex machina scene, have been criticized since Aristotle.[4] In addition, the play's complexity, with its many unanticipated plot twists, has prompted the conclusion that such episodes must be later interpolations.[5] As with other alphabet plays, it is difficult to establish the tragedy's performance date.[6] Statistical analysis recommends sometime between 425 and 420 BCE; however, with an eye to history, some scholars suggest a later date between 421 and 415 BCE, as they interpret references in the tragedy to the Athenian-Argive alliance of 420 BCE.[7] Other scholars suggest 423 BCE, as the theme of unburied dead mimics the Boeotian refusal to allow the Athenians to bury their dead after the battle of Delium in 424 BCE.[8] Other political interpretations focus less on dating than on understanding the main theme as reflecting the ongoing historical debate in Athens between the anti-imperialistic or "quietist" faction versus those who supported imperialistic policies and expansionist "activism."[9]

The dating controversy, however, draws attention to an important element of interpretation. Athenian tragedy was political not only because the Great Dionysia festival became a political event but also because all dramatic works often dealt with broader themes and concepts rooted in Athenian political reality.[10] Yet, the *Suppliant Woman* is even more political than most tragedies: as Burian argues, "[It] more than any other in the canon cries out for a political interpretation."[11] Many contemporary scholars echo early *scholia* that see it as another "encomium of Athens" and celebration of democracy. Zuntz, for example, suggests the tragedy explores the problems of human political fellowship and ends with an optimistic view of "a world surveyable and rational, held together by wholesome laws."[12] Echoing this idea, Jones emphasizes the main theme is a "plea against inhumanity, especially in wartime" and concludes that democracy provides the best chance of observing the decencies of life.[13] More recently, Tzanetou suggests it reveals a "commit[ment] to representing Athens as acting in concert with allied interests."[14] Perhaps Hall puts it most explicitly: "In no [other] Greek tragedy are the Athenians more clearly portrayed as the 'moral policemen' of Greece."

By contrast, other scholars dismiss this celebration of Athens by stressing that the tragedy is deliberately ambivalent concerning the possibility of rational action, political activism on behalf of common humanity, or even the safety found in just and kindly gods.[15] Mendelsohn, for example, in his analysis of the play through the lens of gender, concludes it is not an encomium but a warning against unregulated and violent extremes.[16] Both Michelini and Smith emphasize its dramatization of the limits of intelligence for accomplishing the good or inoculating against violence and danger.[17] Along similar lines, Burian suggests that through the confrontation between intellect and emotion, the tragedy exposes a new political *logos* that offers neither optimistic nor heroic solutions but underscores the reality of an imperfect society.[18] This analysis adopts this critical perspective, which understands the tragedy as undermining a straightforward celebration of Athens and the superiority of democratic values; instead, Euripides offers a complex, multifaceted story highlighting justice in what we call the "global" or "international" community. Such global justice is possible but only in reiterative actions on behalf of others. Most importantly, Euripides questions the idea that justice is found in individualism without proper regard for group identity and the obligations of social community.

The Mythological Context and Plot of the *Suppliant Women*

Background Myth

Although told from a different perspective, the *Suppliant Woman* is Euripides's reworking of the final chapter of the famous story of the ill-fated ruling family of Thebes. This family was first cursed when the city's founder, the Phoenician Cadmus, slaughtered Ares's son, the Boeotian dragon who guarded its sacred spring.[19] Following Athena's advice, Cadmus sowed the dragon's teeth into the ground from which sprung the famous Sown Men. Generations later, Jocasta (a female descendant of this autochthonous line) married Cadmus's great-grandson Laius. Despite Apollo's prophecy that their son would kill his father and marry his mother, they still had a son named Oedipus. Sophocles tells the most well-known version of Oedipus's story. In his *Oedipus Rex*, the infant was left to die but rescued by a shepherd and raised by the Corinthian royal family.[20] Not knowing his true identity, when he hears of the prophecy Oedipus leaves Corinth. He kills an old man on the road (who is, of course, Laius), solves the riddle of the sphinx that plagued Thebes, and marries the Queen Jocasta. They have four children: Eteocles, Polynices, Antigone, and Ismene. There are conflicting versions of what happens in the aftermath of Oedipus's discovery of his patricide and incestuous marriage. In *Oedipus Rex*, Jocasta commits suicide and Oedipus blinds himself. By contrast, Homer tells us he continued to reign until he was killed in battle.²¹ In Sophocles's *Oedipus in Colonus* he is exiled by Creon and, accompanied by Antigone, finds sanctuary in Colonus near Athens.²²

More germane to our present story is the conflict between Oedipus's two sons. In Euripides's *Phoenician Women*, Jocasta, Antigone, and Oedipus are still living in Thebes. Polynices and Eteocles have wrested power from Oedipus who, in response, cursed them to die by mutual slaughter.²³ Oedipus's sons agreed to share the rule of Thebes by alternating their rule annually. When it came time, however, Eteocles refused to hand over power. In exile, Polynices marries the daughter of the Argive king and brings this allied army to reclaim Thebes. This was the famous battle of the Seven against Thebes where Polynices and Eteocles kill each other. The "Seven" are the Argive generals killed at each of the seven gates of Thebes. Like Polynices, they remained unburied by decree of Jocasta's brother Creon, the new king of Thebes.

In this tragedy, Euripides connects this famous story of Thebes to the myth of Theseus. This early king of Athens languished as a minor mythological figure until a form of ancient "spin" transformed him into the city's greatest hero.²⁴ Theseus is most famous for slaying the Minotaur and freeing Athens from its yearly tribute of seven girls and seven boys sent as sacrifices to this monster. His story, however, begins in Troezen, where he is raised by his mother, Aethra, who became pregnant either by King Aegeus of Athens (who was on his way to Troezen when we encountered him in Euripides's *Medea*) or Poseidon, since she had sex with both of them on the same night. Similar to his more famous cousin, Heracles, Theseus underwent a series of labors in which he succeeded using various ingenious tricks, including winning a wrestling match against Cercyon, the king of Eleusis. We also encounter him in stories about Medea, when she tries to trick Aegeus into poisoning Theseus but, luckily, the king recognizes his son in time. Soon afterward, Theseus performed his famous act of killing the Minotaur with the aid of Ariadne, whom he later abandoned. He had several adventures with Heracles, such as when Heracles rescued him from the Underworld after Theseus's failed attempt to abduct Persephone.²⁵ Theseus was also the first abductor of an adolescent Helen, who was later rescued by her brothers the Dioscuri.

For the Athenians, Theseus represented a founder-hero who could be propped up as a rival to the Panhellenic Heracles. Some of the most notable accomplishments attributed to Theseus include the unification of the many Attic communities into a single state (*synoikismos*), building a stronghold on the Acropolis, establishing democracy, and capturing the city of Eleusis from Megara.[26] Depending on the source, Theseus either lost favor with the Athenians, or he left to follow more adventures, including perhaps those involving Jason and the Argonauts.[27] In most versions, Theseus dies a rather anticlimactic death, such as the story of the king of Scyrus pushing him off a cliff. Although this increased attention to Theseus's story can be traced back to the tyrannical period under Peisistratus, the innovative Cleisthenes used Theseus to legitimize the new tribes under his democratic reforms in 508 BCE. In particular, his cult rose in importance after the battle of Marathon in 490 BCE. Plutarch tells a story where Athenian soldiers reportedly saw his ghost leading the charge against the invading Persians.[28] Later in 475 BCE, Cimon of Athens brought home "the bones" of Theseus to be reburied and made into a shrine in Athens. He was celebrated during the festival of Theseia, which was an ephebic celebration of transitions and initiation to manhood.[29] Importantly, such revamped stories brought Theseus into the forefront of mythology and gave Athens a more prominent role in Greek tradition.

EURIPIDES'S *SUPPLIANT WOMEN*

The play opens with Aethra, the Queen-Mother, performing a ceremony in front of Demeter's sanctuary in Eleusis.[30] This town, which was mythologically conquered by Theseus, was approximately fourteen miles from Athens. The setting of the play in Eleusis is significant. The sanctuary was thought to be in the very spot where Demeter, the goddess of grain, the harvest, and fertility, was reunited with her kidnapped daughter Persephone.[31] As told in the *Hymn to Demeter*, Persephone was abducted by her uncle Hades to be his Underworld Queen. In despair, Demeter ceased granting fertility to all living things. Eventually, Zeus was forced to return Persephone to her mother; however, since the young girl had already eaten the food of the dead, she was forced to return for several months each year to the Underworld.[32] This story is a mythical explanation of the seasons, which follow the same pattern of death and rebirth. The reunion of mother and daughter was celebrated in the Eleusinian Mysteries, the most popular mystery cult in Greece. The central building in Eleusis, the Telesterion, could hold up to ten thousand participants. Although we know very little about mystery rites, as they were open only to initiates (*mystai*), anyone could join these mysteries as long as they spoke Greek and had not committed homicide.[33] The Greater Mysteries did begin with open public purification rituals in Athens, followed by a long procession to Eleusis for the closed nocturnal session. What happened in the inner sanctum is purely speculative, but it is possible that the rituals commemorated the natural cycle of life and death.[34] Another possibility was that the mysteries provided an intense personal experience of the divine through the contrast of death, darkness, and terror with life, light, and joy.[35]

Although Aethra is at Eleusis, the event interrupted is likely not the Greater Mysteries but the yearly Proerosia festival to Demeter to ensure her blessing for a successful agricultural season.[36] Into this sacred setting—with its overt associations of fertility, death, and renewal—enter grieving mothers seeking the bodies of their lost children.[37] The chorus that supplicates the Queen Mother is divided into two groups.[38] The main chorus, which represents the Argive mothers of the dead generals, surrounds Aethra as she performs the sacred rites. The only surviving general of the Argive army, King Adrastus, lies prostrate in front of the Telesterion surrounded by the second choral group of his slain comrades' sons. The act of supplication had great significance in Greek culture. Poetic depictions were common. Homer, for example, describes Thetis supplicating Zeus on behalf of her son Achilles.[39] The act of supplication (or *hiketeia*) was under the protection of Zeus Hikesios. It included several rituals, such as a grasping of the knees or beard of the person being supplicated, the wearing of wreaths, and pleading for favors. Physical contact was necessary for the act to be considered complete. If accepted, supplication could establish a guest-friendship (*xenia*) with all its ritualized reciprocal expectations. As is noted in the tragedy, supplication and overt expressions of grief during the fertility festival would have been inappropriate, but this opening scene locates the supplication within the larger theme of the cycle of life and death.[40]

From this point, the tragedy is told in two parts with a middle messenger scene. Into this sober setting at Eleusis, the first part (lines 90–635) begins with the entrance of King Theseus who immediately interrogates Adrastus as to why Argos attacked Thebes.[41] Theseus concludes that Adrastus was an imprudent king who misinterpreted oracles, married his daughters to bestial men, followed the same rash young men into battle, and ignored the warning of his own prophets. As such, he rejects the Argive supplication because their current misfortune was due to their own negligence.[42] Pitying the suppliant women, his mother intervenes to convince her son to change his mind. She provides three arguments for the justice of their cause: first, it is the gods' will; second, it is a courageous labor to punish violators of the Panhellenic law to bury the dead; third, it is cowardice for cities to keep quiet (*hēsuchos*) if they can win glory on behalf of justice.[43] Theseus agrees and leaves to confirm this decision with the Athenian Assembly.

Following a choral ode celebrating the protection of the laws of mortals and those unfortunate, a Theban herald arrives with a message from King Creon.[44] Quickly a debate (*agōn*) over the best form of government erupts.[45] Ironically, for a king, Theseus criticizes the one-man rule of tyrants for "mowing down the best young men like summer wheat" and defends the superiority of democracy, as it ensures office holders rule in turn as well as open or honest speech (*parrhēsia*).[46] By contrast, although a commoner, the Theban herald criticizes democratic freedom as susceptible to demagogues, the rule of better by worse men, and "excessive activism."[47] Although praising democratic open speech, Theseus censures the herald for speaking his mind and rejects his suggestion that peace would represent "quietism at the right time." The attempt to negotiate a peaceful solution fails. Leaving behind the accursed Adrastus, Theseus and the Athenians march off to war.

The middle section begins at line 635 with the arrival of a messenger.[48] His report tells us that Theseus again tried diplomacy, but Creon replied with silence. Mirroring the gruesome language of war in the *Iliad*, the messenger describes the battle of chariots and men marked by rivers of blood as soldiers were cut down. He focuses on Theseus's heroism as the king single-handedly clubbed a path to the gates of Thebes. Surprisingly, Theseus did not pillage the city; instead, he washed and buried the bodies of the regular Argive soldiers. He now returns to Eleusis with the bodies of the seven generals. The chorus of mothers sings a short ode to the misfortune of being deprived of beloved children.

The second part (lines 795–1235) begins with the focus of events turning away from Athenian glory toward Argive grief.[49] Reflecting the Athenian practice of funeral oration, Adrastus gives an epideictic speech praising the previously reproached young generals for the virtues of moderation, generosity, physical courage, and sharing the same likes and dislikes as the rest of the city.[50] His "white-washing" eulogy ends with praising the democratic notion that courage is not inherited by aristocratic blood but can be taught. The eulogy is interrupted by the sudden appearance of the fallen general Capaneus's wife, Evadne. She is pursued by her father Iphis, who attempts to convince her to let go of her desire to join her husband in death. He fails and, shockingly, Evadne leaps to her death in the only onstage suicide in extant tragedy.[51] In uncontrollable despair, Iphis is led away while the second chorus of young Argive sons begins an *exodos* parade with their father's ashes.

At this point, the story appears to have been brought to its sad but noble conclusion.[52] Theseus calls for Adrastus and the city of Argos to remember, honor, and hold gratitude (*kharis*) for Athenian benevolence. Yet into this emotional scene, at line 1185, the goddess Athena unexpectedly appears in a deus ex machina. She corrects Theseus's call for gratitude and orders him to exact a more binding treaty in the form of a civic oath of nonaggression and defense in exchange for Athens's labors. In addition, the goddess further undermines the peaceful ending with instructions to the chorus of young Argive sons who are to become the *Epigoni* (the successors). They must attack Thebes and avenge their fathers—"as soon as their beards grow." With this prophecy, the audience is left with the promise of a renewed cycle of violence, and the chorus departs with praise for Athenian labors on their behalf.

Euripides's Potential Innovations

Euripides's main source for his story—that Theseus was involved in recovering the bodies of the dead Argive generals—likely came from the lost epic the *Thebaid*, which was written in the late sixth century BCE.[53] Aeschylus also tells a version of these events in a tragedy called the *Eleusinians*, which survives only in fragments; in this version violence is avoided when Theseus successfully negotiates a treaty to recover the bodies.[54] Other surviving versions of events include Pindar's account where Adrastus negotiates the recovery of the bodies and buries them in Thebes, not Eleusis. Herodotus's account is similar to that of Euripides, as he suggests that the Athenians fought a battle to retrieve the bodies to bury in Eleusis.[55] As we are uncertain of the date of Euripides's production, it is unclear whether his tragedy predates Herodotus's account of Theseus's military victory.

Despite the uncertainty of source material, Euripides appears to make four potential innovations to the mythological events in his *Suppliant Women*.[56] First, unlike most alternative variations where persuasion is successful in retrieving the bodies, Theseus has to engage in battle. Although this is similar to Herodotus, the historian describes the Athenians as using this event as a "proud boast." By contrast, Euripides's Theseus is reluctant to engage in a military intervention and was content to receive only gratitude in return. Second, although there is usually uncertainty concerning Theseus's illegitimacy, Aethra is firmly presented as the widow of Aegeus, which not only legitimizes Theseus but also privileges her opinions on the suppliants' cause. Third, in a small but potentially symbolic innovation, Euripides may have invented the idea that the tripod mentioned at the end of the play belonged to Heracles. Finally, Euripides likely invented the character of Evadne as well as her suicide.[57] As will be developed in the next section, this scene is shocking for many reasons, including its rare onstage death. Again, it is important to stress that poetic innovations to myth were typical in the ancient tragic art form; however, such unique plot elements draw attention to unexpected elements important for interpreting the playwright's dramatic narrative.

International Justice: War and Panhellenic Law

It is fairly uncontroversial to suggest that war and its repercussions on the family and political community is a unifying theme of the tragedy.[58] The Argive supplication and the unburied dead provide the backdrop to Euripides's portrayal of the underlying causes of conflict and war.[59] The purpose of the Argive supplication is to gain support for retrieving the bodies from those who died in the failed attempt to subjugate Thebes. As noted above, this situation reflects historical events such as the Boeotian refusal to allow the Athenians to retrieve their dead after the battle of Delium in 424 BCE; it also foreshadows the political crisis in Athens resulting from the failure to recover the bodies of the dead from the battle of Arginusae.[60] The theme of violating burial laws is a major preoccupation of many ancient tragedies, especially those dealing with the myth of the Theban royal family. Unlike Sophocles's more famous *Antigone*, in which this theme is often interpreted to highlight the tension between the public and private, Euripides's drama draws attention away from domestic conflict to questions concerning just war and the possibility of broader community ties beyond the polis.[61]

Much of the first part of the tragedy deals directly with the question of just war. In his dialogue with Adrastus, for example, Theseus tells us that there are three motivations that lead to an unjust war: glory-loving young men, ambition for power, and greed.[62] According to

Theseus, these causes are unjust because they fail to account for the common good and, as such, "spoil the townsmen" and "bring harm to the community." Furthermore, in what might be an interpolation in the text, Theseus echoes a later account by Aristotle when he adds that ambition and love of glory and wealth are exaggerated by extremes of rich and poor: only the middle class saves cities, as it is the guardian of order (*kosmos*).[63] Euripides's causes of war are similar to Thucydides's understanding of martial motivations found in honor, self-interest, and fear.[64] Unlike Thucydides, who suggests the Spartans' fear of Athenian power was the main cause of the war, Euripides's account of unjust war does not mention fear; instead, war is caused by the self-interested motives of glory, power, and wealth.

Theseus, at first, also refuses to aid Adrastus for the reason of justice as merit. Again, according to Theseus, the Argive king's actions were rash and ill-advised for two reasons: first, Adrastus foolishly gave his daughters to men who were criminals; second, he followed those same rash men into an ill-advised war of aggression.[65] As Theseus later points out, a war on behalf of the suppliants would be "to mix" the fate of Athens with "the deserved misfortune" of Argos. The herald echoes this same sentiment by emphasizing that Athens should not support those who were destroyed by their own unjust actions. Theseus's original rejection of the suppliants' plea emphasizes a perspective that an unjust war is motived by the desire for glory and driven by ambitions that harm the community. As this war was ill-advised, the Argives now suffer deservedly and are punished according to the principles of justice as merit: in other words, justice has been done. Thus, for Theseus, aiding the suppliants would be equally ill-advised as it would mix the pure with the impure akin to Adrastus's error of marrying his daughters to bestial men.[66]

Added to these human motivations, in several instances in the tragedy, Euripides alludes to divine judgment in the outcome of unjust causes.[67] In his initial interrogation of Adrastus, Theseus also rejects the Argive supplication as consistent with divine judgment: the defeat of the Argive army was merited because of their failure to respect ill omens and divine will. Again, the herald echoes this position in his claim that the gods "destroy the wicked," such as the Argive general Capaneus, who was determined to scale the walls of Thebes "whether the gods wanted him to or not." It was Zeus himself who struck down this general with a lightning bolt. It was Zeus who determined the Argive's defeat. In addition, as noted previously, the Argive supplication during the festival in Eleusis was impious. Thus, the tragedy indicates that unjust war arises from extremes: excessive rashness of youth, extremes of wealth and poverty, and hubris or disproportionate desire for glory beyond human limits. Simply put, the Argives were the aggressors in an offensive war, and they deserve and ought to bear their fate. As Adrastus puts it later in the play: foolish are mortals "who shoot beyond the mark . . . richly you deserve your many woes."

In contrast to this straightforward claim that the Argives deserve their fate, the tragedy also highlights a contrasting claim to justice in their present situation. In several instances, for example, the chorus emphasizes the justice of retrieving the dead because the "lawless men" of Thebes violated Panhellenic law in their refusal to allow burial rites; the chorus also rejoices in news that these hubristic Theban men have paid the price.[68] In contrast to her son, Aethra stresses that supporting the supplicants is justified on political principles: those who refuse to bury the dead, she notes, violate what "all Greece holds lawful." Aethra also counters the political assumption that "an activist" city is always unjust. Rather than dismissing action on behalf of others as "busybody" injustice, she argues that cities flourish in strenuous action, and "quiet" cities (*hēsuchoi*) dishonorably "work in stealth and darkness." If such action is honorable, it is cowardice to back down from a glorious labor (*ponos*). She concludes by reiterating that there is "no fear" in such labor for a just cause. From this perspective, the just war on behalf of burying the dead is founded in the honor of acting nobly, without fear, on behalf of those wronged.

In the end, Theseus is convinced by his mother's argument that it would be cowardice to refuse a glorious labor (*ponos*) to retrieve the bodies as it is "his manner to be a punisher of wicked deeds."[69] Nevertheless, Theseus does not take back his assessment that the Argives deserved their fate, as he refuses to allow Adrastus to participate either in the debate with the Theban herald or accompany the Athenian army into battle. Unlike Adrastus's "unwise mating of just with unjust," Theseus remains steadfast in his refusal to taint his just cause by mingling it with the unjust cause of the war against Thebes. Theseus's perspective underscores the belief that just and unjust should remain separate and unadulterated, which is symbolized in the *Ion* by Creusa's twin vials of Gorgon's blood.[70] Significantly, Theseus's distinction also contrasts the deserved suffering of Adrastus with the unmerited suffering of the suppliant women and unburied dead. As Theseus emphasizes to the herald: the dead generals have already suffered for their injustice, and the Thebans claim that which does not belong to them but to the earth. In other words, the Thebans have exchanged their just defense of their city for an unjust violation of the dead.

Theseus's change of mind can be traced to two important points in Aethra's argument. His intervention is just because it is an act on behalf of those who do not deserve their circumstances of being denied burial rites. Second, political action as opposed to quietism is just, if the "activism" is just and vice versa—if the cause is unjust, then quietism is defensible. This distinction is drawn most vividly in Adrastus's unjust war against Thebes (in which Adrastus should have followed quietism) in contrast to Theseus's honorable activism on behalf of a just cause. The herald's parting shot, that Athens is always a "busybody" involved in the affairs of other states, is countered by Theseus's claim that the happiness of cities arises from noble activism. This language, as Michelini points out, mimics Athenian political debate during the Peloponnesian War between those who favored active intervention and the "isolationists" who saw such foreign intervention as meddling in the affairs of others.[71] Euripides's contribution to this debate stresses that activism and quietism are not categorically just or unjust—but just or unjust relative to the merits of the particular cause.

The first part of the play, which focuses on the question of whether supporting the suppliant women is a just cause, also points out several issues concerning the just relationship between cities. First, Aethra stresses that Athenian intervention is just because Thebes violated the custom (*nomima*) that all Greece holds; it is this custom, she continues, that "holds all communities together."[72] Her son adopts this same argument in his exchange with the herald: "I am asking you," he says, "to allow the burial of the dead, because it is the law of all the Greeks (*ton panellēnōn nomon*)."[73] This custom may have its root in religious dictates, but in this tragedy, what is stressed is not divine law but secular Panhellenic custom. Importantly, what holds any community together, whether among citizens or the possibility of community among cities, is revealed to be an acceptance and respect for common laws or practices.

The debate concerning whether Theseus's intervention is just also reflects two other important aspects that might contribute to bonds of community beyond the polis. First, the play explores several political emotions that unite human beings regardless of their political affiliation. The most obvious of these emotions is pity; Aethra tells us that she is "bound without chains" by her pity for the women and their unburied sons.[74] Despite the fact that Theseus is confused by his mother's weeping because "she is not one of them [an Argive mother]," it is plausible that, as a mother, Aethra identifies with their suffering because she can see herself in the same situation.[75] Such identification is not unlike Achilles in the *Iliad*: Achilles finally weeps with Priam when he recognizes his own father's situation in the suffering of his adversary.[76] In Aethra's case, the suppliant women are not enemies, but her ability to identify with their suffering highlights the fact that pity is not, as Theseus understands it, limited by the boundaries of one's own community.

In addition, after Theseus agrees to support the supplication, the chorus rejoices in the Athenian tie of friendship (*philia*) with Argos; for this, they say, Athens wins its "gratitude (*kharis*) for all time."[77] With this comment, the chorus connects the Athenian support for their supplication to the mutual tie of friendship (*philia*).[78] Importantly, supplication included a crucial role for reciprocity, which was initiated and maintained by the reciprocal favors (*kharis*) between suppliant and supplicated. In the specific example of supplication in this tragedy, although the chorus notes a blood tie to Theseus, it is not this distant kinship but the justice of their cause that is pressed in their supplication.[79] When Theseus is convinced by his mother to accept their request, this formalized bond of *philia* with its reciprocal favors transcends the boundaries of the political community. Theseus recognizes this reciprocity in his request at the end of the tragedy that the Argives remember with gratitude his actions on their behalf.

Although Aethra is motivated by pity, and friendship beyond narrow community is formed with the suppliants, Theseus is not convinced to support the supplication for these community-expanding reasons. By contrast, it is his mother's claim—that it would be a "glorious labor" to punish those who do wrong—that carries the weight of her argument. Theseus lives up to his new and improved role of civilizing hero, undertaking glorious labors similar to the Panhellenic but foreign Heracles.[80] He is interested in keeping a clear line between this just war and the unjust war of the Seven against Thebes. In this part of the story, his glorious labor coincides with just activism on behalf of the deserving weak, and these efforts protect and uphold Panhellenic law. As such, Theseus stands as an Athenian rival to Heracles (and his Spartan descendants) as promoter and defender of wider Greek security and unity. Thus, Nicklin can argue Theseus represents moderation and the ideal of Greek civilization.[81]

Political Justice: International Community and the Next Generations

As with many of Euripides's plays, the apex of the story, which meticulously places Athens on a pedestal, is revealed to be unstable. Following tragic norms, all the bloodletting takes place offstage and is reported by a messenger who watched from one of the infamous gates of Thebes. This final section concentrates mainly on the Argives, so much so that Smith argues that this "second movement" recontextualizes the healthy results of Athenian action and "negates what was positive and hopeful in their first presentation."[82] The clearest case of such a reversal or negation is found in Adrastus's funeral speech: the Argive generals who suffered deservedly for their hubristic unjust war on Thebes are given a substantial persuasive "make-over." In addition, the new improved hero Theseus fulfills his mission to retrieve the bodies. But for all his labors he establishes no enduring Panhellenic unity, and the gods are forced to intervene. In the end, the tragedy's final episodes of old heroes, reinvented heroes, and promising new heroes set the stage to see Athena's deus ex machina commandments not only as limiting human attempts to forge broader cosmopolitan ties but also returning us full circle to the Eleusinian symbolism of rebirth.[83]

At the zenith of the story, the messenger's report of the battle mimics similar heroic descriptions in the *Iliad*.[84] First, like Helen and Priam standing on the ramparts of Troy, the messenger stood on the Electran gate and peered at the heroes below.[85] He describes the array of hoplites, cavalry, chariots, and "how the red blood flowed in rivers as men were cut down . . . and others were thrown into the earth." At the moment when all seems lost, appearing in his "shining armor," Theseus took up "his terrifying club . . . swung it about, snapping necks and harvesting helmeted heads." Despite such violence, surprisingly Theseus stops when he reaches the Theban gates. Unlike the heroes of Troy, he does not sack the city, slaughter all the men, and enslave the women and children. Then, Theseus does another more surprising thing: he performs the ritual washing and burial of the regular Argive soldiers. Thus, in contrast to the Argives who were active for the wrong reasons, or the Thebans who overstepped the proper boundary of victory by refusing to bury the dead, Theseus embodies the moderate form of activism: he acts in a just cause and no further. This is his finest moment, as he is "the kind of general one should choose [who] is brave in the hour of danger and hates insolent men."

From this climatic set-up, it is still easy to see the *Suppliant Women* as a patriotic play promoting Theseus as this moderate and "righteous leader fighting valiantly against the perpetuators of injustice."[86] This laudatory view of Theseus, however, misses two important ways in which his heroism undermines the possibility of establishing justice among cities. First, Theseus's activism or heroic labor on behalf of Panhellenic law is not as "wholesome" as Zuntz suggests. Although Theseus notes in his exchange with the herald that burial is an ancient divine right, he argues the refusal to bury the dead harms all of Greece because "if such actions become customary, it will turn brave men into cowards."[87] In other words, the Panhellenic custom is less about respecting divine law than the pragmatic concern that without such a guarantee of burial, no city in Greece would be able to marshal soldiers into battle. Theseus's burial of the regular soldiers also symbolizes a democratic assurance in the right of burial for all men, noble or common. Thus, Theseus fights to uphold "the law of all of Greece" which "holds all communities together" to ensure that there will be many future soldiers to fight future wars on behalf of their kings. Second, the heroic Theseus reveals that any governance between political communities would be tyrannical. Euripides makes this connection most vividly in the echo between Theseus's previous critique of the tyrant "who culls and cuts away the boldest of the young as one does the towering stalk in the springtime meadow" and the messenger's description of Theseus wielding his mace above his head, "snapping necks and harvesting helmeted heads."[88] Although Theseus's decision to stop at the gates of Thebes does display a prudent activism, he is also an individualistic hero or tyrant harvesting bold young men. In addition, even though he might be a wise tyrant who pragmatically "is a quietist at the right time," the true purpose of his actions is to lay the foundation for future war.

This theme of heroism blends into the next episode as Adrastus's funeral speech praises the moderation and virtue of the fallen generals of Argos.[89] As has often been noted, the funeral speech offers a very different view of the generals than presented earlier in the play.[90] The most noteworthy revisionist history is given to Capaneus, who was struck down by Zeus for his hubris of "climbing too high . . . [without regard as to] whether the gods wanted him to or not."[91] In the funeral oration,

Capaneus is transformed into the most moderate of men, who had "no more pride than a poor man," ate modest fare, and did not know how to lie. The other generals are similarly transmuted: previously deserving of their deaths, they now hate unjust rulers and share the same likes and dislikes as others in the city. Even Polynices' friend, the exiled beastlike murderer Tydeus is praised for honor in deeds and not speech.

It is possible this speech has ironic undertones satirizing the dishonest exaggerations typical of the Athenian practice of funeral orations; however, this scene is more than simply ironic as it is essential to the dramatic context of the play.[92] When Theseus returns to Eleusis, he asks Adrastus to make a funeral oration not about the generals' actions but about their temperament or personality. In other words, the eulogy is framed specifically to highlight their character or dispositions.[93]

The primary audience of the funeral speech is the second chorus consisting of the generals' young sons, which makes the primary function of this epideictic speech educational. This purpose is reinforced by Adrastus's own assertion that "courage is teachable."[94] Second, this educative speech dislocates the dead generals' tainted "international" action of storming the walls of Thebes and restores them to their "domestic" role in their *oikos* and polis: The Seven have come home.[95] Thus, Capaneus's merited death by Zeus's thunderbolt can be inverted to make him a "sacred corpse" set apart from the others for a more honorable burial. The Seven are restored to their former domestic roles, with "undeserved deaths at undeserving hands." We must not forget that we are at Eleusis after all: the site of renewal and rebirth. In other words, the dead are removed from the international stage and reborn as good citizens of their political community.

This focus on the domestic role of the Argive heroes also provides a context for the tragedy's most criticized episode: the suicide of Evadne. Many commentators have either completely ignored this episode, regard it as a later interpolation, or "merely take it on face value."[96] From the perspective that the funeral oration has reversed the tragedy's lens from international concerns to the domestic world, Evadne's unanticipated arrival is not entirely out of context. As a woman and the wife of notable Capaneus, Evadne represents the ultimate site of the most domestic sphere: the *oikos*. Her arrival is a literal break from the constraints of the Athenian ideal of the *oikos*, which promoted female invisibility; in such a world, a woman was visible in the public only at weddings, funerals, and certain festivals.[97] Evadne's sudden arrival fits into the dramatic context in several respects. First, her suicide reverses the positive Aethra-Theseus (or mother-son) dramatic encounter that ended with successful persuasion, with a negative daughter-father (Evadne-Iphis) encounter dramatizing the failure of persuasion.[98] In addition, similar to the funeral oration's reversal of the cursed and the sacred, the Evadne scene obscures the shameful and the glorious. Fleeing from her father's authority, she appears on high and announces her intention to "end weary life" by joining with the "radiant flame" of her husband in the "marriage chamber of Persephone."[99] Through her bold action, Evadne rejects grieving in an act that appropriates the Seven's heroic (and now sanitized) activism.[100]

In contrast to her view of appropriated glory, her father regards her action as shameful. For Iphis, Evadne's suicide cannot be glorious, as a woman's virtue is prudence, silence, and the arts of weaving and craft.[101] Her action also cannot be activism at the right time because it reveals her excessive identification with her husband's exogenous family and neglects her natal family obligations.[102] Although Greek women did leave their father's family to join their husband's *oikos*, women were understood to remain perpetually "in-between" and crossed boundaries of loyalty. Evadne dismisses her father's argument as "an unwise judgment of her intention"; she does, however, acknowledge that her suicide is unkind to him and is an individualistic labor for the sake of self-identification with her husband's glory. The father-daughter *agōn* ends, not with the positive resolution of the Theseus-Aethra debate but echoing the hostility of Theseus and the herald. Persuasion fails, as it did in that case, on the question of whether activism is appropriate or not.[103] The herald argued against activism on others' behalf, as he stresses: "You have no connection to the city [of Argos]." Iphis's perspective identified the loss of his daughter with the emptiness of his *oikos*; thus, like a "busybody," she ignored her "own" natal family in her identification with the affairs of "others." By harming her father, she also violated the ancient ethic of helping friends and harming enemies.[104] Similar to Medea's murder of her children, Evadne's suicide harms friends, not enemies.[105] Significantly, in doing so, no enemy like Jason is simultaneously harmed, nor does her suicide "help" any friend.

Nevertheless, Evadne's great leap shifts the neat and tidy package of the triumph of Theseus and "re-marketing" the Seven. Immediately following her death, the chorus of young sons begins the *exodos* with their father's bones.[106] Theseus interrupts this solemn Argive ceremony to ask for the reciprocal favor (*kharis*) that these boys remember with gratitude and honor that "we deemed you worthy to merit such benefits."[107] At this point the renewal of the Argive fortune seems complete: even Theseus has moved beyond judging the Argives as deserving of their fate. The tragedy's ending appears as if it will reflect the prediction of the chorus that friendship between poleis can be accomplished by pious toil that wins gratitude. But at this happy moment, Athena enters from above, and she turns the conclusion around once more.

Athena produces this reversal with two major pronouncements. First, she insists that Argive remembrance of gratitude was too light an exchange and insists Theseus exact an oath of alliance in compensation for his labor.[108] The requested oath is unusual as it is a one-sided nonaggression pact in which the Argives agree "to never to invade the land [of Athens], and that, if others do so, they [the Argives] will use their power to stop them."[109] More typically, such alliance oaths would be reciprocal with both sides agreeing to not invade but aid the other.[110] Also atypically, this oath was inscribed on the tripod of Heracles, which was to be set up in Delphi. Usually tripods set up in Delphi did not establish oaths but commemorated victories over enemies. Typical Greek civic oaths did involve sacred rituals (such as dipping hands in blood) and almost always involved inscriptions on standing stone (*stele*) set up in a public place. In this case, and likely invented by Euripides for this tragedy, the specific use of Heracles's tripod brings to mind his journey to the Underworld of Persephone to rescue the stranded Theseus.[111] We find ourselves back in Eleusis again.

In addition, the two parties are to bury the knife used for the oath's sacrifice "in the ground." This burial of the knife was also unusual. One possibility is that the knife represented the bones of the dead heroes, which had protective powers.[112] In this case, the knife was a substitute for the bones of the Seven, which were to be buried in Argos. Another possibility is that this act of "sowing" the knife brought to mind Cadmus's sowing of dragon teeth, which engendered the Sown Men.[113] This act of burial also mirrored ritualistic entombments during religious ceremonies, such as the mysteries, which summoned the fertility goddess.[114] Importantly, Athena goes beyond the typical oath of allied agreements by using two objects—the tripod and "sown" knife, reminiscent of Demeter's festivals; the ending thus mimics the beginning that opened with a prayer to the same fertility goddess. As a result, the final episode returns the story full circle to Eleusinian themes of the cycle of nature in death, fertility, and rebirth.

This symbolic rebirth is also reflected in Athena's second command to the young sons of the fallen Argive soldiers. Calling them "young lion cubs," she commands that as soon as their beards grow, they should seek vengeance by marching an army to sack the descendants of the Theban Sown Men.[115] Theseus's moderation and restraint during the battle, therefore, does not set up an enduring paradigm for limited war but merely delays this vengeance for future Argive warriors. The war really was not, as the herald pointed out, Athens's concern. Thus, Athena's final order is more than a simple corrective of Theseus's request for nothing stronger than emotional bonds of favor and gratitude between cities. By contrast, this goddess of war sets into motion another cycle of renewed violence. There is no cure for cycles of violence between states; at most, there may only be hope that in the future Athens is not part of this particular cycle.[116] The young sons are fated to become the new generation with whom Theseus taunted the herald: they have sprung from the dead to avenge their fathers. Thus, these boys, known as the *Epigoni*—the next generation—represent the next rebirth or cycle emerging from the sacred soil of Eleusis.[117]

As several commentators point out, this final scene is reminiscent of the ending of Aeschylus's *Oresteia*.[118] That story, our only extant trilogy, ends with the *Eumenides* where Athena also descends from on high to sit in judgment over the matricide trial of Orestes.[119] Unlike our tragedy, in that case Athena bequeaths an institutional solution to stop the cycle of retributive violence: the Athenian Areopagus court. Originally an aristocratic council, the powers of the Areopagus declined during the democratic period, but as dramatized by Aeschylus, it remained a court for cases of homicide.

If Euripides is consciously imitating Aeschylus's trilogy, it is not a trivial satirical mimicry. Like Aeschylus, Euripides gives Athena a major role in performing justice; yet, in our case, Athena does not set up a perpetual institution to resolve cycles of violence. At most, justice between cities in the *Suppliant Women* requires separate or repetitive acts of prudent activism or labor, such as Theseus's just cause on behalf of the suppliant women. Theseus's example of a new *nomos* of limited war fails to endure and only delays the inevitable sacking of the city by the *Epigoni*. This setup for forthcoming war is echoed earlier in one of Theseus's motives to retrieve the Seven: to protect the Panhellenic burial law that ensured the conditions for future cycles of war. It is also echoed in the purpose of the funeral oration, which was to educate the boys to act courageously. Nothing in this play establishes any corresponding judicial institution like the Areopagus, intended to end cycles of violence between cities. In fact, Athena does the opposite: she descends from on high to ensure the cycle of violence begins anew. There is no hint of an institutionalized solution to injustice between communities. As the chorus reminds us, in the relationships among cities, justice is reiterative: "Justice calls for justice, like murder calls forth murder."[120]

Conclusion

Despite Zuntz's optimism that Euripides fashions a world in which life is secure, ordered, and rational, the tragedy does not end with such a confident tone.[121] Yet, the tragedy's ending of a new cycle of violence is not simply an "anti-militarist satire" critical of Athenian democratic institutions or unequivocal support for political "quietism."[122] By contrast, Euripides appears to be taking a complicated and ambiguous stance regarding the still-important question of whether justice is found in "a sense of common humanity."[123] On the one hand, Euripides does offer up Theseus as a hero who displays prudent activism and limited military intervention only after the failure of diplomacy; on the other hand, Theseus's activism only accomplishes a specific goal and no more. There is no triumph of institutions or universal principles. The only thing that seems to endure is a renewed cycle of life and death.

Thus, Euripides questions the possibility of establishing enduring "global" justice among cities. His example of such justice is a "one-off" support on behalf of those who suffer undeservedly, but Theseus's determination to keep the just separate from unjust is undermined by the revisionist history of the Seven, who come home renewed as courageous and moderate. Similar to the *Ion*, there is no stable boundary between those who fight just or unjust wars or those who are guilty or innocent.[124] Even the common *nomos* (or principle) of Panhellenic law, which "binds communities together," is upheld only to ensure the conditions for the next cycle of war. With his dramatization of the continuing cycles of violence in the relationship among cities, at most, Euripides might support the idea that what remains crucial in international justice is the power of enforcement.[125] In Euripides's world, as in our own, global justice remains precarious.

Euripides's story reveals not only the limitation of enduring solutions to questions of international justice but also the weakness of bonds that tie human beings together. In responding to the chorus's act of supplication, Aethra exposed the potential for emotional bonds such as pity and relational obligations that could tie communities together with reciprocal gratitude (*kharis*) and friendship (*philia*). Yet it is not pity and reciprocity but glorious labor that convinces Theseus to aid the suppliants. After his intervention, Athena appears from on high to ensure the bonds between communities are made of stronger stuff than favors remembered. Thus, pity, friendship, and acts of benevolence are not adequate to inspire just action nor to ensure others will reciprocate—and they are not sufficient to establish a community between cities. We may recognize common humanity, but this recognition provides no universal duty to aid others and is an insecure foundation for global justice.[126]

Finally, the dramatic events of the play also draw attention to the larger question of whether such a community among cities is even desirable. This question is dramatized in Evadne's rare onstage suicide that reveals excessive desire for glory and rejection of one's own "brings harm to communities."[127] Her death can be seen as a stand-in or metaphor for what might be disquieting in a global community among cities: there is something potentially unjust in identifying too much with those outside "one's own" community. In contemporary terms, Euripides would support the "particularists" or "statists" who think there is a specific duty to support compatriots to the more cosmopolitan "universalists" who think morality requires an equal concern for all.[128] Or, as Sandel describes it, the "obligations of solidarity" to the group identity, such as family, religion, and political community, cannot be discounted in questions of justice.[129] From the perspective of this tragedy, the international story of the Seven ends where it began, in a renewed cycle of violence. And, with Evadne's leap, the play reminds us that in the call to just activism we cannot overlook the needs of, and obligations to, one's own.

Part III
JUSTICE IN THE WILDERNESS

Chapter 7

The *Hecuba*

Justice as Autonomy

> No mortal is free.
> For he is a slave to money, or chance,
> To the multitude of his city, or its written laws;
> All things which prevent him from acting
> According to his own judgment.[1]

The *Hecuba* is the story of an aging woman who has lost everything: youth, husband, crown, city, freedom, and almost all her children. The prologue reveals the loss of her final hope: a trusted friend has murdered her last surviving son, and her favorite daughter is about to be sacrificed on the grave of her greatest enemy. As the plot unfolds, Hecuba is crushed by the weight of her grief until her mourning transforms into a song of justice. Using all the tactics of her enemies—rhetoric, trickery, and merciless violence—she leaves behind her former self and previous reliance on political authority to enact her own measure of justice. Yet such justice is not without cost. Hecuba's final transformation will be into a dog whose gravestone becomes a nautical marker of dangerous waters. Although the date of first performance is unknown, most scholars estimate a date between 425–421 BCE. This suggests the *Hecuba*'s troubling ending may reflect the audience's fatigue with the ongoing war with the Spartans.[2] Even if produced earlier, it is hard to avoid the *Hecuba*'s ominous antiwar theme.

Interpreting this play is also akin to wading into dangerous waters without the security of a nautical marker. Despite its dark subject matter and troubling finale, the *Hecuba* was immensely popular in antiquity as part of the Byzantine Triad.[3] Early classical scholarship criticized the play for violating conventions of "unity of plot" by seemingly combining two different tragic stories into one story.[4] More recent scholarship focuses on the shift or reversal in Hecuba's character from sympathetic victim to dreadful avenger. Corey and Eubanks, for example, argue that the fragmented play signals the necessity of finding a middle ground between public and private demands.[5] Wohl focuses on the empty stage of the *exodos* as signifying a new beginning with a new demand for justice.[6] Other scholars suggest Hecuba's descent into vengeance is symbolic of her loss of humanity.[7] Building on these recent interpretations, this chapter explores the meaning of justice during political disintegration and warfare. In such circumstances, justice proves multifaceted and contradictory as Euripides invites us to reject any clear demarcations between victim and persecutor. His conclusion is also disturbing, as the tragedy undermines the possibility of confidence in political authority and institutions. In the face of such distrust, the *Hecuba* exposes the necessity of self-imposed limitations in the search for a more just world.

The Mythological Context and Plot of the *Hecuba*

Background Myth

This tragedy is connected to the most famous of all stories in Greek mythology: the battle of Troy.[8] Although the siege of Troy lasted over a decade, the most famous part of this story is found in Homer's *Iliad*, which recounts a fifty-day period that ends with Achilles's return of the corpse of the Trojan prince Hector for burial. As told in other accounts, this war began when the Trojan Prince Paris (also called Alexander) judged a beauty contest among Hera, Athena, and Aphrodite. Although each goddess attempted to bribe the young mortal with gifts, he accepted Aphrodite's prize of the most beautiful woman in the world: Zeus's half-divine daughter Helen. Unfortunately, Helen was already married to Menelaus, the Spartan king. Depending on the version, while Paris is a guest of Menelaus, he either kidnaps or seduces Helen and spirits her away to Troy.[9] Either way, having previously sworn an oath to defend the chosen husband of Helen, the Greek heroes assembled for war. Their venture is stalled until the leading king, Agamemnon, sacrifices his daughter Iphigenia to gain favorable winds. Then the Greeks launch their thousand ships.

Other episodes in this story, such as Odysseus's ruse with the wooden horse or Achilles's death by Paris's well-aimed arrow to his heel, is told in tragedies such as this one, the *Epic Cycle*, and later texts such as Apollodorus's *Library* or Virgil's *Aeneid*. This tragedy, like his *Andromache* or *Trojan Women*, focuses on events after the fall of Troy.[10] In a linear timeline, the *Hecuba* would take place between these two other extant plays: the *Andromache* takes place many years after the war and outlines the continuing threats to Hector's widow, who became a concubine to Achilles's son Neoptolemus. The *Trojan Women* narrates the horrific events immediately following the Greek victory, including the throwing of Hector's infant son from the battlements and the burning of the city. By contrast, the events of this tragedy take place after the Greeks have departed. This time the Greeks find themselves beached by unfavorable winds in the "in-between" lands of Thrace (situated in the modern Balkans).[11] According to our version, the Greeks remain idle in this alien territory as they debate whether to appease Achilles's ghost with a human sacrifice.[12] Two of the major Greek leaders, Agamemnon and Odysseus, make an appearance. As we know from other tragedies such as Euripides's *Electra* and *Orestes* or Aeschylus's trilogy the *Oresteia*, Agamemnon and his concubine, the Trojan Princess Cassandra, will die by the hands of his wife, Clytemnestra, and her new lover, Aegisthus.[13] And the wily Odysseus, of course, is fated to be blown further off course to wander many years, as told by Homer in the *Odyssey*.

Euripides's *Hecuba*

The setting of the *Hecuba* is the camp of the captive Trojan women who were being taken to Greece as concubines. The story is told in two distinctive parts. The first part, from lines 1–630, opens with the unusual prologue of a ghost. This ghost, Hecuba's son Polydorus, tells us that the family guest-friend Polymestor, the King of Thrace, killed him for his inheritance and threw his body into the sea.[14] His mother has been warned in a dream that she is fated this very day to bury not only his body but also that of his sister Polyxena. The Greeks have decided to offer Polyxena as a sacrifice to appease the dead Achilles in hopes of turning the unfavorable winds. Thus, from the very beginning of the tragedy, Hecuba's hope is hollow, and her fate is sealed.

The elderly, distraught Hecuba arrives on stage to be confronted first with the second fate of her daughter's imminent death.[15] The chorus of Trojan women enters with the news that supported by the sons of Theseus, Odysseus secured a vote to sacrifice her daughter.[16] Polyxena enters to lament her unspeakable fate, and Odysseus arrives to escort Polyxena to the pyre. Hecuba initiates the first *agōn* (debate) with Odysseus to argue her daughter's case with three traditional appeals to justice.[17] First, she appeals to *kharis* or justice as reciprocity: Odysseus owes her a favor because she saved his life during the war.[18] Second, she appeals to pity because her turn from glory to misfortune can happen to anyone. Finally, she reminds him of the justice of Greek custom or law (*nomos*), which forbids human sacrifice. Odysseus is unmoved. He agrees to her first point but is only willing to spare her life, not Polyxena's, in exchange for past favors. In addition, he counters with additional arguments concerning justice: sacrificing Polyxena respects both the concept of justice as helping friends and the principle of justice as merit. Most cities fail, Odysseus suggests, because they neglect friendship and the principle that "worthy men should receive more than their inferiors."[19]

Hecuba implores her daughter to supplicate Odysseus, but the girl refuses.[20] Echoing other Euripidean sacrificial maidens, Polyxena insists that she would rather die than live dishonorably. As she is led away, from lines 455–85, the chorus of Trojan women sings a mourning song of their own enslavement, as strangers far from their hearths. At this point, unable to bear her grief, Hecuba utterly collapses. The messenger Talthybius arrives to report Polyxena's noble death: refusing to be tied down like an animal, the princess bared her breasts and stretched her neck high to the sword. Moved by her courage, the Greek army built a funeral mound to honor her noble death. At this news, Hecuba responds with her famous line: "Noble natures are always noble, and no misfortune can turn such a nature from what is always good."[21] With that, she sends a servant to collect sea water to wash her daughter for the burial ceremony.

The second part of the tragedy (lines 630–1295) returns to the ghost's first message: the gruesome discovery of the corpse of young Polydorus.[22] Under the weight of this new misfortune, Hecuba realizes that her guest-friend (*xenos*) Polymestor was false: he killed her son to steal Trojan gold. The play's second *agōn* begins when Agamemnon arrives to escort her to Polyxena's funeral. Hecuba argues that as political leader, Agamemnon must punish this gross violation of guest-friendship (*xenia*). She supplicates him by, again, appealing to pity. Sensing his reluctance, she changes strategy and demands the private reciprocity (*kharis*) he owes in exchange for the sexual favors he enjoys with her last surviving daughter, Cassandra. For his part, Agamemnon recognizes his pity for Hecuba and her son's death as a violation of law.[23] Yet he refuses to act because honoring a private favor will risk his public reputation. Since the Greeks still lack favorable winds (despite sacrificing Polyxena), and he thinks little of a woman's strength, Agamemnon agrees to grant Hecuba the favor (*kharis*) of her own private justice.[24] Seizing this opportunity, Hecuba acts. She and her fellow enslaved women lure Polymestor with the promise of more Trojan gold. In the dark shadows of their tent, they kill his sons and blind Polymestor with their broaches.

The final scene begins with Agamemnon returning to sit as judge in a final forensic *agōn* between Polymestor and Hecuba.[25] Reduced to crawling blindly on stage, Polymestor argues from political expediency: he killed Polydorus so he would not grow up to retaliate against the Greeks; in exchange for this favor to his Greek friends, the evil race of women destroyed him. Such logic echoes Odysseus's earlier statement that cities fall when they neglect to honor friendship. For her part, "using language as a weapon," Hecuba stresses a violator of *xenia* is no friend to anyone, and, in truth, her son was killed for profit.[26] Unsurprisingly, since he permitted Hecuba's private justice, Agamemnon pronounces Polymestor guilty. Perhaps as an allusion to the blind prophet Teiresias—or, as Planinc suggests, the blinded Cyclops Polyphemus—Polymestor retaliates with a strange Dionysian prophecy: Hecuba will be turned into a dog and jump to her death on her way to captivity in Greece.[27] Her gravestone will become a nautical marker signifying dangerous waters. Polymestor also foretells the more famous impending doom of Cassandra and Agamemnon, who will be slaughtered on their homecoming by Clytemnestra and her new lover. Having had her justice, Hecuba appears unfazed by this prophecy. More alarmed, Agamemnon has Polymestor gagged and, similar to the exile of Philoctetes, banishes him to a deserted island.[28] The tragedy ends with an empty stage: the army has finally departed on favorable winds, and the chorus reminds us that necessity is unrelenting.

Euripides's Potential Innovations

Since Euripides's *Hecuba* deals with the fall of Troy, it draws from well-known mythology but, like all tragedies, transforms the story. Scholarship is divided on Euripides's use of his source material. Callen King, for example, argues that Euripides reconstitutes Homer to critique masculine heroic values and "destroy the authority" of the *Iliad* and its hero Achilles."[29] Drawing from the *Odyssey*, Planinc associates Hecuba with Odysseus's escape from the Cyclops as a way to expose the "injustice of acting against injustice" as a Cyclopean aspect of human nature.[30] By contrast, others see Euripides's allusions to the Trojan myth not in response to Homer but to Aeschylus's *Oresteia*, especially in its portrayal of the insufficiency of institutional solutions to private vengeance.[31] Such metatextual analysis remains conjectural as important source material is now lost, and it is unclear how ancient poets transformed mythology for their own dramatic purposes.[32]

Despite these difficulties, Euripides appears to have made four important innovations in the story of the Trojan survivors.[33] First, Euripides changed the typical genealogy of Polydorus and Hecuba.[34] In Homer, Polydorus is Priam's youngest son, but with his consort Laothoë; also already a young man, he is killed by Achilles in battle and never sent to Thrace. Second, Euripides also changes Hecuba's genealogy from the daughter of the Phrygian Dymas to that of the Thracian Kisseus. This innovation anchors Hecuba's story in Thrace. Her new Thracian connections provide additional kinship bonds, beyond guest-friendship (*xenia*), with its current king, Polymestor. Such associations also connect Hecuba with Dionysus, who is the source of Polymestor's final prophecy. Like Pentheus in Euripides's *Bacchae*, the Thracian king, Lycurgus, was torn apart for denying the god's divinity.[35] In addition, the Dionysian mysteries, which celebrated a liberation from behavioral and cultural norms, originated in Thrace.[36] Finally, Hecuba's new lineage highlights her connection to the ancient Thracian witch goddess Hekate, who held the keys to the crossing between life and death and to whom worshippers sacrificed black dogs.[37]

Second, and also associated with the new location of Thrace, is the role of King Polymestor. It unclear whether Polymestor belongs to the local mythology of the Thracian Chersonese or is purely a Euripidean invention. Polymestor is not mentioned in Homer nor in any other known version of the Trojan story prior to Euripides. Euripides probably invented this character because his name closely represents his personality: *polymestor* means "many councils," "much planning," and, as Mossman notes, is "highly suggestive of a tricky."[38] Although this play most certainly was performed before the Thracian army massacred the defenseless Mycalessians in 413 BCE, in the Greek imagination Thrace was a brutal and barbaric land.[39]

Two other possible innovations in Euripides's plot concern the female heroines. The story of Polyxena's sacrifice can be traced to the sixth-century fragmentary *Epic Cycle* where it is stated that she is slaughtered on the tomb of Achilles.[40] In that version, there is no mention of appeasing his ghost, and his tomb is located near Troy at Sigeum. Once again, with this change of location, Euripides emphasizes the wild, uncivilized Thracian setting.[41] There is a famous sixth-century amphora (ca. 570–50 BCE) that, in contrast to Euripides's depiction, represents her as fully clothed and physically held down by three warriors as Neoptolemus cuts her throat.[42] In other versions, Polyxena is killed during the siege of Troy and buried (not killed) by Neoptolemus. When she does survive the final battle, stories of her fate are varied. Fragments from Sophocles's earlier *Polyxena* include Achilles's ghost but no evidence of a sacrifice. Thus, Euripides possibly invented not only Achilles's demand for her sacrifice but also the description of her as a "willing" and noble victim.

Finally, there are conflicting mythological versions of the fate of Hecuba, which is central to this tragedy.[43] Although Homer is silent on what happened to Hecuba, she sometimes is rescued by Apollo during the destruction of Troy. Later in the Roman period, Ovid will have the Thracians stone her to death for her act of vengeance against their king.[44] What is most controversial is whether Euripides invented her prophesied metamorphosis into a dog or subsequent transformation into a sailor's sign. There was a Thracian promontory known as Cynossema (the Dog's Grave), which suggests Euripides did not invent her metamorphosis de novo but incorporated local Thracian mythology.[45] Importantly, no evidence before Euripides connects her transformation to an act of vengeance. Hence, Euripides appears to have invented Polymestor, altered the genealogy of two major characters, relocated events to a wild and hostile land, and probably introduced the idea of Hecuba's fated metamorphosis.

Justice: As Rhetoric

Euripides's complex dual plot interweaves a story of bloody human sacrifice with an avaricious murder in a setting far away from civilized Athens. The brutality of the plot, as noted above, was one reason early classicists found the tragedy an overblown "calamity" with a "great deal of bloodshed."[46] Similar to other Euripidean war tragedies, this story is not simply violent but encompasses carefully crafted debates (the *agōnes*) that reflect serious questions concerning war and the treatment of the vanquished. Although such debates generally fail to convince the opposing disputant, they raise important questions concerning justice in the conditions of warfare.[47] The three *agōnes* in the tragedy all involve the main character Hecuba: first, Hecuba and Odysseus; second, Hecuba and Agamemnon; and the forensic dispute between Hecuba and Polymestor with Agamemnon presiding as judge.

The debates highlight several competing conceptions of justice, but two conceptions of justice are most prominent. First, in all of the debates, characters appeal to the ancient view of justice as helping friends and harming enemies.[48] In particular, Euripides portrays the obverse of this code: the injustice of harming friends and helping enemies. In this context, Euripides connects justice as helping friends with two interrelated traditions in ancient Greek culture: supplication (*hiketeia*) and the reciprocal relationship of guest-friendship (*xenia*).[49] Significantly, as both supplication and guest-friendship were under the protection of Zeus, violations were considered not only unjust but also impious. Second, the *agōnes* also introduce another ancient understanding of justice: justice as merit or getting what one deserves.[50] Significantly, the debates expose the failure of both established law or custom (*nomos*) and political authority (*archē*) to uphold or enforce such principles of justice.

The understanding of justice as helping friends and harming enemies is asserted in all three debates. In the first *agōn* between Odysseus and Hecuba, Odysseus justifies the sacrifice of Polyxena by suggesting it "would it be disgraceful if we would serve him [Achilles] as a friend while alive, but serve him no longer when he perished."[51] In the second *agōn*, Agamemnon refuses to punish Polymestor, because "the army considers this man a friend and the one who died [Polydorus] an enemy; if this [dead boy] is my friend, this is [a private and] separate concern from the common affairs of the army." Finally, Polymestor employs his friendship with the Greeks to justify harming Polydorus: he murdered the boy because "killing your enemy [Agamemnon and the Greeks] . . . furthered your interest." All three arguments ground this ancient view of justice in the expectation of preferential treatment—or help—from those considered friends. Although the Greeks considered close associates and relatives as "friends," two kinds of formalized relationships expanded the scope of friendship beyond those nearby.

First, supplication (*hiketeia*) rituals could form bonds of friendship. Some form of supplication is portrayed in most extant plays and is a major theme in Euripides's *Suppliant Women* and *Children of Heracles*.[52] The traditional practice of supplication was widespread and could occur at politically controlled sanctuary sites or privately between individuals. Although suppliants could be family or community members, they could also be foreigners, exiles, or criminals. Supplication was protected by divine sanction and political leaders were obligated to defend those whose supplication they accepted.[53] As is dramatized by Hecuba, the ritual act included gestures of kneeling and touching of the benefactor's knees, right hand, and chin. It was considered less problematic to prevent the ritual act than to reject it.[54] This explains why Odysseus physically turns away from Polyxena when her mother begs her to supplicate him.

In addition, although supplication could form expectations of friendship and reciprocity (*kharis*), the tragedy highlights the limitations of extending friendship beyond family and community members. During their *agōn*, Hecuba reminds Odysseus of his reciprocal obligation (*kharis*) to her for the past favor of saving him when he was captured during the war. As someone connected by neither blood ties nor friendship (in fact, he was her enemy), her previous act of benevolence demands "justice . . . as a return for the favor (*kharis*) I showed you then."[55] Odysseus is willing to acknowledge "the good fortune he received" by freeing her but refuses to extend the favor to Polyxena because a personal obligation cannot overrule the public interest of the Greeks. Similarly, in her second supplication of Agamemnon, this king rejects punishing Polymestor because his "friendship" with Cassandra cannot take precedence over Greek alliances. Clearly, the Greek characters reinforce public interest over personal or private obligations. Odysseus ruthlessly taunts her failure to recognize this narrower view of friends as "one's own." Troy fell, he tells her, because the Trojans disrespected the principle of "treating friends as friends." Importantly, it was Hecuba's violation of this principle when she saved Odysseus that sealed the fate of her city and family. This crafty rhetorician lived to fabricate the ruse of the wooden horse; and, more recently, he convinced the army to violate their own norms and sacrifice Hecuba's daughter. Odysseus clearly would not make the same mistake of confusing friends and enemies by aiding her rather than giving preference to the Greek Achilles.

Violations of the ancient practice of formalized guest-friendship (*xenia*) are even more relevant to this plot. Similar to formal supplication, *xenia* was a ritualized hereditary relationship protected by Zeus that created bonds of obligations beyond blood kin and close community ties.[56]

Guest-friendship was created by prior supplication, exchanges of gifts (including women in marriage), and official oaths and pledges. During the classical period, political elites across different poleis continued the practice of *xenia*. At the beginning of the Peloponnesian War, for example, Pericles transferred his private property in Attica to the control of the city. Since the Spartan king Archidamus was his *xenos*, Pericles's own lands would be spared out of respect for this relationship. Thus, this transfer of land avoided an obvious conflict of interest with Pericles's policy of allowing the Spartans to ravage Attic territory unopposed.[57]

Significantly, the *xenia* bond imposed similar obligations to blood kinship, such as acting as foster parents for the other's children. Hecuba stresses Polymestor's violation of this obligation in her formal lament: he, who was "my *xenos*," she cries, committed "a crime without name . . . [w]here is the justice of guest-friends (*xenōn*)?"[58] Supplicating Agamemnon, she emphasizes that customs such as *xenia* establish the standards that determine "how we judge unjust from just . . . [and] if those who murder their guest-friends or dare to steal from the god's temples do not receive justice, then there is no equality (*ison*) among human beings."[59] Explicitly, Hecuba connects *xenia* to accepted norms of behavior that transcend civic law or private gain.[60]

Although Agamemnon agrees that Hecuba's case against Polymestor is valid, he refuses to enact justice on her behalf because he is concerned with his own reputation. His army would fault favoring a private concern (injustice to his mistress's family) over the public good of the Greek political alliance with Polymestor.[61] He does allow her, however, the latitude to act on her own behalf but only because the wind is still not favorable, and he assumes that Hecuba is too powerless to accomplish anything. In the final forensic *agōn*, however, Agamemnon explicitly agrees with Hecuba's position: Polydorus's murder was "not for my sake or for that of the Achaeans, but in order to keep the gold in your [Polymestor's] house . . . perhaps you think killing guests is insignificant, but for the Greeks this is a disgraceful act."[62] Hence, although unwilling to act, Agamemnon permits Hecuba to punish the violation of guest-friendship.

The tragedy also dramatizes the concept of justice as merit. Justice as merit can overlap with the ethic of helping friends and harming enemies—if friends merit such help. Yet, the *Hecuba* challenges such a simplistic conflation of friendship with merit.[63] At the end of the second *agōn*, Agamemnon suggests: "All—each man and each city—in common know this: that bad things should happen to bad men and good fortune should be enjoyed by those who are decent."[64] In other words, we should help friends but only when friends are decent men. What Agamemnon does not reveal are the criteria used to judge whether someone is decent or bad. Is it determined by birth, character, or great actions on behalf of the community? Furthermore, what is this "good thing" that decent men merit but bad men do not?[65]

Euripides explores competing ideas of merit in the first *agōn* between Hecuba and Odysseus. Although Hecuba raises the point that murdering slaves is against Greek law, she makes two claims based on higher principles of justice as merit.[66] First, she argues that human sacrifice is wrong because justice as merit requires an appropriate or commensurate exchange of things. As human beings are not oxen, it is "an improper measure" to substitute a human being for a sacrificial animal. Second, Hecuba suggests that if Achilles demands some kind of "payback" in exchange for his death, then justice requires a judgment of responsibility.[67] In this case, the sacrifice should be Helen (who is responsible for the war) and not Polyxena (who has done nothing wrong). Leaving aside the veracity of Hecuba's judgment of Helen, her point echoes the necessity of responsibility in the idea of corrective justice.[68] Or, as we would now say: punishment should fit the crime. Thus, Hecuba offers two reasons why the sacrifice is unmerited: the treatment of Polyxena must consider her shared and equal humanity and, furthermore, since she committed no crime, she does not deserve to be put to death.

By contrast, Odysseus understands the question of merit differently. For Odysseus, Polyxena's sacrifice is appropriate because Achilles merits (*axios*) an extraordinary sacrifice as "the most courageous man in the army."[69] Communities fail, he further argues, when they "do not give more to a man who is noble and vigorous, than to those who are worthless."[70] From Odysseus's perspective, human beings are not simply equal and thus do not deserve equal treatment. In fact, it is unjust (and destructive to the community) to treat unequals as equals. Second, Odysseus entirely ignores Hecuba's argument associating merit with responsibility. As Achilles demanded Polyxena, her guilt or innocence is immaterial. Thus, Odysseus remains committed to the principle that those who merit more should be given more, even if what they "merit" goes against the law (like human sacrifice).[71] Crucially, this *agōn* highlights not only disputes concerning what is meant by "merit" but, as will be further developed in this chapter, puts a human face on the sophistic justifications of those in power.[72]

Justice: As Pity?

Odysseus's silence concerning Hecuba's second point associating merit with responsibility highlights the potential (but ultimately failed) role of pity in questions of justice as merit.[73] Pity in ancient Greece denoted the sorrow of seeing another suffer but was also often associated with a judgment of whether such suffering was deserved.[74] Hecuba appeals to pity several times in her failed attempts to secure aid.[75] Each time her appeals fall on deaf ears. Other characters refuse to appeal to pity. Polyxena declines, since she prefers to "die before meeting undeserved disgrace" of life as a concubine.[76] Even the ruined Polymestor does not appeal to pity in the forensic *agōn*.[77] Instead, Polymestor stresses his and Agamemnon's shared self-interest: Polydorus was a Greek enemy, and Hecuba should be punished because "no one is more treacherous, on land or sea, than women."[78] Polymestor's appeal rests not in pity but in the chauvinistic self-interest of the community of men.

Although there is a clear conflict of interest, Agamemnon's judgment confirms that Polymestor deserves his misfortune. Yet despite this verdict, the tragedy's finale still seems particularly brutal with offstage cries of murdered children and Polymestor crawling blindly on stage. The question of whether Hecuba's actions are just or excessive has been the subject of a long debate. Eighteenth-century classicists such as Bellegarde were convinced that the spectacle of Polymestor "diminished the sorrow evoked by Hecuba's misfortune."[79] Later Grube emphasized "the savagery of her vengeance, and the bodies of the children that lie before us, have dried up the springs of our pity for Hecuba."[80] Others see our capacity to pity Hecuba dry up because she delights too much in Polymestor's suffering.[81] This potential audience discomfort echoes a similar situation in Alcmene's ecstatic triumph over her enemy Eurystheus in the *Children of Heracles*. In that case, Alcmene kills a prisoner of war in violation of Athenian law.[82]

The context of the tragedy also raises questions as to whether Polymestor merited this violent ending. Contemporary audiences may view Hecuba's actions as excessive because our cultural norms condemn blinding criminals and killing innocent children.[83] By contrast, the ancient Greek audience might judge her actions as entirely appropriate for Polymestor's crime. The plot raises no doubt concerning Polymestor's guilt: from the prologue, we know he murdered Polymestor out of greed.[84] Polymestor is also guilty of violating the sanctity of guest-friendship, which is "a law (*nomos*) above the gods."⁸⁵ Finally, by killing Hecuba's last surviving son, Polymestor also destroyed Priam's bloodline. In exchange for such a horrific crime, Hecuba blinded Polymestor and killed his bloodline with the death of his sons.⁸⁶ Since the ancient Greeks understood the "eyes [as] symbolic of offspring and the family lineage," this double act could be seen as an appropriate and literal exchange for his violation of guest-friendship and destruction of Priam's legacy.⁸⁷

By contrast, however, Hecuba raises the alarm concerning the appropriateness of her action. In her *agōn* with Odysseus, she is the one to introduce the argument that it is unjust to kill innocent children, like Polyxena, who "did nothing wrong."⁸⁸ In addition, although Agamemnon claims that "it is the common wish of [all] . . . that bad men should get bad treatment," it is not only contemporary scholars but other characters in the tragedy who express extreme discomfort at the sight of Polymestor's suffering. The chorus, who previously lamented Polymestor's "terrible and shameful deeds" and acted as co-conspirators with Hecuba, cry out upon seeing the blinded Polymestor: "Oh, wretched man (*tlēmon*), what oppressive evils bear down upon you." Even after consenting to Hecuba's personal justice, Agamemnon is surprised at the sight of Polymestor's misery and shouts in horror: "*Ea!*"

Of course, both the chorus and Agamemnon may simply be acting with exaggerated pretense, since they are all implicated in the act. Agamemnon's surprise may also be genuine, as he doubted a woman could enact such vengeance.⁸⁹ It is also possible he is feigning astonishment to protect his reputation with the army (the reason he refused to enact justice himself). Yet it is not implausible that despite acting or knowing beforehand, the chorus and Agamemnon are simply overcome by the sight of such human misery, deserved or not. At the very least, as Easterling notes, Hecuba's brutal response draws attention to "the problematic nature of the violent deeds."⁹⁰

Such a strong reaction to this final scene, both textually by Euripides's characters and by the tradition of scholarship, emphasizes that human beings can and do experience some kind of discomfort at the sight of suffering, even if such suffering is merited and even if we all agree that bad men deserve bad things. It is not clear what to call this painful discomfort. Grube earlier called it "horror." Hogan suggests our discomfort is not due to Polymestor's suffering but is caused by Euripides's confounding of our emotional response, which creates a "distrust [in] any feeling."⁹¹ Yet it is possible that Euripides is indicating an insufficiency in the Greek understanding of pity.[92] We certainly do not have the same feelings for Polymestor as we did for Hecuba earlier in the play, but it is hard not to feel something at the sight of a blind man crawling in search of his murdered sons, even if he is a greedy child murderer.[93] Thus, it is possible to judge Polymestor's fate as warranted but additionally recognize that Hecuba's "corrective" justice still has an emotional cost.

Justice: As Power

Added to this already somber message Euripides raises the possibility that justice is not based on any standard (or law higher than even the gods, as Hecuba would say) but only reflects the interest of the strongest. Plato depicts this sophistic view of justice as "the advantage of the stronger" with Thrasymachus in the *Republic* and Callicles in the *Gorgias*.[94] Thucydides attributes the statement "the strongest take what they can and weak give way" to the Athenians in his Melian dialogue."[95] In this tragedy, Euripides explores this sophistic or relativist view of justice as power in two ways. First, all three *agōnes* employ rhetorical persuasion as an instrument of power. Although Odysseus represents this tragedy's quintessential rhetorician, Hecuba learns to employ similar tactics to obtain her own goals. Second, by placing an archetypal outsider—an elderly female slave—at the epicenter of questions of justice as power, Euripides reminds us of the consequences of the failure of authority to perform its central enforcement role in questions and enactments of justice.[96]

The first *agōn* prominently presents this relativist view of justice as nothing more than the interest of the strongest. Upon arrival, Odysseus immediately indicates that he will take Polyxena away—by force if necessary.[97] Hecuba asks permission to speak freely (*parrhēsia*): "If slaves may question free men."[98] Odysseus acquiesces since, as he nonchalantly puts it, "He has the time."[99] As Hecuba's freedom to speak frankly is not based on an equal right of speech (*isēgoria*) but on Odysseus's whim, the conclusion to the first *agōn* is a foregone one. Yet despite her lack of power, Hecuba points out the potential weakness of all political speech: political authorities are ungrateful friends, she says, "as they are willing to do anything to please the *dēmos*, including harming friends."[100] As noted above, in this *agōn* Hecuba argued from the position of law and justice as merit; however, in his usual wily manner, Odysseus enforced another custom (*nomos*): "to grant more to great men than inferiors even if this custom is bad (*kakos*)." Dismissing ethical concerns of right and wrong as irrelevant to real questions of political security, like a modern-sounding realist, Odysseus reduces justice to political expediency and the interest of the powerful. Importantly, this exchange also highlights the requirement that genuine political speech depends on an openness to persuasion.[101] Odysseus may have allowed Hecuba to speak, but he is not listening. Departing with Polyxena, he reminds Hecuba that words are "meaningless" as he, not she, is the master.

The second *agōn* also highlights the role of power and justice. In this case, unlike Odysseus who did not listen, Agamemnon will not act. By supplicating Agamemnon, Hecuba recognizes his political authority to enact vengeance (*timōrein*) upon Polymestor.[102] When he rejects her supplication, she turns to an argument vested in Agamemnon's private interest: Agamemnon "owes" her for his sexual enjoyment of Cassandra. With a seeming new flair for amoral reasoning, Hecuba appears to be transformed into Odysseus.[103] Yet as earlier comments betray Agamemnon's genuine feelings for Cassandra, Hecuba's shift in argumentation reinforces a view of justice located in the private ties of friendship.[104] In addition, as she points out, as a private individual Agamemnon has an obligation "to serve justice and to give bad things always to bad men." Thus, she conflates an argument of justice as merit with the ancient code of private obligations to help friends and harm enemies.

Hecuba only half-wins her case. Agamemnon is not indifferent to her various claims to justice: he agrees that justice demands that an impious host should be punished.[105] Yet he refuses to act precisely because his ties to Cassandra are personal. Instead, confirming her earlier comment to Odysseus that politicians are terrible friends, he prioritizes the political alliance with Polymestor and refuses to act "if [he is] to be criticized before the Achaeans." What matters most is not private obligation but political power. The chorus echoes this point: "Political law (*nomos*) determines our closest ties, rending the greatest foes friends and making enemies of those who were once well-disposed."[106] Hence, unlike Odysseus, Agamemnon is convinced by the righteousness of her cause; however, like Odysseus, he prioritizes power and political expedience.

At this point, one might expect an elderly slave woman to concede defeat, but she does not. She presses on. As previously noted, Agamemnon grants her an attempt at vengeance for two reasons: first, he doubts an old woman has the power to subdue a man; and second, "the god still does not release fair winds."[107] Thus, like Odysseus, Agamemnon simply has "the time" to placate her. Scholars have long dismissed Agamemnon's cowardice, but his failure to act is not due to weakness but to his prioritizing political (or public) interest over principled justice. For Reckford, the priority of political expediency highlights a broken or meaningless universe in which justice is nothing but the interest of the strongest.[108] Euripides's point, however, may be less pessimistic. In her clash with political authority, Hecuba did fail to find justice: her daughter was slaughtered, and no one will punish her son's murderer. Hecuba, though, does not accept the decisions of the powerful or "strongest." She does not act as if justice is meaningless. By contrast, she recognizes that justice is not equated with political authority. For Hecuba, justice remains possible because even though she is only an elderly slave woman, she has a freedom to act that has escaped the kings of Greece.

Justice: As Autonomy and Freedom

Thus far, the conceptualization of justice in the play is a complex tapestry of conflicting and overlapping understandings that seem to depend upon the whims of political authority. Unlike many of Euripides's tragedies, the *Hecuba* lacks a miraculous deus ex machina symbolizing some sort of divine will.[109] At best, the mutilated Polymestor foretells a Dionysian prophecy of the fates concerning Hecuba, Agamemnon, and Cassandra. The only hint of divine purpose is the continuing lack of propitious winds. Although the plot intimates that Achilles stopped the winds to force the sacrifice of Polyxena, it is not clear this is the case.[110] The still-beached ships are the reason Agamemnon grants Hecuba her own justice. Only after Hecuba achieves this justice do the winds return. Yet it is not clear these are propitious winds. Do they indicate divine sanction of Hecuba's actions? Or are they inauspicious, as the audience knows they carry the Greeks not to a joyous return but to homecoming slaughter (or, for the wily Odysseus, many years of delay)? With this "obscurity of the gods," Euripides abandons Hecuba to human authorities who either fail to listen or listen but fail to act.[111]

Yet precisely at the moment of Agamemnon's refusal to act, Hecuba underscores one reason for the existence of injustice. She asserts that "no mortal is free . . . for he is a slave to money, or chance, or to the multitude of his city, or its written laws. All things which prevent him from acting according to his own judgment."[112] Clearly, Polymestor is the slave to money, and Agamemnon is a slave to public opinion. Odysseus appears to be free, as he convinces the army to violate their own laws regarding human sacrifice; yet, despite his rhetorical flair Odysseus is still dependent on the opinion of the multitude.[113] Importantly, the literal slave—Hecuba—is the one free from greed, the opinion of the multitude, and legal constraints. For the ancient Greeks, the concept of freedom (*eleutheria*) had several different dimensions: the condition of a free individual in opposition to a slave, citizenship freedom in opposition to tyrannical rule within the polis, and the city's freedom from foreign domination.[114] Hecuba is not free according to any of these meanings. Although she requires Agamemnon's agreement not to obstruct her, she acts according to her own judgment, free from what limits political authority: greed, chance, written law, and the will of the people.

In contemporary terminology, Hecuba has found a kind of freedom that we might now call "autonomy." Although autonomy (*autonomia*) is an ancient Greek word, it is used to describe the latter two kinds of freedom: domestic self-rule and the independence of a city to define its own laws. Euripides never uses this word, but from this moment on in the play, Hecuba is acting freely on a meaning of justice independent of civic law, public opinion, or political authority.[115] Furthermore, she is not constrained by the cultural conventions (*nomos*) of women's behavior. Most importantly, she does not endorse a relativistic moral autonomy; instead, her actions are directed from higher moral principles, such as the sanctity of guest-friendship. These are the laws that rule over even the gods and are the reason that "we believe in the gods and can distinguish between injustice and justice."[116] Thus, Hecuba's autonomy is located in acting despite her circumstances as slave, woman, and citizen of a lost world. Hecuba is not merely challenging political authority for private interests (as perhaps Antigone does in Sophocles's play) but is forced to act after those in power fail to uphold such higher principles.

Hecuba is not alone in her autonomy, as Polyxena can also be seen as embodying this form of freedom.[117] It is important to stress that neither Hecuba nor Polyxena is free in the sense that they act without any constraints or are wholly self-governing. Like all human beings they are still subject to chance and the countering power of other human beings: Polyxena surely would have chosen to be freed rather than sacrificed; Hecuba requires Agamemnon to look the other way. Although bounded by the constraints of their circumstances, both women still make choices central to their self-understanding and "act according to their own judgment."[118] Polyxena chooses to be led away "both for the sake of necessity and because I wish to die;" she demands not to be held down like an animal, but to die a "free-woman." Free of the opinion of the multitude, Hecuba acts for the sake of her murdered son. Despite chance, both mother and daughter act nobly, thus proving Hecuba's statement: "Always for human beings, the villain (*ponēros*) does nothing except bad things (*kakos*) but a noble person is noble, his nature is not destroyed by misfortune, but it always is decent (*chrēstos*)."

This conclusion, that Hecuba and Polyxena make some kind of free choice consistent with noble character, is highly controversial. Certain types of scholarship continue to view Polyxena's sacrifice as an eroticized fetish in which she becomes a spectacle for the gaze of Greek soldiers; by contrast, other scholars regard her death as noble but distinct from Hecuba's actions.[119] Along this latter line, Nussbaum argues the tragedy reveals the fragility of noble characters such as Hecuba, who sings a "new *nomos*" that is corrupted by revenge.[120] Or, as Meagher puts it: "Hekabe is living proof that powerlessness, like power, corrupts and absolute powerlessness corrupts absolutely." The important question is whether Hecuba's new melody is "complete moral ruin," "moral destruction," "a fatal change," or "dehumanizing."[121] Or, as Mossman and Meridor argue, is Euripides condemning the precariousness of justice rather than Hecuba's actions?[122]

The answer to this debate might lie in Hecuba's prophesied metamorphosis. As discussed previously, this version of her fate may have been invented by Euripides. What is not clear is the meaning of her metamorphosis into a dog, her subsequent suicide, and the transformation of her burial spot into a signpost for sailors. One line of argument, put most eloquently by Carson, is that she had already been transformed into a "vengeance maniac," and "there is nowhere for her to go but out of the species."[123] In other words, her metamorphosis is simply a physical transformation of her already transformed soul. Hence, the tragedy is a reversal of Aeschylus's *Eumenides*, which ends with Athena establishing judicial institutions and transforming the ancient personal vengeance maniacs—the Erinyes—into the kindly ones.[124] In our tragedy, Hecuba appeals first to those with institutional authority but is permanently transformed into her own "vengeance hound" when such authority fails.[125]

Yet it is not clear that her vengeance is the act of a mad dog. Polymestor's blinding and the death of his children are reciprocal exchanges for the destruction of a guest-friend's bloodline. Agamemnon's judgment (as biased as it may be) confirms Polymestor's guilt. Perhaps Hecuba is too vicious, as even her co-conspirators exclaim upon seeing Polymestor. The significant question seems to be the meaning of her metamorphosis into a dog. Such animal metamorphoses in ancient Greece were not necessarily punishment for moral transgressions.[126] Human beings were turned into all sorts of animals (birds, snakes, pigs, horses, bulls) and even into trees, flowers, and rocks. Some of these metamorphoses were punishments but usually for transgressions against the gods. Other transformations were a divine reward for services or a means of escaping the pursuit of lustful gods.

Perhaps the real question is—why a dog? From one perspective, the ancient Greeks regarded dogs as representative of an absence of *nomos* or concern for the community: dogs could be symbols of the bestial, vicious, and vengeful private punishment—thus, symbolic again of the doglike Erinyes.[127] Calling a woman "dog-eyed" was an insult that implied shamelessness or lack of control.[128] Dogs could be considered impure; for example, it was forbidden to keep dogs on the sacred island of Delos, the birthplace of Apollo and Artemis.[129] Yet, the meaning of canine imagery in ancient Greek culture is more ambiguous than simply negative. The burning doglike gaze of Hecuba could, for example, allude to Orion and his dog Sirius, whose fiery eyes protect us from the heavens.[130] Other examples of canine faithfulness include Odysseus's dog Argus or the many-headed Cerberus, protector of Hades.[131] In Book V of the *Republic*, Socrates compares his guardian class to dogs because both share the same unswerving loyalty to friends and viciousness to enemies.[132] In addition, Socrates frequently swears "by the dog," likely referencing the Egyptian dog-god Anubis as a way to emphasize the truth of his statements. Such faithfulness might explain why Hecuba would morph into an animal so devoted to its own that she no longer cared about her fate.[133]

Dogs were also sacrificial animals in two major cults: to Asclepius, the god of healing who had a sanctuary adjacent to the theater of Dionysus, and to Hekate, that ancient moon-goddess of the Thracians. Hecuba's new genealogy and transformation into a dog may be a veiled reference to Hekate, who was often accompanied by the Erinyes and whose cult sacrificed black dogs at the crossroads.[134] A mysterious figure, Hekate was associated with the underworld, transitions, and the use of poisons and witchcraft. She was identified with other *chthonic* figures, such as Persephone (for whom she carried the keys of Hades), Artemis, and the Thracian goddess Bendis—that new goddess alluded to at the beginning of Plato's *Republic*.[135] Other avenging women who punish violations of helping friends, such as Medea, were also associated with Hekate.[136] In postclassical era mythology, Hecuba remains a transformed dog and becomes an attendant of this goddess. Finally, the sacrifice of dogs may also draw symmetry to Polyxena as they both are turned into some kind of sacrificial animal.

Whatever meaning the fifth-century audience found in her metamorphosis, her final transformation is not into a dog but into the rocky outcrop that marks her grave. This landmark, called the Cynossema—the dog's grave—is a promontory on the Thracian Chersonese where the Hellespont narrows, near modern Kilitbahir. As noted previously, Euripides may have used this metamorphosis into a dog to explain the origin of this well-known naval marker.[137] Yet there might be a further meaning of this final transformation. Gregory argues it "signals that the desire for justice is rooted deep in human nature and cannot be torn out by force."[138] Kovacs sees the Cynossema as a hero's tomb, in which Hecuba is honored as both sub- and superhuman, having overstepped the boundary of humanity. Thus, the dog's grave is "a mark for the Greek sailor, the most sensible and rational of mortals, to sail by."[139] Nussbaum rejects Hecuba's heroism but suggests the sign is "a marker of the boundary of social discourse."[140] The signpost, however, remains ambiguous. Is Hecuba transformed into a figure whose example we should steer clear of, as she represents a loss of boundaries essential to our humanity? Or, in this ever-shifting tragedy, is this a sign that justice sometimes requires stepping over these boundaries, especially when political authority is a slave to greed and public opinion?

Conclusion

As with all his tragedies (and most literature in general), Euripides poses rather than answers such questions. The view that Hecuba represents a warning sign against the cost of transgressing boundaries assumes that she lost her humanity in the pursuit of vengeance. Yet if her metamorphosis into a dog is a symbol of her faithfulness, her transformation signals the high cost of the institutional failure to protect justice.[141] That leaders would instead pursue their own political self-interest is no surprise to modern and (most likely) ancient Greek audiences. Such a conclusion, however, does not imply that "anarchy is loosed upon the world," or that Euripides leaves no understanding of justice outside of human authority.[142] In fact, the play emphasizes the opposite—the justice Hecuba seeks is not created by, or contingent upon, political authority or civic law.

The idea that there is a higher status to principles of justice resonates across the history of political thought. Hecuba's understanding of such principles, such as not treating Polyxena as a sacrificial animal, hints at later developments in political theory. Cicero, for example, develops the idea of *dignitas*, and the concepts of "human dignity" and "autonomy" in Kant become central to contemporary human rights theory.[143] Hecuba relates such higher principles to divine imperatives, such as the sanctity of guest-friendship. Although she does not elaborate, Hecuba suggests such principles are even above the gods.[144] This idea that the principles of justice preexist and are not determined by the gods is reflected in the famous dilemma in Plato's *Euthyphro*: is something pious because the gods command it? Or do the gods hold pious things dear because those things are pious?[145] Such questions are still important in divine commandment theory, which is less popular in contemporary philosophy but endures in some strains of deontological ethics.[146]

Even if Hecuba points to principles higher than political authority and written law, for many, this tragedy still ends on an uncomfortable note.[147] Again, our modern sensibilities may find her still too narrowly focused on one's own, her punishment too extreme, or her application of the distinction between good and bad too blurry.[148] Yet one final possible meaning of the dog's grave might be to symbolize the high cost of challenging institutional authority and going it alone. As flawed as our political leaders and institutions are, they can provide a less biased and more measured response to injustices. They can stop cycles of violence by tempering Hecuba's close identification with helping loved ones. Going it alone implies, at the very least, that one must take seriously the questions raised concerning justice in this play: Why is someone a friend or enemy? What does a good or bad person merit? Or what makes a person bad or good? Perhaps Hecuba's final transformation serves as an eternal reminder that if we act as autonomous individuals fighting for justice, we must temper the vengeance of our personal Erinyes with a touch of something like compassion.

Chapter 8

The *Alcestis*

Justice as Generosity, or Too Much of a Good Thing

> Phoebus Apollo are you again acting unjustly
> in the dividing of boundary lines and hindering
> the honors due those below?[1]

The *Alcestis* is an obscure and unusual story about a woman who agrees to die her husband's death but is eventually rescued by the strong-arm heroics of Heracles. Although likely written early in Euripides's career, the *Alcestis* is one of his most original and innovative tragedies and has become "a touchstone of Euripidean criticism."[2] Past scholarship pointed to the *Alcestis* as an exemplar of Euripides's supposed assault on the grandeur of Greek tragedy; however, when changing attitudes began to appreciate "Euripides portraying men as they really are," the play became one of his most celebrated tragedies.[3] Other scholarship focuses on the question of why a husband would allow his wife to die in his place or the meaning of the dual leitmotifs of *kharis* (favor and gratitude) and *xenia* (guest-friendship).[4] Connecting these themes specifically to justice, this chapter explores the extent to which we owe obligations to those closest to us, such as our spouses, children, and friends.[5] It questions whether helping others, such as Alcestis's generosity in dying another's death, represents a form of injustice. Euripides also uses the general question of "what is too much" to explore broader metaphysical issues, such as the distinction between being and non-being. Even though this intense drama "leaves us never sure of what we feel," Euripides forces a confrontation not only with how to make judgments of appropriate limits but also how the search to find such boundary lines is inexorably linked to the uncertainty embedded in human experience.[6]

The *Alcestis* is unique in many ways. First, we know more about this play than is typical because of an Alexandrian "second *hypothesis*," which contains information from the original *didascaliae*.[7] This *hypothesis* indicates that Euripides's entry came second to Sophocles at the Great Dionysia in 438 BCE. It also notes that this play was performed fourth, after the trilogy of *The Cretan Women*, *Alcmaeon in Psophis*, and *Telephus*.[8] Except for the most likely spurious *Rhesus*, this makes the *Alcestis* Euripides's earliest surviving manuscript. As his earliest production at the festival was probably in 455 BCE, by the time of this performance he was already a seasoned playwright in his forties.[9] This early production date, however, distinguishes the *Alcestis* as his only really extant pre–Peloponnesian War tragedy, which makes it less susceptible to interpretations of pro-Athenian propaganda or political commentary on the decline of Athenian democratic decision making.

Importantly, this *hypothesis* also highlights the main quandary of this play because it labels the conclusion *kōmikōteran*—comedic-like.[10] Indeed, the play is "comical," although not in the modern sense of being humorous but rather in the ancient meaning of ending positively or in revelry (*kōmos*). The enduring puzzle for classical scholars is the meaning of this comment, especially as the *Alcestis* also occupied the "fourth" position. As mentioned in the introduction, normally the Great Dionysia tragedy competition was a series of three tragedies followed by a fourth satyr play. As the name suggests, the satyr plays involved those half-human horselike creatures who were part of Dionysus's *kōmos* or "band of revelers" and were famous for their excessive desires for food, alcohol, and human women.[11] As Euripides's *Cyclops* is the only extant "true" satyr play, we know little about this genre; however, the choruses were most likely satyrs, and plots concerned themes of hospitality, magical events, and the overthrow of villains or the escapes of heroes.[12] Heracles often performed the role of a drunken glutton who battles local monsters. The function of a satyr play is unknown, although it may have been a "way to cheer up an emotionally drained audience" after the psychological tension of three grim, terrifying, and catastrophic-filled tragedies.[13]

One main question of the *Alcestis* is whether it was intended as a satyr play. As noted above, the *hypothesis* suggests it was performed fourth, in the normal position of a satyr play. As will be discussed below, the story reflects common themes of a satyr play, such as hospitality, the escape of a heroine, and antics of a drunken Heracles. Also similar to satyr plays (the *Cyclops* has 710 lines), the *Alcestis* is relatively short (1160 lines) in comparison to other Euripidean tragedies, such as the *Medea* (1420 lines) or *Hippolytus* (1465 lines). The *Alcestis*, however, lacks the essential ingredient of a satyr play: satyrs. By contrast, its chorus consists of men from Thessaly as supportive friends of the king. It also involves serious subject matter, including metaphysical ideas: all of which suggest a more emotionally draining tragedy than Dionysiac "cheering up."[14] As the *Alcestis* is the only extant play performed in the fourth position but not an obvious satyr play, previous classical scholarship suggested it was a unique genre called "pro-satyric." Dale, for example, argued Euripides adapted satyric themes in order to present "a wider range of mood than any other extant Greek tragedy."[15] By contrast, Kitto suggests, along with the *Ion*, *Helen*, and *Iphigenia among the Taurians*, it is a genre of "tragicomedy" or "melodrama."[16]

More recent scholarship rejects the idea that the *Alcestis* represents a unique genre, since tragic variations may have been more commonplace than we think.[17] It is also possible that the *Alcestis* was produced in response to a decree in 440–39 BCE that outlawed slanderous or ad hominem attacks in dramatic *kōmōdein*.[18] From this perspective, Euripides wrote a satyr-less play because "he could claim he had been forbidden to so by law;" in other words, he uses this play to dramatize the Athenian debate concerning what constitutes appropriate speech. Without more conclusive evidence, however, we are unlikely to know why Euripides wrote this shorter ambiguous play with other uncharacteristic tragic elements, such as an onstage death or a child speaking part. Significantly, the play appears to be neither strictly tragedy nor satyr play but incorporates elements of both. Euripides will return again and again, up until his posthumous *Bacchae*, to explore this theme or the way that "definitions blur."[19] This time, Euripides focuses on the consequences of blurring the boundaries of the meaning of virtues, such as generosity and gratitude, necessary for relationships of family and friends.

The Mythological Context and Plot of the *Alcestis*

Background Myth

This play is also unusual, focusing as it does on the House of Admetus and not the typical source material of the doomed Houses of Atreus or Laius—or the events surrounding the fall of Troy.[20] The appearance of

Heracles on his way to steal Diomedes's man-eating horses places the story within the "common myth kitty," but the main elements of the story are obscure.[21] A fragment of Hesiod refers to Admetus: Zeus forces Apollo to serve Admetus as a herdsman as punishment after Apollo killed the Cyclopes.[22] Homer mentions Eumelus, a son of Admetus and Alcestis, in the catalogue of ships in the *Iliad*.[23] The poet Phrynichus probably produced an *Alcestis* sometime between 511–490 BCE. Little is known about that version, except a possible reference to a wrestling match between Heracles and Death. Finally, Aeschylus's *Eumenides* may refer to this story with the suggestion that Apollo was known to trick the Fates into sparing men's lives.[24]

Most of the known story about Admetus and Alcestis either comes from this play or from later sources. Plato has Phaedrus comment on Alcestis's self-sacrifice in the *Symposium*, but in that version, the gods return Alcestis as a reward for her own selflessness.[25] In this play, Heracles mentions that if he fails to win Alcestis by force, he will convince the gods to release her; this may suggest that Euripides knew of this alternative version of the story.[26] Apollodorus's *Library* provides more details of Admetus's story, such as more explanation of Apollo's period of servitude to Admetus.[27] In this case, the feud between Zeus and Apollo began when Apollo's son Asclepius, who is taught the healing arts by the centaur Chiron, uses the "good" Gorgon blood to resurrect the dead.[28] Fearing that human beings would begin to reverse the natural order of life, Zeus smites Asclepius with a thunderbolt.[29] In retaliation, Apollo kills the Cyclopes who made his thunderbolts; and, in return, Zeus condemns him to servitude to the human Admetus.

Admetus proves a pious master, and Apollo rewards him several times. First, he helps Admetus win the hand of Alcestis, the daughter of Pelias. In Apollodorus's version, Pelias is still alive and sets up a task to win his daughter: potential suitors must yoke together a lion and boar.[30] Apollo accomplishes this on Admetus's behalf. Unfortunately, during the wedding the special rites to Artemis are forgotten, and this goddess condemns Admetus to an early death. Apollo steps in again and convinces the Fates to allow another to die in Admetus's place. Alcestis is the only one to agree. Apollodorus suggests both endings: she either is returned by the gods or rescued by Heracles in a struggle with Hades.

Other possible source material for Alcestis's sacrifice and rescue derives not from Greek myth but from popular folktales found across Europe.[31] Although there are many versions of this particular folktale, the main storyline has Death arrive to take the bridegroom on his wedding day. Death is convinced to accept a substitute, but the young man cannot convince his parents, and only his new bride is willing. In some versions of this folktale, the husband struggles with Death in a physical battle. In other versions, the wife is faced with a choice of saving her husband or her brother. She chooses her father's lineage over that of her husband, emphasizing her position as "outsider" with a potential conflict of loyalties. Conacher suggests that Euripides may have brought together two myths of fundamentally different origins: the Olympian mythology of the enslavement of Apollo to Admetus and this separate folktale story of a wife substitution and struggle with Death.[32]

Euripides's *Alcestis*

Euripides divides the plot into two clearly distinctive parts. The first part (lines 1–475) focuses on the death of Alcestis; the second part (lines 475–1165) shifts to Heracles's subsequent rescue. In the prologue, Apollo tells the backstory of how the House of Admetus came to this moment of losing its mistress.[33] Apollo was sent by Zeus as a slave to the mortal Admetus as punishment to end the cycle of retributive killings that began with Zeus's murder of Asclepius. As Admetus was a reverent man (*hosios*), Apollo blessed his House with miraculous births of twin livestock, and he tricked the Fates into allowing Admetus to substitute his appointed death.[34] When it came time to find a replacement, among those dear (*philoi*) to him, only his wife Alcestis was willing to die in his place. As Apollo is about to depart, he is confronted by Death who has arrived to claim Alcestis.[35] In a short debate (*agōn*), Apollo attempts to convince Death to grant him a favor (*kharis*) by allowing Alcestis to live until old age. Death refuses and stresses the injustice of Apollo's violation of boundary lines (*aphorizō*) and the rights of the ancient *chthonic* gods; he also points out the injustice of this new Olympian god's unequal treatment of Admetus and of the rich. Unable to convince Death, Apollo foretells the arrival of a guest who will take back Alcestis by force since persuasion has failed.[36]

The choral *parodos* of Thessalian citizens enters. Confused by the silence of the House, they wonder as to whether the mistress is still alive or dead.[37] The maidservant's arrival is unhelpful as she describes Alcestis as both "alive and dead." She also describes Alcestis's activities on this fateful day: mimicking funeral rituals, she washed with water from running streams, clothed herself in finery, prayed to Hestia (the goddess of the hearth), and sacrificed on the altars of the House of Admetus.[38] Alcestis does not break down in grief until she enters the privacy of her bed chamber. The also-grieving Admetus begs her not to abandon him.

Alcestis enters, followed by Admetus and an entourage of her children and servants.[39] As she begins to fade, she reminds her husband that she alone (and not his parents) willingly dies his death. In return, she asks for a favor (*kharis*): he should not remarry and subject her children to a stepmother. Admetus promptly agrees and promises more: he will live in perpetual mourning without entertaining guests, disown his parents for failing to save him, make an image (*eikasthen*) of her to embrace at night, visit her in his dreams, and spend the rest of his life waiting to join her in death. Unusual for an ancient Greek play, Alcestis dies on stage, and her young son sings a dirge of grief.[40] Admetus orders a year-long public mourning, and the chorus concludes with an ode to Alcestis as "the bravest of wives" whose death will inspire poets.

The second part of the play (lines 475–1165) begins when the Panhellenic hero Heracles arrives as a guest-friend (*xenos*) on his way to complete the labor of capturing the man-eating horses of Diomedes.[41] As it would be inappropriate to entertain while the House is in mourning, Admetus convinces Heracles to remain by arguing that Alcestis "is and is no more;" and that it was an outsider (*othneios*), not kin, who died. Heracles disagrees with Admetus's collapse of the distinction of being and non-being, but they agree to disagree. Maintaining his reputation as a superlative host (but already breaking his promise to ban the entertaining of guests in perpetuity) Admetus literally divides his House into two separate halves: grief and celebration. On the side of grief, Admetus's father, Pheres, arrives to pay respects to the dead. A debate (*agōn*) breaks out between father and son over whether Pheres was wrong to refuse to die for his child. Pheres points out that there is something shameless and perhaps criminal in Admetus allowing his wife to die in his place.[42] Admetus disagrees and fulfills his promise to disown his parents. Admetus departs for the funeral.

Meanwhile, on the side of celebration, a bawdy and drunken Heracles argues with the servant that he is too long faced and should live for today as "death is an obligation that we all must pay."[43] The servant finally breaks down and tells Heracles the truth: Admetus was "too hospitable," since it was Alcestis who died. Heracles is scandalized to have been tricked by his friend into being shamefully entertained.

Yet he also recognizes the nobility behind Admetus's ruse and so decides to wrestle Death and take Alcestis back by force (following them into Hades, if necessary).[44]

Admetus and the chorus return from the funeral.[45] The chorus advises Admetus to bend to necessity and honor Alcestis's grave not as a monument to her death but with reverence as a shrine to a god.[46] Finally, Admetus recognizes the reality of the situation: his wife's action won her glory, and his life is tainted with the reputation of cowardice and ill-treatment of parents. Suddenly Heracles arrives on the stage accompanied by a veiled woman. He criticizes Admetus for not "speaking freely (*legein eleutherōs*)" or being honest to a friend. He demands Admetus accept the veiled woman, whom he won as a "prize," as a gift of exchange for his act of hospitality. At first, Admetus refuses, citing his mourning, his promise to Alcestis, and the inappropriateness of accepting a woman whose shape (*morphēs*) resembles his dead wife.[47] Heracles insists and Admetus bows to the pressure of his famous guest-friend and takes (in an action mimicking the marriage rite) the young veiled woman by the right hand.[48] Finally, Heracles asks Admetus to really "look at her," and she is revealed to possess the face and form of Alcestis. Due to the pollution of her death, the veiled woman is forced to remain silent for three days. The play ends with Heracles calling Admetus a pious and righteous man, and the chorus echoes the familiar refrain that "the gods find a way to achieve the unexpected."[49]

Euripides's Potential Innovations

Since most of what we know about this story is based on either this play or Apollodorus's later account, it is difficult to speculate on potential Euripidean innovations. Yet certain interesting features of Euripides's version contrast with the European folktale stories of wrestling Death. In the folklore tradition, for example, the substitution of another's death takes place on the wedding night; in our story, Alcestis and Admetus have been married long enough to have children. Importantly, Alcestis's primary concern is that her children do not have to endure a stepmother.[50] Second, Euripides also made his own substitution by having Heracles, an outside agent, take on the role of the husband who typically foils Death and rescues his wife. This second substitution emphasizes the passive role of Admetus as his wife does his dying, and his friend does his rescuing. This makes Admetus a rather ironic candidate for a heroic figure.[51] Finally,

Euripides focuses attention not only on a straightforward story of sacrifice and rescue but on the more complicated subject of indistinct binaries and blurred boundaries such as between generosity and self-interest. To investigate such confused distinctions, Euripides set this story of death substitution and resurrection not in a civilized polis but in the wilderness of Thessaly. And in this wilderness, where even the distinction between life and death is not clear, he highlights one of the enduring questions regarding justice: how much do we owe one another?

Justice: What Do I Owe You, My Friend?

The play opens with Apollo's statement that because he found Admetus a pious host (*xenos*), he tricked the Fates into exchanging Admetus's corpse for another.[52] Upon examining all those dear to him, Admetus found only his wife willing to die in his place. In this way, the prologue introduces the two main interconnected ethical questions of the play. First, although Admetus has a virtuous reputation because he is a good host and friend (the reason for Apollo's extraordinary "favor" of tricking the Fates), the play questions the proper measure of the virtue of hospitality: is his hospitality of Heracles, for example, not really extraordinary but inappropriate and excessive? Second, although Apollo does not use the word "favor," both Apollo's deceit of the Fates and Alcestis's willingness to die another's death are consistent with an act of *kharis* or outwardly directed favor or grace. In general, *kharis* describes both actions of generosity as well as the gratitude of the recipient.[53] Like Admetus's hospitality, both acts of *kharis* in the play (as well as potentially Heracles's favor of returning Alcestis) could be considered not simply favors but excessively virtuous acts.[54] Thus, the play brings to the forefront the question of the limits or proper boundaries of the virtues of generosity and friendship. In particular, Euripides draws attention to the proper boundary of obligation and the limits of a just reciprocity of exchange for hospitality or the generosity of *kharis*.

Justice: Generosity and Gratitude (*Kharis*)

We encounter the first example of questioning appropriate limits to reciprocity in the *agōn* between Apollo and Death. Entering the stage, Death immediately questions the justice of Apollo's deceit of the Fates in order to reward Admetus for his hospitality: "What are you doing in the political community Phoebus? Are you again acting unjustly (*adikeis*) in the dividing of boundary lines (*aphorizomenos*) and hindering the honors due to those below?"[55] Although Apollo claims to engage with "respectful words," Death is concerned, since Apollo carries the weapons that he used in his past "unjust giving of aid to this House."[56] Apollo's main argument is an appeal to self-interest: Death, he claims, would reap a richer burial if Alcestis lived to a ripe old age. Death finds this appeal unjust, since it would benefit only the rich who could pay for a long life. Apollo tries again by asking Death to grant a favor (*kharis*) of allowing Alcestis to live. Death simply replies: "You cannot possibly have all things, as some you ought not to have."[57] The encounter ends with Apollo's prediction that he will get his own way: a guest will come to take Alcestis by force, and Death will receive not reciprocal gratitude (*kharis*) but hatred. This time Apollo may not have used his weapons, but Death was right to see the threat of force if persuasion failed.[58]

Many commentators see a dualism in this exchange: Death represents darkness in contrast with Apollo "the bright savior god."[59] Yet, in this antagonistic encounter, which will repeat in tone in the *agōn* between Admetus and his father, Death is not really contrasted with a shining and pure Apollo. Of the two, Death appears to have the stronger argument, especially concerning questions of equality and justice.[60] Apollo's former act of *kharis* with Admetus contains two forms of injustice: first, Apollo's "favor" to Admetus is not within his authority to grant; we know this because Apollo must deceive the Fates and attempt to save Alcestis through either persuasion or force. Second, Death points to Apollo's unjust overstepping of proper boundaries several times: he acted unjustly in his division of the boundary lines (*aphorizomenos*) between life and death, hindered the honors due the gods below, and argued that the rich should be able to bribe their way into a longer life.

In contrast, Death insists upon the only great equalizer in human life: rich or poor, we all die our own deaths at our own appointed times.[61] Unlike the newer Olympian god, Death insists on respecting what has been long ordered or arranged (*tetagmetha*). Death may be hateful to mortals, but it has long been his proper function to consecrate the dead. Apollo may have tricked the Fates, but he cannot deceive Death. Thus, Apollo's extraordinary return favor to Admetus was not Apollo's to grant. It is not the dark lord but the shining god Apollo who has committed an injustice of overreaching a proper appropriation of reward and honor. Apollo's deceit, the indirect threat of weapons, and foretold violence underline the tension in this exchange. The Olympian god will use force and fraud to exercise his will and go beyond any proper and established boundaries. The play is not a clear-cut battle between the forces of light and dark.

Another way in which Euripides blurs boundaries of what another owes in gratitude, concerns the heroine Alcestis. For her willingness to die in Admetus's place, she is called "beyond all women, the most noble," "a faithful wife," "the best of women," and she is "celebrated."[62] After her death, she will be honored with a grave monument (*tumbos*) to be worshiped by travelers in the same manner as the great hero shines or sacred spaces of gods. A *tumbos* (mound tomb) represented not only a physical burial spot but also a meeting place that encouraged a continuous familiarity and interpretation of the glorious deeds of the dead; in this way, the warrior's *tumbos* became a durable bridge between the hero's death and the cultural memory or collective relevance of the hero's sacrifice.[63] Alcestis's action, therefore, is placed within a context comparable to the warrior's death. Euripides uses this theme of sacrificed woman as glorified hero across several of his plays: Macaria (or the maiden) in the *Children of Heracles*, Polyxena in *Hecuba*, and Evadne in the *Suppliant Women*.[64] Unlike these other heroines, however, Alcestis's choice is fully voluntary, and her remembrance is assured. Even Admetus finally recognizes her newly transformed heroic status.

Yet, Alcestis's transformation into a glorified civic hero is ambiguous. On the one hand, her self-sacrifice is comparable to a war hero's, and she is described in terms of typical male heroism; on the other hand, there is something qualitatively distinctive in the celebration of a woman as "the best of women," whose death does not save the city or her family (e.g., the maiden in the *Children of Heracles*) but is a simple exchange for her husband's death. Vellacott, points out that her action reflects Athenian norms as women would be expected to die for their husbands; thus, Admetus's honor would be unaffected by his wife dying in his place.[65] Alcestis's action, however, is seen as exceptional within the world of the play. Both Alcestis and Pheres make it clear that she, or any wife, has no obligation to die in her husband's place.[66] This could mean, that Alcestis represents not the norm but an "exemplar . . . for excellence in womanhood."[67] Euripides's language certainly emphasizes Alcestis's action of exchanging her life for another as an act that can be glorified, similar to the actions of heroic men who die for honorable causes in war.

Despite scholarship connecting her sacrifice to matrimonial love, Alcestis provides little insight into the reasons for her decision.[68] She tells us that she did not have to die and had much to live for, including the prospect of future husbands and more children.[69] Yet, in the maidservant's description of her final preparations, Alcestis breaks down at the sight of her marriage bed and weeps at the thought of being replaced. It is possible this outburst reveals her love for Admetus and fear of being replaced in his affection; her breakdown, however, may not be out of love or sexual jealousy but concern for her own status and that of her children.[70] This option is reflected in her dying wish to Admetus: "Now, remember to show your gratitude (*kharis*) to me for this [favor]. I shall not pretend to ask for a worthy exchange (for nothing is more precious than a life), but for what is just (*dikaia*) . . . keep these children as rulers of my House and do not remarry."[71] Thus, in exchange for an incommensurate act, she demands the extraordinary act of gratitude that Admetus not remarry.[72] He readily agrees but promises much more, such as living his entire life in mourning, rejecting his parents, banning all hospitality, and sleeping with a statue made in her image. Alcestis is unmoved by his other grand gestures and only repeats her demand that he not remarry or, as Dellner puts it, "fill her space" with someone who could produce new children (and replace hers) or reproduce her extraordinary act of dying in his place.[73] Importantly, she understands that her generosity is an extraordinary act beyond any measurement of reciprocity; the only partial reciprocal justice is that Admetus guarantee not to replace the replacer.

If Alcestis is an irreplaceable exemplar and her death is a substitution glorified in terms of male heroism, it further draws attention to Admetus's passivity. How, as Grube suggests, could he "be such a cad" to have allowed his wife to die in his place?[74] This is not simply an anachronistic concern but textually is alluded to in the *agōn* between Admetus and his father Pheres.[75] Echoing Alcestis's anger that his aged parents should have agreed to die, Admetus calls his father a coward for not saving his only son. In response, Pheres points out that he gave Admetus everything expected of a father—life, property, and kingship—and that no tradition exists where fathers are obligated to take on their son's death.[76] Furthermore, echoing Death in the prologue, Pheres notes that Admetus's exchange of his death for another is also unjust: "We are obligated to live one life, not two." Finally, similar to Grube, he concludes by calling Admetus the coward: "You let your woman out dare you and die for her magnificent young man."[77]

Admetus ignores Pheres but after the funeral recognizes the truth of father's words: Alcestis has been glorified, and he is disgraced. All of these interactions focus on larger questions of expected gender roles, the value of the elderly, and the expectation that family members ought to sacrifice everything, including their own lives, for their relatives. Although Alcestis is celebrated as a hero in the play, her sacrifice rests uncomfortably with the ancient heroic expectations that young men die a noble death on behalf of their city and family. Thus, Alcestis's death both reinforces and confounds this heroic value system: the new female excellence is dying for a male relative, which challenges the traditional male excellence of dying for family and city.[78] Furthermore, if Euripides is suggesting we ought to question the virtue and glorification of Alcestis's death, he might be hinting at the same for the traditional sacrifices expected of young men. In hindsight, this questioning is even more profound, since this play was staged many years prior to the great sacrifices made by the city's young men during the Peloponnesian War.

In any case, the willingness to sacrifice one's life—which, as Pheres puts it, is "short but sweet"—is presented in the play as extraordinary and beyond measure. As Alcestis pointed out, there is no true balance or recompense that can be offered in return for such a sacrifice. Maybe the best we can do is to set up sacred tombs and write honorific poems as some form of reoccurring remembrance. In this way, Alcestis's action underscores the maiden's demand in the *Children of Heracles* to be "remembered always" or Theseus's pragmatic agreement in the *Suppliant Women* to retrieve the bodies of the unburied Seven because without the guarantee of burial honors, no city would be able to marshal soldiers into battle.[79]

Justice: Generosity of Friendship (*Xenia*)

The second example of an extraordinary action concerning the question of what we owe another is represented by the ancient Greek practice of guest-friendship (*xenia*).[80] The relationship of *xenia* was a highly formalized hereditary relationship that emphasized reciprocal obligations and was under the divine protection of Zeus Xenios.[81] The formal initiation that preceded this relationship could include acts of benevolence (*kharis*), supplication (*hiketeia*), exchanges of gifts (including women in marriage), and formal oaths. One important function of *xenia* was that it expanded friendship bonds (*philoi*) beyond close relatives and associates to include outsiders and strangers. Following a ritualized initiation, the duties of guest-friends toward each other was similar to the obligations to family; for example, harming a *xenos* was prevented by the same sense of *aidōs* (respect or reverence) that prevented harm to kin, spouse, or supplicant.[82] The cultural importance of this relationship was found in its mutual and reciprocal obligations, which allowed allegiances to form beyond blood ties and created peaceful exchange between members of different political communities. These ties could also be problematic, especially during war; Alcibiades's *xenia* connections to Sparta during the Peloponnesian War emphasized a real-world occurrence of such complications.[83]

Admetus understands his own self-identity in his extraordinary commitment to the virtue of *xenos*.[84] Most importantly, Apollo rewarded him with a substitution death because of his reverent *xenia* toward the god. Yet, with Heracles's arrival, Admetus is faced with a series of *xenia*-related dilemmas: on the one hand, he had just promised the dying Alcestis to give up the kind of guest-host carousing for which Heracles is famous; on the other hand, Heracles had always been the best of hosts when Admetus visited "thirsty Argos," and turning him away would leave Admetus with an unfulfilled reciprocal obligation.[85] In addition, entertaining Heracles is problematic because as this hero himself points out: "It is disgraceful for guests to be entertained when the House is mourning."[86] By contrast, the neglect of *xenia* reciprocity would taint Admetus with the title "spurner of guests" and undermine the one thing for which he was famous. Thus, if Admetus is to maintain his reputation for being an extraordinary host, he must not only break his promise to the dying Alcestis but also dishonor his friend by lying about the identity of her corpse. Heracles remains uncomfortable with being entertained and begs Admetus "to allow him to leave for which I will be enormously grateful (*kharis*) to you." Admetus still refuses; instead, he solves his dilemma by dividing his House into two halves: the grieving and the celebrating. With this artificial division, he is able to create a façade in which he is neither breaking his promise nor lying since each part of the House honors its respective occupant.

Even though Admetus's partition creates this spatial and conceptual division, it is not an unequivocal or discrete act. It is possible, as some scholars argue, to see Admetus as choosing the male virtue of *xenia* over the promise to his dying wife; for example, in order to enact the separation, he must renounce her as a member of his *oikos*.[87] This view, however, glosses over the fact that Alcestis never asked for such perpetual mourning or for the banishment of revelry. In reciprocity (*kharis*), she only asked that her husband remain widowed and ignored without comment this promise to forgo hosting and his other pledges. Admetus does uphold one of his superfluous pledges. In his *agōn* with this father, he disowns the man who gave him life and status. In Greek culture, this rejection of the honors owed parents was particularly shameful, which Admetus comes to recognize after returning from the funeral.[88] This action, however, indicates that if Admetus prefers anything, it is guest-friendship (*xenia*) over blood ties (*oikos*). His inability to turn Heracles away highlights that Admetus "did not know how to reject or dishonor guests (*xenos*)."[89] Admetus suffers from a kind of immoderation of being "too friendly."[90] Or, as the servant more precisely puts it: "He has much, too much love of guest-friends."[91]

Again, Admetus's extraordinary generosity as a host is not presented as an unambiguous virtue. Importantly, it is because of his extraordinary generosity in *xenia* that Apollo rewards him by deceiving the Fates; yet this and other extraordinary acts of *xenia* put him into conflict with his *oikos* and his *xenos*. Admetus knows this, as he is very careful in his false speech to Heracles: he never admits that Alcestis is dead but speaks in riddles of a "double tale," in which "she is and is no more," and that "those doomed to die are already dead."[92] Furthermore, he calls the woman who died merely an "outsider" who came to live with him after her father died. The word he uses for outsider—*othneios*—means a stranger or someone not related by blood.[93] Cleverly, Admetus speaks the literal truth when he describes Alcestis as not blood but "closely connected to the family." The servant, in his confrontation with the drunken Heracles, clarifies that this unrelated orphan girl was the mistress of the House of Admetus. Euripides often uses such doublespeak to draw attention the duality of meaning throughout his tragedies: in the *Ion*, for example, the double-talk surrounding Ion's genealogy reveals a similar usage of the duality of words to simultaneous reveal and cover meaning.[94]

Recognizing that he (like the Fates) has been tricked, Heracles acknowledges this deceit as a "terrible thing done to him."[95] It might be expected that Heracles would respond with some reciprocal retribution. Yet although Admetus's extraordinary act of hospitality went beyond proper boundaries, Heracles decides to show his "gratitude (*kharis*) to Admetus by restoring Alcestis once more to the House." When he returns from the wrestling match, Heracles does make his displeasure clear. There is also perhaps some retribution in the delayed recognition scene: using his extraordinary virtue of *xenia* against him, Heracles forces Admetus to take the veiled woman, thus breaking the one true promise given in reciprocity to Alcestis.[96] As mentioned previously, this exchange between guest-friends, in which a silent veiled woman is given by one man and taken by her right hand by another man, is a simulation of the ancient Greek wedding ritual.

When the woman is revealed to be a returned Alcestis, Admetus's extraordinary generosity culminates in this equally extraordinary exchange of a "gift" of his wife's restoration. Hence, it is possible that the previously heroic and glorified Alcestis is reinstated to her proper feminine role. And Admetus, no longer shamed by her noble sacrifice, similarly is returned to his proper glory as a manly host. Heracles appears to confirm this final exchange with his departing declaration that Admetus "is just and should remain pious concerning guest-friends."[97] With such words, this Panhellenic hero appears to endorse the idea that Admetus is an extraordinary host.

From this perspective, the play celebrates a "happy ending" by reversing grief to joy and sanctioning the virtue of Admetus's extraordinary hospitality.[98] This reversal takes place over a series of several extreme actions of *xenia* and *kharis*. The prologue opens with the tale of Admetus's extraordinary *xenia* to the god. Apollo responds with extraordinary reciprocal gratitude of a replacement death. Alcestis grants an equally extraordinary favor of dying in Admetus's place. Admetus responds with the extraordinary gratitude to not remarry; he also performs a second act of *xenia* by entertaining Heracles. Finally, Heracles performs the most extraordinary favor of all: wrestling Alcestis away from Death. This final act of *kharis* returns Alcestis to her former position as a veiled and silent wife. With her rescue, "the dominant patriarchal order [is] restored" and Alcestis loses her status as a "blessed spirit—her tomb and glory have become hollow."[99] All these instances of extreme generosity and guest-friendship appear to come full circle by fulfilling Apollo's recognition of Admetus's generosity. Hence, the *Alcestis* is a simple "morality play on the reward of virtue."[100] Or is it?

Justice: The Boundary In-Between

Euripides's presentation of the *Alcestis*'s reversal from grief to joy is not unequivocal nor has Admetus been entirely vindicated. By contrast,

Euripides offers each example of extraordinary virtue—through *xenia* or *kharis*—with ambiguous overtones that question whether the act of generosity remains within the proper measure of what is owed to another.[101] Although difficult to judge a god's act of gratitude as extraordinary (since gods always do astonishing things), Death points to the injustice of Apollo's overstepping the boundaries between the gods above and those below. Alcestis's agreement to die for Admetus is equally problematic since there is no measured reciprocity for her taking on his death; instead, she takes on his heroic space and he makes the culturally discordant promise to remain a widower. Also problematic for the happy ending interpretation, it is not clear we should celebrate Admetus's extraordinary generosity. After the funeral, Admetus recognizes the disgrace of allowing his wife to die his death as well as dishonoring his father. He easily breaks his oaths and, to protect his reputation, tells clever falsehoods and places his guest in a shameful position. Even though Heracles does restore Alcestis, his displeasure with Admetus is unequivocal: "I find fault with this [deceit], I find fault."[102] Admetus may receive a great favor from Heracles, but he does not escape the hero's criticism for going too far.

Second, also problematic for the happy ending interpretation is the assumption that the play actually ends happily. The finale, however, appears unresolved, and several scholars have questioned whether the celebration is premature.[103] Has Death really been overcome, for example, and will no one die this day? Is the "wife" he receives really Alcestis or only a similar-looking woman? If it is Alcestis, what will be the consequences of the fact that he accepted this woman prior to recognizing her?[104] Rabinowitz is certainly not the only one who wonders what Alcestis will say to him when her three days of silence are over.[105] It may be anachronistic to point out, but Euripides's version also undermines Alcestis's heroism by having Heracles rescue her; in other versions of her story, such as the one used by Plato, she is rewarded for her virtue and restored by the gods.[106] In Euripides's version, Heracles drags her across the bridge between life and death, but unlike other heroes, such as Theseus, whom Heracles also saves from Hades, did the silent woman come willingly?[107] Despite Admetus recognizing his poor treatment of parents, it is not clear whether he and Pheres will reconcile. In other words, will the House remain permanently divided?

In another line of critique, scholars have pointed out how the tragedy's two-part structure mirrors the dual content of grief and joy. Thus rather than a straightforward happy ending, the play highlights the difficulty underlying the human capacity to "be of two minds."[108] This theme of duality challenges established binaries and ways of thinking that shape the understandings of human existence.[109] Attempts to create new boundaries in the play, such as the literal division of the House, also remain conspicuously artificial and insecure. By collapsing, distorting, and blurring such boundaries, Euripides openly explores the meaning and purpose of virtues, especially those necessary for the community such as generosity, gratitude, and friendship.

The blurring of the distinction between binaries occurs several times and throughout the play. It is found, as previously mentioned, in the very fabric of its dramatic genre: the *Alcestis* was performed in the fourth position normally reserved for satyr plays. The play contains several elements of a satyr play, such as predominance given to the theme of hospitality and the vanquishing of a villain by a rowdy Heracles; however, the *Alcestis* lacks satyrs and has a darker mood with an atypical onstage death scene and portrayal of lamenting children. Like the amalgamate creatures symbolized by satyrs themselves, the play appears to be an admixture. It is neither a typical tragedy nor a satyr play: it is neither and both. Thus, as the contemporary preoccupation with classifying the play as pro-satyr, melodrama, or tragicomedy reveals, this is a play that does not fit comfortably into any categorizations or definitions. The play itself is a dramatization of a lack of secure boundaries.

As already alluded to, several aspects of the story focus on the blurring and confounding of typical dualisms, such as distinctions between men and women or human and god. Similar to many other of his tragedies, including the *Bacchae*, *Medea*, and *Hecuba*, this story challenges the idea of distinctive virtues for men and women.[110] In this case, Alcestis receives the glorification normally reserved for courageous men who die in battle, and Admetus performs the typical feminine role of lamenting the dead.[111] Importantly, even though this gender reversal is further reversed (or restored by coming full circle) with Heracles's resurrection of Alcestis, the boundary between the virtues of male and female is never firmly resolved. Beyond his extraordinary *xenia*, for example, Admetus remained passive throughout and required a substitute hero to win the day.

In another example of unresolved blurred distinctions, our drunken Heracles represents the always ambiguous figure: the hero. Ancient Greek heroes were half-divine and half-human hybrids whose very nature "redefines the boundaries between man and god" and confuses the distinction between mortal and immortal.[112] In the *Alcestis*, the carousing half-divine Heracles also blurs the most significant human boundary: the one between life and death. This act overturns the proper order of human life and cheats what is owed to the gods below. Even Apollo, the shining god, was unwilling to cross this line; instead, when persuasion failed, he needed a substitute hero to restore her by force.

Importantly, the inappropriateness of blurring the line of life and death is apparent from the start. Like Admetus's lie of omission, Apollo's prologue tells only the partial truth of his servitude.[113] The piece left unstated is the reason for the retributive cycle of violence. Zeus killed Asclepius because the healer overstepped the natural boundaries of life and death by using the Gorgon Medusa's good blood to resurrect the dead. Considering the overarching theme of the play is the death and resurrection of Alcestis, Apollo's silence considering the reason for Asclepius's punishment speaks volumes. Importantly, the chorus rectifies this omission when they indicate that Zeus punished Asclepius for going beyond the prescribed boundary between mortal and immortal. As we know from other tragedies, only those like the *Bacchae*'s Dionysus are truly resurrected: the humans, like Pentheus, remain permanently dismembered.[114] Our play's ending underscores the same point: Alcestis's resurrection obscures the very meaning of mortal. Asclepius was killed for this same inappropriate act.

Equally problematic and ambiguous, as pointed out previously, is whether Alcestis's resurrection succeeds in cheating Death of his corpse. On the one hand, by winning Alcestis from Death, Heracles might ensure that no one dies this day; on the other hand, nothing suggests her restoration is a "second suspension of the rules of death."[115] Instead, since "mathematically, death is down one soul," the play resets time: Admetus is again bound to the necessity of dying his own death.[116] Death may return for him today, or maybe tomorrow, or the next day; as Heracles eloquently puts it: "Death is an obligation we all must pay. There is not one man living who can truly say if he will be alive or dead on the next day."[117] At the end of the play, we do not know what will happen to Admetus. Now, like all of us, he lacks foreknowledge of his own death. Admetus's ignorance of his death, ironically, may be the "happy" in Euripides's ending. If it is happy, it is not because Death has been cheated but because Euripides appears to establish at least one clear boundary: the distinction between mortals and the gods.

This exploration of boundaries between life and death is prominent throughout the play not in only in the action of Alcestis's resurrection but also in the dialogue between characters.[118] Although little is known about what influenced Euripides's work, as noted in the introduction, his tragedies reflect the intellectual interests of the sophists and possibly even Socrates.[119] In this play, Euripides explores the typical sophistic question of whether being and non-being are the same or different, as well as the problematic use of such thinking for rhetorical purposes. Twice in the plot, for example, there is confusion over whether Alcestis is alive or dead. In the *parodos*, the confused chorus asks: "Should there not be cries of mourning?" "Perhaps they have left for the funeral?" and "Maybe she is not dead yet?"[120] The maidservant is little help: "You might say she is living and dead." To which the chorus replies: "How can the same person be living and dead?" For the maidservant, Alcestis is alive and dead, because she is "already sinking" or is dying. She is, in philosophic terms, "becoming" dead. Thus, this opening exchange sets the tone for the tragedy's exploration of what is supposed to be the clearest cut of all binaries: life and death.

In the second instance, Admetus echoes the same ambiguity concerning life and death but employs such indefiniteness for rhetorical purposes. In this case, as we saw Alcestis die on stage, she is no longer becoming but is definitely dead. Yet, Admetus still tells Heracles that "she is and no longer is."[121] Admetus employs such clever rhetorical statements to deceive Heracles in order to perform his extraordinary virtue of hospitality. His statement, however, indicates another intellectual dilemma: he can maintain that Alcestis is and is no longer because, as a human being, she was doomed to die. In other words, no human being "really is," as we are all only becoming dead. As Admetus sums it up: "The one who will be dead and the dead both no longer are." Heracles rejects this collapse of the distinction between life and death; instead, he insists on a strict separation between being and non-being. As he states: "To be and to not be are acknowledged as separate or distinct (*khōris*)." Furthermore, because human nature is mortal, Heracles can later make his famous live-for-today speech to the servant. From Heracles's perspective, human existence implies that "today belongs to you [the living]."

Heracles and Admetus agree to disagree, perhaps because Heracles is deceived into thinking the corpse is not Alcestis. The difference in their positions, however, is significant for the plot's resolution. Admetus's position that those who will be dead are already dead, of course, describes all mortal beings. By contrast, Heracles insists that being and non-being are fundamentally separable and distinct. Ironically, both Admetus's and

Heracles's actions are reversals of their philosophic positions. Admetus tries to establish a discrete, clear, and firm distinction by dividing his House between being and non-being. Heracles's restoration of the dead Alcestis turns what was non-being into being. In other words, Heracles reverses his own argument and appears to prove Admetus right: there is no clear boundary between life and death.[122] Yet, Heracles's reversal again reverses Apollo's extraordinary gift of gratitude to Admetus. In doing so, Heracles reestablishes the boundaries between the living and the dead. Necessity really will allow no substitution.[123]

What are we to make of Heracles's reestablishment of the proper order between life and death? For one thing, it may be important that it is Heracles, the in-between creature, who is successful in restoring or re-creating the boundary line. The human attempt to create a division between life and death is symbolized in Admetus's spatial partition of his House. As Luschnig points out, the House in the *Alcestis* is more than just the *skēnē* but reflects a character whose actions are located in the various exits and entrances.[124] From the maidservant's description of Alcestis's last day, we know much more about what is happening inside the House than is typical in Greek tragedy.[125] Importantly, Alcestis dies, not hidden inside as usual, but outside. Also, unusual is that Admetus sings a lament to the House: although physically unchanged, the House now seems to him "empty" or "hollow." In order to accommodate the entertaining of Heracles, Admetus divides this House into two halves, which spatially and psychologically divide mourning and celebration, life and death, or being and non-being. This dissection is further realized in his violent quarrel with Pheres, which terminates a break in the continuity between the past and present of the *oikos*.[126] This division is tantamount to an act of dismemberment that exposes the whole as more than the sum of its parts.

Therefore, Euripides exposes persuasion and force, the twin powers of politics, at the heart of the attempts to confound or create boundaries. Throughout the plot, persuasion is connected to the confounding of or attempt to step beyond boundaries. The two main *agōnes*, between Apollo and Death and Admetus and Pheres, challenge established boundaries.[127] In the first *agōn*, Apollo tries but fails to convince Death to postpone Alcestis's sacrifice by privileging the rich. In the second *agōn*, between Admetus and Pheres, Admetus is partially successful as he prevents Pheres from attending the funeral; however, his victory disrupts the proper relationship between father and son. As Pheres notes (and Admetus eventually recognizes), he goes too far by insulting (*hubris*) his father. A complicated word, *hubris* can mean pride, insult, or violence associated with overstepping one's proper position. In Greek drama, it is often used in cases where human beings do not properly respect the gods. Admetus, in this instance, oversteps the proper boundary of respect for his father, including his right to be at the funeral.

Physical force or violence proves far more ambiguous with regard to the violation and creation of limits or boundaries. Importantly, the threat of violence is never far off. In the opening scene, Death alludes to the threat of Apollo's weapons. Although Apollo only employs persuasion and not force, he foretells that violence will win the day. Alcestis's death is unusual, not only for being enacted onstage but also because it is one of the only "nonviolent" deaths in extant tragedy. Thus, the only real use of force is Heracles's offstage wrestling match with Death. This match is not even fair, as Heracles "rushed from ambush and caught him [Death] in his side-crushing grip . . . until he released the woman."[128] As stated previously, it is not clear what to make of this act of violence. Heracles clearly is violating the rights and honors of those below by taking Alcestis by force; yet, since everyone now appears to be dying their own deaths, his action reverses Apollo's earlier deceit of the Fates. Thus, force reestablishes the natural boundary between mortal and immortal.[129] Violence, therefore, both violates and restores boundaries, and it may not always be clear from the violent act which of the two it is—destructive or creative.

Conclusion

The *Alcestis*, a dramatization of someone dying another's death, raises questions concerning the appropriateness of extraordinary acts of generosity of favors (*kharis*) and guest-friendship (*xenia*). By definition, an extraordinary act must be atypical: thus, Apollo's gift of exchanging a life, Alcestis's dying another's death, Admetus's promise to never remarry, and Heracles's violent struggle to reverse Alcestis's death are all beyond normal expectations. Although other tragedies, such as the *Suppliant Women* or *Children of Heracles*, raise questions about obligations to strangers, this play refocuses the question on how much we are obligated to help those nearby. This question and the status of such duties or obligations have a long history. Cicero will side with Pheres, as he places duties to parents above the duty to children.¹³⁰ Since Grotius, the duties of generosity have been understood as a matter of virtue but not justice.¹³¹ Mill, for example, understands charity and generosity as imperfect duties; since they are left up to our discretion, they belong to the sphere of benevolence, and thus (reflecting Pheres) are not enforceable.¹³² More recently, Boot argues for a revival of the virtues as duties in the human rights perspectives as they are "an indispensable complement to the sphere of justice."¹³³

Significantly, this dramatization of extraordinary generosity raises an additional question: what are the limits of such obligations or duties to those closest to us? Are parents obligated to die for their children? Was Admetus a "cad" to ask his wife to die in his place? Certainly, the virtues of generosity and reciprocity make family and community possible. It is still a virtue to be a good host. Individuals still continue to make the ultimate sacrifice: parents jump into swollen rivers to save their children; soldiers die on the battlefield; and police and firefighters run toward dangers from which others flee. Yet, the series of reciprocal acts of extraordinary generosity from Apollo's tricking the Fates to Heracles's wrestling death is an overstepping of boundaries that overturns this virtue. It is a dramatization that too much generosity is a bad thing.¹³⁴ Thus, echoing the Greek wisdom highlighted in the Delphic Oracle's inscription to do "nothing in excess," Euripides hints that virtue without moderation proves to be no virtue at all.¹³⁵

Set outside Greece in the wilds of Thessaly, Euripides's story of extraordinary generosity brings to the forefront not only a conceptualization of justice but an experience of being "outside" boundaries and limits. This is not to suggest that Euripides disrupts traditional boundaries to reveal that there are no boundaries.¹³⁶ Again, the play seems to do the opposite. From the outset, Euripides links the overstepping of boundaries with injustice. Death alerts us to what is at stake: "You commit injustices," he says to the shining Apollo, "in the dividing (*aphorizomenos*) of boundary lines and hindering the honors due those below."¹³⁷ The Greek participle *aphorizomenos* means to mark off by boundaries, appropriate for oneself, determine, or define. Apollo's redefinition of what it means to be human provokes the intellectual debate concerning being and non-being. Is human existence simply "becoming" as suggested by the maidservant? Is being and non-being indistinguishable, as proposed by Admetus? By contrast, as Heracles insists, are they separate and finite? This question of existence also preoccupied ancient thinkers from Parmenides and Heraclitus through Plato and Aristotle and continues in contemporary political thought, most famously in Heidegger.[138] For this play, Apollo's blurring of the distinction between life and death is not simply an intellectual debate but infects the boundaries or proper limits of those actions that hold family and community together: generosity, gratitude, and friendship. Without boundaries or limits, such virtues distort and blur into vices. Finally, by highlighting the omnipresence of persuasion and force, Euripides reminds us that this activity of challenging and marking boundary lines (*aphorizō*) is inherently political. Heracles, perhaps, won the day but the struggle to clearly define or distinguish when virtues, like generosity, are too much remains ongoing.

Chapter 9

The *Electra*

The Justice of Good and Bad Judgment

> In making distinctions, how does anyone judge
> such things in a straight line?[1]

Euripides's *Electra* has the "distinction of being the best abused and not best understood of ancient tragedies."[2] It tells a familiar story: the siblings Electra and Orestes plot revenge against their mother Clytemnestra for murdering their father, Agamemnon. This family saga was so popular in ancient Athens that we have extant versions by all three playwrights, including the only surviving trilogy: Aeschylus's *Oresteia*. For both Sophocles and Euripides, only the story of sibling vengeance has survived. This part of the family saga is laden with moral paradox. So horrific is matricide that the ancient goddesses of vengeance, the Erinyes (Furies in Latin), pursue violators to the end of time. Yet, the mother is no saint: she bedded Agamemnon's greatest rival, murdered their father, and usurped Orestes's political inheritance. To complicate matters, the Olympian Apollo contradicts these vengeance goddesses by commanding matricide. Euripides throws open the question of justice in this play: no moral standard is certain, no action is straightforward, and no one is innocent.

Another of the alphabet plays, the performance date and companion tragedies are uncertain. Traditional scholarship dates the *Electra* to 413 BCE, as the mention of rescuing ships in Sicily is considered an allusion to the ill-fated Sicilian Expedition.[3] Other scholars see an anticipation of Euripides's *Helen* of 412 BCE or a response to Sophocles's also undated *Electra*, which was probably produced between 416 and 410

BCE.⁴ Although the performance date of this tragedy remains elusive, Sewell suggests it "almost certainly was written between the sailing [to Sicily] and news of its miserable end . . . but, [one] can imagine him writing it even later, when so many young friends and kin were dead, maimed, or hostage slaves."⁵

These possible allusions to the real world, no matter how opaque, have long been the source of Euripidean criticism.⁶ Certainly, Euripides's "fondness for de-mythologicalization . . . jars us abruptly out of the mythical world [and] into . . . the late fifth-century Athenian reality."⁷ Other scholarship investigates wider possibilities of Euripidean realism.⁸ Lush, for example, explores how the disruption of norms establishes Euripides's dramatic world.⁹ Adding to this perspective, this analysis focuses on how an understanding of justice requires confronting the uncertainty embedded both in authority and standards of judgment. Most importantly, the very act of thinking about justice forces us to question what influences our own judgment of circumstances, other people, and ourselves. Thus, Euripides turns his audience away from a question of "what is justice?" toward the first steps of an unfolding journey of self-examination.

The Mythological Context and Plot of the *Electra*

Background Myth

Euripides's *Electra* is part of a larger narrative concerning the fall of the House of Atreus. Of all the doomed families in Greek mythology, the story of House of Atreus was unrivaled as inspiration for the ancient poets.¹⁰ In most accounts, Atreus was the son of Pelops and Hippodamia. He was a grandson of the infamous Tantalus, who slaughtered Pelops and served up his own son in a banquet to the gods. The gods rejuvenated Pelops, who became the founder of the Peloponnese. Pelops's twin sons, Atreus and Thyestes, are eventually exiled for murdering their half-brother, Chrysippus. Finding refuge in Mycenae/Argos, these twins agree to allow the gods to choose the successor to King Eurystheus, who is killed fighting the Heracleidae.¹¹

The sign from the gods, a golden ram, was born into Atreus's flock; however, with the help of Atreus's wife Aerope (with whom he was having an affair), Thyestes stole the lamb and took control of the kingdom.¹² Atreus is able to reclaim his throne, but in retaliation he also served to Thyestes a banquet consisting of his slaughtered sons (this time there was no rejuvenation). Seeking revenge, Thyestes consulted the Delphic Oracle, which prophesied that Atreus would be killed if Thyestes fathered a son with his own daughter. The child of this incestuous union is Aegisthus, who does kill Atreus, exiles Atreus's sons Agamemnon and Menelaus (who meet their future wives while exiled in Sparta), and rules Mycenae with his father/grandfather, Thyestes. Eventually, Agamemnon returns, kills Thyestes, and forces Aegisthus from power.

Electra's maternal lineage is also mythologically significant. Her mother, Clytemnestra, was the daughter of King Tyndareus and Leda of Sparta.[13] As was often the case, Zeus became enamored with Leda, but she resisted his advances. Not to be denied, Zeus turned himself into a swan and, depending on the version, either raped or successfully seduced Leda on the same night she had intercourse with her husband. Although there are many versions of their birth, one popular account had Leda lay two eggs: out of one egg came the half-divine children Helen and Polydeuces; the other egg produced Tyndareus's human children, Clytemnestra and Castor. Clytemnestra and Helen, however, are usually considered twins, and their brothers (commonly known as the Dioscuri) were deified and transformed into the constellation Gemini (Latin for "twins").[14] Electra's aunt Helen was the most famous of all the siblings. As a daughter of Zeus, Helen's beauty was divine and caused many misadventures, such as an early kidnapping by Theseus. Tyndareus finally agreed to Helen's marriage to Menelaus but only if all her other suitors took an oath to support the marriage. Hence, when Helen either was abducted, or willingly accompanied Paris, the other suitors were obligated to support Menelaus in Troy.

Clytemnestra is often painted as a kind of anti-Penelope, the faithful wife of Odysseus. During Agamemnon's long absence in Troy, Clytemnestra took his rival Aegisthus as a lover. Upon his return, they murder Agamemnon and Cassandra, the doomed Trojan princess. Clytemnestra's role in this murder is a point of disagreement: some say she only submitted to Aegisthus, but others suggest she ensnared Agamemnon with a net and stabbed him herself.[15] Electra, or sometimes a servant (as told in this play), saves her infant brother Orestes by spiriting him away; in other versions, an older Orestes is exiled. Our tragedy picks up the story when Orestes returns to fulfill Apollo's instructions to seek retribution against his father's murderers.

Importantly, Clytemnestra's motive is more complex than simple adultery. In some versions, such as that told by Euripides in *Iphigenia at Aulis*, Clytemnestra was married to Tantalus (another grandson of the more famous Tantalus mentioned previously) and had an infant son.[16] To claim her for himself, Agamemnon killed Clytemnestra's husband and son and then rapes her. She becomes Queen of Mycenae and, depending on the source, she and Agamemnon have several children. Their son Orestes is a consistent figure in the story. However, in the *Iliad*, the list of Agamemnon's daughters does not include an Electra but Chrysothemis, Laodice, and Iphianassa.[17] Iphianassa is probably a variation of Iphigenia, who is also still alive in Homer's account. In other versions, Agamemnon is forced to sacrifice Iphigenia to appease Artemis who stalled the Greek ships on their way to Troy.[18] Electra is thought to be identified with Laodice by emphasizing her virginal status: *alektros* or "the unbedded."

Three important features of this background story are important to keep in mind. First, Aegisthus is not a simple pretty boy but an essential figure born for vengeance in the long dynastic rivalry between two lines of the same family. Second, this is not the first time someone in Aegisthus's family has usurped power from Agamemnon's family: the affair between Thyestes and Aerope started this long blood feud. Finally, Apollo's command of matricide is not his first impious suggestion: it was on his advice that Thyestes rapes his daughter to conceive Aegisthus. Thus, the story told in the *Electra* is part of a long-standing, bloody, occasionally cannibalistic, and unholy cycle of familial curse and revenge.[19]

Euripides's Electra

Compared to many of Euripides's tragedies, the *Electra* is "a close-knit, powerful, well-constructed play."[20] The play's setting is not a typical grand palace but a workman's cottage in the rustic outlands. The tragedy is organized into three parts separated by three choral odes. The first part (lines 1–430) opens with a prologue by Electra's husband, the farmer (*Autourgos*), who tells the backstory: Agamemnon's high status as king of kings in Troy, Clytemnestra's adultery, and his murder at the hands of the two lovers.[21] Although Aegisthus wanted to kill the children, an old servant spirited Orestes to Phocis, and the farmer was married to Electra to ensure her offspring would be too powerless for vengeance. Even though born of noble heritage, the farmer believes it would be an outrage (*hubris*) to touch such an esteemed daughter; thus, she remains a virgin true to her name. Electra enters and the husband chastises her for her shabby appearance and laboring like a servant, rather than behaving like a princess.

As these two characters exit, Orestes and his cousin Pylades (a silent character) arrive and reveal the mission to avenge Agamemnon.[22] After secretly honoring his grave, they now have come to find Orestes's sister or, if necessary, make a quick escape. They hide when Electra reenters but spy on her lamentation for her murdered father and exiled brother.[23] The chorus of rural women arrives to invite Electra to the festival of Hera; she refuses, citing her shameful status as a poor farmer's wife.[24] The women uncover the hidden men, and Orestes convinces them that he is not a bandit but a messenger from her brother. Electra tells him to report her increasingly dire circumstances: a "dead" marriage (*thanasimon gamon*), ignobly shorn hair and ragged clothing, the need to labor, an inability to attend festivals, and their father's neglected tomb.[25]

The farmer reappears and, after a debate (*agōn*) about how to judge nobility (*gennaios*), he extends hospitality (*xenia*).[26] Dismayed by their living conditions, Electra sends the old man for provisions, and the chorus finally makes the long-delayed *parodos*. Known as Achilles's ode, the choral song opens with imagery of the famous ships on route to Troy followed by dancing dolphins.[27] They sing of Achilles's shield with images of Perseus's heroic slaying of the Gorgon and other monstrous female sphinxes and chimeras. Their song ends with a wish for retribution against Tyndareus's evil daughter.[28]

The second part (lines 485–695) focuses on the delayed recognition scene. The old man returns and tells Electra that he found the remains of a sacrifice, including a lock of hair and footprint, on her father's tomb.[29] In a scene often considered a parody of Aeschylus's *Libation Bearers*, the old man tries to convince Electra that the so-called messenger is her brother.[30] Electra finds it ridiculous that her hair or footprint would resemble her brother or that he would come in secret. Orestes returns, and the old man identifies him by a childhood scar (*oulēn*). After a brief joyful reunion, they plot revenge: Orestes and Pylades will seek an invitation to Aegisthus's rural sacrifice; and Electra will lure Clytemnestra with the false news of a grandson.

While the murder of Aegisthus takes place offstage, the chorus sings a short choral ode that takes the story back a generation to the crimes of Aegisthus's father, Thyestes.[31] They sing of Zeus's fury at his ignoble act of stealing the golden lamb, which results in changing the direction of the sun and stars (which formerly rose in the west and set in the east). Although the chorus doubts whether gods care enough for mortals to change the direction of the sun, they suggest that such tales encourage respect for the gods.

The final section (lines 750–1360) begins with the arrival of a messenger who announces their success: Aegisthus invited the young men to a sacrifice, and Orestes stabbed him in the back while his victim was examining a sacrificial animal.[32] Orestes returns for an epinician celebration, and he is crowned in victory.[33] Relishing in her newfound freedom, Electra kills Aegisthus a second time: not in deed but in word.[34] She repeats his crimes and dismisses him as a greedy, unstable, "girly-boy" (*parthenōpos*) who is bossed by his wife. At this moment, Clytemnestra appears in total splendor. At the sight of his mother, Orestes's resolve falters, which sparks a second heated debate (*agōn*) with Electra concerning the justness of Apollo's divine commandment.[35] Electra prevails. Orestes hides inside the farmer's house.

Clytemnestra and her daughter immediately attack each other in the final *agōn*.[36] In her defense, Clytemnestra emphasizes two reasons justifying Agamemnon's murder: first, she was avenging his murder of Iphigenia; second, she highlights the double standard of her being criticized for adultery while Agamemnon introduced a Trojan concubine into her house. Retaliating, Electra points out that Clytemnestra was an adulteress long before Agamemnon returned with Cassandra; and, in addition, Electra accuses her of neglecting her surviving children, who live a life worse than death. The *agōn* resolves nothing, but agreeing to perform the purification ritual for her newborn "grandson," Clytemnestra and walks into the humble cottage to her death.[37] Bringing the bodies on stage, the siblings face the horror of their vengeance: Orestes admits he shielded his eyes, but Electra grasped the sword to share in the final blow. In contrast to the unrestrained joy at Aegisthus's death, there is no celebratory song.

In the deus ex machina, their now divine uncles Castor and Polydeuces descend from above and place the blame squarely on Apollo: "Even though he [Apollo] is wise, he did not possess wise things for you."[38] Despite this, the siblings are to be exiled: Electra will remarry the more suitable Pylades; and, pursued by the Erinyes, Orestes will stand trial at the court of the Areopagus in Athens. This time, Castor prophesies a less definitive outcome than Aeschylus. In Aeschylus's *Eumenides*, Athena decides the case in the favor of the male (Orestes), establishes institutions to end cyclical blood feuds, and convinces the vengeful Erinyes to transform and support the city.[39] In our story, there is no prophesied Athena, no institutionalization of justice, nor a taming of the Erinyes. Instead, acquitted on a legal technicality in which a tied vote grants exoneration, Orestes is released but to permanent exile.[40] Thus, the play ends with the extinction of the House of Atreus's power in Mycenae. The Dioscuri depart with the warning to uphold the holy and refrain from injustice.

Euripides's Potential Innovations

Since we have extant texts from all three major tragedians focusing on the matricide, the potentiality for intertextuality is difficult to resist.[41] This is especially true for Euripides's disputed "recognition scene" and Aeschylus's version.[42] Similarly, despite the impossibility of knowing which tragedy came first, scholars see Euripides "inspired by Sophocles" to push his characterization to its logical extreme.[43] Such potential inferences may not be mockery or ancient literary critique but are intended to draw attention to what is unique in Euripides's version.[44] With this in mind, Euripides appears to make four potential innovations.

First, and most significantly, Euripides relocates the dramatic setting from a grand palace to a rural dwelling on the boundary of Argolid territory. This change of locale repositions the action away from the heroic world to a typical Athenian home.[45] Euripides further accomplishes his "realistic details" by providing stage props "of everyday objects," which bring the real world on stage and make the play "directly relevant to the lives of his contemporary audience."[46] Although his changing the "space" of the tragedy is controversial, such dramatic realism allows the possibility of representing the concerns of a democratic "common man."[47]

Secondly, and closely related to the rural setting, is the novelty of Electra's sham marriage to the poor rural farmer. In the other extant versions, she is unmarried and still living in the palace when Orestes returns. By contrast, the disingenuous marriage protects Electra's mythic status as the "unbedded" (*alektros*) but inserts the farmer into the story. Although Euripides often violates Aristotle's expectation that the best tragedies portrayed men of status, his "common man" provides a sense of realism.[48] It also provides a necessary contrast to judge whether the common farmer or high-born Orestes is nobler.[49]

Third, and the target of the most vehement criticism, is Euripides's characterizations of the traditional heroes.[50] His depiction of Electra contrasts sharply with Aeschylus's or Sophocles's portrayal of the noble heroine as "almost a symbol of the family and dynasty awaiting deliverance;" instead, our Electra is egocentric, self-pitying, and malicious.[51] She participates in the fatal blow.[52] Various scholars have called her "self-indulgent," "morbidly embittered," or (surprisingly, since she is a virgin) possessing a "subtle streak of nymphomania."[53] Her new characterization, however, also provides a strong female voice that challenges gender expectations.[54] Similarly, Orestes is considered less than heroic: he is a "timorous young ruffian," "feeble and irresolute," and "ha[s] no particular character at all."[55] Allan suggests that the greatest innovation with the siblings' new portrayal is their willingness to admit their wrongdoing.[56] In contrast to these negative portrayals of the heroes, the villains of Clytemnestra and Aegisthus are more sympathetic and come across "less heinous," "less villainous," with surprisingly "redeeming features."[57] Aegisthus, for example, is a good host who properly extends hospitality to strangers. Clytemnestra expresses regret for murdering Agamemnon and is more maternal than expected; she saves Electra's life by arranging the sham marriage (Aegisthus wanted to kill her) and is unhappy to find out it is friendless. She is easily lured to her death with the promise of a grandson. Euripides's depiction of these well-known characters with more contradictory attributes, emotional complexity, and rational hesitation also contributes to the play's overall realism.

Finally, as another departure from versions by Aeschylus and Sophocles, the play ends with a deus ex machina scene.[58] The *Electra*'s machina scene is unusual as it involves deified family members who simultaneously affirm and deny the expected resolution. Predictably, Electra will remarry the more appropriate Pylades and become the wife she's known as according to the typical mythology. Unpredictably, Orestes will remain in a kind of culpability limbo: he is exonerated on a human legal technicality, but exiled. Most unexpectedly, the Dioscuri deem Apollo responsible for the matricide, which was "just, but not just for Orestes."[59] Other tragedies dramatize a critique of Apollo, such as in the *Ion*, but in that case Athena arrives with Olympian authority and only indirectly hints at Apollo's culpability.[60] Here, Apollo's mistake is unambiguous and prominently displayed.

One overall effect of Euripides's sense of realism is a series of unanswered questions: if Clytemnestra is not so "evil," and it was not just for Orestes to get revenge, then for whom would it be just? What criteria determines who justly punishes? Or, how do we know if we are justly punishing? Most importantly, the play reveals how such ambiguity turns the question from "what is justice?" to "how does one judge?" then finally, with an inward twist, to the question of "who is judging?"[61] And with this last turn, Euripides reminds us of the importance of what we already know: human justice always is limited by the biases or preconceptions of the judges.

Questions of Justice: Orestes's Moral Conundrum

Although Electra is the primary protagonist, Orestes is hardly a mere foil, as he is central to the tragedy's moral questions. To put it bluntly: Orestes is damned if he does and damned if he doesn't. On the one hand, his mother and her lover have murdered his father, driven him into exile, and stolen his political inheritance. He consulted the "secret rites of the god" and was directed to fulfill his sacred duty to "pay back" the murder with murder.[62] On the other hand, even more ancient gods prohibit matricide as the most horrific of all crimes.[63] The Erinyes, who will pursue Orestes to Athens, emerged as vengeance goddesses from the blood that dripped when the Titan Cronos castrated his father, Ouranos. Their mission was to pursue anyone who violated the natural order of the cosmos. Orestes was thus caught in a moral conundrum of punishing a parent for an injustice.[64] From this perspective, the tragedy foregrounds the moral problem of polytheism: since the gods are not in agreement, which god should be obeyed? In other words, the focus of this tragedy is the dilemma of moral decision making in the conditions of competing moral claims.

First, Orestes is damned if he fails to avenge his father's murder. The Olympian Apollo ordered the matricide and, as Electra frequently reminds him, he would be guilty of impiety if his vengeance fails.[65] Second, added to these divine orders and threats, the play offers human expectation and validation for his actions. Introduced first in the prologue of the farmer is the importance of noble (*eugenēs*) status. Electra was married off to the farmer ("a man of no authority") because a powerless grandson would be unable to pursue the cycle of revenge. By contrast, as the son of the king of kings and grandson of the man for whom Zeus changed the direction of the sun, Orestes is expected to act upon his inborn authority. "It is shameful," Electra emphasized, "if, on the one hand, his father destroyed the Trojans; but, on the other hand, being a young man born from a better father, he would not be able kill one man." Thus, nobility, authority, and power equate justice with a kind of self-reliant vengeance reflected in the long-standing family blood feud. The political question underlying Orestes's return to Mycenae is whether he is truly his father's son or the false coin of "the many who are born noble but are worthless (*kakoi*)."

Second, Orestes is damned when he succeeds in avenging his father. Unlike his sister, who sees only one side of these competing values, Orestes struggles with doubt: "How can I kill her, the one who bore and raised me?"[66] He even questions the Oracle as "ignorant" (*amathian*) and "not good" (*ou eu*), as it "pronounced me to kill my mother, whom it is not right to kill."[67] Unlike his current political exile, he fears legitimate exile for murdering his own mother. Orestes finally submits to "what seems necessary by the gods" (and to Electra's taunts of cowardice) and performs the dreadful deed; yet, when the time came, Orestes "hid his eyes," and it was Electra that guided the final killing thrust.

Beyond Orestes's doubts concerning the wisdom and propriety of the matricide, Euripides portrays Clytemnestra as dissimilar from the choral ode to Achilles which is populated with images of evil, monstrous females.[68] First, Clytemnestra turns out to be far more maternal than expected. Electra knows her mother will not be able to resist seeing her grandchild and will weep for his diminished status.[69] Second, also in contrast to irrational monsters, Clytemnestra provides a reasoned justification for her retaliation against Agamemnon: her husband killed their daughter, not to save the city but because Menelaus could not control his own wife; in addition, he dishonored her by introducing a younger rival into their home. Sounding rather like a modern feminist, Clytemnestra points to the double standard that praises men for the same behavior condemned in women. She also admits that she has no joy "for the things done by my hands" but "my plans (*bouleumatōn*) made me wretched."[70] She is rational and shows remorse for her actions. Electra and the chorus are not convinced, but Clytemnestra raises doubt whether, with the murder of Aegisthus, justice truly demands her death at the hands of her children.[71]

In the final scene, Euripides returns to the moral paradox. After luring Clytemnestra with the promised grandchild, Orestes and Electra reappear on stage with the bodies of their mother and Aegisthus. As noted previously, this time there is no joyful victory celebration but the realization of the meaning of their action. For the first time, Electra is no longer single-minded but recognizes the consequences of her "burning" anger and culpability in her mother's death.⁷² Orestes tries to reconcile their action by suggesting Apollo's justice is simultaneously "invisible, but clearly seen." Only the chorus continues to maintain that "their father's murderer was killed justly (*dikaiōs*)." Into this dark atmosphere of a murdered mother "who is loved and not loved," the Dioscuri come suspended on the *mēchanē* and pronounce that their sister's death "was just, but your action was not." To this they add that even though Apollo is wise, "his prophecy to you was not." Adding to the moral conundrum of determining justice when gods quarrel, these newly minted gods admit that an Olympic god can simply be wrong. To confuse the situation even more, they suggest that Zeus purposely "caused strife (*eris*)" among men, such as when he sent an image of Helen to Troy.⁷³ This means the gods disagree, err, and purposefully deceive.⁷⁴ In the end, fate (*moira*), necessity (*anagkē*), and Apollo's "unwise utterances of the tongue" drove events to this horrific conclusion.

Fulfilling mythological expectations, the Dioscuri foretell the Erinyes will pursue Orestes to stand trial on the Athenian Areopagus. Unlike in Aeschylus, this time the trial is determined by the legal rule: "Votes placed equally will save you justly from being destroyed."⁷⁵ In this human vision of justice, which Zuntz calls "the finite reality of justice," the Euripidean Orestes is not absolved, nor does he regain the power of Mycenae.⁷⁶ Although not guilty, he remains tainted with the pollution (*miasma*) of matricide and is exiled to a "wretched" life "full of groaning."⁷⁷ The siblings' future, however, is not entirely grim: Orestes will establish a town in Arcadia; Electra will remarry the silent Pylades. Thus, the play concludes with this sort of half-happy ending.⁷⁸

What kind of conclusion can be drawn from Euripides's apparent resolution to Orestes's moral conundrum? Does the Dioscuri's surprising pronouncement that Apollo was "not wise" imply that Orestes should have followed his own misgivings and disobeyed Apollo's command?⁷⁹ If so, then the moral paradox might be straightforwardly resolved: justice would be served if someone other than Orestes—let's say an impartial judicial institution—committed the deed: thus reflecting a rather modern view that justice requires the recusal of judgment in one's own case.⁸⁰ This view also protects justice from excessive and later regrettable emotions, such as the cases highlighted by Clytemnestra and Electra, who admit their anger "burned" too hot.

There remain, however, three unsettling issues that undermine this tidy deus ex machina resolution to Orestes's moral dilemma. First, even if the god's commandment was unwise, it was not only the Delphic Oracle that compelled Orestes to avenge his father. Several characters, especially his sister, emphasized the connection between true nobility and acting justly.[81] The implicit question of the first half of the tragedy is whether Orestes is truly noble or is well-born but possessing a "worthless character." If Orestes allowed another, such as let's say Pylades to seek his justice, wouldn't he be "false coin?" Again, such issues could be resolved with the modern opinion that nobility is a worthless notion, along with its concerns for individualistic status and action. In this case, Euripides could be reconciled to Aeschylus's solution: establish judicial institutions that place civilization and law above obscure oracles, the ancient goddess of vengeance, and claims to nobility.[82] Only fair and just institutions can break the Atreidae's cycle of vengeance fueled by deceptive oracles and outdated claims of nobility.

This tidy resolution, however, depends upon Euripides's portrayal of the superiority of institutionalized judicial decision making to private acts of vengeance. By contrast, there is something rather unsettling about Orestes's partial exoneration. Without Athena to break the tie, the decision is left in human hands; the deadlock votes of 6–6 triggered the human rule that a tied vote results in an acquittal. Importantly, this is not a clear judgment in Orestes's favor: he is not really exonerated. Furthermore, despite the Dioscuri's pronouncement that Apollo is ultimately responsible, Orestes does not return to rule Mycenae (as Aeschylus suggests) but remains exiled. The institutional court system can be set up, as it still is today, to take vengeance out of the hands of individuals, but without divine exoneration, Orestes's guilt and pollution of matricide remain. Instead of indicating the superiority of institutionalized justice, Euripides underscores the limitations of human judicial institutions.[83]

The deadlocked human jury also reintroduces Orestes's moral dilemma: half of his judges condemned his act of matricide as unjust, and the other half determined it just. So, was killing Clytemnestra just or not? As is the case in any complex moral dilemma, it is not clear which of the two actions is the just action. Also unsettling is what might have been the outcome if Clytemnestra had faced a real jury and not Electra and the chorus. Would human judges make the same determination as the Dioscuri that her death was just (but not just by Orestes's hand)? Or would they have been convinced by her eloquent argument that she, too, sought retribution for Iphigenia? Or that she was judged more harshly because she was a woman? Clytemnestra's case is not without merit.

The tragedy reveals that something intangible, but potentially essential, is lost with de-personalized institutionalized justice. The establishment of institutional rules substitutes one problem of justice (passionate personalized justice) with another (the imperfections of judicial procedures). Thus, as is still common in our modern justice system, the rules create manufactured legal victories, such as Orestes "getting off" on a technicality. Why doesn't a tie vote equal condemnation and not release? Such arbitrary rules are, of course, necessary to establish judicial proceedings; yet such procedures rarely satisfy injured parties. Although the Dioscuri suggest the Erinyes will be swallowed by the earth after their defeat, we are left wondering if they will rise again to renew their pursuit of Orestes, as dramatized in Euripides's *Iphigenia among the Taurians*.[84] Hence, Euripides's portrayal is not a celebration of founding civic institutions but reveals how judicial courts are limited by human judgment and the inability to truly exonerate lingering guilt. Importantly, such limitations reflect backward toward the other main question of the play: if human judgment is limited "when making distinctions, how does anyone judge such things in a straight line (*orthōs*)?"[85]

Justice: Judgment and Justification

The Dioscuri's pronouncement that Apollo's oracle was not wise has a backward rippling effect on the events of the tragedy. Foremost, of course, is that it vindicates Orestes's doubt of the god's command.[86] The god was unwise. His pronouncement was unjust. In addition, the Dioscuri confirm that the gods, including Zeus, purposely lie to send men to their doom. Hence, it is not only human institutions that are problematic but also divine standards of justice. Importantly, is not clear what replaces divine standards. As Electra puts it: "Where Apollo is foolish, who is wise?"[87] The play proposes several alternative sources for standards of judging the just from unjust: noble birth, wealth, courage, reputation, beauty, good character, and generosity.[88] Through this exploration of possible standards, the tragedy brings to the forefront the enduring question of making judgments in the face of uncertain standards and doubtful authority.

Orestes's distrust of the Oracle dramatizes the experience of lost confidence in divine authority. As his mother's chariot approaches, he cries: "There was much ignorance (*pollēn amathian*) in your [Apollo's] insight" that "I cannot believe such things were prophesied well."[89] He begins to suspect that he has been duped: "Did an avenger (*alastōr*) speak such things disguised as a counterfeit (*apeikastheis*) god." He submits under his sister's pressure but still finds the upcoming conflict odious (*pikron*). Orestes's doubt confirms two possible reasons for false prophecy: the Oracle was wrong because either (1) the god is not wise (*amathia*); or (2) it was not Apollo, but a fake simulacrum sent to destroy him. Orestes's hesitation is often seen as indicative of his timorous disposition, but Orestes was correct to hesitate.[90] The gods can be wrong and do send fake images, like that of Helen, to trick men. Yet, Orestes also does not trust his own judgment. Thus, if the gods cannot be trusted, and we do not trust ourselves, then who or what authority should be trusted?

The easiest place to find a nondivine authority is human nobility. This, of course, merely raises the question: Who is noble? Is nobility simply equated with status such as old-fashioned noble birth? Importantly, this idea is rejected several times in the tragedy. In the early *agōn* with the farmer, for example, Orestes admits that "there is no accurate measure of nobility for the natures of mortals are confused."[91] Later, as the old man suggests, Orestes and Pylades may "look" like noblemen, but "many who are well-born are bad men (*kakoi*)." In other words, inherited aristocracy is unreliable, as noble birth is no guarantee of goodness or good judgment.

Several other alternative sources for nobility are also raised and rejected. In the exchange with the farmer, Orestes also suggests that both wealth and poverty are poor indications of nobility. Wealth is esteemed, he tells us, only by those who have "poverty of mind" and poor men often learn to do bad things out of necessity.[92] Second, Orestes dismisses courage in war as an unreliable guide, since no man facing a spear can testify to the courage of someone else. Third, those with great beauty or athletic ability also can be "long on muscle and short on brains" and, therefore, useless for administering governments or conducting war. Finally, family reputation, like noble birth, offers no guarantee that subsequent children are concerned with the good. Thus, we cannot rely on noble birth, wealth, courage, beauty, bodily strength, or reputation as indicators of true nobility. It appears, as if "we can only toss our judgments random on the wind."

Orestes, however, suggests one final possible foundation for true nobility (*eugeneia*) "in the habits (*ēthesin*) of how mortals live together."[93] For men who are noble in this way are "good at administering cities and households." In other words, nobility is not a trait of birth, wealth, or reputation but found in good character of living together well in a community. Such a definition sounds anachronistic for the heroic setting of the play. But reflecting the realism of the setting, this view is echoed in later Greek philosophers, especially Aristotle, who also understood ethics as the habitual disposition of naturally social human beings.[94] Importantly, the Greek word *eugeneia* can also mean "generosity" or "kindness." Hence, there is one surprising candidate for nobility of character: the farmer. Although poor, the farmer is a generous host and embodies the idea that the truly noble are unfazed by circumstances of poverty or loss.[95] We know from the prologue that he refuses to touch a wife given to him illegitimately. Even Electra calls him a friend (*philos*). The farmer also reveals his prudence as he stresses that anyone claiming nobility based on birth, wealth, or other kinds of status "measures wisdom by a crooked line."

Euripides appears to offer a resolution to the problem of determining an authority to provide wise judgment. Human beings are to judge and be judged by what Martin Luther King Jr. would later call "the content of one's character," rather than false signs of wealth, courage in battle, or family reputation.[96] However, yet again, the play undermines this straightforward resolution. First, there is the farmer himself. In his exchange with Orestes, the farmer agrees that wealth is not the measure of nobility; and, he adds, even if wealth has some advantages, it is unnecessary for most daily needs in which "the rich and the poor are the same."[97] Such statements confirm his view that wealth is not a "straight measure" of a man. Yet the farmer is inconsistent in his commitment to this principle. He suggests poverty "ruined his inherited noble status," and he also did not touch Electra because he is "not her equal." Most problematically, however, is the Dioscuri's command that in exchange for giving up Electra, the farmer would be rewarded with great piles of wealth (*ploutou baros*) and live with the new couple in high society in Pylos.[98] Thus, the farmer is not fully committed to the principle that nobility is found in one's character and not in status and great wealth.[99] It is possible that the farmer was simply wrong to consider himself unworthy of Electra; yet this does not resolve the issue. If the farmer is wrong, he also "measures with a crooked line." Even the best candidate for nobility of character proves to have faulty judgment.

Importantly, beyond the farmer's poor judgment, Euripides's innovative characterizations further destabilize the standard of good character and, as previously noted, are contrary to mythological expectation. The case of the usurper Aegisthus is a revealing illustration. On the one hand, the old man is extremely confident that Aegisthus will be a pious host, since he has a reputation honoring Zeus as god of hospitality.[100] Taking advantage of Aegisthus's piety, the son of the king of kings strikes him down while he inspects a sacrificial animal. Orestes's action seems cowardly, or at least inappropriate, as he kills a defenseless man during a sacrifice.[101] On the other hand, Aegisthus is certainly not consistently pious: he is the "uncivilized" type who gets drunk and both dances on and throws stones at Agamemnon's grave. Again, the ambiguity of his character only highlights the obvious but real difficulty of judging a noble character from "false coin."[102] Like the farmer, we may not always act according to our best principles. Like Aegisthus, no one is a one-dimensional evil villain. Unsurprisingly, the very best man has flaws, and the most horrendous tyrant has some redeeming qualities.

Added to the immense difficulty of determining what human authority makes "straight" judgment, Euripides adds another dimension to the mix: certain actions are just for certain individuals but not for others. In other words, moral judgment involves not only what is done (the act) but an assessment of the agent (the who) and circumstances (the where and the when). In this tragedy, the complexity of such judgment is manifested in unfair double standards. As Clytemnestra stresses, she is condemned as "monstrous" for taking a lover and killing Agamemnon, but he is considered a great hero, even though he murdered their daughter (as if he "had no choice") and brought home a new wife.[103] The chorus is quick to condemn Clytemnestra's argument as "shameful"; yet her argument does reflect the same double standard underlying the play's moral dilemma.[104] Clytemnestra's death was just, but not just at the hands of her son. In other words, what is just for one is unjust for another.

The dramatic events work to undermine both the certitude of divine authority and confidence in human authorities to establish and make straight judgments. By rejecting all standards, it is possible to see the play as ending in despair. Morwood, for example, argues the play concludes that "death and defilement are deepest truths, the ultimate realities."[105] O'Brien suggests all conventional ways of judging good from evil are irrelevant with "no sure standard that separates oppressor from oppressed."[106] Hence similar to other plays with dark themes, such as the *Hecuba* or the *Medea*, such interpretations suggest Euripides is a kind of proto- or ancient nihilist whose vision reinforces the absolute subjectivity of moral judgment. It is true that this tragedy undermines the certitude of authority and confidence in judgment. Yet the pronouncement that Clytemnestra's death was just confirms that justice exists. Nevertheless, the Dioscuri's assertion that the act was not just for Orestes then turns the inquiry inward toward the subject and begs one final question: how do we judge or recognize the "self" who is judging?

Justice: Seeing with Free Eyes

The theme of recognition runs throughout the tragedy. It is, for example, at the heart of the much-discussed delayed recognition scene.[107] As noted previously, the Aeschylean recognition signs, such as a footprint, are raised but rejected here; instead, Orestes is identified by a childhood scar. This draws attention to two important issues lingering in the story. First, even though after such a long absence Electra believes she "would not know him if [she] saw him," the delayed recognition allows her to expound on her romantic conception of Orestes as the "brave brother who would [never] come hidden to this land because he feared Aegisthus."[108] What the audience knows, of course, is that Orestes has been lurking in the borderland so that he can make a quick escape if necessary. In other words, Electra is wrong: he is in hiding and is afraid of Aegisthus. Furthermore, the whole situation is more of an "anti-recognition" scene, since it takes the intervention of the old man for her to see—really see—her brother.[109] The problem highlighted is Electra's "double vision" or the distinction between "[her] image of the truth and the truth itself."[110] Underscored is the difficulty of recognizing that others are never who they seem to be.[111] Second, Electra never recognizes Orestes by the familial signs of identity such a lock of hair or footprint; instead, she identifies him by a scar.[112] Unlike hair color, a scar is not inherited. It literally "marks" him as unique.[113] Thus, this scene highlights not only the dissimilarity between how one imagines the other and who the other is but also the importance of seeing the other, not in relationship to the self, but for their uniqueness.

This idea of really "seeing" or recognizing another is repeated throughout the play. In Electra's antifuneral oration, for example, she uses her newfound "free eyes" to speak frankly (*parrhēsia*) about the "real" Aegisthus.[114] In the *agōn* with her mother, Electra rejects her mother's argument, as she "sees" her mother clearly. She points to her mother's similarity to Helen, whose "willing abduction" started the Trojan War, necessitated Iphigenia's death, and culminated in the murder of Agamemnon. In turn, Clytemnestra also sees Electra: her daughter is one of those children who "belong to the male," "reignite quarrels anew," and "have a nature that is self-willed." The *agōn* ends in a stalemate of irreconcilable differences: they see each other, but there is no indication that they see themselves.

The final *agōn*, therefore, draws attention to this kind of double vision. What Electra ultimately fails to see or recognize is herself: her own character and her own motivations that fueled her judgment. In other words, her critique that Clytemnestra is not so different from Helen could also be applied to Electra's own personality.[115] Although Electra knows, for example, that Clytemnestra preens to draw attention to her appearance, the tragedy opens with Electra's drawing attention to her poor appearance (which, as the farmer notes, is unnecessary). In her antifuneral oration, she finds it shameful for a woman to be seen outdoors and mocks Aegisthus for "being ruled by a woman"; yet Electra is seen on stage for most of the tragedy and treats her husband similarly. She forces Orestes into matricide. Most significantly, like her mother, Electra actively thrusts the sword. Hence, she is not so dissimilar from the woman she hates. It is not until she is faced with the horror of killing her mother that Electra recognizes the truth: she finally sees herself.[116]

Thus, the tragedy reveals that correct judgment requires truly "seeing freely" others and oneself.[117] And on this final point, the story hints at the ultimate inward turn. As noted previously, we know very little about the *Electra*, including its production date or how Euripides's fellow citizens reacted to his innovative version of their heroes and villains. There is, however, a long history of strong reactions in modern scholarship: Electra is "self-indulgent," "morbidly embittered," with a hint of "nymphomania"; her brother is "feeble and irresolute" with "no character." Perhaps the most important question of the tragedy is: why are these characters so disliked?[118] Why do we prefer Aegisthus or Clytemnestra to be more one-dimensionally evil? What does our reaction to these characters reveal about ourselves or what we are hiding, like Orestes, from those closest to us? Or, like Electra, what are we hiding from ourselves? In this way, Euripides's perplexingly ambiguous characterizations invite us to move beyond the role of spectator to that of self-examiner. Most importantly, if the tragedy is a kind of pedagogy, through the example of his flawed characters in their pursuit of flawed justice, it models the great difficulty by which we come to understand—to see—the complexity of all moral judgment.

Conclusion

Euripides's portrayal of the famous story of family blood feud, matricide, and revenge reveals the complexity at the heart of making judgments concerning justice and injustice. This complexity highlights how difficult it is to judge without firm authority or an absolute standard of right and wrong. Moral judgment requires more than a set of divine pronouncements but knowledge of the individuals and circumstances involved. What is just for one person in one set of circumstances is not just for another.[119] To further complicate matters, in order to judge what is just for one but not another, we must go beyond our double vision and really see the other. And to do this, we need to see that crooked judgment can lie in the blurred vision of our own "eyes." As judges, we fail to recognize how our own double vision blurs our judgment of other people, of the circumstances, and of ourselves.

This version of *Electra* is dark and troubling. It undermines authority and standards of judgment and, unlike Aeschylus's more famous account, offers no security in institutionalized justice. Perhaps this is why Aeschylus's story of divinely established courts and the transformation of the Erinyes into civilized kindly goddesses is more comforting. Yet, even as Beccaria, that promoter of certitude in criminal justice, several centuries later poetically put it: "Strictly speaking, moral certitude is nothing but a probability."[120] Without such certitude, the tragedy's hint to focus inward in questioning our own bias continues to resonate. It echoes in Elgin's attempt to mediate a way between absolute knowledge set on firm foundations and arbitrary relativity.[121] It finds purchase in the many arguments against racial, class, and gender bias in the courts and in our own lives.[122] Importantly, Euripides's suggestion of self-examination does not lead to justice as impartiality, rather it is a call to see—really *see*—the motivations underlying our calls to justice.[123]

Thus, despite the condemnation that Euripides offers nothing but despair and doubt, the tragedy's realism can be an invitation to think through the complexity of justice. It can be seen as a call for vigilance toward those considered moral enough not to measure "by a crooked line." Like the farmer, even the noblest among us are flawed. We often fail in our judgment because we are too easily led by false ideas of others and ourselves. This story reminds us, as Badger argues, that the tragic is a recognition of the limitations of a demand for perfect justice.[124] If the experience of ambiguity behind the "double vision" portrayed in the tragedy still feels uncomfortable and negative, Euripides would not be surprised. As Orestes tells his sister, the very wise "pay a high penalty for understanding (*gnōmēn*)."[125]

Conclusion

Considering the breadth, depth, and complexity of Euripides's treatment of justice, it is safe to conclude that he is concerned with "justice and the other virtues."[1] His tragedies explore several perspectives of justice from the traditional norms such as helping friends and harming enemies, oath keeping, and merit—to sophistic arguments of relativism. This exploration of justice uncovers the difficulty of judgment: how we define, or literally draw boundaries around, what is and is not just. Euripides also raises questions about the limitations of making such distinctions, as we lack crucial knowledge of circumstances, of others involved, and of our own personal bias. Sometimes we overreach and turn justice into its opposite. Sometimes we aim for impossible rectifications. Although Euripides's tragedies are set in mythological times with grand noble families facing extreme circumstances, his presentations of justice reflect the ideas of justice held by his fifth-century BCE audience and explored by the intellectual environment of classical Athens. These works encourage his fellow citizens to see and infer "likenesses" or similarities between the representations of justice and their own ideas of justice.[2] They make the audience think and "see all sides of everything."[3] Euripides's tragedies are playful and entertaining, but they are also useful examples for good government: they reveal some knowledge of what makes cities better, and they also nourish prudence as well as promote an understanding of what justice might mean.

Although this analysis focused on the question of justice, Euripides's tragedies are not about justice or, for that matter, any specific topic: instead, these tragedies, like all examples of good storytelling, depict the complexity of human interaction and community, of which justice is an important part. Unfortunately, the reaction of Euripides's contemporary audience to his tragedies is unknown. Yet it is not a stretch to assume that much like our own audiences, his fellow citizens left the theater debating the plot and arguing about the questions the tragedies raised.[4] His audience would likely have also raised different questions than the ones presented in this analysis about the stories or about the meaning of justice. This is to be expected, as the tragedies encourage us to think about ideas and concepts rather than offer answers intended to close discussion. At most, his tragedies hint that because the complexity of thinking about the question of justice is difficult—that is, never fully realized—it is a continuous and essential aspect of human community.

Justice in Euripides's Tragedies

Justice: Helping Friends and Harming Enemies

The tragedies bring up several different perspectives on the question of justice. The most common is the ancient idea of helping friends and harming enemies.[5] Importantly, a "friend" (*philos*) in ancient Greece included not only our definition of close acquaintance but also kin-based relationships and formalized bonds, such as guest-friendship (*xenia*), supplication (*hiketeia*), and reciprocal relationships based on benevolence (*kharis*). Violations of this ancient ethic—harm to friends—is a "central element of the plot structure of nearly all the extant tragedies."[6] Thus, it is no surprise that some form of violation of this ancient code is found in all the plays under examination, either as a direct or secondary plot point. This sample of Euripides's tragedies reveals, for example, problematized friendships of direct kinship: Creusa almost murdering her son in the *Ion*; Agave succeeding in the *Bacchae*; the fratricide in the *Phoenician Women*; the matricide in the *Electra*; and Medea's infamous sacrifice of her own children. Euripides's tragedies also reveal the dilemmas and limitations of formalized relationships such as supplication, guest-friendship, and expectations of reciprocal relationships. Even though this ethic appears a simplistic foundation of justice (what could be easier than helping friends and harming enemies?), Euripides explores the complications, limitations, and difficulties of this deceptively simple case. Most importantly, he reveals the interconnections of this ancient ethic with broader questions, such as: what is a friend?

With a view to formalized relationships, the ethic of helping friends established by supplication is found in several plays, most notably *Hecuba*, *Suppliant Women*, and *Children of Heracles*.[7] Although an ancient practice, the act of supplication (*hiketeia*) remained a cultural practice in the classical era; it involved formalized rituals that established a kind of friendship based on reciprocal obligations.[8] Both the *Suppliant Women* and *Children of Heracles* focus on the connection between reciprocity and the political question of when and under what circumstances the political community should help noncitizens or other political regimes. In the case of the *Suppliant Women*, convinced to be an "activist" for the sake of his own self-interested glory, Theseus retrieves the unburied bodies of the Argive generals.[9] In the *Children of Heracles*, Demophon quickly agrees to the supplication but support for the refugees fails in the Athenian Assembly, and the children end up helping themselves.[10] Supplication is also important to the *Hecuba*, where the titular character fails in her supplication of Odysseus and only partially succeeds with Agamemnon.[11] Reflecting contemporary political issues, Euripides's tragedies reveal how helping noncitizens, even refugee children, can be politically unpopular, and "helping" others conceals the self-interested motivations of political leaders.

The ending of the *Suppliant Women* emphasizes another potential form of friendship created by bonds of gratitude and reciprocity (*kharis*). In ancient Greece, *kharis* invoked a kind of reflective relationship found both in the benevolence of helping others and in the gratitude of future obligations.[12] In the *Suppliant Women*, Theseus succeeds in retrieving the bodies of the Argive generals and is content with personal gratitude in exchange; Athena, however, overrides reciprocity to ensure a formal political alliance with Athens.[13] In the *Children of Heracles*, Iolaus argues that Demophon owes reciprocity because Heracles helped his father; Demophon agrees but is more concerned with safeguarding Athenian political independence.[14] This play also highlights gratitude in the maiden's sacrifice, but she is immediately forgotten and the categories of friends and enemies become subverted. The significance of memory in acts of *kharis*—which must be remembered to be reciprocated—is also highlighted in the *Alcestis*. In this tragedy, *kharis* figures prominently in a series of favors: Apollo's favor to substitute Admetus's death; Alcestis's willingness to die her husband's death; and Heracles's rescuing Alcestis from Death.[15] Unlike the maiden, Alcestis is not forgotten, but her favor reveals that *kharis* can be not only extraordinary but also excessive. In other words, there are limitations to such acts of benevolence, generosity, and reciprocal favors, even to those closest to us.

Another interrelated practice connected to helping friends is the ancient formal relationship of hospitality or guest-friendship (*xenia*). Like supplication and gratitude, guest-friendship (*xenia*) was a highly formalized hereditary relationship that remained important in the classical era.[16] Helping guest-friends is prominent in several plays, most notably the *Alcestis*, *Electra*, and *Hecuba*. In the *Alcestis*, Heracles is entertained as a guest-friend (inappropriately, as Alcestis has died), and in exchange he rescues her from Admetus's fate. If viewed as "happy," the ending appears to redeem the ethic of guest-friendship; yet the ambiguous finale also reveals this ethic can be equally excessive.[17] The *Hecuba* presents a more clearly problematic example.[18] Priam's youngest son Polydorus was sent to their guest-friend Polymestor for safekeeping during the Trojan war; however, he kills the boy to steal his Trojan gold. In response to such injustice, Hecuba kills his sons and blinds Polydorus. Euripides reveals how the bonds of *xenia* prove doubtful and fragile.

Friendship is also found in kinship ties of blood and marriage. Although helping relatives seems undemanding, Euripides exposes how such ties are also unreliable, problematic, and also potentially excessive. Helping kin can become problematic, for example, when individuals identify so completely with certain relationships that they neglect all other obligations. Hence, Alcestis dies her husband's death, or Evadne kills herself to share her husband's glory.[19] In both these cases, helping friends collapses the distinction between "self" and friend. In an opposite example, the *Medea* focuses on another failure of the ethic: when friends harm friends. This reversal of the ethic begins with Jason harming Medea but ends with her harming those dearest to her.[20] Hence, the *Medea* reveals how categories of friends and enemies, or helping and harming, are not fixed but can become confused and confounded.

The concept of friendship is also complicated, as the *Ion* shows, when human beings lack crucial self-knowledge. In that play, ignorant that they are mother and son, the protagonists try to kill each other.[21] A similar lack of self-knowledge is responsible for the incestuous relationship of Jocasta and Oedipus in the *Phoenician Women*, as well as the *Bacchae*'s portrayal of Agave's act of madness during which she tore her son limb from limb.[22] Yet knowledge does not eliminate the problem of kin becoming enemies. In the *Electra*, for example, Orestes faces a dilemma of competing obligations (revenge [his father] and respect [his mother]) and doubtful oracles; yet he kills his mother anyway.[23] Antigone, at the end of the *Phoenician Women*, is faced with the dilemma of choosing to die in order to ensure her brother is properly buried or accompanying her father into exile; she cannot do both actions.[24] Thus, even with the low bar of the ethic of helping friends who are close relations, we still err due to lack of knowledge and contradictory obligations to different family members.

Euripides's exploration of justice as helping friends and harming enemies raises problems and limits regarding this seemingly straightforward ethic. The tragedies reveal the blatant self-interest often underlying the ethic of helping others, even defenseless refugees. Euripides's tragedies also underscore that the ethic can be inverted, especially if one identifies either too little (as did Medea or Electra) or too much (as did Alcestis or Evadne) with their loved ones. Most importantly, Euripides's stories of violated friendships connect this ancient view of justice to broader moral questions. His tragedies dramatize how relationships and ties of friendship are fragile and unreliable. As Creusa's twin vial of good and bad symbolize, it is difficult to make clear and permanent distinctions between friend and enemy or actions that are helpful or harmful.[25] The ethic requires thinking about subsequent questions, such as "who is my friend?," "what is a friend?," or "what is a helpful or harmful action?" Such questions are certainly philosophical, but they also are central to Euripides's tragedies.[26]

JUSTICE OF OATHS, MERIT, AND CORRECTION

Euripides's dramatizations also explore justice between unassociated individuals in the broader community. Although often overlapping with the ethic of helping friends and harming enemies, the idea that justice has something to do with keeping oaths or getting what is deserved was demonstrated in literature across the classical period.[27] In the *Republic*, for example, Plato introduces justice as merit with the aging Cephalus who defines justice as "speaking the truth" and fulfilling obligations of "giving to each what is owed" either to gods or men.[28] Xenophon's *Anabasis* contains a condemnation of perjury.[29] Aristotle's *Nicomachean Ethics* defines the just man as someone who does not take more than what is fair or is merited.[30] Similar to these philosophers, Euripides explores the interconnections between justice as keeping one's word (i.e., oath making as obligation) and other forms of justice as merit (what we are owed and owe others). His tragedies also reveal the difficulties of this broader view of justice, especially the limitations of measuring incommensurate goods or determining recompense for past injustices.

Like other cultural norms, oath making (*horkos*) has ancient roots.[31] Under the protection of Zeus Horkios, it was impious to break one's word, and punishment included "rooting out all traces of a man who had sworn falsely."[32] Although important in the plots of several plays, such as the finale of the *Suppliant Women*, oaths are most significant in the *Medea* and *Phoenician Women*. The *Medea* revolves around the breaking of an oath (Jason's oath to Medea) and the making of an oath (King Aegeus's oath of sanctuary).[33] Jason's oath to Medea, which reflected a military alliance, gave her the assurance for which she betrayed her natal family; in this light, when Jason breaks his word, she acts as her own divine avenger (*alastōr*) by making Jason childless. In the *Phoenician Women*, the war between the brothers comes to a head in part because Eteocles unjustly broke his oath with his brother to alternate ruling power yearly.[34] Like the *Medea*, this tragedy emphasizes the vulnerability underlying oath making and speaking the truth: in both cases, such broken oaths end in violence and self-destruction.

Beyond the obligations arising from oath making, Euripides explores justice as merit as a form of receiving what is deserved. Euripides examines the complexity of determining what one deserves in several of his tragedies. In the *Phoenician Women*, the brothers' war is also caused by Eteocles's claim to more than his fair share of Oedipus's inheritance.[35] As Jocasta stresses, since the brothers are equal, Polynices deserves equal rule. In the *Ion*, Euripides exposes the opposite kind of justice as merit: unequal people deserve unequal outcomes. In his frustrated reaction to the sanctuary law that protects everyone, including criminals, Ion cries out: "It is wrong that good and bad men receive the same thing."[36] In this case, Ion underscores the idea that what someone "deserves" is not strict equality but should include an assessment of an individual's actions or character. The importance of character as essential to what one deserves is also highlighted in *Hecuba* as a reason against the sacrifice of Polyxena: as a human being, Polyxena cannot be sacrificed like an animal.[37] Such assessments require subsequent inquiries: If equals should be given equal things, then what is equality? Or, if only good men deserve good things, then what does it mean to be good?

Added to this complication, justice as merit involves other kinds of assessments. The *Alcestis* focuses on the importance of determining not only what is owed but also how much we owe others. The nasty debate between Admetus and his father questions parental obligations: Are parents obligated to die for their children? Or, as Pheres maintained, is this expectation "out of measure"?[38] If asking someone to die for others is too much, what does this say about Menoeceus's sacrifice in the *Phoenician Women* or the maiden in *Children of Heracles*? In other words, what seems "out of measure" in one case may be considered noble in the next. Thus, Euripides lays bare the complex calculation underlying justice as merit. It requires judgments of whom, what, when, and how much another person deserves in variable and ever-changing circumstances.

Ion's belief that bad men do not deserve the same treatment as good men also reveals justice as merit as a form of corrective reciprocity.[39] This proportional view of justice is an attempt to restore what is unmerited or underserved. At its most basic level, corrective justice is a comparable exchange, such as the compensation of a life, money, or labor in the ancient concept of blood price.[40] Euripides highlights this view of justice in Menoeceus's self-sacrifice in the *Phoenician Women* and the finales of the *Hecuba* and *Medea*. In the *Phoenician Women*, there is a literal exchange of compensation of Menoeceus's life for the life of Ares's son.[41] In the finale of the *Hecuba*, the Trojan Queen blinds her former guest-friend and kills her sons as "the price of satisfaction" or in exchange for his destruction of Priam's House.[42] Medea's attempt to exact similar compensation by destroying Jason's House reveals the impossibility of true compensation or restoration. Whatever Jason suffers, it cannot undo the past; no corrective is truly commensurate in exchange.

The calculation of justice as merit is even further complicated by whether someone deserves the degree of such punishment. In the *Hecuba*, although his argument is dismissed by Agamemnon, Polymestor insists that he did not deserve Hecuba's corrective justice, as he killed her son to help his Greek allies.[43] The supplication plays also reflect similar evaluations. In the *Children of Heracles*, even though the chorus emphasizes that the refugees suffer undeservedly from Eurystheus's persecution, contrary to their own laws protecting prisoners of war, they permit his execution.[44] In the *Suppliant Women*, Theseus initially rejects the supplication because the Argives pursued an unjust war. Although he changes his mind and agrees to retrieve the dead, Theseus never reconsiders that the Argives deserved their destruction.[45] There are many other examples of such judgments: Medea argues that Jason abandoned her without merit; or, in the *Electra*, Clytemnestra asserts Agamemnon deserved his fate because he killed their daughter and brought home a concubine.[46] Underlying any question of merit, these tragedies suggest, are complicated questions concerning whether someone merits some good or suffers undeservedly.

Beyond such assessments of merit, corrective justice also involves an assessment of the proper measure of compensation. Euripides explores proper compensation most visibly in the *Bacchae*. Dionysus drives the women of Thebes "out of their minds" and they tear Pentheus to pieces because he failed to recognize the god. Cadmus admits Dionysus was owed worship but suggests the god's punishment was "too much."[47] Or, in an example from the *Hecuba*, does Polymestor merit blindness and the death of his two sons? Similarly, in the *Children of Heracles*, does Eurystheus deserve to die in violation of divine rules of sanctuary and laws protecting prisoners of war? And what about the *Medea*'s Jason: does he deserve such total annihilation?

In these tragedies, each idea of justice proves problematic and unreliable. Justice as oath making is undermined; justice as merit requires judgments that are multifaceted and variable; corrective justice requires a judgment of the proper proportional amount, often of incommensurate things. Each case of justice requires a fresh evaluation of the complex circumstances and individuals involved. What is just for one person, as we learn from the *Electra*, is not just for another.[48] Euripides's tragedies, therefore, reveal the multitude of layers of assessments connected to the question of justice. Thus, Eteocles is only half-right: certainly, quarrel and strife are the result of our disagreements concerning the meaning of justice.[49] Yet quarrels also arise from the application of the exact same idea of justice when we misjudge or disagree with the assessment of the circumstances and the character of those involved.

Justice: Boundaries and Limits

Cadmus may be out of line to judge a god's punishment, yet his point remains salient: excessive punishment becomes its opposite. The same idea echoes in justice as helping friends and harming enemies. Medea reveals that harming an enemy can blur into harming friends. Yet the line determining the proper measure of justice is rarely obvious, and it is easy to cross over or transgress such boundaries. Euripides also explores the connection of justice to boundaries, especially in the making, enforcing, or crossing of such barriers. Visually and conceptually boundaries have important dramatic significance. Certain plays, such as the *Ion*, dramatize the boundaries of sacred spaces that draw attention to what should not be transgressed (*parabainomen*).[50] The *Alcestis* can be seen as blurring the boundaries of the genre of tragedy as it reflects elements of a satyr play. Several tragedies, such as the *Hecuba* and *Medea*, invoke liminal divinities, such as Hekate, who rule over borderlands and transitional spaces. The *Bacchae* even relocates Dionysus from "watching" the tragedy through his statuary image to appearing on stage.[51] This god of the Great Dionysia festival, perhaps more than any other, represented liminality: he was the god of paradox, metamorphosis, and the freedom to "be what is not."[52]

Through such allusions to boundaries and liminality, Euripides reveals that the question of "what is justice?" invokes setting and crossing boundaries. To answer this question is to draw a boundary around and between what is and is not justice. It is a judgment of who is a friend and who is not. Or who is worthy and who is not. His tragedies also dramatize the limitations and contradictions inherent in our attempts to place fixed boundaries on justice. In some cases, the boundary line between just and unjust is opaque: the same action can be, as the Dioscuri in the *Electra* pronounced, just and not just.[53] In other cases, such as Creusa in the *Ion*, a lack of knowledge confounds the desire to keep the just separate from the unjust. Or, in the case of Admetus in the *Alcestis*, being "too good" or too generous can turn a just action into its opposite.

Euripides's portrayal of boundaries raises additional questions about justice. First, beyond what is deserved or how much, the important question is this: who has the authority to define and enforce the boundary between the just and unjust? The tragedies dramatize different sources of authority from the gods and cultural traditions to political leaders and institutions. Divine authority remains a source of the enforcement of justice, such as Zeus's authority to protect oaths (central to the *Medea*), sanctuary (*Ion* and *Children of Heracles*), and supplication (*Hecuba*, *Suppliant Women*, and *Children of Heracles*). In the *Suppliant Women*, Athena's divine authority replaces human gratitude (*kharis*) with a stronger oath of military alliance.[54] By contrast, other tragedies, such as the *Bacchae*, assert the authority of tradition as a way to stabilize conflicts.[55] Tradition is also significant in the Panhellenic custom respecting burial rites (*Suppliant Women* and *Phoenician Women*) or protecting belligerent heralds. Hecuba also appeals to Panhellenic norms forbidding human sacrifice.[56]

Finally, political authority also establishes justice in the form of positive laws and decrees. In the *Phoenician Women*, for example, Creon's decree exiles Polynices's corpse.[57] The *Children of Heracles* ends with a violation of Athenian law of protecting prisoners of war. Importantly, not only does Euripides present such authorities in conflict, but he also portrays all authority, including the gods, as unreliable.

Euripides, however, is most critical of political authority as a firm foundation for justice. The *Bacchae* highlights the disintegration of political power that is too rigid in the face of the "new" or change.[58] Athena is particularly active in correcting human misjudgment: she arrives deus ex machina to prevent Ion from forcing Apollo to "uncover" what should remain hidden; she overrules Theseus's self-interested request for gratitude rather than a military oath.[59] The *Suppliant Women* also hints at the importance of traditional Greek norms, as Theseus's upholding of Panhellenic law is victorious over Creon's political decrees. Predictably, in conflicts between human and divine (or traditional) authority, human power is humbled.

Political authority's limited ability to determine the just from the unjust receives a great deal of attention. As dramatized by Athena's correction of Theseus's judgment, tyrannical rulers, in particular, reveal poor judgment: Pentheus in the *Bacchae*; Admetus in *Alcestis*; Agamemnon in the *Hecuba*; Creon (and Jason) in *Medea*; and Eteocles in the *Phoenician Women*. Yet democracies fair only marginally better. The *Children of Heracles*, for example, dramatizes the limitations of democratic decision making: the debate over helping suppliants almost causes a civil war and, in the end, the citizens violate their own law and Panhellenic traditions of sanctuary for future self-interest.[60] In the *Hecuba*, the reported debate concerning Polyxena's sacrifice is undermined by greed and political scandal.[61] Euripides offers little optimism that discursive deliberation is the solution to determining just outcomes.

It is not only political leaders but other individuals who lack judgment. Medea's horrific act of filicide is motivated by the impossible desire to erase the past. Ion and Creusa's near homicides expose the erroneous judgment of insufficient information. The *Electra* ends with one of the most decent characters, the farmer, rejecting true nobility for a life of riches. In addition, political institutions offer no mitigating panacea to such poor human judgment. In contrast to Aeschylus's celebrated establishment of institutionalized justice in the *Eumenides*, Euripides ends his *Electra* with a judicial system that is clearly arbitrary and does not fully exonerate Orestes.⁶² All forms of human judgment are imperfect and provide an unreliable distinction between just and unjust.

The failure of human judgment is not unique. Divine and traditional authority proves equally limited and fallible. The most obvious example is the *Ion*, in which human beings foil Apollo's prophetic plan and expose his limited foresight.⁶³ Similarly, in the *Electra*, the Dioscuri declare Apollo was wrong to command matricide.⁶⁴ Cadmus's judgment of Dionysus's excessive punishment exposes potential divine fallibility. Even traditional norms, which the *Bacchae* reveals can be stabilizing, can also be questionable. In the *Suppliant Women*, for example, Panhellenic burial rites are revealed to protect the continuing cycle of warfare by ensuring young men continue to die for their kings.⁶⁵ This cycle of war is reinforced at the end of that tragedy when Athena commands the Argive boys to avenge their fathers. Thus, neither the gods nor tradition can serve as a reliable foundation for justice. Traditions conceal unsavory motivations; the gods can deceive and simply be false.

Euripides's portrayal of the limited capacity of all authority to distinguish the just from the unjust triggers the impression of a relativistic or proto-nihilistic perspective of justice. As his tragedies often conclude without a reliable authority or clear distinction between the just and unjust, justice appears arbitrary and thus subject only to human power. This conclusion reflects the view famously proposed by the sophist Thrasymachus in Plato's *Republic*, but Euripides also raises this idea most notably with Pentheus in the *Bacchae* and Eteocles in the *Phoenician Women*.⁶⁶ Yet, Euripidean characters who endorse such relativistic positions do not fare well. Pentheus, the self-claimed "more authoritative man," is easily manipulated and literally ripped apart by his mother.⁶⁷ Dismissing justice as a meaningless word and tyranny as the "most beautiful injustice," Eteocles and his brother slaughter each other like wild beasts.⁶⁸ Euripides dramatizes the characters promoting or supporting such an extreme position of "might makes right" as coming to a gruesome end.

Yet despite this seeming rejection of the relativist position, Euripides's tragedies over and over again question the possibility that any authority is reliable or can make firm distinctions between the just and the unjust. From this perspective, Euripides reflects what we know of certain sophists who also challenged the certitude of political law and norms.⁶⁹ Yet, Euripides's similar questioning of such foundations does not lend support to the sophistic "reconstruction of a new morality . . . centered on man alone."⁷⁰

There is nothing in his tragedies that suggests Euripides thinks man is the measure of all things. Instead, Euripides highlights the importance of questioning all authorities and the meaning of standards of justice. He seems fully aware of the danger of such investigations, as symbolized by the dismemberment of Pentheus in the *Bacchae*. Yet the one constant in his tragedies is that human knowledge is always limited. This does not mean that there is no justice, only that the onus is on each of us to investigate justice by questioning not only those in authority but also ourselves.

This requirement to question brings us back full circle to the beginning and Plato's suggestion that there is a quarrel between poetry and philosophy. Certainly, Euripides takes seriously questions of justice and virtue. Although the goal of this analysis was not a comparison of Euripides and Plato, his tragedies raise and explore many opinions of justice found in Plato, such as helping friends and harming enemies, keeping oaths, giving what is owed, and even justice as not being a busybody. Through the debates and plots of his tragedies, Euripides points to the important questions related to the meaning of justice but does not provide an answer to such questions. As such, Euripides's approach reflects an interpretation of Plato's dialogues that suggests Platonic philosophy is about testing the truth of opinions not to arrive at certainty but *aporia*. Or, as Socrates puts it in the *Apology*: "Human wisdom is worth a small amount or nothing."[71] Thus, reflecting one interpretation of Platonic dialogues, Euripides reveals that there is no clear or straightforward answer to the question "what is justice?"[72]

There is, however, at least one important difference between Plato's philosophic investigations and Euripides's tragedies. Euripides appears less interested in the question of whether there is an abstract idea of justice that is universally valid. By contrast, taking the realism of his tragedies as his foundation, Euripides is more interested in exploring the human experience of determining justice in a world of limited knowledge and changing circumstances. In this way, Euripides's investigations are not about determining the truth concerning justice but reflect Aristotle's suggestion that there is no exactitude in moral actions that require prudential assessments of the right time, right circumstances, and right amount.[73] The division of this analysis into different "spaces" reflects the importance of particular circumstances. The tragedies set in sacred spaces (*Ion*, *Suppliant Women*, and *Children of Heracles*), for example, tend to focus on questions of justice regarding noncitizens; however, this theme is also important in the *Hecuba*. The tragedies of the city (*Medea*, *Bacchae*, and *Phoenician Women*) tend toward themes of justice and the self, but then so do the *Ion* and *Electra*. Thus, place matters, but justice is more than an evaluation concerning "where." It requires a broader understanding of who, what, how much, and the right time.

Importantly, Euripides's tragedies also differ from Aristotle's philosophic account. As works of drama, Euripides does not present a logical or philosophic argument concerning what justice is. Instead, his storytelling presents an experience of how justice encompasses what is always imprecise and paradoxical.[74] We may desire an understanding of justice with clear boundaries, as symbolized by Creusa's separate vials of good and evil, but Euripides's tragedies point out that for human decision making in an uncertain world, there is no absolute, unchanging boundary between the just and unjust. The just and unjust can be subverted, confused, and confounded—boundaries blur. We may desire exactitude, but all such judgments, such as what one merits or the proper measure of justice, are always incomplete and partial. Although human community requires the marking of boundaries between the just and unjust, Euripides's tragedies emphasize that such community boundaries are always limited and provisional. This does not mean justice does not exist, only that our understanding is incomplete. Whatever justice is, it appears to reflect and embrace the patron of the theater himself: the god of paradox and contradiction.

Final Thoughts

Euripides's plays offer a complex and serious examination of the multifaceted elements and limitations involved in an answer to the question: what is justice? Although various definitions are raised, and authorities claimed, Euripides does not promote a definitive answer to this question. This lack of systematic definition and logical argumentation is predictable, since Euripides is a poet working in a medium not confined by linear logic and orderly thinking. As a poetic account, his exploration highlights the inexactitudes and paradox at the heart of justice. Importantly, such poetry allows contradictions and inconsistencies to be held simultaneously. In the spirit of this liminal space of tragedy, three final observations can be drawn from Euripides's portrayal of justice.

First, although Euripides never defines justice, the ambiguities and inexactitudes of the various perspectives hint at a possible approach to understanding justice. Definitions of justice are not firm but unbounded, and justice in the world is incomplete and partial. Again, this does not suggest justice is merely arbitrary and relative; instead, it implies that justice is not something that one "possesses." There is no definitive or absolute definition or judgment to be found in a book, be it religious or philosophical. Although Euripides never uses this word, perhaps the best metaphor to describe his understanding of justice is the Greek concept of *sōros*: a pile or heap.[75] In contrast to the ancient Greek *metron*, which implies a more exact measurement, a pile is unmeasured, unlimited, and unbounded. A modern equivalent might be the difference between a teaspoon and a pinch. A teaspoon of salt is precise; a pinch is not. As a fixed measure, a teaspoon is an agreed-upon amount; by contrast, there is no fixed agreement as to exactly how much a pinch is. You can add a bit or take away a bit, but a pinch is a pinch and pile is still a pile. Since justice in Euripides's tragedies is not something that can have an agreed-upon definition, it seems more akin to a pile than a fixed measure.

Second, if justice is a like a pile, then determining what justice means or establishing a firm boundary between the just and unjust always remains an open investigation. One constant in Euripides's tragedies is that judgment of the just and unjust is plagued by a biased perspective, lack of understanding, and limited knowledge. Even the most simplistic view of justice, such as helping friends, is never straightforward. The complexity of judgment increases exponentially with more complicated assessments of merit and correction. Our modern versions of justice are not immune to these problems. Justice may be fairness, social equality, redistributive, or restorative, but it is never clear as to what is "fair" or "equal" in each circumstance. Any attempt at redistributive or restorative justice faces the same limitations in determining what one deserves and how much. We still judge with bias and insufficient knowledge. Like determining a pile, our perspective is always partial and conditional. We may, like Electra or Pentheus, invoke a self-righteous claim to justice, but Euripides's tragedies are a lesson in the consequences of thinking we know more than we do. His tragedies are a reminder of the need for humility and openness to others with whom we disagree.

Third, Euripides's tragedies reveal the extent to which steadfastly enforcing a particular definition or questioning those same community norms of justice can be equally disruptive to the community. The *Phoenician*

Women's Eteocles is not wrong to suggest that debate on the meaning of justice causes strife. Pentheus's insistence in the *Bacchae* on enforcing firm distinctions dissolves into violence and chaos. Yet because justice is always incomplete and conditional, a political community cannot escape the necessity of an ongoing and continual discussion of the meaning of justice. Such discussion is informed by debates of philosophy. Today, it is also found in political speeches, media analyses, public demonstrations, and various online forums. Importantly, however, Euripides's tragedies underscore another vital questioning medium: the storytelling genres that are the legacies of ancient poetry. Today, when we open a novel, we find stories highlighting the paradoxes of justice and crises raised by incomplete knowledge of the circumstances, of others, and of ourselves. We debate the meaning of justice in our conversations concerning our latest television binge-watching marathon. Finally, gathered together in our own "seeing places," we still encounter the complex web of human relationships that complicate justice every time we are told to turn off our cellphones as the lights dim.

Notes

Introduction

1. "15 Life Terms and No Parole for Dahmer," *New York Times*, February 18, 1992. https://www.nytimes.com/1992/02/18/us/15-life-terms-and-no-parole-for-dalmer. Video is available on YouTube: https://www.youtube.com/watch?v=utjj H7vDpi8. Accessed March 21, 2019.

2. For examples, see Jon Elster, *Reason and Rationality*, trans. Steven Randall (Princeton, NJ: Princeton University Press, 2009); T. K. Seung, *Intuition and Construction* (New Haven, CT: Yale University Press, 1993); David Gauthier, *Morals by Agreement* (Oxford: Oxford University Press, 1986); and Mary Gibson, "Rationality," *Philosophy & Public Affairs* 6, no. 3 (1977): 193–225.

3. John Rawls, *A Theory of Justice* (Cambridge, MA: Harvard University Press, 1971), 14.

4. John Locke, *The Two Treatises of Government* (Cambridge: Cambridge University Press, 1988), II.6–12, VII.87.

5. Aristotle, *The Nicomachean Ethics*, trans. H. Rackham (Cambridge, MA: Harvard University Press, 1934), 1144a1–b10, 1098a15–20, 1102b1–03a, 1104a1–15, 1107a1–5, 1139a1–b15, 1177a1–30.

6. Plato, *Republic*, trans. Paul Shorey (Cambridge, MA: Harvard University Press, 1925), 423c–24b, 433a, 331b–38d, 532a–e.

7. For example, Allan Bloom, "Interpretive Essay," in *The Republic of Plato* (New York: Basic Books, 1968), 346–51; Karl Popper, *Open Society and Its Enemies* (Princeton, NJ: Princeton University Press, 1971), esp. chap. 6–9; and David N. McNeill, *An Image of the Soul in Speech* (University Park: Pennsylvania State University Press, 2010), 216–18, 301.

8. Plato, *Republic*, 391d, 401a–e, 475b–78e, 485a–87a, 509a–11a, 595b–608b, 611a–12b.

9. All ancient Greek translations are the author's unless otherwise noted. See Plato, *Republic*, 608b.

10. Plato, *Republic*, 607b. See, for instance, *Laws*, trans. R.G. Bury (Cambridge, MA: Harvard University Press, 1926), 12.967a–d.

11. For example, Plato, *Ion*, trans. Harold North Fowler (Cambridge, MA: Harvard University Press, 1925), 531a–34c; Plato, *Phaedrus*, trans. Harold North Fowler (Cambridge, MA: Harvard University Press, 2005), 244b–45a, 248e; Plato, *The Apology*, trans. Harold North Fowler (Cambridge, MA: Harvard University Press, 2005), 22b–d. For discussion of Plato's critique of poetry see Timothy W. Burns, "Philosophy and Poetry," *American Political Science Review* 109, no. 2 (2015): 326–38; Kalliopi Nikolopoulou, "Plato and Hegel on an Old Quarrel," *Epoché* 13, no. 2 (2009): 249–66; Ramona A. Naddaff, *Exiling the Poets* (Chicago: University of Chicago Press, 2002); Susan B. Levin, *The Ancient Quarrel between Poetry and Philosophy Revisited* (Oxford: Oxford University Press, 2001); Julius A. Elias, *Plato's Defense of Poetry* (Albany: State University of New York Press, 1984); and Walter Kaufmann, *Tragedy and Philosophy* (Princeton, NJ: Princeton University Press, 1968).

12. For examples of this perspective Javier Aguirre, "Téchne and Enthousiasmós in Plato's Critique of Poetry, "*Revista Portuguesa de Filosofia* 72, no. 1 (2016): 181–97; Eric A. Havelock, *Preface to Plato* (Cambridge: Belknap, 1963); and Popper, *Open Society and Its Enemies*.

13. There are numerous poetic quotes (i.e., 328e, 334a–b, 404c, 411b, 501b, 605c) throughout the *Republic*; at 595b, Socrates admits he has a "friendship" with Homer. For discussion Peter J. Ahrensdorf, *Greek Tragedy and Political Philosophy: Rationalism and Religion in Sophocles' Theban Plays* (Cambridge: Cambridge University Press, 2009), 152–53; and Stephen Halliwell, "The Subjection of Muthos to Logos: Plato's Citations of the Poets," *The Classical Quarterly* 50, no. 1 (2000): 94–112.

14. For this interpretation see Leo Strauss, *Persecution and the Art of Writing* (Chicago: University of Chicago Press, 1988); Leon Craig, *The War Lover* (Toronto: University of Toronto Press, 1996); Dorrit Cohn, "The Poetics of Plato's *Republic*: A Modern Perspective," *Philosophy and Literature* 24 (2000): 24–48; and Arlene Saxonhouse, "On Socratic Narrative," *Political Theory* 37, no. 6 (2009): 728–53.

15. For an overview of Platonic myths see Catalin Partenie, *Plato: Selected Myths* (Oxford: Oxford University Press, 2009). For debate, see Julia Annas, "Plato's Myths of Judgement," *Phronesis* 27, no. 2 (1982): 119–43; Charles Segal, "The Myth Was Saved: Reflections on Homer and the Mythology of Plato's *Republic*," *Hermes* 106, no. H.2 (1978): 315–36; and Popper, *Open Society and Its Enemies*, 142–43.

16. For example, Jonathan N. Badger, *Sophocles and the Politics of Tragedy* (New York: Routledge, 2015), 22–23; and Robert L. Fowler, "Mythos and Logos," *Journal of Hellenic Studies* 131 (2011): 62–66.

17. See Levin, *The Ancient Quarrel between Poetry and Philosophy Revisited*; Elliot Bartky, "Plato and the Politics of Aristotle's *Poetics*," *Review of Politics* 54, no. 4 (1992): 589–619; and Leo Strauss, *The Rebirth of Classical Political Rationalism* (Chicago: University of Chicago Press, 1989), esp. 141–90.

18. For this interpretation see Saxonhouse, "On Socratic Narrative," 728–53; Jill Frank, *Poetic Justice: Rereading Plato's Republic* (Chicago: University of Chicago Press, 2018); Rebecca Bensen Cain, *The Socratic Method* (London: Continuum, 2007); Ian Kidd, "Socratic Questions," in *Socratic Questions*, ed. Barry S. Gower and Michael C. Stokes (London: Routledge, 1992), 82–92; Todd S. Mei, "Justice and the Banning of the Poets: The Way of Hermeneutics in Plato's *Republic*," *The Review of Metaphysics* 60, no. 4 (2007): 775–78. See also Marlene K. Sokolon, "Poetic Questions in the Socratic Method," in *The Socratic Method Today*, ed. Lee Trepanier (London: Routledge, 2018), 9–21.

19. Plato, *Republic*, 607e. For another defense of tragedy's philosophy, see Simon Critchley, *Tragedy, The Greeks, and Us* (New York: Pantheon, 2019).

20. For ancient poetic education see Neil T. Croally, "Tragedy's Teaching," in *A Companion to Greek Tragedy*, ed. Justina Gregory (Oxford: Blackwell, 2008), 55–70.

21. Aristophanes, *The Frogs*, trans. Jeffrey Henderson (Cambridge, MA: Harvard University Press, 2002), 970–75. For Euripides's pedagogy see Justina Gregory, *Euripides and the Instruction of the Athenians* (Ann Arbor: University of Michigan Press, 1991), 1–12.

22. Fyfe's translation. Aristotle, *The Poetics*, trans. W. Hamilton Fyfe (Cambridge, MA: Harvard University Press, 1932), 1460b.

23. For example see Georg W. F. Hegel, *Hegel on Tragedy*, ed. Anne Paolucci and Henry Paolucci (Westport, CT: Greenwood, 1962). For examples of recent Sophoclean political thought see Jonathan Strauss, *Private Lives, Public Deaths: Antigone and the Invention of Individuality* (New York: Fordham University Press, 2013); Bonnie Honig, *Antigone Interrupted* (Cambridge: Cambridge University Press, 2013); Ahrensdorf, *Greek Tragedy and Political Philosophy*; Badger, *Sophocles and the Politics of Tragedy*; Michael Vickers, *Sophocles and Alcibiades* (Ithaca, NY: Cornell University Press, 2008). For exceptions to this trend see Elizabeth K. Markovits, *Future Freedoms* (New York: Routledge, 2018); Mark Ringer, *Euripides and the Boundary of the Human* (Lanham, MD: Lexington, 2016); and Victoria Wohl, *Euripides and Politics of Form* (Princeton, NJ: Princeton University Press, 2015).

24. For the seminal critiques see Friedrich Nietzsche, *The Birth of Tragedy*, trans. Walter Kaufmann (New York: Vintage, 1967); A.W. Verrall, *Euripides the Rationalist* (Cambridge: Cambridge University Press, 1895). For discussion of Euripidean formalism and rationality, especially in the formal debates, see Michael Lloyd, *The Agon in Euripides* (Oxford: Clarendon, 1992); Ann Norris

Michelini, *Euripides and the Tragic Tradition* (Madison: University of Wisconsin Press, 1987), 95–116; Matthew Wright, "The Tragedian as Critic: Euripides and Early Greek Poetics," *The Journal of Hellenic Studies* 130 (2010): 165–84; and Richard Buxton, *Persuasion in Greek Tragedy: A Study in Peitho* (Cambridge: Cambridge University Press, 1982), 147–86.

25. As will be developed, the sophists were not a unified school or intellectual movement. This term refers to intellectual thinkers in the fifth century BCE that focused on rhetorical training, questioning traditional values, and developing empirical thinking. Euripides's identity as a sophist has been challenged in recent scholarship, despite many sophistic ideas in his plays. For discussion, see Critchley, *Tragedy, The Greeks, and Us*, 114–19; Mary Lefkowitz, *Euripides and the Gods* (Oxford: Oxford University Press, 2016), 24–48; William Allan, "Tragedy and the Early Greek Philosophic Tradition," in *A Companion to Greek Tragedy*, ed. Justina Gregory (Oxford: Blackwell, 2008), 71–82; John Dillon, "Euripides and the Philosophy of His Time," *Classics Ireland* 11 (2004): 47–73; Desmond J. Conacher, *Euripides and the Sophists* (London: Duckworth, 2003); William Allan, "Euripides and the Sophists," *Illinois Classical Studies* 24/5 (1999–2000): 145–56; and Jacqueline de Romilly, *The Great Sophists in Periclean Athens*, trans. Janet Lloyd (Oxford: Oxford University Press, 1992), 8, 16,144–7.

26. Conacher, *Euripides and the Sophists*, 10. For a contrary argument that posits Euripides as a traditional thinker, see Ringer, *Euripides and the Boundary of the Human*, 1–14, 345–47.

27. For the debate on the development of tragedy and politics, especially with democracy see Peter Wilson, "The Glue of Democracy?," in *Why Athens?*, ed. D. M. Carter (Oxford: Oxford University Press, 2011), 19–44; Peter Burian, "Athenian Tragedy as Democratic Discourse," in *Why Athens?*, ed. D. M. Carter (Oxford: Oxford University Press, 2011), 95–118; Richard Seaford, "The Social Function of Attic Tragedy," *Classical Quarterly* (2000): 30–44; John Gibert, "Greek Drama and Political Thought," in *A Companion to Greek and Roman Political Thought*, ed. Ryan K. Balot (Oxford: Wiley-Blackwell, 2009), 440–55; Malcolm Heath, "Should There Have Been a Polis in Aristotle's *Poetics*?," *Classical Quarterly, New Series* 59, no. 2 (2009): 468–85; D. M. Carter, *The Politics of Greek Tragedy* (Exeter: Bristol Phoenix, 2007); P. J. Rhodes, "Nothing to Do with Democracy," *Journal of Hellenic Studies* 123 (2003): 104–19; Simon Goldhill, "The Great Dionysia and Civic Ideology (Revised)," in *Nothing to Do with Dionysus*, ed. John J. Winkler and Froma I. Zeitlin (Princeton, NJ: Princeton University Press, 1990), 97–129; Paul Cartledge, "Deep Plays: Theatre as Process in Greek Civic Life," in *Cambridge Companion to Greek Tragedy*, ed. P. E. Easterling (Cambridge: Cambridge University Press, 1997), 3–35; Edith Hall, "The Sociology of Athenian Tragedy," in *Cambridge Companions to Greek Tragedy*, ed. P.E. Easterling (Cambridge: Cambridge University Press, 1997), 93–126; and Joshua Ober and Barry Strauss, "Drama, Political Rhetoric, and the Discourse

of Athenian Democracy," in *Nothing to Do with Dionysus*, ed. John J. Winkler and Froma I. Zeitlin (Princeton, NJ: Princeton University Press, 1990), 237–70.

28. For discussion see Wohl, *Euripides and the Politics of Form*; Marc Chou, *Greek Tragedy and Contemporary Democracy* (New York: Bloomsbury Academic, 2012); Robert C. Pirro, *The Politics of Tragedy and Democratic Citizenship* (New York: Continuum International, 2011); and Hal Brands and Charles Edel, *The Lessons of Tragedy: Statecraft and World Order* (New Haven, CT: Yale University Press, 2019).

29. See also Daniel DiLeo, "Tragedy against Tyranny," *Journal of Politics* 75, no. 1 (2013): 254–65; Chou, *Greek Tragedy and Contemporary Democracy*, 115–52.

30. For further information on the development of the Great Dionysia Festival and Theater of Dionysus see Laura Swift, *Greek Tragedy* (London: Bloomsbury, 2016), 1–12; David Kawalko Roselli, *Theater of the People* (Austin: University of Texas Press, 2011); Richard C. Sewell, *In the Theatre of Dionysos* (London: McFarland, 2007), 5–30; David Kovacs, "Introduction to the Series," in *Euripides I*, ed. Jeffrey Henderson (Cambridge, MA: Harvard University Press, 2001), 1–50; Ruby Blondell et al., "Introduction," in *Women on the Edge*, ed. Ruby Blondell et al. (London: Routledge, 1999), 27–44; Rush Rehm, *Greek Tragic Theatre* (London: Routledge, 1992), 3–74; and Bernhard Zimmermann, *Greek Tragedy*, trans. Thomas Marier (Baltimore, MD: Johns Hopkins University Press, 1991), 1–20.

31. For a contrasting view to the Athenocentric tradition of the origin of Greek theater see Edmund Stewart, *Greek Tragedy on the Move: The Birth of a Panhellenic Artform* (Oxford: Oxford University Press, 2017), 9–18, 93–97.

32. For more on the controversial term *tragōdia* see Walter Burkert, "Greek Tragedy and Sacrificial Ritual," *Greek, Roman, and Byzantine Studies* 7, no. 2 (1966): 87–121.

33. Peisistratus also developed the Great Panathenaea festival held every four years as a rival to the more famous Panhellenic games of Olympia. On his use of cultural programs to provide a sense of national unity see Ian C. Storey and Arlene Allan, *A Guide to Ancient Greek Drama* (Oxford: Blackwell, 2005), 15; and H. W. Parke, *Festivals of the Athenians* (Ithaca, NY: Cornell University Press, 1977), 32–33.

34. The remains of such a monument, dedicated to Lysikrates in 334 BCE, can still be seen on Vironos Street in Athens.

35. For discussion of controversial evidence of the audience's composition see Roselli, *Theater of the People*, 63–86; Roger Brock, "Citizens and Non-Citizens in Athenian Tragedy," in *Law and Drama in Ancient Greece*, ed. Edward M. Harris, Delfim F. Leao, and P. J. Rhodes (London: Bloomsbury, 2010), 94–107; Simon Goldhill, "The Audience of Greek Tragedy," in *Cambridge Companion to Greek Tragedy*, ed. P. E. Easterling (Cambridge: Cambridge University Press, 1997), 54–68; Jeffrey Henderson, "Women and the Athenian Dramatic Festivals," *Transactions of the American Philological Association* 121 (1991): 133–47.

36. Plato, *The Symposium*, trans. W. R. M. Lamb (Cambridge, MA: Harvard University Press, 1925), 175e.

37. Plato, *The Gorgias*, trans. W. R. M. Lamb (Cambridge, MA: Harvard University Press, 1925), 502b–d; Plato, *Laws*, 817c.

38. Although the Romans represented the satyrs as half-goat, images from ancient Greece portray them as more human but with a horse tail and long ears. The chapter on the *Alcestis* will focus directly on the significance of satyr plays. See Gilbert Murray, "Introduction," in *Euripides: The Alcestis* (London: George Allen and Unwin, 1915), vii.

39. Similar to its political elements, the relationship of the tragedies to Dionysian religion is very controversial. A key text is the edited volume John J. Winkler and Froma I. Zeitlin, eds., *Nothing to Do with Dionysos?* (Princeton, NJ: Princeton University Press, 1990). For other examples see P. E. Easterling, "A Show for Dionysus," in *Cambridge Companion to Greek Tragedy*, ed. P. E. Easterling (Cambridge: Cambridge University Press, 1997), 36–53; Scott Scullion, "Tragedy and Religion: The Problem of Origins," in *A Companion to Greek Tragedy*, ed. Justina Gregory (Oxford: Blackwell, 2008), 23–37; Christiane Sourvinou-Inwood, *Tragedy and Athenian Religion* (Lanham, MD: Lexington, 2003); William Storm, *After Dionysus* (Ithaca, NY: Cornell University Press, 1998); and Rehm, *Greek Tragic Theatre*, 3–20.

40. One important exception is Euripides's *Bacchae*, which will be examined in detail in chapter 2.

41. C. A. E. Luschnig, "Introduction," in *Euripides: Electra, Phoenician Women, Bacchae, Iphigenia at Aulis*, ed. Cecelia Eaton Luschnig and Paul Woodruff (Indianapolis, IN: Hackett, 2011), xxii.

42. Aristotle, *Poetics*, 1447a, 1448b.

43. For more information on the life of Euripides and the transmission of his texts see David Kawalko Roselli, "Vegetable-Hawking Mom and Fortunate Son: Euripides, Tragic Style, and Reception," *Phoenix* 59, no. 1/2 (2005): 1–49; Storey and Allan, *A Guide to Ancient Greek Drama*, 131–50; Kovacs, "Introduction to the Series," 1–22; Zimmermann, *Greek Tragedy*, 86–89; Shirley A. Barlow, "General Introduction to the Series," in *Phoenician Women*, ed. Elizabeth Craik (Warminster, UK: Aris & Phillips, 1988), 1–20; Donald J. Mastronarde and Jan Maarten Bremer, *The Textual Tradition of Euripides' Phoinissai* (Berkeley: University of California Press, 1983); Mary Lefkowitz, "Euripides' Vita," *Greek, Roman, and Byzantine Studies* 20 (1979): 187–210; Kjeld Matthiessen, "Manuscript Problems in Euripides' Hecuba," *Greek, Roman, and Byzantine Studies* 10, no. 4 (1969): 307–24; Günther Zuntz, *An Inquiry into the Transmission of the Plays of Euripides* (Cambridge: Cambridge University Press, 1965).

44. Aristotle, *The Art of Rhetoric*, trans. J. H. Freese (Cambridge, MA: Harvard University Press, 1926), 1416b.

45. For discussion of tradition that Euripides died in exile see Scott Scullion, "Euripides and Macedon, or the Silence of the Frogs," *The Classical Quarterly*

53, no. 2 (2003): 389–400; Mary Lefkowitz, *The Lives of Ancient Greek Poets* (Baltimore: Johns Hopkins University Press, 2012), 103–104.

46. These were the Athenian war prisoners captured by Syracuse during the disastrous Sicilian Expedition in 415–13 BCE. Plutarch, "Life of Nicias," in *Lives* (Cambridge, MA: Harvard University Press, 1916), 29.2–3.

47. Although Euripides did write a play entitled *Rhesus*, the extant tragedy included in the works of Euripides has been considered spurious since antiquity. For discussion see David Kovacs, "Introduction to the *Rhesus*," in *Rhesus* (Cambridge, MA: Harvard University Press, 2002), 352–53.

48. The ten pedagogical plays include: *Hecuba, Orestes, Phoenician Women, Alcestis, Medea, Hippolytus, Andromache, Trojan Women, Bacchae,* and the likely spurious *Rhesus*.

49. The nine alphabet plays include: *Helen, Electra, Children of Heracles, Hercules, Suppliant Women, Iphigenia in Aulis, Iphigenia among the Taurians, Ion,* and the sole surviving satyr play *Cyclops*.

50. Greek plays were written in the five-foot iambic trimeters. Later in his career, Euripides was more flexible and employed more substitution or "resolution" of this typical metrical pattern. For more information on metrical analysis see Sylvia G. Brown, "Metrical Innovations in Euripides' Later Plays," *The American Journal of Philology* 95, no. 3 (1974): 207–34; E. B. Ceadel, "Resolved Feet in the Trimeters of Euripides and the Chronology of the Plays," *The Classical Quarterly* 35, no. 1/2 (1941): 66–89.

51. As Gregory argues, reducing a play to one theme results in a "flattened picture of Euripides, and there is no question that a concentration upon other elements of his dramaturgy would yield a different result." Gregory, *Euripides and the Instruction of the Athenians*, 9. For a discussion of how tragedy generally resists straightforward interpretation see Karl Heinz Bohrer, Sean Nye, and Rita Felski, "The Tragic: A Question of Art, Not Philosophy of History," *New Literary History* 41, no. 1 (2010): 35–51; Critchley, *Tragedy, the Greeks, and Us*, 1–27.

52. Erich Segal, "Euripides: Poet of Paradox," in *Oxford Readings in Greek Tragedy*, ed. Erich Segal (Oxford: Oxford University Press, 1983), 244.

53. Scholars have long noted the similarity of Euripides's open style, which raises more questions than it answers, to Plato's dialectical approach. See Donald J. Mastronarde, *The Art of Euripides* (Cambridge: Cambridge University Press, 2010), 311; David Sansone, "Plato and Euripides," *Illinois Classical Studies* 21 (1996): 35–57; Francis M. Dunn, *Tragedy's End: Closure and Innovation in Euripidean Drama* (Oxford: Oxford University Press, 1996), 26–44; Martha C. Nussbaum, *The Fragility of Goodness* (Cambridge: Cambridge University Press, 1986), 91; and Günther Zuntz, *The Political Plays of Euripides* (Manchester, UK: Manchester University Press, 1955), 3–18, 51–4.

54. For discussion on the Greek use of *sōros* see Steven Johnstone, *A History of Trust in Ancient Greece* (Chicago: University of Chicago Press, 2011), 1–2, fn 6, 173.

55. Although Aeschylus's *Persians* is a notable exception, tragedies focused on mythological stories. The early tragedian Phrynichus dramatized the Persian destruction in his *Capture of Miletus*, shortly after the fall of that city to the Persians. Apparently, this play so affected the audience, a law might have been passed prohibiting the use of contemporary material in the tragic competition. In contrast, comedy made free use of public figures and current events. See Storey and Allan, *A Guide to Ancient Greek Drama*, 91–92. For discussion of the controversy and development of the concept of myth in ancient Greece, see Fowler, "Mythos and Logos," 45–66.

56. For discussion see Ken Dowden and Niall Livingstone, "Thinking through Myth, Thinking Myth Through," in *A Companion to Greek Mythology*, ed. Ken Dowden and Niall Livingstone (Chichester, UK: Blackwell, 2011), 1–23; Jean Alaux, "Acting Myth: Athenian Drama," in *A Companion to Greek Mythology*, ed. Den Dowden and Niall Livingstone (Chichester, UK: Blackwell, 2011), 141–55; Arlene Saxonhouse, "Another Antigone," *Political Theory* 3, no. 4 (2005): 473; Michelini, *Euripides and the Tragic Tradition*, 86, 185–86; Shirley A. Barlow, *The Imagery of Euripides: A Study in the Dramatic Use of Pictorial Language* (London: Methuen, 1974), 197.

57. Emma Stafford, *Herakles* (London: Routledge, 2012), 24–30.

58. The *Oresteia* refers to Aeschylus's three plays the *Agamemnon*, the *Libation Bearers*, and *Eumenides*. This is the only surviving complete trilogy from the Great Dionysia festival, as Sophocles's Theban plays (*Oedipus Rex*, *Antigone*, and *Oedipus at Colonus*) were produced at different times. The trilogy ends with the establishment of the Athenian court of the Areopagus and taming the Erinyes, the ancient vengeance goddesses. For more on this interpretation see Helen H. Bacon, "The Furies' Homecoming," *Classical Philology* 96, no. 1 (2001): 48–59.

Chapter 1

1. Euripides, *Medea*, trans. David Kovacs (Cambridge, MA: Harvard University Press, 2001), 410–11.

2. This date of performance and other information is found in the Alexandrian scholar Aristophanes of Byzantium's *hypothesis*. For information on textual transmission see David Kovacs, "Text and Transmission," in *A Companion to Greek Tragedy*, ed. Justina Gregory (Malden, MA: Blackwell, 2005), 394–86; and Judith Mossman, "Introduction," in *Euripides' Medea* (Oxford: Aris & Phillips, 2011), 11–14.

3. Thucydides, *The History of the Peloponnesian War*, trans. C. F. Smith (Cambridge, MA: Harvard University Press, 1919), 1.68.1–1.71.7.

4. Mossman suggests a unifying theme of "water" as all the stories revolve around images of the sea. See Mossman, "Introduction," 13.

5. For discussion see David Kovacs, "Introduction to *Medea*," in *Medea* (Cambridge, MA: Harvard University Press, 2001), 277.

6. For examples see Nancy Sorkin Rabinowitz, *Anxiety Veiled: Euripides and the Traffic in Women* (Ithaca, NY: Cornell University Press, 1993), 68–75; Froma I. Zeitlin, *Playing the Other* (Chicago: University of Chicago Press, 1996), 63–64; Sue Blundell, "The Play Explores Social Conflict between Men and Women," in *Readings on Euripides' Medea*, ed. Don Nardo (San Diego, CA: Greenhaven, 2001), 68–75; and Eva Cantarella, "Misogyny in *Medea*," in *Readings on Euripides' Medea*, ed. Don Nardo (San Diego: Greenhaven), 64–67.

7. Emily A. McDermott, *Euripides' Medea: The Incarnation of Disorder* (University Park: Pennsylvania State University Press, 1989), 43–64.

8. For examples, see Bernard Knox, "The *Medea* of Euripides," in *Oxford Readings in Greek Tragedy*, ed. Erich Segal (Oxford: Oxford University Press, 1983), 87–120; Anne Pippin Burnett, *Revenge in Attic and Later Tragedy* (Berkeley: University of California Press, 1998), 192–224; Elizabeth Bongie, "Heroic Elements in the *Medea* of Eurpides," *Transactions of the American Philological Association* 107 (1977): 27–56; Kenneth Reckford, "Medea's First Exit," *Transactions of the American Philological Association* 99 (1968): 329–59; Sue Blundell, *Women in Ancient Greece* (Cambridge, MA: Harvard University Press, 1995), 173–77; G. B. Kerferd, *The Sophistic Movement* (Cambridge: Cambridge University Press, 1981), 161–62; and Markovits, *Future Freedoms*, 108–16.

9. Denys L. Page, "Introduction," in *Euripides' Medea*, ed. Denys L. Page (Oxford: Clarendon, 1938), xiv. For further discussion on the theme and pervasiveness of maternal violence see Lilian Corti, *The Myth of Medea and the Murder of Children* (Westport, CT: Greenwood, 1998), 177–220.

10. For more discussion on the mythology of Medea and Jason, see Emma Griffiths, *Medea* (New York: Routledge, 2006); Ruth Morse, *The Medieval Medea* (Martlesham, UK: D. S. Brewer, 1996), 19–58; Siegfried Melchinger, "The Story Told in *Medea*," in *Readings on Euripides' Medea*, ed. Don Nardo (San Diego, CA: Greenhaven, 2001), 32–39; Karl Kerenyi, *Goddesses of Sun and Moon* (Irving: Spring, 1979), 20–40; Simon Spence, *The Image of Jason in Early Greek Myth* (Seattle, WA: CreateSpace, 2010); and C. A. E. Luschnig, *Granddaughter of the Sun* (Boston: Brill, 2007), 37–62.

11. George Leonard Huxley, *Greek Epic Poetry* (London: Faber, 1969), 40.

12. Jason's panther skin signifies him as a seducer because he has mastered the most cunning of animals. See Henry J. Walker, *Theseus and Athens* (Oxford: Oxford University Press, 1995), 102.

13. These teeth are from the dragon slain by Cadmus in the founding of Thebes. Athena and Ares gave some teeth to Medea's father Aeetes and others to Cadmus, which were sown to become famous Theban Sown Men. See Spence, *The Image of Jason in Early Greek Myth*, 82–84.

14. As will be developed later, this murder also severs her ties to her natal city and home. See, Jan N. Bremmer, "Why Did Medea Kill Her Brother Apsyrtus?," in *Medea: Essays on Medea in Myth, Literature, Philosophy and Art*, ed. James J. Clauss and Sarah Iles Johnston (Princeton, NJ: Princeton University Press, 1997), 83–100.

15. For discussion, see Mossman, "Introduction," 14–15.

16. Except for Alcestis, who is either too young to participate or already married to Admetus. For Alcestis's story of rejuvenation see Euripides, *Alcestis*, trans. David Kovacs (Cambridge, MA: Harvard University Press, 2001), 1075–1160.

17. Theseus is the great Athenian hero who, in Euripides's *Suppliant Women*, agrees to retrieve the bodies of the fallen Argive generals who died at the battle of the Seven against Thebes. Euripides, *The Suppliant Women*, trans. David Kovacs (Cambridge, MA: Harvard University Press, 1998), 380–95,

18. Herodotus, *The Histories*, trans. Robert Strassler (Toronto: Anchor, 2009), 7.61.3. For discussion see Griffiths, *Medea*, 7–10.

19. Jason's ship—the Argo—was thought to be the first Greek sailing vessel. Made with the help of Athena, its prow was fitted with the prophetic or speaking timber of the sacred oak tree of Dodona. See David M. Gaunt, "Argo and the Gods in Apollonius Rhodius," *Greece and Rome* 19, no. 2 (1972): 117–26; and William Hansen, *Classical Mythology* (Oxford: Oxford University Press, 2004), 212.

20. Knox, "Medea of Euripides," 283–86; and Mossman, "Introduction," 9.

21. By contrast, Sophocles apparently stressed her exotic foreignness. For more on Medea as goddess, see Kerenyi, *Goddesses of Sun and Moon*, 20–40; Christian Rogowski, "Mad with Love," in *Madness in Drama*, ed. James Redmond (Cambridge: Cambridge University Press, 1993), 171–73.

22. Hesiod also suggests that Medus is Jason's son and not her son with Aegeus. See Hesiod, *Theogony*, trans. Norman O. Brown (Upper Saddle River, NJ: Prentice Hall, 1953), 993–1002.

23. Homer, *The Odyssey*, trans. A. T. Murray (Cambridge, MA: Harvard University Press, 1995), 10.1–635.

24. Apollodorus, *The Library of Greek Mythology*, trans. Robin Hard (Oxford: Oxford University Press, 2008), 1.9.24.

25. Euripides also connects Hekate with Hecuba. See Euripides, *Hecuba*, trans. David Kovacs (Cambridge, MA: Harvard University Press, 1995), 1265–75.

26. Bengt Ankarloo and Stuart Clark, *Witchcraft and Magic in Europe* (Philadelphia: University of Pennsylvania Press, 1999), 111–13; and Zeitlin, *Playing the Other*, 74–81.

27. Tyro is symbolic of the tension between exogamous and endogamous offspring that causes the dynastic struggles of the Argonautic saga. See Margalit

Finkelberg, *Greek and Pre-Greeks* (Cambridge: Cambridge University Press, 2005), 101–102.

28. It is strange that the chorus can only think of Ino, as there are many examples, such as Agave (who dismembers her son in Euripides's *Bacchae*), Althaea (who kills her son Meleager because he killed her brothers), and Procne who also kills her children to punish a faithless father. See Rick M. Newton, "Ino in Euripides' *Medea*," *American Journal of Philology* 106, no. 4 (1985): 496–502.

29. Lora Holland, "Pas Domos Erroi: Myth and Plot in Euripides' Medea," *Transactions of the American Philological Association* 133 (2003): 255–79.

30. Holland, "Pas Domos Erroi," 270.

31. Euripides, *Medea*, 135–40, 1–2.

32. Kovacs, "Introduction to *Medea*," 278.

33. To allow the vessel through, Athena forced apart the moving rocks that would crush ships. See Apollodorus, *Library of Greek Mythology*, 1.9.22.

34. For the interpretation of the play "as a tragedy of immigration" see Ringer, *Euripides and the Boundary of the Human*, 52.

35. Aristotle, *The Poetics*, 1461b. For discussion see Luschnig, *Granddaughter of the Sun*, 157–77.

36. For discussion see William Allan, *Euripides: Medea*, Duckworth Companions to Greek and Roman Tragedy (London: Duckworth, 2002), 33–34; David Kovacs, "Zeus in Euripides' *Medea*," *American Journal of Philology* 114 (1993): 45–70; and Pavlos Sfyroeras, "The Ironies of Salvation," *Classical Journal* 90 (1994): 125–42.

37. For discussion of "mirrored" scenes as a reversal of the action see Oliver Taplin, *Greek Tragedy in Action*, 2nd ed. (London: Routledge, 2003), 122–39.

38. Medea's ability to enact her plans contrasts with Euripides's Apollo of the *Ion*. In that tragedy, Hermes reveals the prophetic god's plans; however, the events do not unfold as directed, and Athena has to intervene. See, for instance, Euripides, *Ion*, trans. David Kovacs (Cambridge, MA: Harvard University Press, 1999), 50–80, 1550–1650.

39. *Medea*, 1020–80, especially lines 1079–80.

40. Aristotle uses the word *epikhairekakia* to describe the "malicious enjoyment" of another's undeserved suffering. Along with envy and shamelessness, it is always bad (*phaulotētos*). See Aristotle, *Nicomachean Ethics*, 1107a10–15.

41. Schlesinger suggests that Medea, the person, died only to be replaced by Medea the goddess exiting in triumph. Jenkyns similarly notes Medea is her own ex machina. Or, as Raeburn points out, Medea's escape entirely usurps the masculine domain. See Eilhard Schlesinger, "On Euripides' *Medea*," in *Oxford Readings in Greek Tragedy*, ed. Erich Segal (Oxford: Oxford University Press, 1983), 310; Richard Jenkyns, "Medea and the Divided Mind," in *Euripides Talks*, ed. Alan Beale (London: Bristol Classical, 2008), 59–60; and David Raeburn, *Greek Tragedies as Plays for Performance* (Oxford: John Wiley-Blackwell, 2016), 154.

42. Also called the *geranos* (crane) or the *kradē* (branch), the first introduction of the *mēchanē* into theatrical performances is not known. It is also not clear whether it was used in this play. Another possibility is that the *mēchanē* was invented for the *Medea*. If true, this would make Medea's divine escape all the more shocking and unexpected. For discussion see Donald J. Mastronarde, "Actors on High," *Classical Antiquity* 9, no. 2 (1990): 269–72; Rehm, *Greek Tragic Theatre*, 72–73; John Davidson, "Theatrical Production," in *A Companion to Greek Tragedy*, ed. Justina Gregory (Malden, MA: Blackwell, 2005), 201–203; and Graham Ley, *A Short Introduction to the Ancient Greek Theater*, rev. ed. (Chicago: University of Chicago Press, 2006), 20–21.

43. This exact same choral ending is found in five of Euripides's extant plays: *Medea, Helen, Andromache, Bacchae*, and *Alcestis*. For discussion see McDermott, *Euripides' Medea*, 112–13.

44. Pindar mentions Medea's involvement in Pelias's death in the Fourth Pythian Ode. The earliest surviving visual evidence of this event is a black figure vase in the British Museum dated to approximately 520 BCE. See Spence, *Image of Jason in Early Greek Myth*, 112–15; and Allan, *Euripides: Medea*, 21.

45. Allan, 113, fn 55.

46. For further discussion see McDermott, *Euripides' Medea*, 9–24; Donald J. Mastronarde, "Introduction," in *Euripides Medea*, ed. Donald J. Mastronarde (Cambridge: Cambridge University Press, 2006), 57–63; Ann Norris Michelini, "Neophron and Euripides' *Medea*," *Transactions of the American Philological Association* 119 (1989): 115–35; and Mossman, "Introduction," 23–28.

47. Her rejuvenation power also associates Medea with Persephone. As the goddess of the Underworld, Persephone personified the rejuvenation of nature, and her return from the dead marked the beginning of spring. See Hugh Bowden, *Mystery Cults of the Ancient World* (Princeton, NJ: Princeton University Press, 2010), 17–20; and John Pedley, *Sanctuaries and the Sacred in the Ancient Greek World* (Cambridge: Cambridge University Press, 2006), 93–95.

48. In this version, Medea had seven boys and seven girls. Although the Corinthian cult's rites are obscure, there is some indication that seven boys and seven girls would spend a year at the cult site on the Acrocorinthus. See Burkert, "Greek Tragedy and Sacrificial Ritual," 117–9; Sarah Iles Johnston, "Corinthian Medea and the Cult of Akraia," in *Medea: Essays on Medea in Myth, Literature, Philosophy, and Art*, ed. James J. Clauss and Sarah Iles Johnston (Princeton, NJ: Princeton University Press, 1997), 44–70; and McDermott, *Euripides' Medea*, 74–75.

49. The *Medea's hypothesis* suggests the sources for this plagiarism are Dicaearchus's *Life of Greece* and (pseudo) Aristotle's *Hypomnemata*. We have several fragments of Neophron's version, but many scholars think it is a later copy of Euripides's play. See Easterling, "Form and Performance," 151–52; McDermott, *Euripides' Medea*, 21–24; and Martin Cropp, "Lost Tragedies: A Survey," in *A*

Companion to Greek Tragedy, ed. Justina Gregory (Oxford: Blackwell, 2005), 271–92.

50. Kovacs, "Introduction to *Medea*," 277; McDermott, *Euripides' Medea*, 10, 18–20; Mastronarde, "Introduction," 57–63; Mossman, "Introduction," 23–28. See also Anne Pippin Burnett, *Catastrophe Survived* (Oxford: Oxford University Press, 1971), 9–10; and Burkert, "Greek Tragedy and Sacrificial Ritual," 119–20.

51. Another piece of evidence for Euripides's invention of her filicide is the *scholia*'s condemning accusation that Euripides accepted a bribe of five talents from the Corinthians to transfer the blame to Medea. See Mossman, "Introduction," 7, fn 23.

52. McDermott, *Euripides' Medea*, 25.

53. For discussion of the ancient understanding of friends and enemies see Mary Whitlock Blundell, *Helping Friends and Harming Enemies* (Cambridge: Cambridge University Press, 1991), 26–60.

54. In the *Republic*, Polemarchus defines justice as helping friends and harming enemies. Similar to issues in this play, Socrates challenges the underlying identification of friends with virtue and enemies with vice. See Plato, *Republic*, 332a–35b.

55. Aristotle states that the friendship between parents and children is the strongest and most natural. Aristotle, *Nicomachean Ethics*, 1155b15–25. For more on how the murder of children is the ultimate perversion of the ethic, see Allan, *Euripides: Medea*, 98; and McDermott, *Euripides' Medea*, 55–60.

56. Elizabeth S. Belfiore, *Murder among Friends* (Oxford: Oxford University Press, 2000), xv.

57. Aristotle, *Poetics*, 1453a–b.

58. For a discussion of this meaning of "tragic," see Badger, *Sophocles and the Politics of Tragedy*, 20–21.

59. Euripides, *Medea*, 1365,10–20, 205–10, 575–80, 695–700, 70–75.

60. Euripides, *Medea*, 540–45, 84–85, 85–90.

61. There is little surviving evidence of divorce rates or ancient Greek attitudes concerning divorce, but we know Athenian women regularly remarried after divorce, so it may have not been considered particularly problematic. See Roger Just, *Women in Athenian Law and Life* (New York: Routledge, 1991), 40–75.

62. Luschnig, *Granddaughter of the Sun*, 21–22. Medea is not the only granddaughter of Helios abandoned by her Greek hero. In the *Odyssey*, Ariadne (the daughter Pasiphaë) is abandoned on Dia after saving Theseus. See Walker, *Theseus and Athens*, 16–17; and Homer, *Odyssey*, 9.370–780.

63. This argument is based on the law of 451/50 BCE that restricted citizenship to children born of two Athenian parents. Logically, the foreigner Jason could not bear legitimate Corinthian children. To complicate matters, the tragedy may also reflect the Hittite influence of pre-Greek culture in which kingship was derived by marriage through the female line. See Allan, *Euripides:*

Medea, 49; McDermott, *Euripides' Medea*, 45–46; Michael Collier and Georgia Machemer, "Introduction," in *Euripides' Medea*, ed. Michael Collier and Georgia Machemer (Oxford: Oxford University Press, 2006), 22–23; Mark Griffith, "Families and Inter-city Relations," in *Why Athens?*, ed. David M. Carter (Oxford: Oxford University Press, 2011), 206; Finkelberg, *Greek and Pre-Greeks*, 71–79; and Luschnig, *Granddaughter of the Sun*, 21.

64. Euripides, *Medea*, 585, 85–90, 1145–50, 559, 565–75.

65. Even if the male Athenian citizens still sided with Jason's new marriage to a Greek woman, it was shameful for him to exile his sons with their mother. In ancient Athens, children always remained with their father's *oikos*. See David M Schaps, *Economic Rights of Women in Ancient Greece* (Edinburgh: University of Edinburgh Press, 1979), 48–88.

66. *Amathia* (overwhelming insensitivity) seems to be his main character trait. See Raeburn, *Greek Tragedies as Plays for Performance*, 145.

67. Luschnig, *Granddaughter of the Sun*, 21–22.

68. Euripides, *Medea*, 850, 10–15, 1390–95, 230–65, 65–70, and 470–520.

69. Luschnig, *Granddaughter of the Sun*, 23.

70. Luschnig, *Granddaughter of the Sun*, 11–18. See also Rabinowitz, *Anxiety Veiled*, 149.

71. The problem of wives as outsiders is also a central focus of the *Alcestis*. For further discussion see Anne Carson, "Putting Her in Her Place," in *Before Sexuality*, ed. David M. Halperin, John J. Winkler, and Froma I. Zeitlin (Princeton, NJ: Princeton University Press, 1990), 135–36; Richard Seaford, "The Structural Problem of Marriage in Euripides," in *Euripides, Women, and Sexuality*, ed. Anton Powell (London: Routledge, 1990), 152–68; Daniel Mendelsohn, *Gender and the City in Euripides' Political Plays* (Oxford: Oxford University Press, 2002), 140–48.

72. Euripides, *Medea*, 230–65.

73. For further discussion see Margaret Williamson, "A Woman's Place in Euripides' *Medea*," in *Euripides, Women, and Sexuality*, ed. Anton Powell (London: Routledge, 1990), 18; Nancy Sorkin Rabinowitz, *Greek Tragedy* (Oxford: Blackwell, 2008), 149; and Griffith, "Families and Inter-city Relations," 220.

74. For example, see Knox, "The *Medea* of Euripides," 272–93. See also Ruby Blondell, "Medea: Introduction," in *Women on the Edge*, ed. Ruby Blondell, et al. (New York: Routledge, 1999), 162–66.

75. Euripides, *Medea*, 465–520.

76. It also confuses the "meaning" of categories. See Morse, *Medieval Medea*, 31–32.

77. This questioning of traditional categories, such as friend and enemy, was associated with sophistic thinking. Euripides's interest in the imprecision of ethical language is one reason why he was later associated with the sophists. See Conacher, *Euripides and the Sophists*, 10, 29, 42–44; and de Romilly, *Great Sophists in Periclean Athens*, 95–103.

78. Euripides, *Medea*, 695–700, 85–90, 1360.

79. Aristotle, *The Politics*, trans. H. Rackham (Cambridge, MA: Harvard University Press, 1944), 1252a25–30; and Aristotle, *Nicomachean Ethics*, 1155a20–25.

80. McDermott, *Euripides' Medea*, 83–84.

81. Herodotus, as quoted in Paul Cartledge, *The Spartans* (New York: Vintage, 2004), 120. Another Spartan custom was to have their wives bear children for childless friends. See Xenophon, "Constitution," in *Aristotle and Xenophon on Democracy and Oligarchy*, ed. J. M. Moore (Berkeley: University of California Press, 1975), 1, 7–9.

82. Euripides, *Medea*, 1305–30.

83. Knox was talking primarily of Sophocles's heroes. See Knox, "Medea of Euripides," 274.

84. Euripides, *Medea*, 1135, 540, 290–305, 249–50. See also Sophocles, *Ajax*, trans. Hugh Lloyd-Jones (Cambridge, MA: Harvard University Press, 1994), 365–480.

85. Luschnig, *Granddaughter of the Sun*, 33, see also 35.

86. Euripides, *Medea*, 805–10.

87. Thucydides, *History of the Peloponnesian War*, 2.45.2.

88. As McDermott notes, our Creon was imprudent for listening. This contrasts him with Sophocles's Creon in the *Antigone* who was imprudent because did not listen to arguments. See McDermott, *Euripides' Medea*, 100–5.

89. Rabinowitz suggests this highlights the tension between the masculine heroic temper and feminine love for children. In other words, Medea's masculine side wins. See Rabinowitz, *Greek Tragedy*, 150–51.

90. For the interpretation that Medea's struggle is between reason and emotion, see Bruno Snell, *The Discovery of the Mind* (New York: Dover, 1960), 124–9; W. M. Fortenbaugh, "On the Antecedents of Aristotle's Bipartite Psychology," *Greek, Roman, and Byzantine Studies* 11 (1970): 233–50; Julia Annas, *Ancient Philosophy* (Oxford: Oxford University Press, 2000), 1–12; Jenkyns, "Medea and the Divided Mind," 63; H. D. F. Kitto, "The *Medea* of Euripides," in *Medea: Myth and Dramatic Form*, ed. James L. Sanderson and Everett Zimmerman (Boston: Houghton Mifflin Company, 1957), 296–97. As Hall points out, Aristotle in the *Politics* 1260a will use the same root (*bouleu*) to refer to an ability to deliberate (something he also claims lacks authority in women). Incidentally, Medea's name is connected to the verb *mēdomai*, which means "she who plans." See Edith Hall, "Medea and the Mind of a Murderer," in *Unbinding Medea*, ed. Heike Bartel and Anne Simon (London: Routledge, 2010), 22.

91. Helene P. Foley, "Medea's Divided Self," *Classical Antiquity* 8, no. 1 (1989): 244–57; Mossman, "Introduction," 46; and Schlesinger, "On Euripides' *Medea*," 294–97. See also Allan, *Euripides: Medea*, 91–92.

92. This access to the internal life of someone else was an important innovation of the theater, which allows privileged access to what cannot be assessed from external actions or words. See Ruth Padel, "Making Space

Speak," in *Nothing to Do with Dionysos*, ed. John J. Winkler and Froma I. Zeitlin (Princeton, NJ: Princeton University Press, 1990), 340–41; and Sewell, *In the Theatre of Dionysos*, 127.

93. This point does not undo the fact that *thumos* is a problematic choice, only that she was not overcome by passion. For a discussion of the play's presentation of the problematic nature of *thumos*, especially for a city on the brink of war, see Aristide Tessitore, "Euripides' *Medea* and the Problem of Spiritedness," *Review of Politics* 53, no. 4 (1991): 587–601; Rabinowitz, *Greek Tragedy*, 153–54. For a discussion of her deliberate choice, see Christopher Gill, *Personality in Greek Epic, Tragedy, and Philosophy* (Oxford: Oxford University Press, 1996), 154–68.

94. It also represents the potential destruction of what Medea is willing to sacrifice to achieve sovereign selfhood or agency. See Markovits, *Future Freedoms*, 95–110.

95. Griffiths, *Medea*, 72–75; Page DuBois, *Centaurs and Amazons* (Ann Arbor: University of Michigan Press, 1982), 110–24; Williamson, "A Woman's Place in Euripides' *Medea*," 26–28; and Luschnig, *Granddaughter of the Sun*, 35–36.

96. Euripides, *Medea*, 20–30, 50–60, 375–85, 865–925, 15–20.

97. Allan, *Euripides: Medea*, 63. See also Laura McClure, *Spoken Like a Woman* (Princeton, NJ: Princeton University Press, 1999), 27; Markovits, *Future Freedoms*, 95.

98. In some versions of his story, Dionysus was disguised as a girl to save him from Hera. Euripides uses Dionysus's gender liminality in his last play, *The Bacchae*, in the famous cross-dressing scene. See Euripides, *The Bacchae*, trans. David Kovacs (Cambridge, MA: Harvard University Press, 2002), 825–50. See also Jan N. Bremmer, "Transvestite Dionysos," in *Rites of Passage in Ancient Greece: Literature, Religion, Society*, ed. Mark William Padilla (Lewisburg, PA: Bucknell University Press, 1999), 183–200.

99. Euripides, *Medea*, 520–25, 85–90.

100. Mossman, "Introduction," 40–44, also 35. See also Foley, "Medea's Divided Self," 83; Shirley A. Barlow, "Euripides' *Medea*: A Subversive Play," in *Stage Directions*, ed. Allan Griffiths (London: Institute of Classical Studies, 1989), 39; and Luschnig, *Granddaughter of the Sun*, 9–10.

101. McDermott, *Euripides' Medea*, 26–27; and Allan, *Euripides: Medea*, 98.

102. Aristotle understands regimes as held together by a kind of political friendship (*philia*) with timocracies as a relationship among "brothers." See Aristotle, *Nicomachean Ethics*, 1159b25–61b30.

103. Euripides focuses on the story of Athenian autochthony in the *Ion*, which is discussed in chapter 4.

104. Using a quote from a lost Euripidean play, Aristotle thinks we become angrier with those closest to us, which explains why "civil wars are more brutal." See Aristotle, *Art of Rhetoric*, 1379b; and Aristotle, *Politics*, 1328a15–20.

105. For a description of this parallel see Thucydides, *History of the Peloponnesian War*, 2.47.3–2.54.5 and 3.82.1–3.84.3. For discussion see Roger

Brock, *Greek Political Imagery: From Homer to Aristotle* (London: Bloomsbury, 2013), 74–75.

106. Cephalus includes speaking the truth as an aspect of justice in the *Republic*, but it is dropped when his son inherits the argument. See Plato, *Republic*, 331c. For a discussion of the importance of oaths in Greek society see Alan H. Sommerstein, "Introduction," in *Horkos: The Oath in Greek Society*, ed. Alan H. Sommerstein and Judith Fletcher (Bristol, UK: Bristol Phoenix, 2007), 1–6; Joseph Plescia, *The Oath and Perjury in Ancient Athens* (Tallahassee: Florida State University Press, 1970), 15–32, 75–82. For discussion of the significance of oath making in the *Medea*, see Mossman, "Introduction," 41–43. Kovacs, "Zeus in Euripides' *Medea*," 59–60; Burnett, *Revenge in Attic and Later Tragedy*, 196–205; and Ernest Heinrich Klotsche, *The Supernatural in the Tragedies of Euripides* (Lancaster, UK: New Era Printing, 1919), 8–14.

107. Burnett, *Revenge in Attic and Later Tragedy*, 201.

108. Fiona McHardy, *Revenge in Athenian Culture* (London: Duckworth, 2008), 7–8, 119–20.

109. Kerenyi, *Goddesses of Sun and Moon*, 21.

110. Euripides, *Medea*, 20–25, 435–40, 90–95.

111. Mossman, "Introduction," 228; Plescia, *Oath and Perjury in Ancient Athens*, 15–32, 75–82.

112. As noted previously, divorced women normally returned to their natal family and often remarried. For further discussion of the uniqueness of Medea's situation see Williamson, "A Woman's Place in Euripides' *Medea*," 18–22; Collier and Machemer, "Introduction," 29; and Blondell, "Medea," 160–62.

113. Just, *Women in Athenian Law and Life*, 40–75.

114. For further discussion of the status of their marriage see Douglas M. MacDowell, *The Law in Classical Athens* (Ithaca, NY: Cornell University Press, 1986), 67; Allan, *Euripides: Medea*, 60–61; Burnett, *Revenge in Attic and Later Tragedy*, 195, fn 11.

115. Blondell, "Medea," 161.

116. Euripides, *Medea*, 710–60.

117. For a discussion of the economic and political significance of trust and distrust in Athens, see Johnstone, *A History of Trust in Ancient Greece*.

118. Euripides, *Medea*, 820–35, 1371.

119. Zeus also sends the Erinyes as avenging spirits against those who commit kin murder, such as Medea does. Euripides deals more extensively with the Erinyes in his *Electra* discussed in chapter 9. At the end of this play, Jason also says the children will transform into spirits of vengeance to punish her crime. See Euripides, *Medea*, 1370–75.

120. Euripides, *Medea*, 760–810, 110–15.

121. Griffiths, *Medea*, 76.

122. Holland, "Pas Domos Erroi," 270–272.

123. Burnett, *Revenge in Attic and Later Tragedy*, 200.

124. Euripides, *Medea*, 165, 690–95, 795–800, 10–15, 1370–75.

125. A similar moral impasse is the focus of Euripides's *Electra*, which ends with the Dioscuri declaring Orestes's action just but not just. See *Electra*, trans. David Kovacs (Cambridge. MA: Harvard University Press, 1998), 1245–50. Whether justice and piety are the same thing is also at the core of Socrates's debate with Protagoras; see Plato, *Protagoras*, trans. W. R. M. Lamb (Cambridge, MA: Harvard University Press, 1924), 325a–34c.

126. McHardy, *Revenge in Athenian Culture*, 61–64, 119–20; and Eva Cantarella, "Private Justice and Public Justice," *Punishment and Society* 3, no. 4 (2001): 273–83.

127. Homer, *The Iliad*, trans. A. T. Murray (Cambridge, MA: Harvard University Press, 1996), 18.560–710.

128. See also Bongie, "Heroic Elements in the *Medea* of Eurpides," 41.

129. Euripides, *Medea*, 1369.

130. For a more discussion of Hekate's rejuvenation power or embodiment of the three *chthonic* phases of womanhood see Griffiths, *Medea*, 45–46; R. Gordon Wasson, Albert Hofmann, and Carl A. Ruck, *The Road to Eleusis*, 30th Anniversary Edition ed. (Berkeley, CA: North Atlantic, 2008), 54.

131. In *Alcestis*, Heracles wins a wrestling match with Death and returns Alcestis to the world of the living. In another miraculous rejuvenation, in the *Children of Heracles*, the aged Iolaus is rejuvenated to his prime by the now divine Heracles and his latest wife Hēbē, the goddess of youth. See Euripides, *Alcestis*, 1125–55; and Euripides, *The Children of Heracles*, trans. David Kovacs (Cambridge, MA: Harvard University Press, 1995), 840–65.

132. Martha C. Nussbaum, *Anger and Forgiveness* (Oxford: Oxford University Press, 2016), 4–5, 76, 92–93, 123.

133. In Seneca's play on the same theme, this point is made more obvious by having Medea actually announce, at line 984, that with the death of her children her virginity has been restored. As quoted in Mossman, "Introduction," 56.

134. Burnett, *Revenge in Attic and Later Tragedy*, 207.

135. Euripides, *Medea*, 1–5, 1410–15, 410–11.

136. For more discussion of the reversals as a challenge of "civilized" norms see John Ferguson, "The Play Is Structured around Scenes of Confrontation," in *Readings on Euripides' Medea*, ed. Don Nardo (San Diego, CA: Greenhaven, 2001), 40–45; and Pietro Pucci, *Euripides' Revolution under Cover* (Ithaca, NY: Cornell University Press, 2016), 26–30.

137. Euripides, *Medea*, 520. Burns suggests that such bitterness continues because we still idealize a patriarchal and procreative ideal family. See Angela J. Burns, "A Thoroughly Modern Medea," in *Unbinding Medea*, ed. Heike Bartel and Anne Simon (New York: Routledge, 2010), 263–82.

138. Sanderijn Cels, "Interpreting Political Apologies: The Neglected Role of Performance," *Political Psychology* 36, no. 3 (2015): 352.

139. As quoted in Lisa Blomgren Amsler, Janet K. Martinez, and Stephanie E. Smith, *Dispute System Design* (Stanford, CA: Stanford University Press, 2020), 259.

140. Nussbaum, *Anger and Forgiveness*, 24, 10–13, 31.

Chapter 2

1. Euripides, *Bacchae*, 330–35.

2. Robert Emmet Meagher, *The Essential Euripides: Dancing in Dark Times* (Wauconda, IL: Bolchazy-Carducci, 2002), 554.

3. The information on the *Bacchae* comes from the *scholia* in the manuscript, and its late date in Euripides's career is supported by metrical analysis. For discussion, see Sophie Mills, *Euripides: Bacchae* (London: Duckworth, 2006), 7–20; Andrew Darby, *Bacchus* (London: British Museum, 2003), 138–39; and Richard Seaford, "Introduction," in *Euripides' Bacchae* ed. Richard Seaford (Warminster, UK: Aris & Phillips, 1997), 25.

4. As noted in the introduction, although there is no evidence that Euripides associated with the sophists, his plays often concern many of their radical ideas and concerns. For discussion see Conacher, *Euripides and the Sophists*.

5. See Lefkowitz, "Euripides' Vita," 87–103.

6. Damen and Richards argue that the play itself represents the birth of theatrical performance similar to the Homeric *Hymn to Hermes* as foundation for the lyre. Significantly for us, it is the only surviving play about Dionysus as a principal character; see Mark L. Damen and Rebecca A. Richards, "Sing the Song of Dionysus," *American Journal of Philology* 133, no. 3 (2012): 366–67; Luschnig, "Introduction," xxii; Jean-Pierre Vernant, "The Masked Dionysus," in *Myth and Tragedy in Ancient Greece*, ed. Jean-Pierre Vernant and Pierre Vidal-Naquet (New York: Zone, 1990), 381–82.

7. For an overview of the extensive interpretative tradition, see Sophie Mills, *Euripides: Bacchae* (London: Duckworth, 2006), 80–102.

8. This interpretation relies on a straightforward reading of Nietzsche's *The Birth of Tragedy*. For examples and debate concerning this interpretation see E. R. Dodds, "Euripides the Irrationalist," *Classics Review* 43, no. 2 (1929): 97–104; Verrall, *Euripides the Rationalist*; Hans Diller, "Euripides' Final Phase: The *Bacchae*," in *Oxford Readings in Greek Tragedy*, ed. Erich Segal (Oxford: Oxford University Press, 1983), 357–69.

9. For an overview of this long-standing interpretation that Euripides was irreligious see Gilbert Norwood, *The Riddle of the Bacchae* (Manchester, UK: Manchester University Press, 1908), 1–17; Mary Lefkowitz, "Impiety and Atheism in Euripides' Dramas," *Classical Quarterly* 39, no. 1 (1989): 70–82. For his change of heart see William Arrowsmith, "Introduction," in *Euripides V*, eds.

David Grene and Richmond Lattimore (Chicago: University of Chicago Press, 1959), 142–53; and Gilbert Norwood, *Essays in Tragedy* (Toronto: University of Toronto Press, 1954), 52–73.

10. Nancy Evans, *Civic Rites* (Berkeley: University of California Press, 2010), 199. Another alternative is that the tragedy exposes the consequences of failing to regulate intergenerational claims. See Matthew Shipton, *The Politics of Youth in Greek Tragedy: Gangs of Athens* (London: Bloomsbury Academic, 2018), 77–93.

11. See Charles Segal, *Dionysiac Poetics and Euripides' Bacchae* (Princeton, NJ: Princeton University Press, 1997), 7–26; Chiara Thumiger, "Animal World, Animal Representation, and the Hunting Model," *Phoenix* 60, no. 3/4 (2006): 191–210; and Arlene Saxonhouse, "Freedom, Form and Formlessness," *American Political Science Review* 108, no. 1 (2014): 88–99.

12. As Meagher poetically notes, the attempt to explain the fluid and elusive *Bacchae* is akin to trying to "pin it to a board like a butterfly spread for labeling." See Meagher, *Essential Euripides*, 534.

13. For more details on the complex myth of Dionysus see Seaford, "Introduction," 1–17; Andrew Darby, *Bacchus* (London: British Museum, 2003), 1–51, 119–31; and Bowden, *Mystery Cults of the Ancient World*, 105–36.

14. The founding of Thebes and the Sown Men is significant also in Euripides's *Phoenician Women*, which focuses on the war between Oedipus's sons Eteocles and Polynices. See Euripides, *Phoenician Women*, trans. David Kovacs (Cambridge, MA: Harvard University Press, 2002), 1–30, 635–90, 815–950.

15. The "di" in Dionysus's name indicates a "doubling," which is also found in his cult hymns of the dithyrambs and the "double birth" of initiates into his cult. See Armand D'Angour, *The Greeks and the New* (Cambridge: Cambridge University Press, 2011), 139–40.

16. Pausanias, *Guide to Greece 1: Central Greece*, trans. Peter Levy (New York: Penguin Classics, 1979), IX.12.1–4.

17. Ino is one of the only filicides the chorus can bring to mind in the *Medea*. See Euripides, *Medea*, 1280–90. For discussion see Newton, "Ino in Euripides' *Medea*," 496–502.

18. In some versions, Persephone was also abducted on Mount Nysa while gathering the *narkissos* flowers. The ending—issos—indicates the potential archaic source of these stories as it is derived from the pre-Greek language prior to the Indo-European migrations. See Wasson, Hofmann, and Ruck, *Road to Eleusis*, 48–49.

19. Homer, *Odyssey*, 11.320–25.

20. Although Dionysus is understood as a "new god" imported from the East, his name appears in Linear B tablets from around 1200 BCE. This means he was worshiped in Greece as long as other Olympians, so his "newness" is not a literal or historical late introduction. It may be psychologically easier, as Evans suggests, to approach this formless god as if he were from "someplace else." See

Mills, *Euripides: Bacchae*, 22; Evans, *Civic Rites*, 174–75; Luschnig, "Introduction," xxiii; Barbara Graziosi, *The Gods of Olympus* (New York: Picador, 2014), 20.

21. Mills, *Euripides: Bacchae*, 22–23; Marcel Detienne, *Dionysos at Large*, trans. A. Goldhammer (Cambridge, MA: Harvard University Press, 1989), 9–12.

22. Apollo's oracle at Delphi was active nine months a year. When Apollo was absent during the winter months, Dionysus was thought to inhabit Delphi and his secret rites were performed in the hills around the Korykian Cave. William J. Broad, *The Oracle* (New York: Penguin, 2006), 41–44; and Mills, *Euripides: Bacchae*, 33.

23. Darby, *Bacchus*, 123. For more discussion on the details of Dionysian worship see Charles Segal, "The Raw and the Cooked in Greek Literature: Structure, Values, Metaphor," *Classical Journal* 69, no. 4 (1974): 301.

24. The actor wore a mask of a man but in the end appears as "himself" in the mask of Dionysus. The actor is, of course, never himself but disguised as another. In this way, the *Bacchae* is a tragedy about tragedy or about a blurring of illusion and reality. See Luschnig, "Introduction," xxiii–xxvi; and Sewell, *In the Theatre of Dionysos*, 24.

25. There is significant disagreement as to whether cult practices in *The Bacchae* represented ritual, such as the ripping apart of sacrificial animals (*sparagmos*) and eating raw meat (*ōmophagia*), which is atypical of known ritual practices. As they were likely restricted to women, it is not clear if Euripides could have had accurate information. What we know of Dionysian cult practices is speculative and based on painted representations on pottery and on the much later Roman friezes of the Villa of Mysteries in Pompeii. See E. R. Dodds, "Introduction," in *Euripides' Bacchae*, ed. E. R. Dodds (Oxford: Clarendon, 1960), xi–lix; Walter Burkert, *Ancient Mystery Cults* (Cambridge, MA: Harvard University Press, 1987), 33, 78–79; Dirk Obbink, "Dionysus Poured Out," in *Masks of Dionysus*, ed. Thomas H. Carpenter and Christopher A. Faraone (Ithaca, NY: Cornell University Press, 1993), 65–86; Charles Segal, "Female Mourning and Dionysiac Lament in Euripides' *Bacchae*," in *Orchestra*, ed. Anton Bierl and Peter von Möllendorff (Wiesbaden, Germany: Springer, 1994), 12–18; Seaford, "Introduction," 25–54; *The Villa of Mysteries in Pompeii* (Pompeii: Edizioni Spano, 2001); Barbara Goff, *Citizen Bacchae* (Berkeley: University of California Press, 2004), 374–87; Bowden, *Mystery Cults of the Ancient World*, 121–24.

26. For more discussion on festivals to Dionysus see Parke, *Festivals of the Athenians*, 77–80, 106–20; Walker, *Theseus and Athens*, 99–101; Mills, *Euripides: Bacchae*, 20–25; Bowden, *Mystery Cults of the Ancient World*, 121–30; and Evans, *Civic Rites*, 170–207.

27. Although most festivals, including the Lenaea (which is an alternative name for the Bacchae) included "secret ceremonies," there is no evidence the Great Dionysia incorporated such rites. See Seaford, "Introduction," 39.

28. Euripides, *Bacchae*, 235–40, 300–85.

29. In the *Republic*, Plato suggests justice in the city in speech requires the "noble lies" (*gennaion pseudōn*) of the myth of metals. See Plato, *Republic*, 414b.

30. Actaeon was the son of Pentheus's aunt Autonoë. For discussion of the myth of Actaeon see John Heath, *Actaeon, the Unmannerly Intruder* (New York: Peter Lang, 1993).

31. This ode is controversial. It may be evidence that the god reserves his anger only for clever men; in contrast, it could symbolize the male "fantasy" of an idealized eroticism. See Herbert Musurillo, "Euripides and Dionysiac Piety: *Bacchae* 370–433," *Transactions and Proceedings of the American Philological Association* 97 (1966): 308; and Laura Swift, "The Symbolism of Space in Euripidean Choral Fantasy," *Classical Quarterly* 59, no. 2 (2009): 364–65, 382.

32. This escape may allude to the temple of Dionysus Liberator located in Thebes near its theater. See Seaford, "Introduction," 38.

33. The question of "who one is" connects this tragedy to Euripides's *Ion*, which also focuses on the problem of "knowing oneself." See Euripides, *Ion*, 1550–1620. Similarly, it is the first question of the *Gorgias*, in which Socrates has Chaerephon ask Gorgias: "Who is he?" See Plato, *Gorgias*, 447c.

34. Euripides, *Bacchae*, 810. The Greek word, *idea*, which can mean the appearance, form, or "look" of something is one of the terms (along with the related *eidos*) Plato uses to describe his theory of the forms (*idea*). See Plato, *Republic*, 505a–11d.

35. Euripides, *Bacchae*, 860–75, 890–900, 920–30, 945–50, 970–75. Segal argues that Dionysus has become the director of a "play within a play," as he dresses up characters and controls the action. See Segal, *Dionysiac Poetics and Euripides' Bacchae*, 225–34.

36. Although especially significant in this play, doubling is typical in tragedy, which is a world that both is and is not there. For discussion see Padel, "Making Space Speak," 354–55.

37. For discussion of tragedy as symbolic of the transition rites into manhood, see John J. Winkler, "The Ephebes's Song: *Tragoidia* and *Polis*," in *Nothing to Do with Dionysos?*, ed. John J. Winkler and Froma I. Zeitlin (Princeton, NJ: Princeton University Press, 1990), 20–62.

38. Euripides, *Bacchae*, 990–1010, 1040, 1045–65.

39. Aristotle calls this enjoyment of another's suffering *epikhairekakia*. Along with envy and shamelessness, he considers it always a negative emotion. See Aristotle, *Nicomachean Ethics*, 1107a10–15.

40. With obvious phallic symbolism, this tree may represent a giant *thyrsus* or erection symbolic of Dionysus's powers of fertility. Conversely, the phallic emblem may represent a symbolic gestation with Pentheus as a sacrificial surrogate. For more discussion see Christine M. Kalke, "The Making of a Thyrsus," *American Journal of Philology* 106 (1985): 409–26; and Wasson, Hofmann, and Ruck, *The Road to Eleusis*, 130–31. For a discussion of what might have occurred on stage

see Victor Castellani, "The Troubled House of Pentheus in Euripides' *Bacchae*," *Transactions and Proceedings of the American Philological Association* 106 (1976): 61–83; and Mary Stieber, "The Wheel Simile in the *Bacchae*, Another Turn," *Mnemosyne* 59, no. 4 (2006): 585–95.

41. For discussion of the so-called psychoanalysis scene see William Sale, *Existentialism and Euripides* (Berwick, UK: Aureal, 1977), 80–123.

42. All copies of *The Bacchae* come from a damaged medieval manuscript. Speculative reconstructions use the twelfth-century *Christus Patiens*, which was based on a complete text. Nussbaum includes it in her analysis of the play as a representation of grief over lost unity. For a discussion, see Richard Seaford, "Introduction," 52–54; and C. W. Willink, "On the Transmission of the *Bacchae*," *Classical Quarterly* 16, no. 2 (1966): 347. See also Martha C. Nussbaum, "Introduction," in *The Bacchae of Euripides* (New York: Noonday, 1990), 1–38.

43. This play never mentions Cadmus's son Polydorus, whose great-grandson Oedipus has his own famous tragedy.

44. The exact same ending is also found in Euripides's plays *Alcestis*, *Andromache*, *Medea*, and *Helen*. See Dodds, "Introduction," 242.

45. For Dionysus's mythology of rejection and retaliation, see P. McGinty, "Dionysos's Revenge and the Validation of the Hellenic World-View," *Harvard Theological Review* 71, no. 1–2 (1978): 77–94; Seaford, "Introduction," 25–26; Mills, *Euripides: Bacchae*, 32–36; Darby, *Bacchus*, 65–70, 118–20; Zeitlin, *Playing the Other*, 180–83; and Jennifer R. March, "Euripides' *Bacchae*: A Reconsideration in Light of Vase Paintings," *Bulletin of the Institute of Classical Studies* 36, no. 2 (1989): 33–65.

46. As Seaford points out, kin murder or cross-dressing are traditional themes, so it is also possible Euripides incorporates elements of a common or widespread story. The fifth-century iconography also depicts, in all but two examples, Dionysus as older with a beard. See Seaford, "Introduction," 27, fn 16; Thomas H. Carpenter, "On the Beardless Dionysus," in *Masks of Dionysus*, ed. Thomas H. Carpenter and Christopher A. Faraone (Ithaca, NY: Cornell University Press, 1993), 185–206. These potential innovations are pointed out by Mills, *Euripides: Bacchae*, 35–37; March, "Euripides' *Bacchae*," 33–65.

47. Ovid, *Metamorphoses*, trans. Rolfe Humphries (Bloomington: Indiana University Press, 1955), IV.563–603.

48. J. Peter Euben, *The Tragedy of Political Theory* (Princeton, NJ: Princeton University Press, 1990), 130.

49. The *Oresteia* tells the story of Agamemnon's homecoming, his death at the hands of his wife Clytemnestra, and her death at the hands of their children Electra and Orestes. The final play, the *Eumenides*, is often interpreted as representing the triumph of rationality and judicial institutions over vengeance and revenge cycles. See Aeschylus, *The Eumenides*, trans. Hugh Lloyd-Jones (Cambridge, MA: Harvard University Press, 1960), 700–900. See H. D. F. Kitto,

Greek Tragedy: A Literary Study, 3rd ed. (New York: Barnes and Noble, 1961), 64–95; Keith J. Dover, "The Political Aspect of Aeschylus' *Eumenides*," *Journal of Hellenic Studies* 77 (1957): 230–37; and Simon Goldhill, *Reading Greek Tragedy* (Cambridge: Cambridge University Press, 1986), 38–41.

50. Raeburn, *Greek Tragedies as Plays for Performance*, 175.

51. Euripides, *Bacchae*, 990–1015, 1340–45, 970–75, 45–50.

52. Aristotle suggests justice as merit, for example, involves taking the proper amount or measure (*isos*) of good and bad things. See Aristotle, *Nicomachean Ethics*, 1129a–30b15.

53. Plato discusses this idea of whether the virtues, such as piety and justice, are the same thing or whether one can be impious but still just in the *Protagoras*. See Plato, *Protagoras*, 329d–34d.

54. Chiara Thumiger, *Hidden Paths: Self and Characterization in Greek Tragedy* (London: Institute of Classical Studies, 2007), 11–18; and Richard Seaford, *Tragedy, Ritual and Money in Ancient Greece* (Cambridge: Cambridge University Press), 178–81.

55. Euripides, *Bacchae*, 305–15, 890–905.

56. Euripides, 385–90, 264–80, 330–35, 440–45. Vickers suggests a political dualism by arguing Euripides is reflecting factional strife with Pentheus as a stand-in for the Critias, a leader of the Thirty Tyrants, and Dionysus as an Alcibiades in his ability to captivate and alter his appearance. See Vickers, *Sophocles and Alcibiades*, 104–14.

57. In the *Rhetoric*, for example, Aristotle describes young men as prone to loving honor, irascible, overconfident, and more powerless (*akrateis*) in controlling sexual desires; whereas old men are fearful, fond of life, and shameless. Some scholars see this contrast further highlighted in the almost comic attempt of the old men to find vigor in Dionysus's new festivities. See Thomas M. Falkner, *The Poetics of Old Age in Greek Epic, Lyric, and Tragedy* (Norman: University of Oklahoma Press, 1995), 185–90; and Aristotle, *Art of Rhetoric*, 1388b–1391a.

58. Euripides, *Bacchae*, 665–70, 340–45, 775–80, 505–10, 305–15. Foucault reads this passage very differently. Since he allows the messenger to speak, Foucault argues that Pentheus agrees to a "parrhesiastic contract" and, in doing so, is a "wise king." For discussion see Michel Foucault, *Fearless Speech* (Los Angeles: Semiotext[e], 2001), 31–33; Kalliopi Nikolopoulou, "Parrhesia as Tragic Structure in Euripides' *Bacchae*," *Epoche* 15, no. 2 (2011): 249–61. For comparison to the messenger speech see Sophocles, *Antigone*, trans. Hugh Lloyd-Jones (Cambridge, MA: Harvard University Press, 1994), 240–525.

59. Seaford, "Introduction," 47–48; Nussbaum, "Introduction," 20; Dodds, "Introduction," i–lix.

60. Saxonhouse, "Freedom, Form and Formlessness," 89–94. For further discussion see Segal, *Dionysiac Poetics and Euripides' Bacchae*, 27–150; Charles Segal, "Euripides' Bacchae: Conflict and Mediation," *Ramus* 6 (1961): 103–20; Charles

Segal "The Menace of Dionysus," *Arethusa* 1 (1978): 185–203; Felix Martin Wassermann, "Man and God in the *Bacchae* and in the *Oedipus at Colonus*," in *Studies Presented to D. M. Robertson*, ed. G. E. Mylonas (St. Louis: Washington University Press, 1953), 559–69; Adam B. Seligman and Robert P. Weller, *Rethinking Pluralism* (Oxford: Oxford University Press, 2012), 39–51; and Thumiger, "Animal World, Animal Representation, and the Hunting Model," 205–8.

61. Euripides, *Bacchae*, 215–50, 450–55, 495–500, 650–55, 805–10.

62. Saxonhouse, "Freedom, Form and Formlessness," 90. For more discussion on the language of Pentheus and Dionysus see Thumiger, "Animal World, Animal Representation, and the Hunting Model," 205–8; Charles Segal, *Interpreting Greek Tragedy* (Ithaca, NY: Cornell University Press, 1986), 308–10.

63. Euripides, *Bacchae*, 675–775, 650–55.

64. See, for instance, the golden age of Hesiod, *Works and Days*, trans. David Tandy and Walter C. Neale (Berkeley: University of California Press, 2008), 90–150. For a discussion of the Greek preoccupation of defining "what is civilized" see Segal, "Raw and the Cooked in Greek Literature," 298–308.

65. Thumiger, "Animal World, Animal Representation, and the Hunting Model," fn 45, 204.

66. Euripides, *Bacchae*, 20–60, 230–40, 450–60.

67. On this aspect of Dionysus see Michael Jameson, "The Asexuality of Dionysus," in *Masks of Dionysus*, ed. Thomas H. Carpenter and Chirstopher A. Faraone (Ithaca, NY: Cornell University Press, 1993), 44–64.

68. In Soyinka's version of *The Bacchae*, he envisions this civilization-nature dichotomy as culminating in a barbaric banquet as a way of "re-affirming man's indebtedness to the earth." See Wole Soyinka, "Introduction," in *The Bacchae of Euripides* (New York: W. W. Norton, 1973), x–xi.

69. Euripides, *Bacchae*, see 280–85, 445–50, 495, 505, 645–55, 600–605; Segal, *Interpreting Greek Tragedy*, 308–10; Thumiger, "Animal World, Animal Representation and the Hunting Model," 206–10; and Valdis Leinieks, *The City of Dionysus* (Stuttgart, Germany: Teubner, 1996), 300–25.

70. For more on the twinning of Demeter and Dionysus, see Robert Parker, *On Greek Religion* (Ithaca, NY: Cornell University Press, 2011), 250–52.

71. Segal, *Dionysiac Poetics and Euripides' Bacchae*, 8–26. Podlecki suggests an additional dichotomy between the individual and community, especially as an individual always is an "outsider" or "outside" a group. See Anthony J. Podlecki, "Individual and Group in Euripides' *Bacchae*," *L'antiquité classique* 43 (1974): 143–65.

72. Euripides, *Bacchae*, 185–90, 245–50, 260–65. Although his worshipers are predominately women, Cadmus and Teiresias leave to worship him on the mountain; however, since Cadmus only hears of Pentheus's murder after returning to the city, the male rites appear to be separate from the female. See Nussbaum, "Introduction," 25–26.

73. As a divine figure Dionysus represented the power of sexuality in human life both as a generating but also destructive force. See Wendy Berg and Mike Harris, *Polarity Magic* (St. Paul, MN: Llewellyn, 2003), 276–77.

74. Cephalus quotes the tragedian Sophocles as his authority on how the elderly escape from the tyrannical pleasures of sexuality. See Plato, *Republic*, 328c–29e. In a similar defiance of old age, Euripides miraculously has the elderly Iolaus rejuvenated in battle. See Euripides, *Children of Heracles*, 680–745, 840–70.

75. A great deal has been written about gender and the blurring of male and female in this play. For a sample see Goff, *Citizen Bacchae*, xxv–xxvi; Olga Taxidou, *Tragedy, Modernity, and Mourning* (Edinburgh: University of Edinburgh Press, 2004), 159–92; Segal, *Dionysiac Poetics and Euripides' Bacchae*, 31–77; Allison Hersh, "How Sweet the Kill," *Modern Drama* 35, no. 3 (1992): 409–23; Zeitlin, *Playing the Other*, 341–43; and Luschnig, "Introduction," xxv–xxix.

76. Euripides, *Bacchae*, 710–80, 300–305. At first, the women are described as *eukosmios*—or "in good order" (693) rather than frenzied. For discussion see Barbara Gold, "Eukosmia in Euripides' *Bacchae*," *American Journal of Philology* 98, no. 1 (1977): 3–15.

77. See Saxonhouse, "Freedom, Form and Formlessness," 91. See also Thumiger, "Animal World, Animal Representation, and the Hunting Model," 194.

78. Arrowsmith's translation. Euripides, "The Bacchae," in *Euripides V*, eds. David Grene and Richmond Lattimore (Chicago: University of Chicago Press, 1959), 760–65.

79. Homer, *Iliad*, IV.530–40.

80. Angry that Odysseus was chosen to inherit Achilles's armor, Ajax intended to kill his Greek allies; instead, driven mad by Athena, he mistook Apollo's sacred cattle for his companions and slaughtered them. When he came to his senses (much like Agave in this play), he commits suicide. See Sophocles, *Ajax*, 201–690.

81. Much has also been written on the topic of cross-dressing; see Zeitlin, *Playing the Other*, 341–65; Eric Csapo, "Riding the Phallus for Dionysus: Iconology, Ritual, and Gender-Role De/Construction," *Phoenix* 51, no. 3/4 (1997): 253–95; Bremmer, "Transvestite Dionysos," 322–25; and Robert Parker, *Polytheism and Society at Athens* (Oxford: Oxford University Press, 2005), 206–7, 323.

82. Euripides, *Bacchae*, 820–45, 910–65, 850–55, 315–20, 995–1005.

83. This self-concealment also draws attention to the tragedy as a "play in a play." See Froma I. Zeitlin, "Playing the Other: Theater, Theatricality, and the Feminine in Greek Drama," in *Nothing to Do with Dionysos?*, ed. John J. Winkler and Froma I. Zeitlin (Princeton, NJ: Princeton University Press, 1990), 83.

84. Segal, *Interpreting Greek Tragedy*, 308–309.

85. Thomas G. Rosenmeyer, "Tragedy and Religion: The Bacchae," in *Oxford Readings in Greek Tragedy*, ed. Erich Segal (Oxford: Oxford University Press, 1983), 385.

86. As noted in the play, Pentheus's name is related to the noun *penthos* or verb *pentheō*, which means grief, sorrow, misfortune. See Luschnig, "Introduction," xxvii.

87. Although this punishment affects the city, it appears to be restricted to the royal family. See Leona MacLeod, "Marauding Maenads: The First Messenger Speech in the *Bacchae*," *Mnemosyne* 59, no. 4 (2006): 582–83.

88. Aristotle suggests something similar in the *Rhetoric* in his discussion of indignation: "Ancient things appear nearly something by nature." Aristotle, *The Art of Rhetoric*, 1387a.

89. Euripides, *Bacchae*, 360–430, 1240–1400, 34–45, 195.

90. As Vernant states, no other play is so obsessively repetitive with words indicating seeing and visibility. See Vernant, "The Masked Dionysus," 393–94.

91. A *paradochia* is something that has been handed down or received. See Euripides, *Bacchae*, 200–205, 305–10.

92. Other scholars argue the wisdom highlighted by Teiresias and the chorus reveals only Pentheus's "false" wisdom. See R. P. Winnington-Ingram, *Euripides and Dionysus* (Cambridge: Cambridge University Press, 1948), 62; Patricia Reynolds-Warnoff, "The Role of *To Sophoron* in Euripides' *Bacchae*," *Quaderni Urbinati di Cultura Classica* 57, no. 3 (1997): 77–103.

93. Euripides, *Bacchae*, 200–205, 890–900, 480–85.

94. As noted previously, although some scholars suggest the play represents "an actual historical event—the introduction into Hellas of a new religion," the worship of Dionysus was long established. It is possible the tragedy alludes to the inclusion of new minor foreign deities such as Sabazius who was a counterpart of Dionysus. See Dodds, "Introduction," xi; and Raeburn, *Greek Tragedies as Plays for Performance*, 173.

95. Plato suggests something similar in his noble lie. See Plato, *Republic*, 414b–c.

96. Euripides, *Bacchae*, 510–15, 265–70, 310–15, 330–35.

97. For Protagoras's quote see Plato, *Cratylus*, trans. Harold North Fowler (Cambridge, MA: Harvard University Press, 1926), 386a.

98. Euripides, *Bacchae*, 45–50, 1345–50. Burnett notes that this order is intended to be peaceful. Anne Pippin Burnett, "Pentheus and Dionysus: Host and Guest," *Classical Philology* 65, no. 1 (1970): 23.

99. As Evans notes, such temporary inversions of "normal" relationships in ritual are used to "reinforce established social structures." Evans, *Civic Rites*, 203.

100. Euripides, *Bacchae*, 920–25.

101. Christian Wolff, "Design and Myth in Euripides' *Ion*," *Harvard Studies in Classical Philology* 69 (1965): 169–94; Emily A. McDermott, "Double-Meaning and Mythic Novelty in Euripides' Plays," *Transactions of the American Philological Association* 121 (1991): 123–32; and Daniel W. Berman, "The Double Foundation

of Boiotian Thebes," *Transactions and Proceedings of the American Philological Association* 134, no. 1 (2004): 1–22.

102. René Girard, *Things Hidden since the Foundation of the World*, trans. Stephen Bann and Michael Metteer (Stanford, CA: Stanford University Press, 1987). See also René Girard, *Violence and the Sacred*, trans. Patrick Gregory (Baltimore: Johns Hopkins University Press, 1977); and Walter Burkert, *Homo Necans*, trans. P. Bing (Berkeley: University of Califonia Press, 1983). For discussion of this approach see Seaford, "Introduction," 32–33.

103. As will be discussed in chapter 4, The *Ion* tells an Athenian foundation story. A half-divine son of Apollo and a "double" of his autochthon grandfather Erichthonius, Ion is not destroyed but saved by his father to refound Athens. See Euripides, *Ion*, 1550–1600. For discussion see Diller, "Euripides' Final Phase," 366–69; Zeitlin, *Playing the Other*, 300–307.

104. Compare Pentheus's threats of beheading (235–40) and stoning (355) to the description of the attack on Pentheus at 1090–1150.

105. For example, Dodds, "Introduction," i–lix; Segal, *Dionysiac Poetics and Euripides' Bacchae*, 158–214; Vernant, "Masked Dionysus," 268–334. For examples of contrasting views see Kitto, *Greek Tragedy*, 377–78; and Seaford, "Introduction," 47–48.

106. Sewell, *In the Theatre of Dionysos*, 183.

107. Nussbaum points out that since gods such as Dionysus do not die or live with the omnipresent "unexpected," they cannot identify with the sufferings of human beings. By contrast, pity is essential to human community since it inspires human beings to support each other in the face of the violent and arbitrary reversals of life, including those "unexpected things" brought by the gods. See Nussbaum, "Introduction," 9–14. For more discussion on the role of pity in this tragedy, see W. B. Stanford, *Greek Tragedy and the Emotions* (London: Routledge, 1983), 40–52; C. Fred Alford, "Greek Tragedy and Civilization," *Political Research Quarterly* 46, no. 2 (1993): 259–80; and Simon Perris, "Perspectives on Violence in Euripides' *Bacchae*," *Mnemosyne* 64 (2011): 54–55.

108. Nikolopoulou, "Parrhesia as Tragic Structure in Euripides' *Bacchae*," 257.

109. See, for instance, Sale, *Existentialism and Euripides*, 96–99. By contrast, see Mills, *Euripides: Bacchae*, 79; and Nikolopoulou, "Parrhesia as Tragic Structure in Euripides' *Bacchae*," 249–61.

110. Euripides, *Bacchae*, 1215–25, 1330–40.

111. Winnington-Ingram, *Euripides and Dionysus*, 178.

112. Vernant, "Masked Dionysus," 411.

113. Euripides, *Bacchae*, 1295–1350, 1000–1005, 385–430, 970–75, 1390–95, 10–65.

114. Similar to the women in the hills, the god only turns violent when threatened. For interpretations of whether justice was served, see Musurillo,

"Euripides and Dionysiac Piety," 308–309; Burnett, "Pentheus and Dionysus," 15–29; and Mills, *Euripides: Bacchae*, 84–85.

115. Saxonhouse, "Freedom, Form and Formlessness," 92.

116. Such thinking is reflected in Plato's portrayal of the sophists Thrasymachus and Callicles. See Plato, *Republic*, 336b–e; Plato, *The Gorgias*, 482c–84c.

117. Meagher, *The Essential Euripides*, 542–545; Nikolopoulou, "Parrhesia as Tragic Structure in Euripides' *Bacchae*," 249–61; Saxonhouse, "Freedom, Form and Formlessness," 88–99; and Thumiger, "Animal World, Animal Representation, and the Hunting Model," 204.

118. Barrett suggests the play as "meta-theater" transforms the theater into a site of public discourse on the life of the city. See James Barrett, "Pentheus and the Spectator in Euripides' *Bacchae*," *American Journal of Philology* 119, no. 3 (1998): 358.

119. There were wide variations in ancient Greece on the meaning and method of dialectics. In the *Phaedrus*, Plato suggests dialectics includes a "gathering together of something scattered" and "a dividing things into natural parts." See Plato, *Phaedrus*, 265c–66c. See, for instance, Aristotle, *Topica*, trans. Hugh Tredennick (Cambridge, MA: Harvard University Press, 1960), 100a18–101b; and Xenophon, *Memorabilia*, trans. E. C. Marchant (Cambridge, MA: Harvard University Press, 2002), iv.6.13–7.2.

120. See, for instance, Plato's description of the dialectical process in the divided line and allegory of the cave. See Plato, *Republic*, 511a–e, 514a–17d.

121. Aristotle in the *Poetics* will suggest that this discovery that something is "this" and "not that" is part of our natural pleasure of learning through imitation. See Aristotle, *Poetics*, 1448b1–10.

122. For discussion of the interpretation that Socratic approach is also a "trial and error" based on fallible reading, see Frank, *Poetic Justice*, 9–18.

123. The potential danger in philosophic or dialectical questioning is reflected in Strauss's understanding of esoteric interpretations. See Strauss, *Persecution and the Art of Writing*, 22–37.

124. Euben, *Tragedy of Political Theory*, 130, 141.

125. We also lack Medea's magical knowledge of how to rejuvenate something that has been dismembered. See Mossman, "Introduction," 17–18.

126. Strauss makes a similar observation: "Philosophy strives for knowledge of the whole . . . [but] the whole eludes us but we know parts: we possess partial knowledge of parts." See Leo Strauss, *What Is Political Philosophy?* (Chicago: University of Chicago Press, 1959), 39.

127. Emphasis in the original. See Meagher, *Essential Euripides*, 553.

128. Plato, of course, suggests something very similar with his noble lie in the *Republic*.

129. Loraux suggests political turmoil is expected since a "Dionysian politics" would involve political metamorphosis of some kind. See Nicole Loraux,

The Mourning Voice, trans. Elizabeth Trapnell Rawlings (Ithaca, NY: Cornell University Press, 2002), 25.

130. Meagher, *Essential Euripides*, 552–53. See also Nikolopoulou, "Parrhesia as Tragic Structure in Euripides' *Bacchae*," 249–61; and Saxonhouse, "Freedom, Form and Formlessness," 88–99.

131. Edmund Burke, *Reflections on the Revolution in France* (Indianapolis: Liberty Fund, 1999), 181–83.

132. Michael Oakeshott, *Rationalism in Politics and Other Essays* (Indianapolis, IN: Liberty Fund, 1991), 60–66.

133. The language of justice as "straight" and injustice as "crooked" can be traced back to Homer's famous depiction of judgment on the shield of Achilles. See Homer, *Iliad*, 18.480–510.

134. Seligman and Weller, *Rethinking Pluralism*, 44–45.

135. Euripides, *Bacchae*, lines 860–65, 280–85, 260–65.

136. Jerome Mazzaro, "Mnema" and Forgetting in Euripides' the *Bacchae*," *Comparative Drama* 27, no. 3 (1993): 302.

Chapter 3

1. Euripides, *Phoenician Women*, 499–505.

2. Elizabeth Wyckoff, "Introduction to the Phoenician Women," in *Euripides V*, eds. David Grene and Richmond Lattimore (Chicago: University of Chicago Press, 1959), 68.

3. The Byzantine Triad (*Hecuba*, *Orestes*, and the *Phoenician Women*) are found in the oldest codices. To attest to the popularity of the *Phoenician Women*, it has the most detailed *scholia* (ancient commentary), the most surviving fragments, and approximately 115 extant manuscripts dated from the tenth to the seventeenth centuries. See Donald J. Mastronarde, *Euripides' Phoenissae* (Cambridge: Cambridge University Press, 1994), 49–52; Luschnig, "Introduction," xv–xvi; and Thalia Papadopoulou, *Euripides: Phoenician Women* (London: Duckworth, 2008), 24–26.

4. As discussed in the introduction, Aristophanes's *Frogs* dramatizes a competition for the best poet between the recently deceased Euripides and the older playwright Aeschylus, who satirizes Euripides's poetic style. See Aristophanes, *Frogs*, 1185–90, 1350–60; Euripides, *Phoenician Women*, 1495–1500, 1565–70. For the *hypotheseis* (ancient prefaces) of this play, see Elizabeth M. Craik, "Ancient Prefaces" in *Euripides' Phoenician Women*, ed. Elizabeth Craik (Warminster, UK: Aris & Phillips, 1988), 58–59.

5. For the critique of A. W. and Friedrich Schlegel, see Ernst Behler, "A. W. Schlegel and the Nineteenth Century '*Damnatio*' of Euripides," *Greek, Roman, and Byzantine Studies* 27, no. 4 (1986): 335–67; and Michelini, *Euripides and the Tragic Tradition*, 3–19.

6. Falkner, *Poetics of Old Age in Greek Epic, Lyric, and Tragedy*, 193; A. C. Pearson, *Euripides: The Phoenissae* (Cambridge: Cambridge University Press, 1909), xxviii; and Kitto, *Greek Tragedy*, 354.

7. For discussion on the many suspect passages see Pearson, *Euripides: The Phoenissae*, xxviii; Anthony J. Podlecki, "Some Themes in Euripides' *Phoenissae*," *Transactions of the American Philological Association* 93 (1962): 355–56; Desmond J. Conacher, "Themes in the "Exodus" of Euripides' *Phoenissae*," *Phoenix* 21, no. 2 (1967): 92–101; H. D. F. Kitto, "The Final Scenes of the *Phoenissae*," *Classical Review* 53, no. 3 (1939): 104–11; Donald J. Mastronarde, "Are Euripides *Phoinissai* 1104–1140 Interpolated?," *Phoenix* 32, no. 2 (1978): 105–28; C. W. Willink, "The Goddess Eulabeia and Pseudo-Euripides in Euripides' *Phoenissae*," *Proceedings of the Cambridge Philological Society* 36, no. 216 (1990): 182–201; Elizabeth M. Craik, "Euripides: *Ion* and *Phoenissae*," in *The Passionate Intellect*, ed. Lewis Aryes (New Brunswick, NJ: Transaction, 1986), 105–15; Storey and Allan, *A Guide to Ancient Greek Drama*, 171; Dana L. Burgess, "The Authenticity of the Teichoskopia of Euripides' *Phoenissae*," *Classical Journal* 83, no. 2 (1987–88): 103–113; and Chiara Meccariello, "The Opening of Euripides' *Phoenissae* between Anecdotal and Textual Tradition," *Zeitschrift für Papyrologie und Epigraphik* 190 (2014): 49–56.

8. Although not a trilogy (as they were performed at different festivals) three of Sophocles's surviving plays, *Oedipus Rex, Antigone*, and *Oedipus at Colonus* deal with this family cycle. The events of this tragedy are closest to *Antigone*. On the enduring cultural influence of Sophocles's *Antigone*, see George Steiner, *Antigones* (New York: Oxford, 1984).

9. Mastronarde, *Euripides' Phoenissae* 3, 4–11. Lamari uses the term "flexi-narrative" to describe its purposeful arrangement of multiple plots. See Anna A. Lamari, *Narrative, Intertext, and Space in Euripides' Phoenissae* (Berlin: De Gruyter, 2010), 17–18.

10. Ringer, *Euripides and the Boundary of the Human*, 256.

11. Swift argues the chorus's centrality to the unifying theme of mismanaged sexuality and shared community values. See Podlecki, "Some Themes in Euripides' *Phoenissae*," *Transactions of the American Philological Association* 93 (1962): 357–62, 369–73; and Laura Swift, "Sexual and Familial Distortion in Euripides' *Phoenissae*," *Transactions of the American Philological Association*, 139, no. 1 (2009): 81–84.

12. Thalia Papadopoulou, "The Prophetic Figure in Euripides' *Phoenissae* and *Bacchae*," *Hermes* 129, no. H.1 (2001): 24–26; and Elizabeth Rawson, "Family and Fatherland in Euripides' *Phoenissae*," *Greek, Roman, and Byzantine Studies* 11, no. 2 (1970): 109–27.

13. For discussion see Mastronarde, *Euripides' Phoenissae*, 11–14; Elizabeth M. Craik, "Introduction to the *Phoenician Women*" in *Euripides' Phoenician Women*, ed. Elizabeth Craik (Warminster, UK: Aris & Phillips, 1988), 40–41, 61; and Papadopoulou, *Euripides: Phoenician Women*, 23–26.

14. The Athenians maintained their calendar year by the name of a religious official called the Archon. We have no mention of a Nausikrates on

the existing Archon lists. For discussion of Athenian calendars see W. Kendrick Pritchett, "The Calendar of the Athenian Civic Administration," *Phoenix* 30, no. 4 (1976): 337–56.

15. For more discussion of Theban mythology see H. J. Rose, *A Handbook of Greek Mythology* (New York: Dutton, 1958), 99–160; and Daniel W. Berman, *Myth, Literature, and the Creation of the Topography of Thebes* (Cambridge: Cambridge University Press, 2015), 14–60.

16. Six (of thirty-three) extant plays focus on the Theban myth: Aeschylus's *Seven against Thebes*; Sophocles's *Oedipus the King*, *Antigone*, and *Oedipus at Colonus*; and Euripides's *Phoenician Women* and *Suppliant Women*. As the Theban foundation mythology is central, Euripides's *Bacchae* on the Dionysian connection can be included.

17. For the Greeks, autochthony (from *autochthōn* or born of the earth) refers both to those who sprung from the earth and those who have "always ruled" without invasion. Euripides deals with the myth of Athenian autochthony in his *Ion*. For discussion see Nicole Loraux, *Born of the Earth*, trans. Selina Stewart (Ithaca, NY: Cornell University Press, 2000), 13–27; Craige B. Champion, "Imperial Ideologies, Citizenship Myths, and Legal Disputes," in *A Companion to Greek and Roman Political Thought*, ed. Ryan K. Balot (Chichester, UK: John Wiley, 2009), 90–6; Arlene Saxonhouse, "Reflections on Autochthony in Euripides' Ion," in *Greek Tragedy and Political Theory*, ed. Peter J. Euben (Berkeley: University of California Press, 1986), 252–73.

18. In another version, this marriage is not a reward but another curse on the House of Thebes. When Hephaestus learned of his wife Aphrodite's affair with Ares, he cursed Harmonia and her descendants with a magical necklace that destroyed anyone who wore it. See Christopher Matthew Chinn, "Statius, Orpheus, and Callimachus *Thebaid* 2.269–96," *Helios* 38, no. 1 (2011): 79–101.

19. In the *Bacchae*, there is no mention of Polydorus. Cadmus abdicates in favor of his grandson Pentheus. See Euripides, *Bacchae*, 40–50.

20. As developed later, in this tragedy Jocasta only reports that Oedipus was fated to kill his father. As the iniquity occurred while Laius is drunk, it also reasserts their kin Dionysus as god of wine into the story. See C. A. E. Luschnig, *The Gorgon's Severed Head* (Leiden, The Netherlands: E. J. Brill, 1995), 177. See also Euripides, *Phoenician Women*, 15–20.

21. Sophocles, *Oedipus Tyrannus*, trans. Hugh Lloyd-Jones (Cambridge, MA: Harvard University Press, 1994), 770–800.

22. The Sphinx was a monstrous female creature represented with the head of a woman, body of a lion, and usually wings. Like the Erinyes, she brought plague as punishment. In this version, the riddle is not specified, and Oedipus solves the riddle by chance and not cleverness. In earlier versions Oedipus defeats her in a typical heroic battle. See Mastronarde, *Euripides' Phoenissae*, 19–21; and Luschnig, *Gorgon's Severed Head*, 181.

23. For more discussion of mythical variation see Papadopoulou, *Euripides: Phoenician Women*, 27–53; Craik, "Introduction to the *Phoenician Women*," 35–40; and Mastronarde, *Euripides' Phoenissae*, 17–30.

24. Homer, *The Odyssey*, 11.270–80; and Homer, *Iliad*, 23.670–80.

25. Sophocles, *Oedipus Tyrannus*, 1351–1684; and Sophocles, *Oedipus at Colonus*, trans. Hugh Lloyd-Jones (Cambridge, MA: Harvard University Press, 1994), 1750–80.

26. Zeitlin argues the prominence of Thebes in Athenian tragedy sets it up as the "other" or a kind of anti-Athens. See Zeitlin, "Playing the Other," 144–45.

27. Papadopoulou, *Euripides: Phoenician Women*, 28, 38. For intertextuality with Aeschylus, see Isabelle Torrance, *Metapoetry in Euripides* (Oxford: Oxford University Press, 2013), 94–96.

28. In *Seven against Thebes*, Polynices does not debate with his brother, but his shield is decorated with an image of the goddess Justice; Eteocles dismisses the idea that Justice would ally against one's fatherland. See Aeschylus, *Seven against Thebes*, trans. Alan H. Sommerstein (Cambridge, MA: Harvard University Press, 2009), 631–85.

29. Euripides, *Suppliant Women*, 215–50, 334–40, 585–90, 1210–26.

30. In Stesichorus's fragments, the quarrel seems to not result from a curse but a prophecy of Teiresias. For further discussion see Arnd Kerkhecker, "Euripides, *Phoenissae* 64f," *Classical Quarterly* 46, no. 2 (1996): 567–72; and Deborah MacInnes, "Gainsaying the Prophet: Jocasta, Tiresias, and the Lille Stesichorus," *Quaderni Urbinati di Cultura Classica* 86, no. 2 (2007): 105–106.

31. In this play, the command to not bury the dead bodies mentions only Polynices and not his Argive allies. Euripides, *Phoenician Women*, 770–80, 1625–35.

32. Sophocles, *Antigone*, 1155–1295.

33. Jocasta mentions Ismene once in the monologue, and she is forgotten thereafter. See Craik, "Introduction to the *Phoenician Women*," 43.

34. Falkner, *Poetics of Old Age in Greek Epic, Lyric, and Tragedy*, 194.

35. Papadopoulou, *Euripides: Phoenician Women*, 90–92. For difficulties with the logic of the exits, entrances, and stage directions see Erez Natanblut, "Two Problems of Staging in Euripides' *Phoenissae*," *Rheinisches Museum für Philologie* 149, no. 3/4 (2006): 429–31; and Herman Altena, "Text and Performance: On Significant Actions in Euripides' "Phoenissae," *Illinois Classical Studies* 24/25 (1999–2000): 303–23.

36. The use of the rooftop for human characters is unusual. Mastronarde makes a textual case for Antigone and the tutor on stage climbing the ladder to a flat roof. The location of a roof may also be significant, as Luschnig points out, since it is a private space (as part of the House) but is also public: it is a space where one looks beyond the city's walls but also where one is seen. It is also possible they either appeared from a window or climbed on the roof offstage. See Mastronarde, "Actors on High," 247–94; Joe Park Poe, "*Phoenissae*

88–201 and Pollux' Distegia," *Classical Philology* 95, no. 2 (2000): 187–90; and Luschnig, *Gorgon's Severed Head*, 184–90.

37. Jocasta's role as a maternal figure is emphasized throughout the play: she is a surrogate mother to her nephew Menoeceus; she bears her breasts in the traditional entreaty to prevent her sons' duel; and she refers to Oedipus primarily as a son and not a husband. See Nicole Loraux, *The Experience of Tiresias* (Princeton, NJ: Princeton University Press, 1995), 135; Luschnig, *Gorgon's Severed Head*, 230; and Papadopoulou, *Euripides: Phoenician Women*, 37–38.

38. See Homer, *Iliad*, 3.121–244. As this scene mimics Homer and is not anticipated in the text, it is sometimes identified as a later interpolation. By contrast, the intertextuality with both Homer and possibly Aeschylus is also seen as critical to the plot's action. For discussion, see Papadopoulou, *Euripides: Phoenician Women*, 19, 24–25, 44–47; Anna A. Lamari, "Aeschylus' *Seven against Thebes* vs. Euripides' *Phoenissae*: Male vs. Female Power," *Wiener Studien* 120 (2007): 15–16; Saxonhouse, "Another Antigone," 480; and Barlow, *Imagery of Euripides*, 58–60.

39. Luschnig argues this scene establishes the process by which we come to name or define things: first, we see indistinguishable masses, then recognizable outlines; then we provide identity or definitions. See Luschnig, *Gorgon's Severed Head*, 191–94.

40. Polynices's exile may be a commentary on ostracism as a form of political catharsis. See Robin Mitchell-Boyask, *Plague and the Athenian Imagination* (Cambridge: Cambridge University Press, 2008), 147–52. For discussion of the significance of frank speech (*parrhēsia*) in this play, see Foucault, *Fearless Speech*, 11–24; Saxonhouse, "Another Antigone," 476–77; Loren J. Samons, "Forms and Forums of Public Speech," in *A Companion to Ancient Greek Government*, ed. Hans Beck (Oxford: John Wiley, 2013), 279–81.

41. For Saxonhouse, one lesson of the play is that speaking the truth or revealing what one hides is not unambiguous and can unveil truths that lead to tragedy. See Arlene Saxonhouse, *Free Speech and Democracy in Ancient Athens* (Cambridge: Cambridge University Press, 2006), 138–45, 210.

42. These foolish stratagems could be allusions to the failed attacks at dinner or at night during the disastrous Sicilian Expedition. See Thucydides, *History of the Peloponnesian War*, 7.39.1–7.45.2.

43. Falkner, *Poetics of Old Age in Greek Epic, Lyric, and Tragedy*, 204.

44. The audience would have understood the reference to Eumolpus, who was defeated when Erechtheus sacrificed his daughters to secure victory. For discussion see Sourvinou-Inwood, *Tragedy and Athenian Religion*, 379–80; Papadopoulou, "Prophetic Figure in Euripides' *Phoenissae* and *Bacchae*," 22–23.

45. Human sacrifice was alien to Greek religion in the classical period but may have been practiced in the Mycenean period. Menoeceus is a rare male example of such a sacrifice which highlights the polluted nature of the Theban

royal family. See Sourvinou-Inwood, *Tragedy and Athenian Religion*, 379–82; John Wilkins, "The State and the Individual: Euripides' Plays of Voluntary Self-Sacrifice," in *Euripides, Women, and Sexuality*, ed. Anton Powell (London: Routledge, 1990), 178–82; Nicole Loraux, *Tragic Ways of Killing a Woman*, trans. Anthony Forster (Cambridge, MA: Harvard University Press, 1985), 35–43; Rabinowitz, *Anxiety Veiled*, 64–67; and Dennis D. Hughes, *Human Sacrifice in Ancient Greece* (London: Routledge, 1991), 13–48, 71–138.

46. Euripides, *Phoenician Women*, 1380–1425.

47. Jocasta's death is a rare example of a woman's suicide by sword, not hanging. It can be interpreted as the completion of her leaving behind the female sphere for the male sphere of the battlefield. See Loraux, "The Experience of Tiresias," 41–42; Falkner, *Poetics of Old Age in Greek Epic, Lyric, and Tragedy*, 206. For an overview of suicide in Greece tragedy, see Elise P. Garrison, *Groaning Tears: Ethical and Dramatic Aspects of Suicide in Greek Tragedy* (New York: E. J. Brill, 1995); and M. D. Faber, *Suicide and Greek Tragedy* (New York: Sphinx, 1970).

48. This passage may be an interpolation. As Luschnig points out, the victory is ignoble as the Thebans "through good foresight (1465)" took their armor during the truce to the winner-take-all battle. See Luschnig, "Introduction," xix.

49. It is possible the play ended before Antigone's personality become more "Sophoclean" with her informing Oedipus of the fate of his sons and Jocasta. For discussion see Wyckoff, "Introduction to the Phoenician Women," 68–69; Conacher, "Themes in the "Exodus" of Euripides' *Phoenissae*," 92–101; Martin Cropp, "Euripides, *Phoenissae* 1567–76," *Classical Quarterly* 47, no. 2 (1997): 570–4; Kitto, "The Final Scenes of the *Phoenissae*," 104–111; Mastronarde, "Are Euripides *Phoinissai* 1104–1140 Interpolated?," 105–28; and David Kovacs, "Introduction to *Phoenician Women*," in *Phoenician Women* (Cambridge, MA: Harvard University Press, 2002), 208–209, see also fn 55, 373.

50. Oedipus is an exemplar of an old man as, like Athenian women, he is "shut in" the house. Or, as Lamar puts it, he is more of a specter or "ghostly figure, coming from the darkness of the abyss." See Falkner, *Poetics of Old Age in Greek Epic, Lyric, and Tragedy*, 198; and Lamari, "Aeschylus' *Seven against Thebes* vs. Euripides' *Phoenissae*," 18.

51. Leading away her blind father, they mirror the blind Teiresias and his daughter in the middle scene. See Jacques Jouanna, "Texte et espace théâtral dans les Phéniciennes d'Euripide," *Ktéma* 1, no. 19 (1976): 92–96.

52. For discussion this final episode, including potential textual corruptions see Wyckoff, "Introduction to the Phoenician Women," 60; Conacher, "Themes in the "Exodus" of Euripides' *Phoenissae*," 92–101; Kitto, "The Final Scenes of the *Phoenissae*," 104–111; and Dunn, *Tragedy's End*, 180–90.

53. For more discussion of alternative myth and potential innovations see Craik, "Introduction to the *Phoenician Women*," 35–40; Mastronarde, *Euripides'*

Phoenissae, 19–30; Saxonhouse, "Another Antigone," 473–74; Storey and Allan, *A Guide to Ancient Greek Drama*, 271; and Luschnig, "Introduction," xviii–xx.

54. Euripides also gives Jocasta a more central connection to the main characters, including nursing Menoeceus after Eurydice's death. See Luschnig, "Introduction," xx; and MacInnes, "Gainsaying the Prophet," 95–108.

55. Although it is not known whether the audience had foreknowledge of tragic plots prior to the festival, the title of this play disguises its storyline and enhances the appearance of Jocasta. For discussion see Marchinus van der Valk, *Studies in Euripides: Phoenissae and Andromache* (Amsterdam: A. M. Hakkert 1985), 16; Papadopoulou, "Prophetic Figure in Euripides' *Phoenissae* and *Bacchae*," 21–31; Page duBois, "Toppling the Hero: Polyphony in the Tragic City," *New Literary History* 35, no. 1 (2004): 71–73; Bernadette Morin, "Pourquoi des Phéniciennes?" *L'antiquité classique* 78 (2009): 25–30; and Niall W. Slater, *Euripides: Alcestis* (London: Bloomsbury, 2013), 5–6.

56. It is possible Euripides changed the name of this character to emphasize his Spartoi heritage. Aeschylus also uses the name Megareus for one of the seven Theban generals. See Aeschylus, *Seven against Thebes*, 474. In no other extant Greek version does Menoeceus sacrifice himself to atone for the founding. For discussion see Papadopoulou, *Euripides: Phoenician Women*, 31–32.

57. Mastronarde, *Euripides' Phoenissae* 17–20, 29; MacInnes, "Gainsaying the Prophet," 95–96; and Papadopoulou, *Euripides: Phoenician Women*, 36–38.

58. The delayed duel between the brothers is also a possible Euripidean innovation. In most versions, the brothers kill each other during the general battle for the city. See Mastronarde, *Euripides' Phoenissae*, 29.

59. This incongruity between the character's name and deeds is another example of the mismatch between words and actions or the way in which we fail to name things properly. See Efi Papadodima, "The Term Ὄνομα and the Theme of Naming in *Seven against Thebes* and *Phoenician Women*," *Acta Classica* 56 (2013): 146–49; and Torrance, *Metapoetry in Euripides*, 97–98.

60. Euripides, *Phoenician Women*, 10–20, 35–50; and Luschnig, "Introduction," xviii.

61. Euripides, *Phoenician Women*, 465–70. Although Sophocles introduced a third actor into tragic scenes, Euripides expanded the dynamism of this role. See Michelini, *Euripides and the Tragic Tradition*, 98–99; Luschnig, "Introduction," xix; Carter, *Politics of Greek Tragedy*, 122–28; and Lloyd, *Agon in Euripides*, 1–18.

62. Euripides, *Phoenician Women*, 469–95, 390–95. The concept of *kairos* is crucial in Greek literature, aesthetics, and ethics. Although it is usually translated as "the right time" it can mean the right opportunity, correct proportion, or due measure. In questions of truth, *kairos* implies the proper context. For discussion see, Phillip Sipiora, "Introduction: The Ancient Concept of *Kairos*," in *Rhetoric and Kairos*, eds. Phillip Sipiora and James S. Baumlin (Albany: State University of New York Press, 2002), 1–22; and Pucci, *Euripides' Revolution under Cover*, 30–32.

63. The injustice of breaking oaths is also central to Euripides's version of *Medea* as it is the core reason for her vengeance against Jason. See Euripides, *Medea*, 20–95, 155–75, 435–40, 730–55.

64. For the importance of oath making in ancient Greece, see Sommerstein, "Introduction," 1–6; and Plescia, *Oath and Perjury in Ancient Athens*, 15–32.

65. Foucault, *Fearless Speech*, 28–29; and Saxonhouse, "Another Antigone," 482–89.

66. Euripides, *Children of Heracles*, 200–35; and Euripides, *Hecuba*, 250–80.

67. Euripides, *Phoenician Women*, 470–90.

68. Plato opens his *Apology* with Socrates rejecting the claim he is a clever speaker; instead, he will speak truthfully in the simple speech of the common man. Like Polynices, Socrates also uses medical metaphors for discussions of ethics. Plato, *Apology*, 17a–18a; and Pucci, *Euripides' Revolution under Cover*, 30–31.

69. In this passage, young Cyrus is asked to determine whether it is just to take away a large coat belonging to a small boy and give it to a larger boy. In the end, Cyrus is chastised for thinking the larger boy merits the coat, as justice of merit understood as the "right fit" does not honor justice as meriting what rightly belongs to someone. Xenophon, *Cyropaedia*, trans. Walter Miller (Cambridge, MA: Harvard University Press, 1914), 1.3.17.

70. Aristotle, *Nicomachean Ethics*, 1130b–31b.

71. Plato, *Republic*, 330a–331e.

72. The term *ergon* means a deed or action. As will be developed later, this term can contrast what is said (*logos*) with what is done (*ergon*) or the difference between ideas and reality. See Euripides, *Phoenician Women*, 499–505.

73. This passage is (purposefully?) ambiguous and difficult to translate. Saxonhouse interprets the sentence to mean "equality or fairness is not the same except in name: the deed does not exist." By contrast, Papadodima interprets this passage to mean that conflicts arise because our understanding of abstract terms in general (and not just "equality") does not correspond to reality or to how other people understand or assess the deeds that accompany these terms. See Saxonhouse, "Another Antigone," 484; and Papadodima, "Term Ὄνομα and the Theme of Naming," 149.

74. Euripides, *Phoenician Women*, 500–525.

75. The sophists were not a homogenous school of thought but professional intellectuals who challenged conventional thinking. Most of their work has not survived, except for fragments in often hostile sources, such as Plato. Morin suggests the chorus of wandering Phoenicians also would remind the audience of these itinerant sophists. For discussion see Conacher, *Euripides and the Sophists*, 7–25; de Romilly, *Great Sophists in Periclean Athens*, 213–32; Morin, "Pourquoi des Phéniciennes?," 27–29; and Jacqueline de Romilly, "Les Phéniciennes d'Euripide ou l'actualité dans la tragédie grecque," *Revue de Philologie, de Littérature et d'Histoire Anciennes* 39 (1965): 29–47.

76. Thucydides, *History of the Peloponnesian War*, 5.89.

77. Plato, *Republic*, 344a–d. For discussion of intellectual parallels with Plato, see Sansone, "Plato and Euripides," 35–67.

78. In this dialogue, Socrates also challenges the notion that the shameful can be distinguished from injustice. Plato, *Gorgias*, 475a–77d, 482c–86d.

79. Euripides, *Phoenician Women*, 530–90.

80. Jocasta's celebration of equality may be ironic since her family's unique perversion is to level or "make equal" all kinship distinctions. See Falkner, *Poetics of Old Age in Greek Epic, Lyric, and Tragedy*, 207.

81. As Papadodima points out, Jocasta's concern for the city challenges gender stereotypes that women are only interested in the good of the family. See Papadodima, "Term Ὄνομα and the Theme of Naming," 149–51. See Falkner, *Poetics of Old Age in Greek Epic, Lyric, and Tragedy*, 194–97.

82. *Sophrosyne* is one of the most important Greek virtues and is found across all literary forms from Homer and Heraclitus to Xenophon, Plato, and Aristotle. The meaning of this term was contested in the fifth century BCE and could mean chastity, temperance, moderation, prudence, or self-control; it is often seen in opposition to ambition and foolishness. For discussion of this term in Greek thought and in Euripides, see Helen F. North, *Sophrosyne: Self-Knowledge and Self-Restraint in Greek Literature* (Ithaca, NY: Cornell University Press, 1966), esp. 68–84.

83. Plato, *Gorgias*, 470b–480a. For further discussion of Jocasta's argument as reflecting political ideas, especially in Plato see Jacqueline de Romilly, "D'Euripide à Platon," *Estudios Clásicos* 26 (1984): 259–65.

84. Aristotle, *The Politics*, 1311a–1312b40.

85. John Lomardini, "*Isonomia* and the Public Sphere in Democratic Athens," *History of Political Thought* 34, no. 3 (2013): 417–19. There may be some form of democratic equality with the "interchangeability" between Eteocles and Polynices. See Arlene Saxonhouse, *Fear of Diversity* (Chicago: University of Chicago Press, 1995), 74–76.

86. Euripides, *Electra*, 420–30; Euripides, *Suppliant Women*, 235–45; and Aristotle, *Politics*, 1295b1–1296a25.

87. Euripides, *Phoenician Women*, 587–637. For discussion of the typical failure of Euripidean *agōnes* see Lloyd, *Agon in Euripides*, 16–17. Jocasta may have delivered the best speech, yet she accomplished nothing more than proving that justice or equality is "just another word." See Luschnig, *Gorgon's Severed Head*, 205–20.

88. Aristotle suggests that deliberative speeches concern questions of future utility more than whether the actions are just or unjust. See Aristotle, *Art of Rhetoric*, 1358b.

89. Euripides, *Phoenician Women*, 505–25.

90. The connection between the breakdown of the meaning of the words signifying community values and the breakdown of the community itself is also found in Thucydides's description of Corcyra's civil war whereby, after "words changed their ordinary meaning," all violence was permissible. See Thucydides, *History of the Peloponnesian War*, 3.82.4.

91. Polynices's exchange with his mother is full of contradictions (he trusts and does not trust her) and, like Eteocles, his experience is more important than words. For all his talk of justice, Polynices never thinks about Thebes as a community of people but as walls, towers, and gates. See Luschnig, *Gorgon's Severed Head*, 202–207.

92. Eteocles's claim of tyranny as the "highest good" reasserts a claim to universal validity. Similarly, although he inversed values, he makes definitive claims to what is shameful and prays to the "most beneficial" goddess Eulabeia (Caution) to save the city. See Euripides, *Phoenician Women*, 690–785. For discussion see Willink, "Goddess Eulabeia and Pseudo-Euripides in Euripides' *Phoenissae*," 183–84; Barbara Goff, "The Shields of the *Phoenissae*," *Greek, Roman, and Byzantine Studies* 29, no. 2 (1988): 136; and Luschnig, *Gorgon's Severed Head*, 208–209, see also 11.

93. Aristotle, *Politics*, 1279b1–10.

94. Euripides also interconnects the brothers linguistically by using the dual form. Ancient Greek grammar has a singular, plural, and a dual number. The dual is used for a pair of things or to connect two close subjects of a verb.

95. Other than the second messenger speech, the play makes no references to citizens of Thebes. The chorus consists of foreigners and the tutor looks for, but cannot see, any citizens in the *teichoskopia* scene. See Luschnig, *Gorgon's Severed Head*, 206, 174, 183–85.

96. This ancient event is represented by the chorus in the *parodos* and subsequent odes. Marilyn B. Arthur, "The Curse of Civilization," *Harvard Studies in Classical Philology* 81 (1977): 163–85.

97. Homer, *Iliad*, 18.490–590. For further discussion of blood price see Cantarella, "Private Justice and Public Justice," 473–83.

98. Euripides explores blood price as an extreme form of reciprocal justice in the *Hecuba*. In this case, Hecuba kills Polymestor and his sons in compensation for the murder of her son. See Euripides, *Hecuba*, 1130–1295. For discussion see Burnett, *Revenge in Attic and Later Tragedy*, 170–76.

99. Euripides, *Phoenician Women*, 865–895, 910–15, 930–50.

100. Menoeceus's death is a *pharmakon* or drug that cures the disease affecting the city. However, since the brothers still fulfill the curse of mutual self-destruction, the city's salvation seems to still require the "best *pharmakon*" of purging the line of Cadmus. For discussion see Mitchell-Boyask, *Plague and the Athenian Imagination*, 134–37.

101. Euripides, *Phoenician Women*, 950–55, 915–20.

102. Creon here stands in contrast to the *Alcestis*'s Pheres who refuses to die for his son. See *Alcestis*, 615–735.

103. Euripides, *Phoenician Women*, 990–1015.

104. In social terms, Menoeceus's act is a noble suicide that subsumes individuality (or the private) into the community (or public). See Elise P. Garrison, "Attitudes toward Suicide in Ancient Greece," *Transactions of the American Philological Association* 121 (1991): 32–33.

105. Aristotle, *Nicomachean Ethics*, 1111b5–1112a20, 1115a25–35.

106. Euripides, *Phoenician Women*, 900–1020. See also Plato, *Crito*, trans. H. N. Fowler (Cambridge, MA: Harvard University Press, 1908), 50b–51d.

107. Plato, *Republic*, 433a.

108. By contrast, Menoeceus could be more concerned with avoiding the evils of exile, which would make him less altruistic and more self-interested. See Rawson, "Family and Fatherland in Euripides' *Phoenissae*," 111–14.

109. Storey and Allan, *A Guide to Ancient Greek Drama*, 171. For further discussion, see Wilkins, "State and the Individual," 177–94; David Sansone, "Iphigenia Changes Her Mind," *Illinois Classical Studies* 16 (1991): 166–67; and de Romilly, "Les Phéniciennes d'Euripide," 29–47.

110. Or, as Rawson puts it, the play is not suggesting that "duty before country must always come before duty towards family or its reverse." See Rawson, "Family and Fatherland in Euripides' *Phoenissae*," 125.

111. It is not clear whether the ending is a textual corruption. Following Orwin's argument that inconsistencies may be essential, this interpretation approaches the text as transmitted. See Clifford Orwin, "Feminine Justice: The End of the *Seven against Thebes*," *Classical Philology* 75, no. 3 (1980): 187–88. For discussion of the possible textual interpolations see Wyckoff, "Introduction to the Phoenician Women," 68–69; Cropp, "Euripides, *Phoenissae* 1567–76," 570–74; Kitto, "Final Scenes of the *Phoenissae*," 104–111; Conacher, "Themes in the 'Exodus' of Euripides' *Phoenissae*," 92–101; and Meccariello, "Opening of Euripides' *Phoenissae* between Anecdotal and Textual Tradition," 49–56.

112. Euripides, *Phoenician Women*, 1485–1535, 1625–1640.

113. She becomes, as Falkner puts it, "*the* Antigone" [italics in the original]. See Falkner, *Poetics of Old Age in Greek Epic, Lyric, and Tragedy*, 208. See also Goff, "Shields of the *Phoenissae*," 141; Lamari, "Aeschylus' *Seven against Thebes* vs. Euripides' *Phoenissae*," 21–23; Luschnig, *Gorgon's Severed Head*, 130; and Saxonhouse, "Another Antigone," 486–90.

114. Saxonhouse, "Another Antigone,"486.

115. Euripides, *Phoenician Women*, 385–95, 1645–1680, 1730–60.

116. Literally, Antigone threatens that such a marriage will transform her into a Danaid. See Euripides, *Phoenician Women*, 1675. The Danaids were the fifty daughters of the Argive king Danaus who were forced to marry the

fifty sons of his twin brother Aegyptus. Danaus commanded them to kill their husbands. All obeyed, except Hypermnestra, who was in love with Lynceus, and the couple became the ancestors of the royal line of Argos. Her sisters faced the eternal punishment of trying to fill water jugs that have no bottom. See Kovacs, "Introduction to *Phoenician Women*," fn 59, 389; and Rose, *Handbook of Greek Mythology*, 67.

117. Euripides, *Phoenician Women*, 1585–95, 1650–60.

118. Violation of burial norms was a preoccupation of many Greek tragedies. This may be a critique of restrictions on public mourning during the war. It is also possible it reflects historical incidents, such as the Athenian defeat at Delium in 424 BCE. After this battle, the Theban-led Boeotians refused to allow Athens to retrieve their dead for seventeen days. For discussion see Honig, *Antigone Interrupted*, 85–119; Kerri J. Hame, "Female Control of Funeral Rites in Greek Tragedy," *Classical Philology* 103, no. 1 (2008): 1–15; and Christopher Coker, *Ethics and War in the 21st Century* (New York and London: Routledge, 2008), 161–62.

119. Euripides, *Suppliant Women*, 120–25, 300–15. In Sophocles's *Antigone*, it is not Creon but Antigone who associates burial practices with divine laws. See Sophocles, *Antigone*, 450–75.

120. This order reflects fifth-century BCE Athenian law, which prohibited traitors from formal burial rites within the city limits. Euripides may be criticizing this practice. For discussion see Sourvinou-Inwood, *Tragedy and Athenian Religion*, 385–86; Astrid Lindenlauf, "Thrown Away Like Rubbish: Disposal of the Dead in Ancient Greece," *Papers from the Institute of Archaeology* 12 (2001): 88–90; and Jon D. Mikalson, *Honor Thy Gods* (Chapel Hill: University of North Carolina Press, 1991), 127–29.

121. Or, more cynically, Creon may doubt whether Menoeceus's sacrifice was responsible for the victory. See Helene P. Foley, *Ritual Irony: Poetry and Sacrifice in Euripides* (Ithaca, NY: Cornell University Press, 1985), 109–10; and Papadopoulou, "Prophetic Figure in Euripides' *Phoenissae* and *Bacchae*," 25–26.

122. For discussion of Creon's "superficial patriotism" see Luschnig, *Gorgon's Severed Head*, 166–67.

123. Euripides, *Phoenician Women*, 960–70, 950–55.

124. Euripides, 1655–80, 1745–50, 1760–65. One could object that Antigone clandestinely plans to bury her brother and then escape with her father before getting caught. This resolution, however, would make her very unlike her Sophoclean counterpart, who may have buried the body the first time but laments loudly enough a second time to ensure she gets caught. See Sophocles, *Antigone*, 245–75, 385–445.

125. Badger suggests that tragedy is this "clash of right actions" or the negotiation of "mutually negating necessities." See Badger, *Sophocles and the Politics of Tragedy*, 21.

126. Arthur, "Curse of Civilization," 184.

127. Luschnig, *Gorgon's Severed Head*, 180–94.

128. There are many versions and nuances of utilitarianism, for discussion see David Johnston, *A Brief History of Justice* (Oxford: Wiley-Backwell, 2011), 116–41.

129. Thomas Nagel, *The Possibility of Altruism* (Princeton, NJ: Princeton University Press, 1979).

130. Melvin J. Lerner, "Doing Justice to the Justice Motive," in *Current Societal Concerns About Justice*, ed. Leo Montada and Melvin J. Lerner (New York: Plenum, 1996), 1–9. The idea that self-interest motivates justice is common to certain strains of modern liberal political thought and especially contemporary rational choice theory. For an overview, see Johnston, *A Brief History of Justice*, 7–14. For examples of the contemporary discussion of the potential relationship between self-interest and justice see Jane Mansbridge, ed. *Beyond Self Interest* (Chicago: University of Chicago Press, 1990); Melvin J. Lerner and Susan Clayton, *Justice and Self-Interest* (Cambridge: Cambridge University Press, 2011); and Lode Walgrave, *Restorative Justice, Self-Interest and Responsible Citizenship* (New York: Routledge, 2012).

131. Euripides, *Phoenician Women*, 585, 745.

132. Sophocles's tragedy, at least in Hegel's interpretation, identifies Antigone with divine law versus the public law of Creon. See G. W. F. Hegel, *Lectures on the Philosophy of Religion: The Lectures of 1827*, trans. R. F Brown, P. C. Hodgson, and J. M. Stewart (Berkeley: University of California Press, 1988), 353.

133. For discussion of the infinite possible interpretations of "open form" see Mastronarde, *Euripides' Phoenissae*, 3–4; Dunn, *Tragedy's End*, 200; and Lamari, *Narrative, Intertext, and Space in Euripides' Phoenissae*, 75–117.

134. Euripides, *Phoenician Women*, 550–55, 585, 745.

135. Plato, *Charmides*, trans. W. R. M. Lamb (Cambridge, MA: Harvard University Press, 1955), 167a–b.

Chapter 4

1. Euripides, *Ion*, 1015–20.

2. Aristotle, *Poetics*, 1452a–b. Kitto classifies the *Ion* as a "pure tragi-comedy" since the tragic is reduced to the pathetic. Knox suggests it is a "full-fledged comedy"; Lucas suggests it is a "melodrama." See D. W. Lucas, *The Ion of Euripides* (London: Cohen and West, 1949), 1–9; Kitto, *Greek Tragedy*, 311–29; and Bernard Knox, *Word and Action* (Baltimore: Johns Hopkins University Press, 1979), 257.

3. For examples of this perspective see Anne Pippin Burnett, "Human Resistance and Divine Persuasion in Euripides' Ion," *Classical Philology* 57 (1962):

89–103; Brian Vickers, *Towards Greek Tragedy* (London: Longman, 1973), 330–5; W. Geoffrey Arnott, "Realism in the *Ion*," in *Tragedy and the Tragic*, ed. M. S. Silk (Oxford: Oxford University Press, 1996), 110–18; and Gary S. Meltzer, *Euripides and the Poetics of Nostalgia* (Cambridge: Cambridge University Press, 2006), 146–87.

4. See Marlene K. Sokolon, "Euripides' *Ion*: Identity, Legitimacy and the Ties That Bind," in *Socrates and Dionysus*, ed. Ann Ward (Newcastle-upon-Tyne, UK: Cambridge Scholars, 2013), 33–53. For examples, see George B. Walsh, "Rhetoric of Birthright and Race in Euripides' *Ion*," *Hermes* 106, no. 2 (1978): 301–15; Dora C. Pozzi, "The Polis in Crisis," in *Myth and the Polis*, ed. Dora C. Pozzi and John M. Wickersham (Ithaca, NY: Cornell University Press, 1991), 135–44; and Demetra Kasimis, "Tragedy of Blood-Based Membership: Secrecy and the Politics of Immigration," *Political Theory* 41 (2013): 231–56.

5. For examples see Nicole Loraux, *The Children of Athena*, trans. Caroline Levine (Princeton, NJ: Princeton University Press, 1993), 184–236; Loraux, *Born of the Earth*, 1–39; Rabinowitz, *Anxiety Veiled*, 189–217; Saxonhouse, "Reflections on Autochthony in Euripides' *Ion*," 252–73; and Zeitlin, *Playing the Other*, 285–338.

6. John Gibert, "Introduction," in *Euripides: Ion*, ed. John Gibert (Cambridge: Cambridge University Press, 2019), 63–66.

7. Zacharia's argument relies on the conjecture that the intense political crisis following the Athenian failure of the Sicilian Expedition (415–413 BCE) during the Peloponnesian War made Euripides's theme of reconciling autochthony and Ionianism more prominent. Metrical analysis of the play dates it to about 415 BCE. Scholars critical of dating tragedies in reference to historical events suggest a range between 420–410 BCE. See Katerina Zacharia, *Converging Truths* (Boston: Brill, 2003), 1–11; and discussion in Laura Swift, *Euripides' Ion* (London: Duckworth Companions, 2008), 28–30.

8. Pozzi, "The Polis in Crisis," 135–36; Carol Doughtery, "Democratic Contraditions and the Synoptic Illusion of Euripides' *Ion*," in *Demokratia*, ed. Joshiah Ober and Charles Hedrick (Princeton, NJ: Princeton University Press, 1996), 252; Kevin H. Lee, "Introduction to Euripides' *Ion*," in *Euripides' Ion*, ed. K. H. Lee (Warminister, UK: Aris & Phillips, 1997), 38–39; Jonathan Hall, *Ethnic Identity in Greek Antiquity* (Cambridge: Cambridge University Press, 1997), 46–54; David Kovacs, "Introduction to *Ion*," in *Ion* (Cambridge, MA: Harvard University Press, 1999), 318–19; and Swift, *Euripides' Ion*, 16–23.

9. Thucydides, *The History of the Peloponnesian War*, 1.2.5–1.2.6, 1.6.3, 2.15.1–2.16.2. The only passage where Ionians are mentioned in the *Iliad* is at 13.685, which many scholars point out is "anachronistic-looking." See T. F. R. G. Braun, "The Greeks in the Near East," in *Cambridge Ancient History*, ed. John Boardman and N. G. L. Hammond (Cambridge: Cambridge University Press, 1982), 1–30; Hall, *Ethnic Identity in Greek Antiquity*, 53; and Finkelberg, *Greek and Pre-Greeks*, 127–28.

10. This version can be traced to *the Catalogue of Women*, traditionally attributed to Hesiod, *Catalogue of Women*, trans. Glenn Most (Cambridge, MA: Harvard University Press, 2007), 9–10.

11. Herodotus, *Histories*, 1.145, 7.94, 8.44.

12. Pausanias, *Description of Greece*, trans. W. H. S. Jones (Cambridge, MA: Harvard University Press, 1933), 7.1.

13. Loraux, *Born of the Earth*, 13–27; Champion, "Imperial Ideologies, Citizenship Myths, Legal Disputes," 92–93. For ancient examples see Thucydides, *History of the Peloponnesian War*, 1.2.5; Lysias, "Funeral Oration," in *Athenian Funeral Orations*, ed. Judson Herrman (Newburyport, MA: Focus, 2004), 17; Demosthenes, *On the Embassy* (Cambridge, MA: Harvard University Press, 1930), 261.

14. This autochthony implied that the Athenians (and other autochthonous people) were different than the humans fashioned from Prometheus's clay. See Zacharia, *Converging Truths*, 56–60; Hansen, *Classical Mythology*, 69–70; V. J. Rosivach, "Autochthony and the Athenians," *Classical Quarterly* 37, no. 2 (1987): 294–305.

15. Joan Breton Connelly, *The Parthenon Enigma* (New York: Vintage, 2014), 202.

16. Hall, *Ethnic Identity in Greek Antiquity*, 53; David Rosenbloom, "The Panhellenism of Athenian Tragedy," in *Why Athens?*, ed. D. M. Carter (Oxford: Oxford University Press, 2011), 365–66; Matthew Clark, *Exploring Greek Myth* (Chichester, UK: Blackwell, 2012), 88.

17. The *Republic*'s "noble lie" is also a story about earthborn origins, as Socrates refers to the myth of metals as a Phoenician tale. See Saxonhouse, "Reflections on Autochthony in Euripides' *Ion*," 252–73; and Plato, *Republic*, 414c.

18. For a discussion see Saxonhouse, "Reflections on Autochthony in Euripides' *Ion*," 252–73; Rosivach, "Autochthony and the Athenians," 294–305; Nicole Loraux, "Kreousa the Autochthon," trans. Janet Lloyd in *Nothing to Do with Dionysos?*, ed. John J. Winkler and Froma I. Zeitlin (Princeton, NJ: Princeton University Press, 1990), 178–90; Lee, "Introduction to Euripides' *Ion*" 21–41; Loraux, *Born of the Earth*, 58–61; Zacharia, *Converging Truths*, 56–99; and Swift, *Euripides' Ion*, 88–90.

19. Euripides also wrote a tragedy on this Athenian autochthonous story, which survives in fragments. See Euripides, "Erechtheus," in *Fragments: Ageus-Meleager* (Cambridge, MA: Harvard University Press, 2008), 362–405.

20. Eumolpus was the son of Poseidon and Chione. Like Creusa, Chione bore Eumolpus in secret and threw the child into the Ocean, but his father the sea-god Poseidon saved the boy, who became a founder of the famous Eleusinian Mysteries. The sanctuary site at Eleusis figures prominently in the *Suppliant Women*. To confuse matters, there was a later version of Ion's story where, during this war with Eleusis, an adult Ion is rewarded with kingship for saving Athens. See

Parke, *Festivals of the Athenians*, 53; Vincent J. Rosivach, "Earthborn Olympians: The Parados of the *Ion*," *Classical Quarterly* 27, no. 2 (1977): 291–93.

21. For discussion see Kovacs, "Introduction to *Ion*," 317; Connelly, *Parthenon Enigma*, 303, 232, 132–42. See also Loraux, *Children of Athena*, 30–32. Others have focused on the significance of the Delphic location and the tragedy's connection to Dionysus and the Eleusinian Mysteries. See Burnett, *Catastrophe Survived*, 107–9; Zeitlin, *Playing the Other*, 285–338; and Doughtery, "Democratic Contradictions and the Synoptic Illusion of Euripides' *Ion*," 249–70.

22. Euripides, *Ion*, 1–80.

23. Euripides, *Ion*, 80–675. This song is an example of the new music of Euripides. See Luigi Battezzato, "Lyric," in *A Companion to Greek Tragedy*, ed. Justina Gregory (Oxford: Blackwell, 2008), 163–65.

24. Donald J. Mastronarde, "Iconography and Imagery in Euripides' *Ion*," in *Oxford Reading in Classical Studies: Euripides*, ed. Judith Mossman (Oxford: Oxford University Press, 2003), 294–308; and Rosivach, "Earthborn Olympians," 294–305.

25. Euripides, *Ion*, 360–80, 675, 810–20, 1055–60. Ion suggests he will "cross-examine (*xelegche*)" Apollo at line 367. A cognate of *elenchus*, this word indicates a questioning of the veracity of myth or revealing what is "hidden." See Meltzer, *Euripides and the Poetics of Nostalgia*, 152–53.

26. Ion's continuing anxiety over not knowing his mother might reflect the possible Hittite origins of ancient kingship lineage in Greece. This tradition descends through the female line by providing a king through his marriage to a female inheritor. See Finkelberg, *Greek and Pre-Greeks*, 71–79.

27. Euripides, *Phoenician Women*, 390–95.

28. Euripides, *Ion*, 675–1100.

29. Euripides, *Ion*, 1110–1555.

30. Euripides, *Ion*, 1555–1620.

31. Carpenter notes that this ending "seals" the view that the unjust are punished. See Rhys Carpenter, *The Ethics of Euripides* (New York: Columbia University Press, 1916), 28.

32. Euripides may have invented Ion's divine lineage, but it is possible that Apollo was considered a progenitor of the Ionians as established by the cult of *Apollo Patroos*. Corroborating evidence for Apollo's parental link to Ion only appears in later sources, such as Plato's *Euthyphro*. See Desmond J. Conacher, "The Paradox of Euripides' *Ion*," *Transactions of the American Philological Association* 90 (1959): 24–25; Desmond J. Conacher, *Euripidean Drama* (Toronto: University of Toronto Press, 1967), 267–85; Charles W. Hedrick, "The Temple and Cult of Apollo Patroos in Athens," *American Journal of Archeology* 92 (1988): 185–210; Doughtery, "Democratic Contradictions and the Synoptic Illusion of Euripides' *Ion*," 249–70; A. Thomas Cole, "The *Ion* of Euripides and Its Audience," in *Poet, Public, and Performance in Ancient Greece*, ed. Lowell Edmunds and Robert

W. Wallace (Baltimore: Johns Hopkins University Press, 1997), 87–96; and Zacharia, *Converging Truths*, 103–49.

33. Like the revamping of Theseus, the Athenians became more interested in their autochthony in the first half of the fifth century in tandem with the rise of democracy. See Connelly, *Parthenon Enigma*, 290–91.

34. In more common mythology, Zeus's son Hellen had three sons: Xuthus, Dorus, and Aeolus. As the progenitor of the Dorians, Dorus was a major figure in Spartan mythology and the founder of the House of Atreus. Athens and the Ionians, in general, were less significant in the stories of the heroic period and may not have been considered "Achaeans." See Hesiod, *Catalogue of Women*, 9–10. For discussion see Loraux, *Born of the Earth*, 28–36; Hansen, *Classical Mythology*, 73–74; and Finkelberg, *Greek and Pre-Greeks*, 138.

35. Kovacs, "Introduction to *Ion*," 318.

36. Doughtery, "Democratic Contraditions and the Synoptic Illusion of Euripides' *Ion*," 249–70; Lee, "Introduction to Euripides' *Ion*," 21–41; Zacharia, *Converging Truths*, 1–7, 183–86; Paul Woodruff, *First Democracy: The Challenge of an Athenian Ideal* (Oxford: Oxford University Press, 2005), 47–49; Meltzer, *Euripides and the Poetics of Nostalgia*, 146–87; and Wohl, *Euripides and the Politics of Form*, 1–28.

37. For discussion of the Athenian autochthony myth see Saxonhouse, "Reflections on Autochthony in Euripides' *Ion*," 252–73; Rosivach, "Autochthony and the Athenians," 294–305; Lee, "Introduction to Euripides' *Ion*," 21–41; Loraux, *Born of the Earth*, 13–27; Zacharia, *Converging Truths*, 56–99; and Swift, *Euripides' Ion*, 73–8.

38. See Mastronarde, "Iconography and Imagery in Euripides' *Ion*," 302–305; Zacharia, *Converging Truths*, 56–60; and Swift, *Euripides' Ion*, 76–77.

39. For an overview of the Apollo-Python mythology see Joseph Fontenrose, *Python* (Berkeley: University of California Press, 1959), 1–24.

40. The autochthonous myth became more prominent in the fifth century after the citizenship reforms of 451 BCE, which required both parents to be Athenians. For discussion see Walsh, "Rhetoric of Birthright and Race in Euripides' *Ion*," 301–15; Edwin Carawan, "Pericles the Younger and the Citizenship Law," *Classical Journal* 103 (2008): 383–406.

41. In the *Iliad* at line 2.547 Homer calls Erechtheus "the earthborn." For discussion, see Robert Parker, "Myths of Early Athens," in *Interpretations of Greek Mythology*, ed. Jan Bremmer (London: Routledge, 1987), 187–214; Rosivach, "Autochthony and the Athenians," 294–305; Hall, *Ethnic Identity in Greek Antiquity*, 53; and Zacharia, *Converging Truths*, 44–102.

42. There are other versions that attempt to "straighten out" the lineage of these first kings. In Apollodorus, the autochthon lineage went from Erichthonius-Pandion-Erechtheus-Creusa. For discussion see Rosivach, "Autochthony and the Athenians," 288.

43. The reconciliation also establishes not only a noble line but Ion as refounder of the city. See Walker, *Theseus and Athens*, 61; Doughtery, "Democratic Contraditions and the Synoptic Illusion of Euripides' *Ion*," 249–70; Saxonhouse, "Reflections on Autochthony in Euripides' *Ion*," 252–73; Rosivach, "Autochthony and the Athenians," 294–305; Hall, *Ethnic Identity in Greek Antiquity*, 36–56; and Zacharia, *Converging Truths*, 44–102.

44. Zacharia, *Converging Truths*, 60.

45. The image of Medusa as a beautiful woman with snakes for hair is Roman. For discussion see Stephen R. Wilk, *Medusa: Solving the Mystery of the Gorgon* (Oxford: Oxford University Press, 2000), 20–22.

46. Euripides, *Ion*, 985–1010.

47. Euripides, *Ion*, 250–60, 805–10, 585–95, 670–75, 720–25, 1055–60.

48. In Athens, resident foreigners or metics (*metoikos*) enjoyed some privileges but had no political rights. For discussion see Champion, "Imperial Ideologies, Citizenship Myths, Legal Disputes," 99; Kasimis, "Tragedy of Blood-Based Membership," 231–56; and Brock, "Citizens and Non-Citizens in Athenian Tragedy," 99.

49. Euripides, *Ion*, 1620–25.

50. For discussion see Blundell, *Helping Friends and Harming Enemies*, 26–60; Elizabeth S. Belfiore, "Harming Friends," in *Reciprocity in Ancient Greece*, ed. Christopher Gill, Norman Postlethwaite, and Richard Seaford (Oxford: Oxford University Press, 1988), 138–58; and Belfiore, *Murder among Friends*, xv–xix, 1–20.

51. Homer, *Odyssey*, 6.180–85; Plato, *Republic*, 334–36a.

52. Hesiod, *Works and Days*, 709.

53. Xenophon, *Memorabilia*, 2.6.21.

54. Lysias, *Against Andocides*, trans. W. R. M. Lamb (Cambridge, MA: Harvard University Press, 1930), 6.7.

55. Aristotle, *Poetics*, 1452a30, 1453a15–20.

56. Belfiore, *Murder among Friends*, 3–20.

57. In the *Republic*, Socrates points out several limitations of this ancient perspective, such as it assumes all friends are good people and worthy of good things and that good men would still harm others. See Plato, *Republic*, 334a–36e.

58. Euripides, *Ion*, 655–70, 810–20, 975–80.

59. For example, Heracles's human stepfather Amphitryon. See Paul Neumarkt, "The Amphitryon Legend," *American Imago* 34, no. 4 (1977): 359.

60. Just, *Women in Athenian Law and Life*, 120–21; Loraux, *Children of Athena*, 10–12; Sarah B. Pomeroy, *Goddess, Whores, Wives, and Slaves*, 2nd ed. (New York: Schocken, 1995), 79–88.

61. For discussion of the tragedy as symbolic of transitions into manhood see R. F. Willetts, "Action and Character in the *Ion* of Euripides," *Journal of Hellenic Studies* 93 (1973): 207; Pozzi, "Polis in Crisis," 135–44; Goldhill, "Great Dionysia and Civic Ideology (Revised)," 97–129; Winkler, "Ephebes's Song,"

24–37; Charles Segal, "Euripides' *Ion*: Generational Passage and Civic Myth," in *Rites of Passage in Ancient Greece*, ed. Mark W. Padilla (Lewisburg, PA: Bucknell University Press, 1999), 67–108; and Swift, *Euripides' Ion*, 124–25.

62. This quietist position of rejecting political participation was considered antidemocratic. See L. B. Carter, *The Quiet Athenian* (Oxford: Oxford University Press, 1986), 52–75.

63. Theseus was another founder-king of Athens. Most famous for killing the Minotaur, he is credited with the political unification of Attica and defeating local monstrous beasts. Euripides tells stories of Theseus and his son Demophon in his *Suppliant Women* and *Children of Heracles*. For discussion see Harry C. Avery, "Euripides' Heracleidae," *American Journal of Philology* 92, no. 4 (1971): 539–65.

64. Euripides, *Ion*, 375–80. Ion's continuing need for empirical evidence also implies new sophistic thinking. See de Romilly, *Great Sophists in Periclean Athens*, 144–47.

65. As Wohl points out, this desire reveals that passionate attachment is essential to all political systems, including open systems such as democracies. See Wohl, *Euripides and the Politics of Form*, 37.

66. Euripides, *Ion*, 985–1000.

67. Although not part of this story, even using the good blood of this Gorgon has negative consequences. Asclepius uses Medusa's good blood to resurrect the dead. For this violation of the natural order, Zeus kills Asclepius, which starts a cycle of retributive killings that ends with Apollo granting Admetus the favor of allowing another to die in his place. This story is told in Euripides's *Alcestis*. For discussion see Burnett, "Human Resistance and Divine Persuasion," 98.

68. Euripides, *Ion*, 1250–1320.

69. For discussion of the inviolability of sanctuary and sanctuary architecture see R. A. Tomlinson, *Greek Sanctuaries* (London: Paul Elek, 1976), 17–20; Ulrich Sinn, "Greek Sanctuaries as Places of Refuge," in *Greek Sanctuaries: New Approaches*, ed. Nanno Marinatos and Robin Hagg (London: Routledge, 1993), 88–109.

70. In *Children of Heracles*, Euripides puts the same argument in the mouth of the impious herald. See Euripides, *Children of Heracles*, 135–40, 235–50.

71. See, for example, Aristotle, *Nicomachean Ethics*, 1131a20–30.

72. Euripides, *Ion*, 340–45, 430–50, 325, 885–900, 970–75, 1315–20, 250–55.

73. Some scholars argue that Ion is holding the gods accountable to human standards. See Felix Martin Wassermann, "Divine Violence and Providence in Euripides' *Ion*," *Transactions of the American Philological Association* 71 (1940): 590–91; Burnett, "Human Resistance and Divine Persuasion," 93–4, 99. By contrast, it could be the lack of human understanding that makes it only appear that the gods are doing wrong. See Lefkowitz, *Euripides and the Gods*, 107–9.

74. Ion's critique of depictions of gods behaving immorally as ridiculous stories mirrors Socrates's critique in Book III of the *Republic*. See Plato, *Republic*, 377b–86a.

75. This is true of the tragic space in which the play occurs; the theater is a sacred space that is symbolic of the tension between secrecy and revelation as it exposes images and ideas to the audience. Boundaries, of course, are also what epic heroes fight over. See Padel, "Making Space Speak," 354–58; and Brock, *Greek Political Imagery*, 91.

76. Euripides, *Ion*, 185–235.

77. For discussion of the temple's geography see Pedley, *Sanctuaries and the Sacred in the Ancient Greek World*, 135–53; and Tomlinson, *Greek Sanctuaries*, 6–9.

78. Themis represents divine custom or practice (*nomos*) that is more sacrosanct and Panhellenic than civic law. See M. I. Finley, *The World of Odysseus* (New York: Viking, 1978), 78.

79. Euripides, *Ion*, 1045–1105, 1095–1100.

80. As a distinctive goddess, Enodia probably originated in Thessaly. She was worshiped at various sites in Greece, such as Euboea, Epidaurus, and as far away as Dalmatia. Like Hekate, she was a goddess of witchcraft and signified crossroads, boundaries, and transitions; her name literally means "the one on the road." For discussion Stephen G. Miller, "The Altar of the Six Goddesses," *California Studies in Classical Antiquity* 7 (1974): 251–54; and Sorita D'Este and David Rankine, *Hekate Liminal Rites* (London: Avalonia, 2009), 42–48.

81. Similar to Creusa, Hades abducted Persephone while she was picking flowers. Her mother, the fertility goddess Demeter, denied the prosperity of crops until a compromise was found whereby Persephone returns to life (as does nature) for the summer months. This allusion recalls the retaliatory death of Erechtheus in exchange for Poseidon's son Eumolpus. See Rosivach, "Earthborn Olympians," 303–4.

82. One of Hekate's many titles included "Hekate Enodia." See, for instance, Euripides, *Medea*, 400–20; Euripides, *Ion*, 1096.

83. As Wolff notes, "Doublings are one of the most characteristic features of mythological stories." See Wolff, "Design and Myth in Euripides' *Ion*," 172. For discussion, see Zacharia, *Converging Truths*, 76–8; Loraux, *Born of the Earth*, 1–13; Stanley E. Hoffer, "Violence, Culture, and the Workings of Ideology in Euripides' *Ion*," *Classical Antiquity* 15, no. 2 (1996): 289–318; and McDermott, "Double-Meaning and Mythic Novelty in Euripides' Plays," 123–32.

84. Berman, "Double Foundation of Boiotian Thebes," 16.

85. Spenser Cole, "Annotated Innovation in Euripides' *Ion*," *Classical Quarterly* 58 (2008): 313–15; and McDermott, "Double-Meaning and Mythic Novelty in Euripides' Plays," 125–5.

86. See Girard, *Things Hidden*, 105–26.

87. For example, women are essential for reproduction and foreigners, such as Xuthus, can save the community. For discussion see Zeitlin, *Playing the Other*, 80–5; Rabinowitz, *Anxiety Veiled*, 192–93; Saxonhouse, *Fear of Diversity*, 78–79; Loraux, "Kreousa the Autochthon," 179–96; Hoffer, "Violence, Culture, and the Workings of Ideology," 289–319; and Swift, *Euripides' Ion*, 88–90.

88. Saxonhouse, "Reflections on Autochthony in Euripides' *Ion*," 252–73; Champion, "Imperial Ideologies, Citizenship Myths, Legal Disputes," 90–2; Doughtery, "Democratic Contradictions and the Synoptic Illusion of Euripides' *Ion*," 249–70; Walsh, "Rhetoric of Birthright and Race in Euripides' *Ion*," 301–15; and Kasimis, "Tragedy of Blood-Based Membership: Secrecy and the Politics of Immigration," 231–56.

89. Euripides, *Ion*, 515–65 and 1395–1490, 1175–1220 and 1260–1320, 10–25 and 70–75. For discussion see Wassermann, "Divine Violence and Providence in Euripides' *Ion*," 600; Wolff, "Design and Myth in Euripides' *Ion*," 170–76, 180; and Carl A. P. Ruck, "On the Sacred Names of Iamos and Ion," *Classical Journal* 71, no. 3 (1976): 235–52.

90. Euripides, *Ion*, 1395 and 210–15, see also 335–85, 1600–1605.

91. Euripides, *Ion*, 1335–55, 1415–45. Zacharia calls this effect "twinning" Zacharia, *Converging Truths*, 66–70. See also Burnett, "Human Resistance and Divine Persuasion," 71–72; Swift, *Euripides' Ion*, 30–5.

92. Euripides, *Ion*, 465.

93. Ion's monody may not simply be a celebration of dawn, but "his" dawning into manhood. See Willetts, "Action and Character in the *Ion* of Euripides," 207–8.

94. For discussion of the Heracles myth see Stafford, *Herakles*, 27–78.

95. Mastronarde, "Iconography and Imagery in Euripides' *Ion*," 169.

96. Euripides, *Ion*, 150–80, 900–20, 1185–1210.

97. Burnett, "Human Resistance and Divine Persuasion," 97. See also John P. Harris, "The Swan's Red-Dipped Foot," *Classical Quarterly* 62 (2012): 510–12.

98. For discussion see Andrew Farrington, "*Gnothi Seauton*: Social Self-Knowledge in Euripides' *Ion*," *Rheinisches Museum für Philologie* 134, no. 2 (1991): 120–36.

99. Plants were "wild beings" and thought to be hunted similar to animals. They also were often identified with sexual forces and the power of Mother Earth. The virgins, like Creusa, who are attacked by the gods, are also often out picking wildflowers. See Ruck, "On the Sacred Names of Iamos and Ion," 243, 235–36; Wasson, Hofmann, and Ruck, *Road to Eleusis*, 52.

100. *Iōn* is the participle of *eimi*, a verb meaning "I will go." An "ion" is also the Greek word for a violet. Euripides, *Ion*, 660–70.

101. In another story that reflects Creusa's, the laurel became sacred to Apollo after he fell in love with Daphne (another daughter of Mother Earth). To escape from Apollo's unwanted advances, her mother turned Daphne into the laurel tree. See Wolff, "Design and Myth in Euripides' *Ion*," 180; Willetts, "Action and Character in the *Ion* of Euripides," 206.

102. Ruck, "On the Sacred Names of Iamos and Ion," 240.

103. Hoffer, "Violence, Culture, and the Workings of Ideology," 308–309. See also Jene Larue, "Creusa's Monody 859–922," *Transactions of the American*

Philological Association 94 (1963): 128; and Wassermann, "Divine Violence and Providence in Euripides' *Ion*," 598.

104. Euripides, *Ion*, 250–55, 440–45.

105. Polynices makes a similar point in the *Phoenician Women*. For example, compare Euripides *Ion*, 670–75 and Euripides, *Phoenician Women*, 390–95. For discussion of *parrhēsia* see Saxonhouse, *Fear of Diversity*, 14–15, 129–45.

106. This doubling of meaning is also found in Socratic irony, in which one says one thing but means another. For a seminal explanation see Gregory Vlastos, *Socrates, Ironist and Moral Philosopher* (Cambridge: Cambridge University Press, 1991), 21–44.

107. For discussion see Broad, *The Oracle*, 9–70; Pedley, *Sanctuaries and the Sacred in the Ancient Greek World*, 135–38. One of the most famous of the Oracle's riddles was that a "wooden wall" would protect Athens during the Second Persian War. Themistocles convinces the Athenians to interpret this to mean building a navy. See Herodotus, *The Histories*, 7.143.

108. Zeitlin, *Playing the Other*, 315.

109. Ruck, "On the Sacred Names of Iamos and Ion," 239.

110. Loraux, *Born of the Earth*, 39–46. See also Doughtery, "Democratic Contradictions and the Synoptic Illusion of Euripides' *Ion*," 254–55. In contrast, Saxonhouse argues that the earthborn myth reinforces aristocratic and imperialistic forces, especially after the people vote to abandon their mother-soil during the Persian invasion in 480 BCE. See Saxonhouse, "Reflections on Autochthony in Euripides' *Ion*," 252–73.

111. Hall, *Ethnic Identity in Greek Antiquity*, 54–56; Julia C. Kindt, "Review of Converging Truths," *International Journal of the Classic Tradition* 13, no. 1 (2006): 125–27.

112. Euripides, *Ion*, 1560–70, 335–40. From this perspective, like the *Eumenides*, Athena's diplomatic skills are necessary to bring about a peaceful ending. See Mary Lefkowitz, *Greek Gods, Human Lives* (New Haven, CT: Yale University Press, 2003), 150–51.

113. See Burnett, "Human Resistance and Divine Persuasion in Euripides' *Ion*," 98–99; Wolff, "Design and Myth in Euripides' *Ion*," 188–89.

114. Creusa, thus, is likened to a male who is not secure in his paternity. See Loraux, *The Children of Athena*, 10–12; and Just, *Women in Athenian Law and Life*, 137–53.

115. Zacharia, *Converging Truths*, 176–83.

116. Farrington, "*Gnothi Seauton*," 133. See also Ringer, *Euripides and the Boundary of the Human*, 215–34.

117. For a discussion of contemporary nationalism see Benedict Anderson, *Imagined Communities*, 2nd ed. (New York: Verso, 2006). For discussion of nationalism as tribal or ethnic identity in the tragedy see Ernest L. Hettich, *A Study in Ancient Nationalism* (Williamsport, PA: Bayard, 1933); Johann P.

Arnason, "Nationalism, Globalism, and Modernity," *Theory, Culture and Society* 7, no. 2 (1990): 207–35; and Sokolon, "Euripides' *Ion*," 33–53.

118. For discussion see Alex Gottesman, *Politics and the Street in Athens* (Cambridge: Cambridge University Press, 2014), 169–76; and Mark Munn, *The School of History* (Berkeley: University of California Press, 2000), 36–37, 180.

119. For examples of this extensive literature see Anke Bartels et al., eds., *Postcolonial Justice* (Leiden, The Netherlands: Brill, 2017); Juan Carlos Velasco, "Beyond the Borders," in *Spheres of Global Justice*, eds. Jean-Christophe Merle et al. (New York: Springer, 2013), 293–306; Peter W. Higgins, *Immigration Justice* (Edinburgh: Edinburgh University Press, 2013); and Ryan Pevnick, *Immigration and the Constraints of Justice* (Cambridge: Cambridge University Press, 2011).

120. Berman, "Double Foundation of Boiotian Thebes," 19.

121. Hoffer, "Violence, Culture, and the Workings of Ideology," 306.

122. Jill Frank, *Democracy and the Death of Shame* (Cambridge: Cambridge University Press, 2016), 11. For other examples see Myra Mendible, ed. *American Shame* (Bloomington: Indiana University Press, 2016); and Martha C. Nussbaum, *Hiding from Humanity* (Princeton, NJ: Princeton University Press, 2004).

123. For example, see Peter N. Stearns, *Shame* (Urbana: University of Illinois Press, 2017); Christina H. Tarnopolsky, *Prudes, Perverts, and Tryants* (Princeton, NJ: Princeton University Press, 2010); and Saxonhouse, *Free Speech and Democracy in Ancient Athens*.

124. For a discussion of shame in ancient Greece, see Douglas L. Cairns, *Aidos: The Psychology and Ethics of Honour and Shame in Ancient Greek Literature* (Oxford: Clarendon, 1993).

125. Euripides, *Ion*, 230–40, 335–40, 1600–1605, 1555–60, 1045–50.

Chapter 5

1. *Children of Heracles*, 1–5.

2. For discussion of textual corruption in possible lacuna and later interpolations see Günther Zuntz, "Is the *Heracleidae* Mutilated?," *Classical Quarterly* 41, no. 1/2 (1947): 46–52; Peter Burian, "Euripides' *Heraclidae*: An Interpretation," *Classical Philology* 22, no. 1 (1977): 1–6. For examples of critiques see John H. McLean, "The *Heracleidae* of Euripides," *American Journal of Philology* 55, no. 3 (1934): 197–224; J. W. Fitton, "The *Suppliant Women* and the *Herakleidai* of Euripides," *Hermes* 89, no. 4 (1961): 430–61; and G. M. A. Grube, *The Drama of Euripides* (London: Methuen, 1961), 166–76.

3. See Zuntz, *Political Plays of Euripides*, 52; Anne Pippin Burnett, "Tribe and City: Custom and Decree in the *Children of Heracles*," *Classical Philology* 71, no. 1 (1976): 4–26; and Peter Burian, "Euripides' *Heraclidae*," 1–21.

4. As an alphabet play, the *Children of Heracles* lacks *scholia*, so little is known about the production date of the trilogy and satyr play. For more discussion see Zuntz, *An Inquiry into the Transmission of the Plays of Euripides*, 3–16; William Allan, "Introduction to the *Children of Heracles*," in *Euripides: The Children of Heracles*, ed. William Allan (Warminster, UK: Aris & Phillips, 2001), 54–58.

5. For the political significance of the Spartans as descendants of Heracles see Stafford, *Herakles*, 135–42.

6. For discussion of the Heracles myth see Stafford, *Herakles*, 79–103; Alastair Blanshard, *Hercules: A Heroic Life* (London: Granta, 2005); Roberto Calasso, *The Marriage of Cadmus and Harmony*, trans. Tim Parks (New York: Vintage International, 1993), 20–3, 60–76; and Frank Brommer, *Heracles: The Twelve Labors of the Hero in Ancient Art and Literature*, trans. Shirley J. Schwarz (New Rochelle, NY: Aristide D. Caratzas, 1986).

7. Euripides tells another version of these events in his tragedy *Heracles*. In that play, Euripides reverses the order of Heracles's madness by placing this event after the completion of the twelve labors. See Euripides, *Heracles*, trans. David Kovacs (Cambridge, MA: Harvard University Press, 1998), 1–15.

8. Identification of specific twelve labors (called the *Dodekathlos*) was not "canonized" until the third century. In Euripides's time there were wide variations of what was included in the list of Heracles's labors. For discussion see Brommer, *Heracles*, 12, 78; and Blanshard, *Hercules*, 90.

9. Although authorship is not certain, Aeschylus tells the early part of this story in Aeschylus, *Prometheus Bound*, trans. Alan H. Sommerstein (Cambridge, MA: Harvard University Press, 2009), 1–127. Fragments of a play called *Prometheus Unbound*, which may also be an Aeschylean play, suggest Heracles kills the eagle that eats his liver and frees him. See Stafford, *Herakles*, 66–68, 80.

10. Mendelsohn suggests this geography allows for literal and symbolic distance through which Athens can investigate its "self" and the "other" in the neutral space of the suburb "between." See Mendelsohn, *Gender and the City*, 51–57, 62. For the significance of Marathon in Athenian cultural memory see Shipton, *Politics of Youth in Greek Tragedy*, 79–80.

11. Euripides, *Children of Heracles*, 15–55.

12. The herald is called "Copreus" in the *Iliad*, although this might be a later addition to the manuscript. See David Kovacs, "Introduction to *Children of Heracles*," in *Children of Heracles* (Cambridge, MA: Harvard University Press, 1995), fn 3, 14–15.

13. The chorus of elderly citizens is unusual as most choruses comprise women, foreigners, or elites. This might indicate that the chorus is a metaphor for the views of the common citizens. For discussion see Jean-Pierre Vernant, "Tensions and Ambiguities in Greek Tragedy," in *Myth and Tragedy in Ancient Greece*, ed. Jean-Paul Vernant and Pierre Vidal-Naquet (New York: Zone, 1990),

33–34; John Gould, "Tragedy and the Collective Experience," in *Tragedy and the Tragic: Greek Theater and Beyond*, ed. M. S. Silk (Oxford: Oxford University Press, 1996), 217–43; Peter Wilson, *The Athenian Institution of the Khoregia: The Chorus, the City, and the Stage* (Cambridge: Cambridge University Press, 2000), 144–93; Carter, *The Politics of Greek Tragedy*, 48–49; Sheila Murnaghan, "Choroi Achoroi: The Athenian Politics of Tragic Choral Identity," in *Why Athens?*, ed. David M. Carter (Oxford: Oxford University Press, 2011), 245–52; and Ian Ruffell, "Response to Murnaghan and Visvardi," in *Why Athens?*, ed. David M. Carter (Oxford: Oxford University Press, 2011), 299–301.

14. Following the convention of only three speaking parts, Acamas is a nonspeaking role. See Allan, "Introduction to the *Children of Heracles*," 31–32.

15. Jaroslav Danes, "*Amēchania* in Euripides' *Heraclidae*," *Classical Quarterly* 65, no. 1 (2015): 367.

16. Demophon and the children are related in two ways. First, they are second cousins as their grandfathers, Zeus and Poseidon, were brothers. Second, their mortal grandmothers, Aethra and Alcmene, were cousins through their shared grandfather, Pelops. Although unstated, Iolaus is also a military ally (*sumploos*). See Calasso, *Marriage of Cadmus and Harmony*, 60–64; John Wilkins, "Introduction and Commentary," in *Euripides: Heracleidae*, ed. John Wilkins (Oxford: Clarendon, 1993), 78; and Griffith, "Families and Inter-City Relations," 198. For discussion of Theseus's rescue see Walker, *Theseus and Athens*, 25–26.

17. The meaning of "Panhellenism" is not clear, but Rosenbloom suggests that, in tragedy, it can denote Athens as synecdoche for Hellenes. See Rosenbloom, "The Panhellenism of Athenian Tragedy," 353–58, 361–64.

18. Although violating sanctuary is not a "sensational" crime, representing the herald as violent reduces the moral ambiguity of his actions. See Burnett, *Revenge in Attic and Later Tragedy*, 146–48.

19. As will be developed, this Athenian self-identity of defenders of justice and place of sanctuary is found in both the tragedy and rhetoric of the classical period. For example, Isocrates in his *Panegyricus* and Alcibiades's speech in Thucydides's history connect the idea of helping of others to Athenian power. See Isocrates, *Panegyricus*, trans. George Norlin (Cambridge, MA: Harvard University Press, 1928), 4.50–90; and Thucydides, *History of the Peloponnesian War*, 6.18.1–6.19.1. For discussion see Walker, *Theseus and Athens*, 172; Angeliki Tzanetou, "Supplication and Empire in Athenian Tragedy," in *Why Athens?*, ed. D. M. Carter (Oxford: Oxford University Press, 2011), 305–11, 321–4; Matthew Christ, *The Limits of Altruism in Democratic Athens* (Cambridge: Cambridge University Press, 2012), 143–45; and Bernd Steinbock, *Social Memory in Athenian Public Discourses* (Ann Arbor: University of Michigan, 2013), 198–206.

20. Kovacs's translation. See Euripides, *Children of Heracles*, 500–505.

21. Euripides, *Children of Heracles*, 840–50, 880–85.

22. Euripides, *Children of Heracles*, 890–900, 935–40.

23. Eurystheus's first justification, compulsion of the gods, reflects the sophist Gorgias's argument defending Helen as not culpable because the gods are too powerful to resist. See Gorgias, *Encomium of Helen*, trans. D. M. MacDowell (London: Bristol Classical, 2005), 6–7.

24. The aging of Iolaus also emphasizes his symmetry with Alcmene. They represent a gender reversal, with Iolaus originally depicted as frail in contrast to Alcmene's energetic pursuit of private vengeance. See Falkner, *Poetics of Old Age*, 180–91.

25. Another problem with the "elderly" Iolaus is that he was worshiped as a patron of the young, especially in Thebes where his cult celebrated the vigor of youth and athletics. See Avery, "Euripides' *Heracleidae*," 553–54; and Allan, "Introduction to the *Children of Heracles*," 27–28.

26. McLean, "*Heracleidae* of Euripides," 204–12; Zuntz, "Is the *Heracleidae* Mutilated?," 50–51. There are several versions that include the maiden's role, but these are dated after Euripides's play, including Pausanias's account that reports seeing a spring named after Macaria. See J. A. Spranger, "The Political Element in the *Heracleidae* of Euripides," *Classical Quarterly* 19, no. 3/4 (1925): fn 4, 128; and Pausanias, *Guide to Greece 1: Central Greece*, 1.32.6.

27. Spranger, "Political Element in the *Heracleidae* of Euripides," 120–24.

28. Avery, "Euripides' *Heracleidae*," 544–45. The sons of Heracles are referred to, but not named, in the *Hecuba*, as supporters of the sacrifice of Polyxena. Euripides, *Hecuba*, 110–15.

29. Burnett, "Tribe and City," fn 29, 22; Zuntz, *Political Plays of Euripides*, 83–88. In the second century AD, Pausanias suggests Iolaus killed Eurystheus and buried him on the Skironian road. See Pausanias, *Guide to Greece 1: Central Greece*, 1.44.10.

30. For discussion see Allan, "Introduction to the *Children of Heracles*," 55–56.

31. McLean, "*Heracleidae* of Euripides," 203–205, 211.

32. For discussion see Zuntz, "Is the *Heracleidae* Mutilated?," 50–52; Philip Vellacott, "Introduction," in *Orestes and Other Plays* (Toronto: Penguin, 1972), 22–24; Burian, "Euripides' *Heraclidae*," fn 3, 2. Spranger suggests that the "utter absence of any lament for Macaria" is evidence that the sacrifice must not have taken place. Spranger, "Political Element in the *Heracleidae* of Euripides," 122–23.

33. For examples, see McLean, "*Heracleidae* of Euripides," 215; Ralph Gladstone, "An Introduction to the *Heracleidae*," in *Euripides I*, eds. David Grene and Richmond Lattimore (Chicago: University of Chicago Press, 1955), 112; Grube, *The Drama of Euripides*, 175–76. For discussion, A.E. Haigh, *The Tragic Drama of the Greeks* (New York: Dover, 1968), 291; and Storey and Allan, *A Guide to Ancient Greek Drama*, 260.

34. McLean, "The *Heracleidae* of Euripides," 215–17; Zuntz, *Political Plays of Euripides*, 35–37; Fitton, "*Suppliant Women* and the *Herakleidai* of Euripides," 457–58; and Avery, "Euripides' *Heracleidae*," 558.

35. Burian, "Euripides' *Heraclidae*," 11–12; S. E. Smethurst, "Heracles and Iolaus, Part I," *Classical Journal* 45, no. 6 (1950): 288–93. For a critique of this scene as "comic" see Donald J. Mastronarde, "Euripidean Tragedy and Genre," *Illinois Classical Studies* 24/25 (1999): 36.

36. Kitto, *Greek Tragedy*, 252; and Fitton, "*Suppliant Women* and the *Herakleidai* of Euripides," 460.

37. The Athenians are so "eclipsed" by the Heracleidae's glory that Spranger suggests they must have not taken part in the victory. See Spranger, "Political Element in the *Heracleidae* of Euripides," 122–23.

38. Based on Aristotle's influence, the "closed form" of tragedy tends toward order, coherence, and self-containment of a single theme in contrast to the "open form," which lacks hierarchy and involves multiple characters and events. See Mastronarde, *Euripides' Phoenissae* 3–4.

39. Danes, "*Amēchania* in Euripides' *Heraclidae*," 370.

40. The title is rare. Of our existing plays, only this tragedy and *Seven against Thebes* are not named for a main character, the chorus, or the major event in the tragedy. See Avery, "Euripides' *Heracleidae*," 39–40, 564.

41. Burian, "Euripides' *Heraclidae*," 19–20.

42. Euripides, *Children of Heracles*, 1–5.

43. Thucydides, *History of the Peloponnesian War*, 1.68.1–1.71.3. The term "busybody" (*polupragmosynē*) referred to the "faction" in Athens that advocated active engagement in foreign affairs as opposed to the more conservative "quietists." Plato also uses this term (*polupragmosynē*) in the *Republic* to describe injustice as opposed to the justice of "minding one's own business" by performing one's natural function. See Plato, *Republic*, 452b.

44. In the *Republic*, this ethical norm is raised as Polemarchus's definition of justice. See *Republic*, 331e–36a. For discussion of the pervasiveness of this ethic see Blundell, *Helping Friends and Harming Enemies*, 26–60.

45. Belfiore, *Murder among Friends*, 19.

46. Tzanetou suggests that as a stand-in for the "weak," the Heracleidae are given a voice not possible in Athenian oratory. By contrast, Saxonhouse points out how this conflict reveals the exclusionary possibility of freedom of speech. See Tzanetou, "Supplication and Empire in Athenian Tragedy," 324; Saxonhouse, *Free Speech and Democracy in Ancient Athens*, 99.

47. In the *Suppliant Women*, Theseus supports the mothers of the fallen Argive generals after the battle of the Seven against Thebes. In this version, Creon decreed that these fallen generals (like his nephew Polynices) are to remain unburied. See Euripides, *Suppliant Women*, 300–400.

48. See, for example, Plato, *Republic*, 327a–28b. For discussion of this idea in the *Republic* see Leo Strauss, *The City and Man* (Chicago: University of Chicago

Press, 1964), 64; Bloom, "Interpretive Essay," 310; and Laurence Lampert, *How Philosophy Became Socratic* (Chicago: University of Chicago Press, 2010), 248–50.

49. During the Peloponnesian War, there were many violations of the sacred law protecting supplication on both sides, including starving or burning to death those who claimed sanctuary. The Spartans, for example, killed several hundred suppliant Plataeans. Despite celebrating protecting the weak in tragedies such as this one, the Athenians had a guard post that prevented refugees from claiming sanctuary on the Acropolis. See Sinn, "Greek Sanctuaries as Places of Refuge," 92–93. See also Paul Bentley Kern, *Ancient Siege Warfare* (Bloomington: Indiana University Press, 1999), 143–47; Fred S. Naiden, *Ancient Supplication* (Oxford: Oxford University Press, 2006), 171–218; and Tzanetou, "Supplication and Empire in Athenian Tragedy," 307.

50. Euripides, *Children of Heracles*, 55–60, 105–10, 135–80, 255–60.

51. Zuntz, *Political Plays of Euripides*, 33–34.

52. This argument is echoed in the *Ion*, when Ion criticizes that the sanctuary protection of criminals is wrong because "good and bad men receive the same thing from the gods." Euripides, *Ion*, 1310–20.

53. Euripides, *Children of Heracles*, 70–80, 180–230.

54. The sanctuaries were inviolable both for valuable votive offerings as well as supplicants (*hiketai*) who took refuge on the god's altar. See Sinn, "Greek Sanctuaries as Places of Refuge," 88–94, 100. See also Tomlinson, *Greek Sanctuaries*, 9–14; Belfiore, *Murder among Friends*, 41–44; and Josiah Ober, "Law and Political Theory," in *Cambridge Companion to Ancient Greek Law*, ed. Michael Gagarin and David Cohen (Cambridge: Cambridge University Press, 2005), 403–405.

55. Michael Gagarin, "Laws and Legislation in Ancient Greece," in *A Companion to Ancient Greek Government*, ed. Hans Beck (London: John Wiley, 2013), 225–26.

56. Mendelsohn, *Gender and the City*, 67–72.

57. Steinbock, *Social Memory in Athenian Public Discourses*, 158–80. For discussion on kinship and supplication see Belfiore, *Murder among Friends*, 41–42.

58. For discussion of this reciprocal relationship see Robert Parker, "Pleasing Thighs," in *Reciprocity in Ancient Greece*, ed. Christopher Gill, Norman Postlethwaite, and Richard Seaford (Oxford: Clarendon, 1998), 105–27.

59. Euripides, *Children of Heracles*, 100–15, 125–30, 230–35, 325–35.

60. Kovacs's translation. Euripides, *Children of Heracles*, 230–35. Aristotle defines pity as "a kind of pain at the sight of another person suffering from undeserved misfortune." See Aristotle, *Art of Rhetoric*, 1385b.

61. Euripides, *Children of Heracles*, 235–40, 260–65, 270–75.

62. Supplication could be rejected or prevented by blocking sacred spaces. Murderers, for example, were not allowed to participate in mystery rites. Third parties, however, were not permitted to drag the suppliant away. See Sinn, "Greek Sanctuaries as Places of Refuge," 91; Sir Frank Adcock and D. J. Mosley,

Diplomacy in Greece (London: Thames and Hudson, 1975), 10–11; and Naiden, *Ancient Supplication*, 177–83.

63. Euripides, *Children of Heracles*, 270–75.

64. Sinn, "Greek Sanctuaries as Places of Refuge," 90; and Ober, "Law and Political Theory," 403–405.

65. Euripides, *Children of Heracles*, 310–35.

66. See, for example, Joseph William Hewitt, "Gratitude and Ingratitude in the Plays of Euripides," *American Journal of Philology* 43, no. 4 (1922): 340–41.

67. Although *kharis* is a unifying theme, there is considerable scholarly disagreement as to whether this ethical norm is reversed in the finale. See Conacher, *Euripidean Drama*, 115–24; and Zuntz, *The Political Plays of Euripides*, 27–28, 48–54.

68. Burian, "Euripides' Heraclidae," 16–21; Fitton, "The *Suppliant Women* and the *Herakleidai* of Eurpidies," 458–59; and Burnett, "Tribe and City," 22–26.

69. Euripides, *Children of Heracles*, 400–420.

70. Sinn, "Greek Sanctuaries as Places of Refuge," 92.

71. Angeliki Tzanetou, *City of Suppliants* (Austin: University of Texas Press, 2012), 86.

72. Euripides, *Children of Heracles*, 540–95; and Avery, "Euripides' Heracleidae," 541–46.

73. The motif of a sacrificial victim that saves a people is, of course, not unique to Euripides nor Greek mythology but common across mythological and religious traditions. For discussion see Connelly, *Parthenon Enigma*, 335–37. For Euripides's use of this motif see Garrison, *Groaning Tears*, 129–67; Helene P. Foley, *Female Acts in Greek Tragedy* (Princeton, NJ: Princeton University Press, 2001), 145–200; Rabinowitz, *Anxiety Veiled*, 31–65; Mendelsohn, *Gender and the City*, 89–104; and Brands and Edel, *The Lessons of Tragedy*, 15–16.

74. Gladstone's translation. Euripides, "The Heracleidae," in *Euripides I*, eds. David Grene and Richmond Lattimore (Chicago: University of Chicago Press, 1955), 545–50, see also 500–535.

75. McLean, "Heracleidae of Euripides," 211; Avery, "Euripides' Heracleidae," 539–40; Fitton, "Suppliant Women and the Herakleidai of Euripides," 452. The maiden's speech is ambiguous as it simultaneously challenges and reinforces gender norms as well as proclaims and disavows her position of moral authority. For discussion see McClure, *Spoken Like a Woman*, 25.

76. Tzanetou argues that her sacrifice is a metaphor for the tribute expected from the subject states of the empire in return for Athenian military protection. This tribute was offered and displayed at the Great Dionysia. Tzanetou, *City of Suppliants*, 89.

77. Burnett, "Tribe and City," 18–21.

78. Euripides, *Children of Heracles*, 530–35.

79. Rabinowitz, *Anxiety Veiled*, 63–66.

80. Euripides, *Children of Heracles*, 590–95.

81. Compare the extended onstage lament for Alcestis in Euripides, *Alcestis*, 390–475. Mendelsohn argues that the maiden's disappearance is a parody of her attempt to enter the world of men. The lack of lament is also cited as a reason for a suspected lacuna in the text. For discussion see McLean, "*Heracleidae* of Euripides," 204–12; Mendelsohn, *Gender and the City*, 93–94, 104.

82. Burian, "Euripides' *Heraclidae*," 8, 7–11. See also Burnett, "Tribe and City," 16–17; Danes, "*Amēchania* in Euripides' *Heraclidae*," 367–70.

83. Euripides, *Children of Heracles*, 645–715.

84. As noted previously, see Fitton, "*Suppliant Women* and the *Herakleidai* of Euripides," 430–61; Kitto, *Greek Tragedy*, 252; and McLean, "The *Heracleidae* of Euripides," 197–224.

85. This scene could also contrast Iolaus with Eurystheus, who is never portrayed as courageous or heroic. For example, one popular image of Heracles completing the labor of delivering the Erymanthian boar shows Eurystheus so fearful that he jumps in a jar to hide. See Brommer, *Heracles*, 19–20.

86. Aeschylus may have had a similar rejuvenation scene in a lost play. See Avery, "Euripides' *Heracleidae*," 552–54; Ralph Gladstone, "An Introduction to the *Heracleidae*," 113. As the attendant of Athenian *ephēboi* in their transitional rites, Hēbē's appearance might also symbolize Iolaus's transformation into an Athenian *ephēbos*. See Mendelsohn, *Gender and the City*, 119, 133–34; and Shipton, *Politics of Youth in Greek Tragedy*, 77–78, 91–92.

87. In Book 24 of the *Odyssey*, Athena rejuvenates Laertes so he can help his son and grandson defeat the suitors. Homer, *The Odyssey*, 24.580–90. For Medea's rejuvenation stories see Kerenyi, *Goddesses of Sun and Moon* 30–36; Griffiths, *Medea*, 41–48; Luschnig, *Granddaughter of the Sun*, 80–84, 182.

88. Euripides, *Children of Heracles*, 935–40, 345–55. For discussion see Burian, "Euripides' *Heraclidae*," 14; Fitton, "*Suppliant Women* and the *Herakleidai* of Euripides," 454; and Burnett, "Tribe and City," 18–21.

89. Heracles also required divine support, especially from Hermes and Athena, to complete his famous labors. See Blanshard, *Hercules*, 79.

90. Avery, "Euripides' *Heracleidae*," 555.

91. The Athenians promoted the self-ideal that their city helped the weak and was a place of sanctuary. The Theseion temple (now often called the Hephaisteion) dedicated to Demophon's father in the agora, for example, was a famous site for asylum. For discussion see Tzanetou, "Supplication and Empire in Athenian Tragedy," 305–12; and Walker, *Theseus and Athens*, 22–24, 172–73.

92. Zuntz, *Political Plays of Euripides*, 85. See also J. T. Sheppard, "*Tyrannos, Kerdos*, and the Modest Measure in Three Plays of Euripides," *Classical Quarterly* 11, no. 1 (1917): 3–4; Kovacs, "Introduction to *Children of Heracles*," 6; Haigh, *Tragic Drama of the Greeks*, 291–92; and Tzanetou, "Supplication and Empire in Athenian Tragedy," 89.

93. Even scholars who critique such idealism typically suggest the finale is the main reversal of the action. See Burian, "Euripides' Heraclidae," 15–16; and Burnett, "Tribe and City," 22–23.

94. Euripides, *Children of Heracles*, 1025–30.

95. See also Avery, "Euripides' Heracleidae," 561.

96. Euripides, *Children of Heracles*, 230–35.

97. This scene contrasts with Athena's deus ex machina in the *Suppliant Women* where the goddess insists on an oath because promises of reciprocity are insufficient. See Euripides, *Suppliant Women*, 1180–1215. For discussion of the importance of oath taking, especially between states, see Alan H. Sommerstein and Andrew J. Bayliss, *Oath and State in Ancient Greece* (Boston: Walter de Gruyter, 2013), 147–280.

98. Tzanetou, *City of Suppliants*, 100; Tzanetou,"Supplication and Empire in Athenian Tragedy," 308; and Stafford, *Herakles*, 93.

99. Burian, "Euripides' Heraclidae," 20; and Avery, "Euripides' Heracleidae," 563. Euripides deals with the problem of this reversal of enemies and friends in several plays, most notably in Euripides, *Medea*, 465–520.

100. Burian, "Euripides' Heraclidae," 20.

101. Euripides, *Children of Heracles*, 970–75.

102. Euripides, *Children of Heracles*, 325–35.

103. Euripides, *Children of Heracles*, 890–920.

104. Aristotle would not be surprised by this reversal, as he also interconnects pity for the undeserved misfortune of others with either a lack of emotion or the joy of seeing the deserved success of others. See Aristotle, *Art of Rhetoric*, 1386b. For discussion see my Marlene K. Sokolon, *Political Emotions: Aristotle and the Symphony of Reason and Emotion* (DeKalb: Northern Illinois University Press, 2006), 143–47.

105. McLean, "*Heracleidae* of Euripides," 213; and Gladstone, "Introduction to the *Heracleidae*," 112.

106. Euripides, *Children of Heracles*, 980–1020, 465–70.

107. Haigh, *Tragic Drama of the Greeks*, 292; Burian, "Euripides' Heraclidae," 20.

108. Avery, "Euripides' Heracleidae," 557; and Burnett, "Tribe and City," 26.

109. Haigh, *Tragic Drama of the Greeks*, 292.

110. For discussion of the possibility of this critique of vengeful women as a modern problem see Malcolm Heath, "Iure Principem Locum Tenet: *Hecuba*," in *Oxford Readings in Classical Studies: Euripides*, ed. Judith Mossman (Oxford: Oxford University Press, 2003), 256–60; Grube, *Drama of Euripides*, 227; and Ernst L. Abrahamson, "Euripides' Tragedy of *Hecuba*," *Transactions and Proceedings of the American Philological Association* 83 (1952): 128.

111. For discussion of Medea's killing of her children as inappropriate punishment of Jason see Foley, "Medea's Divided Self," 83; Mossman, "Introduction," 40–43.

112. Euripides, *Children of Heracles*, 980–85.

113. Carpenter, *Ethics of Euripides*, 21–22.

114. In this sense, Alcmene may represent the typical female concern with private or individual vengeance. See Falkner, *Poetics of Old Age*, 180–85.

115. Euripides, *Children of Heracles*, 890–915, 935–40.

116. Burnett, "Tribe and City," 26.

117. Euripides, *Children of Heracles*, 1045–55.

118. Vernant, "Tensions and Ambiguities in Greek Tragedy," 33.

119. There is a vast literature on contemporary duty or obligation of care, which often builds on Kant's understanding of universal human dignity. For example, in the *Law of Peoples*, Rawls includes a duty to assist noncitizens in unfavorable conditions. See Immanuel Kant, *Groundwork for the Metaphysics of Morals*, trans. H. J. Paton (London: Routledge, 1948), 67–72; and John Rawls, *Law of Peoples* (Cambridge, MA: Harvard University Press, 1999), 37.

120. Robert E. Goodin, "What Is So Special About Our Fellow Countrymen?," *Ethics* 98, no. 4 (1988): 663–86; and Thomas W. Pogge, "Cosmopolitanism and Sovereignty," *Ethics* 103, no. 1 (1992): 48–49.

121. For examples of this extensive debate see Kyrie Kowalik, "Defining Refugees in Terms of Justice," *Peace Review* 29, no. 1 (2017): 68–75; Max Cherem, "Refugee Rights: Against Expanding the Definition of a 'Refugee' and Unilateral Protection Elsewhere," *Journal of Political Philosophy* 24, no. 2 (2016): 183–205; and Joseph H. Carens, "Refugees and the Limits of Obligation," *Public Affairs Quarterly* 6, no. 1 (1992): 31–44.

122. Euripides, *Children of Heracles*, 110–15.

123. Michel de Montaigne, *The Complete Essays*, trans. M. A. Screech (New York: Penguin, 2003), 480–81.

124. Nussbaum, *Anger and Forgiveness*, 14–56.

125. Pablo de Greiff, "Theorizing Transitional Justice," in *Transitional Justice*, eds. Melissa Williams, Rosemary Nagy, and Jon Elster (New York: New York University Press, 2012), 48–51.

126. "Global Trends Report," ed. Statistics and Demographics Section (Copenhagen: United Nations High Commissioner for Refugees [UNHCR], 2019).

Chapter 6

1. Euripides, *Suppliant Women*, 615.

2. For example, see Frank William Jones, "Introduction to the *Suppliant Women*," in *Euripides IV*, eds. David Grene and Richmond Lattimore (Chicago: University of Chicago Press, 1958), 53.

3. See Wesley D. Smith, "Expressive Form in Euripides' *Suppliants*," *Harvard Studies in Classical Philology* 71 (1967): 151–53; and Ann Norris Michelini, "Political Themes in Euripides' *Suppliants*," *American Journal of Philology* 115, no. 2 (1994): 249–50.

4. Aristotle, *Poetics*, 1456b.

5. Norwood, *Essays in Tragedy*, 112–84; and Kitto, *Greek Tragedy*, 222. For discussion of potential interpolations see Smith, "Expressive Form in Euripides' *Suppliants*," 151–53.

6. For the debate on the dating of the play, including metrical evidence, see Zuntz, *Political Plays of Euripides*, 3–4, 56–78; and James Morwood, "Introduction," in *Euripides: Suppliant Women* (Oxford: Aris & Phillips, 2007), 26–30.

7. See, for example, Jones, "Introduction to the *Suppliant Women*," 53; Christopher Pelling, "Conclusion," in *Greek Tragedy and the Historian*, ed. Christopher Pelling (Oxford: Oxford University Press, 1997), 213–23; and A. M. Bowie, "Tragic Filters for History," in *Greek Tragedy and the Historian*, ed. Christopher Pelling (Oxford: Clarendon, 1997), 39–62.

8. The Thebans of this tragedy belong to the same Boeotian cultural group. The Battle of Delium is also famous since Socrates saved Alcibiades's life during this disastrous Athenian campaign. For discussion, see Bowie, "Tragic Filters for History," 46–56.

9. Carter, *Quiet Athenian*, 44–45; Michelini, "Political Themes in Euripides' Suppliants," 228; Jaroslav Danes, "The Political Thought of the *Suppliant Women*," *Greco-Latina Brunensia* 16, no. 2 (2011): 17–30.

10. For discussion of the potential political significance of tragedy see Goldhill, "Great Dionysia and Civic Ideology (Revised)," 97–129. See also Seaford, "Social Function of Attic Tragedy," 30–44; Rhodes, "Nothing to Do with Democracy," 104–19; Gregory, *Euripides and the Instruction of Athens*, 1–12; and Carter, *Politics of Greek Tragedy*.

11. Peter Burian, "Logos and Pathos: The Politics of the Suppliant Women," in *Directions in Euripidean Criticism*, ed. Peter Burian (Durham, NC: Duke University Press, 1985), 129. See also Zuntz, *The Political Plays of Euripides*, 55; and Wohl, *Euripides and the Politics of Form*, 90.

12. Zuntz, *Political Plays of Euripides*, x, 20–21.

13. Jones, "Introduction to the *Suppliant Women*," 32.

14. Tzanetou, *City of Suppliants*, 24; see also 67–69; and Edith Hall, *Greek Tragedy: Suffering under the Sun* (Oxford: Oxford University Press, 2010), 260.

15. Desmond J. Conacher, "Religious and Ethical Attitudes in Euripides' *Suppliants*," *Transactions and Proceedings of the American Philological Association* 56 (1956): 10–14, 26; R. B. Gamble, "Euripides' *Suppliant Women*: Decision and Ambivalence," *Hermes* 98, no. 4 (1970): 25, 404–405; and Walker, *Theseus and Athens*, 164.

16. Mendelsohn, *Gender and the City*, 221–23.

17. Smith, "Expressive Form in Euripides' *Suppliants*," 151–53; and Michelini, "Political Themes in Euripides' Suppliants," 249–50.

18. Burian, "Logos and Pathos," 129, 154–55.

19. For discussion of the House of Laius in mythology see Lowell Edmunds, *Oedipus* (London: Routledge, 2006); James Morwood, "Euripides' *Suppliant Women*, Theseus and Athenocentrism," *Mnemosyne* 65 (2012): 2–5, fn.150, 155.

20. Sophocles, *Oedipus Tyrannus*, 573–953, 997–1194.

21. Homer, *The Odyssey*, 11.310–20.

22. Sophocles, *Oedipus at Colonus*, 1750–55.

23. Jocasta outlines this version in the prologue of the *Phoenician Women*. See Euripides, *Phoenician Women*, 60–70.

24. Walker, *Theseus and Athens*, 35–81; Saxonhouse, *Free Speech and Democracy in Ancient Athens*, 47–48; Steinbock, *Social Memory in Athenian Public Discourses*, 160–75. For further discussion of the myth of Theseus and archeological evidence for possible child sacrifices in Crete see "Theseus and His Parents and Stepmother," *Bulletin of the Institute of Classical Studies* 26, no. S40 (1979): 18–28; Peter Warren, "Knossos: New Excavations and Discoveries," *Archaeology* 37, no. 4 (1984): 48–55; John S. Rundin, "Pozo Moro, Child Sacrifice, and the Greek Legendary Tradition," *Journal of Biblical Literature* 123, no. 3 (2004): 425–47; and Ruby Blondell, *Helen of Troy: Beauty, Myth, and Devastation* (Oxford: Oxford University Press, 2013), 29–30, 230–33.

25. The reciprocal obligation for this favor is one of the reasons his sons rescue Heracles's children from their archenemy, Eurystheus. See Euripides, *Children of Heracles*, 210–20.

26. The festival of Synoikia celebrated a united Attica, although there remained unique customs and festivals throughout the Athenian territory. Theseus was connected to the unification story only after the reforms of Cleisthenes in 503 BCE. It is also possible this tragedy is the source of the tradition crediting Theseus with the establishment of democracy. See Parke, *Festivals of the Athenians*, 30–31; Walker, *Theseus and Athens*, 145, 196–97, 351–52; Ian C. Storey, *Euripides: Suppliant Women* (London: Duckworth, 2008), 11–15; Evans, *Civic Rites*, 42; and Steinbock, *Social Memory in Athenian Public Discourses*, 158–80.

27. There are versions that suggest Theseus was a member of the Argonauts, which would make the linear history of Medea's story problematic, as Jason's adventures would have had to occur after the events of the *Medea*. See "Theseus and His Parents and Stepmother," 18–28.

28. Plutarch, "The Life of Theseus," in *Lives* trans. Bernadotte Perrin (Cambridge, MA: Harvard University Press, 1914), 35.4–5; Plutarch, "Life of Cimon," in *Lives* trans. Bernadotte Perrin (Cambridge, MA: Harvard University Press, 1914), 8.1–2. For discussion, Morwood, "Introduction," 13–14; and Evans, *Civic Rites*, 80.

29. This festival, established in 475 BCE, also connect Theseus to Dionysus, another figure of transition. His numerous connections to Dionysus include the famous story of Ariadne, who sometimes is married to Dionysus after Theseus abandons her. For discussion see Walker, *Theseus and Athens*, 101–104; Graziella

Vinh, "Athens in Euripides' *Suppliants*," in *Why Athens?*, ed. D. M. Carter (Oxford: Oxford University Press, 2011), 338–39, 343; and Adrienne Mayor, *The Amazons* (Princeton, NJ: Princeton University Press, 2014), 283.

30. For discussion of Eleusis and the Mysteries see Parke, *Festivals of the Athenians*, 54–72; Mara Lynn Keller, "The Eleusinian Mysteries of Demeter and Persephone: Fertility, Sexuality, and Rebirth," *Journal of Feminist Studies in Religion* 4, no. 1 (1988): 27–54; Nancy Evans, "Sanctuaries, Sacrifices, and the Eleusinian Mysteries," *Numen* 49, no. 3 (2002): 227–54; Morwood, "Introduction," 17–20; Bowden, *Mystery Cults of the Ancient World*, 26–48; and Parker, *On Greek Religion*, 251–55.

31. Barbara Goff, "Aithra at Eleusis," *Helios* 22, no. 1 (1995): 67–9.

32. *Homeric Hymn to Demeter*, ed. and trans. Helene P. Foley (Princeton, NJ: Princeton University Press, 1993), 2–28.

33. Although most civic rites were obligatory, exclusionary, and focused on the polis community, the mysteries were voluntary, inclusionary (open to all Greek-speaking people), and focused on individual experience. The festival still had political and community undertones, as Eleusis was where human beings were taught cultivation. Thus, Athens was "the seat of civilization." For discussion see, Evans, *Civic Rites*, 116–17, 126–27.

34. There is speculation that new initiates were blindfolded before entering the Telesterion, which was brightly lit with torches. The meaning of the experiences is elusive since the practices were so sacrosanct that centuries later Pausanias refused to describe the inner sanctum. It is also possible Persephone's descent and return may have been acted out, which connects the mysteries to theatrical Dionysian festivals. See Pausanias, *Description of Greece*, 1.14.1–3. For potential meaning of the experience of the mysteries see Dag Oistein Endsjo, "To Lock up Eleusis," *Numen* 47 (2000): 351–86; Pedley, *Sanctuaries and the Sacred in the Ancient Greek World*, 92–95; Sewell, *In the Theatre of Dionysos*, 33; Wasson, Hofmann, and Ruck, *Road to Eleusis*, 142.

35. In a fragment attributed to Aristotle (fr. 15), initiates went to Eleusis to learn by experience something intensely personal that could not be learned by rote memorization. For discussion see Evans, *Civic Rites*, 126.

36. Sometime around the estimated production date of this play, Athens expanded the Proerosia into a Panhellenic festival that required their allies to pay a tribute of first fruits to the goddess Demeter. See David Kovacs, "Introduction to *Suppliant Women*," in *Suppliant Women* (Cambridge, MA: Harvard University Press, 1998), 15, n. 4. See also Parke, *Festivals of the Athenians*, 72–75; and Morwood, "Introduction," 19.

37. For more on the significance of Eleusis, especially as connected to the Great Dionysia, see Sourvinou-Inwood, *Tragedy and Athenian Religion*, 180, 250, 310–11.

38. As Vinh points out, the chorus in this tragedy evolves to become a significant character, having over a third of the lines in the second part. See Vinh, "Athens in Euripides' *Suppliants*," 327.

39. Storey, *Euripides: Suppliant Women*, 29–32. For discussion of supplication see Walker, *Theseus and Athens*, 185; Naiden, *Ancient Supplication*, 3–21. For Thetis's supplication of Zeus see Homer, *The Iliad*, I. 490–520; for discussion see Christos Tsagalis, "Style, Construction, Sound and Rhythm: Thetis' Supplication of Zeus," *Arethusa* 34, no. 1 (2001): 1–29.

40. For discussion of the imagery of the female in Eleusis and inappropriateness of supplication during the festival see Bowie, "Tragic Filters for History," 54; Mendelsohn, *Gender and the City*, 135–48; and Morwood, "Introduction," 17–20.

41. Euripides, *Suppliant Women*, 90–365.

42. For discussion of how Adrastus's responsibility points to a sophistic view of a disordered universe, see Segal, "Raw and the Cooked in Greek Literature," 301; and Kerferd, *Sophistic Movement*, 141–43.

43. Although the term "Panhellenic" is imprecise, unlike a political regime's positive law it requires cooperation from all Greek people. The idea of Panhellenic norms was likely a byproduct of the Persian wars. See Walker, *Theseus and Athens*, 161–62; Evans, *Civic Rites*, 75–78; Rosenbloom, "Panhellenism of Athenian Tragedy," 355–61. For discussion of Panhellenic law applied to war see Adriaan Lanni, "The Laws of War in Ancient Greece," *Law and History Review* 23, no. 3 (2008): 469–89.

44. Euripides, *Suppliant Women*, 365–595.

45. As Saxonhouse points out, this is one of the only explicit examples in Greek literature of a defense of democracy. See Saxonhouse, *Free Speech and Democracy in Ancient Athens*, 132. For discussion of whether Euripides intends Theseus to represent a political figure such as Pericles, see Storey, *Euripides: Suppliant Women*, 21; and James Morwood, "Euripides and the Demagogues," *Classical Quarterly* 59, no. 2 (2009): 356–60.

46. Although it seems anachronistic to attribute democracy to Theseus, the Athenians did not see their democratic regime as an "event" but in continuity with the past. See Walker, *Theseus and Athens*, 64.

47. By using the outsider herald as a "stand-in" for oligarchic views, Euripides displaces this perspective from the "true" Athenian opinion in support of democracy. See Rosenbloom, "Panhellenism of Athenian Tragedy," 367; and Wohl, *Euripides and the Politics of Form*, 97–98. For discussion on potential reactions of the democratic audience to the herald's speech see Morwood, "Euripides and the Demagogues," 356–60.

48. Euripides, *Suppliant Women*, 635–95.

49. Euripides, *Suppliant Women*, 795–1113.

50. Funeral orations were an important feature of Athenian democracy. The most famous example is Thucydides's account of Pericles's Funeral Oration in 431 BCE. See Thucydides, *History of the Peloponnesian War*, 2.35.1–2.46.2. For discussion see Nicole Loraux, *The Invention of Athens: The Funeral Oration in the Classical City*, trans. Alan Sheridan (Cambridge, MA: Harvard University Press, 1986); and John Ziolkowski, *Thucydides and the Tradition of Funeral Speeches in Athens* (New York: Arno, 1981).

51. Mendelsohn, *Gender and the City*, 197. Wohl suggests that this new explosion of grief is a staging of "tragedy doing tragedy." See Wohl, *Euripides and the Politics of Form*, 102. For a discussion of cultural views of suicide see Garrison, "Attitudes toward Suicide in Ancient Greece," 1–13.

52. Euripides, *Suppliant Women*, 1113–1235.

53. For discussion of the *Thebaid* see Morwood, "Introduction," 23–24.

54. Steinbock, *Social Memory in Athenian Public Discourses*, 176–79.

55. Pindar, *Olympian Odes*, trans. William H. Race (Cambridge, MA: Harvard University Press, 1997), 6.15; Pindar, *Nimean Odes*, trans. William H. Race (Cambridge, MA: Harvard University Press, 1997), 9.22; and Herodotus, *Histories*, 9.27. For further discussion of the controversy concerning the Athenian involvement and the location of the Seven's funeral pyres see Steinbock, *Social Memory in Athenian Public Discourses*, 165–70.

56. For further discussion of innovations see Storey, *Euripides: Suppliant Women*, 11–15; and Morwood, "Introduction," 23–24.

57. J. H. Kim On Chong-Gossard, *Gender and Communication in Euripides' Plays: Between Song and Silence* (Leiden, The Netherlands: Brill, 2008), 216–17. See also Morwood, "Introduction," 24.

58. Despite their piteous situation, the suppliants are less desperate than defeated women and their children during the Peloponnesian War, who were sold into slavery. One of the most infamous examples of this policy was the Athenians' total destruction of the neutral city Melos. See Thucydides, *History of the Peloponnesian War*, 5.84.1–5.115.4. For discussion of the escalating violence of this war see Donald Kagan, *The Peloponnesian War* (New York: Penguin, 2003), 366–86.

59. In the historical case at Delium, as in this mythological story, the Theban violation of the norm to allow the burial of the dead made them not "Greek" but indistinguishable from barbarians. See Coker, *Ethics and War in the 21st Century*, 161–62.

60. The battle of Delium took place in 424 BCE and Arginusae in 406 BCE, the year after Euripides died. Both battles are famous for their association with Socrates; he fought in the battle of Delium as a hoplite and was the *prostatēs* (presiding officer) on the day of the trial of the Arginusae generals. In the *Apology*, Socrates reports that he was the only official to insist on the legality of the generals' trial. See Plato, *Apology*, 32b–c. See also Kagan, *Peloponnesian War*, 169–70, 463–66.

61. This interpretation that the Antigone reveals irreconcilable duality, such as public and private, is most famously made in Hegel, *Lectures on the Philosophy of Religion*, 353. For a contemporary account, see Strauss, *Private Lives, Public Deaths*, 36–48; and Honig, *Antigone Interrupted*, 20–46, 126–9.

62. Euripides, *Suppliant Women*, 230–45, 470–75, 495–500.

63. See, for example, Aristotle, *Politics*, 1295b1–1293a.

64. Thucydides, *History of the Peloponnesian War*, 1.75.3–4.

65. Euripides, *Suppliant Women*, 145–60, 215–45, 470–75.

66. Morwood links the failure of supplication to these ill-advised marriages as symbolizing Theseus's narrow nationalism in the rejection of foreigners. See Morwood, "Euripides' *Suppliant Women*, Theseus and Athenocentrism," 558–59.

67. Euripides, *Suppliant Women*, 300–5, 160–65, 495–500, 745–50.

68. Euripides, *Suppliant Women*, 40–45, 730–35, 310–15, 320–25.

69. Euripides, *Suppliant Women*, 340–45, 355–60, 510–40, 585–90, 220–25. As Ringer points out, "as the ultimate female insider" Theseus's mother knows how to manipulate her son. See Ringer, *Euripides and the Boundary of the Human*, 133–34.

70. In this tragedy, the separation of good and bad was undermined by the inability to strictly determine the good from the bad. See Euripides, *Ion*, 985–1015. From another perspective, Fitton argues that Theseus is not won over by arguments for just war but by nationalism, egotism, and maternal compulsion. See Fitton, "*Suppliant Women* and the *Herakleidai* of Eurpidies," 435.

71. The terms quietist (*hēsuchos*) and "busybody" (*polla prattein* or *polupragmōn*) referred to the "factions" of those who opposed Athenian imperialism and meddling in the affairs of other states versus those who supported the expansion of the empire. Domestically the activist faction also tended to support the poorer or farming classes in the democracy. See Michelini, "Political Themes in Euripides' Suppliants," 226–30. For further discussion see Carter, *Quiet Athenian*, 26–52; Roger Brock, "Mythical Polypragmosyne in Athenian Drama and Rhetroic," *Bulletin of the Institute of Classical Studies* 42, no. S71 (1998): 227–38. These are the terms Plato uses in the *Republic* in Socrates's definition of justice as "minding one's own business" or not being a "busybody." See Plato, *Republic*, 443a–d.

72. Euripides, *Suppliant Women*, 310–15.

73. For discussion of the political significance of Greek norms of burial see Ahrensdorf, *Greek Tragedy and Political Philosophy*, 100–103; and Mark Toher, "Euripides' *Supplices* and the Social Function of Funeral Ritual," *Hermes* 139 (2001): 332–43.

74. Euripides, *Suppliant Women*, 30–40, 290–95.

75. Aristotle defines pity as a kind of pain on seeing the misfortunes of an unrelated person where such misfortunes can be imagined happening to oneself. By contrast, *kharis* is a two-sided emotion motivating benevolence to help others

in need (whether deserved or not) and the feeling of gratitude arising from such favor. See Aristotle, *Art of Rhetoric*, 1385b, 1385a.

76. In another example of an unburied corpse, at the end of the *Iliad*, Achilles allows King Priam of Troy to retrieve the body of his son Hector. When he sees the old king weep, Achilles also weeps, as he recognizes his father will suffer similarly as Achilles, too, is now fated to die. See Homer, *Iliad*, 24.505–15.

77. Euripides, *Suppliant Women*, 370–80, 260–65, 1165–75.

78. In ancient Greece, *philia* represented not only kinship or blood-based ties but the relationship bonds of ritualized guest-friendship (*xenia*) and supplication (*hiketeia*). For discussion of supplication, *kharis*, and friendship see Belfiore, *Murder among Friends*, 5–19, 154–55; and Naiden, *Ancient Supplication*, 87.

79. The chorus notes that Theseus, through his mother, Aethra, and the suppliants shared a blood tie with Pelops, who was the conquering founder of the Peloponnese and progenitor of the House of Atreus. See Euripides, *Suppliant Women*, 260–65.

80. Greg Anderson, *The Athenian Experiment* (Ann Arbor: University of Michigan Press, 2003), 134–46. See also Blanshard, *Hercules*, 52; and Steinbock, *Social Memory in Athenian Public Discourses*, 26–28, 50–68. Significantly, for example, pictorial images of Heracles on pottery drop off in the fourth century in favor of Theseus. See Brommer, *Heracles*, 51–52; and Stafford, *Herakles*, 167–70.

81. T. Nicklin, "Introduction," in *The Suppliant Women of Euripides* (London: Oxford University Press, 1936), viii. By contrast, Greenwood understands this early part of the play as pure irony. See L. H. G. Greenwood, *Aspects of Euripidean Tragedy* (Cambridge: Cambridge University Press, 1953), 92–103.

82. Smith, "Expressive Form in Euripides' *Suppliants*," 152–53. Conacher also suggests the second half is "the Argive section." See Conacher, "Religious and Ethical Attitudes in Euripides' *Suppliants*," 23.

83. Tzanetou, *City of Suppliants*, 18–19.

84. Euripides, *Suppliant Women*, 635–730.

85. For a discussion of the realism of this description to the actual topography, see Christopher Collard, "Notes on Euripides' *Supplices*," *Classical Quarterly* 13, no. 2 (1963): 178–87.

86. Zuntz, *Political Plays of Euripides*, 16–22.

87. Euripides, *Suppliant Women*, 545–60, 310–15, 445–50, 710–15, 505–510.

88. The imagery of wheat is significant, as Eleusis was the place human beings were taught to cultivate grain. It also could allude to the autochthony myth of Athens, in which the citizens literally sprang from the soil. For discussion see Smith, "Expressive Form in Euripides' *Suppliants*," 161; Walker, *Theseus and Athens*, 157–60; Mendelsohn, *Gender and the City*, 183–85; and Brock, *Greek Political Imagery*, 164.

89. Euripides, *Suppliant Women*, 835–930.

90. Gamble, "Euripides' *Suppliant Women*," 403; and Kovacs, "Introduction to *Suppliant Women*," 6.

91. Euripides, *Suppliant Women*, 495–505; see also 860–70, 835–40, 915–20, 935–40, 810–15.

92. For a discussion of this episode as an ironic critique of the heroic code see Conacher, "Religious and Ethical Attitudes in Euripides' *Suppliants*," 23–25. For an opposing view in which the funeral oration is significant for community solidarity and reflects legitimacy of empire, see Collard, "Notes on Euripides' *Supplices*," 185; Christopher Collard, "The Funeral Oration in Euripides' *Supplices*," *Bulletin of the Institute of Classical Studies* 19, no. 1 (1972): 43–5, 49; John E. G. Whitehorne, "The Dead as Spectacle in Euripides' *Bacchae* and *Supplices*," *Hermes* 114 (1986): 68–72; Eleni Kornarou, "The Display of the Dead on the Greek Tragic Stage," *Bulletin of the Institute of Classical Studies* 51, no. 1 (2008): 31–8; and Tzanetou, "Supplication and Empire in Athenian Tragedy," 331–33, 343.

93. For discussion on the theme of disposition (*ēthos*) see Michael H. Shaw, "The Ethos of Theseus in the *Suppliant Women*," *Hermes* 110 (1982): 3–19.

94. Euripides, *Suppliant Women*, 910–15. The *Hecuba* focuses on the question of the "teachablity" of virtue, which was a popular topic among the sophists and is the main question in Plato's *Protagoras*. Euripides, *Hecuba*, 585–610; Plato, *Protagoras*, esp. 316a–20a, 360e–62a. For discussion see de Romilly, *Great Sophists in Periclean Athens*, 45–56; and Kerferd, *Sophistic Movement*, 131–38.

95. Mendelsohn sees this oration as assigning appropriate aristocratic values for the Athenian *dēmos*. See Mendelsohn, *Gender and the City*, 192–95.

96. For example, Conacher omits the scene as an extreme and intrusive dramatization of the chorus's grief. See Conacher, "Religious and Ethical Attitudes in Euripides' *Suppliants*," 23. For more discussion see Garrison, *Groaning Tears*, 121; Mendelsohn, *Gender and the City*, 197; and Wohl, *Euripides and the Politics of Form*, 102–3.

97. As discussed in the introduction, women may have attended the Great Dionysia. For further discussion of the feminine and marriage in this tragedy see Rush Rehm, *Marriage to Death: The Conflation of Wedding and Funeral Rituals in Greek Tragedy* (Princeton, NJ: Princeton University Press, 1994), 110–121; and Mendelsohn, *Gender and the City*, 197–211.

98. Garrison, *Groaning Tears*, 121–25.

99. Euripides, *Suppliant Women*, 990–1025, 1060–65. See Goff, "Aithra at Eleusis," 67–69.

100. Although there is no prophecy or salvation of the city that would justify her act, with her self-appointed decision to die, Evadne is mimicking the glory of the acts of the maiden in the *Children of Heracles* or Menoeceus in *Phoenician Women*. See Euripides, *Children of Heracles*, 500–35; and *Phoenician Women*, 990–1020.

101. Euripides, *Suppliant Women*, 1050–55, 470–75, 1095–1100, 1080–85.

102. In this situation, Athenian norms would expect Evadne to return to her father's house and eventually remarry. See Mendelsohn, *Gender and the City*, 202–5.

103. The critique of the failure of persuasion, especially to come to good or valid conclusions, was part of the intellectual debate of fifth-century Athens. For discussion see Bettany Hughes, *The Hemlock Cup* (New York: Vintage, 2012), 47. Also see Burian, "Logos and Pathos," 17–18; and Brands and Edel, *Lessons of Tragedy*, 16–17.

104. For discussion of this ancient heroic code see Blundell, *Helping Friends and Harming Enemies*, 26–59; and Belfiore, *Murder among Friends*, 3–20.

105. See Euripides, *Medea*, 1075–80, 1370–75.

106. Euripides, *Suppliant Women*, 1120–60, 1170–75, 370–75, 330–40.

107. Euripides, *Suppliant Women*, 1165–75, 1180–1225.

108. Her "correction" of Theseus on this point may also be a result of his youth and need for guidance. Athenian festivals celebrating Theseus were often associated with "growing up rituals." See Parker, *On Greek Religion*, 28–29.

109. Euripides, *Suppliant Women*, 1180–95.

110. For discussion of typical oath practices see Judith Fletcher, *Performing Oaths* (Cambridge: Cambridge University Press, 2012), 1–34; Christina Williamson, "As God Is My Witness," in *Cults, Creeds and Identities in the Greek City after the Classical Age*, ed. R. Alston, O.M. van Nijf, and C. G. Williamson (Leuven, Belgium: Peeters, 2013), 119–74.

111. Although civic oaths were common in the classical period, the use of a tripod is archaic. Torrance, *Metapoetry in Euripides*, 172–73; Sommerstein and Bayliss, *Oath and State in Ancient Greece*, 148–50; and Lefkowitz, *Euripides and the Gods*, 79–81. See also Morwood, "Introduction," 12–14.

112. Such a shine was dramatized, for example, by Eurystheus's tomb as protection against future attacks from the descendants of Heracles. See Euripides, *Children of Heracles*, 1025–35. For discussion see Michael J. Anderson, "Myth," in *A Companion to Greek Tragedy*, ed. Justina Gregory (Oxford: Blackwell, 2008), 127–28.

113. Mendelsohn goes as far as to argue that as Athena was goddess of war, her intervention represents victory over Demeter. See Mendelsohn, *Gender and the City*, 219–21. See also Morwood, "Introduction," 12–14.

114. If the knife is mimicking the sowing of seeds, Athena's harvest is bloodthirsty, which contrasts the Realpolitik of war with Demeter as goddess of fertility. See Stephen Scully, "Orchestra and Stage and Euripides' *Suppliant Women*," *Arion* 4, no. 1 (1996): 70–71.

115. Euripides, *Suppliant Women*, 1220–25, 470–75, 540–50.

116. Burian, "Logos and Pathos," 153–55; and Smith, "Expressive Form in Euripides' *Suppliants*," 167. By contrast, Kennedy understands the prophecy as forestalling a premature attack to ensure vengeance is within the boundaries of justice and reaffirms Athens's position as arbitrator of justice. See Rebecca Futo Kennedy, *Athena's Justice* (New York: Peter Lang, 2009), 76–79.

117. The presence of the next generation preset for war may have symbolized the parade of Athenian orphans at the beginning of the Great Dionysia

festival. See Goldhill, "The Great Dionysia and Civic Ideology (Revised)," 123; Shipton, *Politics of Youth in Greek Tragedy*, 77–78. For more on the Eleusinian connection, see Goff, "Aithra at Eleusis," 65–78.

118. For examples of the comparison of this tragedy to the *Oresteia*, see Smith, "Expressive Form in Euripides' *Suppliants*," 166; Zuntz, *Political Plays of Euripides*, 3–4; and Mendelsohn, *Gender and the City*, 219–20.

119. Aeschylus, *Eumenides*, 700–900.

120. Euripides, *Suppliant Women*, 610–15.

121. Zuntz, *The Political Plays of Euripides*, 20. For more on this optimistic view see also Morwood, "Introduction," 4–5.

122. Greenwood, *Aspects of Euripidean Tragedy*, 102–3. This pessimistic perspective includes the idea that the tragedy is a warning against relying on just gods or that Athens, not immune to violence, should choose anti-imperialistic peace. See Conacher, "Religious and Ethical Attitudes in Euripides' *Suppliants*," 22–26; Smith, "Expressive Form in Euripides' *Suppliants*," 20; Mendelsohn, *Gender and the City*, 221–23; and Tzanetou, "Supplication and Empire in Athenian Tragedy," 324.

123. Gamble, "Euripides' *Suppliant Women*," 405.

124. Burian, "Logos and Pathos," 155.

125. Euripides is silent on the idea of international institutions. For discussion of the contemporary view of this issue see Charles Beitz, "Social and Cosmopolitan Liberalism," *International Affairs* 75 (1999): 125–40; Fred Dallmayr, "Cosmopolitanism," *Political Theory* 31 (2003): 421–42; and Thomas Nagel, "The Problem with Global Justice," *Philosophy & Public Affairs* 33, no. 2 (2005): 113–47.

126. Euripides contrasts with cosmopolitan positions that base global justice in shared humanity. For examples of this contemporary position, see Simon Caney, *Justice beyond Borders* (Oxford: Oxford University Press, 2005); and Samuel Black, "Individualism at an Impasse," *Canadian Journal of Philosophy* 21, no. 3 (1991): 347–77.

127. Euripides, *Suppliant Women*, 225–30.

128. Richard W. Miller, "Cosmopolitan Respect and Patriotic Concern," *Philosophy and Public Affairs* 27, no. 3 (1998): 202–24. See also Kok-Chor Tan, *Justice without Borders* (Cambridge: Cambridge University Press, 2004).

129. Michael J. Sandel, *Justice: What Is the Right Thing to Do?* (New York: Farrar, Straus and Giroux, 2009), 208–43.

Chapter 7

1. Euripides, *Hecuba*, 860–70.

2. The first performance date and titles of other tragedies in the trilogy or its satyr play are unknown. Metrical dating places it sometime around the

Suppliant Women, which is thought to have been performed around 423 BCE. Scholars who interpret the plot as alluding to external events, such the "revival" of Maiden Dances at the Delian festival of Apollo, or mimicry to Aristophanes's *Clouds* date it earlier from 426 to 428 BCE; others who see it reflecting the Peace of Nicias suggest 421–420 BCE. For discussion, see William Arrowsmith, "Introduction to the *Hecuba*," in *Euripides III*, eds. David Grene and Richmond Lattimore (Chicago: University of Chicago Press, 1958), 67; and Christopher Collard, "Introduction to the *Hecuba*," in *Hecuba*, ed. Christopher Collard (Warminster, UK: Aris & Phillips, 1991), 34–35.

3. The Euripidean Byzantine Triad of the *Hecuba*, *Orestes* and *Phoenician Women* was used for special educational purposes. More than 250 manuscript copies of the *Hecuba* survive. For discussion see Matthiessen, "Manuscript Problems in Euripides' *Hecuba*," 293, 295–97.

4. See Kitto, *Greek Tragedy*, 216–23; Kenneth Reckford, "Pity and Terror in Euripides' *Hecuba*," Arion 1, no. 2 (1991): 29; David Kovacs, "Introduction to Hecuba," in *Hecuba* (Cambridge, MA: Harvard University Press, 1995), 393. For discussion of plot unity see Desmond J. Conacher, "Euripides' *Hecuba*," *American Journal of Philology* 82, no. 1 (1961): 12–4. See also Aristotle, *Poetics*, 51a–b.

5. David D. Corey and Cecil L Eubanks, "Private and Public Virtue in Euripides *Hecuba*," *Interpretations* 30, no. 3 (2003): 225, 226–27.

6. The empty stage is rare in Greek tragedy. See Wohl, *Euripides and the Politics of Form*, 57, 61–62.

7. See C. A. E. Luschnig, "Euripides' *Hekabe*: The Time Is Out of Joint," *Classical Journal* 71, no. 3 (1976): 227–34; Kenneth Reckford, "Concepts of Demoralization in the *Hecuba*," in *Directions in Euripidean Criticism*, ed. Peter Burian (Durham, NC: Duke University Press, 1985), 112–28; and Charles Segal, *Euripides and the Poetics of Sorrow* (Durham, NC: Duke University Press, 1993), 170–91.

8. For discussion of the mythological context see Collard, "Introduction to the *Hecuba*," 32–33; Judith Mossman, *Wild Justice: A Study of Euripides' Hecuba* (London: Bristol Classical, 1999), 19–47; and Helene P. Foley, *Euripides' Hecuba* (London: Bloomsbury, 2015), 14–23.

9. Stesichorus may be the source of the alternative version where a simulacrum of Helen is taken to Troy while the real Helen is spirited off by the gods to Egypt. Euripides tells this version in his *Helen*, and it is also found in Herodotus. See Euripides, *Helen*, trans. David Kovacs (Cambridge, MA: Harvard University Press, 2002), 1–65; and Herodotus, *Histories*, 2.113–20. For discussion see Blondell, *Helen of Troy*, 117–22.

10. Euripides, *Andromache*, trans. David Kovacs (Cambridge, MA: Harvard University Press, 1995), 1–55; and Euripides, *Trojan Women*, trans. David Kovacs (Cambridge, MA: Harvard University Press, 1999), 1–40, 71–75, 1305–35.

11. As Rabinowitz points out, the location highlights the marginality of location since Thrace is not quite Greece but not quite Troy, either. See Rabinowitz, *Greek Tragedy*, 139.

12. By raising this sympathy for the conquered, Euripides parallels the sympathy for the enemy in the *Iliad*. See Sewell, *In the Theatre of Dionysos*, 75–6.

13. The *Agamemnon*, the first tragedy in Aeschylus's trilogy, outlines the deaths of Agamemnon and Cassandra. Like Aeschylus's other two tragedies in this trilogy, Euripides's two plays follow the fates of their children Electra and Orestes, who avenge their father's murder by killing their mother. The *Electra* concerns the return of Orestes from exile and the murder; the *Orestes* relates the continuing events before Orestes is judged at the Athenian Aeropagus. See Aeschylus, *Agamemnon*, trans. Alan H. Sommerstein (Cambridge, MA: Harvard University Press, 2009), 1365–1605; Euripides, *Electra*, 80–105, 1220–30; and Euripides, *Orestes*, trans. David Kovas (Cambridge, MA: Harvard University Press, 2002), 1–70, 1625–90.

14. Euripides, *Hecuba*, 1–60.

15. Euripides, *Hecuba*, 60–330. Hecuba's old age can be seen as a metaphor for fallen Troy. See Falkner, *Poetics of Old Age in Greek Epic, Lyric, and Tragedy*, 173.

16. For discussion D. M. Carter, "Reported Assembly Scenes in Greek Tragedy," *Illinois Classical Studies* 38 (2013): 34–39. Although human sacrifice was not practiced in the classical era, it is unclear whether this was a practice of the Mycenean period depicted in the tragedies. For discussion of the Greek view of human sacrifice, see Wilkins, "State and the Individual," 195–50; and Hughes, *Human Sacrifice in Ancient Greece*, 13–48, 71–138.

17. Euripides, *Hecuba*, 220–375.

18. See, for example, Socrates's discussion with Cephalus and Polemarchus in Book I of Plato, *Republic*, 331a–d, 335b–e.

19. Euripides, *Hecuba*, 305–10. Odysseus's refusal to acknowledge her appeal to pity reflects Cleon's famous speech to destroy Mytilene in 427 BCE. See Thucydides, *History of the Peloponnesian War*, 3.36.1–3.49.4. For discussion see, Corey and Eubanks, "Private and Public Virtue in Euripides *Hecuba*," 237.

20. Euripides, *Hecuba*, 330–660.

21. Euripides, *Hecuba*, 595–600. This echoes what Aristotle says of a supremely virtuous man who could encounter the misfortunes of her husband Priam but still not be miserable. See Aristotle, *Nicomachean Ethics*, 1101a5–10. By contrast, as Hecuba is altered in the tragedy, she seems her own exception to this principle. See Emily Katz Anhalt, *Enraged: Why Violent Times Need Ancient Greek Myths* (New Haven, CT: Yale University Press, 2017), 181–83.

22. Euripides, *Hecuba*, 660–1055.

23. For Agamemnon's recognition of higher principle see Meltzer, *Euripides and the Poetics of Nostalgia*, 139.

24. Agamemnon's comment is doubly ironic since the reference to unfavorable winds mimics the sacrifice of his own daughter, Iphigenia. In addition, his dismissal of a woman's strength will be his own downfall as he will be slaughtered by Clytemnestra. See David Kovacs, *The Heroic Muse* (Baltimore: Johns Hopkins University Press, 1987), 105.

25. Euripides, *Hecuba*, 1055–1295.

26. Pucci, *Euripides' Revolution under Cover*, 32.

27. Zdravko Planinc, "Expel the Barbarian from Your Heart: Intimations of the Cyclops in Euripides's *Hecuba*," *Philosophy and Literature* 42, no. 2 (2018): 406–7.

28. Philoctetes, who inherited Heracles's famous bow, was abandoned by the Greeks on an island because of his festering wound. They return only after learning he and the bow were necessary to defeat the Trojans. This story is told in Sophocles, *Philoctetes*, trans. Hugh Lloyd-Jones (Cambridge, MA: Harvard University Press, 1994), 1–85.

29. Katherine Callen King, "The Politics of Imitation: Euripides' *Hekabe* and the Homeric Achilles," *Arethusa* 18, no. 1 (1985): 47, 59–60.

30. Planinc, "Expel the Barbarian from Your Heart," 407, 411–12.

31. William G. Thalmann, "Euripides and Aeschylus: The Case of *Hekabe*," *Classical Antiquity* 12, no. 1 (1993): 126–59.

32. Mossman, *Wild Justice*, 19–20. See also Peter Burian, "Myth into Muthos: The Shaping of Tragic Plot," in *The Cambridge Companion to Greek Tragedy*, ed. P. E. Easterling (Cambridge: Cambridge University Press, 1997), 178–210; and Saxonhouse, "Another Antigone," 473–74.

33. For discussion of innovations see Conacher, "Euripides' *Hecuba*," 2–8; Mossman, *Wild Justice*, 19–47; Foley, *Euripides' Hecuba*, 14–23; and Collard, "Introduction to the *Hecuba*," 32–35.

34. For discussion see Justina Gregory, "Genealogy and Intertexuality in *Hecuba*," *American Journal of Philology* 116, no. 3 (1995): 92–93. See, for instance, Homer, *Iliad*, 21.84–91, 11.223–26.

35. Darby, *Bacchus*, 65–70. See, for example, Euripides, *Bacchae*, 1085–1150.

36. For a discussion of Dionysiac rites see Bowden, *Mystery Cults of the Ancient World*, 105–36.

37. Hekate often bore the cult title of "protector of the dogs" and was associated with magic, crossroads, and the boundaries of life and death. Medea invokes this goddess as her personal guardian of the hearth. See Euripides, *Medea*, 395–400. For Hecuba's connection see Mossman, *Wild Justice*, fn 39, 35, 197–99.

38. Mossman, 30. See also Conacher, "Euripides' *Hecuba*," 7.

39. Charles Segal, "Violence and the Other: Greek, Female, and Barbarian in Euripides' *Hecuba*," *Transactions and Proceedings of the American Philological*

Association 120 (1990): 110. When a group of Thracian allies missed the Athenian fleet's departure on the Sicilian Expedition, they attacked the town of Mycalessus and slaughtered every living creature, including beasts of burden. Thucydides describes this massacre as the greatest example of brutality during the Peloponnesian War. See Thucydides, *History of the Peloponnesian War*, 7.29.1–7.30.3.

40. For discussion of the myth of Polyxena see Calasso, *Marriage of Cadmus and Harmony*, 119–21; Collard, "Introduction to the *Hecuba*," 33–34; and Jonathan S. Burgess, *The Tradition of the Trojan War in Homer and the Epic Cycle* (Baltimore: Johns Hopkins University Press, 2001), 139–42.

41. Collard, "Introduction to the *Hecuba*," fn15, 8. Scholars, such as Zeitlin, argue that this setting of stories in "other" places provides a frame for self-examination. See Froma I. Zeitlin, "Thebes: Theater of Self and Society in Athenian Drama," in *Greek Tragedy and Political Theory*, ed. J. Peter Euben (Berkeley: University of California Press, 1986), 101–41.

42. This Attic black-figured amphora (BM GR 1897.7–27.2), labeled as painted by Timiades, is currently in the British Museum. See Segal, "Violence and the Other," fn 32, 118. See also Mossman, *Wild Justice*, 256–59.

43. For discussion Foley, *Euripides' Hecuba*, 29–34.

44. In Ovid's version, she is transformed into a dog who spends eternity howling and biting at stones thrown at her. See Ovid, *Metamorphoses*, 323–24. See also Burnett, *Revenge in Attic and Later Tragedy*, 173.

45. A *sēma* can mean a tomb but also a boundary marker or omen. See Mossman, *Wild Justice*, 35–36. Also see, for example, Burnett, *Revenge in Attic and Later Tragedy*, 174–75.

46. Heath, "Iure Principem Locum Tenet," 240–50.

47. For discussion see Christopher Collard, "Formal Debates in Euripides' Drama," *Greece & Rome* 22, no. 1 (1975): 72–73; Buxton, *Persuasion in Greek Tragedy*, 147–53, 170–86; and Lloyd, *Agon in Euripides*, 1–36, 95–110.

48. In the *Republic*, Polemarchus attributes the idea of "helping friends and harming enemies" to the poet Simonides. See Plato, *Republic*, 334b–36a.

49. For discussion of *xenia* see Belfiore, *Murder among Friends*, 14–18, 147–51. For the justice of *hiketeia* see Naiden, *Ancient Supplication*, 171–218.

50. For Aristotle's view of justice as merit see Aristotle, *Nicomachean Ethics*, 1131a–32a.

51. Euripides, *Hecuba*, 310–15, 855–60, 1130–40, 1175–80.

52. In three of four tragedies specifically on the theme of supplication, suppliants also claim blood ties. Belfiore, *Murder among Friends*, 14–16. As examined in other chapters, Euripides's supplication tragedies dramatize the question of defending noncitizens. See Euripides, *Suppliant Women*, 1–40; and Euripides, *Children of Heracles*, 225–30.

53. For discussion of the failure of leadership to protect suppliants see Froma I. Zeitlin, "Euripides' *Hekabe* and the Somatics of Dionysiac Drama," *Ramus* 20 (1991): 83.

54. During the Peloponnesian War, the Athenians created a special police force to prevent suppliants from reaching sanctuary sites. See Walker, *Theseus and Athens*, 184–85; and Naiden, *Ancient Supplication*, 43–64.

55. This story of Odysseus being caught and Hecuba's benevolence toward him is not found in any other existing mythology and might be another Euripidean invention. See Euripides, *Hecuba*, 270–75, 300–305, 855–65.

56. Belfiore, *Murder among Friends*, 7–8, 18; and Griffith, "Families and Inter-City Relations," 106.

57. Thucydides, *History of the Peloponnesian War*, 2.43.1. See also Sarah Brown Ferrario, "Reading Athens," in *Thucydides between History and Literature*, ed. Antonis Tsakmakis and Melina Tamiolaki (Berlin: De Gruyter, 2013), 181–98.

58. Euripides, *Hecuba*, 710–15, see also 795–805, 885–90, 1240–50.

59. Euripides, *Hecuba*, 800–805. Although not mentioned in this play, failure to bury Polydorus also violates Panhellenic norms, as dramatized in Euripides's *Suppliant Women*, 310–15.

60. Segal, *Euripides and the Poetics of Sorrow*, 192.

61. Euripides, *Hecuba*, 850–905, 1240–50.

62. It is also disgraceful, of course, to seduce or kidnap your host's wife as did Paris. See McHardy, *Revenge in Athenian Culture*, 45–64.

63. The tragedy's challenge reflects Socrates's exchange with Polemarchus, where Socrates points out that it would only be just to help friends—if friends were also good men—and it would be unjust to harm anyone. See Plato, *Republic*, 334a–34d.

64. Euripides, *Hecuba*, 900–905.

65. As Aristotle suggests, the real issue is not that just distribution is according to merit but what merit should be. See Aristotle, *Nicomachean Ethics*, 1131a–b.

66. Euripides, *Hecuba*, 251–95, 300–30.

67. This "payback" could refer to the practice of blood price, which could be a literal exchange of a life for a life but more often was compensation in kind, such as in labor or cattle. For discussion of blood price in ancient Greece see Cantarella, "Private Justice and Public Justice," 473–83.

68. See also Aristotle, *Nicomachean Ethics*, 1132a.

69. In other versions of this story that postdate Euripides, Achilles was ambushed when he came to retrieve his betrothed, Polyxena. His ghost's demand for her sacrifice could allude to the symbolic death in Greek marriage ritual. See Conacher, "Euripides' *Hecuba*," fn 5, 3; Greg R. Stanton, "Aristocratic Obligation in Euripides' *Hekabe*," *Mnemosyne* 48, no. 1 (1995): fn 28, 19. For death imagery in Greek marriage ritual see Rehm, *Marriage to Death*, 11–30; Michelini, *Euripides and the Tragic Tradition*, 158–70; Segal, "Violence and the Other," 11–13; and Rabinowitz, *Anxiety Veiled*, 94–6.

70. Odysseus's point is rather anachronistic since Achilles fought not for the community but himself. See Foley, *Euripides' Hecuba*, 41.

71. Unlike Odysseus, Cyrus is taught to respect the law above fitness. See Xenophon, *Cyropaedia*, 1.3.17.

72. See Thalmann, "Euripides and Aeschylus," 136–40; and Meltzer, *Euripides and the Poetics of Nostalgia*, 108–109.

73. Gregory, *Euripides and the Instruction of the Athenians*, 102–5.

74. In the *Rhetoric*, for example, Aristotle defines pity as "a kind of pain . . . [at observing] destructive or painful things, happening to another person, undeserved." In the *Poetics*, Aristotle suggests we feel pity when "someone suffers undeservedly." This idea that pity is a judgment of merit is by no means universal, even in Aristotle, who suggests we also feel pity for those who are sick or old that contains no evaluation of merit. See Aristotle, *Art of Rhetoric*, 1385b–86b. See also Aristotle, *Poetics*, 1453a. For discussion David Konstan, *Pity Transformed* (London: Duckworth, 2001); and Douglas L. Cairns, "Pity in the Classical World," *Hermathena* 176 (2004), 59–74.

75. Euripides, *Hecuba*, 285–95, 805–10, 335–45, 365–75, 1110–1115. Visvardi suggests pity for human beings generally stems from "a consciousness shaped by participation in the *polis*." In Greece, pity was also seen as a recourse of the weak. See Eirene Visvardi, "Pity and Panhellenic Politics," in *Why Athens?*, ed. D. M Carter (Oxford: Oxford University Press, 2011), 273.

76. In this way she resembles Penthesilea, the Amazon warrior killed by Achilles but afterward grieved as a "beautiful corpse." See Mayor, *Amazons*, 297–98.

77. Other scholars disagree and see his crawling blindly about as an "emotional figure who needs justice and demands pity." See Foley, *Euripides' Hecuba*, 54.

78. Euripides, *Hecuba*, 1130–40, 1180–85.

79. As cited in Heath, "Iure Principem Locum Tenet," 240–41. Kitto will suggest that we are disguised and not edified. See Kitto, *Greek Tragedy*, 219–20.

80. Grube, *Drama of Euripides*, 227. See, for example, Segal, *Euripides and the Poetics of Sorrow*, 165; and Wohl, *Euripides and the Politics of Form*, 60–61.

81. Euripides, *Hecuba*, 255–60. Hecuba's reaction also conforms to Aristotle's understanding that we feel either joy or nothing at the suffering of those who deserve it. See Aristotle, *Art of Rhetoric*, 1386b. For discussion see Abrahamson, "Euripides' Tragedy of *Hecuba*," 128.

82. Euripides, *Children of Heracles*, 935–1055.

83. Heath, "Iure Principem Locum Tenet," 256–60.

84. Carpenter understands the ethics of the play as "devoted to the punishment of avarice." Carpenter, *Ethics of Euripides*, 26. See also Ringer, *Euripides and the Boundary of the Human*, 129–30.

85. Euripides, *Hecuba*, 795–810, 900–905.

86. Although shocking to us, killing the enemy's children was not unusual in ancient literature. In contrast, Wohl argues Hecuba is "unmeasured" because she kills two sons for her one; by contrast, Segal sees these two children measured against her recently murdered two children. See Ra'anana Meridor, "Hecuba's Revenge: Some Observations on Euripides' *Hecuba*," American Journal of Philology 99, no. 1 (1978): 35, fn 24; Burnett, *Revenge in Attic and Later Tragedy*, 169–71; Wohl, *Euripides and the Politics of Form*, 60–61; and Segal, *Euripides and the Poetics of Sorrow*, 165.

87. McHardy, *Revenge in Athenian Culture*, 44.

88. Euripides, *Hecuba*, 255–70, 900–905, 1085–90, 1115–20.

89. Euripides, *Hecuba*, 880. Agamemnon, of course, learns nothing and will fall to an equally vengeful woman. For discussion, Abrahamson, "Euripides' Tragedy of *Hecuba*," 126–27; Grube, *Drama of Euripides*, 227; James L. Kastely, "Violence and Rhetoric in Euripides' *Hecuba*," PMLA 108, no. 5 (1993): 1044; and Mossman, *Wild Justice*, 193.

90. Easterling, "Form and Performance," 155. See also Planinc, "Expel the Barbarian from Your Heart," 406.

91. James C. Hogan, "Thucydides 3.52–68 and Euripides' *Hecuba*," Phoenix 26, no. 3 (1972): 257.

92. The Greek word *philanthrōpia*, which means literally love of humanity, might be a candidate; yet, although it can prompt aid to others, as Sternberg stresses, it does not imply sorrow for others' suffering. See Rachael Hall Sternberg, *Tragedy Offstage: Suffering and Sympathy in Ancient Athens* (Austin: University of Texas Press, 2006), 13–15. See also Malcolm Heath, *The Poetics of Greek Tragedy* (Stanford, CA: Stanford University Press, 1987), 82–83; and Heath, "Iure Principem Locum Tenet," 257.

93. This emotional response is something closer to what the Romans and later Christians might call "compassion." For discussion see Martha C. Nussbaum, "Compassion: The Basic Social Emotion," Social Philosophy and Policy 13, no. 1 (1996), 17–58; Brian Carr, "Pity and Compassion as Social Virtues," Philosophy 74, no. 289 (1999), 411–29; and Sternberg, *Tragedy Offstage*, 1–20.

94. Plato, *Republic*, 343a–46a; and Plato, *Gorgias*, 452a–e. Although sophists such as Antiphon and Gorgias did promote this view, there is no evidence that real sophists made as strong a claim as Callicles in the *Gorgias*. See de Romilly, *Great Sophists in Periclean Athens*, 124–33. See Michael Gagarin, *Antiphon the Athenian: Oratory, Law and Justice in the Age of the Sophists* (Austin: University of Texas Press, 2002), 73–78; and Gorgias, *Encomium of Helen*, 6.

95. Thucydides, *History of the Peloponnesian War*, 5.89, see also 1.76. For similarities between Thucydides and this tragedy see Gregory, *Euripides and the Instruction of the Athenians*, 85–120; Walker, *Theseus and Athens*, 177; and Meltzer, *Euripides and the Poetics of Nostalgia*, 111–14, 122–23.

96. Scholarship has long focused on the alterity of dualistic pairs, especially those with the political "other" such as barbarian-Greek, female-male, old-young, and slave-free. See Zeitlin, *Playing the Other*, 1–18; Paul Cartledge, *The Greeks: A Portrait of the Self and Others*, 2nd ed. (Oxford: Oxford University Press, 2002).

97. Euripides, *Hecuba*, 220–40, 320–35, 395–400.

98. Euripides similarly highlights the importance of free speech and justice in the *Phoenician Women*. See Euripides, *Phoenician Women*, 380–635.

99. Odysseus does not always permit free speech. In the *Iliad*, he beats a regular soldier named Thersites for speaking openly. One defining feature of democratic Athens was this equal right of male citizens (*isēgoria*) to speak openly in the Assembly. For discussion, Woodruff, *First Democracy*, 33; Saxonhouse, *Free Speech and Democracy in Ancient Athens*, 7–10, 94. See Homer, *Iliad*, 2.210–280.

100. Euripides, *Hecuba*, 240–95. As Corey and Eubanks suggest tragedy occurs when the demands of the public or the private are ignored. Corey and Eubanks, "Private and Public Virtue in Euripides *Hecuba*," 225, 246.

101. Kastely, "Violence and Rhetoric in Euripides' *Hecuba*," 1043–46.

102. Euripides, *Hecuba*, 725–845, 110–15, 840–45.

103. This argumentative turn has been the source of contemporary criticism. Kirkwood, for example, finds her use of her daughter's sexual oppression as "repulsive"; Reckford finds it "shocking"; Segal suggests it reflects Odysseus's amoral rhetoric. See Gordon M. Kirkwood, "*Hecuba* and Nomos," *Transactions and Proceedings of the American Philological Association* 78 (1947): 66; Reckford, "Pity and Terror in Euripides' *Hecuba*," 35; and Segal, "Violence and the Other," 310. For further discussion see also Planinc, "Expel the Barbarian from Your Heart," 406.

104. The sons of Theseus, who figure prominently in the *Children of Heracles*, used Agamemnon's relationship with Cassandra against him in the army's debate concerning the sacrificing of Polyxena. Euripides, *Hecuba*, 125, 825–45.

105. Euripides, *Hecuba*, 251–60, 850–905.

106. For discussion of law and friendship see Belfiore, *Murder among Friends*, 8–9, 19–20.

107. Euripides, *Hecuba*, 895–900. As will be demonstrated, since the winds have not turned, the demand for the sacrifice of Polyxena may not be the cause of the beached army. See Collard, "Introduction to the *Hecuba*," 29.

108. Reckford, "Concepts of Demoralization in the *Hecuba*," 114. See also Abrahamson, "Euripides' Tragedy of *Hecuba*," 128; Hogan, "Thucydides 3.52–68 and Euripides' *Hecuba*," 257; and Mossman, *Wild Justice*, 40–41.

109. Reckford, "Pity and Terror in Euripides' *Hecuba*," 39.

110. For dispute regarding the winds, see Hogan, "Thucydides 3.52–68 and Euripides' *Hecuba*," 252.

111. Segal, *Euripides and the Poetics of Sorrow*, 225.

112. Euripides, *Hecuba*, 860–70.

113. The idea of being a slave to written law is not pursued in the story; presumably, this only causes problems when such law is unjust. Since Odysseus convinces the people to break a just law (not murdering slaves), this could be seen as a critique of democracy's susceptibility to demagogues. Foley, *Euripides' Hecuba*, 51; and Gregory, *Euripides and the Instruction of the Athenians*, 98–102.

114. Plato further develops the notion of internal freedom from the tyranny of one's desires. See, for example, Plato, *Republic*, 576c–78a. For further discussion of the concept of freedom in ancient Greece see Janet Coleman, *A History of Political Thought* (Malden, MA: Blackwell, 2000), 34–37; Woodruff, *First Democracy*, 61–79. See also Stephen G. Daitz, "Concepts of Freedom and Slavery in Euripides' *Hecuba*," *Hermes* 99, no. 2 (1971): 218.

115. For evidence that Euripides does not use *autonomia*, see James T. Allen and Gabriel Italie, *A Concordance to Euripides* (Groningen, The Netherlands: Bouma's Boekhuis, 1970).

116. Euripides, *Hecuba*, 795–805. See, for example, Neil T. Croally, *Euripidean Polemic* (Cambridge: Cambridge University Press, 1994), 101–102.

117. See also Daitz, "Concepts of Freedom and Slavery in Euripides' *Hecuba*," 220.

118. Euripides, *Hecuba*, 345–50, 545–55, 860–75, 595–600. For discussion of the importance of choice in such actions see Anhalt, *Enraged*, 168–74.

119. See Loraux, *Tragic Ways of Killing a Woman*, 56; Rabinowitz, *Anxiety Veiled*, 54–62; Wohl, *Euripides and the Politics of Form*, 54–55. For the contrast between Polyxena and Hecuba see Grube, *Drama of Euripides*, 220; Kastely, "Violence and Rhetoric in Euripides' *Hecuba*," 1038–39; and Conacher, "Euripides' *Hecuba*," 113–14.

120. As Hecuba sings her revenge song (lines 685–90) Euripides plays on the double-meaning of the word *nomos*, which can mean law or custom but also a melody or song. Nussbaum, *Fragility of Goodness*, 397–421; and Meagher, *The Essential Euripides*, 153. See also Burnett, *Revenge in Attic and Later Tragedy*, 162.

121. Kirkwood, "*Hecuba* and Nomos," 67; Conacher, "Euripides' *Hecuba*," 123; and Abrahamson, "Euripides' Tragedy of *Hecuba*," 129.

122. Meridor, "Hecuba's Revenge: Some Observations on Euripides' *Hecuba*," 34; and Mossman, *Wild Justice*, 204–209.

123. Anne Carson, "Preface to *Hecube*," in *Grief Lessons*, ed. Anne Carson (New York: New York Review of Books, 2006), 90.

124. Aeschylus, *Eumenides*, 950–1040. For this potential intertextuality see Thalmann, "Euripides and Aeschylus," 137, 153–7.

125. Euripides's cynicism regarding the effectiveness of judicial systems and transformation of the Erinyes is explored in *Iphigenia among the Taurians* where we find Orestes still pursued by unsatisfied Erinyes. See Euripides, *Iphigenia among the Taurians*, trans. David Kovacs (Cambridge, MA: Harvard University Press, 1999), 75–105.

126. Kovacs agrees that it is not necessary for her to have a physical manifestation to indicate loss of humanity, especially since Hecuba understands the metamorphosis as a rescue from slavery. See Kovacs, "Introduction to Hecuba," 397; Kovacs, Heroic Muse, 108–11; Mossman, Wild Justice, 205; and Anhalt, Enraged, 181. For further discussion of the significance of metamorphosis in ancient Greece, see Richard Buxton, Forms of Astonishment: Greek Myths of Metamorphosis (Oxford: Oxford University Press, 2009).

127. Segal suggests her bestial transformation is a shameful monstrosity. See Segal, Euripides and the Poetics of Sorrow, 159. See also Nussbaum, Fragility of Goodness, 414–15; Gregory, Euripides and the Instruction of the Athenians, 110; and Planinc, "Expel the Barbarian from Your Heart," 413.

128. Blondell, Helen of Troy, 16–18.

129. David Stuttard, Nemesis (Cambridge, MA: Harvard University Press, 2018), 91.

130. Zeitlin, Playing the Other, 185–86.

131. Euripides may be the originator of the version of Heracles's labors when he returns Cerberus to protect the underworld. See Brommer, Heracles, 45–48.

132. Plato, Republic, 373e–76c, 392e.

133. For further discussion of dog imagery see Mossman, Wild Justice, 194–202; Foley, Euripides' Hecuba, 33; Meltzer, Euripides and the Poetics of Nostalgia, 144–45, fn 102; and Wasson, Hofmann, and Ruck, Road to Eleusis, 113–14.

134. Hecuba is called "the dog of fire-bearing Hekate" in a lost Euripidean tragedy. See Burnett, Revenge in Attic and Later Tragedy, 176.

135. For discussion of Hekate see Ankarloo and Clark, Witchcraft and Magic in Europe, 147–51; D'Este and Rankine, Hekate Liminal Rites, 19–47; and Zeitlin, Playing the Other, 74–81. For discussion of the introduction of the new gods Bendis and Asclepius see D'Angour, Greeks and the New, 96–98. For Bendis in the Republic, see Plato, The Republic of Plato, trans. Allan Bloom (New York: Basic Books, 1968), 354a, note 5.

136. Medea invokes this goddess in the place of Hestia, the traditional goddess of the hearth. See Euripides, Medea, 395–400.

137. In 411 BCE, presumably many years after the performance of this tragedy, the Cynossema was the site of a famous battle during the Peloponnesian War. See Thucydides, History of the Peloponnesian War, 8.101.1–8.106.1.

138. Gregory, Euripides and the Instruction of the Athenians, 112.

139. Kovacs, Heroic Muse, 108–109. According to Burnett, it marks "the place where men change course as they move from wild justice to a tamer kind." See Anne Pippin Burnett, "Hekabe the Dog," Arethusa 27 (1994): 152–53.

140. Nussbaum, Fragility of Goodness, 420–21. See also Planinc, "Expel the Barbarian from Your Heart," 413.

141. Anhalt notes that the failure of rulers to uphold justice in a democracy reflects upon the choices of the audience members themselves. See Anhalt, Enraged, 165–68.

142. Reckford, "Concepts of Demoralization in the *Hecuba*," 122–23; and Meltzer, *Euripides and the Poetics of Nostalgia*, 104–105.

143. Marcus Tullius Cicero, *De Officiis*, trans. Walter Miller (Cambridge, MA: Harvard University Press, 1913), 1.30. Also see Kant, *Groundwork for the Metaphysics of Morals*, 67–72. For discussion about the development of the concept of human dignity see Christopher McCrudden, "Human Dignity and Judicial Interpretations of Human Rights," *European Journal of International Law* 19, no. 4 (2008): 655–724; and Erin Daly, *Dignity Rights* (Philadelphia: University of Pennsylvania Press, 2013).

144. Euripides, *Hecuba*, 795–805. See Zeitlin, "Euripides' *Hekabe* and the Somatics of Dionysiac Drama," 83.

145. Euthyphro is a mirrored image of Hecuba, as he is prosecuting his own father for the murder of a slave. See Plato, *Euthyphro*, trans. Harold North Fowler (Cambridge, MA: Harvard University Press, 1914), 7a–8e.

146. For example, see Michael Beaty, Carlton Fisher, and Mark Nelson, eds., *Christian Theism and Moral Philosophy* (Macon, GA: Mercer University Press, 1998); and William J. Wainright, *Religion and Morality* (Burlington, VT: Ashgate, 2005).

147. Segal suggests that there is a possibility of universal moral laws but that we are not ready for them. See Segal, *Euripides and the Poetics of Sorrow*, 211.

148. Rabinowitz, *Greek Tragedy*, 138–46.

Chapter 8

1. Euripides, *Alcestis*, 25–35.
2. Michelini, *Euripides and the Tragic Tradition*, 324.
3. Sophocles's quote in Aristotle, *Poetics*, 1460b. For the nineteenth-century interpretation, see Behler, "A.W. Schlegel and the Nineteenth Century 'Damnatio' of Euripides," 335–67.
4. For example, Wesley D. Smith, "The Ironic Structure in *Alcestis*," *Phoenix* 14, no. 3 (1960): 127–45; Grube, *Drama of Euripides*, 129–46; Charles Segal, "Admetus' Divided House: Spatial Dichotomies and Gender Roles in Euripides' *Alcestis*," *Materiali e discussioni per l'analisi dei testi classici* 28 (1992): 9–26; and Mark Padilla, "Gifts of Humiliation: *Charis* and the Tragic Experience in *Alcestis*," *American Journal of Philology* 121, no. 2 (2000): 179–211.
5. For examples of this interpretation see Hewitt, "Gratitude and Ingratitude in the Plays of Euripides," 331–43; Nancy Sorkin Rabinowitz, "Introduction to the *Alcestis*," in *Women on the Edge*, ed. Ruby Blondell et al. (New York: Routledge, 1999), 103–113.
6. Charles Rowan Beye, "Introduction," in *Alcestis by Euripides* (Englewood Cliffs, NJ: Prentice Hall, 1974), 10.

7. An ancient *hypothesis* is an introduction included with medieval manuscripts that includes an outline of the plot. The ancient *didascaliae* was the performance production record that contained the names of the plays, authors, and victories of the festivals. For discussion see Desmond J. Conacher, "Introduction to *Alcestis*," in *Euripides: Alcestis* (Warminster, UK: Aris & Phillips, 1988), 29–30.

8. As Slater notes, *Telephus* may be the most famous lost tragedy, as it was later parodied by Aristophanes. See Slater, *Euripides: Alcestis*, 2.

9. Prior to the production of this play, we think Euripides produced three other tetralogies (trilogy, plus satyr play) in the years following his first production of the *Daughters of Pelias* at the Great Dionysia in 455 BCE. Alcestis was also a daughter of Pelias, but unlike her sisters, she was either too young or already married to Admetus when Medea tricked her sisters into killing her father. See A. M. Dale, "Introduction," in *Euripides: Alcestis* (Oxford: Clarendon, 1961), v–vii; and Moses Hadas, "Introduction to *Alcestis*," in *Ten Plays by Euripides* (Toronto: Bantam, 1960), 1.

10. The second *hypothesis* also calls the play *saturikōteron* (satyr-like), but this comment is believed to be a later addition. See Conacher, "Introduction to *Alcestis*," 30.

11. Murray, "Introduction," vii.

12. For discussion of satyr plays see Storey and Allan, *Guide to Ancient Greek Drama*, 156–68; Edith Hall, "Introduction," in *Euripides: Alcestis, Heracles, Children of Heracles, Cyclops* (Oxford: Oxford University Press, 2003), xii, xxvii.

13. Storey and Allan, *Guide to Ancient Greek Drama*, 156.

14. Based on Aristotle, tragedies are supposed to evoke emotions of fear and pity. Aristotle, *Poetics*, 1453b. For discussion see Dana LaCourse Munteanu, *Tragic Pathos* (Cambridge: Cambridge University Press, 2012), 1–28.

15. Dale, "Introduction," xxi. See also Murray, "Introduction," vii–x; and Dana Ferrin Sutton, *The Greek Satyr Play* (Hain, Germany: Meisenheim-am-Glan, 1980).

16. Kitto, *Greek Tragedy*, 327–47. See also M. A. Bayfield, "Introduction," in *The Alcestis of Euripides* (New York: Macmillian, 1902), x–xi; Richmond Lattimore, "Introduction to the *Alcestis*," in *Euripides I*, eds. David Grene and Richmond Lattimore (Chicago: University of Chicago Press, 1955), 4–5; and William Arrowsmith, "Introduction," in *Euripides: Alcestis* (Oxford: Oxford University Press, 1974), 29.

17. David Kovacs, "Introduction to *Alcestis*," in *Alcestis* (Cambridge, MA: Harvard University Press, 2001), 151. For contemporary bias in "classifying" the *Alcestis* see Richard Seaford, *Euripides: Cyclops* (Oxford: Oxford University Press, 1984), 24; and Mastronarde, "Euripidean Tragedy and Genre," 35.

18. This decree might have been directed at Aristophanes. See C. W. Marshall, "*Alcestis* and the Problem of Prosatyric Drama," *Classical Journal* 95, no. 3 (2000): 220–31; 233.

19. Anne Carson, "Preface to the *Alcestis*," in *Grief Lessons*, ed. Anne Carson (New York: New York Review of Books), 247. Or, as Segal notes, although Euripides typically deals with paradoxes, "nowhere does he do this more deliciously than in the *Alcestis*." See Segal, *Euripides and the Poetics of Sorrow*, 37.

20. For discussion of the background myth and sources see Dale, "Introduction," ix, xii–xix; Desmond J. Conacher, "Introduction to *Alcestis*," in *Euripides: Alcestis* (Warminster, UK: Aris & Phillips, 1988), 30–35; L. P. E. Parker, "Introduction and Commentary," in *Euripides' Alcestis* (Oxford: Oxford University Press, 2007), xiv–xix; and Slater, *Euripides: Alcestis*, 1–14.

21. In extant literature (except for a fragment in Pindar), the *Alcestis* is also the first mention of Heracles's labor of stealing the Thracian horses. See Brommer, *Heracles*, 34. The phrase "myth kitty" is from Philip Larkin. As quoted in Mossman, *Wild Justice*, 19–20; fn 1.

22. Hesiod's Fragment, 1759. As quoted in Conacher, "Introduction to *Alcestis*," 50, fn 4.

23. Homer, *Iliad*, 2.710. In some versions, they also have a daughter named Perimele who marries Argo, the builder of the eponymously named famous ship.

24. Aeschylus, *Eumenides*, 720–30.

25. Plato, *Symposium*, 179b–108b.

26. Euripides, *Alcestis*, 845–50.

27. Apollodorus, *Library of Greek Mythology*, 3.10.3, 1.9.15. For discussion see Hansen, *Classical Mythology*, 153, 260.

28. This was the same blood that Creusa had in her twin vials in the *Ion*. In that tragedy, the "bad" blood was unjustly used in an attempted murder; by contrast, Asclepius inappropriately or unjustly uses the "good" blood. See Euripides, *Ion*, 895–1040.

29. Asclepius was also a new god who arrived in Athens from Epidaurus (the site of the most intact Greek theater today). In the 420s during the Peace of Nicias, the Athenians built a shrine to him close to the theater of Dionysus. See Evans, *Civic Rites*, 38–39.

30. Alcestis's father Pelias sent Jason on his adventure to retrieve the Golden Fleece. The *Medea* alludes to the story of Medea's deceit of Alcestis's sisters who are tricked into killing Pelias because he refused to return power to Jason. This is why Medea and Jason are exiled to Corinth. See Euripides, *Medea*, 1–15.

31. The folklore origins of this play were first explained by Albin Lesky. See Parker, "Introduction and Commentary," xvi–xlviii. For discussion, Michelini, *Euripides and the Tragic Tradition*, 324–29.

32. Conacher, "Introduction to *Alcestis*," 32.

33. Euripides, *Alcestis*, 1–75.

34. This allusion to twinning and substitutions connects this play to others, like the *Ion* and the *Bacchae*, which also draw on the idea of doubling. For a seminal discussion of the significance of the double in mythology see Girard, *Things Hidden since the Foundation of the World*, 105–26, 141–79.

35. For discussion of the contrast of Apollo, the god of light, with the darkness of Death see Ringer, *Euripides and the Boundary of the Human*, 37.

36. Apollo has accurate foresight in this tragedy, while Death does not. See Lefkowitz, *Euripides and the Gods*, 101.

37. Euripides, *Alcestis*, 75–240, esp. 140–43.

38. The ritual duties Alcestis performs, such as washing with river water and adorning herself, are performed by the family of the deceased. These rituals bear similarities to those performed by the bride on her wedding day, which represent the death of her maidenhood before marriage. See Rehm, *Marriage to Death*, 29, 85.

39. Euripides, *Alcestis*, 230–475.

40. She also dies a "natural" death, which is rare in Greek tragedy. For discussion see Segal, *Euripides and the Poetics of Sorrow*, 53–58; Pucci, *Euripides' Revolution under Cover*, 8–12.

41. Euripides, *Alcestis*, 475–745, esp. 520, 615–70.

42. Although Pheres was disliked by twentieth-century scholars, this scene highlights Admetus's abandonment, which allows Heracles to "adopt" him. See Maria do Ceu Fialho, "Paidotrophia and Gerotrophia: Reciprocity and Disruption in Attic Tragedy," in *Law and Drama in Ancient Tragedy*, ed. Edward M. Harris, Delfim F. Leao, and P. J. Rhodes (London: Bloomsbury, 2010), 117–19; D. M. Jones, "Euripides' *Alcestis*," *Classical Review* 62, no. 2 (1948): 52–54; Lattimore, "Introduction to the *Alcestis*," 3; Grube, *Drama of Euripides*, 139–41; and Beye, "Introduction," 9–10.

43. Euripides, *Alcestis*, 745–860, esp. 745–85, 805–810.

44. Heracles frequently does Apollo's "dirty work," as he fights on the god's behalf in several mythological stories. See Fontenrose, *Python*, 36–37.

45. Euripides, *Alcestis*, 860–1165, 860–960, 1005–1010, 1120–1125, 1160–1164.

46. For the importance of necessity in Euripides see Ringer, *Euripides and the Boundary of the Human*, 37–38.

47. This "shape" reflects the "image" Admetus claimed he would fashion. It could also refer to the "statuary motif" of Greek tombs. See Mary Stieber, "Statuary in Euripides' *Alcestis*," *Arion* 5, no. 3 (1998): 70. By contrast, such visual imagery might suggest the statue of Dionysus that was set up in the theater to "watch" the drama unfold. See Parker, *On Greek Religion*, 183–84.

48. Many images in Greek art survive that depict the husband leading his new wife away with his right hand. See Rehm, *Marriage to Death*, 12–17, 84–85.

49. The exact same choral ending is found in five of Euripides's extant plays: *Medea*, *Helen*, *Andromache*, *Bacchae*, and *Alcestis*.

50. Children were considered part of the father's family (*oikos*) and would remain with their father in cases of divorce or the mother's death. Conacher, "Introduction to *Alcestis*," 33; Parker, "Introduction and Commentary," xiii–xiv.

51. Segal, "Admetus' Divided House," 6. See also Mendelsohn, *Gender and the City*, 225–26.

52. Euripides, *Alcestis*, 1–25.

53. In the *Rhetoric*, Aristotle describes *kharis* as providing a service to another in need without expectation of something in return. See Aristotle, *Art of Rhetoric*, 1385a. For discussion of *kharis* in ancient Greece see Parker, "Pleasing Thighs," 105–27.

54. According to Padilla, the play is a performance of a series of extraordinary gifts of *kharis* that disrupt social relationships with the ultimate lesson that death is necessary for moral understanding. See Padilla, "Gifts of Humiliation," 179–211.

55. Euripides, *Alcestis*, 25–35, 40–75.

56. This insinuation might be a reference to the story later told by Apollodorus that Apollo yoked the boar and lion, but Admetus claimed it as his own victory to claim Alcestis as wife. See Conacher, "Introduction to *Alcestis*," 32; Parker, "Introduction and Commentary," xvii–xviii.

57. Euripides, *Alcestis*, 63.

58. The reference to weapons also may allude to Apollo's murder of the Python of Delphi, which guarded the oracle site. Apollo killed this giant snake because it tormented his mother during her pregnancy. An alternative version suggests Apollo was sent into servitude for killing Python and not the Cyclopes. See Fontenrose, *Python*, 13–22.

59. For example, Arrowsmith understands the play rhythms of contrasting moods established with this first scene of the dark lord of death and the bright savior god. See Arrowsmith, "Introduction," 12; and Richard Garner, "Death and Victory in Euripides' *Alcestis*," *Classical Antiquity* 7, no. 1 (1988): 59.

60. Euripides, *Alcestis*, 25–70.

61. Euripides, *Alcestis*, 55–60, 45–50.

62. Euripides, *Alcestis*, 80–85, 510–52, 900–995, 240–45, 990–1005, 930–40.

63. One of the most important Athenian burial mounds commemorated the dead of Marathon (which can still be visited today). See Katherine Derderian, *Leaving Words to Remember: Greek Mourning and the Advent of Literacy* (London: Brill, 2001), 43–52. There is also some similarity between the description of Alcestis and the deaths of Patroclus and Hector in the *Iliad*. For example, Hector and Alcestis have a "hollow" (*koilē*) grave. See Garner, "Death and Victory in Euripides' *Alcestis*," 63–67.

64. Euripides, *Children of Heracles*, 475–595; Euripides, *Hecuba*, 340–80; and Euripides, *Suppliant Women*, 1010–70.

65. Philip Vellacott, *Ironic Drama* (Cambridge: Cambridge University Press, 1975), 100.

66. Euripides, *Alcestis*, 280–90, 685–705; Jennifer Dellner, "Alcestis' Double Life," *Classical Journal* 96, no. 1 (2000): 6.

67. Rabinowitz, "Introduction to the *Alcestis*," 93. See also Helene P. Foley, "Anodos Drama: Euripides *Alcestis* and *Helen*," in *Innovations in Antiquity*, ed. Daniel Selden and Ralph Hexter (New York: Routledge, 1992), 133–34.

68. For the motive of love for her husband see Grube, *Drama of Euripides*, 134–35. See also Dale, "Introduction," xxvi.

69. For discussion on whether to see Alcestis's action as a form of suicide see Garrison, "Attitudes toward Suicide in Ancient Greece," 20–33.

70. For discussion of sexual jealousy in Greek plays, see Dana LaCourse Munteanu, "Notes on Women's Responses to Infidelity in Greek Tragedy," *International Society for the Study of European Ideas* 13 (2012): 1–12.

71. Euripides, *Alcestis*, 300–305, 330–65, 370–75.

72. Although such a promise may not seem so extraordinary to modern audiences, in ancient Greece this promise violated crucial cultural norms, as men would have an obligation to remarry and produce more children for their *oikos*. See Stephanie Lynn Budin, *The Ancient Greeks* (Oxford: Oxford University Press, 2009), 142–49.

73. Dellner, "Alcestis' Double Life," 8–10.

74. Grube, *Drama of Euripides*, 129.

75. This *agōn* also highlights the dualism of old age and youth. See Falkner, *Poetics of Old Age in Greek Epic, Lyric, and Tragedy*, 175–76. Euripides, *Alcestis*, 615–750, 860–70.

76. Although several characters—Alcestis, Admetus, and the chorus—point out that as an old man he should have died for his son, Pheres insists there is no law or custom of such a duty of parents or the elderly. For discussion of this point see Hewitt, "Gratitude and Ingratitude in the Plays of Euripides," 335–37; Ruth Scodel, "Admetou Logos and the *Alcestis*," *Harvard Studies in Classical Philology* 83 (1979): 55; Falkner, *Poetics of Old Age in Greek Epic, Lyric, and Tragedy*, 176. For ancient perspectives on old age see M. I. Finley, "The Elderly in Classical Antiquity," *Greece & Rome* 28, no. 2 (1981): 156–71.

77. Lattimore's translation. Euripides, *Alcestis*, eds. David Grene and Richmond Lattimore, trans. Richmond Lattimore, *Euripides 1* (Chicago: University of Chicago Press, 1955), 695–700.

78. Rabinowitz, "Introduction to the *Alcestis*," 98–99.

79. Euripides, *Children of Heracles*, 585–90; Euripides, *Suppliant Women*, 545–60.

80. Padilla, "Gifts of Humiliation," 195–96.

81. For discussion of *xenia* practices see Belfiore, *Murder among Friends*, 7–8, 11, 18; Gabriel Herman, *Ritualised Friendship and the Greek City* (Cam-

bridge: Cambridge University Press, 2002), 31–36, 120–42; and Naiden, *Ancient Supplication*, 86–88.

82. Euripides dramatized an example of violated *xenia* in his *Hecuba* with the murder of Polydorus at the hands of the family *xenos* Polymestor. See Euripides, *Hecuba*, 725–905, 1020–85.

83. Alcibiades's family had long-standing *xenia* ties with Sparta (Alcibiades, for example, is a Spartan name), which aided his exile to Sparta after he fled Athenian prosecution in 415 BCE for the mutilation of the herms (*hermēs*) and profaning the Eleusinian Mysteries. While in exile, he influenced the Spartans' strategy against Athens. See Thucydides, *History of the Peloponnesian War*, 8.6.1–8.6.5; 6.88.10–6.93.3. For discussion see Munn, *School of History*, 67–68, 123–24; and Stuttard, *Nemesis*, 170–73, 18–21.

84. For examples, see Murray, "Introduction," xiv–xv; and Hadas, "Introduction to *Alcestis*," 1.

85. This carousing reflects Heracles's role as an "outsider" hero who is civilizing but never civilized. See Blanshard, *Hercules*, 32–40.

86. Euripides, *Alcestis*, 555–60, 505–45, 950–60.

87. Segal, "Admetus' Divided House," 25.

88. Euripides, *Alcestis*, 955–60. For discussion Falkner, *Poetics of Old Age in Greek Epic, Lyric, and Tragedy*, 176–77; Hallvard Fossheim, "Aristotle on Happiness and Old Age," in *The Quest for the Good Life*, ed. Oyvind Rabbas et al. (Oxford: Oxford University Press, 2015), 125.

89. Dale, "Introduction," xxvii.

90. The idea that virtue requires some sort of moderate amount reflects Aristotle's later view of a mean between two extreme vices. This idea of "too friendly" is comparable to Aristotle's virtues of "friendliness" and possibly liberality, which describes a kind of generosity of things measurable by money. See Aristotle, *Nicomachean Ethics*, 1106b5–25, 1127a1–15, 1121a25–1122a15.

91. Euripides, *Alcestis*, 805–10.

92. Euripides, *Alcestis*, 550–60, 1145–50.

93. Segal, "Admetus' Divided House," 10–16. For details on the role of the wife as an "outsider" see Rehm, *Marriage to Death*, 7–9.

94. Euripides, *Ion*, 405–10. For discussion see Hoffer, "Violence, Culture, and the Workings of Ideology in Euripides' *Ion*," 308–10; and Larue, "Creusa's Monody 859–922," 126–36.

95. Euripides, *Alcestis*, 1075–1155.

96. As Heracles is surprised by Admetus's extreme decision to remain a widower, his forcing Admetus to accept the veiled women seems premeditated. See Euripides, *Alcestis*, 1080–90.

97. Euripides, *Alcestis*, 1145–50.

98. This is in contrast to Aristotle's comment that tragedy is a reversal from joy or safety to ruin and disgrace. See Aristotle, *Poetics*, 1452a–b. This

position is most strongly endorsed by Burnett, *Catastrophe Survived*, 240–55; Anne Pippin Burnett, "The Virtues of Admetus," *Classical Philology* 60 (1965): 240–55.

99. Although not his last word on the play, see Segal, *Euripides and the Poetics of Sorrow*, 81.

100. Also definitely not his last word on the play, see Conacher, "Introduction to *Alcestis*," 42.

101. Conacher suggests that Euripides goes as far as to propose the relativity of such virtues. See Conacher, *Euripides and the Sophists*, 108–109.

102. Euripides, *Alcestis*, 1015–20.

103. See, for example, Michael Lloyd, "Euripides' *Alcestis*," *Greece & Rome* 32, no. 2 (1985): 129; and Beye, "Introduction," 10.

104. Smith, "Ironic Structure in *Alcestis*," 127, 144–45.

105. Rabinowitz, "Introduction to the *Alcestis*," 103.

106. The reason for Alcestis's muteness in the final scene is not clear. It is possible this was simply a theatrical convention, but her silence may suggest the three-day rebirth ritual of the Eleusinian Mysteries. Although little is known about the Eleusinian Mysteries, one theory is that these rites provided an experience of liminal time through the contrast of terror and darkness with light and joy. For discussion of mute Alcestis see G. G. Betts, "The Silence of Alcestis," *Mnemosyne* 18, no. 2 (1965): 181–82; Rehm, *Marriage to Death*, 95; and Erna P. Trammell, "The Mute Alcestis," *Classical Journal* 37, no. 3 (1941): 144–50. For discussion of the Mysteries see Pedley, *Sanctuaries and the Sacred in the Ancient Greek World*, 93–95; and Endsjo, "To Lock Up Eleusis," 354–61.

107. One reason Demophon accepts the Heracleidae supplication is in return for the "favor" of their father rescuing him. See Euripides, *Children of Heracles*, 210–20. See Blanshard, *Hercules*, 147.

108. Garner, "Death and Victory in Euripides' *Alcestis*," 70–71.

109. Dellner, "Alcestis' Double Life," 5; Arrowsmith, "Introduction," 3–29; Justina Gregory, "Euripides' *Alcestis*," *Hermes* 107, no. 3 (1979): 268–70. See also Lloyd, "Euripides' *Alcestis*," 123–25, 129.

110. See, for instance, Euripides, *Bacchae*, 820–60, 925–65; Euripides, *Medea*, 280–90, 790–810, 870–95; and Euripides, *Hecuba*, 1015–1110, 1145–80. Alcestis's adoption of male warrior virtues also reflects Plato's discussion of female guardians in Plato, *Republic*, 451b–61e.

111. Men rarely grieve in tragedy and Admetus's extended grieving blurs lines of gender. See Segal, *Euripides and the Poetics of Sorrow*, 62–72.

112. Arrowsmith, "Introduction," 5.

113. Euripides, *Alcestis*, 1–25, 120–30.

114. The *Bacchae* does not mention Dionysus's resurrection. In other mythological versions, Dionysus is resurrected by Demeter after being torn apart by the Titans. Euripides probably ended his story with Agave attempting to reassemble her son's body which she, in a fit of madness, tore into pieces. See Nussbaum,

"Introduction," 1–38; and Willink, "On the Transmission of the *Bacchae*," 347.

115. Gregory, "Euripides' *Alcestis*," 269. Another possibility is that since Heracles beats Death, like Asclepius, he will pay the price. Interestingly, Heracles does eventually die from poisoned blood (similar to Medusa's bad blood) but from the tainted blood of the centaur Nessus. See Mitchell-Boyask, *Plague and the Athenian Imagination*, 139–41.

116. Carson, "Preface to the *Alcestis*," 248.

117. Lattimore's translation. See Euripides, *Alcestis*, 780–90.

118. Lloyd, "Euripides' *Alcestis*," 123–24.

119. Although biographic information on Euripides comes from later sources, he appears concerned with similar intellectual ideas to the sophists, such as the role of circumstance in determining virtue. See Philip Vellacott, "Introduction," in *Euripides: Three Plays* (Toronto: Penguin Press, 1953), 7–9. See also Lefkowitz, *Lives of Ancient Greek Poets*, 87–103; and Conacher, *Euripides and the Sophists*, 42–49.

120. Euripides, *Alcestis*, 85–150, 515–30.

121. Euripides, *Alcestis*, 515–30, 775–90.

122. The very existence of this heroic half-god violates his insistence on clear boundaries. He is fated to die a mortal death, become immortal, and live forever with the Olympian gods. In another example, in the *Children of Heracles*, the now immortal Heracles and his new wife, Hēbē (the goddess of youth), miraculously rejuvenate Iolaus, thus blurring the boundary between old and young. See *Children of Heracles*, 840–65. See also Stafford, *Herakles*, 104–36, 170–80.

123. Gregory, "Euripides' *Alcestis*," 269–70.

124. C. A. E. Luschnig, "Interiors: Imaginary Spaces in *Alcestis* and *Medea*," *Mnemosyne*, 45, no. 1 (1992): 23–34. See also Smith, "Ironic Structure in *Alcestis*," 135–38; and Segal, "Admetus' Divided House," 16–20. In Euripides's time the *skēnē* was a painted building from which actors could arrive and exit the "scene." See Ley, *Short Introduction to the Ancient Greek Theater*, 17–22.

125. Euripides, *Alcestis*, 155–290, 385–95, 860–70, 545–50, 730–40.

126. This disruption also breaks biological continuity in favor of the friendship of husband and wife or ethical continuity. See Fialho, "Paidotrophia and Gerotrophia," 119.

127. Euripides, *Alcestis*, 25–70, 675–740, 950–60, 280–370.

128. Euripides, *Alcestis*, 840–50, 775–85. Heracles's wrestling match with Death, without the use of weapons, mirrors stories of his barehanded capture of Cerberus, the dog protecting Hades. Thus, Heracles's defeat of Death could be seen as another labor that blurs the line between life and death. See Brommer, *Heracles*, 46.

129. Gregory, *Euripides and the Instruction of the Athenians*, 19–47.

130. Cicero, *De Officiis*, 1.45.160.

131. Hugo Grotius, *The Rights of War and Peace*, ed. Jean Barbeyrac (Indianapolis: Liberty Fund, 2005), II.XXII.xvi.

132. John Stuart Mill, "Utilitarianism," in *On Liberty and Other Essays* (Oxford: Oxford University Press, 2008), 184–85.

133. Eric R. Boot, *Human Duties and the Limitations of Human Rights Discourse* (Leiden, The Netherlands: Springer, 2017), 9. See also Liam Murphy, *Moral Demands in Nonideal Theory* (Oxford: Oxford University Press, 2000), 117–34.

134. Despite the extraordinary case of Alcestis's generosity, it highlights the injustice of cultural expectations that women sacrifice their own self-interest for their children and husbands. For examples of this perspective, see Nancy Folbre, "Should Women Care Less? Intrinsic Motivation and Gender Inequality," *British Journal of Industrial Relations* 50, no. 4 (2012): 597–619; and Karen Korabik, "The Intersection of Gender and Work–Family Guilt," in *Gender and the Work-Family Experience*, ed. Maura J. Mills (New York: Springer, 2015), 141–57.

135. Moderation (*sōphrosunē*) was a preoccupation of ancient ethics. Along with the more famous "know thyself," this statement was inscribed on the *pronaos* of the temple in Delphi. For examples of the widespread discussion of moderation in Greek thought see Plato, *Republic*, 427b–28a, 433a–c; Plato, *Charmides*, 158c–67b; Aristotle, *Nicomachean Ethics*, 1118a1–19b15; Aristotle, *Art of Rhetoric*, 1390a–b; Xenophon, *Memorabilia*, IV.1–6; Isocrates, *Panathenaicus*, trans. George Norlin (Cambridge, MA: Harvard University Press, 1929), 12.151, 197; Thucydides, *History of the Peloponnesian War*, 8.24.4, 8.86.7; and Hesiod, *Works and Days*, 694.

136. For discussion of the debate concerning the potential nihilism of Euripides see McDermott, *Euripides' Medea*, 3–4; Meltzer, *Euripides and the Poetics of Nostalgia*, 223–24; Thumiger, *Hidden Paths*, 214–7; and Ruth Scodel, *Introduction to Greek Tragedy* (Cambridge: Cambridge University Press, 2010), 67–70.

137. Euripides, *Alcestis*, 30, 140, 520–30.

138. Only fragments of Parmenides and Heraclitus survive. For discussion of their ideas see John Palmer, *Parmenides and Pre-Socratic Philosophy* (Oxford: Oxford University Press, 2009), 137–89; Edward Hussey, "Heraclitus on Living and Dying," *Monist* 74, no. 4 (1991): 517–21. For examples of this discussion of being and not being, see Plato, *Sophist*, trans. Harold North Fowler (Cambridge, MA: Harvard University Press, 1921), 237b–39c, 240b–d; Plato, *Timaeus*, trans. R. G. Bury (Cambridge, MA: Harvard University Press, 1929), 27d–28a; Plato, *Protagoras*, 338e–48c; Aristotle, *Metaphysics*, trans. John H. McMahon (Amherst: Prometheus, 1991), 1003a21–1012b. Also see Martin Heidegger, *Being and Time*, trans. Joan Stambaugh (Albany: State University of New York Press, 2010). See also Étienne Gilson, *Being and Some Philosophers* (Toronto: Pontifical Institute of Mediaeval Studies, 1952); and William Desmond, *Being and the Between* (Albany: State University of New York Press, 1995).

Chapter 9

1. Euripides, *Electra*, 370–75.
2. Gilbert Murray, "Introduction," in *Collected Plays of Euripides*, ed. Gilbert Murray (London: George Allen & Unwin, 1954), 5.
3. For example, Zuntz, *Political Plays of Euripides*, 64–71; Luschnig, "Introduction," ix–x; Emily Vermeule, "Introduction to Electra," in *Euripides V*, eds. David Grene and Richmond Lattimore (Chicago: University of Chicago Press, 1959), 204–5. David Kovacs, "Introduction to *Electra*," in *Electra* (Cambridge, MA: Harvard University Press, 1998), 142.
4. For discussion see J. D. Denniston, "Introduction," in *Euripides' Electra*, ed. J. D. Denniston (Oxford: Clarendon, 1939), xxxiii–xxxix.
5. Some Athenian captives of this ill-begotten expedition reportedly won their freedom by reciting Euripides and, possibly, even this choral *parados*. Sewell, *In the Theatre of Dionysos*, 168. See also Edith Hall, "Introduction," in *Euripides: Medea, Hippolytus, Electa, Helen*, ed. James Morwood (Oxford: Clarendon, 1997), xx.
6. For examples see Moses Hadas, "Introduction to *Electra*," in *Euripides' Electra*, ed. Moses Hadas (New York: Liberal Arts, 1950), vi–vii; Grube, *Drama of Euripides*, 297–314; Martin Cropp, "Introduction to *Electra*," in *Euripides' Electra*, ed. M. J. Cropp (Warminster, UK: Aris & Phillips, 1988), xli–xliii; and David Raeburn, "The Significance of Stage Properties in Euripides' *Electra*," *Greece & Rome*, 47, no. 2 (2000): 14951.
7. Victoria Wohl, "How to Recognize a Hero in Euripides' *Electra*," *Bulletin of the Institute of Classical Studies* 58, no. 1 (2015): 62; and Victoria Wohl, *Euripides and the Politics of Form*, 86.
8. For examples see, Froma I. Zeitlin, "The Argive Festival of Hera and Euripides' *Electra*," *Transactions and Proceedings of the American Philological Association* 101 (1970): 645–69; Michael Lloyd, "Realism and Character in Euripides' *Electra*," *Phoenix* 40, no. 1 (1986): 1–19; Judith Mossman, "Women's Speech in Greek Tragedy: The Case of Electra and Clytemnestra in Euripides' *Electra*," *Classical Quarterly* 51, no. 2 (2001): 374–84.
9. Brian Lush, "What Sacrifices Are Necessary: The Corruption of Ritual Paradigms in Euripides' *Electra*," *College Literature* 42, no. 2 (2015): 566–67.
10. For a general discussion of the House of Atreus see Hansen, *Classical Mythology*, 79–91.
11. The ancient sites of Argos and Mycenae are approximately fourteen miles apart and are considered interchangeable in tragedy. Euripides tells the story of Eurystheus's persecution of Heracles's children and his death at the hands of Heracles's mother in his *Children of Heracles*. Euripides, *Children of Heracles*, 980–1050.

12. This is a different golden lamb than the ram's golden fleece that Jason was sent to retrieve in the *Medea*. See Vincent J. Rosivach, "The "Golden Lamb" Ode in Euripides' *Electra*," *Classical Philology* 73, no. 3 (1978): 189–90. See also Burnett, *Revenge in Attic and Later Tragedy*, 246.

13. For discussion of Clytemnestra's family story see Blondell, *Helen of Troy*, 27–52; Bettany Hughes, *Helen of Troy* (New York: Vintage, 2005), 49–50; 118–19.

14. Castor and Polydeuces together are known as the Dioskouroi (or, in Latin, "Dioscuri"), which means the sons of Zeus. Only Polydeuces (in Latin, "Pollux") was originally immortal. The twins are unique for splitting or sharing together Polydeuces's fate of immortality. For discussion see Rosa Andujar, "Uncles Ex Machina," *Ramus* 45, no. 2 (2016): 165, 177–78.

15. Homer blames Aegisthus, but Aeschylus portrays Clytemnestra as killing him with her own hands. Homer, *The Odyssey*, 3.25–35; and Aeschylus, *Agamemnon*, 1125–30, 1400–10.

16. Euripides, *Iphigenia at Aulis*, trans. David Kovacs (Cambridge, MA: Harvard University Press, 2002), 1145–1205.

17. Homer, *Iliad*, 9.280–90. For discussion see Cropp, "Introduction to *Electra*," xiii–xiv; and Jasper Griffin, "Hope Deferred Makes the Heart Sick," in *Euripides Talks*, ed. Alan Beale (London: Bristol Classical, 2008), 104.

18. In Euripides's *Iphigenia at Aulis*, Artemis substitutes Iphigenia with a deer at the last minute. In his *Iphigenia among the Taurians*, Iphigenia is discovered living as a priestess sacrificing foreigners to the same goddess. In the *Electra*, Euripides reflects the more traditional telling of a genuine human sacrifice or, at least, Clytemnestra remains unaware of Artemis's potential deceit. See Euripides, *Iphigenia at Aulis*, 1575–1610; and Euripides, *Iphigenia among the Taurians*, 1–65.

19. Griffin, "Hope Deferred Makes the Heart Sick," 104–6.

20. Murray, "Introduction," 5.

21. Euripides, *Electra*, 1–80.

22. Euripides, *Electra*, 80–340. Pylades is Orestes's usual companion on this act of revenge, but in this tragedy he is a silent character. This is probably due to the convention for only three speaking parts at the same time. For discussion see Charles Haines Keene, "Introduction," in *The Electra of Euripides*, ed. Charles Haines Keene (London: Bell, 1898), lxxi.

23. For discussion of potential corruption of this passage see Mark Alonge, "Standing in a Chorus in Euripides' *Electra*, 178 and *Iphigenia in Tauris* 1143," *Mnemosyne* 65 (2012): 116–24.

24. The festival referred to here was the Heraea that honored Hera as goddess of marriage and domestic stability. Electra's refusal to join them draws attention to the tragedy's inversion of this ritual. See Zeitlin, "Argive Festival of Hera and Euripides' *Electra*," 650–52; Naomi A. Weiss, *The Music of Tragedy: Performance and Imagination in Euripidean Theater* (Berkeley: University

of California Press, 2018), 67–72; Christopher A. Pfaff, "Artemis and a Hero at the Argive Heraion," *Hesperia* 82, no. 2 (2013): 277–99; and Lush, "What Sacrifices Are Necessary," 571–72.

25. Electra's "dead" marriage refers to her continuing virginal status. As Greek marriage reflects the death of maidenhood, her virginity highlights again her reversal of ritual. See Rehm, *Marriage to Death*, 117; and Rabinowitz, *Greek Tragedy*, 117–21. For further discussion see Kitto, *Greek Tragedy*, 336–37; Evert van Emde Boas, *Language and Character in Euripides' Electra* (Oxford: Oxford University Press, 2017), 57–58. For potential textual corruption in these passages see Luigi Battezzato, "Euripides' *Electra* 300–301," *Mnemosyne* 54, no. 6 (2001): 731–33.

26. Euripides, *Electra*, 340–485. For potential textual corruption see Simon Goldhill, "Rhetoric and Relevance," *Greek, Roman, and Byzantine Studies* 27, no. 2 (1986): 158–63.

27. Weiss draws attention to this passage as an example of Euripides's new music that correlates the verbal, dancing dolphins with choreographic elements. Weiss, *Music of Tragedy*, 78–79, 88.

28. For discussion of parallels to the *Iliad* see Luschnig, "Introduction," xii; Katherine Callen King, "The Force of Tradition: The Achilles Ode in Euripides' *Electra*," *Transactions and Proceedings of the American Philological Association* 110 (1980): 205, 211–12; and Torrance, *Metapoetry in Euripides*, 76–81.

29. Euripides, *Electra*, 485–700.

30. In Aeschylus's *Libation Bearers*, Electra recognizes Orestes by the very same signs (a lock of hair, a footprint, and a bit of cloth) that she rejects here. Aeschylus, "The Libation Bearers," in *Aeschylus I*, eds. David Grene and Richmond Lattimore (Chicago: University of Chicago Press, 1953), 83–300. For discussion of potential parody see Froma I. Zeitlin, "A Study in Form: Recognition Scenes in the Three Electra Plays," *Lexis* 30 (2012): 361–78; Isabelle Torrance, "In the Footprints of Aeschylus: Recognition, Allusion, and Metapoetics in Euripides," *American Journal of Philology* 132, no. 2 (2011): 177–204; and Malcolm Davies, "Euripides' *Electra*: The Recognition Scene Again," *Classical Quarterly* 48, no. 2 (1998): 389–403.

31. For discussion see Rosivach, "The "Golden Lamb" Ode in Euripides' *Electra*," 189–99; and Weiss, *Music of Tragedy*, 91.

32. Euripides, *Electra*, 750–990. According to Henrichs, this is "the most graphic description of homicide in the extant plays of Euripides." Albert Henrichs, "Drama and Dromena: Bloodshed, Violence, and Sacrificial Metaphor in Euripides," *Harvard Studies in Classical Philology* 100 (2000): 187.

33. An epinicion was a victory ode normally dedicated to those who triumphed in athletic events or war. For discussion see Raeburn, "Significance of Stage Properties in Euripides' *Electra*," 160–62; Raeburn, *Greek Tragedies as Plays for Performance*, 165; and Weiss, *Music of Tragedy*, 70–73.

34. This mirrors Orestes who proclaims (at line 893) to kill Aegisthus in "deed." See Mossman, "Women's Speech in Greek Tragedy," 377.

35. Euripides, *Electra*, 990–1235. For the significance of Electra's "non-hesitation," see Keene, "Introduction," xl; Janet Lembke and Kenneth J. Reckford, "Introduction," in *Euripides' Electra*, ed. Janet Lembke and Kenneth J. Reckford (New York: Oxford University Press, 1994), 3–4.

36. Euripides, *Electra*, 990–1235.

37. Thus, Electra again perverts ritual for revenge. See Sourvinou-Inwood, *Tragedy and Athenian Religion*, 348–50.

38. Euripides, *Electra*, 1245–55.

39. Aeschylus, *Eumenides*, 735–45.

40. The "tied votes" rule was a legal norm in Athenian trials; see Antiphon, *On the Murder of Herodes*, trans. K. J. Maidment (Cambridge, MA: Harvard University Press, 1941), 51. For discussion, Walter Woodburn Hyde, "On the Homicide Courts of Ancient Athens," *University of Pennsylvania Law Review and American Law Register* 66, no. 7/8 (1918): 319–62, esp. 336.

41. Storey and Allan, *A Guide to Ancient Greek Drama*, 265. Metatextual comparison with Aeschylus can be traced to August W. von Schlegel. For discussion see Michael J. O'Brien, "Orestes and the Gorgon: Euripides' *Electra*," *American Journal of Philology* 85, no. 1 (1964): 14–15; Raeburn, "Significance of Stage Properties in Euripides' *Electra*," 149–51; and Denniston, "Introduction," ix–xxxiii. The intertextuality also may reveal Euripides's reflection on dramatic conventions. See Wright, "The Tragedian as Critic," 180–82; and Torrance, "In the Footprints of Aeschylus," 177–204.

42. Such metatextual references may have been more widespread than found in our limited evidence from surviving texts. Emily A. McDermott, "Euripides' Second Thoughts," *Transactions and Proceedings of the American Philological Association* 130 (2000): 241. See also Torrance, *Metapoetry in Euripides*, 14–32.

43. Vermeule, "Introduction to Electra," 205. For discussion the contrast of this play with Sophocles's version see Murray, "Introduction," 5–7. Or further comparison to Homer, see John Davidson, "Euripides, Homer, and Sophocles," *Illinois Classical Studies* 24/25 (1999–2000): 119–22.

44. Barlow, *Imagery of Euripides*, 197.

45. For potential innovations see Loukas Papadimitropoulos, "Causality and Innovation in Euripides' *Electra*," *Rheinisches Museum für Philologie, Neue Folge* 151, no. 2 (2008): 113–26; and Cropp, "Introduction to *Electra*," xliii–l. For innovations of his language and new music see Burnett, *Revenge in Attic and Later Tragedy*, 229–31; and Weiss, *Music of Tragedy*, 61–62.

46. Zeitlin, "Argive Festival of Hera and Euripides' *Electra*," 645; Luschnig, "Introduction," x; Denniston, "Introduction," xii–xiii; Hadas, "Introduction to *Electra*," vi, xi; and Chris Carey, "Country Matters: The Location of Euripides' *Electra*," in *Euripides Talks*, ed. Alan Beale (London: Bristol Classical, 2008), 94–102.

47. Zeitlin, "Argive Festival of Hera and Euripides' *Electra*," 646. Or, the allusion to the "common man" represents a not-yet-realized equality of Athenian democracy. For this perspective see Wohl, *Euripides and the Politics of Form*, 87.

48. Aristotle, *Poetics*, 1453a. For the effect of portraying a common man, see Keene, "Introduction," xi. See also J. T. Sheppard, "The *Electra* of Euripides," *Classical Review* 32, no. 7–8 (1918): 137–38.

49. This juxtaposition of expectation and reality is reflected in the debate (*agōn*) on true nobility. See Goldhill, "Rhetoric and Relevance," 167–71.

50. For discussion see Lloyd, "Realism and Character in Euripides' *Electra*," 2–6.

51. Cropp, "Introduction to *Electra*," xxxvi. See also Carey, "Country Matters," 100–102; and Kitto, *Greek Tragedy*, 333–37.

52. This action may be another intertextual reflection, as Aeschylus may have invented Clytemnestra's similar participation. See Hughes, *Helen of Troy*, 394, fn 6.

53. Hadas, "Introduction to *Electra*," vii; Raeburn, *Greek Tragedies as Plays for Performance*, 158; Vermeule, "Introduction to Electra," 205. See also Sheppard, "*Electra* of Euripides," 138–39; Grube, *The Drama of Euripides*, 298–99. By contrast, other scholars are more sympathetic to her diminished circumstances. See N. G. L. Hammond, "Spectacle and Parody in Euripides' *Electra*," *Greek, Roman, and Byzantine Studies* 25, no. 4 (1984): 377–81.

54. Mossman, "Women's Speech in Greek Tragedy," 374–84. For discussion see also van Emde Boas, *Language and Character in Euripides' Electra*, 188–228; Lloyd, "Realism and Character in Euripides' *Electra*," 216; and J. H. Kim On Chong-Gossard, "Song and the Solitary Self: Euripidean Women Who Resist Comfort," *Phoenix* 57, no. 3/4 (2003): 209–31.

55. Hadas, "Introduction to *Electra*," vii; Lembke and Reckford, "Introduction," 4; Cropp, "Introduction to *Electra*," xxxiii. See also Kitto, *Greek Tragedy*, 338.

56. William Allan, "The Ethics of Retaliatory Violence in Athenian Tragedy," *Mnemosyne* 66 (2013): 611.

57. Keene, "Introduction," vi; Sheppard, "*Electra* of Euripides," xxx. See also Kitto, *Greek Tragedy*, 336–37; Denniston, "Introduction," xxix–xxxi; Lembke and Reckford, "Introduction," 14.

58. As we know from Aristotle, Euripides was more creative in resolving plots "mechanically" (i.e., with the *mēchanē*). See Aristotle, *Poetics*, 1454a.

59. Euripides, *Electra*, 1265, 1240–50. For discussion of how the doubt of this tragedy is linked to the idea that Euripides destroyed tragedy see Badger, *Sophocles and the Politics of Tragedy*, 181.

60. Euripides, *Ion*, 335, 485–50, 1535–40. Such critique has been used as evidence of Euripides's irreligious views. For discussion, see Conacher, "Religious and Ethical Attitudes in Euripides' *Suppliants*," 8–26; Kovacs, "Introduction to

Electra," 149; O'Brien, "Orestes and the Gorgon," 30–34; and Ringer, *Euripides and the Boundary of the Human,* 147–63.

61. This kind of "twisting" and "turning" is also represented acoustically. See Weiss, *Music of Tragedy,* 96.

62. Euripides, *Electra,* 85–90.

63. For more discussion of the Erinyes see Elizabeth Meier Tetlow, *Women, Crime, and Punishment in Ancient Law and Society,* vol. 2 (London: Continuum, 1985), 124–27; and Albert Henrichs, "Anonymity and Polarity: Unknown Gods and Nameless Altars at the Areopagos," *Illinois Classical Studies* 19 (1994): 38–8, 53–54.

64. This is similar to the moral question (i.e., the piety of prosecuting parents) proposed in Plato, *Euthyphro,* 6b–8e.

65. Euripides, *Electra,* 970–80, 20–40, 255–60, 430–85, 335–40, 85–90, 550.

66. Euripides, *Electra,* 960–85, 1205–20.

67. Matricide is also an extreme violation of the ancient code of helping friends and harming enemies. See Rabinowitz, *Greek Tragedy,* 116–17; and Belfiore, "Harming Friends," 152–54.

68. Cropp, "Introduction to *Electra,*" xxxii–xxxvi; and King, "Force of Tradition," 203–10.

69. Euripides, *Electra,* 655–60, 1125–50, 1100–1110.

70. Clytemnestra's regret that her anger at her husband influenced her plans (*bouleumatōn*) reflects Medea's famous speech that she chooses her spirit (*thumos*) rather than love for her children—an act she also knows she will suffer for. See, for instance, Euripides, *Medea,* 1020–80.

71. Cropp, "Introduction to *Electra,*" xxxii; and Hall, "Introduction," xxi.

72. Euripides, *Electra,* 1180–1335.

73. The Dioscuri suggest the version found in Euripides's *Helen* where a counterfeit image was sent to Troy, while the real Helen was safe in Egypt. For another example of this version see Herodotus, *Histories* 2.112. For discussion, see Hughes, *Helen of Troy,* 160–63.

74. For discussion, see Lefkowitz, *Greek Gods, Human Lives,* 136–37.

75. Euripides, *Electra,* 1265–70, see also 235–45, 205–15, 1330–15.

76. Zuntz, *Political Plays of Euripides,* 67–70.

77. Thus, Electra's self-imposed exile becomes a reality. See Chong-Gossard, "Song and the Solitary Self," 218.

78. For discussion see Rush Rehm, *The Play of Space* (Princeton, NJ: Princeton University Press, 2002), 199; and Mastronarde, "Euripidean Tragedy and Genre," 36–37. Kitto suggests it is a "grim" species of melodrama. See Kitto, *Greek Tragedy,* 330.

79. Euripides, *Electra,* 980–85, 1110, 1180–85.

80. The audience's pride in their legal system might encourage this conclusion. Allan, "Ethics of Retaliatory Violence in Athenian Tragedy," 612–13.

81. Euripides, *Electra*, 35–45, 265–70, 335–40, 375–90, 550–60, 980–85. This might be the closest staged act of noble revenge. See Burnett, *Revenge in Attic and Later Tragedy*, 243.

82. For the institutionalization of the Erinyes, see Bacon, "The Furies' Homecoming," 57.

83. See, for instance, Cropp, "Introduction to *Electra*," xxxi.

84. Euripides, *Iphigenia among the Taurians*, 75–85.

85. Euripides, *Electra*, 370–75.

86. For discussion of the Oracle's command see Papadimitropoulos, "Causality and Innovation in Euripides' *Electra*," 123–24.

87. Euripides, *Electra*, 970–75.

88. This makes the *Electra* a kind of anti-*Hecuba* as it focuses on nobility of character as opposed to nobility of birth. See Wohl, *Euripides and the Politics of Form*, 64–70. See also W. Geoffrey Arnott, "Double the Vision: A Reading of Euripides' *Electra*," *Greece & Rome* 28, no. 2 (1981): 180–82.

89. Euripides, *Electra*, 960–90. *Alastōrs* were punitive agents, such as the Erinyes. See Burnett, *Revenge in Attic and Later Tragedy*, 119–20.

90. Cropp, "Introduction to *Electra*," xxxiii. See also Hadas, "Introduction to *Electra*," vii.

91. Euripides, *Electra*, 360–400, 550–55.

92. Vermeule's translation, lines 370–85. See also Euripides, *Electra*, 50–55, 405–10.

93. Euripides, *Electra*, 375–85, 405–10, 50–55.

94. Aristotle, *Nicomachean Ethics*, 1106b–07a; and Aristotle, *Politics*, 1253a1–10.

95. This idea that true nobility is unfazed by circumstance is reflected in Euripides, *Hecuba*, 595–600. Aristotle also revisits this idea in Aristotle, *Nicomachean Ethics*, 1100a1–1101a10.

96. King would add the false "color of one's skin" to Euripides's list of potential criteria for judgment. Martin Luther King Jr., *Testament of Hope: The Essential Writings and Speeches* (New York: HarperOne, 2003), 217–20.

97. Euripides, *Electra*, 420–35, 355–75, 25–55, 30–50, 1280–90.

98. Another possibility is that this outcome is the tragedy of the play: the farmer receives such wealth but does not wish for such a life. See Luschnig, "Introduction," xv; and Wohl, *Euripides and the Politics of Form*, 86.

99. See, for instance, O'Brien, "Orestes and the Gorgon," 34.

100. Euripides, *Electra*, 635–40, 320–30, 1110–1120. See O'Brien, "Orestes and the Gorgon," 28; Lloyd, "Realism and Character in Euripides' *Electra*," 15–16; and Lush, "What Sacrifices Are Necessary," 580–81.

101. Health would disagree as Greek heroes were not above using deceit or killing another during a sacrifice. For discussion, see Heath, *Poetics of Greek Tragedy*, 71–80; John R. Porter, "Tiptoeing through the Corpses: Euripides' *Electra*,

Apollonius, and the *Bouphonia*," *Greek, Roman, and Byzantine Studies* 13, no. 3 (1990): 259–60. Also see John Gibert, "Apollo's Sacrifice: The Limits of a Metaphor in Greek Tragedy," *Harvard Studies in Classical Philology* 101 (2003): 161–67; and Henrichs, "Drama and Dromena," 187–88.

102. Aegisthus's behavior as a "good host" may be less an indication of generosity than a simple reflection of cultural norms. For discussion, see Keene, "Introduction," xiv–xv.

103. Denniston, "Introduction," vi. See Euripides, *Electra*, 1035–1140.

104. The chorus's cries of shame are also connected to the double standard, as shame is used to silence and regulate ways of being in the world. See Frank, *Democracy and the Death of Shame*, 3–46.

105. James Morwood, "The Pattern of the Euripides *Electra*," *American Journal of Philology* 102, no. 4 (1981): 370.

106. O'Brien, "Orestes and the Gorgon," 38–39. Or, as Lembke and Reckford suggest, the "deliberately lame" deus ex machina offers no solution. See Lembke and Reckford, "Introduction," 4, 13.

107. Griffin, "Hope Deferred Makes the Heart Sick," 107–109; Goldhill, "Rhetoric and Relevance," 169–71; and Torrance, *Metapoetry in Euripides*, 15–30.

108. Euripides, *Electra*, 280–85, 520–30. For discussion see Lloyd, "Realism and Character in Euripides' *Electra*," 10–12; and van Emde Boas, *Language and Character in Euripides' Electra*, 165–87.

109. Raeburn, "Significance of Stage Properties in Euripides' *Electra*," 157–59. See also Goldhill, "Rhetoric and Relevance," 167. For the disingenuousness of this argument see Robert L. Gallagher, "Making the Stronger Argument the Weaker: Euripides's *Electra* 518–44," *Classical Quarterly* 53, no. 2 (2003): 401–15.

110. Vermeule, "Introduction to Electra," 205–6; and Sheppard, "The *Electra* of Euripides," 138. Or another possibility is that Electra's double vision forces the audience to judge between her distorted view and what they see. See Arnott, "Double the Vision," 182, 190.

111. For discussion, Padel, "Making Space Speak," 344–45.

112. Zeitlin, "A Study in Form," 366–69.

113. As O'Brien emphasizes, this scar is compared to "a stamp of a coin" and highlights the distinction between false coinage and false nobility. See O'Brien, "Orestes and the Gorgon," 35–37.

114. Euripides, *Electra*, 1060–1100.

115. See Cropp, "Introduction to *Electra*," xxxvii; and van Emde Boas, *Language and Character in Euripides' Electra*, 58.

116. This change is also represented in Electra joining with the chorus in song, which contrasts with her former rejection of community. Weiss, *Music of Tragedy*, 97–98.

117. The *skēnē* itself is symbolic of what is hidden within human beings. See Padel, "Making Space Speak," 358.

118. Lembke and Reckford, "Introduction," 7; and Rabinowitz, *Greek Tragedy*, 119.

119. It can be seen as a dramatization of Aristotle's later comment that ethical judgment involves feeling and knowing "the right time, the right circumstance, the right reason, and the right manner." See Aristotle, *Nicomachean Ethics*, 1106b20–25.

120. Cesare Beccaria, *On Crimes and Punishments and Other Writings*, trans. Aaron Thomas and Jeremy Parzen (Toronto: University of Toronto Press, 2008), 82.

121. Catherine Z. Elgin, *Considered Judgment* (Princeton, NJ: Princeton University Press, 1999).

122. For example, see Joan L. Brockman and Dorothy E. Chunn, *Investigating Gender Bias: Law, Courts, and the Legal Profession* (Toronto: Thompson Educational, 1993); and Matthew Clair, *Privilege and Punishment: How Race and Class Matter in Criminal Court* (Princeton, NJ: Princeton University Press, 2020).

123. For a seminal discussion of impartiality and justice see Brian Barry, *Justice as Impartiality* (Oxford: Clarendon, 1995).

124. Badger, *Sophocles and the Politics of Tragedy*, 21.

125. Euripides, *Electra*, 290–300.

Conclusion

1. Plato, *Republic*, 608b.
2. Aristotle, *Poetics*, 1448b.
3. So says the character of Euripides in Aristophanes, *Frogs*, 970–75, 955–60.
4. Socrates suggests the common person does as much when discussing poets. See Plato, *Protagoras*, 347d–48a.
5. Blundell, *Helping Friends and Harming Enemies*, 26–27.
6. Belfiore, *Murder among Friends*, xv.
7. Supplication also is important in Euripides, *Medea*, 320–55, 660–800, 1350–1390.
8. For discussion of supplication see Naiden, *Ancient Supplication*, 3–21; Tzanetou, "Supplication and Empire in Athenian Tragedy," 305–24; and Belfiore, *Murder among Friends*, 14–16.
9. Euripides, *Suppliant Women*, 465–580, 295–345. For connections to Athenian political debates see Carter, *Quiet Athenian*, 26–52; Michelini, "Political Themes in Euripides' Suppliants," 226–30; and Brock, "Mythical Polypragmosyne in Athenian Drama and Rhetroic," 227–38.
10. Euripides, *Children of Heracles*, 330–50, 390–535, 800–70.

11. Euripides, *Hecuba*, 270–335, 785–860, 1045–55.

12. For discussion see Parker, "Pleasing Thighs," 105–27; and Belfiore, *Murder among Friends*, 5–19.

13. Euripides, *Suppliant Women*, 1180–1215.

14. Heracles rescued Demophon's father Theseus from his failed attempt to kidnap Persephone. See Euripides, *Children of Heracles*, 235–75.

15. Euripides, *Alcestis*, 1–15, 1120–1135.

16. Belfiore, *Murder among Friends*, 7–9, 14–19; Blundell, *Helping Friends and Harming Enemies*, 48–49; and Victoria Wohl, *Intimate Commerce: Exchange, Gender and Subjectivity in Greece* (Austin: University of Texas Press, 1998), xiix–xxvi.

17. Euripides, *Alcestis*, 1070–1160. Guest-friendship also plays a minor role in *Ion*, 60–80, 515–65, 770–830, 1120–1230.

18. Euripides, *Hecuba*, 1–60, 1130–80.

19. Euripides, *Suppliant Women*, 990–1120.

20. Euripides, *Medea*, 1–50, 1235–50, 1350–60.

21. Euripides, *Ion*, 245, 380, 1260–1445.

22. Euripides, *Phoenician Women*, 30–50; Euripides, *Bacchae*, 1230–1325.

23. The Dioscuri confirm that Clytemnestra's death was just but not by Orestes's hand. See Euripides, *Electra*, 965–85, 1235–45.

24. Euripides, *Phoenician Women*, 1685–1760.

25. Euripides, *Ion*, 1000–1030.

26. This question is central in Books 8 and 9 of Aristotle, *Nicomachean Ethics*, 1155a1–1172a15. It is also the main question of Plato's dialogue *Lysis*. Plato, *Lysis*, trans. W. R. H. Lamb (Cambridge, MA: Harvard University Press, 1925), 203a–223c. In the *Memorabilia*, Xenophon devotes the better part of Books 2 and 3 to the question of friendship. See Xenophon, *Memorabilia*, 2.1.27–2.10.6, 3.11.4–3.14.7.

27. See also Homer, *Iliad*, 18.560–800; Hesiod, *Works and Days*, II.10–300.

28. Plato, *Republic*, 331–32a.

29. Xenophon, *Anabasis*, trans. Carleton Lewis Brownson and John Dillery (Cambridge, MA: Harvard University Press, 1998), 3.2.8.

30. Aristotle, *Nicomachean Ethics*, 1130b–1133a5. Justice as reciprocal equality in opposition to "overreaching" (*pleonexia*) is also brought up in Plato, *Republic*, 359a–c.

31. Sommerstein, "Introduction," 1–6; Plescia, *The Oath and Perjury in Ancient Athens*, 1–14.

32. Burnett, *Revenge in Attic and Later Tragedy*, 201.

33. In the whole affair, what Medea laments most is Jason's breaking of his oath. See Euripides, *Medea*, 15–25, 490–95, 710–55.

34. Euripides, *Phoenician Women*, 70–80.

35. Euripides, *Phoenician Women*, 530–45.

36. Euripides, *Ion*, 1310–20. In the *Children of Heracles*, the Argive herald also suggests nonequals do not deserve the same things as equals. See Euripides, *Children of Heracles*, 135–40, 235–50.

37. Euripides, *Hecuba*, 255–70.

38. Euripides, *Alcestis*, 610–740.

39. See, for instance, Aristotle, *Nicomachean Ethics*, 1131b25–1132b25.

40. In the case of murder, blood price could be a literal exchange of life for a life but most often was paid in compensation. See Cantarella, "Private Justice and Public Justice," 473–83.

41. Menoeceus saves Thebes by sacrificing his life in exchange for Cadmus's murder of Ares's son. Euripides, *Phoenician Women*, 850–1050.

42. Euripides, *Hecuba*, 1130–80, 1205–40.

43. Euripides, *Hecuba*, 1175–80.

44. Euripides, *Children of Heracles*, 230–35, 325–35.

45. Euripides, *Suppliant Women*, 220–50, 335–55, 585–95.

46. Euripides, *Medea*, 485–90; Euripides, *Electra*, 1015–40.

47. Euripides, *Bacchae*, 1345–50. As Cephalus asserted in the *Republic*, justice also involves what we owe the gods. Plato, *Republic*, 331b.

48. Euripides, *Electra*, 1240–50.

49. Euripides, *Phoenician Women*, 500–505.

50. Euripides, *Ion*, 225–35.

51. The ancient wooden statue of Dionysus was brought into the theater to watch the spectacle. See Parke, *Festivals of the Athenians*, 130–31.

52. Meagher, *The Essential Euripides*, 554; Darby, *Bacchus*, 123–25; and Segal, "Raw and the Cooked in Greek Literature," 292–93.

53. Euripides, *Electra*, 1240–45.

54. Euripides, *Suppliant Women*, 1185–1215.

55. Euripides, *Bacchae*, 200–205, 480–85, 890–900.

56. Euripides, *Hecuba*, 290–95.

57. Euripides, *Phoenician Women*, 1630–50.

58. Euripides, *Bacchae*, 505–10, 1320–30.

59. Euripides, *Ion*, 370–80, 1545–65; Euripides, *Suppliant Women*, 1180–1235. For discussion of Athena's justice in tragedy generally see Kennedy, *Athena's Justice*.

60. Euripides, *Children of Heracles*, 410–20, 1050–55.

61. Euripides, *Hecuba*, 100–50.

62. See, for example, *Electra*, 1255–75; and Aeschylus, *Eumenides*, 735–800. For this interpretation of the *Eumenides* as establishing institutional solutions to cycles of violence see Kitto, *Greek Tragedy*, 94–95; and Goldhill, *Reading Greek Tragedy*, 38–41.

63. Euripides, *Ion*, 1560–70 and 335–40.

64. Euripides, *Electra*, 1245–50.

65. Euripides, *Suppliant Women*, 540–45.

66. Plato, *Republic*, 344d. See also the herald in Euripides, *Children of Heracles*, 150–60, 906–1060.

67. Euripides, *Bacchae*, 505–10, 1320–30.

68. Euripides, *Phoenician Women*, 495–525, 1380–1400.

69. The sophist Antiphon (fragment D-K 87 B44), for example, questioned whether things that are just according to law are "at variance with nature." As quoted in Conacher, *Euripides and the Sophists*, 43.

70. de Romilly, *Great Sophists in Periclean Athens*, 132.

71. Plato, *Apology*, 23a. For examples of this approach see Vasilis Politis, "Aporia and Searching in the Early Plato," in *Remembering Socrates*, ed. L. Judson and V. Karamanis (Oxford: Oxford University Press, 2006), 88–109; and Saxonhouse, "On Socratic Narrative," 728–53.

72. Zuntz argues that Euripides's tragedies have the "ambiguous conclusion of a Platonic dialogue, [which] leaves the spectator with disquieting questions and thus stirs him to thinking." See Zuntz, *The Political Plays of Euripides*, 38.

73. Aristotle, *Nicomachean Ethics*, 1104a5–20, 1106b20–30.

74. See Segal, "Euripides," 244–53. For the connection of this imprecision to the tragic see Badger, *Sophocles and the Politics of Tragedy*, 21–22.

75. In the *Metaphysics*, Aristotle uses *sōros* to describe an aggregate. Xenophon, in the *Hellenica*, uses this term to describe a pile of wheat or, more prosaically, a heap of dead bodies. Aristotle, *Metaphysics*, 7.1040b, 7.1041b, 8.1045a, 13.1084b; Xenophon, *Hellenica*, trans. Carleton L. Brownson (Cambridge, MA: Harvard University Press, 1918), 4.4.12. For discussion of the ancient Greek concept of *sōros* see Johnstone, *A History of Trust in Ancient Greece*, 1–2, fn 6, 173.

Bibliography

Abrahamson, Ernst L. "Euripides' Tragedy of *Hecuba*." *Transactions and Proceedings of the American Philological Association* 83 (1952): 120–29.
Adcock, Sir Frank, and D. J. Mosley. *Diplomacy in Greece*. London: Thames and Hudson, 1975.
Aeschylus. *Agamemnon*. Translated by Alan H. Sommerstein. Cambridge, MA: Harvard University Press, 2009.
———. *The Eumenides*. Translated by Hugh Lloyd-Jones. Cambridge, MA: Harvard University Press, 1960.
———. "The Libation Bearers." Translated by Richmond Lattimore. In *Aeschylus 1*, edited by David Grene and Richmond Lattimore, 91–132. Chicago: University of Chicago Press, 1953.
———. *Prometheus Bound*. Translated by Alan H. Sommerstein. Cambridge, MA: Harvard University Press, 2009.
———. *Seven against Thebes*. Translated by Alan H. Sommerstein. Cambridge, MA: Harvard University Press, 2009.
Aguirre, Javier. "Téchnē and Enthousiasmós in Plato's Critique of Poetry." *Revista Portuguesa de Filosofia* 72, no. 1 (2016): 181–97.
Ahrensdorf, Peter J. *Greek Tragedy and Political Philosophy: Rationalism and Religion in Sophocles' Theban Plays*. Cambridge: Cambridge University Press, 2009.
Alaux, Jean. "Acting Myth: Athenian Drama." In *A Companion to Greek Mythology*, edited by Den Dowden and Niall Livingstone, 141–55. Chichester, UK: Blackwell, 2011.
Alford, C. Fred. "Greek Tragedy and Civilization." *Political Research Quarterly* (1993): 259–80.
Allan, William. "The Ethics of Retaliatory Violence in Athenian Tragedy." *Mnemosyne* 66 (2013): 593–615.
———. "Euripides and the Sophists." *Illinois Classical Studies* 24/5 (1999–2000): 145–56.
———. *Euripides: Medea*. Duckworth Companions to Greek and Roman Tragedy. London: Duckworth, 2002.

———. "Introduction to the *Children of Heracles*." In *Euripides: The Children of Heracles*, edited by William Allan, 21–58. Warminster, UK: Aris & Phillips, 2001.

———. "Tragedy and the Early Greek Philosophic Tradition." In *A Companion to Greek Tragedy*, edited by Justina Gregory, 71–82. Oxford: Blackwell, 2008.

Allen, James T., and Gabriel Italie. *A Concordance to Euripides*. Groningen, The Netherlands: Bouma's Boekhuis, 1970.

Alonge, Mark. "Standing in a Chorus in Euripides' *Electra* 178 and *Iphigenia in Tauris* 1143." *Mnemosyne* 65 (2012): 116–24.

Altena, Herman. "Text and Performance: On Significant Actions in Euripides' *Phoenissae*." *Illinois Classical Studies* 24/25 (1999–2000): 303–23.

Amsler, Lisa Blomgren, Janet K. Martinez, and Stephanie E. Smith. *Dispute System Design*. Stanford, CA: Stanford University Press, 2020.

Anderson, Benedict. *Imagined Communities*. 2nd ed. New York: Verso, 2006.

Anderson, Greg. *The Athenian Experiment*. Ann Arbor: University of Michigan Press, 2003.

Anderson, Michael J. "Myth." In *A Companion to Greek Tragedy*, edited by Justina Gregory, 121–35. Oxford: Blackwell, 2008.

Andujar, Rosa. "Uncles *Ex Machina*." *Ramus* 45, no. 2 (2016): 165–91.

Anhalt, Emily Katz. *Enraged: Why Violent Times Need Ancient Greek Myths*. New Haven, CT: Yale University Press, 2017.

Ankarloo, Bengt, and Stuart Clark. *Witchcraft and Magic in Europe*. Philadelphia: University of Pennsylvania Press, 1999.

Annas, Julia. *Ancient Philosophy*. Oxford: Oxford University Press, 2000.

———. "Plato's Myths of Judgement." *Phronesis* 27, no. 2 (1982): 119–43.

Antiphon. *On the Murder of Herodes*. Translated by K. J. Maidment. Cambridge, MA: Harvard University Press, 1941.

Apollodorus. *The Library of Greek Mythology*. Translated by Robin Hard. Oxford: Oxford University Press, 2008.

Aristophanes. *The Frogs*. Translated by Jefffrey Henderson. Cambridge, MA: Harvard University Press, 2002.

Aristotle. *The Art of Rhetoric*. Translated by J. H. Freese. Cambridge, MA: Harvard University Press, 1926.

———. *Metaphysics*. Translated by John H. McMahon. Amherst, MA: Prometheus, 1991.

———. *The Nicomachean Ethics*. Translated by H. Rackham. Cambridge, MA: Harvard University Press, 1934.

———. *The Poetics*. Translated by W. Hamilton Fyfe. Cambridge, MA: Harvard University Press, 1932.

———. *The Politics*. Translated by H. Rackham. Cambridge, MA: Harvard University Press, 1944.

---. *Topica*. Translated by Hugh Tredennick. Cambridge, MA: Harvard University Press, 1960.
Arnason, Johann P. "Nationalism, Globalism, and Modernity." *Theory, Culture and Society* 7, no. 2 (1990): 207–36.
Arnott, W. Geoffrey. "Double the Vision: A Reading of Euripides' 'Electra.'" *Greece & Rome* 28, no. 2 (1981): 179–92.
---. "Realism in the *Ion*." In *Tragedy and the Tragic*, edited by M. S. Silk, 110–18. Oxford: Oxford University Press, 1996.
Arrowsmith, William. "Introduction." In *Euripides: Alcestis*, 3–29. Oxford: Oxford University Press, 1974.
---. "Introduction." In *Euripides V*, edited by David Grene and Richmond Lattimore, 142–53. Chicago: University of Chicago Press, 1959.
---. "Introduction to the *Hecuba*." In *Euripides III*, edited by David Grene and Richmond Lattimore, 2–7. Chicago: University of Chicago Press, 1958.
Arthur, Marilyn B. "The Curse of Civilization." *Harvard Studies in Classical Philology* 81 (1977): 163–85.
Avery, Harry C. "Euripides' *Heracleidae*." *American Journal of Philology* 92, no. 4 (1971): 539–65.
Bacon, Helen H. "The Furies' Homecoming." *Classical Philology* 96, no. 1 (2001): 48–59.
Badger, Jonathan N. *Sophocles and the Politics of Tragedy*. New York: Routledge, 2015.
Barlow, Shirley A. "Euripides' Medea: A Subversive Play." In *Stage Directions*, edited by Allan Griffiths, 36–45: Bulletin of the Institute of Classical Studies, 1989.
---. "General Introduction to the Series." In *Phoenician Women*, edited by Elizabeth Craik, 1–31. Warminster, UK: Aris & Phillips, 1988.
---. *The Imagery of Euripides: A Study in the Dramatic Use of Pictorial Language*. London: Methuen, 1974.
Barrett, James. "Pentheus and the Spectator in Euripides' *Bacchae*." *American Journal of Philology* 119, no. 3 (1998): 337–60.
Barry, Brian. *Justice as Impartiality*. Oxford: Clarendon, 1995.
Bartels, Anke, Lars Eckstein, Nicole Waller, and Dirk Wiemann, eds. *Postcolonial Justice*. Leiden, The Netherlands: Brill, 2017.
Bartky, Elliot. "Plato and the Politics of Aristotle's *Poetics*." *Review of Politics* 54, no. 4 (1992): 589–619.
Battezzato, Luigi. "Euripides' *Electra* 300–301." *Mnemosyne* 54, no. 6 (2001): 731–33.
---. "Lyric." In *A Companion to Greek Tragedy*, edited by Justina Gregory, 149–66. Oxford: Blackwell, 2008.
Bayfield, M. A. "Introduction." In *The Alcestis of Euripides*. New York: Macmillian, 1902.

Beaty, Michael, Carlton Fisher, and Mark Nelson, eds. *Christian Theism and Moral Philosophy*. Macon, GA: Mercer University Press, 1998

Beccaria, Cesare. *On Crimes and Punishments and Other Writings*. Translated by Aaron Thomas and Jeremy Parzen. Toronto: University of Toronto Press, 2008.

Behler, Ernst. "A. W. Schlegel and the Nineteenth Century 'Damnatio' of Euripides." *Greek, Roman, and Byzantine Studies* 27, no. 4 (1986): 335–67.

Beitz, Charles. "Social and Cosmopolitan Liberalism." *International Affairs* 75 (1999): 125–40.

Belfiore, Elizabeth S. "Harming Friends." In *Reciprocity in Ancient Greece*, edited by Christopher Gill, Norman Postlethwaite, and Richard Seaford, 139–58. Oxford: Oxford University Press, 1988.

———. *Murder among Friends*. Oxford: Oxford University Press, 2000.

Berg, Wendy, and Mike Harris. *Polarity Magic*. St. Paul, MN: Llewellyn, 2003.

Berman, Daniel W. "The Double Foundation of Boiotian Thebes." *Transactions and Proceedings of the American Philological Association* 134, no. 1 (2004): 1–22.

———. *Myth, Literature, and the Creation of the Topography of Thebes*. Cambridge: Cambridge University Press, 2015.

Betts, G. G. "The Silence of Alcestis." *Mnemosyne, Fourth Series* 18, no. 2 (1965): 181–82.

Beye, Charles Rowan. "Introduction." In *Alcestis by Euripides*, 1–13. Englewood Cliffs, NJ: Prentice Hall, 1974.

Black, Samuel. "Individualism at an Impasse." *Canadian Journal of Philosophy* 21, no. 3 (1991): 347–77.

Blanshard, Alastair. *Hercules: A Heroic Life*. London: Granta, 2005.

Blondell, Ruby. *Helen of Troy: Beauty, Myth, and Devastation*. Oxford: Oxford University Press, 2013.

———. "Medea: Introduction." In *Women on the Edge*, edited by Ruby Blondell, Mary-Kay Gamel, Nancy Sorkin Rabinowtiz, and Bella Zweig, 149–69. New York: Routledge, 1999.

Blondell, Ruby, Mary-Kay Gamel, Nancy Sorkin Rabinowitz, and Bella Zweig. "Introduction." In *Women on the Edge*, edited by Ruby Blondell, Mary-Kay Gamel, Nancy Sorkin Rabinowitz, and Bella Zweig, 1–90. London: Routledge, 1999.

Bloom, Allan. "Interpretive Essay." In *The Republic of Plato*. New York: Basic Books, 1968.

Blundell, Mary Whitlock. *Helping Friends and Harming Enemies*. Cambridge: Cambridge University Press, 1991.

Blundell, Sue. "The Play Explores Social Conflict between Men and Women." In *Readings on Euripides' Medea*, edited by Don Nardo, 68–75. San Diego, CA: Greenhaven, 2001.

———. *Women in Ancient Greece*. Cambridge, MA: Harvard University Press, 1995.

Bohrer, Karl Heinz, Sean Nye, and Rita Felski. "The Tragic: A Question of Art, Not Philosophy of History." *New Literary History* 41, no. 1 (2010): 35–51.
Bongie, Elizabeth. "Heroic Elements in the *Medea* of Eurpides." *Transactions of the American Philological Association* 107 (1977): 27–56.
Boot, Eric R. *Human Duties and the Limitations of Human Rights Discourse*. Leiden, The Netherlands: Springer, 2017.
Bowden, Hugh. *Mystery Cults of the Ancient World*. Princeton, NJ: Princeton University Press, 2010.
Bowie, A. M. "Tragic Filters for History." In *The Cambridge Companion to Greek Tragedy and the Historian*, edited by Christopher Pelling, 39–62. Oxford: Clarendon, 1997.
Brands, Hal, and Charles Edel. *The Lessons of Tragedy: Statecraft and World Order*. New Haven, CT: Yale University Press, 2019.
Braun, T. F. R. G. "The Greeks in the Near East." In *Cambridge Ancient History*, edited by John Boardman and N. G. L. Hammond, 1–30. Cambridge: Cambridge University Press, 1982.
Bremmer, Jan N. "Transvestite Dionysos." In *Rites of Passage in Ancient Greece: Literature, Religion, Society*, edited by Mark William Padilla, 183–200. Lewisburg, PA: Bucknell University Press, 1999.
———. "Why Did Medea Kill Her Brother Apsyrtus." In *Medea: Essays on Medea in Myth, Literature, Philosophy and Art*, edited by James J. Clauss and Sarah Iles Johnston, 83–100. Princeton, NJ: Princeton University Press, 1997.
Broad, William J. *The Oracle*. New York: Penguin, 2006.
Brock, Roger. "Citizens and Non-Citizens in Athenian Tragedy." In *Law and Drama in Ancient Greece*, edited by Edward M. Harris, Delfim F. Leao and P. J. Rhodes, 94–107. London: Bloomsbury, 2010.
———. *Greek Political Imagery: From Homer to Aristotle*. London: Bloomsbury, 2013.
———. "Mythical Polypragmosyne in Athenian Drama and Rhetroic." *Bulletin of the Institute of Classical Studies* 42, no. S71 (1998): 227–38.
Brockman, Joan L., and Dorothy E. Chunn. *Investigating Gender Bias: Law, Courts, and the Legal Profession*. Toronto: Thompson Educational, 1993.
Brommer, Frank. *Heracles: The Twelve Labors of the Hero in Ancient Art and Literature*. Translated by Shirley J. Schwarz. New Rochelle, NY: Aristide D. Caratzas, 1986.
Brown, Sylvia G. "Metrical Innovations in Euripides' Later Plays." *American Journal of Philology* 95, no. 3 (1974): 207–34.
Budin, Stephanie Lynn. *The Ancient Greeks*. Oxford: Oxford University Press, 2009.
Burgess, Dana L. "The Authenticity of the Teichoskopia of Euripides' *Phoenissae*." *The Classical Journal* 83, no. 2 (1987–88): 103–13.
Burgess, Jonathan S. *The Tradition of the Trojan War in Homer and the Epic Cycle*. Baltimore: Johns Hopkins University Press, 2001.
Burian, Peter. "Athenian Tragedy as Democratic Discourse." In *Why Athens?*, edited by D. M. Carter, 95–118. Oxford: Oxford University Press, 2011.

———. "Euripides' *Heraclidae*: An Interpretation." *Classical Philology* 22, no. 1 (1977): 1–21.

———. "Logos and Pathos: The Politics of the Suppliant Women." In *Directions in Euripidean Criticism*, edited by Peter Burian, 129–55. Durham, NC: Duke University Press, 1985.

———. "Myth into Muthos: The Shaping of Tragic Plot." In *The Cambridge Companion to Greek Tragedy*, edited by P. E. Easterling, 178–210. Cambridge: Cambridge University Press, 1997.

Burke, Edmund. *Reflections on the Revolution in France*. Indianapolis: Liberty Fund, 1999.

Burkert, Walter. *Ancient Mystery Cults*. Cambridge, MA: Harvard University Press, 1987.

———. "Greek Tragedy and Sacrificial Ritual." *Greek, Roman, and Byzantine Studies* 7, no. 2 (1966): 87–121.

———. *Homo Necans*. Translated by P. Bing. Berkeley: University of Califonia Press, 1983.

Burnett, Anne Pippin. *Catastrophe Survived*. Oxford: Oxford University Press, 1971.

———. "Hekabe the Dog." *Arethusa* 27 (1994): 154–64.

———. "Human Resistance and Divine Persuasion in Euripides' *Ion*." *Classical Philology* 57 (1962): 89–103.

———. "Pentheus and Dionysus: Host and Guest." *Classical Philology* 65, no. 1 (1970): 15–29.

———. *Revenge in Attic and Later Tragedy*. Berkeley: University of California Press, 1998.

———. "Tribe and City: Custom and Decree in the *Children of Heracles*." *Classical Philology* 71, no. 1 (1976): 4–26.

———. "The Virtues of Admetus." *Classical Philology* 60 (1965): 240–55.

Burns, Angela J. "A Thoroughly Modern Medea." In *Unbinding Medea*, edited by Heike Bartel and Anne Simon, 263–280. New York: Routledge, 2010.

Burns, Timothy W. "Philosophy and Poetry." *American Political Science Review* 109, no. 2 (2015): 326–38.

Buxton, Richard. *Persuasion in Greek Tragedy: A Study of Peitho*. Cambridge: Cambridge University Press, 1982.

———. *Forms of Astonishment: Greek Myths of Metamorphosis*. Oxford: Oxford University Press, 2009.

Cain, Rebecca Bensen. *The Socratic Method*. London: Continuum, 2007.

Cairns, Douglas L. *Aidos: The Psychology and Ethics of Honour and Shame in Ancient Greek Literature*. Oxford: Clarendon, 1993.

———. "Pity in the Classical World." *Hermathena* 176 (2004): 59–74.

Calasso, Roberto. *The Marriage of Cadmus and Harmony*. Translated by Tim Parks. New York: Vintage International, 1993.

Caney, Simon. *Justice Beyond Borders*. Oxford: Oxford University Press, 2005.
Cantarella, Eva. "Misogyny in *Medea*." In *Readings on Euripides' Medea*, edited by Don Nardo, 64–67. San Diego, CA: Greenhaven, 2001.
———. "Private Justice and Public Justice." *Punishment and Society* 3, no. 4 (2001): 473–83.
Carawan, Edwin. "Pericles the Younger and the Citizenship Law." *Classical Journal* 103 (2008): 383–406.
Carens, Joseph H. "Refugees and the Limits of Obligation." *Public Affairs Quarterly* 6, no. 1 (1992): 31–44.
Carey, Chris. "Country Matters: The Location of Euripides' *Electra*." In *Euripides Talks*, edited by Alan Beale, 94–102. London: Bristol Classical, 2008.
Carpenter, Rhys. *The Ethics of Euripides*. New York: Columbia University Press, 1916.
Carpenter, Thomas H. "On the Beardless Dionysus." In *Masks of Dionysus*, edited by Thomas H. Carpenter and Christopher A. Faraone, 185–206. Ithaca, NY: Cornell University Press, 1993.
Carr, Brian. "Pity and Compassion as Social Virtues." *Philosophy* 74, no. 289 (1999): 411–29.
Carson, Anne. "Preface to *Hecube*." In *Grief Lessons*, edited by Anne Carson, 89–97. New York: New York Review of Books, 2006.
———. "Preface to the *Alcestis*." In *Grief Lessons*, edited by Anne Carson, 247–49. New York: New York Review of Books, 2006.
———. "Putting Her in Her Place." In *Before Sexuality*, edited by David M. Halperin, John J. Winkler, and Froma I. Zeitlin, 135–70. Princeton, NJ: Princeton University Press, 1990.
Carter, D. M. *The Politics of Greek Tragedy*. Exeter, UK: Bristol Phoenix, 2007.
———. "Reported Assembly Scenes in Greek Tragedy." *Illinois Classical Studies* 38 (2013): 23–63.
Carter, L. B. *The Quiet Athenian*. Oxford: Oxford University Press, 1986.
Cartledge, Paul. "Deep Plays: Theatre as Process in Greek Civic Life." In *Cambridge Companion to Greek Tragedy*, edited by P. E. Easterling, 3–35. Cambridge: Cambridge University Press, 1997.
———. *The Greeks: A Portrait of the Self and Others*. 2nd ed. Oxford: Oxford University Press, 2002.
———. *The Spartans*. New York: Vintage, 2004.
Castellani, Victor. "The Troubled House of Pentheus in Euripides' *Bacchae*." *Transactions and Proceedings of the American Philological Association* 106 (1976): 61–83.
Ceadel, E. B. "Resolved Feet in the Trimeters of Euripides and the Chronology of the Plays." *Classical Quarterly* 35, no. 1/2 (1941): 66–89.

Cels, Sanderijn. "Interpreting Political Apologies: The Neglected Role of Performance." *Political Psychology* 36, no. 3 (2015): 351–60.
Champion, Craige B. "Imperial Ideologies, Citizenship Myths, and Legal Disputes." In *A Companion to Greek and Roman Political Thought*, edited by Ryan K. Balot, 85–99. Chichester, UK: John Wiley, 2009.
Cherem, Max. "Refugee Rights: Against Expanding the Definition of a 'Refugee' and Unilateral Protection Elsewhere." *Journal of Political Philosophy* 24, no. 2 (2016): 183–205.
Chinn, Christopher Matthew. "Statius, Orpheus, and Callimachus *Thebaid* 2.269–96." *Helios* 38, no. 1 (2011): 79–101.
Chong-Gossard, J. H. Kim On. *Gender and Communication in Euripides' Plays: Between Song and Silence*. Leiden, The Netherlands: Brill, 2008.
———. "Song and the Solitary Self: Euripidean Women Who Resist Comfort." *Phoenix* 57, no. 3/4 (2003): 209–31.
Chou, Marc. *Greek Tragedy and Contemporary Democracy*. New York: Bloomsbury Academic, 2012.
Christ, Matthew. *The Limits of Altruism in Democratic Athens*. Cambirdge: Cambridge University Press, 2012.
Cicero, Marcus Tullius. *De Officiis*. Translated by Walter Miller. Cambridge, MA: Harvard University Press, 1913.
Clair, Matthew. *Privilege and Punishment: How Race and Class Matter in Criminal Court* Princeton, NJ: Princeton University Press, 2020.
Clark, Matthew. *Exploring Greek Myth*. Chichester, UK: Blackwell, 2012.
Cohn, Dorrit. "The Poetics of Plato's *Republic*: A Modern Perspective." *Philosophy and Literature* 24 (2000): 34–48.
Coker, Christopher. *Ethics and War in the 21st Century*. New York and London: Routledge, 2008.
Cole, A. Thomas. "The *Ion* of Euripides and Its Audience." In *Poet, Public, and Performance in Ancient Greece*, edited by Lowell Edmunds and Robert W. Wallace, 87–96. Baltimore: Johns Hopkins University Press, 1997.
Cole, Spenser. "Annotated Innovation in Euripides' *Ion*." *Classical Quarterly* 58 (2008): 313–15.
Coleman, Janet. *A History of Political Thought*. Malden, MA: Blackwell, 2000.
Collard, Christopher. "Formal Debates in Euripides' Drama." *Greece & Rome*, 22, no. 1 (1975): 58–71.
———. "The Funeral Oration in Euripides' *Supplices*." *Bulletin of the Institute of Classical Studies* 19, no. 1 (1972): 31–53.
———. "Introduction to the *Hecuba*." In *Hecuba*, edited by Christopher Collard, 21–42. Warminster, UK: Aris & Phillips, 1991.
———. "Notes on Euripides' *Supplices*." *Classical Quarterly* 13, no. 2 (1963): 178–87.

Collier, Michael, and Georgia Machemer. "Introduction." In *Euripides' Medea*, edited by Michael Collier and Geogia Machemer, 3–32. Oxford: Oxford University Press, 2006.
Conacher, Desmond J. *Euripidean Drama*. Toronto: University of Toronto Press, 1967.
———. "Euripides' Hecuba." *American Journal of Philology* 82, no. 1 (1961): 1–26.
———. *Euripides and the Sophists*. London: Duckworth, 2003.
———. "Introduction to *Alcestis*." In *Euripides: Alcestis*, edited by D. J. Conacher, 29–57. Warminster, UK: Aris & Phillips, 1988.
———. "The Paradox of Euripides' *Ion*." *Transactions of the American Philological Association* 90 (1959): 20–39.
———. "Religious and Ethical Attitudes in Euripides' *Suppliants*." *Transactions and Proceedings of the American Philological Association* 56 (1956): 8–26.
———. "Themes in the "Exodus" of Euripides' *Phoenissae*." *Phoenix* 21, no. 2 (1967): 92–101.
Connelly, Joan Breton. *The Parthenon Enigma*. New York: Vintage, 2014.
Corey, David D., and Cecil L Eubanks. "Private and Public Virtue in Euripides *Hecuba*." *Interpretations* 30, no. 3 (2003): 223–49.
Corti, Lilian. *The Myth of Medea and the Murder of Children*. Westport, CT: Greenwood, 1998.
Craig, Leon. *The War Lover*. Toronto: University of Toronto Press, 1996.
Craik, Elizabeth M. "Ancient Prefaces" in *Euripides' Phoenician Women*, edited by Elizabeth Craik, 58–61. Warminster, UK: Aris & Phillips, 1988.
———. "Introduction to the *Phoenician Women*" in *Euripides' Phoenician Women*, edited by Elizabeth Craik, 35–57. Warminster, UK: Aris & Phillips, 1988.
———. "Euripides: *Ion* and *Phoenissae*." In *The Passionate Intellect*, edited by Lewis Aryes, 105–15. New Brunswick, NJ: Transaction, 1986.
Critchley, Simon. *Tragedy, The Greeks, and Us*. New York: Pantheon, 2019.
Croally, Neil T. *Euripidean Polemic*. Cambridge: Cambridge University Press, 1994.
———. "Tragedy's Teaching." In *A Companion to Greek Tragedy*, edited by Justina Gregory, 55–70. Oxford: Blackwell, 2008.
Cropp, Martin. "Euripides, *Phoenissae* 1567–76." *Classical Quarterly* 47, no. 2 (1997): 570–74.
———. "Introduction to *Electra*." In *Euripides' Electra*, edited by M. J. Cropp, xxix–lvi. Warminster, UK: Aris & Phillips, 1988.
———. "Lost Tragedies: A Survey." In *A Companion to Greek Tragedy*, edited by Justina Gregory, 271–92. Oxford: Blackwell, 2005.
Csapo, Eric. "Riding the Phallus for Dionysus: Iconology, Ritual, and Gender-Role De/Construction." *Phoenix* 51, no. 3/4 (1997): 253–95.
D'Angour, Armand. *The Greeks and the New*. Cambridge: Cambridge University Press, 2011.

D'Este, Sorita, and David Rankine. *Hekate Liminal Rites*. London: Avalonia, 2009.
Daitz, Stephen G. "Concepts of Freedom and Slavery in Euripides' *Hecuba*." *Hermes* 99, no. 2 (1971): 217–26.
Dale, A. M. "Introduction." In *Euripides: Alcestis*, v–xl. Oxford: Clarendon, 1961.
Dallmayr, Fred. "Cosmopolitanism." *Political Theory* 31 (2003): 421–42.
Daly, Erin. *Dignity Rights*. Philadelphia: University of Pennsylvania Press, 2013.
Damen, Mark L., and Rebecca A. Richards. "Sing the Song of Dionysus." *American Journal of Philology* 133, no. 3 (2012): 343–63.
Danes, Jaroslav. "*Amēchania* in Euripides' *Heraclidae*." *Classical Quarterly* 65, no. 1 (2015): 366–71.
———. "The Political Thought of the *Suppliant Women*." *Greco-Latina Brunensia* 16, no. 2 (2011): 17–30.
Darby, Andrew. *Bacchus*. London: British Museum, 2003.
Davidson, John. "Euripides, Homer, and Sophocles." *Illinois Classical Studies* 24/25 (1999–2000): 117–28.
———. "Theatrical Production." In *A Companion to Greek Tragedy*, edited by Justina Gregory, 194–211. Malden, MA: Blackwell, 2005.
Davies, Malcolm. "Euripides' *Electra*: The Recognition Scene Again." *Classical Quarterly* 48, no. 2 (1998): 389–403.
de Greiff, Pablo. "Theorizing Transitional Justice." In *Transitional Justice*, edited by Melissa Williams, Rosemary Nagy, and Jon Elster, 31–77. New York: New York University Press, 2012.
de Romilly, Jacqueline "D'Euripide à Platon." *Estudios Clásicos* 26 (1984): 259–65.
———. *The Great Sophists in Periclean Athens*. Translated by Janet Lloyd. Oxford: Oxford University Press, 1992.
———. "Les Phéniciennes d'Euripide ou l'actualité dans la tragédie grecque." *Revue de Philologie, de Littérature et d'Histoire Anciennes* 39 (1965): 28–47.
Dellner, Jennifer. "Alcestis' Double Life." *Classical Journal* 96, no. 1 (2000): 1–25.
Demosthenes. "On the Embassy." Translated by J. H. Vince. Cambridge, MA: Harvard University Press, 1930.
Denniston, J. D. "Introduction." In *Euripides' Electra*, edited by J. D. Denniston, ix–xxxv. Oxford: Clarendon, 1939.
Derderian, Katherine. *Leaving Words to Remember: Greek Mourning and the Advent of Literacy*. London: Brill, 2001.
Desmond, William. *Being and the Between*. New York: State University of New York Press, 1995.
Detienne, Marcel. *Dionysos at Large*. Translated by A. Goldhammer. Cambridge, MA: Harvard University Presss, 1989.
DiLeo, Daniel. "Tragedy against Tyranny." *Journal of Politics* 75, no. 1 (2013): 254–65.
Diller, Hans. "Euripides' Final Phase: The *Bacchae*." In *Oxford Readings in Greek Tragedy*, edited by Erich Segal, 357–69. Oxford: Oxford University Press, 1983.

Dillon, John. "Euripides and the Philosophy of His Time." *Classics Ireland* 11 (2004): 47–73.
Dodds, E. R. "Euripides the Irrationalist." *Classics Review* 43, no. 2 (1929): 97–104.
———. "Introduction." In *Euripides' Bacchae*, edited by E. R. Dodds, i–lix. Oxford: Clarendon, 1960.
Doughtery, Carol. "Democratic Contraditions and the Synoptic Illusion of Euripides' Ion." In *Demokratia*, edited by Joshiah Ober and Charles Hedrick, 249–70. Princeton, NJ: Princeton University Press, 1996.
Dover, Keith J. "The Political Aspect of Aeschylus' *Eumenides*." *Journal of Hellenic Studies* 77 (1957): 230–37.
Dowden, Ken, and Niall Livingstone. "Thinking through Myth, Thinking Myth Through." In *A Companion to Greek Mythology*, edited by Ken Dowden and Niall Livingstone, 1–23. Chichester, UK: Blackwell, 2011.
DuBois, Page. *Centaurs and Amazons*. Ann Arbor: University of Michigan Press, 1982.
———. "Toppling the Hero: Polyphony in the Tragic City." *New Literary History* 35, no. 1 (2004): 63–81.
Dunn, Francis M. *Tragedy's End: Closure and Innovation in Euripidean Drama*. Oxford: Oxford University Press, 1996.
Easterling, P. E. "Form and Performance." In *Cambridge Companion to Greek Tragedy*, edited by P. E. Easterling, 151–77. Cambridge: Cambridge University Press, 1997.
———. "A Show for Dionysus." In *Cambridge Companion to Greek Tragedy*, edited by P. E. Easterling, 36–53. Cambridge: Cambridge University Press, 1997.
Edmunds, Lowell. *Oedipus*. London: Routledge, 2006.
Elgin, Catherine Z. *Considered Judgment*. Princeton, NJ: Princeton University Press, 1999.
Elias, Julius A. *Plato's Defense of Poetry*. Albany: State University of New York Press, 1984.
Elster, Jon. *Reason and Rationality*. Translated by Steven Randall. Princeton, NJ: Princeton University Press, 2009.
Endsjo, Dag Oistein. "To Lock up Eleusis." *Numen* 47 (2000): 351–86.
Euben, J. Peter. *The Tragedy of Political Theory*. Princeton, NJ: Princeton University Press, 1990.
Euripides. *Alcestis*. Translated by Richmond Lattimore. In *Euripides 1*. Edited by David Grene and Richmond Lattimore. Chicago: University of Chicago Press, 1955.
———. *Alcestis*. Translated by David Kovacs. Cambridge, MA: Harvard University Press, 2001.
———. *Andromache*. Translated by David Kovacs. Cambridge, MA: Harvard University Press, 1995.

———. *The Bacchae*. Translated by David Kovacs. Cambridge, MA: Harvard University Press, 2002.

———. *The Bacchae*. Translated by William Arrowsmith. In *Euripides V*. Edited by David Grene and Richmond Lattimore. Chicago: University of Chicago Press, 1959.

———. *The Children of Heracles*. Translated by David Kovacs. Cambridge, MA: Harvard University Press, 1995.

———. *Electra*. Translated by David Kovacs. Cambridge, MA: Harvard University Press, 1998.

———. *Electra*. Translated by Emily Townsend Vermeule. In *Euripides V*. Edited by David Grene and Richmond Lattimore. Chicago: University of Chicago Press, 1959.

———. "Erechtheus." Translated by Christopher Collard and Martin Cropp. In *Fragments: Ageus-Meleager*, 368–405. Cambridge, MA: Harvard University Press, 2008.

———. *Hecuba*. Translated by David Kovacs. Cambridge, MA: Harvard University Press, 1995.

———. *Helen*. Translated by David Kovacs. Cambridge, MA: Harvard University Press, 2002.

———. *The Heracleidae*. Translated by Ralph Gladstone. In *Euripides I*, edited by David Grene and Richmond Lattimore. Chicago: University of Chicago Press, 1955.

———. *Heracles*. Translated by David Kovacs. Cambridge, MA: Harvard University Press, 1998.

———. *Ion*. Translated by David Kovacs. Cambridge, MA: Harvard University Press, 1999.

———. *Iphigenia among the Taurians*. Translated by David Kovacs. Cambridge, MA: Harvard University Press, 1999.

———. *Iphigenia at Aulis*. Translated by David Kovacs. Cambridge, MA: Harvard University Press, 2002.

———. *Medea*. Translated by David Kovacs. Cambridge, MA: Harvard University Press, 2001.

———. *Orestes*. Translated by David Kovas. Cambridge, MA: Harvard University Press, 2002.

———. *Phoenician Women*. Translated by David Kovacs. Cambridge, MA: Harvard University Press, 2002.

———. *Suppliant Women*. Translated by David Kovacs. Cambridge, MA: Harvard University Press, 1998.

———. *Trojan Women*. Translated by David Kovacs. Cambridge, MA: Harvard University Press, 1999.

Evans, Nancy. *Civic Rites*. Berkeley: University of California Press, 2010.

———. "Sanctuaries, Sacrifices, and the Eleusinian Mysteries." *Numen* 49, no. 3 (2002): 227–54.

Faber, M. D. *Suicide and Greek Tragedy*. New York: Sphinx, 1970.
Falkner, Thomas M. *The Poetics of Old Age in Greek Epic, Lyric, and Tragedy*. Norman: University of Oklahoma Press, 1995.
Farrington, Andrew. "*Gnothi Seauton*: Social Self-Knowledge in Euripides' *Ion*." *Rheinisches Museum für Philologie* 134, no. 2 (1991): 120–36.
Ferguson, John. "The Play Is Structured around Scenes of Confrontation." In *Readings on Euripides' Medea*, edited by Don Nardo, 40–45. San Diego, CA: Greenhaven, 2001.
Ferrario, Sarah Brown. "Reading Athens." In *Thucydides between History and Literature*, edited by Antonis Tsakmakis and Melina Tamiolaki, 181–98. Berlin: De Gruyter, 2013.
Fialho, Maria do Ceu. "Paidotrophia and Gerotrophia: Reciprocity and Disruption in Attic Tragedy." In *Law and Drama in Ancient Tragedy*, edited by Edward M. Harris, Delfim F. Leao, and P. J. Rhodes, 108–21. London: Bloomsbury, 2010.
Finkelberg, Margalit. *Greek and Pre-Greeks*. Cambridge: Cambridge University Press, 2005.
Finley, M. I. "The Elderly in Classical Antiquity." *Greece & Rome* 28, no. 2 (1981): 156–71.
———. *The World of Odysseus*. New York: Viking, 1978.
Fitton, J. W. "The *Suppliant Women* and the *Herakleidai* of Euripides." *Hermes* 89, no. 4 (1961): 430–61.
Fletcher, Judith. *Performing Oaths*. Cambridge: Cambridge University Press, 2012.
Folbre, Nancy. "Should Women Care Less? Intrinsic Motivation and Gender Inequality." *British Journal of Industrial Relations* 50, no. 4 (2012): 597–619.
Foley, Helene P. "Anodos Drama: Euripides *Alcestis* and *Helen*." In *Innovations in Antiquity*, edited by Daniel Selden and Ralph Hexter, 133–60. New York: Routledge, 1992.
———. *Euripides' Hecuba*. London: Bloomsbury, 2015.
———. *Female Acts in Greek Tragedy*. Princeton, NJ: Princeton University Press, 2001.
———. "Medea's Divided Self." *Classical Antiquity* 8, no. 1 (1989): 61–85.
———. *Ritual Irony: Poetry and Sacrifice in Euripides*. Ithaca, NY: Cornell University Press, 1985.
Fontenrose, Joseph. *Python*. Berkeley: University of California Press, 1959.
Fortenbaugh, W. M. "On the Antecedents of Aristotle's Bipartite Psychology." *Greek, Roman, and Byzantine Studies* 11 (1970): 233–50.
Fossheim, Hallvard. "Aristotle on Happiness and Old Age." In *The Quest for the Good Life*, edited by Oyvind Rabbas, Eyjolfur K. Emilsson, Hallvard Fossheim, and Miira Tuominen, 113–26. Oxford: Oxford University Press, 2015.
Foucault, Michel. *Fearless Speech*. Los Angeles: Semiotext(e), 2001.

Fowler, Robert L. "Mythos and Logos." *Journal of Hellenic Studies* 131 (2011): 45–66.
Frank, Jill. *Democracy and the Death of Shame*. Cambridge: Cambridge University Press, 2016.
———. *Poetic Justice: Rereading Plato's Republic*. Chicago: University of Chicago Press, 2018.
Gagarin, Michael. *Antiphon the Athenian: Oratory, Law and Justice in the Age of the Sophists*. Austin: University of Texas Press, 2002.
———. "Laws and Legislation in Ancient Greece." In *A Companion to Ancient Greek Government*, edited by Hans Beck, 221–34. London: John Wiley, 2013.
Gallagher, Robert L. "Making the Stronger Argument the Weaker: Euripides' Electra 518–44." *Classical Quarterly* 53, no. 2 (2003): 401–15.
Gamble, R. B. "Euripides' *Suppliant Women*: Decision and Ambivalence." *Hermes* 98, no. 4 (1970): 385–405.
Garner, Richard. "Death and Victory in Euripides' *Alcestis*." *Classical Antiquity* 7, no. 1 (1988): 58–71.
Garrison, Elise P. "Attitudes toward Suicide in Ancient Greece." *Transactions of the American Philological Association* 121 (1991): 1–34.
———. *Groaning Tears: Ethical and Dramatic Aspects of Suicide in Greek Tragedy*. New York: E. J. Brill, 1995.
Gaunt, David M. "Argo and the Gods in Apollonius Rhodius." *Greece and Rome* 19, no. 2 (1972): 117–26.
Gauthier, David. *Morals by Agreement*. Oxford: Oxford University Press, 1986.
Gibert, John. "Apollo's Sacrifice: The Limits of a Metaphor in Greek Tragedy." *Harvard Studies in Classical Philology* 101 (2003): 150–206.
———. "Greek Drama and Political Thought." In *A Companion to Greek and Roman Political Thought*, edited by Ryan K. Balot, 440–55. Oxford: Wiley-Blackwell, 2009.
———. "Introduction." In *Euripides: Ion*, edited by John Gibert, 1–68. Cambridge: Cambridge University Press, 2019.
Gibson, Mary. "Rationality." *Philosophy & Public Affairs* 6, no. 3 (1977): 193–225.
Gill, Christopher. *Personality in Greek Epic, Tragedy, and Philosophy*. Oxford: Oxford University Press, 1996.
Gilson, Étienne. *Being and Some Philosophers*. Toronto: Pontifical Institute of Mediaeval Studies, 1952.
Girard, René. *Things Hidden since the Foundation of the World*. Translated by Stephen Bann and Michael Metteer. Stanford, CA: Stanford University Press, 1987.
———. *Violence and the Sacred*. Translated by Patrick Gregory. Baltimore: Johns Hopkins University Press, 1977.

Gladstone, Ralph. "An Introduction to the *Heracleidae*." In *Euripides I*, edited by David Grene and Richmond Lattimore, 110–14. Chicago: University of Chicago Press, 1955.
Goff, Barbara. "Aithra at Eleusis." *Helios* 22, no. 1 (1995): 65–78.
———. *Citizen Bacchae*. Berkeley: University of California Press, 2004.
———. "The Shields of the *Phoenissae*." *Greek, Roman, and Byzantine Studies* 29, no. 2 (1988): 135–52.
Gold, Barbara. "Eukosmia in Euripides' *Bacchae*." *American Journal of Philology* 98, no. 1 (1977): 3–15.
Goldhill, Simon. "The Audience of Greek Tragedy." In *Cambridge Companion to Greek Tragedy*, edited by P. E. Easterling, 54–68. Cambridge: Cambridge University Press, 1997.
———. "The Great Dionysia and Civic Ideology (Revised)." In *Nothing to Do with Dionysus*, edited by John J. Winkler and Froma I. Zeitlin, 97–129. Princeton, NJ: Princeton University Press, 1990.
———. *Reading Greek Tragedy*. Cambridge: Cambridge University Press, 1986.
———. "Rhetoric and Relevance." *Greek, Roman, and Byzantine Studies* 27, no. 2 (1986): 157–71.
Goodin, Robert E. "What Is So Special About Our Fellow Countrymen?" *Ethics* 98, no. 4 (1988): 663–86.
Gorgias. *Encomium of Helen*. Translated by D. M. MacDowell. London: Bristol Classical, 2005.
Gottesman, Alex. *Politics and the Street in Athens*. Cambridge: Cambridge University Press, 2014.
Gould, John. "Tragedy and the Collective Experience." In *Tragedy and the Tragic: Greek Theater and Beyond*, edited by M. S. Silk, 217–43. Oxford: Oxford University Press, 1996.
Graziosi, Barbara. *The Gods of Olympus*. New York: Picador, 2014.
Greenwood, L. H. G. *Aspects of Euripidean Tragedy*. Cambridge: Cambridge University Press, 1953.
Gregory, Justina. "Euripides' *Alcestis*." *Hermes* 107, no. 3 (1979): 259–70.
———. *Euripides and the Instruction of the Athenians*. Ann Arbor: University of Michigan Press, 1991.
———. "Genealogy and Intertexuality in *Hecuba*." *American Journal of Philology* 116, no. 3 (1995): 389–97.
Griffin, Jasper. "Hope Deferred Makes the Heart Sick." In *Euripides Talks*, edited by Alan Beale, 103–109. London: Bristol Classical, 2008.
Griffith, Mark. "Families and Inter-City Relations." In *Why Athens?*, edited by David M. Carter, 175–208. Oxford: Oxford University Press, 2011.
Griffiths, Emma. *Medea*. New York: Routledge, 2006.
Grotius, Hugo. *The Rights of War and Peace*. Edited by Jean Barbeyrac. Indianapolis: Liberty Fund, 2005.

Grube, G. M. A. *The Drama of Euripides*. London: Methuen, 1961.
Hadas, Moses. "Introduction to *Alcestis*." In *Ten Plays by Euripides*, 1–2. Toronto: Bantam, 1960.
———. "Introduction to *Electra*." In *Euripides' Electra*, edited by Moses Hadas, v–viii. New York: Liberal Arts, 1950.
Haigh, A. E. *The Tragic Drama of the Greeks*. New York: Dover, 1968.
Hall, Edith. *Greek Tragedy: Suffering under the Sun*. Oxford: Oxford University Press, 2010.
———. "Introduction." In *Euripides: Alcestis, Heracles, Children of Heracles, Cyclops*, translated by Robin Waterfield, vii–liii. Oxford: Oxford University Press, 2003.
———. "Introduction." In *Euripides: Medea, Hippolytus, Electa, Helen*, edited by James Morwood, ix–xxxiv. Oxford: Clarendon, 1997.
———. "Medea and the Mind of a Murderer." In *Unbinding Medea*, edited by Heike Bartel and Anne Simon, 16–24. London: Routledge, 2010.
———. "The Sociology of Athenian Tragedy." In *Cambridge Companions to Greek Tragedy*, edited by P. E. Easterling, 93–126. Cambridge: Cambridge University Press, 1997.
Hall, Jonathan. *Ethnic Identity in Greek Antiquity*. Cambridge: Cambridge University Press, 1997.
Halliwell, Stephen. "The Subjection of Muthos to Logos: Plato's Citations of the Poets." *Classical Quarterly* 50, no. 1 (2000): 94–112.
Hame, Kerri J. "Female Control of Funeral Rites in Greek Tragedy." *Classical Philology* 103, no. 1 (2008): 1–15.
Hammond, N. G. L. "Spectacle and Parody in Euripides' *Electra*." *Greek, Roman, and Byzantine Studies* 25, no. 4 (1984): 373–87.
Hansen, William. *Classical Mythology*. Oxford: Oxford University Press, 2004.
Harris, John P. "The Swan's Red-Dipped Foot." *Classical Quarterly* 62 (2012): 510–22.
Havelock, Eric A. *Preface to Plato*. Cambridge: Belknap, 1963.
Heath, John. *Actaeon, the Unmannerly Intruder*. New York: Peter Lang, 1993.
Heath, Malcolm. "Iure Principem Locum Tenet: *Hecuba*." In *Oxford Readings in Classical Studies: Euripides*, edited by Judith Mossman, 218–60. Oxford: Oxford University Press, 2003.
———. *The Poetics of Greek Tragedy*. Stanford, CA: Stanford University Press, 1987.
———. "Should There Have Been a Polis in Aristotle's *Poetics*?" *Classical Quarterly* 59, no. 2 (2009): 468–85.
Hedrick, Charles W. "The Temple and Cult of Apollo Patroos in Athens." *American Journal of Archeology* 92 (1988): 185–210.
Hegel, Georg W. F. *Hegel on Tragedy*. Edited by Anne Paolucci and Henry Paolucci. Westport, CT: Greenwood, 1962.

———. *Lectures on the Philosophy of Religion: The Lectures of 1827.* Translated by R. F Brown, P. C. Hodgson and J. M. Stewart. Berkeley: University of California Press, 1988.
Heidegger, Martin. *Being and Time.* Translated by Joan Stambaugh. Albany: State University of New York Press, 2010.
Henderson, Jeffrey. "Women and the Athenian Dramatic Festivals." *Transactions of the American Philological Association* 121 (1991): 133–47.
Henrichs, Albert. "Anonymity and Polarity: Unknown Gods and Nameless Altars at the Areopagos." *Illinois Classical Studies* 19 (1994): 27–58.
———. "Drama and Dromena: Bloodshed, Violence, and Sacrificial Metaphor in Euripides." *Harvard Studies in Classical Philology* 100 (2000): 173–88.
Herman, Gabriel. *Ritualised Friendship and the Greek City.* Cambridge: Cambridge University Press, 2002.
Herodotus. *The Histories.* Translated by Robert Strassler. Toronto: Anchor, 2009.
Hersh, Allison. "How Sweet the Kill." *Modern Drama* 35, no. 3 (1992): 409–23.
Hesiod. *Catalogue of Women.* Translated by Glenn Most. Cambridge, MA: Harvard University Press, 2007.
———. *Theogony.* Translated by Norman O. Brown. Upper Saddle River, NJ: Prentice Hall, 1953.
———. *Works and Days.* Translated by David Tandy and Walter C Neale. Berkeley: University of California Press, 2008.
Hettich, Ernest L. *A Study in Ancient Nationalism.* Williamsport, PA: Bayard, 1933.
Hewitt, Joseph William. "Gratitude and Ingratitude in the Plays of Euripides." *American Journal of Philology* 43, no. 4 (1922): 331–43.
Higgins, Peter W. *Immigration Justice.* Edinburgh: Edinburgh University Press, 2013.
Hoffer, Stanley E. "Violence, Culture, and the Workings of Ideology in Euripides' *Ion*." *Classical Antiquity* 15, no. 2 (1996): 289–318.
Hogan, James C. "Thucydides 3.52–68 and Euripides' *Hecuba*." *Phoenix* 26, no. 3 (1972): 241–57.
Holland, Lora. "Pas Domos Erroi: Myth and Plot in Euripides' Medea." *Transactions of the American Philological Association* 133 (2003): 255–79.
Homer. *The Iliad.* Translated by A. T. Murray. Cambridge, MA: Harvard University Press, 1996.
———. *The Odyssey.* Translated by A. T. Murray. Cambridge, MA: Harvard University Press, 1995.
Homeric Hymn to Demeter. Edited and translated by Helene P. Foley. Princeton, NJ: Princeton University Press, 1993.
Honig, Bonnie. *Antigone Interrupted.* Cambridge: Cambridge University Press, 2013.
Hughes, Bettany. *Helen of Troy.* New York: Vintage, 2005.
———. *The Hemlock Cup.* New York: Vintage, 2012.
Hughes, Dennis D. *Human Sacrifice in Ancient Greece.* London: Routledge, 1991.

Hussey, Edward. "Heraclitus on Living and Dying." *Monist* 74, no. 4 (1991): 517–21.
Huxley, George Leonard. *Greek Epic Poetry*. London: Faber, 1969.
Hyde, Walter Woodburn. "On the Homicide Courts of Ancient Athens." *University of Pennsylvania Law Review and American Law Register* 66, no. 7/8 (1918): 319–62.
Isocrates. *Panathenaicus*. Translated by George Norlin. Cambridge, MA: Harvard University Press, 1929.
———. *Panegyricus*. Translated by George Norlin. Cambridge, MA: Harvard University Press, 1928.
Jameson, Michael. "The Asexuality of Dionysus." In *Masks of Dionysus*, edited by Thomas H. Carpenter and Chirstopher A. Faraone, 44–64. Ithaca, NY: Cornell University Press, 1993.
Jenkyns, Richard. "Medea and the Divided Mind." In *Euripides Talks*, edited by Alan Beale, 56–64. London: Bristol Classical, 2008.
Johnston, David. *A Brief History of Justice*. Oxford: Wiley-Backwell, 2011.
Johnston, Sarah Iles. "Corinthian Medea and the Cult of Akraia." In *Medea: Essays on Medea in Myth, Literature, Philosophy, and Art*, edited by James J. Clauss and Sarah Iles Johnston, 44–70. Princeton, NJ: Princeton University Press, 1997.
Johnstone, Steven. *A History of Trust in Ancient Greece*. Chicago: University of Chicago Press, 2011.
Jones, D. M. "Euripides' *Alcestis*." *Classical Review* 62, no. 2 (1948): 50–55.
Jones, Frank William. "Introduction to the *Suppliant Women*." Translated by Frank William Jones. In *Euripides IV*, edited by David Grene and Richmond Lattimore, 52–54. Chicago: University of Chicago Press, 1958.
Jouanna, Jacques. "Texte et espace théâtral dans les Phéniciennes d'Euripide." *Ktèma* 1, no. 19 (1976): 81–97.
Just, Roger. *Women in Athenian Law and Life*. New York: Routledge, 1991.
Kagan, Donald. *The Peloponnesian War*. New York: Penguin, 2003.
Kalke, Christine M. "The Making of a Thyrsus." *American Journal of Philology* 106 (1985): 409–26.
Kant, Immanuel. *Groundwork for the Metaphysics of Morals*. Translated by H. J. Paton. London: Routledge, 1948.
Kasimis, Demetra. "Tragedy of Blood-Based Membership: Secrecy and the Politics of Immigration." *Political Theory* 41 (2013): 231–56.
Kastely, James L. "Violence and Rhetoric in Euripides' *Hecuba*." *PMLA* 108, no. 5 (1993): 1036–49.
Kaufmann, Walter. *Tragedy and Philosophy*. Princeton, NJ: Princeton University Press, 1968.
Keene, Charles Haines. "Introduction." In *The Electra of Euripides*, edited by Charles Haines Keene, iii–xxxi. London: Bell, 1898.

Keller, Mara Lynn. "The Eleusinian Mysteries of Demeter and Persephone: Fertility, Sexuality, and Rebirth." *Journal of Feminist Studies in Religion* 4, no. 1 (1988): 27–54.
Kennedy, Rebecca Futo. *Athena's Justice*. New York: Peter Lang, 2009.
Kerenyi, Karl. *Goddesses of Sun and Moon*. Irving, TX: Spring, 1979.
Kerferd, G. B. *The Sophistic Movement*. Cambridge: Cambridge University Press, 1981.
Kerkhecker, Arnd. "Euripides, *Phoenissae* 64f." *Classical Quarterly* 46, no. 2 (1996): 567–72.
Kern, Paul Bentley. *Ancient Siege Warfare*. Bloomington: Indiana University Press, 1999.
Kidd, Ian. "Socratic Questions." In *Socratic Questions*, edited by Barry S. Gower and Michael C. Stokes, 82–92. London: Routledge, 1992.
Kindt, Julia C. "Review of Converging Truths." *International Journal of the Classic Tradition* 13, no. 1 (2006): 125–27.
King, Katherine Callen. "The Force of Tradition: The Achilles Ode in Euripides' *Electra*." *Transactions and Proceedings of the American Philological Association* 110 (1980): 195–212.
———. "The Politics of Imitation: Euripides' *Hekabe* and the Homeric Achilles." *Arethusa* 18, no. 1 (1985): 47–66.
Kirkwood, Gordon M. "*Hecuba* and Nomos." *Transactions and Proceedings of the American Philological Association* 78 (1947): 61–68.
Kitto, H. D. F. "The Final Scenes of the *Phoenissae*." *Classical Review* 53, no. 3 (1939): 104–11.
———. *Greek Tragedy: A Literary Study*. 3rd ed. New York: Barnes and Noble, 1961.
———. "The *Medea* of Euripides." In *Medea: Myth and Dramatic Form*, edited by James L. Sanderson and Everett Zimmerman, 286–97. Boston: Houghton Mifflin, 1957.
Klotsche, Ernest Heinrich. *The Supernatural in the Tragedies of Euripides*. Lancaster, PA: New Era Printing, 1919.
Knox, Bernard. "The *Medea* of Euripides." In *Oxford Readings in Greek Tragedy*, edited by Erich Segal, 272–93. Oxford: Oxford University Press, 1983.
———. *Word and Action*. Baltimore: Johns Hopkins University Press, 1979.
Konstan, David. *Pity Transformed*. London: Duckworth, 2001.
Korabik, Karen. "The Intersection of Gender and Work–Family Guilt." In *Gender and the Work-Family Experience*, edited by Maura J. Mills, 141–57. New York: Springer, 2015.
Kornarou, Eleni. "The Display of the Dead on the Greek Tragic Stage." *Bulletin of the Institute of Classical Studies* 51, no. 1 (2008): 29–38.
Kovacs, David. *The Heroic Muse*. Baltimore: Johns Hopkins University Press, 1987.
———. "Introduction to *Alcestis*." In *Alcestis*, 146–51. Cambridge, MA: Harvard University Press, 2001.

———. "Introduction to *Children of Heracles*." In *Children of Heracles*, 3–8. Cambridge, MA: Harvard University Press, 1995.

———. "Introduction to *Electra*." In *Electra*, 142–50. Cambridge, MA: Harvard University Press, 1998.

———. "Introduction to *Hecuba*." In *Hecuba*, 393–98. Cambridge, MA: Harvard University Press, 1995.

———. "Introduction to *Ion*." In *Ion*, 315–20. Cambridge, MA: Harvard University Press, 1999.

———. "Introduction to *Medea*." In *Medea*, 276–81. Cambridge, MA: Harvard University Press, 2001.

———. "Introduction to *Phoenician Women*." In *Phoenician Women*, 203–10. Cambridge, MA: Harvard University Press, 2002.

———. "Introduction to *Suppliant Women*." In *Suppliant Women*, 3–10. Cambridge, MA: Harvard University Press, 1998.

———. "Introduction to the *Rhesus*." In *Rhesus*, 347–54. Cambridge, MA: Harvard University Press, 2002.

———. "Introduction to the Series." In *Euripides I*, edited by Jeffrey Henderson, 1–50. Cambridge, MA: Harvard University Press, 2001.

———. "Text and Transmission." In *A Companion to Greek Tragedy*, edited by Justina Gregory, 379–93. Malden, MA: Blackwell, 2005.

———. "Zeus in Euripides' *Medea*." *American Journal of Philology* 114 (1993): 45–70.

Kowalik, Kyrie. "Defining Refugees in Terms of Justice." *Peace Review* 29, no. 1 (2017): 68–75.

Lamari, Anna A. "Aeschylus' *Seven against Thebes* vs. Euripides' *Phoenissae*: Male vs. Female Power." *Wiener Studien* 120 (2007): 5–24.

———. *Narrative, Intertext, and Space in Euripides' Phoenissae*. Berlin: De Gruyter, 2010.

Lampert, Laurence. *How Philosophy Became Socratic*. Chicago: University of Chicago Press, 2010.

Lanni, Adriaan. "The Laws of War in Ancient Greece." *Law and History Review* 23, no. 3 (2008): 469–89.

Larue, Jene. "Creusa's Monody 859–922." *Transactions of the American Philological Association* 94 (1963): 126–36.

Lattimore, Richmond. "Introduction to the *Alcestis*." In *Euripides I*, edited by David Grene and Richmond Lattimore, 1–5. Chicago: University of Chicago Press, 1955.

Lee, Kevin H. "Introduction to Euripides' *Ion*." In *Euripides' Ion*, edited by K. H. Lee, 21–41. Warminster, UK: Aris & Phillips, 1997.

Lefkowitz, Mary. "Euripides' Vita." *Greek, Roman, and Byzantine Studies* 20 (1979): 187–210.

———. *Euripides and the Gods*. Oxford: Oxford University Press, 2016.

———. *Greek Gods, Human Lives*. New Haven, CT: Yale University Press, 2003.
———. "Impiety and Atheism in Euripides' Dramas." *Classical Quarterly* 39, no. 1 (1989): 70–82.
———. *The Lives of Ancient Greek Poets*. Baltimore: Johns Hopkins University Press, 2012.
Leinieks, Valdis. *The City of Dionysus*. Stuttgart, Germany: Teubner, 1996.
Lembke, Janet, and Kenneth J. Reckford. "Introduction." In *Euripides' Electra*, edited by Janet Lembke and Kenneth J. Reckford, 3–5. New York: Oxford University Press, 1994.
Lerner, Melvin J. "Doing Justice to the Justice Motive." In *Current Societal Concerns About Justice*, edited by Leo Montada and Melvin J. Lerner, 1–8. New York: Plenum, 1996.
Lerner, Melvin J., and Susan Clayton. *Justice and Self-Interest*. Cambridge: Cambridge University Press, 2011.
Levin, Susan B. *The Ancient Quarrel between Poetry and Philosophy Revisited*. Oxford: Oxford University Press, 2001.
Ley, Graham. *A Short Introduction to the Ancient Greek Theater*. Rev. ed. Chicago: University of Chicago Press, 2006.
Lindenlauf, Astrid. "Thrown Away Like Rubbish: Disposal of the Dead in Ancient Greece." *Papers from the Institute of Archaeology* 12 (2001): 86–99.
Lloyd, Michael. *The Agon in Euripides*. Oxford: Claredon, 1992.
———. "Euripides' Alcestis." *Greece & Rome* 32, no. 2 (1985): 119–31.
———. "Realism and Character in Euripides' *Electra*." *Phoenix* 40, no. 1 (1986): 1–19.
Locke, John. *The Two Treatises of Government*. Cambridge: Cambridge University Press, 1988.
Lomardini, John. "*Isonomia* and the Public Sphere in Democratic Athens." *History of Political Thought* 34, no. 3 (2013): 393–420.
Loraux, Nicole. *Born of the Earth*. Translated by Selina Stewart. Ithaca, NY: Cornell University Press, 2000.
———. *The Children of Athena*. Translated by Caroline Levine. Princeton, NJ: Princeton University Press, 1993.
———. "The Experience of Tiresias." Translated by Paula Wissing. Princeton, NJ: Princeton University Press, 1995.
———. *The Invention of Athens: The Funeral Oration in the Classical City*. Translated by Alan Sheridan. Cambridge, MA: Harvard University Press, 1986.
———. "Kreousa the Autochthon." Translated by Janet Lloyd. In *Nothing to Do with Dionysos?*, edited by John J. Winkler and Froma I. Zeitlin, 168–206. Princeton, NJ: Princeton University Press, 1990.
———. *The Mourning Voice*. Translated by Elizabeth Trapnell Rawlings. Ithaca, NY: Cornell University Press, 2002.

———. *Tragic Ways of Killing a Woman*. Translated by Anthony Forster. Cambridge, MA: Harvard University Press, 1985.
Loren J. Samons, II. "Forms and Forums of Public Speech." In *A Companion to Ancient Greek Government*, edited by Hans Beck, 267–84. Oxford: John Wiley, 2013.
Lucas, D. W. *The Ion of Euripides*. London: Cohen and West, 1949.
Luschnig, C. A. E. "Euripides' *Hekabe*: The Time Is Out of Joint." *Classical Journal* 71, no. 3 (1976): 227–41.
———. *The Gorgon's Severed Head*. Leiden, The Netherlands: E. J. Brill, 1995.
———. *Granddaughter of the Sun*. Boston: Brill, 2007.
———. "Interiors: Imaginary Spaces in *Alcestis* and *Medea*." *Mnemosyne* 45, no. 1 (1992): 19–44.
———. "Introduction." In *Euripides: Electra, Phoenician Women, Bacchae, Iphigenia at Aulis*, edited by Cecelia Eaton Luschnig and Paul Woodruff, vii–xxxvi. Indianapolis, IN: Hackett, 2011.
Lush, Brian. "What Sacrifices Are Necessary: The Corruption of Ritual Paradigms in Euripides' *Electra*." *College Literature* 42, no. 2 (2015): 565–96.
Lysias. *Against Andocides*. Translated by W. R. M. Lamb. Cambridge, MA: Harvard University Press, 1930.
———. "Funeral Oration." In *Athenian Funeral Orations*, edited by Judson Herrman, 27–44. Newburyport, MA: Focus, 2004.
MacDowell, Douglas M. *The Law in Classical Athens*. Ithaca, NY: Cornell University Press, 1986.
MacInnes, Deborah. "Gainsaying the Prophet: Jocasta, Tiresias, and the Lille Stesichorus." *Quaderni Urbinati di Cultura Classica* 86, no. 2 (2007): 95–108.
MacLeod, Leona. "Marauding Maenads: The First Messager Speech in the *Bacchae*." *Mnemosyne* 59, no. 4 (2006): 578–95.
Mansbridge, Jane, ed. *Beyond Self Interest*. Chicago: University of Chicago Press, 1990.
March, Jennifer R. "Euripides' *Bacchae*: A Reconsideration in Light of Vase Paintings." *Bulletin of the Institute of Classical Studies* 36, no. 2 (1989): 33–65.
Markovits, Elizabeth K. *Future Freedoms*. New York: Routledge, 2018.
Marshall, C. W. "*Alcestis* and the Problem of Prosatyric Drama." *Classical Journal* 95, no. 3 (2000): 229–38.
Martin Luther King, Jr. *Testament of Hope: The Essential Writings and Speeches*. New York: HarperOne, 2003.
Mastronarde, Donald J. "Actors on High." *Classical Antiquity* 9, no. 2 (1990): 247–94.
———. "Are Euripides *Phoinissai* 1104–1140 Interpolated?" *Phoenix* 32, no. 2 (1978): 105–28.
———. *The Art of Euripides*. Cambridge: Cambridge University Press, 2010.
———. "Euripidean Tragedy and Genre." *Illinois Classical Studies* 24/25 (1999): 23–39.

———. *Euripides' Phoenissae*. Cambridge: Cambridge University Press, 1994.
———. "Iconography and Imagery in Euripides' *Ion*." In *Oxford Reading in Classical Studies: Euripides*, edited by Judith Mossman, 294–308. Oxford: Oxford University Press, 2003.
———. "Introduction." In *Euripides Medea*, edited by Donald J. Mastronarde, 1–112. Cambridge: Cambridge University Press, 2006.
Mastronarde, Donald J., and Jan Maarten Bremer. *The Textual Tradition of Euripides' Phoinissai*. Berkeley: University of California Press, 1983.
Matthiessen, Kjeld. "Manuscript Problems in Euripides' *Hecuba*." *Greek, Roman, and Byzantine Studies* 10, no. 4 (1969): 307–24.
Mayor, Adrienne. *The Amazons*. Princeton, NJ: Princeton University Press, 2014.
Mazzaro, Jerome. ""Mnema" and Forgetting in Euripides' the *Bacchae*." *Comparative Drama* 27, no. 3 (1993): 286–305.
McClure, Laura. *Spoken Like a Woman*. Princeton, NJ: Princeton University Press, 1999.
McCrudden, Christopher. "Human Dignity and Judicial Interpretations of Human Rights." *European Journal of International Law* 19, no. 4 (2008): 655–724.
McDermott, Emily A. "Double-Meaning and Mythic Novelty in Euripides' Plays." *Transactions of the American Philological Association* 121 (1991): 123–32.
———. *Euripides' Medea: The Incarnation of Disorder*. University Park: Pennsylvania State University Press, 1989.
———. "Euripides' Second Thoughts." *Transactions and Proceedings of the American Philological Association* 130 (2000): 239–59.
McGinty, P. "Dionysos's Revenge and the Validation of the Hellenic World-View." *Harvard Theological Review* 71, no. 1–2 (1978): 77–94.
McHardy, Fiona. *Revenge in Athenian Culture*. London: Duckworth, 2008.
McLean, John H. "The *Heracleidae* of Euripides." *American Journal of Philology* 55, no. 3 (1934): 197–224.
McNeill, David N. *An Image of the Soul in Speech*. University Park: Pennsylvania State University Press, 2010.
Meagher, Robert Emmet. *The Essential Euripides: Dancing in Dark Times*. Wauconda, IL: Bolchazy-Carducci, 2002.
Meccariello, Chiara. "The Opening of Euripides' *Phoenissae* between Anecdotal and Textual Tradition." *Zeitschrift für Papyrologie und Epigraphik* 190 (2014): 49–56.
Mei, Todd S. "Justice and the Banning of the Poets: The Way of Hermeneutics in Plato's *Republic*." *Review of Metaphysics* 60, no. 4 (2007): 755–78.
Melchinger, Siegfried. "The Story Told in *Medea*." Translated by Samuel R. Rosenbaum. In *Readings on Euripides' Medea*, edited by Don Nardo, 32–39. San Diego, CA: Greenhaven, 2001.
Meltzer, Gary S. *Euripides and the Poetics of Nostalgia*. Cambridge: Cambridge University Press, 2006.

Mendelsohn, Daniel. *Gender and the City in Euripides' Political Plays*. Oxford: Oxford University Press, 2002.
Mendible, Myra, ed. *American Shame*. Bloomington: Indiana University Press, 2016.
Meridor, Ra'anana. "Hecuba's Revenge: Some Observations on Euripides' *Hecuba*." *American Journal of Philology* 99, no. 1 (1978): 28–35.
Michelini, Ann Norris. *Euripides and the Tragic Tradition*. Madison: University of Wisconsin Press, 1987.
———. "Neophron and Euripides' *Medea*." *Transactions of the American Philological Association* 119 (1989): 115–35.
———. "Political Themes in Euripides' Suppliants." *American Journal of Philology* 115, no. 2 (1994): 219–52.
Mikalson, Jon D. *Honor Thy Gods*. Chapel Hill: University of North Carolina Press, 1991.
Mill, John Stuart. "Utilitarianism." In *On Liberty and Other Essays*, 129–201. Oxford: Oxford University Press, 2008.
Miller, Richard W. "Cosmopolitan Respect and Patriotic Concern." *Philosophy and Public Affairs* 27, no. 3 (1998): 202–24.
Miller, Stephen G. "The Alter of the Six Goddesses." *California Studies in Classical Antiquity* 7 (1974): 231–56.
Mills, Sophie. *Euripides: Bacchae*. London: Duckworth, 2006.
———. "Euripides and the Limits of Tragic Instruction." In *War, Democracy and Culture in Classical Athens*, edited by David M. Pritchard, 163–83. Cambridge: Cambridge University Press, 2010.
Mitchell-Boyask, Robin. *Plague and the Athenian Imagination*. Cambridge: Cambridge University Press, 2008.
Montaigne, Michel de. *The Complete Essays*. Translated by M. A. Screech. New York: Penguin, 2003.
Morin, Bernadette. "Pourquoi des Phéniciennes?" *L'antiquité classique* 78 (2009): 25–37.
Morse, Ruth. *The Medieval Medea*. Martlesham, UK: D. S. Brewer, 1996.
Morwood, James. "Euripides and the Demagogues." *Classical Quarterly* 59, no. 2 (2009): 353–63.
———. "Euripides' *Suppliant Women*, Theseus and Athenocentrism." *Mnemosyne* 65 (2012): 552–64.
———. "Introduction." In *Euripides: Suppliant Women*, 1–36. Oxford: Aris & Phillips, 2007.
———. "The Pattern of the Euripides *Electra*." *American Journal of Philology* 102, no. 4 (1981): 362–70.
Mossman, Judith. "Introduction." In *Euripides' Medea*. Oxford: Aris & Phillips, 2011.
———. *Wild Justice: A Study of Euripides' Hecuba*. London: Bristol Classical, 1999.

———. "Women's Speech in Greek Tragedy: The Case of Electra and Clytemnestra in Euripides' *Electra*." *Classical Quarterly* 51, no. 2 (2001): 374–84.
Munn, Mark. *The School of History*. Berkeley: University of California Press, 2000.
Munteanu, Dana LaCourse. "Notes on Women's Responses to Infidelity in Greek Tragedy." *International Society for the Study of European Ideas* 13 (2012): 1–12.
———. *Tragic Pathos*. Cambridge: Cambridge University Press, 2012.
Murnaghan, Sheila. "Choroi Achoroi: The Athenian Politics of Tragic Choral Identity." In *Why Athens?*, edited by David M. Carter, 245–68. Oxford: Oxford University Press, 2011.
Murphy, Liam. *Moral Demands in Nonideal Theory*. Oxford: Oxford University Press, 2000.
Murray, Gilbert. "Introduction." In *Euripides: The Alcestis*, v–xvi. London: George Allen and Unwin, 1915.
———. "Introduction." Translated by Gilbert Murray. In *Collected Plays of Euripides*, edited by Gilbert Murray, 5–8. London: George Allen & Unwin, 1954.
Musurillo, Herbert. "Euripides and Dionysiac Piety: Bacchae 370–433." *Transactions and Proceedings of the American Philological Association* 97 (1966): 299–309.
Naddaff, Ramona A. *Exiling the Poets*. Chicago: University of Chicago Press, 2002.
Nagel, Thomas. *The Possibility of Altruism*. Princeton, NJ: Princeton University Press, 1979.
———. "The Problem with Global Justice." *Philosophy & Public Affairs* 33, no. 2 (2005): 113–47.
Naiden, Fred S. *Ancient Supplication*. Oxford: Oxford University Press, 2006.
Natanblut, Erez. "Two Problems of Staging in Euripides' *Phoenissae*." *Rheinisches Museum für Philologie* 149, no. 3/4 (2006): 429–31.
Neumarkt, Paul. "The Amphitryon Legend." *American Imago* 34, no. 4 (1977): 357–73.
Newton, Rick M. "Ino in Euripides' *Medea*." *American Journal of Philology* 106, no. 4 (1985): 496–502.
New York Times. "15 Life Terms and No Parole for Dahmer." February 18, 1992.
Nicklin, T. "Introduction." In *The Suppliant Women of Euripides*, vii–xii. London: Oxford University Press, 1936.
Nietzsche, Friedrich. *The Birth of Tragedy*. Translated by Walter Kaufmann. New York: Vintage, 1967.
Nikolopoulou, Kalliopi. "Parrhesia as Tragic Structure in Euripides' *Bacchae*." *Epoché* 15, no. 2 (2011): 249–61.
———. "Plato and Hegel on an Old Quarrel." *Epoché* 13, no. 2 (2009): 249–66.
North, Helen F. *Sophrosyne: Self-Knowledge and Self-Restraint in Greek Literature*. Ithaca, NY: Cornell University Press, 1966.
Norwood, Gilbert. *Essays in Tragedy*. Toronto: University of Toronto Press, 1954.
———. *The Riddle of the Bacchae*. Manchester, UK: Manchester University Press, 1908.

Nussbaum, Martha C. *Anger and Forgiveness*. Oxford: Oxford University Press, 2016.
———. "Compassion: The Basic Social Emotion." *Social Philosophy and Policy* 13, no. 1 (1996): 17–58.
———. *The Fragility of Goodness*. Cambridge: Cambridge University Press, 1986.
———. *Hiding from Humanity*. Princeton, NJ: Princeton University Press, 2004.
———. "Introduction." Translated by C. K. Williams. In *The Bacchae of Euripides*, 1–38. New York: Noonday, 1990.
O'Brien, Michael J. "Orestes and the Gorgon: Euripides' *Electra*." *American Journal of Philology* 85, no. 1 (1964): 13–39.
Oakeshott, Michael. *Rationalism in Politics and Other Essays*. Indianapolis, IN: Liberty Fund, 1991.
Obbink, Dirk. "Dionysus Poured Out." In *Masks of Dionysus*, edited by Thomas H. Carpenter and Christopher A. Faraone, 65–86. Ithaca, NY: Cornell University Press, 1993.
Ober, Joshua, and Barry Strauss. "Drama, Political Rhetoric, and the Discourse of Athenian Democracy." In *Nothing to Do with Dionysus*, edited by John J. Winkler and Froma I. Zeitlin, 237–70. Princeton, NJ: Princeton University Press, 1990.
Ober, Josiah. "Law and Political Theory." In *Cambridge Companion to Ancient Greek Law*, edited by Michael Gagarin and David Cohen, 394–411. Cambridge: Cambridge University Press, 2005.
Orwin, Clifford. "Feminine Justice: The End of the *Seven against Thebes*." *Classical Philology* 75, no. 3 (1980): 187–96.
Ovid. *Metamorphoses*. Translated by Rolfe Humphries. Bloomington: Indiana University Press, 1955.
Padel, Ruth. "Making Space Speak." In *Nothing to Do with Dionysos*, edited by John J. Winkler and Froma I. Zeitlin, 336–84. Princeton, NJ: Princeton University Press, 1990.
Padilla, Mark. "Gifts of Humiliation: *Charis* and the Tragic Experience in *Alcestis*." *American Journal of Philology* 121, no. 2 (2000): 179–211.
Page, Denys L. "Introduction." In *Euripides' Medea*, edited by Denys L. Page, vii–lxviii. Oxford: Clarendon, 1938.
Palmer, John. *Parmenides and Pre-Socratic Philosophy*. Oxford: Oxford University Press, 2009.
Papadimitropoulos, Loukas. "Causality and Innovation in Euripides' *Electra*." *Rheinisches Museum für Philologie, Neue Folge* 151, no. 2 (2008): 113–26.
Papadodima, Efi. "The Term Ὄνομα and the Theme of Naming in *Seven against Thebes* and *Phoenician Women*." *Acta Classica* 56 (2013): 136–54.
Papadopoulou, Thalia. *Euripides: Phoenician Women*. London: Duckworth, 2008.
———. "The Prophetic Figure in Euripides' *Phoenissae* and *Bacchae*." *Hermes* 129, no. H.1 (2001): 21–31.

Parke, H. W. *Festivals of the Athenians*. Ithaca, NY: Cornell University Press, 1977.
Parker, L. P. E. "Introduction and Commentary." In *Euripides: Alcestis*, viii–lxxxv. Oxford: Oxford University Press, 2007.
Parker, Robert. "Myths of Early Athens." In *Interpretations of Greek Mythology*, edited by Jan Bremmer, 187–214. London: Routledge, 1987.
———. *On Greek Religion*. Ithaca, NY: Cornell University Press, 2011.
———. "Pleasing Thighs." In *Reciprocity in Ancient Greece*, edited by Christopher Gill, Norman Postlethwaite, and Richard Seaford, 105–27. Oxford: Clarendon, 1998.
———. *Polytheism and Society at Athens*. Oxford: Oxford University Press, 2005.
Partenie, Catalin. *Plato: Selected Myths*. Oxford: Oxford University Press, 2009.
Pausanias. *Description of Greece*. Translated by W. H. S. Jones. Cambridge, MA: Harvard University Press, 1933.
———. *Guide to Greece 1: Central Greece*. Translated by Peter Levy. New York: Penguin Classics, 1979.
Pearson, A. C. *Euripides: The Phoenissae*. Cambridge: Cambridge University Press, 1909.
Pedley, John. *Sanctuaries and the Sacred in the Ancient Greek World*. Cambridge: Cambridge University Press, 2006.
Pelling, Christopher. "Conclusion." In *Greek Tragedy and the Historian*, edited by Christopher Pelling, 213–23. Oxford: Oxford University Press, 1997.
Perris, Simon. "Perspectives on Violence in Euripides' *Bacchae*." *Mnemosyne* 64 (2011): 37–57.
Pevnick, Ryan. *Immigration and the Constraints of Justice*. Cambridge: Cambridge University Press, 2011.
Pfaff, Christopher A. "Artemis and a Hero at the Argive Heraion." *Hesperia* 82, no. 2 (2013): 277–99.
Pindar. *Nimean Odes*. Translated by William H. Race. Cambridge, MA: Harvard University Press, 1997.
———. *Olympian Odes*. Translated by William H. Race. Cambridge, MA: Harvard University Press, 1997.
Pirro, Robert C. *The Politics of Tragedy and Democratic Citizenship*. New York: Continuum International, 2011.
Planinc, Zdravko. "Expel the Barbarian from Your Heart: Intimations of the Cyclops in Euripides's *Hecuba*." *Philosophy and Literature* 42, no. 2 (2018): 403–15.
Plato. *The Apology*. Translated by Harold North Fowler. Cambridge, MA: Harvard University Press, 2005.
———. *Charmides*. Translated by W. R. M. Lamb. Cambridge, MA: Harvard University Press, 1955.
———. *Cratylus*. Translated by Harold North Fowler. Cambridge, MA: Harvard University Press, 1926.

———. *Crito*. Translated by H. N. Fowler. Cambridge, MA: Harvard University Press, 1908.

———. *Euthyphro*. Translated by Harold North Fowler. Cambridge, MA: Harvard University Press, 1914.

———. *The Gorgias*. Translated by W. R. M. Lamb. Cambridge, MA: Harvard University Press, 1925.

———. *Ion*. Translated by Harold North Fowler. Cambridge, MA: Harvard University Press, 1925.

———. *Laws*. Translated by R. G. Bury. Cambridge, MA: Harvard University Press, 1926.

———. *Lysis*. Translated by W. R. H. Lamb. Cambridge, MA: Harvard University Press, 1925.

———. *Phaedrus*. Translated by Harold North Fowler. Cambridge, MA: Harvard University Press, 2005.

———. *Protagoras*. Translated by W. R. M Lamb. Cambridge, MA: Harvard University Press, 1924.

———. *Republic*. Translated by Paul Shorey. Cambridge, MA: Harvard University Press, 1925.

———. *The Republic of Plato*. Translated by Allan Bloom. New York: Basic Books, 1968.

———. *Sophist*. Translated by Harold North Fowler. Cambridge, MA: Harvard University Press, 1921.

———. *The Symposium*. Translated by W. R. M. Lamb. Cambridge, MA: Harvard University Press, 1925.

———. *Timaeus*. Translated by R. G. Bury. Cambridge, MA: Harvard University Press, 1929.

Plescia, Joseph. *The Oath and Perjury in Ancient Athens*. Tallahassee: Florida State University Press, 1970.

Plutarch. "Life of Cimon." Translated by Bernadotte Perrin. In *Lives*. Cambridge, MA: Harvard University Press, 1914.

———. "Life of Nicias." Translated by Bernadotte Perrin. In *Lives*. Cambridge, MA: Harvard University Press, 1916.

———. "The Life of Theseus." Translated by Bernadotte Perrin. In *Lives*. Cambridge, MA: Harvard University Press, 1914.

Podlecki, Anthony J. "Individual and Group in Euripides' *Bacchae*." *L'antiquité classique* 43 (1974): 143–65.

———. "Some Themes in Euripides' *Phoenissae*." *Transactions of the American Philological Association* 93 (1962): 355–73.

Poe, Joe Park. "*Phoenissae* 88–201 and Pollux' Distegia." *Classical Philology* 95, no. 2 (2000): 187–90.

Pogge, Thomas W. "Cosmopolitanism and Sovereignty." *Ethics* 103, no. 1 (1992): 48–75.

Politis, Vasilis. "Aporia and Searching in the Early Plato." In *Remembering Socrates*, edited by L. Judson and V. Karamanis, 88–109. Oxford: Oxford University Press, 2006.

Pomeroy, Sarah B. *Goddess, Whores, Wives, and Slaves*. 2nd ed. New York: Schocken, 1995.

Popper, Karl. *Open Society and Its Enemies*. Princeton, NJ: Princeton University Press, 1971.

Porter, John R. "Tiptoeing through the Corpses: Euripides' *Electra*, Apollonius, and the *Bouphonia*." *Greek, Roman, and Byzantine Studies* 13, no. 3 (1990): 255–80.

Pozzi, Dora C. "The Polis in Crisis." In *Myth and the Polis*, edited by Dora C. Pozzi and John M. Wickersham, 126–63. Ithaca, NY: Cornell University Press, 1991.

Pritchett, W. Kendrick. "The Calendar of the Athenian Civic Administration." *Phoenix* 30, no. 4 (1976): 337–56.

Pucci, Pietro. *Euripides' Revolution under Cover*. Ithaca, NY: Cornell University Press, 2016.

Rabinowitz, Nancy Sorkin. *Anxiety Veiled: Euripides and the Traffic in Women*. Ithaca, NY: Cornell University Press, 1993.

———. *Greek Tragedy*. Oxford: Blackwell, 2008.

———. "Introduction to the *Alcestis*." In *Women on the Edge*, edited by Ruby Blondell, Mary-Kay Gamel, Nancy Sorkin Rabinowitz, and Bella Zweig, 103–13. New York: Routledge, 1999.

Raeburn, David. *Greek Tragedies as Plays for Performance*. Oxford: John Wiley-Blackwell, 2016.

———. "The Significance of Stage Properties in Euripides' *Electra*." *Greece & Rome* 47, no. 2 (2000): 149–68.

Rawls, John. *Law of Peoples*. Cambridge, MA: Harvard University Press, 1999.

———. *A Theory of Justice*. Cambridge, MA: Harvard University Press, 1971.

Rawson, Elizabeth. "Family and Fatherland in Euripides' *Phoenissae*." *Greek, Roman, and Byzantine Studies* 11, no. 2 (1970): 109–27.

Reckford, Kenneth. "Concepts of Demoralization in the *Hecuba*." In *Directions in Euripidean Criticism*, edited by Peter Burian, 112–28. Durham, NC: Duke University Press, 1985.

———. "Medea's First Exit." *Transactions of the American Philological Association* 99 (1968): 188–91.

———. "Pity and Terror in Euripides' *Hecuba*." *Arion* 1, no. 2 (1991): 24–43.

Rehm, Rush. *Greek Tragic Theatre*. London: Routledge, 1992.

———. *Marriage to Death: The Conflation of Wedding and Funeral Rituals in Greek Tragedy*. Princeton, NJ: Princeton University Press, 1994.

———. *The Play of Space*. Princeton, NJ: Princeton University Press, 2002.

Reynolds-Warnoff, Patricia. "The Role of *To Sophorin* in Euripides' *Bacchae*." *Quaderni Urbinati di Cultura Classica* 57, no. 3 (1997): 77–103.
Rhodes, P. J. "Nothing to Do with Democracy." *Journal of Hellenic Studies* 123 (2003): 104–19.
Ringer, Mark. *Euripides and the Boundary of the Human*. Lanham, MD: Lexington, 2016.
Rogowski, Christian. "Mad with Love." In *Madness in Drama*, edited by James Redmond, 171–228. Cambridge: Cambridge University Press, 1993.
Rose, H. J. *A Handbook of Greek Mythology*. New York: Dutton, 1958.
Roselli, David Kawalko. *Theater of the People*. Austin: University of Texas Press, 2011.
———. "Vegetable-Hawking Mom and Fortunate Son: Euripides, Tragic Style, and Reception." *Phoenix* 59, no. 1/2 (2005): 1–49.
Rosenbloom, David. "The Panhellenism of Athenian Tragedy." In *Why Athens?*, edited by D. M. Carter, 353–81. Oxford: Oxford University Press, 2011.
Rosenmeyer, Thomas G. "Tragedy and Religion: *The Bacchae*." In *Oxford Readings in Greek Tragedy*, edited by Erich Segal, 370–89. Oxford: Oxford University Press, 1983.
Rosivach, Vincent J. "Autochthony and the Athenians." *Classical Quarterly* 37, no 2 (1987): 294–305.
———. "Earthborn Olympians: The Parados of the *Ion*." *Classical Quarterly* 27, no. 2 (1977): 284–94.
———. "The "Golden Lamb" Ode in Euripides' *Electra*." *Classical Philology* 73, no. 3 (1978): 189–99.
Ruck, Carl A. P. "On the Sacred Names of Iamos and Ion." *Classical Journal* 71, no. 3 (1976): 235–52.
Ruffell, Ian. "Response to Murnaghan and Visvardi." In *Why Athens?*, edited by David M. Carter, 293–301. Oxford: Oxford University Press, 2011.
Rundin, John S. "Pozo Moro, Child Sacrifice, and the Greek Legendary Tradition." *Journal of Biblical Literature* 123, no. 3 (2004): 425–47.
Sale, William. *Existentialism and Euripides*. Berwick, UK: Aureal, 1977.
Sandel, Michael J. *Justice: What Is the Right Thing to Do?* New York: Farrar, Straus and Giroux, 2009.
Sansone, David. "Iphigenia Changes Her Mind." *Illinois Classical Studies* 16 (1991): 161–72.
———. "Plato and Euripides." *Illinois Classical Studies* 21 (1996): 35–67.
Saxonhouse, Arlene. "Another Antigone." *Political Theory* 3, no. 4 (2005): 472–94.
———. *Fear of Diversity*. Chicago: University of Chicago Press, 1995.
———. *Free Speech and Democracy in Ancient Athens*. Cambridge: Cambridge University Press, 2006.
———. "Freedom, Form and Formlessness." *American Political Science Review* 108, no. 1 (2014): 88–99.
———. "On Socratic Narrative." *Political Theory* 37, no. 6 (2009): 728–53.

———. "Reflections on Autochthony in Euripides' *Ion*." In *Greek Tragedy and Political Theory*, edited by Peter J. Euben, 252–73. Berkeley: University of California Press, 1986.
Schaps, David M. *Economic Rights of Women in Ancient Greece*. Edinburgh: University of Edinburgh Press, 1979.
Schlesinger, Eilhard. "On Euripides' *Medea*." In *Oxford Readings in Greek Tragedy*, edited by Erich Segal, 294–310. Oxford: Oxford University Press, 1983.
Scodel, Ruth. "Admetou Logos and the *Alcestis*." *Harvard Studies in Classical Philology* 83 (1979): 51–62.
———. *Introduction to Greek Tragedy*. Cambridge: Cambridge University Press, 2010.
Scullion, Scott. "Euripides and Macedon, or the Silence of the *Frogs*." *Classical Quarterly* 53, no. 2 (2003): 389–400.
———. "Tragedy and Religion: The Problem of Origins." In *A Companion to Greek Tragedy*, edited by Justina Gregory, 23–37. Oxford: Blackwell, 2008.
Scully, Stephen. "Orchestra and Stage and Euripides' *Suppliant Women*." *Arion* 4, no. 1 (1996): 61–84.
Seaford, Richard. *Euripides: Cyclops*. Oxford: Oxford University Press, 1984.
———. "Introduction." In *Euripides' Bacchae*, edited by Richard Seaford, 25–52. Warminster, UK: Aris & Phillips, 1997.
———. "The Social Function of Attic Tragedy." *Classical Quarterly* (2000): 30–44.
———. "The Structural Problem of Marriage in Euripides." In *Euripides, Women, and Sexuality*, edited by Anton Powell, 151–76. London: Routledge, 1990.
———. *Tragedy, Ritual and Money in Ancient Greece*. Cambridge: Cambridge University Press.
Segal, Charles. "Admetus' Divided House: Spatial Dichotomies and Gender Roles in Euripides' *Alcestis*." *Materiali e discussioni per l'analisi dei testi classici* 28 (1992): 9–26.
———. *Dionysiac Poetics and Euripides' Bacchae*. Princeton, NJ: Princeton University Press, 1997.
———. "Euripides' *Bacchae*: Conflict and Mediation." *Ramus* 6 (1961): 103–20.
———. "Euripides' *Ion*: Generational Passage and Civic Myth." In *Rites of Passage in Ancient Greece*, edited by Mark W. Padilla, 67–108. Lewisburg, PA: Bucknell University Press, 1999.
———. *Euripides and the Poetics of Sorrow*. Durham, NC: Duke University Press, 1993.
———. "Female Mourning and Dionysiac Lament in Euripides' *Bacchae*." In *Orchestra*, edited by Anton Bierl and Peter von Möllendorff, 12–18. Wiesbaden, Germany: Springer, 1994.
———. *Interpreting Greek Tragedy*. Ithaca, NY: Cornell University Press, 1986.
———. "The Menace of Dionysus." *Arethusa* 1 (1978): 185–203.
———. "The Myth Was Saved: Reflections on Homer and the Mythology of Plato's *Republic*." *Hermes* 106, no. H.2 (1978): 315–36.

———. "The Raw and the Cooked in Greek Literature: Structure, Values, Metaphor." *Classical Journal* 69, no. 4 (1974): 298–308.

———. "Violence and the Other: Greek, Female, and Barbarian in Euripides' *Hecuba*." *Transactions and Proceedings of the American Philological Association* 120 (1990): 109–31.

Segal, Erich. "Euripides: Poet of Paradox." In *Oxford Readings in Greek Tragedy*, edited by Erich Segal, 244–53. Oxford: Oxford University Press, 1983.

Seligman, Adam B., and Robert P. Weller. *Rethinking Pluralism*. Oxford: Oxford University Press, 2012.

Seung, T. K. *Intuition and Construction*. New Haven, CT: Yale University Press, 1993.

Sewell, Richard C. *In the Theatre of Dionysos*. London: McFarland, 2007.

Sfyroeras, Pavlos. "The Ironies of Salvation." *Classical Journal* 90 (1994): 125–42.

Shaw, Michael H. "The Ethos of Theseus in the *Suppliant Women*." *Hermes* 110 (1982): 3–19.

Sheppard, J. T. "The *Electra* of Euripides." *Classical Review* 32, no. 7–8 (1918): 137–41.

———. "*Tyrannos, Kerdos*, and the Modest Measure in Three Plays of Euripides." *Classical Quarterly* 11, no. 1 (1917): 3–10.

Shipton, Matthew. *The Politics of Youth in Greek Tragedy: Gangs of Athens*. London: Bloomsbury Academic, 2018.

Sinn, Ulrich. "Greek Sanctuaries as Places of Refuge." Translated by Judith Binder. In *Greek Sanctuaries: New Approaches*, edited by Nanno Marinatos and Robin Hagg, 88–109. London: Routledge, 1993.

Sipiora, Phillip. "Introduction: The Ancient Concept of *Kairos*." In *Rhetoric and Kairos*, edited by Phillip Sipiora and James S. Baumlin, 1–22. Albany: State University of New York Press, 2002.

Slater, Niall W. *Euripides: Alcestis*. London: Bloomsbury, 2013.

Smethurst, S. E. "Heracles and Iolaus, Part I." *Classical Journal* 45, no. 6 (1950): 288–93.

———. "Heracles and Iolaus, Part II." *Classical Journal* 45, no. 7 (1950): 322–26.

Smith, Wesley D. "Expressive Form in Euripides' *Suppliants*." *Harvard Studies in Classical Philology* 71 (1967): 151–70.

———. "The Ironic Structure in *Alcestis*." *Phoenix* 14, no. 3 (1960): 127–45.

Snell, Bruno. *The Discovery of the Mind*. New York: Dover, 1960.

Sokolon, Marlene K. "Euripides' *Ion*: Identity, Legitimacy, and the Ties That Bind." In *Socrates and Dionysus*, edited by Ann Ward, 33–53. Newcastle-upon-Tyne, UK: Cambridge Scholars, 2013.

———. "Poetic Questions in the Socratic Method." In *The Socratic Method Today*, edited by Lee Trepanier, 9–21. London: Routledge, 2018.

———. *Political Emotions: Aristotle and the Symphony of Reason and Emotion*. DeKalb: Northern Illinois University Press, 2006.

Sommerstein, Alan H., and Andrew J. Bayliss. *Oath and State in Ancient Greece.* Boston: Walter de Gruyter, 2013.
Sommerstein, Alan H. "Introduction." In *Horkos: The Oath in Greek Society,* edited by Alan H. Sommerstein and Judith Fletcher, 1–6. Bristol, UK: Bristol Phoenix, 2007.
Sophocles. *Ajax.* Translated by Hugh Lloyd-Jones. Cambridge, MA: Harvard University Press, 1994.
———. *Antigone.* Translated by Hugh Lloyd-Jones. Cambridge, MA: Harvard University Press, 1994.
———. *Oedipus at Colonus.* Translated by Hugh Lloyd-Jones. Cambridge, MA: Harvard University Press, 1994.
———. *Oedipus Tyrannus.* Translated by Hugh Lloyd-Jones. Cambridge, MA: Harvard University Press, 1994.
———. *Philoctetes.* Translated by Hugh Lloyd-Jones. Cambridge, MA: Harvard University Press, 1994.
Sourvinou-Inwood, Christiane. *Tragedy and Athenian Religion.* Lanham, MD: Lexington, 2003.
Soyinka, Wole. "Introduction." In *The Bacchae of Euripides,* v–xi. New York: W. W. Norton, 1973.
Spence, Simon. *The Image of Jason in Early Greek Myth.* Seattle, WA: CreateSpace, 2010.
Spranger, J. A. "The Political Element in the *Heracleidae* of Euripides." *Classical Quarterly* 19, no. 3/4 (1925): 117–28.
Stafford, Emma. *Herakles.* London: Routledge, 2012.
Stanford, W. B. *Greek Tragedy and the Emotions.* London: Routledge, 1983.
Stanton, Greg R. "Aristocratic Obligation in Euripides' *Hekabe.*" *Mnemosyne* 48, no. 1 (1995): 11–33.
Stearns, Peter N. *Shame.* Urbana: University of Illinois Press, 2017.
Steinbock, Bernd. *Social Memory in Athenian Public Discourses.* Ann Arbor: University of Michigan, 2013.
Steiner, George. *Antigones.* New York: Oxford, 1984.
Sternberg, Rachael Hall. *Tragedy Offstage: Suffering and Sympathy in Ancient Athens.* Austin: University of Texas Press, 2006.
Stewart, Edmund. *Greek Tragedy on the Move: The Birth of a Panhellenic Artform.* Oxford: Oxford University Press, 2017.
Stieber, Mary. "Statuary in Euripides' *Alcestis.*" *Arion* 5, no. 3 (1998): 69–97.
———. "The Wheel Simile in the *Bacchae,* Another Turn." *Mnemosyne* 59, no. 4 (2006): 585–95.
Storey, Ian C. *Euripides: Suppliant Women.* London: Duckworth, 2008.
Storey, Ian C., and Arlene Allan. *A Guide to Ancient Greek Drama.* Oxford: Blackwell, 2005.
Storm, William. *After Dionysus.* Ithaca, NY: Cornell University Press, 1998.

Strauss, Jonathan. *Private Lives, Public Deaths: Antigone and the Invention of Individuality*. New York: Fordham University Press, 2013.
Strauss, Leo. *The City and Man*. Chicago: University of Chicago Press, 1964.
———. *Persecution and the Art of Writing*. Chicago: University of Chicago Press, 1988.
———. *The Rebirth of Classical Political Rationalism*. Chicago: University of Chicago Press, 1989.
———. *What Is Political Philosophy?* Chicago: University of Chicago Press, 1959.
Stuttard, David. *Nemesis*. Cambridge, MA: Harvard University Press, 2018.
Sutton, Dana Ferrin. *The Greek Satyr Play*. Hain, Germany: Meisenheim-am-Glan, 1980.
Swift, Laura. *Euripides' Ion*. London: Duckworth Companions, 2008.
———. *Greek Tragedy*. London: Bloomsbury, 2016.
———. "Sexual and Familial Distortion in Euripides' *Phoenissae*." *Transactions of the American Philological Association* 139, no. 1 (2009): 53–87.
———. "The Symbolism of Space in Euripidean Choral Fantasy." *Classical Quarterly* 59, no. 2 (2009): 564–82.
Tan, Kok-Chor. *Justice without Borders*. Cambridge: Cambridge University Press, 2004.
Taplin, Oliver. *Greek Tragedy in Action*. 2nd ed. London: Routledge, 2003.
Tarnopolsky, Christina H. *Prudes, Perverts, and Tyrants*. Princeton, NJ: Princeton University Press, 2010.
Taxidou, Olga. *Tragedy, Modernity, and Mourning*. Edinburgh: University of Edinburgh Press, 2004.
Tessitore, Aristide. "Euripides' *Medea* and the Problem of Spiritedness." *Review of Politics* 53, no. 4 (1991): 587–601.
Tetlow, Elizabeth Meier. *Women, Crime, and Punishment in Ancient Law and Society*. Vol. 2. London: Continuum, 1985.
Thalmann, William G. "Euripides and Aeschylus: The Case of Hekabe." *Classical Antiquity* 12, no. 1 (1993): 126–59.
"Theseus and His Parents and Stepmother." *Bulletin of the Institute of Classical Studies* 26, no. S40 (1979): 18–28.
Thucydides. *The History of the Peloponnesian War*. Translated by C. F. Smith. Cambridge, MA: Harvard University Press, 1919.
Thumiger, Chiara. "Animal World, Animal Representation and the Hunting Model." *Phoenix* 60, no. 3/4 (2006): 191–210.
———. *Hidden Paths: Self and Characterization in Greek Tragedy*. London: Institute of Classical Studies, 2007.
Toher, Mark. "Euripides' *Supplices* and the Social Function of Funeral Ritual." *Hermes* 139 (2001): 332–43.
Tomlinson, R. A. *Greek Sanctuaries*. London: Paul Elek, 1976.

Torrance, Isabelle. "In the Footprints of Aeschylus: Recognition, Allusion, and Metapoetics in Euripides." *American Journal of Philology* 132, no. 2 (2011): 177–204.
——. *Metapoetry in Euripides*. Oxford: Oxford University Press, 2013.
Trammell, Erna P. "The Mute Alcestis." *Classical Journal* 37, no. 3 (1941): 144–50.
Tsagalis, Christos. "Style, Construction, Sound and Rhythm: Thetis' Supplication of Zeus." *Arethusa* 34, no. 1 (2001): 1–29.
Tzanetou, Angeliki. *City of Suppliants*. Austin: University of Texas Press, 2012.
——. "Supplication and Empire in Athenian Tragedy." In *Why Athens?*, edited by D. M. Carter, 305–24. Oxford: Oxford University Press, 2011.
UNHCR. *Global Trends Report*, edited by Statistics and Demographics Section. Copenhagen: United Nations High Commissioner for Refugees (UNHCR), 2019.
van der Valk, Marchinus. *Studies in Euripides: Phoenissae and Andromache*. Amsterdam: A. M. Hakkert, 1985.
van Emde Boas, Evert. *Language and Character in Euripides' Electra*. Oxford: Oxford University Press, 2017.
Velasco, Juan Carlos. "Beyond the Borders." In *Spheres of Global Justice*, edited by Jean-Christophe Merle et al., 293–306. New York: Springer, 2013.
Vellacott, Philip. "Introduction." In *Orestes and Other Plays*, 7–100. Toronto: Penguin, 1972.
——. "Introduction." In *Euripides: Three Plays*, 7–25. Toronto: Penguin Press, 1953.
——. *Ironic Drama*. Cambridge: Cambridge University Press, 1975.
Vermeule, Emily. "Introduction to Electra." Translated by Emily Vermeule. In *Euripides V*, edited by David Grene and Richmond Lattimore, 204–8. Chicago: University of Chicago Press, 1959.
Vernant, Jean-Pierre. "The Masked Dionysus." Translated by Janet Lloyd. In *Myth and Tragedy in Ancient Greece*, edited by Jean-Pierre Vernant and Pierre Vidal-Naquet, 381–412. New York: Zone, 1990.
——. "Tensions and Ambiguities in Greek Tragedy." Translated by Janet Lloyd. In *Myth and Tragedy in Ancient Greece*, edited by Jean-Paul Vernant and Pierre Vidal-Naquet, 29–48. New York: Zone, 1990.
Verrall, A. W. *Euripides the Rationalist*. Cambridge: Cambridge University Press, 1895.
Vickers, Brian. *Towards Greek Tragedy*. London: Longman, 1973.
Vickers, Michael. *Sophocles and Alcibiades*. Ithaca, NY: Cornell University Press, 2008.
The Villa of Mysteries in Pompeii. Pompeii: Edizioni Spano, 2001.
Vinh, Graziella. "Athens in Euripides' *Suppliants*." In *Why Athens?*, edited by D. M. Carter, 325–44. Oxford: Oxford University Press, 2011.

Visvardi, Eirene. "Pity and Panhellenic Politics." In *Why Athens?*, edited by D. M Carter, 269–92. Oxford: Oxford University Press, 2011.

Vlastos, Gregory. *Socrates, Ironist and Moral Philosopher*. Cambridge: Cambridge University Press, 1991.

Wainright, William J. *Religion and Morality*. Burlington, VT: Ashgate, 2005.

Walgrave, Lode. *Restorative Justice, Self-Interest and Responsible Citizenship*. New York: Routledge, 2012.

Walker, Henry J. *Theseus and Athens*. Oxford: Oxford University Press, 1995.

Walsh, George B. "Rhetoric of Birthright and Race in Euripides' *Ion*." *Hermes* 106, no. 2 (1978): 301–15.

Warren, Peter. "Knossos: New Excavations and Discoveries." *Archaeology* 37, no. 4 (1984): 48–55.

Wassermann, Felix Martin. "Divine Violence and Providence in Euripides' *Ion*." *Transactions of the American Philological Association* 71 (1940): 587–604.

———. "Man and God in the *Bacchae* and in the *Oedipus at Colonus*." In *Studies Presented to D. M. Robertson*, edited by G. E. Mylonas, 559–69. St. Louis: Washington University Press, 1953.

Wasson, R. Gordon, Albert Hofmann, and Carl A. Ruck. *The Road to Eleusis*. 30th Anniversary Edition. Berkeley, CA: North Atlantic, 2008.

Weiss, Naomi A. *The Music of Tragedy: Performance and Imagination in Euripidean Theater*. Berkeley: University of California Press, 2018.

Whitehorne, John E. G. "The Dead as Spectacle in Euripides' *Bacchae* and *Supplices*." *Hermes* 114 (1986): 59–72.

Wilk, Stephen R. *Medusa: Solving the Mystery of the Gorgon*. Oxford: Oxford University Press, 2000.

Wilkins, John. "Introduction and Commentary." In *Euripides: Heracleidae*, edited by John Wilkins, xviii–xix. Oxford: Clarendon, 1993.

———. "The State and the Individual: Euripides' Plays of Voluntary Self-Sacrifice." In *Euripides, Women, and Sexuality*, edited by Anton Powell, 195–250. London: Routledge, 1990.

Willetts, R. F. "Action and Character in the *Ion* of Euripides." *Journal of Hellenic Studies* 93 (1973): 201–209.

Williamson, Christina. "As God Is My Witness." In *Cults, Creeds and Identities in the Greek City after the Classical Age*, edited by R. Alston, O. M. van Nijf, and C. G. Williamson, 119–74. Leuven, Belgium: Peeters, 2013.

Williamson, Margaret. "A Woman's Place in Euripides' *Medea*." In *Euripides, Women, and Sexuality*, edited by Anton Powell, 16–31. London: Routledge, 1990.

Willink, C. W. "The Goddess Eulabeia and Pseudo-Euripides in Euripides' *Phoenissae*." *Proceedings of the Cambridge Philological Society, New Series* 36, no. 216 (1990): 182–201.

———. "On the Transmission of the *Bacchae*." *Classical Quarterly* 16, no. 2 (1966): 347.

Wilson, Peter. *The Athenian Institution of the Khoregia: The Chorus, the City, and the Stage*. Cambridge: Cambridge University Press, 2000.

———. "The Glue of Democracy?" In *Why Athens?*, edited by D. M. Carter, 19–44. Oxford: Oxford University Press, 2011.

Winkler, John J. "The Ephebes's Song: *Tragoidia* and *Polis*." In *Nothing to Do with Dionysos?*, edited by John J. Winkler and Froma I. Zeitlin, 12–20. Princeton, NJ: Princeton University Press, 1990.

Winkler, John J., and Froma I. Zeitlin, eds. *Nothing to Do with Dionysos?* Princeton, NJ: Princeton University Press, 1990.

Winnington-Ingram, R. P. *Euripides and Dionysus*. Cambridge: Cambridge University Press, 1948.

Wohl, Victoria. *Euripides and the Politics of Form*. Princeton, NJ: Princeton University Press, 2015.

———. "How to Recognize a Hero in Euripides' *Electra*." *Bulletin of the Institute of Classical Studies* 58, no. 1 (2015): 61–76.

———. *Intimate Commerce: Exchange, Gender, and Subjectivity in Greece*. Austin: University of Texas Press, 1998.

Wolff, Christian. "Design and Myth in Euripides' *Ion*." *Harvard Studies in Classical Philology* 69 (1965): 169–94.

Woodruff, Paul. *First Democracy: The Challenge of an Athenian Ideal*. Oxford: Oxford University Press, 2005.

Wright, Matthew. "The Tragedian as Critic: Euripides and Early Greek Poetics." *Journal of Hellenic Studies* 130 (2010): 165–84.

Wyckoff, Elizabeth. "Introduction to the Phoenician Women." In *Euripides V*, edited by David Grene and Richmond Lattimore, 68–70. Chicago: University of Chicago Press, 1959.

Xenophon. *Anabasis*. Translated by Carleton Lewis Brownson and John Dillery. Cambridge, MA: Harvard University Press, 1998.

———. "Constitution." Translated by J. M. Moore. In *Aristotle and Xenophon on Democracy and Oligarchy*, edited by J. M. Moore, 37–47. Berkeley: University of California Press, 1975.

———. *Cyropaedia*. Translated by Walter Miller. Cambridge, MA: Harvard University Press, 1914.

———. *Hellenica*. Translated by Carleton L. Brownson. Cambridge, MA: Harvard University Press, 1918.

———. *Memorabilia*. Translated by E. C. Marchant. Cambridge, MA: Harvard University Press, 2002.

Zacharia, Katerina. *Converging Truths*. Boston: Brill, 2003.

Zeitlin, Froma I. "The Argive Festival of Hera and Euripides' *Electra*." *Transactions and Proceedings of the American Philological Association* 101 (1970): 645–69.

———. "Euripides' *Hekabe* and the Somatics of Dionysiac Drama." *Ramus* 20 (1991): 53–94.

———. *Playing the Other*. Chicago: University of Chicago Press, 1996.

———. "Playing the Other: Theater, Theatricality, and the Feminine in Greek Drama." In *Nothing to Do with Dionysos?*, edited by John J. Winkler and Froma I. Zeitlin, 63–96. Princeton, NJ: Princeton University Press, 1990.

———. "A Study in Form: Recognition Scenes in the Three Electra Plays." *Lexis* 30 (2012): 361–78.

———. "Thebes: Theater of Self and Society in Athenian Drama." In *Greek Tragedy and Political Theory*, edited by J. Peter Euben, 101–41. Berkeley: University of California Press, 1986.

Zimmermann, Bernhard. *Greek Tragedy*. Translated by Thomas Marier. Baltimore, MD: Johns Hopkins University Press, 1991.

Ziolkowski, John. *Thucydides and the Tradition of Funeral Speeches in Athens*. New York: Arno, 1981.

Zuntz, Günther. *An Inquiry into the Transmission of the Plays of Euripides*. Cambridge: Cambridge University Press, 1965.

———. "Is the *Heracleidae* Mutilated?" *Classical Quarterly* 41, no. 1/2 (1947): 46–52.

———. *The Political Plays of Euripides*. Manchester, UK: Manchester University Press, 1955.

Index

Achilles, 15, 20, 22, 74, 142, 149, 163, 211, 216
activists, political faction versus quietists, 4, 138, 143, 147–49, 151, 153, 156, 290n62, 298n43, 309n71
Aegeus, King of Athens, 22, 24–26, 28, 30, 32–33; oath maker, with Medea, 35–36
Aeropagus, 155–56, 212, 217
Aeschylus, 6, 10, 42, 48, 144, 250n58, 301n86; character in *Frogs*, 4, 272n4; *Agamemnon*, 315n13, 335n15; *Eumenides*, 155, 212, 217, 218, 265n49; *Libation Bearers*, 214, 336n30; *Prometheus Bound*, 295n9; *Seven Against Thebes*, 68, 275n28, 278n56
Aethra, 22, 296n16; *Suppliant Women*, character in, 140–42, 145, 147–49, 153, 157, 310n79
Agamemnon, 80, 171, 173, 177, 229, 233, 236; Clytemnestra, relationship with, 207, 209–10, 212, 214, 216, 222, 223, 234; *Hecuba*, character in, 171, 173, 177; Hecuba's supplication of, 169–70; in debates, 164–65, 168, 176–76, 222, 224, 320n89
agōn. See debate

Alcibiades, 195, 266n56, 296n19, 304n8, 330n83
Alcmene, 1, 172, 296n16; *Children of Heracles*, character in, 114–15, 117–18, 125, 297n24; violator of law, 124, 127, 128–36
alphabet plays, 10–11, 13, 91, 114, 137–38, 207
anger, 14, 15, 31–33, 39–40, 50, 103, 134, 136, 193, 217, 264n31, 339n70. See also rage, righteous indignation
Antigone, 68, 139, 140, 177, 231, 284n132; *Phoenician Women*, character in, 68–69, 71–72, 275n36; moral paradox, debate on, 82–86, 277n49, 282n116, 283n124
Antiphon, 320n94, 337n40, 345n69
Aphrodite, 21, 43, 67, 162, 274n18
Apollo, 67, 145, 167, 179, 236, 268n80, 292n101; *Alcestis*, character in, 183, 186–87, 190–92, 195–97, 200, 202–205; Dionysus, twinned with, 44–45, 52, 57, 263n22; *Electra*, erroneous judgment in, 207, 209–20, 229, 327n44; god of prophecy, 73, 139, 328n58; *Ion*, referred to in, 94–97, 100, 102–103, 105–107, 108–109, 237, 287n32

385

Apollodorus, 163, 186, 189
Apollonius of Rhodes, 21, 23
Aristophanes, 9, 66, 325n8, 325n18;
  Frogs, 4, 6, 10, 65, 66
Aristophanes of Byzantium, 66
Aristotle, 2, 11, 30, 49, 205,
  239; 280n82, 298n38, 306n35;
  Nicomachean Ethics, 2, 74–75, 80,
  221, 231, 238, 253n40, 255n55,
  258n102, 266n52, 315n21, 330n90,
  342n119; Metaphysics, 333n138,
  345n75; Poetics, 4, 9, 25, 27–28,
  91, 99, 137, 213, 271n121; Politics,
  77, 78, 146, 257n90; Rhetoric, 10,
  266n57, 269n88, 280n88, 299n60,
  302n201, 319n81, 328n53; Topica,
  271n119
Artemis, 34, 45–46, 104, 179, 186
Athena, 93, 118–19, 162, 229, 235,
  268n80; Athenian institutions,
  founder of, 178, 212, 213, 218,
  293n112; deus ex machina, role of,
  236–37, deus ex machina, in Ion,
  96, 101, 105, 109, 214; deus ex
  machina, in Suppliant Women, 129,
  144, 150, 154–56, 157; heroes,
  helper of, 24, 43, 115, 251n13,
  252n19, 253n33, 301n87, 301n89;
  Medusa's blood, supplier of, 95,
  97–98, 101, 103, 106
Athenian Assembly, 8, 143, 229
authority, 15, 166, 208, 235–38,
  268n74; divine, 36 109, 191, 235,
  237; divine, in Bacchae 56–58, 6;
  divine, in Electra, 214, 220, 222;
  parental, 153, 328n50; political,
  26, 71, 116, 122–24, 133, 135;
  political, in Bacchae, 50–54, 61;
  political, in Electra, 216, 220, 222;
  political, failure of, in Hecuba,
  161, 162, 168, 174–78, 180–81;
  traditional, in Bacchae, 55–56;
  questions of, in Bacchae, 49,
  61–62; questions of, in Electra,
  215, 219–33, 225
autochthony/autochthonous, 33, 67,
  288n40; Ion, origin story of, 93–97,
  100–101, 104–10, 115
avenger (*alastōr*), 24, 35–37, 220,
  232. See also revenge

Beccaria, Cesare, 225
binaries, 42, 109, 198–99, 20. See
  also dichotomy, duality
blood price, justice as, 37, 78–81, 85,
  233
boundary, justice as, 9, 12, 13, 14,
  15, 180, 234–39, 240, 291n75;
  Alcestis, 183, 185, 187, 190–91,
  196–203, 204–205, 332n122;
  Bacchae, 45, 50–51, 55, 56–58,
  59; Children of Heracles, 116–20,
  136; Electra, 213, 235, 239; Ion,
  94, 103, 104–109, 111; Medea, 24,
  37; Suppliant Women, 150, 156,
  312n116
Burke, Edmund, 62

Cicero, 181, 203
Cleisthenes, 141, 305n26
Clytemnestra, 163, 165, 265n49;
  Electra, character in, 207, 211,
  212, 218, 335n15, 335n18; Electra,
  debate with, 222–24, 234
common good, justice as, 110, 124,
  146; Phoenician Women, 78, 80–81,
  82, 85–87
community, 2, 15, 231, 239, 240–41,
  270n107; Alcestis, 191, 199, 204,
  205; Bacchae, 14, 42, 61, 267n71;
  Children of Heracles, 15, 114, 120,
  124, 126, 131 135–36, 229; Electra,
  221, 227–28, 341n116; Hecuba,
  169, 171–72, 179, 319n70; Ion,

INDEX 387

91, 105, 111, 291n87; *Medea*, 30, 33, 39; *Phoenician Women*, 78–86, 273n11, 281n90, 281n91; *Suppliant Women*, 137, 139, 145–46, 148–49, 152, 157, 306n33, 311n92; theater, necessity of, 5, 6, 9, 12, 108, 111, 134, 240–41

corrective justice, *Children of Heracles*, 115–16; *Hecuba*, 171, 174; *Suppliant Women*, 142, 146–47. *See also* merit

Creusa, 23, 115, 147, 228, 235, 286n20, 288n42; background myth of, 93–94; *Ion*, character in, 94–96, 97–98, 101–103, 105–109; xenophobia, connection to, 99, 100–101, 109–10, 111

custom (*nomos*), 29, 103, 107, 118, 322n120; *Bacchae*, tradition as, 55–56, 62; justice as, 163–65; nature, as opposed to, 56, 76, 120, 135, 180, 267n68, 269n88, 345n69; panhellenic norms of, 121, 148, 151, 155–56, 164, 170, 173, 179, 235, 291n78; unwritten norms, 46, 55–57, 62, 107–108, 168, 175, 177–78, 305n26, 329n76

debate (*agōn*), 4, 25–26, 27, 45, 233, 236, 238, 241; *Alcestis*, 187–88, 190–91, 193, 196, 202, 204, 205; *Children of Heracles*, 116, 118, 121–25; *Electra*, 211, 212, 220, 224–25, 338n49; *Hecuba*, 163, 164, 165, 167–71, 172–76, 321n104; *Ion*, 97, 100–101; *Phoenician Women*, 65, 70, 73–78, 275n28; *Suppliant Women*, 137–38, 143, 147–49, 153

deliberation, 1, 2, 16; *Medea*, 27–28, 30–31, 34, 36, 257n90; *Children of Heracles*, 125–26; *Phoenician Women*, 80–81

Delphic Oracle, 154; characters, on the road to, 24, 25, 68, 69; Dionysus, connection to, 44, 57, 263n22; *Ion*, setting of, 14, 94–95, 97, 105, 106, 108, 287n21; prophecies of, 47, 67, 73, 94–95, 100, 106, 115, 139, 209, 218, 220; sanctuary site, 7, 94, 103, 204

Demeter, 61, 104, 125, 126; Dionysus, twinned with, 43, 47, 52; Eleusis, connection to, 141–42, 291n81

democracy, citizens of, 28, 33, 110, 288n40, 298n48, 309n71; education in, 5–6, 228, 240–41; free speech, necessity for, 108, 322n113; patriotism in, 93, 138, 288n33, 308n50; Theseus, connection to, 140, 141, 143, 305n26

Demophon, 101, 229; *Children of Heracles*, character in, 116–17, 118, 120, 121–26, 128, 129–30, 134–35, 296n16

Demosthenes, 286n13

deus ex machina, 7, 42, 150, 253n41; Athena, role in, 236, 302n97; *Children of Heracles*, 119, 129; *Electra*, 212, 214, 217–18; *Ion*, 94, 96, 101, 105, 109; *Suppliant Women*, 137, 144, 150, 341n106

dialectics, 58–62, 271n119

dichotomy, justice as, in *Bacchae*, 52–53, 56–58, 267n68, 267n71; in *Ion*, 14, 92, 101–104, 108; in *Phoenician Women*, 75; poetry and philosophy as, 3, 227. *See also* binaries, duality

Dionysus, 8, 67, 144, 166, 200, 234, 263n22, 264n32, 265n46, 305n29;

Dionysus *(continued)*
  Bacchae, character in, 14, 41–61,
    63; god of paradox, 2, 9, 32, 235,
    258n98, 262n20; 268n73, 269n94,
    274n20
Dioscuri, 140, 209, 335n14; *Electra*,
  characters in 212–14, 217–21, 223,
  235, 237, 339n73
dismemberment, 202, 238; of
  Apsyrtos, 21; of Dionysus, 47; of
  Pelias, 21–22, 254n44; *Bacchae*, of
  Pentheus, 48, 54, 58, 60, 66
distributive, justice as. *See* merit
divine justice, 35, 42, 54, 55, 58, 60,
  146–47, 148, 151
divine law, 59, 103; 123, 126,
  132–33, 135; burial rites as, 83,
  148, 151, 284n132, supplication,
  protection of, 102, 123, 126;
  boundary of, 59–60, 111, 187, 203
double/doubling, *Bacchae*, 46, 53,
  57–58, 60, 262n15, 264n36;
  Electra, double standard in, 212,
  216, 222, 341n104; *Ion*, 92, 93,
  104–109, 110, 270n103, 293n106;
  vision, seeing double in, 46, 52,
  48, 222–23, 224–26, 341n110;
  words, double meaning of, 196,
  322n120
drug/poison (*pharmakon*), 79; Hekate,
  skilled in, 23, 179: Heracles, death
  by, 115, 332n115; Medea, use of,
  22, 23, 25–26, 32, 35, 140; Gorgon
  blood, used as, 95, 106–107,
  281n100
duality, *Alcestis*, 191–92, 196, 198–
  99, 200, 203, 205; *Bacchae*, 50–51,
  55; *Ion*, 92, 105–107, 110. *See also*
  binaries, dichotomy

Eleusinian Mysteries, 104, 141–42,
  286n20, 287n21, 331n26;
Alcibiades, profanity against,
  330n83
Enodia, 95, 104, 107, 111, 291n80,
  291n82. *See also* Hekate
ephebes (youth), 8, 45, 46, 106, 141,
  301n86
equality, justice as, 12, 240, 338n47;
  Alcestis, 190–91; *Bacchae*, 58;
  Hecuba, 170, 232; *Ion*, 93, 108,
  232; *Phoenician Women*, 70, 73–
  74, 76–77, 85, 87, 279n73,
  280n80, 280n85, 280n87. *See also*
  fairness
Erinyes, 250n58, 259n119, 274n22,
  322n125; *Electra*, 207, 212–13,
  215, 217, 219, 225, 340n89; *Ion*,
  178, 179, 181
Eteocles, 139–40, 241, 232, 234,
  236–37, 275n28; *Phoenician
  Women*, character in, 68, 70–78,
  81, 86–87, 280n85
Euripides, critiques of, 4–5, 20–21,
  26–27, 42, 65, 73, 113, 119, 173,
  183, 207–208, 224; character in
  Frogs, 4, 10; life of, 9–11, 41–42;
  other tragedies, 41–42, 66, 184,
  249n47, *Andromache*, 66, 163,
  249n49, 254n43; *Cyclops*, 184,
  249n49; *Daughters of Pelias*, 20,
  21, 30, 325n9; *Heracles*, 249n49,
  295n7; *Helen*, 66, 105, 185,
  207, 249n49, 254n43, 314n9;
  Hippolytus, 185, 249n48; *Iphigenia
  among the Taurians*, 66, 85, 219,
  322n125, 335n18; *Iphigenia at
  Aulis*, 41–42, 209, 335n18; *Orestes*,
  10, 65, 163, 272n3; *Trojan Women*,
  163–64, 249n48
Eurystheus, 172, 208, 234, 297n29,
  301n85; *Children of Heracles*,
  character in, 115–19, 125, 128–29,
  131–36

Evadne, 125, 192; *Suppliant Women*, character in 143–45, 152–53, 157, 230, 231, 311n100, 311n102
excess, justice, opposition to, 29, 39, 66, 86, 133, 145, 172, 217, 230, 234, 237; emotional, 2, 50, 157, 184; identification, with others, 15, 153; justice, as claims to, 58, 60, 62, 77, 81, 84; middle or mean, as opposed to, 77, 147, 204. *See also* immoderation, moderation
expediency, *Children of Heracles*, 116, 121–22, 124, 132, 135; *Hecuba*, 165, 175–76: political, 45, 122, 312n114

fairness, justice as, 12, 13, 203, 218, 231–32, 240, 279n73. *See also* equality
freedom, 70, 108, 143, 212, 235, 334n5; *Bacchae*, 41, 49, 51, 52, 54; *Children of Heracles*, 124, 135; *Hecuba* 161, 174, 176–80, 322n114
friendship (*philia*), 30, 228–31; *Alcestis*, 190, 194, 199, 205: *Children of Heracles*, 114, 120–24, 129–33, 135; *Hecuba*, 164, 165, 168–70, 175; *Suppliant Women*, 149, 154, 157. *See also* guest-friendship
funeral oration, 141, 150–53, 155, 223, 224; and democracy, 308n50
Furies. *See* Erinyes

gender, as the "other," 91, 138, 225; reversals of, 32, 37, 44, 46, 52, 53, 55, 60, 125, 177, 199, 258n98, 268n75, 277n47, 277n50, 297n24, 331n111; expectations of, 32, 152, 194, 214, 216, 280n81, 300n75, 307n40, 311n102, 329n72, 333n134. *See also* binaries, women

generosity, 143, 219, 221, 230, 330n90; *Alcestis*, 183, 185, 190, 193, 196–97, 198–99, 203–205. *See also* gratitude
Giants, 46, 94, 97–88, 106, 107, 115
Goodin, Robert E., 135
Gorgons, 97–98, 105, 186, 200, 211; Gorgon blood, 95, 101, 106, 115, 290n67. *See also* Medusa
gratitude (*kharis*), as benevolence or reciprocity, 229, 233, 302n97, 309n75; *Alcestis*, 183, 187–88, 190–94, 196–97, 198, 203–205; *Children of Heracles*, 116–17, 122–30, 133, 135; *Electra*, 219, 222; *Hecuba*, 163–66, 159, 318n55; *Suppliant Women*, 144–45, 149, 153–55, 157. *See also* generosity
Great Dionysia festival, 5, 6–9, 10, 19, 20, 41, 45, 138, 184, 235, 263n27, 300n76, 311n97, 312n117, 325n9
Grotius, Hugo, 204
guest-friendship (*xenia*), justice as, 27, 95, 99, 142, 228, 230, 233, 310n78, 330n83; *Alcestis*, 183, 188–89, 194–99, 201, 203, 205; *Electra*, 211, 214, 221–22; *Hecuba*, 163, 164–66, 168–73, 177, 179, 181, 214. *See also* friendship

Hecuba 1, 15, 19, 132, 229–30, 233, 235; *Hecuba*, character in 161–81
Hegel, Georg W. F., 4, 86, 284n132, 309n61
Heidegger, Martin, 205
Hekate, 104, 107, 235, 291n82, 316n37; 323n134; *Medea*, 23, 34, 37; *Hecuba*, 166, 179–80. *See also* Enodia
Helen, 22, 140, 209, 224; image sent to Troy, 217, 220, 314n9, 339n73;

Helen *(continued)*
  Trojan War, role in, 69, 140, 162, 171, 297n23
Helios, 19, 22, 23, 26, 28, 35, 36, 37, 255n62; Zeus, changed direction of, 211–12, 215
helping friends and harming enemies, justice as, 12, 74, 153, 183, 227, 228–23, 234, 240; *Children of Heracles*, 121, 122–24, 124–34; *Hecuba*, 63–64; 168–70, 175, 179–80; 181; *Ion*, 92, 96, 98–101, 104, 109; *Medea*, 14, 20, 27–33, 39; Plato, discussions of, 2, 153, 238, 255n54
Hera, 23, 27, 162, 211, 335n24; Dionysus, persecution of, 43, 48, 258n98; Heracles, persecution of, 114–15, 118, 131
Heracles, 8, 20, 96, 106, 140, 145, 154; 301n89, 323n131, 326n21, 327n44, 332n115, 310n80; *Alcestis*, character in, 183, 184, 186, 188–90, 195–205, 230; background myth of, 114–15; *Children of Heracles*, 113, 116–19, 122, 125, 128, 131–32; Panhellenic hero, 14, 114, 134, 140, 149, 188, 197
Heraclitus, 205, 280n82, 333n138
Hermes, 45, 301n89; *Ion*, character in, 43, 94, 100
Herodotus, 22, 92 144, 293n97, 314n9
Hesiod, 186; *Catalogue of Women*, 92, 288n34; *Theogony*, 23; *Works and Days*, 51, 99, 333n135
Hestia, 23, 188, 323n135
hiketeia. *See* supplication
Homer, 3, 4, 11, 99, 165, 166, 167, 280n82; *Iliad*, 53, 79, 142, 162, 166, 186, 210, 272n133, 310n76, 321n99; *Odyssey*, 21, 44, 139, 163, 301n87

hospitality, 67, 184, 199, 230. *See also* guest-friendship (*xenia*)
household (*oikos*), 20, 29, 33, 51, 100, 105, 152–53, 195–96, 202, 221, 256n65, 329n72
humanity, justice as shared, 138, 156–57

immigration, 97, 110, 111, 253n34
immoderation, 50, 196. *See also* excess, moderation
impiety, 101, 130, 215
Ion, 232, 235, 236, 286n20, 287n32; *Ion*, as character in, 91–111
Iphigenia, 80, 125, 162, 210, 212, 218, 316n24

Jason, 115, 141, 153, 230, 232–34, 235, 251n12, 252n22, 305n27; background myth of, 21–24, 252n19; *Medea*, character in, 19, 25–26, 28, 30–32, 34–40
Jocasta, 139. 140, 230, 232, 276n32, 277n47; 280n80; *Phoenician Women*, character in, 62, 67, 68, 71–73, 76–77, 85, 86
just war, 122, 233, 309n70; *Suppliant Women*, 145–47, 148, 149, 150, 156

kairos. *See* measure
Kant, Immanuel, 181, 303n119
kharis. *See* gratitude

law. *See* custom (*nomos*)
lies, 41, 45, 61, 96, 100, 264n29, 269n9, 271n98, 286n17. *See also* truth
liminal/liminality, 32–33, 104, 106–108, 235, 239, 331n106; Dionysus and, 9, 258n98. *See also* boundary
Locke, John, 2

Lysias, 99

maiden (Macaria), 192, 229, 233, 297n26, 311n100; *Children of Heracles*, character in, 117–20, 125–26, 297n32
malicious enjoyment, 26, 214, 253n40
Marathon, 14, 115, 141, 295n10, 328n63, *Children of Heracles*, chorus in, 116, 122, 130, 134
measure (*kairos*), as measure of right time/right amount, 49, 73–74, 80, 96, 143, 151, 153, 190, 238–39, 278n62
Medea, 1, 24, 132, 140, 180, 230–32, 234, 254n47; background myth of, 21–24, 305n27; *Medea*, character in, 25–40, 253n41
Medes. *See* Persians
Medusa, 97–98, 106, 200, 289n45, 290n67, 322n15. *See also* Gorgons
merit, justice as, 12, 14, 15, 101, 219, 227, 231–34, 240, 266n52, 279n69, 319n74; *Bacchae*, 49, 54; *Children of Heracles*, 114, 123, 125–28, 129, 130–31, 133–34; *Hecuba*, 163, 168, 170–71, 172, 174–75, 181; *Phoenician Women*, 73–76, 78, 80, 85, 87; *Suppliant Women*, 146–48, 152, 154
metamorphosis, 19; Dionysus as god of, 9, 12, 41, 44, 51–52, 235; *Bacchae*, 48, 54, 57, 62; *Hecuba*, 167, 178–80, 323n126; political, 61, 271n129. *See also* transformation
Mill, John Stuart, 204
moderation, justice as, 50, 162, 280n82, 330n135; *Alcestis*, 196, 198, 203–204; *Phoenician Women* 73, 76–77, 86; *Suppliant Women*, 143, 146–47, 149–51, 155. *See also* excess, immoderation
Montaigne, Michel de, 136

Nagel, Thomas, 85, 313n125
nationalism, 92, 110, 309n70
natural justice, 76, 120
Nietzsche, Friedrich, 4, 42
nihilism, 19, 20, 59, 109, 120, 233, 237, 333n136

Oakeshott, 62
oaths, justice as, 55, 95, 129, 144, 154, 162, 209, 227, 231–32, 234–36, 259n106; *Medea*, 20, 25, 27, 33–38, 40; *Phoenician Women*, 72–75, 78
obligation, ethical, 74, 120, 123, 131, 134, 188, 200, 203, 232; familial, 84, 166, 122–23, 135, 153, 157, 169–70, 183, 192, 195, 204, 230–31, 233, 329n72; political, 84, 113, 120, 136, 139, 157, 169; reciprocal, role of, 114, 116, 124, 129, 169, 175, 190, 194–95, 229, 231–32, 305n25
Odysseus, 23, 74, 163, 209, 268n80; *Hecuba*, as character in, 164–77, 229, 315n19, 318n55, 321n99, 322n113
Oedipus, 47, 230, 274n22; background myth of, 67–68, 71, 139–40, 265n43; *Phoenician Women*, as character in, 65, 69, 73, 79, 81–84, 276n31, 277n56
Orestes, 155, 230, 237, 322n125, 336n30; background myth of, 209–10; *Electra*, character in, 207, 210–14, 220–21, 223–24, 226; moral paradox of, 215–19
Ovid, 48, 167

Panhellenic, 126, 150, 235, 291n78, 307n43; burial rites, norms of, 83, 143, 147–49, 151, 155–56, 235–36, 237, 318n59; festivals of, 247n33, 306n36; human sacrifice, violation of, 164–65, 169, 171, 177; sanctuary/supplication, norms of, 116, 121, 123, 236. *See also* Heracles, Panhellenic hero

paradox, Dionysus, as god of, 9, 16, 41, 44, 49, 51, 52, 54, 56, 235, 239; Euripides, tragedian of 12, 236n19; justice as, 16, 239; as moral conundrum, 207, 216, 217

parrhēsia. See speech, frank or honest

patriotism, 91, 98, 113, 119, 128, 134, 151, 283n122

Pausanias, 43, 92, 297n26, 297n29, 306n34

pedagogy, of tragedy, 2–6, 11, 13, 225

Peisistratus, 6, 141, 247n33

Pelias, 21–22, 23, 24, 38, 127, 186; daughters of, 26, 30, 37, 254n44, 325n9

Peloponnesian War, 8, 19, 41–42, 96, 110, 114, 121, 124, 148, 170, 184, 194–95, 285n7, 299n49, 308n58, 317n39, 318n54, 323n137, 330n83

Pelops, 67, 208, 296n16, 310n79

Pericles, 8, 31, 170

Persephone, 43, 104, 117, 126, 179, 254n47; Hades, abduction of, 141, 153, 262n18; Theseus, failed abduction of, 122, 140, 154, 155

Persians, 9, 22, 115, 141, 250n55, 293n107, 293n110, 307n43

pharmakon. See drug/poison

pile (*sōros*), 13, 240, 345n75

Pindar, 34, 144, 254n44, 326n21

pity, 49, 58, 99, 270n107, 299n60, 302n104, 319n74, 319n75, 325n14; *Children of Heracles*, 121–23, 131–32, 136, 142; *Hecuba*, 163, 164–65, 172–74; justice, 172–74; as self-pity, 214; *Suppliant Women*, 148–49, 157

Plato, 11, 120, 205, 249n53, 279n75, 280n82; *Apology*, 279n68, 308n60; *Charmides*, 82, 174; critique of poetry, 2–4, 238, 290n74; *Euthyphro*, 181, 287n32, 324n145; *Gorgias*, 8, 76, 264n33; *Phaedrus*, 271n119; *Protagoras*, 260n125, 266n53, 311n94, 342n4; *Republic*, 2, 27, 28, 75–76, 174, 180, 198, 231, 237, 264n29, 264n34, 271n120, 289n57, 298n43, 322n114; *Symposium*, 7, 186

pluralism, justice as, 62–63

Pogge, Thomas, 135

poison. See drug (*pharmakon*)

polis/poleis, 29, 30, 33, 51, 116, 145, 148, 152, 177, 190, 306n33, 319n75

quietists. *See* activists

rage, 1, 19, 53, 68, 98, 100, 103, 111, 133. *See also* anger, righteous indignation

Rawls, John, 2, 303n119

redistributive justice, 40, 74–75, 128–34, 240, 318n65. *See also* merit

refugees, 13, 15, 229, 231, 233, 299n49; *Children of Heracles*, 113–22, 124–25, 135–36

rejuvenation, 209, 260n130, 260n131, 301n86; *Alcestis*, 197, 200, 202, 208–209, 210; *Children of Heracles*, 113, 119, 127; *Medea*, 21–22, 36–39, 40, 254n47. *See also* resurrection

relativism, justice as, 19, 60, 73, 80, 85, 237, 227; Eteocles, moral relativism of, 76, 77–78, 83; *Hecuba*, 174–76
restorative justice, 13, 240
resurrection, 38, 130, 331n14; *Alcestis*, 190, 199, 200. *See also* rejuvenation
retribution, justice as, 79, 225; *Alcestis*, 187, 196, 200; *Electra*, 208–12, 215–16, 218, 225; *Ion*, 103–104; *Medea*, 26–29. *See also* revenge
revenge, 1, 95, 155, 225, 231, 265n49; *Children of Heracles*, 118, 125, 130–31, 134; *Electra*, 207, 209–11, 214–15, 335n22, 337n37, 340n81; *Hecuba*, 178, 322n120; *Medea*, 36–37
rhetoric, 5, 86, 96, 280n88; *Hecuba*, justice as, 161, 167–72, 321n103
righteous indignation, 109, 111, 136, 240. *See also* anger, rage

Sandel, Michael J., 151
satyr play, 8, 15, 20; *Alcestis*, 184–85, 199, 235, 325n9, 325n10
seeing place (*theatron*), 6–9, 60, 179, 241, 326n29
self-sacrifice, justice as, 229, 233, 236, 274n45; *Alcestis*, 186, 192–94, 197, 202, 204; *Children of Heracles*, 117–18, 120, 125–29, 130–35, 278n56, 300n76; *Phoenician Women*, 71–72, 78–81, 82–83, 85–86
Seneca, 21, 260n133
Sicilian Expedition, 10, 92, 207, 249n46, 276n42, 285n7, 317n39, 334n5
social justice, 12, 13, 73, 76, 93, 170, 240. *See also* equality

sophists, 14, 73, 76, 171, 174, 207, 246n25, 271n116, 279n75, 311n94, 320n94, 345n69; Euripides, potential association with, 5, 11–12, 174, 201, 237, 256n77, 331n101, 332n119
Sophocles, 4, 6, 10, 20, 48, 66, 72, 86, 167, 184, 213, 250n58, 252n21, 257n83, 263n74, 274n16, 324n3; *Antigone*, 68, 86, 145, 177, 257n88, 266n58, 283n119, 283n124; *Ajax*, 31, 268n80; *Oedipus at Colonus*, 68, 140; *Oedipus Tyrannus*, 57–58, 139; *Philoctetes*, 316n28
sōros. *See* pile
speech, frank or honest (*parrhēsia*), 74, 82, 108, 143, 174, 266n58, 276n40, 276n41, 279n68, 231n99, 321n99. *See also* lies
supplication (*hiketeia*), 99, 102, 194, 228–30, 233, 235, 299n49, 299n62, 301n91, 310n78; *Children of Heracles*, 115–16, 118, 121, 123, 125–26, 128; *Hecuba*, 168–70, 175; *Medea* 27, 35; *Suppliant Women*, 142, 145–46, 149, 157

theatron. *See* seeing place
Thebaid, 72, 144
Themis, 34, 103, 111, 291n78
Theseus, 22, 33, 47, 68, 77, 101, 116, 121, 209, 229, 233, 236, 312n108; background myth of, 140–41, 270n63, 305n27, 310n79; democracy, mythological role in, 140–41, 143, 288n33, 305n26, 307n46; Dionysus, connection to, 44, 305n29; Heracles, rival of, 115, 122, 140–41, 198, 288n33, 310n80; *Suppliant Women*, character in,

Theseus (continued)
15, 142–51, 153–56, 194; sons of, 116, 121, 164, 321n104. See also Demophon
Thucydides, 33, 92, 76, 121, 146, 174, 276n42, 281n90, 296n19, 308n50, 308n58, 315n19, 317n39, 323n137, 330n83
tragicomedy, 91, 99, 185, 197–99, 217
transformation, 96, 126, 129, 140, 152, 192, 209, 225, 271n118, 301n86, 322n125; *Bacchae*, 44, 48, 51, 53–54, 61; *Hecuba*, 161, 165–67, 178–80, 181, 323n127. See also metamorphosis
transgression, 27, 52, 61, 103–104, 111, 136, 179–80, 234–37. See also boundary
transitional justice, 39, 136
trust (*pistis*), 35, 39, 124, 220, 281n91
truth (*alētheia*), 44, 61, 63, 68, 69, 109, 110, 133, 136, 194, 222, 223–24, 238, 278n62; philosophy, goal of, 2–3, 4, 179, 231, 238, 259n106, 279n68; speech, possibility of, 73–75, 108, 188, 196, 232, 246n41; gods, source of, 96, 200. See also lies
tyranny/tyrant 6, 23, 177, 222, 236–37, 281n92; *Bacchae*, 41, 50–51, 54–55, 59–60; *Children of Heracles*, 113, 132, 135; human desire for, 62, 268n74, 322n114; *Phoenician Women*, 70, 73–78; *Suppliant Women*, 141, 143, 151, 153
Tyro, 23–24, 36, 252n27

uncertainty, 13, 240; decision making, under conditions of, 120, 144–45, 183, 208; competing moral claims, with, 215–19, 219–23

vengeance. See revenge
Virgil, 163

women, as audience members, 8; Euripides, views of, 10, 20, 104, 125, 165, 192, 216; Medea, famous speech on plight of, 20, 25, 29, 30; status of, 20, 57, 69, 104, 170, 177, 192, 199, 216, 255n61, 256n65, 263n25, 277n50. See also gender

xenia. See guest-friendship
xenophobia, 20, 74, 114; *Ion*, 98–99, 101, 104, 108, 110, 291n87
Xenophon, 11, 280n82; *Anabasis*, 231; *Cyropaedia*, 74, 319n71; *Hellenica*, 345n75; *Memorabilia*, 99, 271n119, 333n135, 343n26

Zeus, 34, 57, 94, 106, 116, 141, 217, 219; father of Dionysus, 43–44, 45, 57; father of Heracles 114–15, 296n16; father of Helen and Polydeuces, 209, 335n14; punisher of injustice, 24, 34, 36, 117, 146, 151, 186–87, 200, 215, 259n119; Zeus Hikesios, guise of, 102, 123, 142; Zeus Horkios, guise of, 34, 35, 74; Zeus Xenios, guise of, 168–69, 187, 222, 232

www.ingramcontent.com/pod-product-compliance
Ingram Content Group UK Ltd.
Pitfield, Milton Keynes, MK11 3LW, UK
UKHW041921140426

5217IPUK00014B/257